The language of Ancient Egypt, with the long
guage, has been the object of careful investig
the nineteenth century, but this is the first ac
insights of modern linguistics. Antonio Lopri
the older phase of the language ("Earlier
Egyptian in the third millennium BCE, the classical literary language of the Middle Kingdom (2000–1750 BCE) and the Late Middle Egyptian of religious texts until the Roman period, to the more recent phase ("Later Egyptian"), which emerged as a vehicle of profane literature and administration during the New Kingdom (1500–1000 BCE), and continued to be in productive use down to Coptic, the language of medieval Christian Egypt. These two main historical forms of the Egyptian language are analyzed combining, wherever possible, diachronic and synchronic viewpoints. Professor Loprieno discusses the hieroglyphic system and its cursive varieties (Hieratic and Demotic), the phonology of Classical Egyptian and Coptic, the phonology and syntax of the literary languages, and semantic and pragmatic constraints on syntax. He also looks at the genetic connections of Egyptian within the Afroasiatic family, especially with Semitic languages such as Akkadian, Arabic and Hebrew.

Ancient Egyptian

ANCIENT EGYPTIAN

A linguistic introduction

ANTONIO LOPRIENO
Department of Near Eastern Languages and Cultures
University of California, Los Angeles

CAMBRIDGE
UNIVERSITY PRESS

PUBLISHED BY THE PRESS SYNDICATE OF THE UNIVERSITY OF CAMBRIDGE
The Pitt Building, Trumpington Street, Cambridge, United Kingdom

CAMBRIDGE UNIVERSITY PRESS
The Edinburgh Building, Cambridge CB2 2RU, UK
40 West 20th Street, New York, NY 10011–4211, USA
10 Stamford Road, Oakleigh, VIC 3166, Australia
Ruiz de Alarcón 13, 28014 Madrid, Spain
Dock House, The Waterfront, Cape Town 8001, South Africa

http://www.cambridge.org

First published 1995
Reprinted 1996, 1998, 2000

Printed in the United Kingdom at the University Press, Cambridge

A catalogue record for this book is available from the British Library

Library of Congress Cataloguing in Publication Data
Loprieno, Antonio.
Ancient Egyptian: a linguistic introduction / Antonio Loprieno.
p. cm.
Includes bibliographical references and index.
ISBN 0 521 44384 9 (hardback) ISBN 0 521 44849 2 (paperback)
1. Egyptian language. I. Title.
PJ1111.L66 1996
493′.1 – dc20 95-14789 CIP

ISBN 0 521 44384 9 hardback
ISBN 0 521 44849 2 paperback

AU

CONTENTS

Preface *page* xi
Major chronological divisions of Egyptian history xiv

1 The language of Ancient Egypt
1.1 The genetic frame 1
1.2 History of the Egyptian language 5
1.3 A brief look at Egyptological linguistics 8
Further reading 10

2 Egyptian graphemics
2.1 Introduction 11
2.2 The basic principles of hieroglyphic writing 12
2.3 Connotational devices in the hieroglyphic system 18
2.4 The historical development of Egyptian writing 19
2.5 The end of the system and its rediscovery 24
Further reading 27

3 Egyptian phonology
3.1 Introduction 28
3.2 Heuristic criteria 29
3.3 The prehistory of Egyptian phonology 31
3.4 The phonological system of earlier Egyptian 32
3.4.1 Consonants 32
3.4.2 Vowels 35
3.4.3 Syllabic structures 36
3.5 The phonological system of later Egyptian 38
3.5.1 Consonants 38
3.5.2 Vowels 38
3.5.3 Syllabic structures 39
3.6 The phonological system of Coptic 40
3.6.1 Consonants 41
3.6.2 Vowels 46

3.6.3 Syllabic structures 48

Further reading 50

4 Elements of historical morphology

4.1 Introduction 51

4.2 Root, stem, word 52

4.3 Nominal morphology

4.3.1 General features 55

4.3.2 Compound nouns 56

4.3.3 The feminine 57

4.3.4 Plural and dual 58

4.3.5 Feminine and plural in later Egyptian 60

4.4 Pronouns

4.4.1 Personal pronouns 63

4.4.2 Personal pronouns in later Egyptian 66

4.4.3 Deictic, interrogative, and relative pronouns 68

4.5 Numerals 71

4.6 The verb

4.6.1 Introduction 72

4.6.2 General features of verbal morphology 73

4.6.3 Verbal morphology in earlier Egyptian 77

4.6.4 Non-finite verbal forms 86

4.6.5 Negative verbal forms 89

4.6.6 Verbal morphology in later Egyptian 90

4.7 Prepositions, conjunctions, particles 99

Further reading 101

5 Nominal syntax

5.1 Introduction 103

5.2 Bipartite vs. tripartite patterns

5.2.1 Classifying and identifying patterns 104

5.2.2 Specifying patterns 106

5.3 Entire clauses as predicate of *pw* : "thetic" statements 109

5.4 Sentences with adjectival predicate and cleft sentences

5.4.1 Qualifying patterns 112

5.4.2 Identifying (cleft) sentences 114

5.5 Possessive and interrogative patterns

5.5.1 Possessive constructions 118

5.5.2 Interrogative constructions 121

5.6 Existential sentences and temporal-modal features 122
5.7 Negative patterns 125
5.8 Nominal sentences in later Egyptian 131
5.9 Old and new cleft sentences 133
5.10 Interrogative, possessive, and existential patterns 137
5.11 Negation in later Egyptian 140
Further reading 142

6 Adverbial and pseudoverbal syntax
6.1 Introduction 144
6.2 Adverbial and pseudoverbal patterns 146
6.3 Adverbial conversions
6.3.1 Adverbial clauses 150
6.3.2 Adverbial phrases 155
6.3.3 Converted vs. unconverted relative clauses 158
6.4 Initial vs. non-initial clauses
6.4.1 General features 162
6.4.2 The proclitic particles jw *and* mk 166
6.5 Negation in adverbial and pseudoverbal patterns
6.5.1 Negation in adverbial and pseudoverbal sentences 168
6.5.2 Negation of adverbial phrases 170
6.6 Adverbial sentences in later Egyptian
6.6.1 The Present I and its conversions 172
6.6.2 The fate of pseudoverbal patterns 176
6.6.3 Main vs. subordinate clauses 178
6.7 Later Egyptian negative patterns 180
Further reading 182

7 Verbal syntax
7.1 Introduction 183
7.2 The independent verbal sentence 184
7.3 Initial vs. non-initial main clauses 186
7.4 Verbal clauses embedded as adverbial phrases 189
7.5 The verbal sentence with topicalized predicate
7.5.1 General characteristics 192
7.5.2 Topicalized vs. adverbialized verbal forms 195
7.5.3 The "balanced" sentence 196
7.5.4 Other focalizing uses of the topicalized VP 198
7.6 Verbal clauses embedded as noun phrases 199

7.7 Converted relative clauses
7.7.1 General features 202
7.7.2 Relative conversion of agentless sentences 204
7.8 Negation in verbal clauses
7.8.1 Contradictory negation in main verbal clauses 209
7.8.2 Modal negation 210
7.8.3 Contrary negation in verbal clauses 213
7.8.4 Negation of verbal predicates embedded as AP 214
7.8.5 Negation of verbal predicates embedded as NP 215
7.8.6 Negation of adjectival conversions 217
7.9 Verbal syntax in later Egyptian
7.9.1 General features 220
7.9.2 Initial verbal clauses and parataxis 221
7.9.3 Non-initial verbal clauses and hypotaxis 225
7.9.4 Dependent clauses and subordination 229
7.9.5 From embedding to conversion 231
Further reading 236

Epilogue 237
Notes 240
References 279
Index of passages 293
Index of morphemes 301
Index of lexemes 304
Index of topics 313

Preface

This book is neither a grammar of Ancient Egyptian for Egyptologists nor a handbook for the study of hieroglyphs. Rather, it has been written aiming at the needs of a multiplicity of audiences. To use a fashionable word, I wanted to address the interdisciplinary interests of linguists and Egyptologists. In order to achieve this result, I had to resort to sometimes quite diverse methodological frames and scholarly conventions, which have been and are at best indifferent to each other, and at times even in overt conflict. On the one hand, the main goal of the book is to provide the linguistic audience with an introduction to the historical grammar of Ancient Egyptian, one of the oldest and longest documented languages of mankind: from its oldest (Old Egyptian) to its most recent phase (Coptic), Ancient Egyptian remained in productive written use for more than four millennia – from about 3000 BCE to the Middle Ages. On the other hand, the book also tries to reach the numerically much smaller public of Egyptologists interested in linguistic issues, i.e. my own professional milieu, offering a global presentation of the language from a structural as well as historical point of view.

Traditionally, the study of Ancient Egyptian has been the monopoly of the latter group of scholars, who operate within the discipline called "Egyptology." In this field of scholarship, the study of the language is necessarily rooted in philology and has been mainly pursued with the aim of editing or translating Egyptian and Coptic texts. The handbooks for the academic and individual study of Egyptian, first and foremost Alan H. Gardiner, *Egyptian Grammar* (Oxford University Press, third edn 1957), share the assumption that potential readers are Egyptologists interested primarily in acquiring the philological tools needed for their professional encounter with Ancient Egypt: Gardiner's grammar bears the appropriate, although certainly modest subtitle *Being an Introduction to the Study of Hieroglyphs*. While much work has been done since then in Egyptian grammar and some of the theoretical foundations of Gardiner's approach to Egyptian have been shaken if not damaged, a linguist interested in the strategies adopted by Egyptian as a language will experience some distress in finding the answers to his or her queries in modern secondary literature.

This distress is not due to a lack of linguistic sophistication among Egyptologists; on the contrary, the presence of Egyptological linguistics as one of the most vital components of the field of Egyptology is one of the reasons for my trying to make its discoveries available to other linguists. But I doubt that the work of the more linguistically inclined Egyptologists has been or is adequately noticed by professional linguists. For one, scholars of Egyptian linguistics tend to follow the conventions of the broader field of Egyptology in terms of attitudes to transliteration (just to quote an example: for a variety of reasons, there still is no universally accepted system for the phonetic rendition of Egyptian) and translations (which address the semantic, rather than the grammatical sphere, interlinear translations being discouraged or unknown). Secondly, over the last decades we have preferred to engage in a dialog among ourselves rather than with the broader audience of comparative and general linguists, and we have developed conceptual and terminological conventions that often appear opaque, if not downright incomprehensible to the non-initiated. This is due in part to the specific methodological frame adopted by modern students of Egyptian, the so-called "Standard theory," in part to the ignorance of Egyptian among linguists. Only recently, thanks to a new generation of Egyptologists also trained in linguistics, has there been a shift towards an increased interest in theoretical issues. The present work is a product of this change of perspectives within my own scholarly community: although I have tried to explain unusual terms when they appear for the first time, a certain familiarity with linguistic terminology is expected from the Egyptological readership of the book; as for general linguists, while no previous Egyptological knowledge is required, I expect them to devote particular attention to the introduction and to the chapter on graphemics, where basic preliminaries on chronology, typology, and notational conventions of Egyptian are discussed at some length.

The concept of "Ancient Egyptian" is taken throughout this book in its broader scope to comprise all the stages of the language from Old Egyptian to Coptic. While focusing on Old and Middle Egyptian, i.e. on the language of classical literature, the analysis proceeds diachronically to investigate the main features of Late Egyptian and Coptic, especially when this evolution displays changes which attract the linguist's attention. In essence, I have tried to present synchronical sketches of the main properties of classical Egyptian, Late Egyptian, and Coptic and to consider the mechanisms of linguistic change inherent in the history of the Egyptian language.

Although philological and not interlinear, the translation of Egyptian and Coptic passages provides in parentheses enough information for the non-specialists to allow them to recognize all the elements of the morpho-syntactic as well as lexical structure of the sentence. Most Egyptian texts are referred to according to the Egyptological conventions as established in the *Lexikon der Ägyptologie* (Wiesbaden: Harrassowitz, 1975–1986), in short *LÄ*; only less commonly quoted texts are accompanied by a reference to their edition. Notes, bibliography and indices try to blend the expectations of the two potential readerships for which the book is intended. In the notes, whose number had to be limited to an acceptable minimum, books and articles are usually referred to in short title; the reference in full detail, however, is given both at first mention and in the bibliography at the end of the volume. While abbreviations are used in the notes, I have tried to avoid them in the final bibliography; for the most common ones, the reader is referred to the list provided in vols. I and IV of the *LÄ*. In the notes, I often mention only the more recent treatments of a particular topic, even if the interpretation offered by the authors differs from mine; this is the reason for the relative paucity of references to older secondary literature. Modern treatments, however, usually contain abundant references to previous studies as well. The index of Egyptian and Coptic passages and of Egyptian grammatical words is intended mainly for the Egyptological audience, whereas the register of topics is conceived with a linguistic public in mind.

I would like to mention and thank those friends and colleagues who in different ways have participated in the completion of this book: first and foremost Wolfgang Schenkel, who followed its development with particular attention and saved me from many inaccuracies, Bernard Comrie, who acted as a careful and inspiring linguistic reader, and Gerald Moers, who provided invaluable help in the preparation of the indices; further Heike Behlmer, Mark Collier, Andrea M. Gnirs, Orly Goldwasser, Sarah I. Groll, Friedrich Junge, Frank Kammerzell, Aldo Piccato, Dana M. Reemes, Deborah Sweeney, and Thomas Ritter for fruitful debates and assistance; and finally Judith Ayling, Hilary Gaskin, and Ann Rex of Cambridge University Press for guiding me in editorial matters. The book was written in part during a sabbatical year funded by a University of California President's Fellowship in the Humanities (1993–94): I would like to acknowledge with sincere thanks the help and generosity of the Office of the President for providing me with ideal research conditions.

This book is dedicated to my wonderful daughter Victoria, who is more often than I can bear away from my eyes, but always closest to my heart.

Major chronological divisions of Egyptian history

Archaic Egypt: Dyn. I–II	ca. 3000–2650 BCE
Old Kingdom: Dyn. III–VIII	ca. 2650–2135
Dyn. III	2650–2590
Dyn. IV	2590–2470
Dyn. V	2470–2320
Dyn. VI	2320–2160
First Intermediate Period: Dyn. VII–XI	ca. 2160–2040
Middle Kingdom: Dyn. XI–XIV	ca. 2040–1650
Dyn. XI	2040–1990
Dyn. XII	1990–1785
Second Intermediate Period: Dyn. XV–XVII	ca. 1785–1550
Dyn. XIII–XIV	1785–1650
Dyn. XV–XVI (Hyksos)	1650–1550
New Kingdom: Dyn. XVII–XX	ca. 1560–1070
Dyn. XVII	1560–1552
Dyn. XVIII	1552–1306
Dyn. XIX	1306–1186
Dyn. XX	1186–1070
Third Intermediate Period: Dyn. XXI–XXV	1070–656
Dyn. XXI	1070–945
Dyn. XXII–XXIV (Libyans)	945–712
Dyn. XXV (Nubians)	712–664
Late Period: Dyn. XXVI–XXX	664–341
Dyn. XXVI	664–525
Dyn. XXVII (Persians)	525–404
Dyn. XXVIII–XXX	404–343
Dyn. XXXI (Persians)	343–332

Greek Period	332–30 BCE
Alexander the Great	332–323
Ptolemaic Period	323–30 BCE
Roman Period	30 BCE – 395 CE
Byzantine Period	395–641
Islamic Egypt	641–present

1

The language of Ancient Egypt

1.1 The genetic frame

Ancient Egyptian represents an autonomous branch of the language phylum called Afroasiatic in the USA and in modern linguistic terminology,[1] Hamito-Semitic in Western Europe and in comparative linguistics,[2] Semito-Hamitic mainly in Eastern Europe.[3] Afroasiatic is one of the most widespread language families in the world, its geographic area comprising, from antiquity to the present time, the entire area of the eastern Mediterranean, northern Africa, and western Asia.

The most important languages of the ancient and modern Near East – with the notable exceptions of Sumerian and Hittite – belong to this family, which is characterized by the following general linguistic features:[4] a preference for the fusional (or flectional) type;[5] the presence of bi- and tri-consonantal lexical roots, capable of being variously inflected; a consonantal system displaying a series of pharyngealized or glottalized phonemes (called *emphatics*) alongside the voiced and the voiceless series; a vocalic system originally limited to the three vowels /a/ /i/ /u/; a nominal feminine suffix **-at*; a rather rudimentary case system, consisting of no more than two or three cases; a nominal prefix *m-*; an adjectival suffix *-ī* (called *nisba*, the Arabic word for "relation"); an opposition between prefix conjugation (dynamic) and suffix conjugation (stative) in the verbal system; a conjugation pattern singular first person **'a-*, second person **ta-*, third person masculine **ya-*, feminine **ta-*, plural first person **na-*, with additional suffixes in the other persons.

The individual branches of the Afroasiatic family are:

(1) ANCIENT EGYPTIAN, to which this book is devoted.

(2) SEMITIC, the largest family of the Afroasiatic phylum.[6] The term derives from the anthroponym "Sem," Noah's first son (Gen 10,21–31; 11,10–26) and has been applied since A. L. Schlözer (1781) to the languages spoken in ancient times in most of western Asia (Mesopotamia, Palestine, Syria, Arabia), and in modern times, as a consequence of invasions from the Arabian peninsula in the first millennium CE, in northern Africa and

Ethiopia as well. The traditional grouping of Semitic languages is in three subgroups:

(a) *Eastern Semitic* in Mesopotamia, represented by Akkadian (2350–500 BCE), further divided into two dialects and four typological phases: Old Akkadian (2350–2000 BCE), Old Babylonian and Old Assyrian (2000–1500 BCE), Middle Babylonian and Middle Assyrian (1500–1000 BCE), New Babylonian (1000–Hellenistic times, the phase from 600 BCE on also called "Late Babylonian") and New Assyrian (1000–600 BCE). A western variety of Old Akkadian was spoken and written in the Early Bronze Age in the kingdom of Ebla in northern Syria ("Eblaite").

(b) *Northwest Semitic* in Syria and Palestine, divided into: (1) Northwest Semitic of the second millennium BCE, which includes inscriptions from Byblos in Phoenicia and from the Sinai peninsula, Amorite (inferred from northwest Semitic proper names and expressions in Old Akkadian and Old Babylonian), Early Canaanite (glosses and linguistic peculiarities in the Akkadian international correspondence from the Late Bronze archive of el-Amarna in Egypt), and especially Ugaritic, the only northwest Semitic literary language of the second millennium BCE; (2) Canaanite in Palestine and Phoenicia during the first millennium BCE, including Hebrew (the most important language of the group, documented in a literature ranging from the Bible to modern times and resurrected as a spoken vehicle in modern Israel), Phoenician and Punic, and Moabite; (3) Aramaic in Syria and progressively in Mesopotamia as well: Old Aramaic (1000–700 BCE), Classical or Imperial – including Biblical – Aramaic (700–300 BCE); for the later phases (from the second century BCE to survivals in modern times), Aramaic is divided into Western Aramaic (Jewish, Samaritan and Christian Palestinian Aramaic, Nabatean, Palmyrene, and modern Western Aramaic in a few present-day Syrian villages) and Eastern Aramaic (Syriac, Babylonian Aramaic, Mandean, and contemporary remnants in eastern Turkey, northern Iraq, and the Caucasus).

(c) *Southwest Semitic* in the Arabian peninsula, including: (1) Arabic, often grouped with Northwest Semitic into a "Central Semitic,",[7] the most widespread Semitic language, spoken at present by 150 million people from Morocco to Iraq; contemporary written Arabic (which overlies a variety of diversified spoken dialects) represents a direct continuation of the language of the Qur'ān and of classical literature; inscriptions from northern and central Arabia in an earlier form of the language (called "pre-classical North Arabic") are known from the fourth century BCE to the fourth century CE; (2) Epigraphic South Arabian, contemporary with pre-classical North Arabic, followed by modern South Arabian dialects; (3) Ethiopic, the result of the emigration to eastern Africa of South Arabian populations, subdivided into classical Ethiopic ("Gəʿəz") from the fourth century CE, the liturgical language of the Ethiopian church, and the modern Semitic languages of Ethiopia (Tigre, Tigriña in Eritrea; Amharic, Harari, Gurage in central Ethiopia).

Some of the most important characteristics of the Semitic languages are: in phonology, the articulation of "emphatic" phonemes as ejectives in Ethiopia and as pharyngealized stops in the Arabic world; in morphology, a tendency to the paradigmatization of the triradical root, which is inflectionally or derivationally combined with a series of consonantal and vocalic phonemes to produce regular, i.e. predictable morphological forms; a preference for the Verb-Subject-Object syntactic order in the older forms of the languages, usually replaced by a SVO (in Arabic and Hebrew) or SOV order (in the modern Semitic languages of Ethiopia, probably under the influence of the Cushitic adstratum) in the later phases.

(3) BERBER, a group of related languages and dialects[8] currently spoken (mostly in competition with Arabic) by at least five million speakers in northern Africa from the Atlantic coast to the oasis of Siwa and from the Mediterranean Sea to Mali and Niger. Although written records exist only since the nineteenth century, some scholars take Berber to represent the historical outcome of the ancient language of the more than 1000 "Libyan" inscriptions, written in autochthonous or in Latin alphabet and documented from the second century BCE onward. The linguistic territory of Berber can be divided into seven major areas: the Moroccan Atlas (Tachelhit, Tamazight), central Algeria (Zenati), the Algerian coast (Kabyle), the Gebel Nefusa in Tripolitania (Nefusi), the oasis of Siwa in western Egypt (Siwi), the Atlantic coast of Mauretania (Zenaga), and the central Sahara in Algeria and Niger (Tuareg). Isolated communities are also found in Mali, Tunisia, and Libya. The Tuareg have preserved an old autochthonous writing system (*tifinaɣ*), ultimately related to the alphabet of the old Libyan inscriptions.

Characteristic for Berber phonology is the presence of two allophonic varieties of certain stops: a "tense" articulation, connected with consonantal length, as opposed to a "lax" one, often accompanied by spirantization. E.g., the two variants of /k/ are [kk] (tense) and [x] (lax). In nominal morphology, masculine nouns normally begin with a vowel, whereas feminine nouns both begin and end with a *t*-morpheme. In the verb, aspectual oppositions (unmarked, intensive, perfect) are conveyed by prefixes, the subject being indicated by a prefix (first person plural and third person singular), a suffix (first person singular and third person plural), or a discontinuous affix consisting of a prefix and a suffix (second person). The unmarked order of the sentence, which can be modified in presence of pragmatic stress, is VSO.

(4) CUSHITIC, a family of languages[9] spoken by at least fifteen million people in eastern Africa, from the Egyptian border in northeast Sudan to Ethiopia, Djibouti, Somalia, Kenya, and northern Tanzania. The existence of the Cushitic languages has been known since the seventeenth century. While this family does not seem to be documented in the ancient world – Meroitic, the still imperfectly understood language used and written in the Kingdom of Napata and Meroe between the third and the sixth cataract of the Nile from the third century BCE to the fourth century CE, was a Nilo-Saharan language – one of its languages, Beja, shows close etymological and typological ties with Ancient Egyptian.[10] Cushitic languages are divided into four major groups: (a) *Northern* (Beja, in coastal Sudan); (b) *Central* (Agaw, in northern Ethiopia); (c) *Eastern*, further subdivided into Saho-Afar in southern Eritrea, Somali in Somalia, Oromo in central Ethiopia, Highland East Cushitic in central and southern Ethiopia, and various other languages in Ethiopia, such as Dullay and Western Omo-Tana, and in northern Kenya, such as Rendille; (d) *Southern* (Alagwa, Burunge, Iraqw, etc.), spoken in southern Kenya and Tanzania.

Cushitic languages are characterized by the presence of a set of glottalized consonants and in some cases, such as Somali, by vowel harmony. Although they display tonal oppositions, these are, unlike for example in Chinese, morphosyntactically determined. In the area of morphology, Cushitic languages tend to be very synthetic; there are two genders (masculine, often covering the lexical areas of "greatness" or "importance", and feminine, often used for the semantic realm of "smallness"), a complex system of plural formations, and a varying number of cases: the Proto-Cushitic binary system with nominative in *ú* or *í* and absolutive case in *a* has either been abandoned, as in southern Cushitic, or has evolved into a more complex system with numerous cases derived from the agglutination of postpositions. The verbal system tends to replace the Afroasiatic prefix conjugation (still present in Beja and Saho-Afar, with remnants in other languages as well) with a suffix conjugation based on the auxiliary verb "to be"; it is very rich in tenses, which are often derived from the grammaticalization of conjunctions and auxiliaries. Cushitic languages grammaticalize pragmatic oppositions such as topic or focus, while the preferred syntactic order is SOV.

(5) CHADIC, a family of about 140 languages and dialects[11] spoken by more than thirty million speakers in sub-Saharan Africa around Lake Chad

(Nigeria, Cameroon, Chad, and Niger). They are currently subdivided into the following groups: (a) *Western* (Hausa, Bole, Ron, Bade/Warji, Zaar, etc.); (b) *Biu-Mandara* (Tera, Bura/Higi, Mandara, Daba, Bata, etc.); (c) *Eastern* (Somrai, Nancere, Kera, Dangla, etc.); (d) *Masa*. The most important language of this family, Hausa, enjoys the status of first language in northern Nigeria and Niger and of second language and regional lingua franca in the entire West Sahara. Chadic languages have a very rich consonantal inventory: like Cushitic, they display glottalized consonants, and they are often tonal. There is no gender distinction in the plural, verbal forms are normally not conjugated for person. The unmarked word order is SVO.

(6) OMOTIC, a family of languages spoken by approximately one million speakers along both shores of the Omo River and north of Lake Turkana in southwest Ethiopia, formerly thought to represent the western branch of Cushitic.[12] It is still a matter of debate whether Omotic really belongs to the Afroasiatic language family. Characteristic features of the Omotic languages are the absence of emphatic phonemes and the almost total loss of gender oppositions.

1.2 History of the Egyptian language

Ancient Egyptian shows the closest relations to Beja (Cushitic), Semitic and Berber, more distant ones to the rest of Cushitic and Chadic. With its more than four millennia of productive history (3000 BCE – 1300 CE), Egyptian proves an ideal field for diachronic and typological investigation. The history of Egyptian[13] can be divided into two main stages, characterized by a major change from synthetic to analytic patterns in the nominal syntax and the verbal system. Each of these two stages of the language can be further subdivided into three different phases, affecting primarily the sphere of graphemics.

(1) EARLIER EGYPTIAN: the language of all written texts from 3000 to 1300 BCE, surviving in formal religious texts until the third century CE. Its main phases are:

(a) *Old Egyptian*, the language of the Old Kingdom and of the First Intermediate Period (3000–2000 BCE). The main documents of this stage of the language are the religious corpus of the "Pyramid Texts" and a sizeable number of so-called "Autobiographies," which are accounts of individual achievements inscribed on the external walls of the rock tombs of the administrative élite.

(b) *Middle Egyptian*, also termed *Classical Egyptian*, from the Middle Kingdom to the end of Dyn. XVIII (2000–1300 BCE). Middle Egyptian is the classical language of Egyptian literature, conveyed in a variety of texts that can be classified according to four main genres: (1) Funerary texts, especially the "Coffin Texts" inscribed on the sarcophagi of the administrative élite. (2) "Instructions," i.e. wisdom texts normally addressed from a father to a son, which conveyed the educational and professional expectations of Egyptian society. The most renowned examples are the "Instructions of the Vizier Ptahhotep" and the "Instructions for Merikare." Some of these moral texts, such as the "Admonitions of Ipu-Wer," are in fact philosophical discussions *ex eventu* on the state of the country taking as a point of departure the political evolution from the Old to the Middle Kingdom, the historical phase generally referred to as First Intermediate Period. (3) "Tales," which are narratives relating adventures of a specific hero and representing the vehicle of individual, as opposed to societal concerns. The most famous specimens of this genre are the "Tale of Sinuhe" and the "Shipwrecked Sailor." (4) "Hymns," poetical texts with religious contents, written in praise of a god or of the king. Famous examples are provided by the "Hymn to the Nile" and by the cycle of "Hymns to King Sesostris III." Some texts, such as the story of Sinuhe and especially the "Eloquent Peasant," combine features and contents of all main genres. Besides literary texts, the Middle Egyptian corpus comprises administrative documents, for example the Kahun papyri, and historical records.

(c) *Late Middle Egyptian*, the language of religious texts (rituals, mythology, hymns) from the New Kingdom to the end of Egyptian civilization. Late Middle Egyptian, also called *égyptien de tradition*, coexisted with later Egyptian (see below) for more than a millennium in a situation of diglossia. From a grammatical point of view, Late Middle Egyptian maintains the linguistic structures of the classical language, but on the graphemic side, especially in the Greco-Roman period (Ptolemaic Egyptian: third century BCE to second century CE), it shows an enormous expansion of the set of hieroglyphic signs.

Linguistically, earlier Egyptian is characterized by a preference for synthetic grammatical structures: for example, it displays a full set of morphological suffixes indicating gender and number: m. s. *nṯr.ø* "god", f. s. *nṯr.t* "goddess", m. pl. *nṯr.w* "gods", f. pl. *nṯr.wt* "goddesses"; it exhibits no definite article: *rmṯ* "the man, a man"; it maintains the VSO order in verbal formations: *sḏm=k n=f* "may you listen to him."

(2) LATER EGYPTIAN, documented from Dyn. XIX down to the Middle Ages (1300 BCE – 1300 CE):

(a) *Late Egyptian* (1300–700 BCE), the language of written records from the second part of the New Kingdom. It primarily conveys the rich entertainment literature of Dyn. XIX, consisting of wisdom and narrative texts, for example the "Tale of the Two Brothers," the "Tale of Wenamun," or the "Instructions of Ani" and the "Instructions of Amenemope," but also of some new literary genres, such as mythological tales or love poetry. Late Egyptian was also the vehicle of Ramesside bureaucracy, such as the archival documents from the Theban necropoleis or of school texts, called "Miscellanies." Late Egyptian is not a completely homogeneous linguistic reality; rather, the texts of this phase of the language show various degrees of interference with classical Middle Egyptian, with the tendency of older or more formal texts, such as historical records or literary tales, to display a higher number of borrowings from the classical language ("literary Late Egyptian"), as opposed to later or administrative texts, where Middle Egyptian forms are much rarer ("colloquial Late Egyptian").[14]

(b) *Demotic* (seventh century BCE to fifth century CE), the language of administration and literature during the Late Period. While grammatically closely akin to Late Egyptian, it differs from it radically in its graphic system. Important texts in Demotic are the narrative cycles of Setne-Khaemwase and of Petubastis and the instructions of Papyrus Insinger and of Onkhsheshonqi.

(c) *Coptic* (fourth to fourteenth century CE),[15] the language of Christian Egypt, written in a variety of Greek alphabet with the addition of six or seven Demotic signs to indicate Egyptian phonemes absent from Greek. As a spoken, and gradually also as a written language, Coptic was superseded by Arabic from the ninth century onward, but it survives to the present time as the liturgical language of the Christian church of Egypt, which is also called the "Coptic" church.

Besides displaying a number of phonological evolutions, later Egyptian tends to develop analytic features: suffixal markers of morphological oppositions tend to be dropped and functionally replaced by prefixal indicators such as the article: Late Eg. and Dem. *pꜣ-nṯr*, Coptic *p-noute* "the god," Late Eg. and Dem. *tꜣ-nṯr(.t)* "the goddess," *nꜣ-nṯr(.w)* "the gods"; the demonstrative "this" and the numeral "one" evolve into the definite and the indefinite article: Coptic *p-rôme* "the man" < "this man", *ou-rôme* "a man" < "one man"; periphrastic patterns in the order SVO supersede older verbal formations: Coptic *ma-re pe=k-ran ouop*, lit. "let-do your-name be-pure" = "your name be hallowed," as opposed to the synthetic classical Egyptian construction *wʿb(.w) rn=k*, lit. "shall-be-purified your-name."

Due to the centralized nature of the political and cultural models underlying the evolution of Ancient Egyptian society, there is hardly any evidence of dialect differences in pre-Coptic Egyptian.[16] However, while the writing system probably originated in the south of the country,[17] the origins of the linguistic type represented by earlier Egyptian are to be seen in Lower Egypt, around the city of Memphis, which was the capital of the country during the Old Kingdom, those of Later Egyptian in Upper Egypt, in the region of Thebes, the cultural, religious and political center of the New Kingdom. Coptic displays a variety of dialects that do not vary very profoundly: they differ mainly in graphic conventions and sporadically in morphology and lexicon, but hardly at all in syntax.

1.3 A brief look at Egyptological linguistics

Since the decipherment of the Egyptian writing systems during the last century (section 2.5), the grammatical study of Egyptian has been treated primarily within four successive approaches:[18] (a) the Berlin School and the recovery of Egyptian morphology; (b) A. H. Gardiner and the fixation of the canon for the study of the Egyptian language; (c) H. J. Polotsky and the "Standard theory" of Egyptian syntax; (d) a contemporary shift to functional linguistic models.

(a) To A. Erman and the so-called "Berlin School" modern Egyptology owes three major contributions: (a) the division of the history of Egyptian into two main phases[19] (called by Erman *[Alt]ägyptisch* and *Neuägyptisch*, roughly corresponding to "earlier" and "later" Egyptian respectively); (b) the basic identification of the morphosyntactic inventory of all the stages of the language; (c) the monumental *Wörterbuch der ägyptischen Sprache* (1926–53), as yet the most complete lexicographical tool available for Egyptian. The approach of Erman and his followers over three generations (K. Sethe, G. Steindorff, E. Edel, W. Westendorf) was in fact modeled upon a historical-philological method similar to the one adopted in contemporary Semitic linguistics, which also conditioned the choices of the Berlin School in terms of grammatical terminology or transliteration.

(b) Although very much in Erman's "neogrammatical" tradition, the contribution by scholars such as A. H. Gardiner[20] and B. Gunn[21] brought to the study of Egyptian a pragmatic approach derived from their Anglo-Saxon tradition; the characteristics of Egyptian are checked against the background of the grammar of the classical languages and of what has come to be referred to as "Standard European": if Erman and the Berlin School were methodologically "semitocentric," Gardiner and the linguistic knowledge he represented were "eurocentric," in the sense that the grammatical study of Egyptian was seen at the same time as the study of the differences between Egyptian and Western "mind,"[22] and its main purpose becomes the correct *translation* of Egyptian texts.

(c) The problem of the adequacy of an Egyptian grammar based on the theoretical categories of standard European languages became acute in the 1940s with the work of H. J. Polotsky,[23] whose broader reception did not begin before the late 1960s, and found its most complete treatments by Polotsky himself in 1976 for classical Egyptian and in 1987–90 for Coptic.[24] The basic feature of Polotsky's "Standard theory"[25] is the systematic application of substitutional rules for syntactic nodes such as nominal phrases (NP) or adverbial phrases (AP): most Egyptian verbal phrases (VP)[26] are analyzed as syntactic "transpositions" of a verbal predication into a NP- or an AP-node. But this syntactic conversion affects dramatically their predicative function. In case of a *nominal* transposition, they lose their predicative force altogether; for example, on the basis of the paradigmatic substitution between an initial verbal form (*jj.n=j m nʔ.t=j* "I came from my city") and a noun in initial position (*zẖ3w m nʔ.t=j* "The scribe is[27] in my city"), the structure of the former Egyptian sentence should be analyzed as "*The-fact-that-I-came (is) from-my-city." In case of an *adverbial* transposition, they acquire the value of a circumstantial predicate: in the sentence *z3-nh.t ḏd=f* "Sinuhe speaks," because of the possibility of paradigmatic substitution between the VP "speaks" and any AP (*z3-nh.t m nʔ.t=j* "Sinuhe is in my city"), the underlying structure is taken to be "*Sinuhe (is) while-he-speaks."

(d) In recent years, due to a certain extent to the increased awareness among Egyptologists of the idiosyncrasies of the Polotskyan system and of methodological developments in the field of general linguistics,[28] the Standard theory seems to have exhausted its innovative potential, being superseded by more verbalistic approaches, i.e. by interpretations of Egyptian syntax in which verbal phrases, rather than being "converted" into other parts of discourse, maintain their full "verbal" character.[29] The present writer understands himself as a member of this latter generation of Egyptological linguists. Although much of the recent production on this topic aims at clarifying the differences between the Polotskyan model and more recent trends,[30] which tend to pay more attention to discourse phenomena and to pragmatics, in this book I have tried to refrain from delving into the historical debate, preferring to suggest in each individual case the solution to a linguistic problem of Egyptian grammar that I find most appealing from a general linguistic as well as diachronic standpoint. In this respect, this book is probably best understood as a historical grammar of Egyptian within the theoretical models provided by the recent tendencies in Egyptological linguistics.

Further reading

Černý, J. and S. I. Groll. *A Late Egyptian Grammar*. Studia Pohl, Series Maior IV (Rome: Pontifical Biblical Institute, third edn 1984) [A structural grammar of "colloquial," i.e. scholastic and administrative Late Egyptian].

Crum, W. E. *A Coptic Dictionary* (Oxford: Clarendon Press, 1939) [The standard dictionary of Coptic, with very detailed philological references].

Erman, A. and H. Grapow. *Wörterbuch der ägyptischen Sprache* (Berlin: Akademie-Verlag, 1926-53) [Still the fundamental dictionary for Old, Middle, and Late Egyptian).

Faulkner, R. O. *A Concise Dictionary of Middle Egyptian* (Oxford University Press, 1962) [A lexicographical aid for the translation of Middle Kingdom texts].

Gardiner, A. *Egyptian Grammar, Being an Introduction to the Study of Hieroglyphs* (Oxford University Press, 1927; third edn 1957) [A detailed tool for the philological study of the classical language].

Graefe, E. *Mittelägyptische Grammatik für Anfänger* (Wiesbaden: Harrassowitz, fourth edn 1994) [A user-friendly manual for academic instruction in classical Egyptian].

Johnson, J. H. *Thus Wrote 'Onchsheshonqy. An Introductory Grammar of Demotic*. Studies in Ancient Oriental Civilization XLV (Chicago: Oriental Institute, second edn 1991) [A short, but comprehensive introduction to Demotic script and grammar].

Junge, F. "Sprachstufen und Sprachgeschichte," in *Zeitschrift der Deutschen Morgenländischen Gesellschaft. Supplement VI* (Stuttgart: Franz Steiner, 1985), 17-34 [The most modern presentation of the history of Egyptian].

Lambdin, Th. O. *Introduction to Sahidic Coptic* (Macon: Mercer University Press, 1983) [The standard academic handbook for teaching classical Coptic].

Polotsky, H. J. *Collected Papers* (Jerusalem: Magnes Press, 1971) [For the development of the "Standard theory" of Egyptian syntax].

Schenkel, W. *Einführung in die altägyptische Sprachwissenschaft*. Orientalistische Einführungen (Darmstadt: Wissenschaftliche Buchgesellschaft, 1990) [The essential companion for the study of the history of linguistic thinking in Egyptology].

2

Egyptian graphemics

2.1 Introduction

The basic graphic system of the Egyptian language for three fourths of its life as a productive language, i.e. from about 3000 BCE to the first centuries of our era, is known as "hieroglyphic writing."[1] This term has been used since the Ptolemaic period (323–30 BCE) as the Greek counterpart (ἱερογλυφικὰ γράμματα "sacred incised letters") to the Egyptian expression *mdw.w-nṯr* "god's words." Throughout Egyptian history, hieroglyphs were used primarily for monumental purposes, their main material support being stone or, less frequently, papyrus. For cursive uses the hieroglyphic system developed two handwriting varieties, called "Hieratic" (ἱερατικὰ γράμματα "priestly writing"), documented from the Old Kingdom through the third century CE, and "Demotic" (δημοτικὰ γράμματα "popular writing"), from the seventh century BCE to the fifth century CE. In a process beginning in Hellenistic times and concluded with the complete Christianization of the country in the fourth century CE, hieroglyphs and their manual varieties were gradually superseded by alphabetic transcriptions of words, and then of whole texts, inspired by the Greek alphabet with the addition of Demotic signs to render Egyptian phonemes unknown to Greek. The final result of this process is the emergence of "Coptic," the name given to the Egyptian language and its alphabet in its most recent form, which remained in productive use from the fourth century to the end of the first millennium CE, when it was superseded by Arabic as the common language of the country.

Unlike other writing systems of the Ancient Near East, for example Mesopotamian cuneiform, hieroglyphs were never used to write down any language other than Egyptian, except for their later adoption in Meroitic.[2] However, the so-called Protosinaitic inscriptions[3] of the second millennium BCE show that hieratic signs may have inspired the shape of Northwest Semitic alphabetic signs. As for Demotic, some of its sign-groups were adopted and phonetically reinterpreted in Nubia for the writing of Meroitic (third century BCE to fourth century CE);[4] this language is still imperfectly understood in both its grammar and its lexicon, but it certainly did not belong to the Afroasiatic phylum.

2.2 The basic principles of hieroglyphic writing

Egyptian hieroglyphs are a variable set of graphemes, ranging from about 1000 in the Old Kingdom (third millennium BCE) down to approximately 750 in the classical language (second millennium BCE), then increasing to many thousands during the Ptolemaic and Roman rule in Egypt, from the third century BCE to the second century CE. They are *pictographic* signs representing living beings and objects, such as gods or categories of people, animals, parts of the human or animal body, plants, astronomical entities, buildings, furniture, vessels, etc.

But these pictograms are not organized within a purely ideographic system; rather, they represent a combination of phonological and semantic principles.[5] An Egyptian word usually consists of two components:

(1) A sequence of *phonograms*, each of which represents a sequence of one, two, or three consonantal phonemes; hence their label as monoconsonantal (such as 𓅓 /m/), biconsonantal (such as 𓉐 /p-r/), or triconsonantal signs (such as 𓊵 /ḥ-t-p/). Phonograms convey a substantial portion of the phonological structure of the word: normally all the consonants, less regularly the semiconsonantal or semivocalic glides /j/ and /w/, vowels remaining for the most part unexpressed. Biconsonantal and triconsonantal signs are often accompanied by other phonograms, mostly monoconsonantal, which spell out one or two of their phonemes, allowing in this way a more immediate interpretation of the intended phonological sequence; these phonograms are called "complements." The phonological value of the phonograms is derived from the name of the represented entity by means of the *rebus principle*, i.e. by applying the same phonological sequence to other entities semantically unrelated to them. For example, from the representation of water 𓈗 **maw* is derived the phonological value of this sign as /m-w/. It needs to be stressed that frequently, in this process of derivation, only a segment of the original sequence of phonemes of the represented entity, usually the strong consonants (*consonantal principle*), is isolated to function as general phonogram: for example the sign for a house 𓉐 **pāruw*, is used for the sequence /p-r/. In later times, the consonantal principle was expanded by the so-called *acrophonic principle*, i.e. by the derivation of a phonological value from the first consonantal sound of the represented entity.

(2) The sequence of phonograms is usually followed by a *semagram*, called in the Egyptological custom "determinative," which classifies a word according to its semantic sphere: for example, a sitting man 𓀀 expresses the lexical realm of "man, mankind," a sitting man touching his mouth 𓀁 the domain of "eating, speaking, thinking, sensing," a scribe's equipment 𓏞 the area of "writing," a stylized settlement 𓊖 identifies the word as a toponym.

While some words of common use (pronouns, prepositions, a few nouns and verbs such as *rn* "name" or *ḏd* "to say") are written only phonologically, i.e. only with a combination of consonantal signs <r> + <n>, <ḏ> + <d> indicating the sequences /r-n/ and /ḏ-d/ respectively, many items of the basic vocabulary of Egyptian are expressed by semagrams which indicate their own semantic meaning. They do this *iconically* (by reproducing the object itself), through *rebus* (by portraying an entity whose name displays a similar phonological structure), or *symbolically* (by depicting an item metaphorically or metonymically associated with the object). These signs are called *logograms* (also labeled *ideograms* by Egyptologists): for example, the hieroglyph which represents the enclosure of a house 𓉐 is used to indicate iconically the concept "house" (**pāruw*); the sign representing a duck 𓅭 means "son" (**ziɜ*) by virtue of the phonetic identity between the Egyptian words for "duck" and for "son"; the cloth wound on a pole 𓊹, a sacred emblem placed on the pylons of Egyptian temples, through symbolic association means "god" (**nāṯar*). In order to distinguish the logographic use (𓉐𓏺 = **pāruw* = "house") from the phonological use of the same sign on the basis of the rebus principle (𓉐 = /p-r/, without any semantic connection to the word in which it appears), logographic uses are often marked by a stroke following the sign.

Egyptian writing also displays a set of twenty-four "alphabetic," i.e. monoconsonantal signs (table 2.1). Although these cover almost completely the inventory of consonantal and semiconsonantal phonemes of the language – the two exceptions being the etymological /ʔ/,[6] which remained unexpressed, and the /l/, originally conveyed by the graphemes <n>, <r>, and <n+r>, for which an autonomous sign, derived from the hieroglyph 𓃭𓏺, appears only in Demotic – hieroglyphs never developed into a genuine alphabet, but always maintained the original combination of word-signs (*logograms*) and sound-signs (*phonograms*). Also, unlike most other systems of pictographic origin, such as Mesopotamian cuneiform or Chinese ideograms, Egyptian hieroglyphs kept their original iconicity throughout their entire history without developing stylized forms. On the contrary, in later periods (section 2.4f) the iconic potential of the system was further unfolded by the addition of new signs and of idiosyncratic phonetic values for existing signs.

This shows that, historically, the development of alphabetic writing is not, as often assumed, the predictable outcome of a non-alphabetic system,[7] but the result of an underlying difference in the "philosophy of writing":[8] with the breakthrough of the Hellenistic cultural *koinē* and, eventually, with the final victory of Christianity in Egypt during the second and third century, when a changed cultural and religious setting favored the adoption of an alphabetic system, hieroglyphs were completely superseded by the Coptic alphabet, which was written from left to right and consisted of the Greek letters and of six (in some dialects seven) Demotic signs for the indication of phonemes absent from Greek. These supplementary letters are in all dialects ϣ = /š/, ϥ = /f/, ϩ = /h/, ϫ = /c/, ϭ = /kʲ/, ϯ = /ti/, plus Bohairic ϧ/Akhmimic ⳉ = /x/. In good Coptic manuscripts in Sahidic – the dialect of classical literature – a superlinear stroke (called in German *Vokalstrich*) marks a syllable which does not display a full vowel in the Greek sense of the word (i.e. ⲁ, ⲉ, (ⲉ)ⲓ, ⲟ, (ⲟ)ⲩ, or ⲱ), but rather a *schwa* or the syllabic pronunciation of a consonant; for example ϩⲱⲧⲃ̄ = /hoːtəb/ or /hoːtḅ/.[9]

Beginning with the late Old Kingdom, from about 2150 BCE, Egyptian developed a subsystem of hieroglyphic orthography to express a sequence of "consonant+vowel." From its beginning, but especially in the New Kingdom, this subsystem was used for the writing of words of foreign – mostly Northwest Semitic – origin, but at times also for the graphic rendition of Egyptian words. This procedure, known as "syllabic orthography,"[10] allowed the rendering of vowels by combining Egyptian monoconsonantal or biconsonantal graphemes displaying a sequence of strong+weak consonant (such as *k+ꜣ*, *r+j*, *p+w*) in sign-groups with specific syllabic values. Thus, glides (*'aleph*, *yod* and *waw*) were used to express vowels, in a procedure similar to the use of *matres lectionis* in Northwest Semitic. While regular correspondences are still elusive and disagreements concerning the vocalic values of specific sign-groups, therefore, are doomed to persist, the general characteristics of syllabic orthography are well understood. The system combines three principles: the so-called "Devanāgari principle" (from the name of the Indian writing system), according to which the unmarked vocalic value of each basic sign is "consonant+/a/" within a word or "consonant+/ø/" at its end (for example *šꜣ* for /ša/ or /š#/), with the optional additional glide read vocalically (i.e. *j* for /i/ and *w* for /u/); the "cuneiform principle," according to which the sign-group is to be read with the vowel phoneme it has in the underlying Egyptian word from which this sign is borrowed (for example the foal  *jw* for /ʔu/ or the

Table 2.1 Monoconsonantal hieroglyphic signs

Sign	Entity depicted	Transliteration	Phonological value
𓄿	vulture	*ꜣ* (aleph)	earlier /ʀ/ > later /ʔ/
𓇋	flowering reed	*j* (yod)	earlier /j/ > later /ʔ/
(1) 𓇌 or (2) 𓏭	(1) two reed flowers (2) two strokes	*jj* or *y*	/j/ as in English *yoke*
𓂝	human forearm	*ʿ* (ayin)	/ʕ/ as in Arabic *kaʿba*
𓅱	quail chick	*w* (waw)	/w/
𓃀	foot	*b*	/b/
𓊪	stool	*p*	/p/
𓆑	horned viper	*f*	/f/
𓅓	owl	*m*	/m/
𓈖	water	*n*	/n/
𓂋	human mouth	*r*	/r/
𓉔	reed shelter	*h*	/h/ as in English *he*
𓎛	twisted wick	*ḥ*	/ḥ/ as in Arabic *aḥmad*
𓐍	placenta	*ḫ*	/x/ as in German *Buch*
𓄡	animal's belly	*ẖ*	/ç/ as in German *ich*
𓊃	bolt	*z*	/z/
𓋴	folded cloth	*s*	/s/
𓈙	pool or lake	*š*	/š/ as in English *she*
𓈎	hill slope	*q*	/q/ as in Arabic *qurʾān*
𓎡	basket with handle	*k*	/k/
𓎼	stand for jar	*g*	/g/
𓏏	bread loaf	*t*	/t/
𓍿	tethering rope	*ṯ*	/c/ as in English *choke*
𓂧	human hand	*d*	/d/
𓆓	snake	*ḏ*	/ɟ/ as in English *joke*

hare over the water *wn* for /wan/); the "consonantal principle" of the conventional hieroglyphic system, in which the sign-group stands only for the consonantal phoneme regardless of the accompanying glide, i.e. it is a mere graphic variant of the consonantal sign (for example *bw* for /b/).[11]

Table 2.1 displays the set of Egyptian monoconsonantal signs, accompanied by their pictographic content, their Egyptological transliteration, and their phonological value. The "alphabetic" signs cover the entire set of consonantal phonemes of the classical language, which will be discussed in section 3.4. The only exception is /l/, a phoneme conveyed by different combinations of signs (see above). In the conventional Egyptological "reading" of an Egyptian text, which does not pay attention to the original pronunciation of the words, a short vowel [e] is inserted between the consonants of a word (*ḥtp* = [ḥetep]); semivocalic glides are mostly read like the corresponding vowel (*jmn* = [imen], *prw* = [peru]); pharyngeal /ʕ/ and laryngeal /ʔ/ are both read as [a].

The writing system also had a set of hieroglyphic signs used to convey logographically the numbers $10^0 \ldots 10^6$ and the fractions 1/2, 1/3, and 1/4.[12] To indicate natural numbers, signs appear repeated and organized sequentially from the highest to the lowest (356 = 3x100, 5x10, 6x1).

Here follows a specimen[13] of how the hieroglyphic system worked. The same text is presented in the four ways in which a hieroglyphic text could be written. Numbers indicate the sequence of the individual signs; phonograms are indicated in *italic*, logograms in SMALL CAPITALS, determinatives in SMALL CAPITALS and "quotes"; additional phonemes necessary to complete the grammatical structure of the corresponding words are added in parentheses.

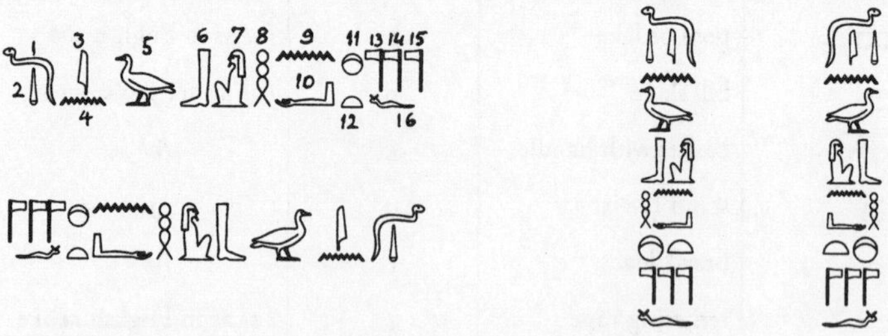

TRANSLITERATION: [1]*ḏ* [2]MDW [3]*j* - [4]*n* [5]*gb* - [6]*b* - [7]"GOD" [8]*ḥ* - [9]*n* - [10]*ꜥ*
[11]PSḎ - [12]*t* - [13-14-15]"GODS" - [16]*f*

TRANSCRIPTION: *ḏ(d)* *mdw(.w)* *jn gbb* *ḥnꜥ* *psḏ.t=f*

TRANSLATION: "To say the words by Geb with his Ennead"

CONVENTIONAL READING: [ɟed me'duu in 'gebeb 'ḥena peseɟe'tef]

Table 2.2 Samples of Hieratic and Demotic writing

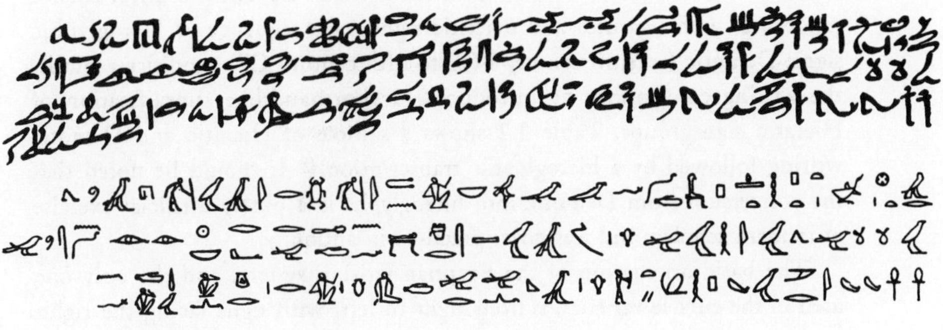

Hieratic of Dyn. XII (Pt. 4,2-4) with hieroglyphic transcription

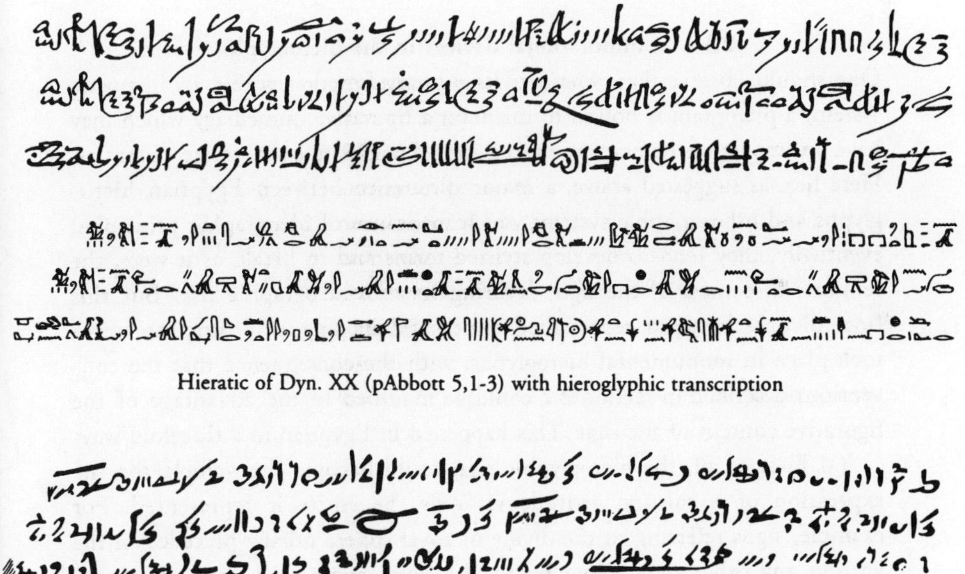

Hieratic of Dyn. XX (pAbbott 5,1-3) with hieroglyphic transcription

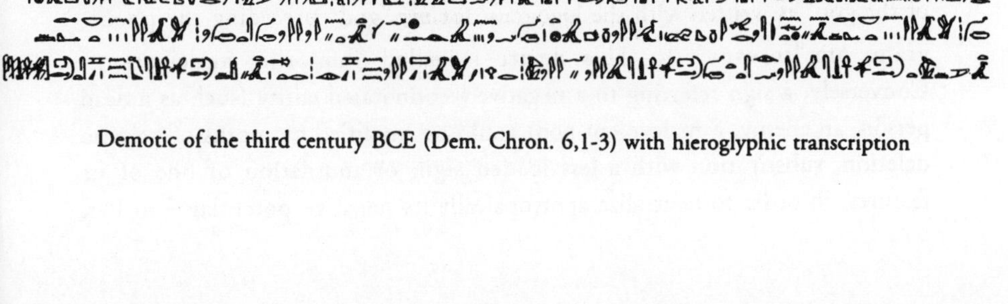

Demotic of the third century BCE (Dem. Chron. 6,1-3) with hieroglyphic transcription

The hieroglyphic system was used mainly for monumental purposes, more rarely (in a cursive form) for religious texts in the Middle and the New Kingdom. During their history, however, hieroglyphs developed two manual varieties: Hieratic (2600 BCE to third century CE) represents a direct cursive rendering, with ligatures and diacritic signs, of a sequence of hieroglyphic signs; Demotic (seventh century BCE to fifth century CE) modifies radically the writing conventions by introducing a shorthand-like simplification of Hieratic sign-groups. Table 2.2 shows a sample of Hieratic and Demotic writing followed by a hieroglyphic transcription.[14] It should be noted that the conversion from Demotic into hieroglyphs is a purely artificial exercise of modern scholars and was never practised in antiquity.

The basic orientation of the Egyptian writing system, and the only one used in the cursive varieties, is from right to left, with signs facing the right; in monumental texts, as in the example above, the order may be inverted to left to right for reasons of symmetry or artistic composition.

2.3 Connotational devices in the hieroglyphic system

One should observe that, whatever its primary function within its linguistic system, a pictogram is bound to maintain a figurative immediacy which may have an impact on its perception as a sign, i.e. on its connotative potential. Here lies, as suggested above, a major difference between Egyptian hieroglyphs and other graphic systems which made use of ideographic principles: eventually, they tend to develop stylized forms and to break, as it were, the semiotic directness of the sign, favoring its non-ideographic use. But this final divorce between represented entity and its linguistic function never took place in monumental hieroglyphs, with the consequence that the conventions described in section 2.2 could be modified to the advantage of the figurative content of the sign. This happened in Egyptian in a threefold way:

(a) First of all, the hieroglyphic sign could become the vehicle for the expression of a cultural attitude vis-à-vis the entity it represented. For example, signs referring to the divine or royal sphere usually preceded in the writing any other sign belonging to the same compound noun, independently of their actual syntactic position: the word *ḥm-nṯr* "priest," lit. "servant of the god" is written with the logogram for *nṯr* "god" preceding the phonogram *ḥm* "servant": . This device is called "honorific anticipation." Conversely, a sign referring to a negatively connotated entity (such as a dead person, an enemy, a malevolent god) could be modified by means of graphic deletion, substitution with a less loaded sign, or mutilation of one of its features, in order to neutralize apotropaically its negative potential:[15] in Pyr.

566c[N] *wnm=f* "he eats," the determinative of a bodiless man who touches his mouth is apotropaically used instead of the more usual , in order to prevent the sign of a man from harming the referent of the third person pronoun, i.e. the dead King.

(b) Secondly, specific sequences of hieroglyphic signs could acquire a function as recitational instruction about the preceding phrase. This happens, for example, in the case of the expression *zp 2* "twice," "two times," which means that the preceding phrase should be read (i.e. recited) twice: *j.gr zp 2* "be silent, be silent."

(c) Thirdly, the array of functional values of a specific sign could be expanded beyond the limits of the fixed convention: a sign could be given a different phonological value from the traditionally established one(s), especially by using it to indicate only the first consonantal phoneme of the corresponding word (*acrophonic principle*). The idiosyncratic use of the sign was bound to attract the observer's attention to the sign itself, opening the way to symbolic interpretations of its figurative content. This second type of connotational expansion of the hieroglyphic system is found sporadically from the Old Kingdom onward, with the emergence of "cryptographic" solutions,[16] but developed dramatically in Ptolemaic times, leading to a radical change in the laws regulating the use of hieroglyphs.

2.4 The historical development of Egyptian writing

The principles described in section 2.2 and the devices discussed in section 2.3 characterize the entire hieroglyphic writing and its manual derivatives in their historical development. They represent the common denominator of this system from its onset at the end of the predynastic period (about 3100 BCE) to the final disappearence of hieroglyphs and Demotic in the fourth and fifth century CE. But in these 3500 years a number of typological evolutions affected the Egyptian writing systems; they correspond to slight modifications or adjustments in the underlying "philosophy of writing." While the principles described above basically apply to each of these typological stages, innovations concern the historical emergence of changes in their *distribution*; these changes are sufficiently meaningful to justify a treatment of the resulting graphic form as a new "type" of hieroglyphic or derivative writing. What is even more significant is that these typological changes take place in concomitance with specific historical events which themselves represent major turning points in other aspects of Egypt's cultural life as well. Accordingly, one can observe a succession of six typological phases in the history of Egyptian writing: (a) the archaic period, (b) the Old Kingdom system, (c) the classical model, (d) the Ramesside orthography, (e) Demotic, (f) the Ptolemaic system.

(a) *The archaic period*. The historical event with which the emergence of writing in Egypt is traditionally associated is the gradual development of a centralized system of government covering the entire country, or at least a large portion thereof: this is the so-called "unification" of Egypt and the parallel emergence of an Egyptian state. Although the details are by no means clear,[17] this historical phase runs simultaneously with the development of a writing system from the last kings of the predynastic period at Abydos (Scorpion, Iri-hor, Ka, Narmer) at the end of the fourth millennium to the establishment of a rather complete set of mono- and biconsonantal phonograms by the end of Dyn. III (about 2700 BCE). In these early inscriptions on seals, seal impressions, palettes, short funerary stelae and other monuments pertaining to the royal or administrative sphere,[18] phonological and semantic principles are already intertwined, with a high number of signs functioning as logograms. For example, the name of the last predynastic king Narmer (about 3000 BCE), in Egyptian *nʿr-mr* "striking catfish (?)" is written with the logogram  *nʿr* "catfish" followed by the biconsonantal sign  indicating the two phonemes /m-r/: this latter sign is a pictogram representing a chisel and bears no transparent etymological connection to its use as phonogram in the word *mr* "sick": the reading is derived by means of the rebus principle. In the archaic writing, the notation of each word allows a degree of flexibility and a variety of options, with more than one concomitant writing for one concept: a possible example is offered by the rosette  *ḥrrt* and the falcon  *ḥrw*, which are both used as alternative writings for the word *ḥrw* "Horus," i.e. "the king."

(b) *The Old Kingdom*. With the emergence of a society strongly founded upon what has been described as "the bureaucratic mind,"[19] the quantity and the complexity of written documents expands dramatically (Dyn. IV–VI, 2650–2150 BCE). From this period we have a wealth of texts exhibiting a full-fledged writing system based on a systematic, rather than random application of the principles described in section 2.2. The inventory of signs is slightly over a thousand and the possibility of substitute writings for the same word is reduced in the case of logograms, but maintained for the phonetic signs: 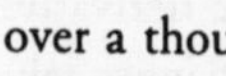 *s-ḏ-sḏm-m*, 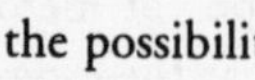 *s-ḏ-m-sḏm*, 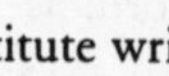 *s-ḏ-sḏm*, and 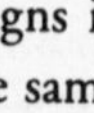 *s-sḏm* are all alternate options for *sḏm* "to hear." Frequent use is made of phonetic complementation both preceding and following the main sign. Texts from this period are mainly documents pertaining to the administration of royal funerary domains, legends on the walls of private tombs of the élite in the necropoleis of the Memphite area, autobiographies on the external walls of the rock-cut tombs in Upper Egypt, and the theological corpus of the "Pyramid Texts" in the burial chambers of the royal tombs from the end of Dyn. V (about 2330 BCE) through the end of the Old Kingdom.

(c) *The classical system*. In the Middle Kingdom (2050–1750 BCE), the authority of the royal court is reaffirmed after about a century of centrifugal tendencies towards provincial centers of power ("First Intermediate Period," 2150–2050 BCE). A newly developed school system for the education of the bureaucratic élite fixes Egyptian orthography by reducing the number of graphic renditions conventionally allowed for any given word: while in the Old Kingdom the spectrum of scribal possibilities was relatively broad, only one or two of the potential options are now selected as the received written form(s) of the word. This conventional orthography of the word usually consists either of a logogram (for the most basic nouns of the lexicon) or of a sequence of phonograms, often complementized, followed by a determinative: for example /sḏm/+/m/+det. "ABSTRACT" for *sḏm* "to hear." When compared with the Old Kingdom system, logograms have become less common and slightly varying hieroglyphic shapes have been reduced to one basic form, for a total of about 750 signs.[20] The classical principles remain in use for monumental hieroglyphs as well as for manual Hieratic until the end of Dyn. XVIII (ca. 1300 BCE).

(d) *Ramesside orthography*. During early Dyn. XIX (from about 1310 to 1195 BCE), major changes affected the writing conventions of hieroglyphs and especially of Hieratic. In monumental texts, the space units within which sequences of hieroglyphs are formally arranged, i.e. the so-called "ideal squares," undergo an aesthetic readjustment: while in earlier epochs signs would contain either one larger sign (such as the owl /m/) or else two rows of flat signs (for example a snake over a human mouth /f-r/), two columns of narrow signs (such as a seat followed by a loaf of bread and a house for the word *s.t* "seat"), with a maximum of *four* flat narrow hieroglyphs (as in the sequence *ptpt*), they are now reorganized within a three-way structure, each "ideal square" containing now up to *nine* smaller fields: see the following example from a private tomb from Dyn. XIX,[21] where the small numbers indicate the order in which individual signs should be read.

Changes are even more significant in manual writing. Ramesside and late New Kingdom hieratic orthography is the product of two conflicting tendencies: on the one hand the need to guarantee the recognizability of words by maintaining in many instances their received orthography, on the other hand the desire to partially render in writing the conspicuous phonetic evolutions that had affected Egyptian since the fixation of classical conventions. The result is a constant interaction of the "ideographic" (i.e. historical) and the phonetic level, often within the same word: while the word *ḏr.t* "hand" is still written with the logogram "HAND" followed by the phonetic complement /t/ and the stroke which usually accompanies ideograms, in spite of the fact that by that time the word had lost the final /t/ (as in Coptic τωρε), when it is followed by the third person possessive pronoun the received writing is completed by an additional /t/ (written <tw>) to indicate its permanence in the pronunciation: "his hand" (as in Coptic τοοτϥ). Similarly, the classical spelling of *ḫpr* "to become," in which the phonetic complement /r/ accompanies the triliteral /ḫ-p-r/, is now often followed by a *new* phonetic complement /p/ (<ḫpr-r> + <p-w>), which mirrors more closely the contemporary pronunciation *[ḫa:pə] or *[ḫo:pə] (Coptic ϣωπε); the verb *mšʿ* "to walk" (Coptic μοοϣε) is written in pAnastasi I 22,1 with a new determinative, which is in fact nothing else but the traditional writing of the verb *šm* "to go" (now pronounced *[šeʔ], see Coptic ϣε) employed in a new function: <m> + <šmt> = *[maʔšə]. For the broader use of syllabic writing, which is now applied to the writing of Egyptian words, see section 2.2 above.

(e) *Demotic.* With the decay of a powerful centralized government in the first millennium BCE, centrifugal tendencies affect writing conventions as well. During Dyn. XXVI (seventh century BCE), a new form of cursive writing called "Demotic" (section 2.1) develops at first in the north of the country, where the royal residence was located, and is gradually extended to the southern regions, where a form of Hieratic survives for about a century ("abnormal Hieratic"). Unlike Hieratic, whose sign groups mirror the shape of the original hieroglyphs rather closely, Demotic signs break away from this tradition and adopt a relatively small set of stylized, conventional forms, in which the connection to the hieroglyphic counterpart is hardly perceivable, and which are therefore more likely to be used in purely phonetic function. Determinatives have now lost to a large extent their function as lexical classifiers. While the demotic system was neither syllabic nor alphabetical, and precisely because the limited number of shapes it used to represent the language required a high degree of professional training on the part of the Late Period scribes, its development marks for Egypt the beginning of a divorce between monumental and cursive writing which will have a dramatic impact on the evolution of the hieroglyphic system as well.

Demotic remained in administrative and literary use until the end of the Roman period; the last dated text gives the year 452 CE.[22]

(f) *The Ptolemaic system.* The increasing consciousness of the symbolic potential inherent in the relation between the signs used to write words and the semantic meaning of the words themselves led already in the Late Period (from Dyn. XXI, ca. 1000 BCE) but particularly in Ptolemaic and Roman times (fourth century BCE to third century CE) to the development of previously unknown phonetic values and also of so-called cryptographic solutions.[23] This evolution, which originated in priestly circles and remained until the end the monopoly of a very restricted intellectual community, threatened on the one hand the accessibility of the system, favoring a dramatic increase in the number of signs, which now reaches many thousands;[24] on the other hand, it exploited the full array of potential meanings of the individual hieroglyphs, making the system more perfect as a pictorial-linguistic form (see section 2.3). And it is exactly this radical change in the nature of the writing system in the Greco-Roman period which is at the origin of the view, held in the Western world from Late Antiquity to the emergence of modern Egyptology (and still surviving to the present day in some aspects of popular culture), of the "symbolic", rather than functional character of the hieroglyphic writing: one need only think of the decorative use of Egyptian hieroglyphs during the Renaissance and the Neoclassical period in Europe.[25]

Unlike earlier conventions, the Ptolemaic system makes abundant use of orthographic, rather than phonetic puns, i.e. of associations of meaning based upon the writing of a word rather the identity of pronunciation between individual hieroglyphs: for example, the signs  and were used in the classical system only to indicate the phonograms /g-s/ and /f/ respectively; in Ptolemaic Egyptian, they are creatively combined to represent the two verbs *ʿq* "to enter" (with the *f*-snake "entering" the *gs*-sign) and *prj* "to come out" (with the snake "coming out" of the *gs*-sign): *'q* "to enter" and *prj* "to exit." The most fundamental criterion followed in this functional expansion of the classical system is the "consonantal principle,"[26] according to which pluriconsonantal signs may acquire a new value: this new value is either based upon the phonetically strongest consonants of the sign (for example the triliteral sign *nfr* may acquire the values /n/ or /f/) or upon the coalescence of homorganic sounds (such as the labials /p/ and /b/ in the sign *jb*, which can be used to indicate /p/) or of neighboring consonants (for example *jmn* for /j-m/). However, the so-called "acrophonic principle," according to which only the first consonant of a pluriconsonantal sign is kept, regardless of its phonetic strength, was applied in some religious contexts[27] and played a higher role in the development of Ptolemaic "cryptography,"[28] i.e. of a form of figurative writing in which the name of a god is written with (and at the same time his theological qualities iconically evoked by) specific hieroglyphic signs used alphabetically. Let us take for example the sequence for the name of the god Khnum.[29] Here the scarab, which is usually read *ḫpr*, is used with the acrophonic value *ḫ*, the lizard (unusual in this shape in the classical system)[30] with the value *n*, and the feather, originally *mꜣ'*, with the acrophonic value *m*; at the same time, this combination of signs evokes specific qualities of the god: his assimilation to the sun god Re through the scarab, to the funerary god Nehebkau through the reptile, and to the principle of Maat (truth, justice) through the feather. Cryptography, which had been sporadically used in religious contexts from the Old Kingdom onward,[31] is culturally similar to the "isopsephy" of classical antiquity and to the Jewish *qabbālâh*, i.e. to a numeric value attributed to alphabetic letters. With very few exceptions,[32] the Ptolemaic system was applied solely to monumental writing.

2.5 The end of the system and its rediscovery

We saw above that already in Hellenistic times there are sporadic instances of a Demotic text accompanied by Greek transcriptions; aimed at favoring a correct pronunciation, these reading helps are the sign of a divorce between Egyptian culture and its traditional writing systems. Gradually, the use of Greek transcriptions became more frequent: the first two centuries of our era saw the development of a whole corpus of mostly magical Egyptian texts in Greek letters (with the addition of Demotic signs to supplement it when phonologically required), known in the literature as "Old Coptic." To this cultural milieu we must also ascribe the only lengthy Egyptian text in Greek

Table 2.3 The Coptic alphabet

Sign	Conventional transliteration	Phon. value (section 3.6)	Coptic name of the letter (of Greek or Demotic origin)
ⲁ	*a*	/a/, /ʔ/	ⲁⲗⲫⲁ
ⲃ	*b*	/b/	ⲃⲏⲧⲁ, ⲃⲓⲇⲁ
ⲅ	*g*	/g/	ⲅⲁⲙⲙⲁ
ⲇ	*d*	/d/	ⲇⲗ̄ⲇⲁ, ⲇⲁⲗⲇⲁ
ⲉ	*e*	/e/, /ʔ/	ⲉⲓ, ⲉⲓⲉ
ⲍ	*z*	/z/	ⲍⲏⲧⲁ, ⲍⲓⲧⲁ, ⲍⲁⲧⲁ
ⲏ	*ê*	/e:/, /ʔ/	ϩⲏⲧⲁ, ⲏⲧⲁ, ϩⲁⲧⲉ
ⲑ	*th*	/th/ /t^h/ (Bohairic)	ⲑⲏⲧⲁ, ⲑⲓⲧⲁ, ⲑⲉⲑⲉ
ⲓ, ⲉⲓ	*i*	/i/	ⲓⲱⲧⲁ, ⲓⲟⲧⲁ, ⲓⲁⲩⲇⲁ
ⲕ	*k*	/k/, /g/	ⲕⲁⲡⲡⲁ, ⲕⲁⲡⲁ
ⲗ	*l*	/l/	ⲗⲁⲩⲇⲁ, ⲗⲁⲩⲗⲁ
ⲙ	*m*	/m/	ⲙⲏ, ⲙⲉ, ⲙⲓ
ⲛ	*n*	/n/	ⲛⲛⲏ, ⲛⲉ, ⲛⲓ
ⲝ	*ks*	/ks/	ⲝⲓ
ⲟ	*o*	/o/, /ʔ/	ⲟⲩ, ⲟ
ⲡ	*p*	/p/	ⲡⲓ
ⲣ	*r*	/r/	ⲣⲱ, ϩⲣⲟ, ⲣⲟ
ⲥ	*s*	/s/	ⲥⲏⲙⲙⲁ, ⲥⲓⲙⲁ
ⲧ	*t*	/t/, /d/	ⲧⲁⲩ
ⲩ, ⲟⲩ	*u*	/u/, /w/	ϩⲉ, ⲩⲉ, ⲩⲁ
ⲫ	*ph*	/ph/ /p^h/ (Bohairic)	ⲫⲓ
ⲭ	*kh*	/kh/ /k^h/ (Bohairic)	ⲭⲓ
ⲯ	*ps*	/ps/	ⲯⲓ
ⲱ	*ô*	/o:/, /ʔ/	ⲱ, ⲁⲩ, ⲱⲟⲩ
ϣ	*š*	/š/	ϣⲁⲓ, ϣⲉⲓ
ϥ	*f*	/f/	ϥⲁⲓ, ϥⲉⲓ
ϧ	*x* (Bohairic)	/x/	ϧⲁⲓ, ϧⲉⲓ
ⳉ	*x* (Akhmimic)	/x/	No name recorded
ϩ	*h*	/h/	ϩⲟⲣⲓ
ϫ	*j*	/c/, /ɟ/	ϫⲁⲛϫⲓⲁ, ϫⲉⲛϫⲉ
ϭ	*c*	/k^j/ /c^h/ (Bohairic)	ϭⲓⲙⲁ
ϯ	*ti*	/ti/, /di/	ϯ

characters, namely pBM 10808,[33] in its grammatical structure a Late Middle Egyptian text, but displaying contemporary phonological outcomes. The pressure to adopt an alphabetic system increased with the christianization of the country, when religious reasons contributed to the divorce between Egyptian culture and its traditional writing system(s). In this respect, the third century CE represents the turning point: hieroglyphic texts exhibit a progressive decay both in their grammatical structure and in the formal appearance of the signs; the last dated hieroglyphic inscription is from the year 394 CE.[34] Demotic texts substantially decrease in number, Egyptian being replaced by Greek as a written language.[35] In the following century, the new convention, which we call "Coptic," appears completely established: the Egyptian language is now written in a Greek-derived alphabet, presented in table 2.3.[36] By the fifth century, the Egyptian élite had lost the knowledge of the nature of hieroglyphs: the *Hieroglyphiká* of Horapollo,[37] a hellenized Egyptian, offer a "decipherment" of the hieroglyphs fully echoing the late antique symbolic speculations.[38]

While the interest in matters Egyptian remained vivid in the West for the following centuries, it was only in modern times that the knowledge of the true nature of the writing system was recovered. In the seventeenth century Athanasius Kircher recognized the linguistic derivation of Coptic from the language of the hieroglyphs (which he still took to be a symbolic writing), and in the eighteenth century Jean Barthélemy suggested that the cartouches which surround some hieroglyphic words contain divine and royal names – an assumption which turned out to be correct. In 1799, during Napoleon's expedition to Egypt, the discovery of the so-called Rosetta Stone, a trilingual (Hieroglyphic, Demotic, and Greek) document from the Ptolemaic period found in the Egyptian town of Rosetta, provided the possibility to compare a text in two unknown writing systems (Demotic and hieroglyphs) with the same text in Greek; this event opened the way to the actual decipherment.

First methodological contributions were made by Silvestre de Sacy (1802), who laid down the criteria to be followed, and more substantial results were reached by Johan David Åkerblad for the Demotic section and especially by the English physician Thomas Young, who, however, did not progress beyond the royal names. The most decisive contribution to the decipherment of the hieroglyphs[39] was achieved by the French scholar Jean-François Champollion in his *Lettre à M. Dacier* (1822), and especially in the *Précis du système hiéroglyphique* (1824). On the basis of the writing of Greek names in the hieroglyphic text, Champollion was able to establish the presence of a phonetic component in the system, breaking away from the traditional symbolic approach that had prevailed in the West since the knowledge of this writing was lost in the first centuries CE. His point of departure were Ptolemaic royal names, traditionally written in hieroglyphic texts within a rope called "cartouche"  . After identifying the name of Ptolemy (Greek Πτολεμαῖος) in the sequence of signs 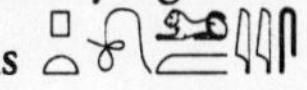, he was able to establish a correspondence between the phonetic values he had ascribed to each hieroglyphic sign, namely <p-t-o-l-m-y-s>, and the values they displayed in royal names on other Ptolemaic monuments, for example Cleopatra (Greek Κλεοπάτρα), spelled <q-l-i-o-p-3-d-r-3-t>: . Thus, he was able to achieve the major breakthrough for a complete decipherment of the system.

With the adoption and expansion of Champollion's work by Richard Lepsius from 1837 onward[40] the decipherment can be considered completed: scholarly attention is now directed towards the study of the features of the Egyptian language. Subsequent generations of students of the language could concentrate primarily on the treatment of Egyptian grammar in terms of both its synchronic features and its historical development (section 1.3).

Further reading

Davies, W. V. *Egyptian Hieroglyphs* (London: British Museum, 1987) [An introductory presentation of the writing system with many examples and references].

Gelb, I. J. *A Study of Writing* (Chicago University Press, revised edn 1963) [An idiosyncratic, but fundamental text for the study of Egyptian writing within a comparative frame].

Iversen, E. *The Myth of Egypt and its Hieroglyphs in European Tradition* (Princeton University Press, 1961) [For the history of the decipherment].

Schenkel, W. "Schrift," in *Lexikon der Ägyptologie* V, 713–35 [A systematic presentation of the features of the hieroglyphic system].

3

Egyptian phonology

3.1 Introduction

At the present state of our knowledge, a discussion of Egyptian phonology must be addressed primarily as an issue of *diachronic*, rather than synchronic linguistics. While it is possible to recognize regular patterns of sound change in the history of the Egyptian language as a whole, including in many cases Afroasiatic antecedents, the synchronic systems of phonological oppositions at any given time in the four millennia of the productive history of this language often defy a clear analysis. Furthermore, our models of historical phonology tend to hide many uncertainties behind the regularity of the reconstructed paradigm, conveying the misleading impression that for each of the different phases of the language (Old, Middle, and Late Egyptian, Demotic, and Coptic) we are able to establish a discrete phonological system.

The actual phonetic realities underlying the abstract reconstructions are even more elusive: the traditional pronunciation and transliteration of many Egyptian phonemes rest upon hardly anything more than scholarly conventions, and even for the relatively well-known Coptic, in which Egyptian sounds are rendered in a Greek-based alphabet, it is difficult to assess reliable phonetic values for some of the Greek signs and the Demotic graphemes that were added to the Greek alphabetic set.

In fact, the main reason for the difficulties in reconstructing the phonology of Ancient Egyptian lies in the nature of the writing system: Hieroglyphs, Hieratic and Demotic represent the mere consonantal skeleton of a word (and sometimes only a portion thereof), followed by indicators of lexical classes, the so-called "determinatives." Semivocalic phonemes are rarely indicated, vowels practically never. As for Coptic, in which vowels are indeed rendered, one should not downplay the methodological difficulty inherent in the widespread assumption of a phonological or phonetic identity between a specific Coptic sign and its original value in the Greek system.

Therefore, the reconstruction of the phonological inventory and of the phonetic values in any period of the history of Egyptian is bound to remain hypothetical, which motivates the constant use of an asterisk (*) before vocalized forms. The full phonological or phonetic shape of an Egyptian word can be reconstructed through a procedure in which three dimensions are checked against each other and mutually verified: the comparative Afroasiatic reconstruction,[1] the information drawn from contemporary sources in other (mostly Semitic) languages with a better investigated phonology,[2] and the laws of phonological evolution leading from earlier Egyptian to Coptic.[3]

3.2 Heuristic criteria

In spite of these difficulties, the study of Egyptian phonology has achieved significant progress since its inception in the late nineteenth century both in the assessment of sound values and in the reconstruction of prosodic rules. Scholars mainly rely on four procedures of linguistic reconstruction:[4]

Comparative Afroasiatic linguistics. Egyptian is a language of the Afroasiatic phylum, and the presence of established etymological equivalents offers a fundamental source for our reconstruction of phonological values. For example, since Eg. <qꜣb> corresponds to Sem. *qrb* meaning "interior part," one can confidently establish that Eg. <q> = /q/ and that <b> = /b/.

Contemporary transcriptions in foreign languages. Many Akkadian texts, especially from the archive of el-ʿAmarna (fifteenth–fourteenth century BCE), contain Egyptian words and phrases in cuneiform transcription. Although the phonology and the graphemics of Akkadian are themselves by no means fully decoded, these transcriptions provide a valuable insight into the contemporary pronunciation of Egyptian. For example Eg. <stpnrʿ> "the-one-whom-(the-god)-Re-has-chosen" (royal name of King Ramses II) appears in cuneiform as *šá-te-ep-na-ri/e-a*, a form on the basis of which one can both posit the contemporary Egyptian pronunciation as */saˌtepnaˈriːʕa/ and observe the correspondence Eg. <s> // Akk. <š>, both of which were probably realized as [s] or as a sound very close to it (at least in some dialects).[5]

Egyptian renderings of foreign words, especially of Northwest Semitic origin. This criterion, the symmetrical counterpart to the preceding one, provides an insight into the phonology of contemporary Egyptian while at the same time offering the possibility to verify scholarly assumptions on Semitic phonology. For example, Northwest Sem. **sōpēr* "scribe" => Eg. <ṯu-pa-r>: on the one hand, this piece of evidence raises questions about the phonological status and the phonetic realization of Eg. /c/, which is the palatal phoneme usually transcribed *ṯ* by Egyptologists, while on the other, it can also be used to shed some light on the value of the phoneme /s/ (*samekh*), which originally must have been an affricate [t͡s] in Semitic.[6]

The evidence provided by Coptic. The latest stage of Egyptian provides the broadest basis for the study of the phonology of older linguistic periods. For example, the three Eg. words spelled uniformly <w‘b>, namely "pure," "to be pure," and "priest," appear in Coptic in the lexemes ⲟⲩⲁⲁⲃ "holy," ⲟⲩⲟⲡ "to be pure," ⲟⲩⲏⲏⲃ "priest." This enables us to reconstruct three different vocalization patterns underlying the same graphic reality of hieroglyphic Egyptian: the stative **wă‘baw* "he is pure," the infinitive **wa‘ắb* "to become pure," and the noun **wī‘ab* "priest" (sections 3.4–3.6). At the same time, this piece of evidence raises questions of consonantism, i.e. the fate of the phoneme /ʕ/ and the reason for the alternance ⲃ vs. ⲡ in the Coptic forms as opposed to <b> in both cases in their Egyptian antecedents.

In the practice of Egyptian phonological reconstruction, these criteria appear constantly combined: while each of them, if considered individually, proves largely inadequate in order to determine a synchronic stage, together they convey a relatively homogeneous picture of the fundamental laws of Egyptian phonological development. What follows in sections 3.3–3.6 is a presentation of the historical phonology of Egyptian from its Afroasiatic roots to Coptic. Transcriptions from Egyptian and Semitic follow the conventions in the respective disciplines and are rendered in *italics*; transliterations of graphemes without reference to their phonological status are indicated in angle brackets (<x>); phonemes (/x/) and tentative phonetic values ([x]) are represented according to IPA conventions, exceptions being the use of /š/ for IPA /ʃ/ and of /ḥ/ for IPA /ħ/. The sign /v/ indicates a short vowel whose color cannot be reconstructed with any reasonable degree of accuracy.

At this point, a methodological warning is necessary: in the case of Ancient Egyptian and of many other "philological" languages known only through written records, the distinction between the *phoneme* as the distinctive minimal unit of the language (/x/), and the often much larger inventory of *sounds* ([x]) representing its physical realizations is less significant than in languages with a better known phonology: while scholars can strive for the reconstruction of the sound units of the language, the technical assessment of their phonological status, which would require in each case the minimal pair test, often proves a very problematic endeavor: on the one hand, our only source of information is represented by a complex writing system in which phonetic and semantic principles are combined; on the other hand, because of the restrictiveness in the use of writing in Egyptian society,[7] our knowledge of certain areas of the lexicon, and especially of their functional evolution throughout Egyptian history, is doomed to remain far from exhaustive.

3.3 The prehistory of Egyptian phonology

Before the emergence of Egyptian as a written language, a few adjustments within the stock of phonemes inherited from "Afroasiatic"[8] seem to have taken place. Three major evolutions from the original phonological stock characterize the Egyptian domain as it begins its recorded history:

(a) In the apical and interdental series, voiced **d, *z,* and **ð* develop into the pharyngeal phoneme /ʕ/,[9] probably going through an intermediate stage with pharyngealized lateral: **d, *z, *ð* (> **ɬ* >) > /ʕ/.[10] For example, Eg. *ʿr.t* "portal," Sem. **dalt* "door"; Eg. *ꜣʿʿ* "to speak a foreign language," Sem. **lɣz* (Ar. *laɣaza* "to speak enigmatically," Hebr. *lʿz* "to speak a foreign language"); Afroas. **ðuṗṗ* "fly" > Eg. *ʿff* */ʕuffvj/ > Coptic ⲁϥ, see Sem. **ḏbb* (Akk. *dubbum*, Ar. *ḏubāb*, Hebr. *zəbûb*).

(b) Among the liquids, the original opposition between nasal **n*, lateral **l*, and vibrant **r* underwent a profound reorganization, not yet fully understood in its specific details, in which a role was also played by dialectal variants. Afroas. **n* and **r* were kept as Eg. /n/ and /ʀ/ – the latter being the phoneme conventionally transcribed *ꜣ* by Egyptologists and traditionally taken to be a variety of glottal stop /ʔ/, but in earlier Egyptian probably a uvular trill;[11] Eg. *jnk* */ja'nak/,[12] Sem. **'anāku*, first person independent pronoun, or Eg. *kꜣm* */kaʀmvw/,[13] Sem. **karm* "vineyard." On the contrary, Afroas. **l* does not display consistent Egyptian correspondences nor is Eg. */l/ indicated by an independent grapheme, in spite of its almost presence in the phonological inventory of the language: Afroas. **l* corresponds to Eg. <n> in Afroas. **lis* "tongue" > Eg. *ns* */lis/, see Coptic ⲗⲁⲥ, Sem. **liš-ān*; to Eg. <r> in *jzr* */jazrvw/ "tamarisk," see Sem. **'aṯl*; to Eg. <ꜣ> in *ꜣʿʿ* "to speak foreign languages," see Sem. **lɣz*; and to Eg. <j> in Afroas. **lib* "heart" > Eg. *jb* */jib/, see Sem. **libb* or Afroas. **lwn* "color" > Eg. *jwn* */ja'win/,[14] see Sem. **lawn*. Presumably, proto-Eg. **l* merged with other sonorants in the dialect which eventually led to the written language, while still being kept in less normative varieties of the language: in the New Kingdom, when Later Egyptian became the written form of the language for the domain of administration and literature, a specific grapheme <n>+<r> was created in order to express the phoneme /l/. In Demotic, /l/ is autonomously indicated by a grapheme <l>, a diacritic variety of <r> = /r/.

(c) The Afroas. velar plosives **k, *g* and **ḳ* display two outcomes in Eg., probably motivated by the phonetic environment: either they are maintained as *k* /k/, *g* /g/ and *q* /q/, or they are palatalized into *ṯ* /c/, *j* /j/ and *ḏ* /ɟ/: see the second person suffix pronoun masc. /k/ < **-ka/-ku* vs. fem. /c/ < **-ki*[15] or the opposition between the two Eg. roots *wꜣḏ* (see *wꜣḏ* */wa:ʀiɟ/ "green"), which displays palatalization, and *jꜣq* (see *jꜣq.t* */juʀqat/ "vegetables"), which does not, both derived from an identical Afroas. root **wrḳ*.

(d) The phonemes corresponding to the "emphatic" series of other branches of the Afroas. phylum lost their phonological status in Egyptian, merging either with the corresponding voiceless fricative, as in the labial series, in which Afroas. **ṗ* develops into Eg. /f/: Afroas. **sṗɣ* "seven" > Eg. *sfḫw* */safχaw/, see Sem. **šb‘*, or with the corresponding voiced plosive: (1) the Afroas. emphatic dentals **ṭ* and **ṣ* merge into Eg. /d/: Eg. *dwn* "to stretch" */daːwan/, see Sem. *ṭwl* "to be long"; Eg. *wdpw* "servant," see Ar. *waṣīf*; (2) in specific phonetic environments, the Afroas. emphatic velars **ḳ* and **x̣* merge into the voiced palatal stop /ɟ/, the phoneme conventionally transcribed *ḏ* by Egyptologists: Afroas. **wrḳ* > Eg. *wꜣḏ* */waːʀiɟ/ "green," see Sem. **warq* "leaf"; Afroas. **nx̣m* > Eg. *nḏm* */naːɟim/ "sweet," see Sem. **n‘m*. As we saw in the preceding paragraphs, in absence of palatalization Afroas. **ḳ* is kept in Eg. as /q/, which was probably articulated as ejective [q'] (see section 3.6 below for the Coptic evidence): from Afroas. **ḳrb/ḳlb* > Eg. *qꜣb* "interior" (see Akk. *qerbum* "inside") and Eg. *ḏnb* "to turn" (see Ar. *qlb* "to turn around"). As for Afroas. **x̣*, when not subject to palatalization it merges into the voiceless pharyngeal fricative /ḥ/: Afroas. **x̣al* > Eg. *ḥr* */ḥar/ "on," see Sem. * *‘al*.

3.4 The phonological system of earlier Egyptian

At the beginning of its written history, i.e. during the historical period known as the "Old Kingdom" (2800–2150 BCE), one can assume that Egyptian displayed the phonological inventory indicated in table 3.1. Here, *x* indicates the traditional Egyptological transcription, /x/ the posited phoneme, [x] a tentative phonetic reconstruction (if different from /x/).

3.4.1 Consonants

Many contemporary scholars, following Rössler[16] and a long tradition going back to the nineteenth century, offer a different analysis of voiced plosives: since Eg. <d> and <ḏ> represent the heirs of Afroas. "emphatics" (**ṭ/ṣ* and **ḳ/x̣* respectively), these phonemes, rather than as "voiced" /d/ and /ɟ/, should be understood as "voiceless emphatic" <d> = /ṭ/ and <ḏ> = /ç̣/, without the possibility to determine whether the actual phonetic realization of the feature [+EMPHATIC] was one of pharyngealization or glottalization. Yet, because of the presence of *two*, rather than *three* phonemes in the respective Egyptian consonantal series, I prefer to analyze them as poles of a simpler binary opposition "voiceless" vs. "voiced."[17] But an important fact must be

Table 3.1 The consonantal phonemes of earlier Egyptian

CONSONANTS	BILABIAL	DENTAL	ALVEO-PALATAL	PALATAL	VELAR	UVULAR	PHARYN-GEAL	GLOTTAL
PLOSIVE								
Voiceless	*p* /p/ [p(^{h})]	*t* /t/ [t(^{h})]		*ṯ* /c/ [c(^{h})]	*k* /k/ [k(^{h})]	*q* /q/ [q']		<[a]> /ʔ/
Voiced	*b* /b/	*d* /d/ [t']		*ḏ* /ɟ/ [c']	*g* /g/ [k']			
FRICATIVE								
Voiceless	*f* /f/	*s* /s/ [s^j]	*š* /š/	*ẖ* /ç/		*ḫ* /χ/	*ḥ* /ḥ/	*h* /h/
Voiced		*z* /z/ [s']					*ʿ* /ʕ/	
NASAL	*m* /m/	*n* /n/						
VIBRANT		*r* /r/ [ɾ]				*ꜣ* /ʀ/[b]		
LATERAL		<[c]> /l/						
GLIDE	*w* /w/			*j* /j/[d]				

a. In very early Egyptian, the glottal stop [ʔ] was probably limited to few words and not expressed by an independent hieroglyphic grapheme; later on, presumably during the Middle Kingdom (2000–1750 BCE), /ʔ/ represents on the one hand the result of the evolution /ʀ/ > /ʔ/ (see the next footnote), on the other hand the outcome of /j/ > /ʔ/ between two vowels in post-tonic position (*/ˈbaːjin/ > */ˈbaːʔən/ "bad") and before an unstressed vowel in initial position (*/jaˈnak/ > */ʔaˈnak/ "I"). Kammerzell, in *Gedenkschrift Peter Behrens*, 186–87 and *LingAeg* 2 (1992), 169–75 prefers a consistent interpretation of <j> as palatal glide /j/ rather than as glottal stop /ʔ/.

b. In the later phases of early Egyptian (i.e. probably during the Middle Kingdom), the uvular trill /ʀ/, which is the Eg. heir of Afroas. **r*, progressively tends to acquire the realization as glottal stop [ʔ] – an evolution which appears almost completed in the New Kingdom (1550–1050 BCE); see, however, note 11.

c. In the hieroglyphic system, the phoneme /l/ is not indicated unambiguously: it is frequently conveyed by <n> and <r>, more rarely by <ꜣ> and <j>, see above.

d. For the writing of this phoneme, the following rules apply (with exceptions): /j/ is rendered by <j> in initial position: <jt> = */ˈjaːtvj/ "father," and immediately following a stressed vowel: <bjn> = */ˈbaːjin/ "bad"; by <jj> within a word, if /j/ immediately precedes the stressed vowel: <ḫʿjjk> = */χaʕˈjak/ "you will appear"; by <ø> at the end of a word: <jt> = */ˈjaːtvj/ "father."

borne in mind and accounted for: on the basis of both comparative evidence[18] and diachronic signals,[19] Egyptian *mediae* appear to have indeed neutralized the feature [+VOICED] and to have been realized – together with the uvular plosive /q/ – as ejective stops.[20] The feature [+EJECTIVE], whose existence can be inferred through Coptic evidence (section 3.6), brought these phonemes in the phonetic proximity of Semitic emphatics: most likely /d/ = [t'], probably also /ɟ/ = [c'], /g/ = [k'] and /q/ = /q'/. A possible explanation of this phenomenon of (especially initial) devoicing[21] is that the feature [+VOICED] must have become redundant under the competition of the optional aspiration which, at least in some varieties of the language and specific environments, characterized Egyptian voiceless stops: /p/ = [p^h] and /t/ = [t^h], probably also /c/ = [c^h] and /k/ = [k^h].[22] This is shown by the fact that Eg. /p/ and /t/ are rendered in the Greek transcriptions by ϕ and θ respectively: *ptḥ* */pi'taḥ/ "(the god) Ptah" > Φθα, and Eg. /c/ and /k/ often by σ and χ respectively: *ṯb-nṯr* */ˌcab'naːcar/ > */ˌcəb'nuːtə/ "(the city of) Sebennytos" > Σεβεννυτος, *bꜣk-n-rn=f* */ˌbaːʀak-vn-'riːnvf/ > */bokko'riː(nv)/ "Bocchoris" (lit. "servant-of-his-name") > Βογχορις, Βοκχορις, Βοχορινις. This aspiration is exhibited by the Bohairic dialect of Coptic (section 3.6).

In the sibilants, Old Kingdom Egyptian displays three phonemes, usually transcribed *z* (or *s*), *s* (or *ś*), and *š*. When subject to palatalization, this last phoneme corresponds etymologically to Afroas. **x* (which, as a rule, evolves to Eg. *ẖ* = /ç/): Eg. *ẖmm*, *šmm* "to become hot," see Sem. **ḥmm*. This seems indeed to indicate an articulation /š/ for Eg. *š*, although both Afroas. **š* and **ś* are continued by Eg. *s* (*ś*), i.e. by the second phoneme in the series listed above: see Afroas. **šuː* "he" > Eg. *sw* */suw/,[23] Sem. **šuwa*; Afroas. **śapat* "lip" > Eg. *sp.t* */'saːpat/,[24] Sem. **śapat*. It is possible, therefore, that Eg. *s* /s/ was characterized by a supplementary feature [+PALATAL], with an articulation close to [s^j]. Eg. *z*, on the other hand, is the heir of Afroas. **θ* and **s*, as shown for example by *jzr* */'jazrvw/ "tamarisk," see Sem. **'aṯl* or Afroas. **sulx̣am* "locust" > Eg. *znḥmw* */zun'ḥuːmvw/,[25] see Hebr. *sol'ām*. For systematic reasons, and in order to keep the symmetry with the ejective articulation of voiced plosives, I reconstruct this phoneme as /z/ = [s'];[26] the phonological opposition between /z/ and /s/ was neutralized by the beginning of the Middle Kingdom, at which time <z> and <s> had become graphic variants of the same phoneme /s/. However, the articulation and the phonological status of sibilants in the whole phylum remains a thorny issue of Afroasiatic linguistics.

The Eg. phoneme /j/ represents the outcome of Afroas. **j* (Eg. *jmn* "right side" > "west," the point of reference being represented by the sources of the Nile, i.e. the south, vs. Sem. **ymn* "right side" > "south," the reference point being the place where the sun rises, i.e. the east) and of Afroas. **l* (Eg. *jwn* "color," see Sem. **lawn*) when subject to palatalization. By the beginning of the Middle Kingdom, as part of the global reorganization of liquid phonemes which took place in Egyptian, with /ʀ/ > /ʔ/ and the neutralization of the opposition between /l/ and other sonorants, /j/ turned into a laryngeal glide /ʔ/ before an unstressed vowel in initial position (*jwn* */ja'win/ > */ʔa'win/ "color") and in postvocalic position following the stress (for example, *ḥjpw* */'ḥujpvw/ > /'ḥeʔp(vw)/ "[the god] Apis").

Among the guttural fricatives, <ẖ> = /ç/ is the heir of Afroas. **x* (Afroas. **xanam* > Eg. *ẖnmw* "[the ram-god] Khnum," Ar. *ɣanam* "sheep"), whereas <ḫ> = /χ/ is the outcome of Afroas. **ɣ* (Afroas. **wsɣ* "wide" > Eg. *wsḫ*, Ar. *wsʿ*), and <ḥ> = /ħ/ derives from Afroas. **x̣* when not subject to palatalization (Afroas. **sulx̣am* "locust" > Eg. *znḥmw*, Hebr. *solʿām*). The phoneme <h> = /h/ does not display any unequivocal Afroas. cognate.

3.4.2 *Vowels*

The vocalic system of earlier Egyptian can be reconstructed as follows:

Table 3.2 The vocalic phonemes of earlier Egyptian

VOWELS	SHORT	LONG
FRONT	/i/	/i:/
CENTRAL	/a/	/a:/
BACK	/u/	/u:/

The three vowels posited for earlier Egyptian are inherited directly from its Afroasiatic prehistory. While never spelled out in writing, vocalic phonemes can be reconstructed with a sufficient degree of systematic reliability on the basis of the four criteria formulated in section 3.2. For the earliest phase of the development of the Egyptian phonological system we do not assume the existence of the vocalic phonemes /e/, /o/ and *schwa*, which on the contrary play an important role in the phonology of later Egyptian (sections 3.5–3.6).

Unlike stressed vocalic phonemes, unstressed vowels cannot be reconstructed with any degree of reliability. For example, in the word *nṯr* */'na:car/ "god," while the stressed vowel is derived directly from Coptic ⲛⲟⲩⲧⲉ (with */na:/ > /nu:/, see section 3.6), the quality of the unstressed vowel in */-car/ can only be inferred indirectly through the feminine form *nṯr.t* */na'ca:rat/ > Coptic -ⲛⲧⲱⲣⲉ (with */ca:/ > /to:/, see section 3.6). The extent to which a whole paradigmatic class should be posited on the basis of analogy is still a matter of intense scholarly debate.

3.4.3 Syllabic structures

As a general rule, the opposition between short and long vowel is not phonological, but determined by the respective syllabic structure: long vowels appear in open stressed syllables, and short vowels in closed syllables and in open unstressed syllables. Major exceptions are represented by the presence of a long vowel in a closed stressed syllable in the infinitive of biconsonantal verbal roots and the possibility of long ($'cv:c#) or doubly-closed syllables ($'cvcc#) in final position. It is known that in many languages word-final position represents an ideal environment for "licensed extrasyllabicity,"[27] i.e. for the presence of a supplementary segment in addition to the standard constitution of a syllabic skeleton: $'cv:c# and $'cvcc# are in fact analyzable as $\sigma + \mathrm{c}]_{\omega}$, where σ indicates the syllable and $]_{\omega}$ the word edge. Accordingly, the following seven patterns of syllabic distribution are licensed in earlier Egyptian words (v: = stressed long vowel, v = stressed or unstressed short vowel, c = consonant, # = word boundary, $ = syllable boundary, ' = syllable affected by tonic stress):

1. $'cvc$ — *jnn* */ja'**nan**/ "we"
2. cvc — *rmṯ* */'ra:**mac**/ "man"
3. $'cv:$ — *ḥtp* */'**ḥa**:tip/ "pleasing"
4. #cv$ — *tpj* */**ta**'pij/ "first"
5. $'cv:c# — *mn* */**ma:n**/ "to stay"
6. $'cvcc# — *mdw.w* */ma'**duww**/ "words"[28]
7. $cv# — *stp.k(w)* */svt'pa:**ku**/ "I chose"[29]

A type of "contingent," rather than "licensed" extrasyllabicity can be invoked in order to explain another problematic feature of the earlier Egyptian phonological system as posited by current scholarship, namely the presence of final semiconsonantal glides /j/ and /w/ in bisyllabic and trisyllabic nouns much in excess of what is even remotely documented by written hieroglyphic or hieratic sources: for example <jt> =: */'ja:tvj/ "father," <hrw> =: */'harwuw/ "day," etc. It is advisable to take these glides to be extrasyllabic additions to final $cv# syllables

$$(\mathrm{cv})_{\sigma} + \mathrm{w/j}]_{\omega}$$

"contingent" upon specific phonetic requirements, such as the presence of a new syllabic rhyme following it, for example a suffix pronoun added to the basic form of the word: */'ja:t(v)/ "father," but */'jatjif/ "his father," or an older morphological marker of subject case: */nib/ "lord," but **/nibu/ > */ni:buw/ "the $\text{lord}_{\text{subj}}$."[30]

Table 3.3 summarizes the syllabic paradigms licensed in earlier Egyptian. Doubly-closed stressed syllables characterize only a certain number of plural forms of bisyllabic nouns; open unstressed syllables in final position are only found in the endings of specific verbal forms and personal pronouns – hence the use of parentheses to indicate these patterns.

Table 3.3 The syllabic structures of earlier Egyptian

SYLLABIC STRUCTURES	PRETONIC	TONIC	POSTTONIC
OPEN	cv	$ˈcvː$	($cv#)
CLOSED	cvc	$ˈcvc$	$cvc#
DOUBLY-CLOSED		($ˈcvcc#)	
LONG		$ˈcvːc#	

Independent of morphological patterns, the stress falls in Egyptian on either the ultimate (oxytone) or the penultimate (paroxytone) syllable of a word. The oxytone patterns[31] are #cvˈcvc# (*wbḫ* */waˈbaχ/ "to become white" > **ⲟⲩⲃⲁϣ**), #cvcˈcvc# (*jfdw* */jafˈdaw/ "four" > **ϥⲧⲟⲟⲩ**), #cvːc# (*ḏd* */ɟaːd/ "to say" > **ϫⲱ**), #cvˈcvcc# (*mdw.w* */maˈduww/ "words" > B-**ⲙⲧⲁⲩ**). The paroxytone patterns are #ˈcvccvc# (*stp.w* */ˈsatpaw/ "is chosen" > **ⲥⲟⲧⲡ**), #ˈcvːcvc# (*stp* */ˈsaːtap/ "to choose" > **ⲥⲱⲧⲡ̄**), #cvˈcvc$cvc# (*ḫprw.w* */χuˈpirwaw/ "transformations," Akk. transcription *(a)ḫ-pe/i-e/ir*),[32] #cvˈcvː$cvc# (*psḏw* */piˈsiːɟvw/ "nine" > **ⲯⲓⲧ**), #cvcˈcvc$cvc# (*wpw.tjw* */wapˈwutjvw/ "messengers," Akk. transcription *ú-pu-ti/ú-pu-ut*), #cvcˈcvː$cvc# (*wpw.tj* */wapˈwuːtij/ "messenger," borrowed in Meroitic as *apote*[33]).

Since the stress can only affect the last two syllables of an Egyptian word, the governing rule of syllabic patterns is known with the German term *Zweisilbengesetz* ("law of the two syllables"). For the prehistory of the Egyptian language, some scholars posit a situation in which, as in the related Semitic languages, the stress could also affect the antepenultimate syllable (*Dreisilbengesetz* , i.e. "law of the three syllables").[34] Following the loss of the short vowel in the open posttonic syllable, words displaying this syllabic pattern were subsequently integrated into the regular patterns with penultimate stress: **/ˈχupiraw/ > */ˈχupraw/ "transformation." Generally speaking, tonic stress played in the history of Egyptian a much more crucial role for the development of prosodic patterns than is the case in related Afroasiatic languages, for example Semitic, for which one could easily posit an original "free" stress. It would be preferable, therefore, to posit the "foot,"[35] rather than the individual word as the basic stress unit in Egyptian.

3.5 The phonological system of later Egyptian

By the end of the New Kingdom (1550–1000 BCE), the phonological system described in the preceding section had undergone a certain number of developments which modified all its components. The phonology of later Egyptian is known to us more precisely than the hypothetical reconstruction of earlier Egyptian thanks primarily to the cuneiform transcriptions of Egyptian words and phrases. The major changes can be delineated as follows:

3.5.1 Consonants

From the velar to the dental series, oppositions between voiced and voiceless phonemes become gradually neutralized: *tꜣ.wj* */ˈtaʀwvj/ > Akk. transcription *-ta-a-wa* "the Two Lands" vs. *dbn* */ˈdiːban/ > Akk. transcription *ti-ba-an* "*dbn*-weight."[36]

While palatal phonemes are regularly kept in a number of lexemes, they often move to the frontal portion of the oral cavity and acquire a dental realization: *psḏw* */piˈsiːɟaw/ > Akk. transcription *pi/e-ši-iṭ* "nine."[37]

The dental phonemes /t/ and /r/ and the glides /j/ and /w/ undergo a process of lenition to /ʔ/ at the end of a stressed syllable, and eventually to /ø/ at the end of a word:[38] *pḏ.t* */ˈpiːɟat/ > Akk. transcription *-pi-ta* "bow"; *hnw* */ˈhiːnaw/ > Akk. transcription *ḫi-na* "jar"; *mrjw* */ˈmarjiw/ > Akk. transcription *ma-aʼ-ia-*, *ma-a-i-* "beloved."[39]

The uvular trill /ʀ/ completes its evolution to glottal stop /ʔ/, merging with /ʔ/ < /j/ (see section 3.4): indirect evidence of this evolution can be drawn from the fact that while in the execration texts of the Middle Kingdom the writings <ʻkꜣm> and <jjjꜣmt> render the Sem. anthroponym **ʻakram* (Hebrew *ʻokrān*) and toponym **yarmuta* (Hebrew *yarmût*) respectively,[40] in the syllabic writing of the New Kingdom <ꜣ> has come to indicate the *a*-vowel.[41]

3.5.2 Vowels

Major developments alter the vocalic system of Egyptian during the late New Kingdom, after the reign of Ramses II, i.e. from around 1200 BCE onward. Parallel to the so-called "Canaanite vowel shift" in contemporary Northwest Semitic, long stressed */ˈaː/ becomes */ˈoː/: *ḥrw* "(the god) Horus" */ˈḥaːruw/ > */ˈḥoːrə/ (Akk. transcription of the Neo-Assyrian period *-ḫuru-*).[42] This sound change provokes other adjustments within the system, notably the change of long stressed */ˈuː/ to */ˈeː/: *šnj* "tree" */ˈšuːnvj/ > */ˈšeːnə/ (Akk. transcription of the Neo-Assyrian period *-sini*).[43]

In the early New Kingdom, short stressed */ˈi/ had become */ˈe/: see the anthroponym *mnj* "Menes" */maˈnij/ > */maˈneʔ/ (Akk. transcription *ma-né-e*);

at a later date, probably around 1000–800 BCE, short stressed */e/ < */i/ and */u/ merged into */e/: see the toponym *ḏ'n.t* "Tanis" */ɟuʕnat/, borrowed in Hebrew at a time when the original vocalization was still productive (**ṣu'n* > *ṣō'an*), but transcribed as *ṣe-e'-nu/ṣa-a'-nu* in the Neo-Assyrian period.[44]

Unstressed vowels, especially in posttonic position, merged into the mid central */ə/ (the so-called *schwa*): *r'w* "(the god) Re" */riːʕuw/ > */reːʕə/ (Akk. transcriptions *-ri-ia, -re-e*), *nfr* "good" */naːfir/ > */naːfə/ (Akk. transcription *-na-a-pa*), *mꜣ'.t* "truth" */muʀʕat/ > */muʔʕə/ (Akk. transcription *-mu-a*).[45]

A phonetic evolution which probably did not affect the phonological level is */iː/ > *[eː] in proximity of /ʕ/ and /j/: *w'w* "soldier" */wiːʕiw/ (Akk. transcription *ú-i-ú*) > *['weːʕə] (later transcriptions *ú-e-eḫ, ú-e-e, ú-e-ú*); *mḥj.t* "Northwind" */ma'ḥiːjvt/ > *[mə'ḥeːʔ] (Akk. transcription *-ma-ḫe-e*).[46]

One can, therefore, posit for later Egyptian around 1000 BCE the vocalic system presented in table 3.4. While at the phonetic level the vocalic sounds have indeed evolved from the earlier system presented in section 3.4, the number of vocalic phonemes (six) remains unchanged.

Table 3.4 The vocalic phonemes of later Egyptian

VOWELS	SHORT	LONG
FRONT	/e/	/iː/
CENTRAL	/ə/	/eː/
BACK	/a/	/oː/

3.5.3 *Syllabic structures*

Because of the loss of the final dentals and of the semivocalic glides caused by a strong tonic stress, the prosodic system underwent a partial reorganization, with the emergence of previously unknown or poorly documented syllabic patterns.

The syllabic structure $'cvːc# could now occur in plurisyllabic words (in earlier Egyptian, this pattern had a restricted functional yield, see section 3.4.3): *mḥj.t* "(the goddess) Mehit" */ma'ḥuːjvt/ > */mə'ḥuːʔ/, Akk. transcription *-ma-ḫu-ú*, Greek -μχης (with */uː/ > η); *ḫmnw* "eight" */χa'maːnvw/ > */χa'maːn/, Akk. transcription *ḫa-ma-an*.[47] The same development affects the pattern $'cvcc#, previously limited to some plurals of the type **maduww*: *zꜣjw.tj* "(the city of) Asyut" */zvʀ'jawtvj/ > */sə'jawt/, Neo-Assyrian cuneiform *ši-ia-a-u-tu*.[48]

The fall of final consonants increases the presence of unstressed open syllables of the pattern $cv#, which in earlier Egyptian were limited to the endings of specific verbal forms and personal pronouns: *ḥrj-pḏ.t* "overseer of the troop" */ḥarij'piːɟat/ > */ḥəri'piːdə/, see cuneiform *a/i/uḫ-ri-pí-ta*.[49]

Table 3.5 The syllabic structures of later Egyptian

SYLLABIC STRUCTURES	PRETONIC	TONIC	POSTTONIC
OPEN	cv	$'cv:$	$cv#
CLOSED	cvc	$'cvc$	$cvc#
DOUBLY-CLOSED		$'cvcc#	
LONG		$'cv:c#	

3.6 The phonological system of Coptic

Unlike ealier stages of the language, Coptic, written in an alphabetic system derived from Greek, is documented in a number of closely related dialects.[50] These dialects, however, do not necessarily reproduce local varieties of the language: they represent, to a large extent, discrete sets of mainly graphic conventions for rendering Egyptian in an inadequate foreign script.[51]

Table 3.6 The consonantal phonemes of Coptic

CONSONANTS	LABIAL	DENTAL	PALATAL	VELAR	GLOTTAL
PLOSIVE					
Palatalized				ϭ /kʲ/	
Voiceless[52]	ⲡ /p/ [p(ʰ)]	ⲧ /t/ [t(ʰ)]	ϫ /c/ [c(ʰ)]	ⲕ /k/ [k(ʰ)]	<[53]> /ʔ/
Ejective		ⲧ /d/ [t']	ϫ /ɟ/ [c']	ⲕ /g/ [k']	
[Voiced]	ⲃ /b/ [β]	ⲇ /d/ [d]		ⲅ /g/ [g]	
FRICATIVE					
Voiceless	ϥ /f/	ⲥ /s/	ϣ /š/	<[54]> /x/	ϩ /h/
[Voiced]		ⲍ /z/			<[55]> /ʕ/
NASAL	ⲙ /m/	ⲛ /n/			
VIBRANT		ⲣ /r/[56]			
LATERAL		ⲗ /l/			
GLIDE	(ⲟ)ⲩ /w/		(ⲉ)ⲓ /j/		

The two major Coptic dialects are *Sahidic*, normally considered to reflect the Theban, upper Egyptian variety of the language, documented from the fourth century CE and representing the language of classical Coptic literature, and *Bohairic*, the dialect of the Nile delta, documented from the fifth century CE and progressively established as the dialect of the liturgy of the Coptic church. For the basic presentation of Coptic phonology I have chosen Sahidic, which is the dialect of classical literature. However, I shall refer to other dialects, especially Bohairic, whenever such references become necessary for the purpose of an historical or a typological analysis. Dialects are indicated by small capitals in superscript preceding the Coptic word: S = Sahidic, B = Bohairic, A = Akhmimic, L = Lycopolitan (alternatively called Subakhmimic and abbreviated A_2), F = Fayyumic. Where no indication is given, the dialect is Sahidic.

3.6.1 Consonants

During the first millennium BCE and the first centuries CE, Egyptian continued to undergo a number of phonological changes.[57] In the consonantal system, the tendencies described in section 3.5.1 led to a neutralization of voiced plosives in the dental, palatal, and velar series: the phonemes /d/, /g/ and /z/ are present only in Greek borrowings, the rare exceptions to this rule being the result of sonorization in proximity of /n/ (for example, ⲁⲛⲧ̄ vs. ⲁⲛⲟⲕ < *jnk* "I," ⲁⲛϫⲏⲃⲉ vs. ⲁⲛⲥⲏⲃⲉ < *ꜥ.t n.t sbꜣ.w* "school").

In the labial series, the situation is more complex: the voiced phoneme /b/, which by this time was probably articulated as a fricative [β],[58] is kept in all initial and medial positions (^{BF}ⲃⲱⲕ "servant," ϩⲓⲃⲱⲓ "ibis," ⲧⲃⲁ "ten thousand"), and in final position whenever it did not immediately follow the tonic vowel of a closed syllable in the earlier stages of the language, although this may indeed be synchronically the case in Coptic: ⲛⲟⲩⲃ < */naːbaw/ "gold." If /b/ followed the tonic vowel of an etymological closed syllable, whether in monosyllabic or plurisyllabic words, it became in Coptic voiceless /p/: ⲟⲩⲟⲡ < */waʕab/ "to be pure," ⲧⲁⲡ < */dib/ "horn."

Guttural fricatives of earlier Egyptian (especially /χ/) merge in Sahidic either into ϣ /š/ (for example *ḫꜣ* "thousand" */χaʀ/ > */χaʔ/ > ϣⲟ) or into ϩ /h/ (mostly /ḥ/ and /ç/, sometimes also /χ/: for example *ḥꜣ.t* "beginning" */ˈḥuːʀit/ > ϩⲏ, *ẖ(w).t* "body" */ˈçuːwat/ > ϩⲏ, *ḫrw* "voice" */χiˈraw/ > ϩⲣⲟⲟⲩ). But other dialects appear more conservative: Bohairic and Akhmimic keep a velar fricative /x/ (written ϧ in Bohairic and ⳉ in Akhmimic, for example ^{B}ϧⲣⲱⲟⲩ, ^{A}ⳉⲣⲁⲩ "voice"). Finally, the glottal stop /ʔ/, which represents on the one hand the regular development of */ʔ/ and */ʕ/, and on the other hand the result of the fall of final /t/, /r/, /j/ and /w/ after stressed vowel, is not expressed by an independent grapheme, but rather rendered by <ø> at the beginning and at the end of a word (for example ⲁⲛⲟⲕ /ʔaˈnok/ "I" < */jaˈnak/, ⲧⲟ /toʔ/ "land" < */taʔ/) and, except in Bohairic, by the reduplication of the vocalic grapheme when immediately following the stressed vowel of a word (for example ^{A}ⳉⲟⲟⲡ /xoʔp/, ^{SL}ϣⲟⲟⲡ, ^{B}ϣⲟⲡ /šoʔp/ "to be" < *ḫpr.w* */ˈχapraw/ "has become").[59]

Bohairic spelling conveys a traditional feature of Egyptian phonetics, namely the aspirated realization of stops, which are expressed by the corresponding *aspiratae* of the Greek alphabet: voiceless stops become aspirated when immediately preceding a tonic vowel, semivowels, and sonorant consonants (including ⲃ):

/p/, /t/, /c/, /k/ → ⲫ [pʰ], ⲑ [tʰ], ϭ [cʰ], ⲭ [kʰ] / __'v, /b/, /m/, /n/, /l/, /r/, /w/, /j/

Examples: Sⲡⲣⲏ vs. Bⲫⲣⲏ "the sun," Sⲧⲁⲓ vs. Bⲑⲁⲓ "this (fem.)," Sϫⲟⲉⲓⲥ vs. Bϭⲱⲓⲥ "lord," Sⲕⲟⲩⲁⲁⲃ vs. Bⲭⲟⲩⲁⲃ "you are holy." This phonetic rule proves that ϭ [cʰ] represents in Bohairic the aspirated variety of the palatal plosive ϫ /c/; the value of the sign ϭ in this dialect, therefore, differs from all other Coptic conventions, where it indicates the palatalized velar /kʲ/.

The Bohairic rule of aspiration, however, exhibits an interesting property: when /t/, /c/ and /k/ represent the outcome of voiced *d* /d/, *d̠* /ɟ/, *g* /g/ and of uvular *q* /q/, no aspiration immediately preceding the tonic vowel takes place:[60] SBⲧⲁⲡ "horn" < Eg. *db* */dib/, Bⲧⲱⲣⲓ ~ Sⲧⲱⲣⲉ "hand" < Eg. *d̠r.t* */ɟaːrat/, Bϫⲓⲙⲓ ~ Sϭⲓⲛⲉ "to find" < Eg. *gmj.t* */giːmit/, SBⲕⲁⲥ "bone" < Eg. *qs* */qes/; in pre-sonorant environments, on the other hand, the rule is upheld: Bⲑⲣⲉϥ- < *dj-jrj=f-*, Bⲑⲃⲁ "ten thousand" < *d̠bʿ* /ɟa'baʕ/, Bϭⲣⲏϫⲓ "dowry" < *grg.t* /ga'ruːgvt/, Bⲭⲃⲟⲃ "to become cool" < *qbb* /qa'bab/.[61]

This phenomenon can be interpreted by assuming that in spite of the forward movement of their point of articulation which took place in later Egyptian (section 3.5) from the palatal to the dental (*d̠* > /d/), from the velar to the palatal (*g* > /ɟ/), and from the uvular to the velar region (*q* > /g/), these three phonemes of earlier Egyptian preserved in fact in prevocalic position their ejective articulation down to Coptic: <d̠> =: /ɟ/ = [c'] > /d/ = [t']; <g> =: /g/ = [k'] > /ɟ/ = [c']; <q> =: /q/ = [q'] > /g/ = [k']. This justifies the use of <ϫ> and of the Greek *tenues*, rather than of the Greek *mediae* to indicate them in the writing: ⲧ for /d/ = [t'], ϫ for /ɟ/ = [c'], ⲕ for /g/ = [k']. On the contrary, etymological *t* /t/, *t̠* /c/ and *k* /k/, which were not ejective but aspirated stops ([tʰ], [cʰ] and [kʰ] respectively), maintained the aspiration in the environments described above. Once again, we can consider this aspiration graphically rendered only in Bohairic, but phonetically present in Coptic as a whole:[62] Sⲧⲁϥ vs. Bⲑⲁϥ "spittle" /taf/ = [tʰaf] < Eg. *tf* */tif/ = [tʰif], Sⲧⲱⲣⲉ vs. Bⲑⲱⲣⲓ "willow" /toːrə/ = ['tʰoːrə] < Eg. *t̠r.t* */caːrvt/ = ['cʰaːrvt], Sϫⲓ vs. Bϭⲓ "to take" /ciːʔ/ = [cʰiːʔ] < Eg. *t̠ꜣj.t* /ciʀjit/ > ['cʰiːʔ(ət)], Sⲕⲏⲙⲉ vs. Bⲭⲏⲙⲓ "Egypt" /keːmə/ = ['kʰeːmə] < Eg. *km.t* */kuːmat/ = ['kʰuːmat]. This points to a phonological, rather than merely allophonic status of the underlying opposition "voiceless vs. ejective,"[63] an opposition graphically conveyed only by Bohairic and displayed by the presence of minimal pairs such as ^{B}τωρι /do:rə/ [ˈt'o:rə] "hand" < *ḏr.t* vs. ^{B}θωρι "willow" /to:rə/ = [ˈtʰo:rə] < *ṯr.t* or ^{B}ϫη "dish" /ɟe:ʔ/ [c'e:ʔ] < *ḏꜣ.t* ~ ^{B}ϭη /ce:ʔ/ [cʰe:ʔ] "quince."

An indirect, but very cogent proof of their actual phonetic articulation as ejectives is offered by the fact that these phonemes behave phonologically as a sequence of "plosive + glottal stop" such as ^{B}πωπ "the account" (consisting of the definite article π followed by the lexeme ωπ), in which no aspiration of the plosive labial is displayed (*φωπ) because /p/ here does not immediately precede the stressed *vowel* /o:/, but rather the first *consonant* of the lexeme, i.e. the glottal stop /ʔ/: πωπ =: /pʔo:p/.[64] Indirect evidence of the ejective character of voiceless stops in Bohairic is also provided by a late medieval Arabic version of the *Apophthegmata Patrum* in Coptic script.[65] While in Arabic transcriptions of Coptic words voiced /d/ and pharyngealized voiced /ḍ/ are used as a rule to indicate <τ>, as in Copt. τεντωρε > Ar. *dandara* "(the city of) Dendera" – meaning that <τ> was neither articulated like Ar. /t/, which was aspirated, nor like Ar. /ṭ/, which was pharyngealized – <τ> and <κ> are used in this text to render Ar. /ṭ/ and /q/, and also <θ> and <χ> for Ar. /t/ and /k/ respectively. Since the feature [+ASPIRATED] is neutralized in final position (for example Eg. *zꜣjw.tj* */zvʀˈjawtvj/ > */səˈjawt/ > Copt. ϲιοογτ > Ar. *ʾasyūṭ* "(the city of) Asyut"),[66] it is not surprising that at the end of a word Ar. /t/ is sometimes rendered by Copt. <τ> and Ar. /k/ as a rule by Copt. <κ>. On the other hand, the letter <δ> =: /d/ = [d], which in standard Coptic appears only in lexical items borrowed from Greek, is used in this text to transliterate Ar. /d/. This asymmetric state of affairs seems to point to the fact that the letter <τ>, at least in a number of cases, stood for a phoneme exhibiting a specific phonetic feature in addition to voicelessness and lack of aspiration: both diachronically (section 3.4) and synchronically (see above), glottalization appears here to be the most likely candidate.

Therefore, as in the case of its Egyptian antecedent, the phonology of Coptic may actually exhibit a higher degree of complexity than is betrayed by a superficial graphemic analysis:[67] in our concrete example, we probably have to posit for the entire Coptic domain (although graphemically mirrored only in Bohairic) the presence of *three* stops in the dental, prepalatal, and velar region: (a) a voiceless series /p/ /t/ /c/ /k/, characterized by an optional aspiration; (b) a voiced series /b/ /d/ /g/, limited to Greek borrowings – with the exception of /b/ and of secondary sonorization due to the proximity on /n/; (c) an ejective series /d/ = [t'], /ɟ/ = [c'] and /g/ = [k'], which never exhibited aspiration and therefore resisted a merging with the corresponding voiceless phonemes. Graphemically, the voiceless series is conveyed by the Greek *tenues*

<ⲡ> <ⲧ> <ⲕ> and Coptic <ϫ> (or by the *aspiratae* <ⲫ> <ⲑ> <ⲭ> and <ϭ> in Bohairic in stressed prevocalic or presonorant environment),[68] the voiced series by the Greek *mediae* <ⲃ> <ⲇ> <ⲅ>, and the ejective series – limited to the Egyptian vocabulary – again by the *tenues* <ⲧ> <ϫ> <ⲕ>, but this time without the Bohairic change to the corresponding *aspirata* in stressed prevocalic or pre-sonorant environment.

The treatment of the glottal stop /ʔ/ also deserves attention. As was pointed out in section 3.5, later Egyptian /t/, /r/, /j/ and /w/ are dropped in final unstressed position, but become /ʔ/ when closing a syllable, often representing the only remnant of an unstressed final syllable of earlier Egyptian dropped in the later phase of the language. However, especially in final position after stressed vowels, glottal stops deriving from the development of final /t/, /r/, /j/ and /w/ are not treated exactly like etymological /ʔ/; one also finds slight differences in the treatment of /eʔ/ < */uʔ/ as opposed to /eʔ/ < */iʔ/.[69]

Different graphic solutions for /ʔ/ are adopted in the dialects. All of them display /ʔ/ = <ø> in initial position (see ^{SB}ⲁⲛⲟⲕ /ʔaˈnok/, ^{ALF}ⲁⲛⲁⲕ /ʔaˈnak/ < */jaˈnak/ "I"). To express a glottal stop following the tonic vowel in plurisyllabic words, all dialects except Bohairic exhibit the reduplication of the vowel's grapheme, whether the glottal stop belongs to the same syllable – the vowel being in this case short: /ˈcvʔ/ = <cvv>, for example ^{S}ⲧⲟⲟⲧϥ̄, ^{B}ⲧⲟⲧϥ /ˈdoʔtəf/, ^{F}ⲧⲁⲁⲧϥ̄ /ˈdaʔtəf/ < */ˈɟartvf/ "his hand," ^{S}ⲙⲟⲟϣⲉ, ^{B}ⲙⲟϣⲓ /ˈmoʔšə/ < */ˈmašʕvj/ "to walk" – or to the following syllable – the tonic vowel being here long: /ˈcvːʔ/ = <cv̄v̄>, see ⲟⲩⲏⲏⲃ /ˈweːʔəb/ < */ˈwiːʕab/ "priest." In this last case, i.e. if /ʔ/ is the first phoneme of a final syllable of the type $ʔvc# following a stressed syllable of the type #ˈcvː$, this phoneme is conveyed in most dialects by the reduplication of the tonic vowel, and in Bohairic by <ø>: ^{S}ϫⲱⲱⲙⲉ, ^{B}ϫⲱⲙ /ˈɟoːʔəm/ < */ˈɟaːmiʕ/ "book." But the presence of a glottal stop in this pattern must be assumed for Bohairic as well, since there seems to be a rule in this dialect that the phoneme /ʔ/ is always rendered by <ø>, regardless of its syllabic surroundings: examples such as ^{SB}ϩⲟⲟⲩ (rather than ^{B*}ϩⲱⲟⲩ) /hoʔw/ "day" show that the phoneme /ʔ/ determines here the appearance of the vowel <ⲟ> rather than <ⲱ>, as would be expected in the presence of a diphthong /ow/, see Eg. */maw/ "water" > ^{S}ⲙⲟⲟⲩ, ^{A}ⲙⲁⲩ, but ^{B}ⲙⲱⲟⲩ.[70]

In most words displaying the phonological sequence /ʔc#/, the glottal stop /ʔ/ derives from an etymological /ʕ/ or /j/ through metathesis: ^{S}ⲧⲱⲱⲃⲉ, ^{B}ⲧⲱⲃ/ⲧⲱⲡ /ˈdoːʔəb/ < *ḏbʿ* */ˈɟaːbaʕ/ "to seal," ^{S}ϫⲟⲟⲣ, ^{B}ϫⲟⲣ /ˈɟoʔr/ "to be strong" < *ḏrj.w* */ˈɟarjaw/ "he is strong." The reason for this metathesis in bisyllabic words ending in /ʕ/ or /j/ is found in the "contact law,"[71] which provides that a syllable contact A$B is the more preferred, the less the consonantal strength of the offset A and the greater the consonantal strength of the onset B; voiceless plosives display the strongest, low vowels the weakest consonantal strength.[72] Since Eg. /ʕ/ was originally an ejective plosive /d/ = [ṭ] (section 3.3), its degree of sonority, which is the reverse of the consonantal strength, was lower than that of a preceding fricative or sonorant phoneme; by turning into a voiced fricative /ʕ/ in *mšʿj*, it acquired, like the glide /j/ in *ḏrj.w*, a higher degree of sonority, favoring in this way the metathesis by virtue of the contact law. Let us consider the examples *mšʿj* **/maš$dvj/ and *ḏrj.w* */ˈɟarjaw/. The syllable contact š$d is rather stable, since the consonantal strength of /d/ is greater than that of /š/. When the sound change /d/ > /ʕ/ took place, **/ˈmašdvj/ became */ˈmašʕvj/, which is the form we posit for classical Egyptian. The syllable contacts š$ʕ and r$j, however, are rather unstable, because the degree of sonority of B (the voiced pharyngeal fricative /ʕ/ and the glide /j/) is higher than that of A (the voiceless fricative /š/ and the sonorant /r/ respectively). As a consequence, an adjustment of the phonetic environment through metathesis occurred, leading to the Coptic forms /ˈmoʔšə/ and /ɟoʔr/. An evidence in this sense is offered by the presence of a Demotic verb *mšd* "to wander," regularly kept in Coptic as ⲙⲟⲩϣⲧ̄ "to examine," most probably a Late Egyptian etymological doublet[73] of *mšʿj* in which the original Afroas. phoneme is maintained: at least in a few instances ⲙⲟⲩϣⲧ̄ occurs with the same meaning of ⲙⲟⲟϣⲉ,[74] a fact which strengthens the hypothesis that the metathesis was caused in similar cases by the "contact law" of phonological environments.

The phonetic contact law can be invoked to explain other cases of metathesis which affected the development of Egyptian and Coptic phonology: one of the plural forms of *nṯr* */naːcar/ "god" was */naˈcurw/.[75] A syllable such as $curw$, however, in which the consonant of the nucleus (/r/ = A) has a lower degree of sonority than the semiconsonantal coda (/w/ = B), is unstable. This instability favored the metathesis of the two phonemes -rw- > -wr- > -jr-, documented by the Coptic forms ⲛⲧⲁⲓⲣ /ntajr/ or ⲛⲁⲉⲉⲣⲉ /nteʔrə/ "gods" < */naˈtejrv/. In this way, we can posit a relative date for the sound changes involved in this evolution: the metathesis must have occurred *before* the sound change from the glide /w/ or /j/ to the glottal stop /ʔ/ took place.

This analysis of the phonological status of /ʔ/ in Coptic is confirmed by two facts: (a) The interesting graphemic opposition found in Bohairic between the writing <-ⲥⲓ> to express a final syllable /-cə/, as in [B]ⲣⲱⲙⲓ /roːmə/ "man" or [B]ⲙⲟϣⲓ /moʔšə/ "to walk," as opposed to the writing <-øⲥ> to express /-ʔəc/, as in [B]ⲙⲏϣ /meːʔəš/ "crowd," whereas in Sahidic both environments are graphically rendered by <-ⲥⲉ>: [S]ⲣⲱⲙⲉ, [S]ⲙⲟⲟϣⲉ, [S]ⲙⲏⲏϣⲉ. (b) The two graphic renditions exhibited by the unstressed syllabic structure $ʔəc# in Sahidic, namely <-v̄v̄cⲉ> as in ϫⲱⲱⲙⲉ /ɟoːʔəm/, but also <-v̄v̄c> as in ⲃⲱⲱⲛ /boːʔən/. There can be no doubt that these two patterns are phonologically identical: see on the one hand the Sahidic variant with final -ⲉ (^Sⲃⲱⲱⲛⲉ), on the other hand the identical treatment of the two structures in the other dialects: see ^Aϫⲟⲩⲟⲩⲙⲉ, ⲃⲟⲩⲟⲩⲛⲉ, ^Bϫⲱⲙ, ⲃⲱⲛ /ɟoːʔəm/, /boːʔən/.

A last problem is represented by the fate of the phoneme /ʕ/. Its existence, although not excluded, is in fact very doubtful. The graphic distribution of etymological /ʕ/ is identical with that of etymological /ʔ/, including /ʔ/ < /j/, /w/, /r/, and /t/, and scholars generally maintain[76] that it had merged with the glottal stop in later pre-Coptic Egyptian, leaving traces in Coptic vocalism, especially in the anteriorization of its vocalic surrounding: unstressed ⲁ instead of ⲉ or <ø> (as in ⲁϣⲁⲓ < *ʿšꜣ* */ʕiˈšiʀ/ > */ʕəˈšiʔ/ "to become many" vs. ⲥϩⲁⲓ < *zẖꜣ* */ziˈçiʀ/ > */səˈçiʔ/ "to write"), stressed ⲁ instead of ⲟ (as in ⲧⲃⲁ < *ḏbʿ* */ɟaˈbaʕ/ > */təˈbaʔ/ "10000" vs. ⲕⲣⲟϥ < *qrf* */qaˈraf/ > */qəˈraf/ "ambush").[77]

3.6.2 Vowels

Table 3.7 captures the vocalic system of Sahidic Coptic around 400 CE:

Table 3.7 The vocalic phonemes of Sahidic Coptic

VOWELS	UNSTRESSED	STRESSED SHORT	STRESSED LONG
FRONT			<(ⲉ)ⲓ> /iː/
		<ⲉ>, <ø> /e/[78]	
	<ⲉ>, <ø> /ə/		<ⲏ> /eː/
CENTRAL		<ⲁ> /a/	
	<ⲁ> /a/		<ⲱ> /oː/
		<ⲟ> /o/	
BACK			<ⲟⲩ> /uː/

When compared with the preceding phases in the history of Egyptian, the vocalic system of Coptic exhibits the further consequences of the Late Egyptian sound change. Late Eg. stressed */ˈa/ becomes /ˈo/ in the two major dialects: Eg. *sn* */san/ "brother" > ^SBⲥⲟⲛ, ^ALFⲥⲁⲛ, following the pattern of */ˈaː/ > /ˈoː/: Eg. *rmṯ* */ˈramac/ "man" > */ˈroːmə/ > ⲣⲱⲙⲉ, which had already taken place around 1000 BCE (section 3.5). Moreover, Late Eg. */ˈe/, whether from original */ˈi/ (as in *rn* */rin/ > */ren/ "name") or from original */ˈu/ (as in *ḫrw* */ˈχurraw/ "Hurrian" > */χel/ "servant"), becomes /ˈa/ in Sahidic and Bohairic, but is kept as /ˈe/ in the other dialects: ^SBⲣⲁⲛ, ^ALⲣⲉⲛ, ^Fⲗⲉⲛ; ^SLϩⲁⲗ, ^Aϩⲉⲗ, ^Fϩⲉⲗ.

These two developments in the quality of the short stressed vowels display a number of exceptions of phonetic (sometimes purely graphemic) character, generally motivated by specific consonantal surroundings. Thus, */ˈa/ is kept as /ˈa/ in the two major dialects and is rendered as <ⲉ> in Fayyumic before etymological guttural fricatives (^{SAL}ⲧⲃⲁ, ^{B}ⲑⲃⲁ, ^{F}ⲧⲃⲉ < *ḏbʿ* */ɟaˈbaʕ/ "10000"); conversely, */ˈa/ becomes /ˈo/ also in Akhmimic and Lycopolitan before etymological /ʔ/ and /ʕ/ (^{S}ⲉⲓⲟⲟⲣ(ⲉ), ^{B}ⲓⲟⲣ, ^{A}ⲓⲟⲟⲣⲉ, ⲓⲱⲱⲣⲉ, ^{F}ⲓⲁⲗⲗ, ⲓⲁⲁⲣ < *jtrw* */ˈjatraw/ > */jaʔr(ə)/ "river"). Also, the diphthongs */ˈaj/ and */ˈaw/, which regularly yield /ˈoj/, /ˈow/ in Sahidic and /ˈaj/, /ˈaw/ in the other dialects, appear written in Bohairic as <ⲱⲓ> (except in final position) and <ⲱⲟⲩ> (in all positions) respectively: ^{S}ⲉⲣⲟⲓ, ⲉⲣⲟⲟⲩ, ^{AL}ⲁⲣⲁⲓ, ⲁⲣⲁⲩ, ^{F}ⲉⲗⲁⲓ, ⲉⲗⲁⲩ, ^{B}ⲉⲣⲟⲓ, ⲉⲣⲱⲟⲩ "to me, to them."

As for */ˈe/, which, as we saw, regularly turns into ^{SB}ⲁ and ^{ALF}ⲉ, the main exceptions are: (a) it is kept also in Sahidic and Bohairic as ⲉ before /ʔ/, whether derived from an etymological /ʔ/ or from the lenition of a /t/, /r/, /j/ and /w/ in the coda of a tonic syllable: ^{S}ⲙⲉ, ^{B}ⲙⲉⲓ /meʔ/ "truth" < */ˈmeʔʕə/ < */muʔʕat/, ^{SB}ⲛⲉ /neʔ/ "to you (fem.)" < */net/ < */nic/, ^{SB}ϣⲛⲉ /šneʔ/ "net" < */šəneʔ/ < */švˈnuw/; (b) it is written before sonorant phonemes (including ⲃ) as <ø>[79] in Sahidic, Akhmimic and Lycopolitan, as <ⲉ> in Bohairic, and as <ⲏ> or <ⲩ> in Fayyumic: *šmsj* */ˈšimsij/ > ^{SAL}ϣⲙ̄ϣⲉ, ^{B}ϣⲉⲙϣⲓ, ^{F}ϣⲏⲙϣⲓ /šemšə/ "to worship." If the following sonorant is not followed by another consonant, it undergoes reduplication in all dialects except Bohairic: *qnj.t* */ˈqinjit/ > ^{S}ⲕⲛ̄ⲛⲉ, ^{A}ⲕⲛ̄ⲛⲓⲉ, ^{B}ⲕⲉⲛⲓ, ^{F}ⲕⲏⲛⲛⲓ "to become fat." Also, in proximity of sibilants one often finds the outcome */ˈe/ > ^{SB}ⲉ or ^{SBAF}ⲓ: for example, *wsḫ.t* */ˈwisχat/ > ^{S}ⲟⲩⲉϣⲥⲉ, ^{S}ⲟⲩⲟϣⲥⲉ, ^{B}ⲟⲩⲉ/ⲏϣⲥⲓ "breadth," *pšs.t* */ˈpušsat/ > ^{S}ⲡⲓϣⲉ, ⲡⲁϣⲉ "half." Diphthongs display slight irregularities as well: instead of the paradigmatic form <ⲁⲩ> (as in *snwj* */siˈnewwvj/ > ^{S}ⲥⲛⲁⲩ "two," *ḥnw* */ḥvˈnew/ > ^{S}ϩⲛⲁⲩ "jar"), */ˈew/ occasionally yields <ⲟⲩ>, and <ⲟ> in Akhmimic in final position: ^{S}ⲥⲛⲟⲩ, ϩⲛⲟⲩ, ^{A}ⲥⲛⲟ. The outcome of */ˈej/ is even more complex: it develops as expected into ^{SL}ⲁ(ⲉ)ⲓ, but it keeps a vocalization closer to the original in ^{A}ⲉ(ⲉ)ⲓ, ^{F}ⲏⲓ; Bohairic exhibits a difference in treatment, depending on whether the original vowel was **u* (i.e., */ˈej/ < */ˈuj/), in which case it goes with Sahidic ⲁⲓ, or **i* (i.e. */ˈej/ < */ˈij/), in which case it goes with Fayyumic ⲏⲓ: for example *zjnw* */ˈzijnvw/ > ^{S}ⲥⲁⲉⲓⲛ, ^{A}ⲥⲉ(ⲉ)ⲓⲛⲉ, ^{BF}ⲥⲏⲓⲛⲓ "physician," *ʿjqj* */ˈʕujqvj/ > ^{SL}ⲁⲉⲓⲕ, ^{B}ⲁⲓⲕ "consecration."

Coptic long vowels display no major phonological development from Late Egyptian. But at the phonetic level, the following phenomena take place: (a) All dialects exhibit the evolution */ˈaː/ > <ⲟⲩ> [uː] (instead of */ˈaː/ > /oː/) after nasal consonants, and occasionally following other consonants as well: *nṯr* */ˈnaːcar/ > ⲛⲟⲩⲧⲉ /ˈnuːte/ "god."[80] Akhmimic displays <ⲟⲩ> in final position or when followed by the glottal stop, i.e. by a reduplication of the vocalic grapheme: Sϫⲱⲱⲙⲉ, Aϫⲟⲩⲟⲩⲙⲉ. We shall see below that these two phonological contexts are in fact identical, final stressed vowels being regularly followed in Coptic by an extrasyllabic /ʔ/. That /uː/, however, has acquired phonemic character in Coptic is shown by the presence of minimal pairs such as ϩⲱⲛ /hoːn/ < *ẖnn* */ˈçaːnan/ "to approach" vs. ϩⲟⲩⲛ /huːn/ < *ẖnw* */ˈçaːnaw/ "inside." (b) The outcome <(ⲉ)ⲓ> [iː] instead of /eː/ from etymological */uː/ > */eː/ (3.5) is frequent in proximity of /r/ and after etymological pharyngeals: SLϩⲓⲣ, Bϧⲓⲣ, Aϩⲓⲣ, Fϩⲓⲗ < */ˈχuːr/ "street," a loanword from Semitic. As in the case of */aː/ > <ⲟⲩ> [uː], Akhmimic displays here <ⲉⲓ> in final position or if the vowel is followed by /ʔ/: Sⲧⲏⲏⲃⲉ, Aϯⲉⲓⲃⲉ "finger." This same */uː/ > */eː/ occasionally appears as <ⲉ> before pharyngeal phonemes: Sϫⲙ̄ⲡⲉϩ < */tapˈpuːḥ/ "apple," also a Semitic loanword. (c) We had already observed in Late Egyptian (section 3.5) the phonetic outcome */iː/ > *[eː] in proximity of /ʕ/ or /j/.

Most Coptic dialects have two unstressed vocalic phonemes,[81] depending on the phonetic context of the original structure of the word: as a general rule, pretonic and posttonic vowels have developed into /ə/,[82] graphically rendered by <ⲉ> or <ø> (<ⲓ> in Bohairic and Fayyumic in final position); pretonic unstressed /a/ owes its origin to an earlier Egyptian unstressed */a/, either etymological or resulting from assimilation of */e/ < */i/ or */u/ in proximity of an etymological pharyngeal or velar phoneme: ⲁϣⲁⲓ "to become many" < *ʿšꜣ* */ʕiˈšiʀ/, or to an unstressed sonorant phonetic surrounding: ⲁⲙⲣⲏϩⲉ "asphalt" < */mvˈriḥjat/. An apparent pretonic unstressed /i/ derives from a pretonic unstressed syllable of the type cvj and is in fact to be analyzed as /j/: Sϩⲓⲃⲱⲓ /həjboːj/ "ibis" < *h(j)bj.w* */hijˈbaːjvw/, originally the plural of *h(j)bw* */hijbaw/ > */hiːb/, see Bϩⲓⲡ.

3.6.3 Syllabic structures

Coptic syllabic patterns[83] are similar to those of Late Egyptian, the only major difference being represented by the emergence of new patterns from the reduction to *schwa* (and eventually to zero) of the short vowel of pretonic open syllables and the development of biconsonantal onsets: *#cv$cv(c)$ > #ccv(c)$. As in the earlier stages of the language, long and doubly-closed syllables are documented only in stressed final position. These rules of syllabic distribution and the ensuing comments apply to the vocabulary of Egyptian stock, not to the Greek words which entered the language especially in the religious sphere.

Table 3.8 The syllabic structures of Sahidic Coptic

SYLLABIC STRUCTURES	PRETONIC	TONIC	POSTTONIC
OPEN	\$cv\$	\$ˈcv:\$	\$cv#
	#ccv\$	#ˈccv:\$	
CLOSED	\$cvc\$	\$ˈcvc\$	\$cvc#
	#ccvc\$	#ˈccvc\$	
DOUBLY-CLOSED		\$ˈcvcc\$	
		#ˈccvcc\$	
LONG		\$ˈcv:c#	
		#ˈccv:c#	

At first sight, a pattern of tonic open syllable with short vowel \$ˈcv\$ is documented in words such as ⲡⲉ "heaven" < *p.t* */pit/, ⲧⲟ "land" < *tꜣ* */taʀ/, ϣⲁϫⲉ "to tell" < *sḏd.t* */ˈsiɟdit/, or ⲉⲓⲟⲡⲉ "occupation" < *wpw.t* */ˈwapwat/. In these patterns, however, one has to assume the presence of a final /-ʔ#/[84] deriving from the lenition of /t/, /r/, /j/ and /w/ in a stressed syllable in later Egyptian (section 3.5). Within an autosegmental approach to Coptic phonology, these syllables can be analyzed as closed \$ˈcvc\$ or doubly-closed \$ˈcvcc\$, by positing the insertion of an extrasegmental glottal stop /ʔ/ as "default consonant" in the final position on the skeletal tier \$cv(c)\$: thus ⲡⲉ = /peʔ/, ⲧⲟ = /toʔ/, ϣⲁϫⲉ = /šaɟʔ/, and ⲉⲓⲟⲡⲉ = /jopʔ/, parallel to the cvc-pattern ⲣⲁⲛ = /ran/ and to the cvcc-pattern ⲥⲟⲧⲡ = /sotp/ "chosen."[85] When this final /ʔ/ appears in closed syllables, it is mostly indicated in the writing by <ø>; in doubly-closed syllables, it is represented graphemically by <-ⲉ> in the dialects of Upper Egypt and by <-ⲓ> in those of Lower Egypt: ^{S}ⲉⲓⲟⲧⲉ, ^{B}ⲓⲟϯ /jotʔ/, ^{AL}ⲉⲓⲁⲧⲉ, ^{ALF}ⲉⲓⲁϯ /jatʔ/ < */ˈjatjaw/ "fathers," ^{S}ϩⲓⲟⲙⲉ, ^{B}ϩⲓⲟⲙⲓ /hjomʔ/, ^{AL}ϩⲓⲁⲙⲉ, ^{F}ϩⲓⲁⲙⲓ /hjamʔ/ < */ḥiˈjamwvt/ "women."[86]

Two important elements in favor of this analysis are: (a) the graphic rendering of this glottal phoneme in dialects other than Sahidic as final <-ⲉ> (in Akhmimic and Lycopolitan) or <-ⲓ> (in Bohairic and Fayyumic), and occasionally in Sahidic itself: see ^{S}ⲙⲉ, ⲙⲉⲉ, ^{SAL}ⲙⲏⲉ, ^{A}ⲙⲓⲉ, ^{B}ⲙⲏⲓ, ⲙⲉⲓ, ^{F}ⲙⲉⲓ, ⲙⲉⲉⲓ, ⲙⲏⲓ "truth," to be analyzed in all cases as /mvʔ/; (b) the Akhmimic (and partially Lycopolitan) raising of etymological */ˈa/ to <ⲟ> or sometimes <ⲉ> (instead of the regular outcome <ⲁ>), of etymological */ˈa:/ to <ⲟⲩ> (instead of the usual <ⲱ>), and of etymological */i:\$ʕ/ to <ⲓ> (instead of <ⲏ>) in final position and before reduplication of the vowel:[87] ^{SAL}ⲧⲟⲟⲧϥ̄, ^{B}ⲧⲟⲧϥ, ^{F}ⲧⲁⲁⲧϥ̄ "his hand"; ^{SBAL}ⲛ̄ⲧⲟ, ^{F}ⲛ̄ⲧⲁ "you (fem.)," ^{SF}ⲕⲱ, ^{B}ⲭⲱ, ^{L}ⲕⲱ(ⲉ), ^{AL}ⲕⲟⲩ "to lay"; ^{S}ϫⲱⲱⲙⲉ, ^{A}ϫⲟⲩⲟⲩⲙⲉ "book." It is evident that these two environments were perceived as sharing a common feature, which is precisely the presence of a /ʔ/

after the tonic vowel: in Akhmimic /daʔtəf/ = [ˈtʼoʔtəf], /ntaʔ/ = [nt(ʰ)oʔ], /koːʔ/ = [k(ʰ)uːʔ], /ˈɟoːʔəm/ = [ˈcʼuːʔəm]. That this final glottal stop is not expressed in the writing should hardly be surprising, since this is the regular fate of /ʔ/ in Coptic in all initial and final positions, unless it represents the last phoneme of a doubly-closed syllable of the type we considered above (**ⲉⲓⲟⲡⲉ** = /jopʔ/). Accordingly, a structure such as **ⲧⲟⲉ** "part" < *dnj.t* */ˈdanjut/[88] should probably be analyzed as /doʔʔ/, the sequence of two glottal stops at the end of the doubly-closed syllable being the reason for the variety of spellings of this word: **ⲧⲟⲓⲉ**, **ⲧⲁ**(**ⲉ**), **ⲧⲟ**, just to mention the Sahidic forms.

Conversely, the apparent and utterly un-Egyptian presence of patterns with long unstressed vowel (pretonic as in **ⲟⲩⲧⲁϩ** "fruit" or posttonic as in **ⲁⲥⲟⲩ** "price") is easily removed from the phonological system of Coptic by interpreting <**ⲟⲩ**> in these cases not as syllabic /uː/, but rather as semiconsonantal /w/: **ⲟⲩⲧⲁϩ** /wdah/, pattern #ccvc# < *wdḥ* */wiˈdaḥ/, pattern #cv$cvc# and **ⲁⲥⲟⲩ** /ʔasw/, pattern #cvcc# < *jsw.t* */ˈjiswat/, pattern #cvc$cvc#. In both cases, the hypothetical [uː] (*[uːˈtʼah] or *[ˈasuː]) would represent the phonetic realization of /w-/ and /-əw/ in those specific environments.

Further reading

Fecht, G. *Wortakzent und Silbenstruktur.* Ägyptologische Forschungen XXI (Glückstadt: Verlag J. J. Augustin, 1960) [The standard analysis of the syllabic patterns of Egyptian].

Hintze, F. "Zur koptischen Phonologie," *Enchoria* 10 (1980), 23-91 [A generative analysis of Coptic phonology].

Hoch, J. E. *Semitic Words in Egyptian Texts of the New Kingdom and Third Intermediate Period* (Princeton University Press, 1994) [A companion for issues of comparative Egyptian-Semitic phonology].

Osing, J. *Die Nominalbildung des Ägyptischen*, 2 vols. (Mainz: Philipp von Zabern, 1976) [The fundamental reference work on the vocalic patterns of the language from Middle Egyptian through Coptic].

Schenkel, W. *Zur Rekonstruktion der deverbalen Nominalbildung des Ägyptischen.* Göttinger Orientforschungen IV/13 (Wiesbaden: Harrassowitz, 1983) [Expands and discusses the methodology of Osing, *Nominalbildung*].

Schenkel, W. *Einführung in die altägyptische Sprachwissenschaft.* Orientalistische Einführungen (Darmstadt: Wissenschaftliche Buchgesellschaft, 1990) [Indispensable tool for the study of the prehistory of Egyptian phonology and its comparative aspects].

4

Elements of historical morphology

4.1 Introduction

Ancient Egyptian is a language of the flectional or *fusional* type,[1] with a diachronic tendency to replace VSO-synthetic structures by SVO-analytic constructions and to move toward the *polysynthetic* type which characterizes Coptic, its more recent phase. Egyptian morphemes are unsegmentable units combining grammatical functions. Morphological forms exhibit a number of correspondences with the patterns of word formation and of flection in other Afroasiatic languages. But although Egyptian is the oldest language of the phylum documented in written form (at least seven centuries before Akkadian), its morphological repertoire differs to a great extent from that of Semitic and of other Afroasiatic languages.[2] This morphological variety can be accounted for in many ways:[3] (a) by suggesting that, in spite of its archaic date, Egyptian had undergone already before its emergence as a written language a considerable number of changes which modified the genetic inventory inherited from Afroasiatic;[4] (b) by considering Afroasiatic a relatively loose language continuum, whose individual branches came to share linguistic features through intensive contact, but were not necessarily derived from a common ancestor;[5] (c) by rejecting the prevailing "semitocentric" approach to Afroasiatic linguistics, proposing that the regular patterns displayed by Semitic, and above all by Arabic, represent a typologically late result of a series of grammaticalizations which created its rich phonology and morphology, rather than the original situation inherited from the *Ursprache*.[6]

In fact, all these approaches have their strong points and contribute to explaining in part the emergence of historical forms. To give one example for each of them: (aa) Egyptian developed already in prehistoric times rigid syntactic forms which favored the neutralization of the function of the original case endings and the loss of vocalic endings. In this respect, Egyptian is typologically more recent than classical Semitic languages such as Akkadian or Arabic, where case endings are kept and productive, although not to the extent in which they played a role in classical Indo-European languages. This is an interpretation according to the first approach. (bb) Conjugational patterns vary considerably within Afroasiatic, displaying prefixal or suffixal forms, but with few regularities beyond the boundaries of a language family. Thus, the presence of two types of suffix conjugation in Egyptian can hardly be regarded as the result of a development following an original state in which prefix and suffix conjugations coexisted, since the Afroasiatic prefix conjugation forms are themselves a fusion of a pronominal clitic anticipating a coreferential NP to a verbal stem.[7] This is an interpretation according to the second model. (cc) Egyptian exhibits a high number of biradical (and possibly monoradical) roots, in contrast to the quasi-universal, although overestimated[8] Semitic triradicalism. Egyptian probably represents the original state preceding the regularizations which took place at a typologically later stage in Semitic. This interpretation follows the third approach.

In spite of the underlying theoretical problems, Egyptian morphology is nonetheless conveniently described within the Afroasiatic frame, which is capable of clarifying both the synchronic structures of the language and the remnants of earlier stages.[9] In addition to the Afroasiatic background, attention must be paid to the patterns of evolution from Egyptian to Coptic. As we saw, the general trend in the history of Egyptian is to replace *synthetic* structures, such as the morphemes of gender and number in the noun and the suffixal deictic markers in the verb, by *analytic* constructions:[10] nominal suffixes are superseded by the definite and the indefinite article, grammatical indicators of specialized semantic functions are replaced by lexicalized expressions, synthetic verbal forms give place to juxtapositions of a conjugational head followed by a verbal lexeme.

4.2 Root, stem, word

The basic structure of an Egyptian word is a lexical *root*, an abstract phonological entity consisting of a sequence of consonants or semiconsonants which vary in number from one (for example 1-rad. *j* "to say") to four (4-rad. *znḥm* "locust"), with an overwhelming majority of biconsonantal (2-rad. *ḏd* "to say"), triconsonantal (3-rad. *rmṯ* "man"), and so-called weak roots, which display a semivocalic ("infirm") last radical (II-inf. *zj* "to go away," III-inf. *mrj* "to love," IV-inf. *ḥmsj* "to sit") or a gemination of the second radical (II-gem. *mꜣꜣ* "to see," III-gem. *sšꜣꜣ* "to land").

Superimposed on the root as a separate morphological tier is a vocalic or semivocalic pattern, which together with the root forms the so-called *stem*, the surface form acquired by the root; the stem determines the functional class to which the word belongs. It is transformed into an actual *word* of the language by means of inflectional affixes (in Egyptian for the most part suffixes), which convey deictic markers and other grammatical functions such as gender, number, tense and aspect, and voice.[11] Table 4.1 offers common examples of derivational patterns of Egyptian words from roots and stems.

Table 4.1 The derivation of Egyptian words

ROOT	STEM	AFFIX	FUNCTION	WORD
sn "brother"	**san-*	.ø	m.s	**san* "brother"
		.at	f.s.	**sānat* "sister"
	**sanu-*	.aw	m.pl.	**sanūwaw* "brothers"
	**sansan-*	.ø	Infinitive	**sansan* "to be friendly with"
ȝbd "month"	**ȝabad-*	.ø	sing.	**ȝabád* "month"
	**ȝabud-*	.aw	pl.	**ȝabūdaw* "months"
nṯr "god"	**naṯar-*	.ø	sing.	**nāṯar* "god"
	**naṯur-*	.aw	pl.	**naṯūraw* "gods"
	**nuṯr-*	.ij	masc. adjective	**nuṯrij* "divine" (masc.)
		.it	fem. adjective	**nuṯrit* "divine" (fem.)
sḏm "to hear"	**saḏam-*	.ø	Infinitive	**sāḏam* "to hear"
		.s	3 p.f.s.	**saḏāmas* "that she hears"
	**saḏma-*	.ø	Subject = NP	**saḏma-NP* "may NP hear"
		.f	3 p.m.s.	**saḏmáf* "may he hear"
	**saḏim-*	.na+f	Past + 3 p.m.s.	**saḏímnaf* "he heard"
		.ø	Active participle	**sāḏim* "the one who hears"
		.iw	Passive participle	**sáḏmiw* "the one who is heard" < ***saḏimiw*
ḏd "to say"	**ḏad-*	.ø	Infinitive	**ḏād* "to say"
	**ḏvdvd-*	.at	Passive part. + f.s.	**ḏvdvdat* "what has been said"
	**ḏid-*	.nu+k	Past rel. + 2 p.m.s.	**ḏídnuk* "which you said"
	**siḏid-*	.it	Causative infinitive	**síḏdit* "to tell"
ʿḥʿ "to stand"	**maʿḥiʿ-*	.wat	f.pl.	**maʿḥíʿwat* "tomb(s)"
mn "(to be) stable"	**man-*	.ø	Infinitive	**mān* "to be stable"
	**simin-*	.t	Causative infinitive	**simīnit* "to establish"
	**jamin-*	.ij	Nominal ending	**jamīnij* "(type of) vessel"
ʿq "to enter"	**ʿaqw-*	.uw	Nominal ending	**ʿaqwuw* "income" (> "food")
wsḫ "(to be) broad"	**saḫ-*	.at	f.s.	**sāḫat* "field" (< "breadth")

Vocalic skeletons generally determine the structure of nominal patterns and of basic conjugational forms, whereas semivocalic suffixes convey the expression of the plural, of adjectival forms of the verb (participles and relative forms), and of some conjugational patterns. The feminine marker is a *t*-suffix added to the basic masculine noun (*sn* "brother" vs. *sn.t* "sister"); the most common derivational pattern of adjectives is a *j*-suffix (*nṯrj* "divine" from *nṯr* "god"). A *j*- or *w*-prefix can be added to biconsonantal roots to form triradical nominal stems;[12] conversely, a triconsonantal root may lose a semivocalic glide and be reduced to a biradical stem.[13] Examples of consonantal additions to a root are *s*- for causative stems,[14] *n*- for singulative nouns and reflexive verbs,[15] and *m*- for nouns of instrument, place, or agent.[16] While many of these morphological features are indeed shared by other Afroasiatic languages, Egyptian stems resulting from the addition of a consonantal phoneme to a root tend to be lexicalized as new autonomous roots rather than treated as grammatical forms of the basic root: Egyptian, therefore, does not possess a full-fledged paradigm of verbal stems conveying semantic nuances of a verbal root similar to the ones we know from Semitic.

The most common modifications of the root are: (1) the *reduplication* of the entire root or of a segment thereof. This pattern affects the semantic sphere, creating new lexemes: from *sn* "brother" *snsn* "to be friendly with," from *gmj* "to find" *ngmgm* "to be gathered" (with the *n*-prefix of reflexivity), from *snb* "to be healthy" *snbb* "to greet"; (2) the *gemination* of the last radical, which affects the grammatical sphere: 2-rad. *ḏd* "to say" > *ḏdd.t* "what has been said," III-inf. *mrj* "to love" > *mrr=j* "that I love," II-gem. *mꜣꜣ* "to see" > *mꜣꜣ=f* "while he sees," 3-rad. *sḏm* "to hear" > *sḏmm=f* "he will be heard."[17]

Table 4.2 From synthetic to analytic patterns

	EARLIER EGYPTIAN	LATER EGYPTIAN
NOUN	*sn* "(a, the) brother" *sn.t* "(a, the) sister" *nfr* "good"	*ou-son* "a brother," *p-son* "the brother" *ou-sône* "a sister," *t-sône* "the sister" *p-et-nanou=f* "good" < *"that-which it is good"
VERB	*sḏm.n=f* "he heard" *mrj.w=f* "may he be loved"	*a=f-sôtm* "he heard" < *"he did the hearing" *ma-r=ou-merit=f* "may he be loved" < *"let them do the loving of him"

The presence of a strong expiratory stress led in late prehistoric times to a change of the inherited syllabic patterns from the prehistoric *Dreisilbengesetz* to the historical *Zweisilbengesetz* (section 3.4.3) and to the reorganization of nominal stems. Following its analytic tendency, later Egyptian morphology displays a variety of inflectional prefixes deriving from the grammaticalization of earlier Egyptian patterns,[18] which have been phonologically reduced and are now followed by the lexeme, as shown in table 4.2.

4.3 Nominal morphology

4.3.1 General features

In our discussion of phonology (section 3.4.3), we saw that one of the major features of Egyptian in its early stages was the presence of a strong expiratory stress, which eventually caused a reduction to /ø/ of short vowels in open syllables in posttonic position, with the resulting change from the *Dreisilbengesetz* to the *Zweisilbengesetz* (***saḏimat* > **saḏmat* "she who hears"). A very important effect of this reduction of short posttonic vowels was the loss of the old Afroasiatic case markers (nominative **-u*, accusative **-a*, genitive-possessive **-i*, possibly locative **-is*):[19] thus, a prehistoric ***san-u* became the form we posit for earlier Egyptian: **san* "brother."

The case markers, however, left traces in the morphological behavior of the corresponding nouns. An example was already given in table 4.1 s.v. **san*: the old case marker **u*, which was dropped in the singular form, reappears in the formation of the plural, attracting stress and vocalic length, developing a glide before the morpheme **-aw*, and generating the form **sanūwaw*. Also, the ending **-u* is still preserved, although functionally reinterpreted, in the forms of some singular patterns as well: when the original stem ended in a vowel, for example **-u* in **ḥāruw* "(the god) Horus," **-a* in **ḫupraw* "form," or **-i* in **masḏiw* "enemy," the ending was maintained as a glide, often written in good orthography as <-w> in the case of **-aw* as opposed to <-ø> in the case of **-iw* or **-uw*:[20] <ḫprw> =: **ḫupraw* "form," <ḥfꜣw> =: **ḥafꜣaw* "snake." Further evidence of survival of the nominative ending was discussed in section 3.4.3 as a form of "contingent extrasyllabicity": there are instances of two variants of the same word, one with consonantal nominal stem (for example Proto-Eg. ***nib-u* > Upper Eg. **nib* > ^{L}ⲛⲉⲡ "lord," **nībif* > Greek -νηφις "his lord") and one in which the old ending **-u* develops an extrasyllabic *w*-glide and keeps the original bisyllabic structure (for example ***nib-u* > Lower Eg. **nībuw* > ^{B}ⲛⲏⲃ "lord," **nibwif* "his lord" > Greek -ναβ-).[21]

Remnants of the accusative (or "absolutive") case in **-a* will be mentioned in sections 4.6.3.2 and 4.7. As for the genitive and possessive **-i*, a survival in historical times is offered by the *i*-pattern before pronominal suffixes (for example Proto-Eg. nominative ***ḥar-u* > *ḥr* */ḥar/ > ϩⲟ /hoʔ/ "face," genitive + *f*-suffix ***ḥar-i-f* > *ḥr=f* */ḥa'rif/ > ϩⲣⲁϥ /hraf/ "his face"), and by the vocalization of the adjectives derived from nouns by means of the pattern known as ***nisbation***, from the Arabic noun *nisba* "relation": a morpheme *-j* is affixed to the genitive of a noun in order to derive the corresponding adjective: nominative ***ḥar-u* > *ḥr* */ḥar/ > ϩⲟ /hoʔ/ "face," genitive + *j*-suffix ***ḥar-i-j* > **ḥaríj* > ϩⲣⲁⲓ /hraj/ *"related to the face" > "upper part"; nominative **taʒaš-u* > *tʒš* */ta'ʀaš/ > ⲧⲟϣ /toš/ "border," genitive + *j*-suffix ***taʒaš-i-j* > *tʒšj* */taʀ'šij/ > ⲧⲉϣⲉ /tə'šeʔ/ *"related to the border" > "neighbor"; **jamin-u* "the right side" > ***jamin-at* > *jmn.t* */'jamnat/ "the right side" > *jmn.tj* */ja'mintij/ > ⲉⲙⲛⲧ /ʔə'ment/ "West."[22]

Egyptian adjectives are syntactically treated as substantives. Nouns can function as appositions to a preceding noun: *zʒ=j ḥrw* */ziːʀaj ḥaːruw/ "my son Horus"; when used attributively, adjectives follow the modified noun: *zʒ=j nfr* */ziːʀij naːfir/ "my beautiful son."

The main innovation in the phonology of later Egyptian nouns is the lenition and the progressive loss of final vocalic and semivocalic endings (section 3.5), which at times provoked the disappearance of the entire final syllable of the word: consonantal stem *nṯr* */'naːcar/ > ⲛⲟⲩⲧⲉ /nuːtə/ "god"; *u*-stem *hrww* */'harwuw/ > ϩⲟⲟⲩ /hoʔw/ "day"; *a*-stem *ḥfʒw* */'ḥafʀaw/ > ϩⲟϥ /hof/ "snake"; *i*-stem *kʒmw* */'kaʀmiw/ > ϭⲙⲉ /kʲmeʔ/ "gardener." On the syntactic level, this phenomenon is paired by the development of an overt marker of determination represented by the definite and indefinite article *pʒ* > ⲡ-, ⲡⲉ- and *wʿ* > ⲟⲩⲁ- respectively: Late Egyptian *pʒ-ntr* > Coptic ⲡ-ⲛⲟⲩⲧⲉ "the god," *wʿ-hʒw* > ⲟⲩ-ϩⲟⲟⲩ "a day," *pʒ-kʒm* > ⲡⲉ-ϭⲙⲉ "the gardener," *wʿ-ḥf* > ⲟⲩ-ϩⲟϥ "a snake." But unlike what happens in the Semitic languages which possess a definite article, where the determined modifier is introduced by a determinative pronoun (for example Hebrew *hā-ʾīš hag-gādôl* "the great man"), later Egyptian displays no such morpheme: Late Egyptian *pʒ-rmt ʿʒ* "the great man."[23] In later Demotic and Coptic, however, the determinative pronoun *n* (Coptic ⲛ̄-) acquires this function: Coptic ⲡⲣⲱⲙⲉ ⲛ̄ⲛⲟϭ "the great man." The morpheme *n* is also used in all stages of the language to express the indirect genitive (section 4.4): earlier Egyptian *rmṯ n(j) km.t*, Late Egyptian *pʒ-rmt n km.t*, Coptic ⲡⲣⲙ̄ⲛ̄ⲕⲏⲙⲉ "the Egyptian man" < "the man of Egypt."

4.3.2 *Compound nouns*

Like many other Afroasiatic languages, earlier Egyptian exhibits a pattern of nominal determination characterized by the direct juxtaposition of a *regens* and a *rectum*, originally in the genitive case; this form of direct genitive is called "construct state" (*status constructus*): *nb jmзḫ* "possessor of veneration" > "venerable." The direct genitive was a productive device in classical Egyptian, although not as frequent as in Akkadian, Hebrew or Arabic, and tended to be replaced by the analytic construction with the determinative pronoun *n(j)*: *rmṯ nj km.t* "man that-of Egypt" > "Egyptian." However, the structure of a set of Egyptian words known as "compound nouns" shows that already in early historical times these compounds were lexicalized and treated as a single lexical item:[24] while in the genitival construction and in the pattern "noun + adjective" the stress falls on the *rectum* (*md.t rmṯ* */ˌmadatˈraːmac/ "the 'thing' of man" > ⲙⲛ̄ⲧⲣⲱⲙⲉ /məntˈroːmə/ "mankind"; *rmṯ* ʿз */ˌramacˈʕaʀ/ "great man" > ⲣⲙ̄ⲙⲁⲟ /rəmmaˈʔoʔ/ "rich"), in the compound nouns it falls on the *regens*: *ḥm-nṯr* */ˈḥamˌnacar/ > ϩⲟⲛⲧ /hont/ "servant-of-god" > "priest"; *zз-tз* */ˈziʀtaʀ/ ("son of the earth" >) "snake" > ⲥⲓⲧⲉ /ˈsiːtə/ "basilisk." The same pattern is shared by a few instances of adjectival or participial constructions, such as *mn-nfr* */ˈminnafvr/ "stable of beauty" (the reference is to King Pepi I) > Μεμφις, ⲙⲛ̄ϥⲉ /ˈmenfə/, originally the name of the king's pyramid, metonymically extended to the whole city of "Memphis," the first capital of Egypt.[25]

Compound nouns are rare and their etymology often unclear; however, they point back to a phase in the history of Egyptian, which probably lasted until the end of the Old Kingdom, in which the old tonic pattern with antepenultimate stress (*Dreisilbengesetz*, section 3.4.3) was still productive.

4.3.3 The feminine

The feminine singular ending of earlier Egyptian was marked by a suffix *-t* preceded by a vowel, frequently **-at*, also **-it* for the *i*-stem and **-ut* for the *u*-stem. The vowel can be reconstructed with a degree of certitude only if it was stressed or – less reliably – if it can be inferred on the basis of Akkadian transcriptions or derivational patterns. A stressed feminine ending is documented by examples such as *ḥṯṯ.t* */ḥacˈcat/ > ᴮⲁϭⲟ /ʔaˈcoʔ/ "armpit," *p.t* */pit/ > ⲡⲉ /peʔ/ "heaven," *pr.t* */puˈrut/ > (ⲉ)ⲃⲣⲁ /(ə)braʔ/ "seed"; transcriptions and derivational patterns show the ending **at* in *pḏ.t* */ˈpiːɟat/ > ⲡⲓⲧⲉ /piːtə/ "bow," see Akk. transcription *-pi-ta*, the feminine adjectival *nisba* ending **-it* as in *jmn.tt* */jaˈmintit/ "West" > ⲁⲙⲛ̄ⲧⲉ /ʔaˈmentə/ "Afterlife," see masc. *jmn.tj* */jaˈmintij/, or the ending **-ut* in *wpw.t* */ˈwapwut/ > */wapʔ/ > ⲉⲓⲟⲡⲉ /jopʔ/ "occupation," see *wpw.tj* */wapˈwuːtij/ "messenger," Meroitic *apote*.[26] In general, posttonic vowels were dropped in later Egyptian (section 3.3); in most cases, therefore, the vocalic color of the feminine endings is retrievable only on systematic grounds. Parallel to the masculine forms discussed above, Egyptian morphology shows cases of feminine words derived from a stem originally ending in

*-u in which the thematic vowel reappears as a semiconsonantal glide before pronominal suffixes: _dp.t_ "boat" (stem *dvpu-), probably */dv:put/, with pronominal suffix _dp.wt=f_ "his boat," probably */dvpwv:tif/.[27]

The feminine ending corresponding to the _nisba_ *-ij is *-it: from the preposition _ẖr_ */çur/ "beneath" one derives the adjective _ẖrj_ */çu'rij/ "which is beneath" > ϩⲣⲁⲓ "lower part," whose feminine form is _ẖr.t_ */çu'rit/ (*what is beneath" > *"what is needed" >) "food offerings" > ϩⲣⲉ /hreʔ/ "food."[28]

4.3.4 Plural and dual

The formation of the plural is more complex. A semivocalic morpheme *-w or *-aw, possibly derived, like the corresponding Semitic plural in *-ū,[29] from a longer form of the singular ending *-u,[30] was added to most singular forms, although a few nouns may have possessed a plural or collective form without external suffixes.[31] An important morphological alternation connected with plural suffixes relates to what is usually called the "broken plural": while in the singular form triradical nouns often display the vocalic pattern *cacac-, their plural stem is *cacuc-, which originally indicated collectiveness, followed by the plural suffix *-w or *-aw.[32] The morphological alternation between singular and plural is known from other Afroasiatic languages,[33] for example Arabic _qalb_ "heart," pl. _qulūb_. But Egyptian broken plurals differ from their Semitic equivalents – being in this respect closer to the African branches of the phylum – in that internal morphological alternation was rarely the only marker of the plural form, but rather coexisted with other morphological devices, such as the affixation of *-w or *-aw.

Examples of *-w are: (a) cons. stem **'anaḫ-u > 'nḫ */ʕa'naχ/ > ⲁⲛⲁϣ /ʔa'naš/ "oath," pl. **'anaḫu-u > 'nḫ.w */ʕa'naχw/ > */ʕa'nawχ/ > ⲁⲛⲁⲩϣ /ʔa'nawš/;[34] (b) u-stem **haru-u > hrww */'harwuw/ "day" > ϩⲟⲟⲩ /hoʔw/, pl. **haruu-u > hrw.w */ha'ruww/ > ᴬϩⲣⲉⲩ /hrew/; **madu-u > mdw "word," pl. **maduu-u > md.w */ma'duww/ > ᴮ-ⲙⲧⲁⲩ /mdaw/; (c) a-stem **ḫupira-u > ḫprw */'χupraw/ "form," Akk. transcription -ḫu-u'-ru[35] (corresponding to a later Egyptian *ḫuprə), pl. **ḫupirau-u > ḫpr.w */χu'pirw/, Akk. transcription (a)ḫ-pe/i-e/ir (for a later Egyptian form *ḫpeʔr);[36] (d) i-stem **jaḥi-u > jḥj */ja'ḥij/ "ox" > ⲉϩⲉ /ʔə'heʔ/, pl. **jaḥiu-u > jḥ.w */ja'ḥiww/ > ⲉϩⲉⲩ /ʔə'hew/.

Examples of *-aw: (a) cons. stem **raꜣ-u > rꜣ */raʀ/ > ⲣⲟ /roʔ/ "mouth," pl. **raꜣ-aw > rꜣ.w */'ra:ʀaw/ > ⲣⲱⲟⲩ /ro:w/;[37] (b) u-stem **radu-u > rdw */'ra:duw/ > ⲣⲱⲧ /ro:t/ "plant," pl. **raduu-aw > rdw.w */'radwaw/ > ᴮⲣⲟϯ /rotʔ/; (c) a-stem **zaẖꜣa-u > zẖꜣw */'zaçʀaw/ > ᴮⲥⲁϧ /sax/ "scribe," pl. **zaẖꜣau-aw > zẖꜣ.w */zaç'ʀa:waw/ > zẖy.w */zəç'ʔa:j(vw)/ > ᴮⲥϧⲟⲩⲓ /sxu:j/; (d) i-stem **taꜣašij-u > tꜣšj

*/tarʀ'šij/ > ⲧⲉϣⲉ /tə'šeʔ/ "neighbor," pl. ***taзašiju-aw* > *tзšj.w* */tarʀ'šijwaw/ > */təʔšejwə/ > ⲧⲉϣⲉⲉⲩ /tə'šeʔw/.[38]

The plural suffix, therefore, caused considerable changes in the syllabic structure of the corresponding singular forms. In many cases these changes affected only the phonological level and the word stress: *tзš* */ta'ʀaš/ > ⲧⲟϣ /toš/ "province," pl. *tзš.w **taзaš-aw* > */'taʀšaw/ > ⲧⲟⲟϣ /toʔš/, *jtj* */'ja:tij/ > ⲉⲓⲱⲧ /jo:t/ "father," pl. *jtj.w **jatij-aw* > */'jatjaw/ > ⲉⲓⲟⲧⲉ /jotʔ/ or *hзbw* */'haʀbuw/ > */haʔb(vw)/ > ϩⲱⲃ /ho:b/ "event," pl. *hзbw.w* */haʀ'bu:waw/ > ϩⲃⲏⲩⲉ /hbe:wə/. In other cases they also involved the morphological level, with the original case markers reinterpreted as thematic vowels with the developement of a *w*-glide: sing. ***haru-u* > *hrww* */'harwuw/ > ϩⲟⲟⲩ /hoʔw/ "day," pl. ***haru-w* > *hrw.w* */ha'ruww/ > ^{A}ϩⲣⲉⲩ /hrew/; sing. ***san-u* > *sn* */san/ > ⲥⲟⲛ "brother," pl. ***sanu-aw* > *sn.ww* */sa'nu:waw/ > ⲥⲛⲏⲩ.[39]

Feminine plurals are of two types.[40] While many feminine words do not show a specific plural ending different from the corresponding singular in *-t*, both hieroglyphic and Coptic evidence indicates the existence of a feminine plural morpheme *.wt* (**-wat*) affixed to the basic stem: for example from the consonantal stem ***ḥijam-* sing. *ḥjm.t* */ḥijmat/ > (ⲥ)ϩⲓⲙⲉ /'(s)hi:mə/ "woman" vs. pl. *ḥjm.wt* */ḥi'jamwat/ > ϩⲓⲟⲙⲉ /hjomʔ/; from the *a*-stem ***ranpa-* sing. *rnp.t* */'ranpat/ > ⲣⲟⲙⲡⲉ /'rompə/ "year" vs. pl. *rnp.wt* */ran'pawwat/ > ⲣⲙ̄ⲡⲟⲟⲩⲉ /rəm'powwə/; from the *i*-stem ***pi-* sing. *p.t* */pit/ > ⲡⲉ /peʔ/ "heaven" vs. pl. *p.wt* */'pi:wat/ > ⲡⲏⲩⲉ /'pe:wə/. A few feminine plurals, especially those belonging to the *a*-pattern **-awwat* > -ⲟⲟⲩⲉ /-owwə/,[41] survive down to Coptic.

Table 4.3 Earlier Egyptian nominal morphology

		STEM			
		CONS.	*U*-STEM	*A*-STEM	*I*-STEM
MASCULINE	SINGULAR	**raʔ* **'anáḫ* **зabád* **sāḫam*	**hárwu-w* **házbu-w*	**ḫúpra-w* **ḥáfзa-w*	**jaḥí-w* **ḥúmwi-w*
	PLURAL	**rāʔ-aw* **'anaḫ-w* **зabúd-w/* **зabūd-aw* **sáḫm-aw*	**harúw-w* **haзbūw-aw*	**ḫupír-w* **ḥafзāw-aw*	**jaḥíw-w* **ḥumwīw-aw*
FEMININE	SINGULAR	**ḥíjm-at*	**purú-t*	**ránpa-t* **subзā-wat*	**pi-t* **tapí-t*
	PLURAL	**ḥijám-wat*		**ranpáw-wat* **subзáw-wat*	**pī-wat* **tapī-wat*

Another suffix *.wt*, morphologically feminine but applied to masculine nouns, is often used in the formation of collectives: from *rd* */ˈraːduw/ "plant" the collective noun *rd.wt* */ˈridwat/ "flora," from *sbꜣ* "star" the collective *sbꜣ.wt* "constellation."[42]

The main features of earlier Egyptian nominal morphology are captured in table 4.3. The reconstructions refer to the formal ("prehistoric") structure of the words, and not necessarily to their actual phonological realization in historical Egyptian.

Earlier Egyptian possessed a recessive morphological category "dual," in classical times limited to natural duals such as the numeral "2," parts of the human body occurring in pairs (eyes, ears, feet, legs, etc.) and semantically related lexemes: the two sandals, the Two Gods. Masculine duals display a semivocalic addition *.j* to the plural form: *sn.wj* */siˈnuwwvj/ > **ⲥⲛⲁⲩ** /snaw/ "two (masc.)," *pḥ.wj* */ˈpaḥwvj/ > **ⲡⲁϩⲟⲩ** /pahw/ "buttocks." Feminine duals also exhibit the ending *.j*, but it is not clear whether this ending was affixed to the singular (as generally assumed), or rather to the plural (as required by the symmetry with the masculine paradigm), since, as we saw, it is difficult to assess in which nominal classes the plural feminine morpheme *.wt* was used:[43] *sn.tj* */ˈsintvj/ > **ⲥⲛ̄ⲧⲉ** /ˈsentə/ "two (fem.)," *sp.tj* */ˈsaptvj/ "lips," Old Coptic <spat> < /saˈpatjaj/ "my lips," Coptic **ⲥⲡⲟⲧⲟⲩ** /spotw/ "lips" < */saˈpatjvw/ "their lips,"[44] *wʿr.tj* */wuʕruːtvj/ "legs" > **ⲟⲩⲉⲣⲏⲧⲉ** /wəˈreːtə/ "foot."[45]

4.3.5 Feminine and plural in later Egyptian

The fall of final vocalic and semivocalic phonemes in later Egyptian (section 3.5) led to a synchronic state in which feminine nouns maintain their syntactic gender, being determined by the feminine article (definite *tꜣ* > **ⲧ-**, **ⲧⲉ-**; indefinite *wʿ.t* > **ⲟⲩ-**) and agreeing with feminine pronouns, but are hardly recognizable on purely morphological grounds: a pattern cōcə < *cācac, for example, is shared by feminine nouns like **ⲥⲱⲛⲉ** /soːnə/ "sister" < **sān.at*, by masculine nouns like **ⲣⲱⲙⲉ** /roːmə/ "man" < **rāmaṯ*, and by verbal infinitives like **ⲕⲱⲧⲉ** /goːtə/ "to turn" < **qādaj*. In rare instances, the feminine of a noun or of an adjective is retained in Coptic as an autonomous lexeme together with its masculine counterpart: **ⲥⲟⲛ** "brother" vs. **ⲥⲱⲛⲉ** "sister," **ϣⲏⲣⲉ** /ˈšeːrə/ (< **šīrij*) "son" vs. **ϣⲉⲉⲣⲉ** /ˈšeʔrə/ (< **šírjit*) "daughter," **ϩⲟϥ** /hof/ (< **ḥafꜣaw*) vs. **ϩϥⲱ** /hfoː/ (< **ḥafꜣāwat*) "snake," **ⲃⲱⲱⲛ** /ˈboːʔən/ (< **bāꜣin*) vs. **ⲃⲟⲟⲛⲉ** /ˈboʔnə/ (< **báꜣnat*) "bad," **ⲥⲁⲃⲉ** /saˈbeʔ/ (< **sabꜣíw*) vs. **ⲥⲁⲃⲏ** /saˈbeːʔ/ (< **sabꜣīwat*) "wise."

A similar phonological outcome affected dual and plural forms as well. As in the case of the feminine, the development of the definite article *nꜣ* > Coptic **ⲛ̄-**, **ⲛⲉ-** is paralleled by a progressive fall of the plural endings. In general, while only a limited number of identifiable feminines and an even smaller number of duals (usually reinterpreted as singulars or plurals)[46] is kept in later Egyptian, the number of plural patterns is much higher, with the loss of final vowels and semiconsonants favoring the emergence of new oppositions based on internal apophonic alternations between singular and plural forms: Late Middle Egyptian sing. <soxm> vs. pl. <saxm> "power";[47] Coptic ⲉⲃⲟⲧ /ʔə'bot/ vs. ⲉⲃⲏⲧ /ʔə'beːt/ "month," ⲕⲁⲥ /gas/ vs. ⲕⲉⲉⲥ /geʔs/ "bone," ϯⲙⲉ /diːmə/ vs. ⲧⲙⲉ /dmeʔ/ "town," ⲁⲛⲁϣ /ʔa'naš/ vs. ⲁⲛⲁⲩϣ /ʔa'nawš/ "oath."

The state of affairs in later Egyptian raises questions about the features of the earlier Egyptian system. While justified within the conjectural Afroasiatic comparative frame and supported to a certain degree by the scanty Coptic evidence, the reconstruction of the nominal system faces nonetheless two methodological difficulties. On the one hand, earlier Egyptian morphological oppositions often appear redundant: for example, if the system did have apophonic alternations between singular and plural forms (as in *ʒabad-* vs. *ʒabud-* in the word for "month"), and if, moreover, this is often the only opposition surviving in the corresponding Coptic forms (ⲉⲃⲟⲧ vs. ⲉⲃⲏⲧ), do we always have to posit the concomitant presence of an external plural suffix in earlier Egyptian? On the other hand, the presence of these morphemes is not always supported by the actual evidence of hieroglyphic texts: the plural *ʒbd.w* "months" is regularly written like the singular *ʒbd* "month," with an ideographic (the three strokes for "PLURAL"), rather than phonetic indication (<w>) of the presence of the plural morpheme.

This divorce between methodological requirements and philological evidence has urged modern scholars to draw a distinction between two realities underlying our historical study of Egyptian: (1) the linguistic system resulting from a regular application of the morphophonological rules of derivation of Coptic forms from Egyptian antecedents, conventionally called "pre-Coptic Egyptian"; (2) the forms which emerge from the actual reality of Egyptian texts, i.e. "hieroglyphic Egyptian."[48]

The reasons for the fact that "hieroglyphic Egyptian" appears much less regular than "pre-Coptic" are twofold. First and foremost, as recognized by all students of the field, the Egyptian graphic system, while not as irregular or inconsistent as suggested by traditional Egyptology, prevents us from acquiring a reliable insight into the underlying morphological patterns (sections 2.2, 3.2). There is also another aspect to this issue: to follow Hjelmslev's terminology, no linguistic code displays a total identity between underlying *system* and historical *norm*.[49] The reconstructed "pre-Coptic Egyptian" is an *idealized* linguistic system: even if the rules for its reconstruction were all correct, which is in itself very doubtful, this redundant system would still not be the mirror of an actual historical reality. Nor can the hieroglyphic evidence be trusted to provide access to the synchronic norms of Egyptian: the use of hieroglyphs, Hieratic and Demotic is highly controlled by social conventions,[50] therefore doomed to convey a constant dialectics between traditional orthography and underlying phonology (section 2.3). Thus, actual historical manifestations of Egyptian were probably less regular than reconstructed "pre-Coptic," but more diversified than is betrayed by "hieroglyphic Egyptian."

To give just some examples of how these methodological concerns may modify the paradigms of nominal morphology given above, I would like to argue that the "systematic" singular and plural ending **-w* (in the singular patterns **-vw* and in the plural patterns **-w* and **-aw* respectively) may have been actually realized as /ø/ in words in which the presence of **-w* was redundant, i.e. where there was no opposition between two homophonic realities: for example *r'(w)* "sun" */riːʕv/ rather than the commonly assumed **rī'uw*. The historical shape of *hrw(w)* was probably from the very beginning */ˈharwv/ rather than */ˈharwuw/;[51] this would fit better both the traditional hieroglyphic writing of this word as <hrw> and its Coptic outcome ϩοου /hoʔw/. This hypothesis implies, however, that the apophonic alternation may have sufficed in some cases to mark the opposition between a singular and a plural form already in earlier Egyptian: sing. *hrw* */ˈharw(v)/ vs. pl. *hr.w* */haˈruw(w)/, which again suits perfectly the hieroglyphic writing of the plural as <hrw> and the Coptic form ᴬϩρηυ /hrew/. Similarly, there is no need to suppose that one of the two plural forms of *ɜbd* */ʀaˈbad/ "month" ever displayed a semiconsonantal ending: while a *w*-plural **ɜabúdw* is documented by Coptic євαтє /ʔəˈbatʔ/, the *aw*-plural **ɜabūdaw* was probably always */ʀaˈbuːdv/, from which both the hieroglyphic writing with <ø> and the Coptic form євнт /ʔəˈbeːt/ are readily derivable. In the word *ḥfɜw* */ˈḥafʀaw/ and generally in the *a*-stem, on the other hand, the presence of a semiconsonantal ending is supported not only by the orthographic frequency of <-w>,[52] but also by the fact that the *w*-glide was eventually palatalized to *j* in the plural pattern, i.e. in an environment in which /w/ was intervocalic: */ḥafˈʀaːwaw/ > */ḥafˈʔaːjv/, as suggested by the presence of the two spellings <ḥfɜw> (the older form) and <ḥfɜjj> (the recent form)[53] and by the Coptic outcome ϩвουι /hbuːj/. What seems less probable is that this word had in fact *two* plural forms, one ending in *-w* and one ending in *-aw*,[54] or that the realized form ever included the second *w*, i.e. the actual ending of the plural *aw*-morpheme: the hieroglyphic evidence does not support it,[55] and its presence also appears functionally redundant. If this hypothesis is correct, the Egyptian *norm* will be found to display a significantly lower number of semi-consonantal endings than the *system* posited by contemporary research.[56]

The evolution of nominal morphology is presented in table 4.4, which captures the later Egyptian counterparts – reconstructed on the basis of Akkadian transcriptions, Late Middle Egyptian evidence, and Coptic – of the lexemes treated in table 4.3.

Table 4.4 Later Egyptian nominal morphology

		STEM			
		CONS.	*U*-STEM	*A*-STEM	*I*-STEM
MASCULINE	SINGULAR	/roʔ/ /ʔanaš/ /ʔəbot/ /soːχəm/	/hoʔw/ /hoːb/	/χuprə/[57] /hof/	/ʔəheʔ/ /ham/
	PLURAL	/roːw/ /ʔanawš/ /ʔəbatʔ/, /ʔəbeːt/ /saχm/	/hrew/ /hbeːwə/	/χpeʔr/[58] /hbuːj/	/ʔəhew/ /hmeːw/
FEMININE	SINGULAR	/hiːmə/	/braʔ/	/rompə/ /sboːʔ/	/peʔ/ /ʔapeʔ/[59]
	PLURAL	/hjomʔ/		/rəmpowwə/ /sbowwə/	/peːwə/ /ʔapeːwə/

4.4 Pronouns

4.4.1 *Personal pronouns*

Earlier Egyptian exhibits four sets of personal pronouns, which share many elements with the pronouns of other Afroasiatic languages:[60]

(1) *Suffix pronouns*. They are used to indicate the possessor in a direct genitival construction (*prw=j* "my house"), the prepositional complement (*jm=f* "in him"), the subject of a verbal form, whether active (*sḏm=k* "you hear") or passive (*sḏm.n.tw=f* "it was heard"), including participles and relative forms (*mrjj=f* "his beloved"), and the highest argument of an infinitive, mostly the agent, but in the case of a transitive verb often the patient (*ḏd=k* "your saying," *rḏj.t=f* "to put him").

The morphological structure of the suffix pronouns is similar to that of their Semitic equivalents:[61] (1) first person *=j* (probably **-aj*); (2) second person masc. =*k* (Proto-Eg. ***-ku*; the final vowel does not appear in historical Egyptian: **-k*), fem. =*ṯ* (Proto-Eg. ***-ki*; the final vowel was also dropped, but left a trace of its earlier presence in the resulting palatalization of the plosive velar: */-ki/ > */-k^{j}i/ > **-ṯ*, i.e. the palatal plosive /-c/); (3) third person masc. =*f* (Proto-Eg. ***-su*; the back vowel /u/ led to a labialization of /s/: */-su/ > */-s^{w}/ > */-ɸ/ > **-f*), fem. =*s* (Proto-Eg. ***-si*, with the dropping of the front vowel /i/: */-si/ > */-s^{j}i/ > **-s*).[62] The plural forms, common to masculine and feminine, show the addition of an element *n* (in the dual *nj*) to the singular: (1) first person plural =*n* (***-ina* > **-in*), dual =*nj* (**-inij*); (2) second person plural =*ṯn* (from ***-kina*; the front vowel led to a palatalization of the velar stop: **-ṯin*), dual =*ṯnj* (**-ṯinij*); (3) third person plural =*sn* (***-sina* > **-sin*), dual =*snj* (**-sinij*).

(2) *Enclitic pronouns*, called by Egyptologists "dependent pronouns." They are used as object of transitive verbal phrases (*mꜣꜣ=j sw* "I see him"), as subject of adjectival sentences (*nfr sw* "he is good"), and as object of initial particles in verbal and adverbial sentences (*mk wj m-bꜣḥ=k* "behold, I am in front of you").

Morphologically, these pronouns show the addition of a morpheme *w* (in the first, second and third person masculine), *j* (third person feminine), or *m/n* (second person feminine) to the original form of the suffix pronoun, whereas plurals and duals show no difference between suffix and enclitic pronouns: first person *-wj* */wvj/, second person masc. *-kw* */kuw/ (in Old Egyptian) > *-ṯw* (in the classical language), fem. ***-km* > *-ṯm* */cim/ > *-ṯn*, third person masc. *-sw* */suw/, fem. *-sj* */sij/ (from the classical language onward also *-st*, the use of which is soon extended to the third person plural). The forms *sw* and *sj* prove that /s/ must have been the original consonantal element in the third person suffix pronouns as well. Enclitic pronouns always occupy the syntactic position after the first prosodic unit of the clause.[63]

(3) *Stressed pronouns*, often called "independent pronouns." They function as subject (or better "topic") of a nominal sentence in the first and second person (*jnk jtj=k* "I am your father," section 4.2), as focalized subject of a cleft sentence (*ntf mdw* "It is he who speaks," *jnk jnj=j sw* "it is I who shall bring it," section 4.4),[64] and in the earliest texts also as subject of an adverbial sentence (Pyr. 1114b^{P} *jnk jr p.t* "I am toward the heaven").[65]

In their structure, stressed pronouns contains three morphs:[66]

(a) An initial element *(j)n*, probably connected with the marker *jn*, which in historical Egyptian is a particle introducing the focalized nominal subject of a cleft sentence, the agent, i.e. the logical subject of a passive predicate,[67] and an interrogative sentence. It has been argued that *jn*, originally a marker of "ergativity," points back to the prehistoric phase still characterized by the presence of cases in the nominal morphology of Egyptian.[68] Traces of ergativity, together with other remnants of a full-fledged case system (section 4.3.1), can be found in Egyptian not only in the variety of uses of the particle *jn*, but also in the identical morphological treatment of the pronominal objects of transitive verbal phrases – whether of finite forms (*sḏm=j sw* "I hear *him*") or of infinitives (*sḏm=f* "hearing *him*") – and of the pronominal subjects of intransitive or adjectival verbs – once again in finite forms (*nfr sw* "*he* is good") as well as in infinitives (*prj.t=f* "*his* coming"). These remnants of an earlier ergativity appear integrated into the nominative-accusative coding (section 4.6.3.3) of historical Egyptian.

(b) A deictic element *k* (in the first persons) or *t* (in the second and third persons), etymologically connected with the pronominal endings of the stative, see (4) below.

(c) A partially modified form of the corresponding suffix pronoun.

The first person pronoun is *jnk* */jaˈnak/, see Akkadian *'anāku*, Hebrew *'ānōkî*.[69] In the second and third person singular there are two sets of independent pronouns, an Old Kingdom form displaying an element *t* following the corresponding form of the enclitic pronoun (second person masc. *ṯwt*, fem. *ṯmt*, third person masc. *swt*, fem. *stt*), and a more recent one, from the late Old Kingdom onward, build according to the pattern described in (a)–(c): second person masc. *ntk* */(ja)nˈtak/, fem. *ntṯ* */(ja)nˈtac/, third person masc. *ntf* */(ja)nˈtaf/, fem. *nts* */(ja)nˈtas/. The plural forms are common to masculine and feminine: first person *jnn* */jaˈnan/ (documented only in postclassical times), second person *ntṯn* */(ja)nˈtaːcin/, third person *ntsn* */(ja)nˈtaːsin/. The third person form has a dual variant *ntsnj*.

(4) *Stative endings*. The pronominal paradigm of personal endings added to the conjugation pattern called *stative* (or *old perfective*, or *pseudoparticiple*)[70] exhibits close kinship to the suffix conjugation of Semitic and Berber, with the addition of a suffix *.j/.w* to the consonantal endings:[71] first person *.kj* > *.kw* (Akk. *-āku*, Berber *-ɣ*), second person *.tj* (Akk. masc. *-āta*, fem. *-āti*), third person masc. *.j* > *.w*, mostly written <ø> (Akk. *-a*), fem. *.tj* (Akk. *-at*); the plural forms show the addition of a morph *n*, which is also found in the independent pronouns and in the Semitic counterparts: first person *.w(j)n* (Akk. *-ānu*), second person *.tw(j)n* (Akk. masc. *-ātunu*, fem. *-ātina*), third person masc. *.wj* (Akk. *-ū*), fem. *.tj* (Akk. *-ā*). A dual form with the addition of an ending *j* to the plural is documented for the second and third person.

The functional array of the Egyptian stative matches the corresponding forms in Semitic and Berber.[72] Although Egyptian stative endings, unlike the Akkadian permansive, cannot be applied to nouns (*šarrāku* "I am a king"),[73] the stative finds its semantic origin in a nominal construction with a conjugated "middle" participle following its subject: *zẖ3w jj.w* "the scribe has gone." The later evolution is characterized by two features: on the one hand, the form maintained its original function with intransitive verbs but was reinterpreted as passive when used with transitive verbs, passive being a semantic subset of the aspectual category of "perfectivity" (*zẖ3w sḏm.w* "the scribe was heard");[74] on the other hand, the stative was integrated into non-stative paradigms such as the narrative use of the first person perfect (*jrj.kj* "I did"), the optative use of the second person prospective (*snb.tj* "may you be healthy" > "Farewell!," CT VI 76c *ḥrj.twn r b3=j pn* "Keep yourselves removed from my soul"), or the use of the third person jussive in eulogies (*nzw-bjt X ʿnḫ.w wḏ3.w snb.w* "the King X – may he be alive, prosperous, and healthy").

All these uses represent a typologically predictable evolution from the original semantic spectrum of the stative as a conjugated nominal form, with a close historical and typological kinship to the grammaticalization of the suffix conjugation form *qatal-a* in Northwest Semitic.[75] Syntactically, the stative is found in classical Egyptian in paradigmatic alternation with the construction "subject + preposition *ḥr* + infinitive" in the so-called pseudo-verbal sentence (*zẖ3w ḥr sḏm* *"the scribe is on hearing" > "the scribe is hearing" vs. *zẖ3w sḏm.w* "the scribe has been heard").

4.4.2 *Personal pronouns in later Egyptian*

In principle, forms and functions of personal pronouns do not change in later Egyptian, the only exception being represented by the form of the third person plural suffix and of the corresponding independent pronoun, which are now *=w* instead of *=sn* and *ntw* instead of *ntsn*. However, because of phonological evolutions and of modified syntactic patterns in adverbial and verbal sentences, four simultaneous phenomena take place:

(a) Vocalic and semivocalic suffixes tend to be dropped. This is particularly the case for the first person suffix **-aj*: *ḏr.t=j* */ɟartaj/ > Coptic ⲧⲟⲟⲧ /doʔt/ "my hand."

(b) The use of enclitic pronouns becomes restricted, until they gradually disappear;[76] while Late Egyptian and Demotic develop a new set of object pronouns (section 4.6.6.5),[77] Coptic exhibits the grammaticalization of a new pattern for the pronominal object, consisting of a prepositional phrase with *m* "in," followed by the direct nominal object or by the suffix pronoun: *a=f-sôtm mmo=i* "he heard me" < *jr=f-sdm jm=j* *"he did the hearing *in* me."[78]

(c) While third person enclitic pronouns are kept as subject of adverbial sentences,[79] the grammaticalization of the conjunction *tj* < *sṯ* "while" (section 4.7) followed by the suffix pronoun creates for this use a new set of proclitic pronouns in the first and second person: **tj-wj* > *twj* > ϯ-; **tj-ṯw*, **tj-ṯn* > *twk*, *twt* > ⲕ-, ⲧⲉ-; **tj-n* > *twn* > ⲧⲛ̄-; **tj-ṯn* > *twtn* > ⲧⲉⲧⲛ̄- : *twtn jm* "you are there."

(d) Finally, the pattern "preposition+infinitive" and the stative are grammaticalized as adverbial constructions, so that they too can be preceded by the new proclitic pronouns *twj*, *twk* etc.; already in Late Egyptian, therefore, stative endings become redundant and are dropped.[80] In Coptic, only the third person stative (either masculine or feminine, depending on the morphological class) is kept for each verbal lexeme and used for all persons and numbers: ϯ-ϩⲕⲁⲉⲓⲧ "I am hungry" < *twj ḥqr.tj* (feminine form), ⲥ-ⲟⲩⲟϫ "she is whole" < *st wḏꜣ.w* (masculine form).[81]

Table 4.5 captures the main morphological features of personal pronouns in both phases of Egyptian.

Table 4.5 Egyptian personal pronouns and their Coptic outcome

NUMBER	PERSON	SUFFIX	ENCLITIC/ PROCLITIC	STRESSED	STATIVE ENDINGS
SINGULAR	1	*=j* > =ⲓ	OEg: *-wj* LEg: *twj-* > ϯ-	*jnk* */ja'nak/ > ⲁⲛⲟⲕ	*.kj* > *.kw*
	2 masc.	*=k* > =ⲕ	OEg: *-kw* > *-ṯw* LEg: *twk-* > ⲕ-	OK: *ṯwt* MK: *ntk* */ntak/ > ⲛ̄ⲧⲟⲕ	*.tj*
	2 fem.	*=ṯ* > =ⲉ	OEg: *-ṯm* > *-ṯn* LEg: *twt-* > ⲧⲉ-	OK: *ṯmt* MK: *ntṯ* */ntac/ > ⲛ̄ⲧⲟ	*.tj*
	3 masc.	*=f* > =ϥ	OEg: *-sw* LEg: *sw-* > *ef-* > ϥ-	OK: *swt* MK: *ntf* */ntaf/ > ⲛ̄ⲧⲟϥ	*.j* > *.w*
	3 fem.	*=s* > =ⲥ	OEg: *-sj/-st* LEg: *st-* > *es-* > ⲥ-	OK: *stt* MK: *nts* */ntas/ > ⲛ̄ⲧⲟⲥ	*.tj*
DUAL	1	*=nj*			
	2	*=ṯnj*	*-ṯnj*		*.twnj*
	3	*=snj*	*-snj*	*ntsnj*	*.wj*
PLURAL	1	*=n* > =ⲛ	OEg: *-n* LEg: *twn-* > ⲧⲛ̄-	*jnn* */ja'nan/ > ⲁⲛⲟⲛ	*.wjn*
	2	*=ṯn* > =ⲧⲛ̄	OEg: *-ṯn* LEg: *twtn-*>ⲧⲉⲧⲛ̄-	*ntṯn* */'nta:cin/ > ⲛ̄ⲧⲱⲧⲛ̄	*.twjn*
	3 OEg	*=sn*	*-sn/-st* > -ⲥⲟⲩ, -ⲥⲉ	*ntsn* */'nta:sin/	masc. *.wj*
	LEg	*=w* > =ⲟⲩ	*st-* > ⲥⲉ-	*ntw* */ntaw/ > ⲛ̄ⲧⲟⲟⲩ	fem. *.tj*

4.4.3 *Deictic, interrogative and relative pronouns*

Earlier Egyptian displays four morphological series for the formation of adjectives with deictic function. In these series, each of which conveys a different demonstrative meaning, morphemes consist of a pronominal base (generally *p* for the masculine, *t* for the feminine, *jp* and *jpt* for the plural patterns), followed by a deictic indicator: *n* for closeness (*rmṯ pn* "this man"), *f* for distance (*ḥjm.t tf* "that woman"), *w* (originally *j*) also for closeness (*nṯr.w jpw* "those gods"), *ꜣ* for vocative reference (*pꜣ mrjj* "O beloved one"). The development in Middle Egyptian displays a tendency for the *pw*-series to be superseded by the *pn*-series in the demonstrative use and to be restricted to the function as copula in nominal sentences (*rmṯ pw* "this is a man," see chapter 4) , and for the *pꜣ*-series to acquire anaphoric function and to become the definite article in later Egyptian (*pꜣ rmṯ* "the man").

Parallel to the adjectival series, earlier Egyptian also exhibits a set of demonstrative pronouns, in which a demonstrative base *n* is followed by the same deictic indicators used in the adjectival paradigm (*n*, *f*, *w*, *ꜣ*). While these pronouns were originally unmarked in gender and number (*nn*, *nf*, *nw*, *nꜣ* "this," "these things") and were treated syntactically in earlier Egyptian as masculine plurals when accompanied by participles and relative forms, but as feminine singulars when referred to by a resumptive pronoun,[82] they replace in Middle Egyptian the old plural adjectival forms and appear in pronominal constructions with the determinative pronoun *n(j)*: *nn n(j) sjrw.w* (*"this of officials" >) "these officials." As in the case of the singular adjectives *pꜣ* and *tꜣ*, the anaphoric pronoun *nꜣ* eventually becomes the plural definite article in later Egyptian: Middle Egyptian *nꜣ n(j) ꜥ.wt* "the aforementioned rooms," Late Egyptian *nꜣ-rmt.w*, Coptic *n-rôme* "the men."

Table 4.6 Deictics in earlier Egyptian

ADJECTIVES				PRONOUNS	ADVERBS
SINGULAR		PLURAL			
MASC.	FEM.	MASC.	FEM.	NEUTER	
pn "this"	*tn*	*jpn*	*jptn*	*nn*	*ꜥn*
pf "that"	*tf*	*jpf*	*jptf*	*nf*	*ꜥf*
pj > *pw* "this"	*tj* > *tw*	*jpw*	*jptw*	*nw*	
pꜣ "the said"	*tꜣ*			*nꜣ*	*ꜥꜣ*

The paradigm of demonstrative elements is completed by a set of adverbs characterized by the formant *ꜥ* (*ꜥayin*) followed by the deictic marker: the most common is *ꜥꜣ* "here." Post-classical Middle Egyptian of Dyn. XVIII also documents the adverbs *'n* and *'f*, which can be pronominalized by means of the derivational morpheme *tj*: *'n.tj* "the one here," *'f.tj* "the one there."[83]

Table 4.6 visualizes the paradigms of earlier Egyptian demonstratives; the most common morphemes or those which play a role in the later diachronic development are underlined.

In later Egyptian, the picture changes considerably. While the *pn*-series is kept in Late Egyptian only in a few bound expressions (*hɜw pn* "this day"), the deictic paradigm is reorganized on the basis of the *pɜ*-series. The bare morphemes *pɜ-* */piʔ/, *tɜ-*, *nɜ-* acquire the function of definite articles,[84] whereas a derived form with suffix *j* (*pɜj*, *tɜj*, *nɜj*) is used as adjective when it precedes the noun it qualifies (*pɜj rmt*, **πει-ρωμε** "this man"), as pronoun in independent use (*pɜj* > **παι**, **πη** "this one") or as copula, in which case it follows a predicate introduced in Coptic by a definite or indefinite article (*rmt pɜj*, **ου-ρωμε πε** "this is a man," *ḥm.t tɜj*, **ου-ϲϩιμε τε** "this is a woman"). Unlike in earlier Egyptian, where the masculine copula *pw* is used regardless of the gender and number of the antecedent, in later Egyptian the copula *pɜj* > **πε**, *tɜj* > **τε**, *nɜj* > **νε** agrees in gender and number with its antecedent. In Coptic bipartite cleft sentences, however (section 4.9), the copula is assimilated to a definite article *pɜ* preceding the second nominal phrase; in the Bohairic dialect, it is invariably the masculine **πε**. The deictic adverb is now *dy* > **ται**, most probably an Upper Egyptian doublette of the earlier Egyptian form *'ɜ*, in which the outcome of Afroasiatic **d* is /d/ rather than /ʕ/ (section 3.6.1).[85]

Table 4.7 Deictics in later Egyptian

ARTICLES			ADJECTIVES AND PRONOUNS		
M.	F.	PL.	MASCULINE	FEMININE	PLURAL
pɜ- > **π(ε)-**	*tɜ-* > **τ(ε)-**	*nɜ-* > **ν(ε)-**	*pɜj* > **παι**, **πη** "this" (pron.)	*tɜj* > **ται**, **τη** "this" (pron.)	*nɜj* > **ναι**, **νη** "these" (pron.)
			πει- "this" (adj.)	**τει-** "this" (adj.)	**νει-** "these" (adj.)
			πε "is" (copula)	**τε** "is" (copula)	**νε** "are" (copula)
			pɜ-n > *pɜ-* > **πα-** "that-of"	*tɜ-nt* > *tɜ-* > **τα-** "that-of"	*nɜ-n* > *nɜ-* > **να-** "those-of"
			pɜj=j > **πα-**, **πω=ι** "my, mine"	*tɜj=j* > **τα-**, **τω=ι** "my, mine"	*nɜj=j* > **να-**,**νω=ι** "my, mine"
			pɜj=k > **πεκ-**, **πω=κ** "your(s)" (m)	*tɜj=k* > **τεκ-**, **τω=κ** "your(s)" (m)	*nɜj=k* > **νεκ-**, **νω=κ** "your(s)" (m)
			etc.		

In accordance with the analytic tendency discussed in section 4.1, later Egyptian demonstratives may also control pronominal possessive suffixes to form complete adjectival and pronominal paradigms: *tȝj=k-jp.t* > ⲧⲉ=ⲕ-ⲉⲓⲟⲡⲉ "your mission," *pȝj=k pȝj* > ⲡⲱ=ⲕ ⲡⲉ "this is yours." In the same pattern, the *pȝ*-series followed by the determinative pronoun *n(j)* is used with a nominal, rather than pronominal possessor: *pȝ-n s nb* "what belongs to every man" (sections 4.5, 4.10). Structures and functions of deictic morphemes in later Egyptian are summarized in table 4.7.

The most common morpheme for the formation of interrogatives is *m* (Arabic *man* "who," *mā* "what"), originally a pronoun "who?," "what?" (CT VI 314b *ṯwt tr m* "who are you then?"), but used most frequently in prepositional compounds (*ḥr-m* "why?," *mj-m* "how?") or with the "ergative" particle *jn* (section 4.4.1) which indicates a focalized subject (*jn-m* > *nm*, ⲛⲓⲙ): Sh.S. 69 *(j)n-m jnj ṯw* "who brought you?" Other interrogative pronouns are *jḫ* > ⲁϣ "what," in earlier Egyptian also *pw*, *p(w)-tr*, *zj*, *jšst*, and in Late Egyptian the interrogative adjective *jṯ* "which?" as focalized subject of a cleft sentence: *jṯ šms pȝ-jj n=k* "which messenger is the one who came to you?"

Determinative and relative pronouns are formed by means of a base *n*, which builds the determinative series masc. sing. *n(j)*, fem. *n.t*, pl. *n.w*, used as genitival marker: *nzw n(j) km.t* "the king of Egypt," *nʔ.t n.t nḥḥ* "the city of eternity." A morph *t(j)* is affixed to the pronominal base *n* to form the relative pronouns *ntj*, *ntt*, *ntj.w*, used in adverbial and verbal sentences and resumed by a resumptive element in the oblique cases: *bw ntj nṯr.w jm* "the place in which the gods are," lit. "that the gods are there"; *jr.wj=kj ntj mȝȝ=k jm=sn(j)* "your eyes with which you see," lit. "that you see with them." The relative pronoun is used only when the antecedent is either morphologically determined or semantically specific; non-specific antecedents are modified by asyndetic constructions without overt expression of the relative pronoun, labeled in Egyptological literature "virtual relative clauses" (section 6.3.3).

Parallel to the positive relative pronoun *ntj*, *ntt*, *ntj.w*, Egyptian also possesses a negative series *jwtj*, *jwtt*, *jwtj.w* "who not, which not." These relative pronouns are functionally equivalent to a positive relative pronoun *ntj* controlling a negative predication: Pt. 235[86] *jwtj sḏm=f n ḏd ẖ.t=f* "who does not listen to what his belly says," semantically equivalent to a clause **ntj nj sḏm.n=f n ḏd ẖ.t=f*;[87] Urk. I 192,14 *jwtj zȝ=f* "who does not have a son," equivalent to **ntj nn zȝ=f*.

Save for the expected phonological developments, determinative and relative pronouns survive unchanged in later Egyptian; the use of the genitival pronoun *n(j)* is gradually expanded, the old construct state being limited in Coptic to few bound constructions. Also, in the later stages of the language a new genitival marker ⲛ̄ⲧⲉ-, originally a prepositional construction (later Eg. *m-dj* = earlier Eg. *m-ʿw* "at, by"),[88] is used in presence of an indefinite, possessive, or compound antecedent: ⲡⲙⲟⲟⲩ ⲉⲧⲟⲛϩ ⲛ̄ⲧⲉ-ⲡⲟⲩⲟⲓⲛ "the living (*et-onh*) water (*moou*) of the light (*nte-p-ouoin*)."

4.5 Numerals

Numerals have often – although by no means always – been considered to be a conservative part of speech:[89] it is not surprising, therefore, that Egyptian words for numbers[90] show a wide array of correspondences with other Afroasiatic languages, most notably with Semitic and Berber. The following table shows the basic forms of Egyptian numerals, each of them accompanied by its fullest hieroglyphic writing, by a phonological reconstruction, and by a comparative reference.

Table 4.8 Egyptian and Coptic numerals

1	*wʿw* */ˈwuʕʕuw/ > ⲟⲩⲁ Sem. *wḥd*	10	*mḏw* */ˈmu:ɟaw/ > ⲙⲏⲧ Berb. *mraw*[91]	100	**š(n)t* */ši(nju)t/[92] > ϣⲉ
2	*sn.wj* */siˈnuwwaj/[93] > ⲥⲛⲁⲩ Sem. *ṯny*	20	**ḏwtj* */ɟaˈwa:taj/[94] > ϫⲟⲩⲱⲧ	200	**š(n).tj* */šinju:taj/[95] > ϣⲏⲧ
3	*ḫmtw* */ˈχamtaw/ > ϣⲟⲙⲛ̄ⲧ	30	*mʿbꜣ* */ˈmaʕbvʀ/[96] > ⲙⲁⲁⲃ	300–900	**ḫmt-š(n.w)t* etc.[97]
4	*jfdw* */jifˈdaw/ > ϥⲧⲟⲟⲩ Hausa *fuɗu*	40	**ḥm.w* */ḥvˈmew/[98] > ϩⲙⲉ	1,000	*ḫꜣ* */χaʀ/ > ϣⲟ
5	*djw* */ˈdi:jaw/[99] > ϯⲟⲩ	50	**dj.w* */ˈdijjaw/[100] > ⲧⲁⲓⲟⲩ	10,000	*ḏbʿ* */ɟvˈbaʕ/[101] > ⲧⲃⲁ
6	*sjsw* */ˈsaʔsaw/ > ⲥⲟⲟⲩ Sem. *šdš*	60	**sjs.w* */saʔˈsew/ > ⲥⲉ	100,000	*ḥfn* see Sem. *ʔlp* "1,000"
7	*sfḫw* */ˈsafχaw/ > ⲥⲁϣϥ̄ Sem. *šbʿ*	70	**sfḫ.w* */safˈχew/ > ϣϥⲉ	1,000,000	*ḥḥ* */ḥaḥ/[102]
8	*ḫmnw* */χaˈma:naw/ > ϣⲙⲟⲩⲛ Sem. *ṯmny*	80	**ḫmn.w* */χamˈnew/ > ϩⲙⲉⲛⲉ		
9	*psḏw* */piˈsi:ɟaw/[103] > ⲯⲓⲧ Sem. *tšʿ*	90	**psḏj.w* */pisˈɟijjaw/ > ⲡⲉⲥⲧⲁⲓⲟⲩ		

The study of the syntactic behavior of numerals is complicated by the early tendency to write them ideographically, using for that purpose a set of hieroglyphic signs expressing the numbers 10^0...10^6 (section 2.2). It is clear, however, that "1" and "2" were adjectives following the noun they modify (in the singular or the dual), whereas the other numerals represented an autonomous part of speech. The numbers "3" through "10" were originally treated as singular substantives, agreeing in gender with the plural noun they refer to, which followed them appositionally: *psḏw zp.w* "nine times," *sfḫ.t=f j'r.wt* "his seven snakes." When written ideographically, which becomes the rule in Middle and Late Egyptian, numbers are written after the noun they refer to; this may appear in the plural form (*pꜣ ẖrd.w 3* "the three children," probably **pꜣ-ḫmtw n(j) ẖrd.w* in the underlying segment of speech), but from Middle Egyptian onwards more often in the singular.

In later Egyptian, the appositional noun is regularly in the singular and it is often introduced by the genitival marker *n* (Coptic ⲛ̄-): *pꜣ 77 n ntr* "the seventy-seven gods," ⲡⲥⲁϣϥ̄ ⲛ̄ϩⲟⲟⲩ "the seven days."

In earlier Egyptian, ordinals from 2 to 9 are formed by means of a suffix *.nw* added to the corresponding cardinal, which may be written as an ideogram: *ḫmt.nw zp* "the third time," *m zp=f 3.nw ḥꜣb-sd* "in his third jubilaeum," probably **m ḫmt.nw zp=f (nj) ḥꜣb-sd* in the underlying segment of speech. The word for "first" is the *nisba* adjective *tpj* */ta'pij/ from *tp* */tap/ "head." In later Egyptian, the derivational pattern for ordinals is a construction with the active participle of the verb *mḥ* "to fill": *pꜣj=w zp mḥ-5* "their fifth time" ("*their filling-five time"), ⲡⲙⲟⲩ ⲙ̄ⲙⲉϩⲥⲛⲁⲩ "the second death." In later Egyptian the adjective "first" is usually *ḥꜣ.tj* */ḥu'ʀiːtij/ (Coptic ϩⲟⲩⲉⲓⲧ) from *ḥꜣ.t* */ḥuːʀit/ "front," in Coptic also ϣⲟⲣⲡ from the root *ḫrp* "to lead."

Distributive numbers are formed through a reduplication of the basic cardinal: *w'w w'w* "one each," ⲥⲛⲁⲩ ⲥⲛⲁⲩ "two each."

4.6 The verb

4.6.1 *Introduction*

The verbal morphology of earlier Egyptian is one of the most intricate chapters of Egyptian linguistics.

(a) First of all, the vocalic patterns for verbal stems are less easily inferred than their nominal counterparts, mainly because the verbal morphology of later Egyptian, which replaces the synthetic verbal forms of earlier phases through periphrastic constructions with a verbal prefix followed by the infinitive, fails to provide a reliable basis for the understanding of vocalic alternations. Akkadian transcriptions, Late Middle Egyptian texts in Greek alphabet and Coptic do provide valuable information, but their paradigmatic value, i.e. the likelihood for individual witnesses to be extended to other verbal classes, remains debatable.

(b) The second difficulty is posed by the relevance of semivocalic affixes and their paradigmatic representativeness. Many verbal forms exhibit a suffix *j* or *w* in some verbal classes, especially those with final weak radical, but not in others. Whether one takes this to be a purely graphic phenomenon or the sign of morphological oppositions affects the general interpretation of verbal morphology.

(c) A third difficulty is that while in the nominal morphology the differences within the main stages of the history of the language (Old Egyptian, Middle Egyptian and Late Middle Egyptian for earlier Egyptian vs. Late Egyptian, Demotic and Coptic for later Egyptian) are marginal, in the morphology and syntax of verbal forms a major evolution takes place between Old and Middle Egyptian on the one hand and between Late Egyptian and Coptic on the other hand. The picture is, therefore, rather complex.

(d) Finally, work on verbal morphology (as opposed to syntax) has been partially neglected in modern approaches to Egyptian grammar (section 1.3), due to a certain extent to the difficulties discussed above, but also to the impression that, because of the rigid syntax of Egyptian, little contribution to our understanding of the language as a whole could be expected from the study of morphological alternations in the verbal system. Only in recent times one can observe a new wave of interest in verbal morphology.[104]

4.6.2 General features of verbal morphology

Egyptian verbal forms[105] can be classified according to whether they convey the indication of the subject, in which case they are ***finite*** (the basic conjugation *sḏm=f* "he hears" and a variety of affixal forms), or they represent subjectless nominal phrases, in which case they are ***non-finite*** (the participle *sḏm* "the hearer," the infinitive *sḏm* "to hear" and the so-called negatival complement NEG-*sḏm.w* "not-to-hear"). Finite verbal forms, which can be treated as predicative VP, as NP (after prepositions), as AdjP (relative forms), or as AP (in clauses of circumstance), are composed of a verbal stem, derived from the lexical root with the addition of suffixes (including *.ø*), followed by the subject, which can be nominal (*sḏm rmṯ* "the man hears") or pronominal (*sḏm=f* "he hears"). Thus, unlike verbal formations in other Afroasiatic languages (Arabic *yasmaʿu* "he hears," *yasmaʿu 'l-rağulu* "the man hears"), the Egyptian suffix conjugation does not display the pronominal affix of the third person in the presence of nominal subjects, a feature which is relevant for our understanding of the origin of this morphological pattern.[106] Non-finite verbal forms are also built on the basis of a verbal stem; they convey the indication of gender and number, and in the case of the participles[107] also markers of tense, aspect, mood, and voice.

Table 4.9 The basic patterns of Egyptian verbal morphology

NUMBER	PERSON	SUFFIX CONJ.	STATIVE	NON-FINITE FORMS
	1	*sḏm=j* "I hear"	*(jw=j) sḏm.kw* "I was heard"	
	2 m.	*sḏm=k*	*(jw=k) sḏm.tj*	INFINITIVE:
	2 f.	*sḏm=ṯ*	*(jw=ṯ) sḏm.tj*	*sḏm* "to hear"
SINGULAR	3 m. pron.	*sḏm=f*	*(jw=f) sḏm.w*	
	3 m. nom.	*sḏm rmṯ*	*(NP) sḏm.w*	NEG. COMPLEMENT:
	3 f. pron.	*sḏm=s*	*(jw=s) sḏm.tj*	*sḏm.w* "(not) to hear"
	3 f. nom.	*sḏm ḥjm.t*	*(NP) sḏm.tj*	PARTICIPLES:
	1	*sḏm=nj*		*sḏm* "hearer"/"heard" (m.)
DUAL	2	*sḏm=ṯnj*		*sḏm.t* fem. s.
	3	*sḏm=snj*	*(jw=snj/NP) sḏm.wj*, fem. *sḏm.tj*	*sḏm.w* masc. pl.
	1	*sḏm=n*	*(jw=n) sḏm.wjn*	*sḏm.t* fem. pl.
PLURAL	2	*sḏm=ṯn*	*(jw=ṯn) sḏm.twjn*	
	3 pron.	*sḏm=sn*	*(jw=sn) sḏm.w/sḏm.tj*	
	3 nomin.	*sḏm rmṯ.w*	*(NP) sḏm.w/sḏm.tj*	

In addition to these two categories of forms, Egyptian displays a suffix conjugation pattern which follows the subject and is marked by a different set of pronominal endings, called *stative* on the basis of its primary semantic function, *old perfective* since it displays similarities with the Semitic suffix conjugation, or *pseudoparticiple* because of its syntactic behavior, which to a certain extent is analogous to that of the participles.[108]

Table 4.9 shows the morphological structure of Egyptian verbal morphology, using as an example, as is the custom in Egyptology, the conjugation of the verbal root *sḏm* "to hear" in the unmarked stem with suffix *.ø*, usually called *sḏm=f* and conventionally pronounced [seɟeˈmef], together with the stative and the non-finite patterns (participles and infinitive).

In general, finite Egyptian verbal forms display a morphologically overt indication of (a) tense and/or aspect, (b) mood and (c) voice.[109]

(a) As far as the first category is concerned, while the traditional assumption, largely derived from the "semitocentric" interpretation of the Egyptian verbal system shared by the Berlin School and its followers (section 1.3), has been that the fundamental reference of Egyptian verbal forms is aspectual, i.e. that they present a predication according to its contextual completeness (*perfective aspect*), or lack thereof (*imperfective aspect*), regardless of the temporal location vis-à-vis the speaker,[110] the trend is now to take them as temporal forms[111] which assess whether the verbal predication takes place before (*past tense* or *preterite*), in concomitance (*present* or *unmarked tense*), or after (*future tense*) the time reference of the speech act.[112]

Apart from terminological quarrels which often overshadow the issue, it seems that Egyptian, like many other languages, combined in its verbal morphology these two temporal dimensions, i.e. the internal composition (*aspect*) and the external location (*tense*) of a verbal predication.[113] Egyptian verbal forms are "relative tenses" or "aspects":[114] their semantic reference can be determined only within the syntactic context of their appearance: while in initial position they tend to be primarily temporal, fixing the time location of the verbal predicate in reference to the moment of the speech act (*jj.n=j* "I came" vs. *jj=j* "I come"), in non-intial position, i.e. within a string of discourse, they derive their temporal reference from the initial form and are more likely to convey aspectual features: *mk wj m jj.t* "look, I am coming" vs. *mk wj jj.kj* "look, I have come."

(b) A similar analysis applies to the category of *mood*:[115] in general, the speaker's attitude to a verbal predication – whether neutral ("indicative") or marked ("epistemic" or "deontic" mood) – applies to events which have not yet taken place;[116] mood will, therefore, apply most frequently to future events. Besides the imperative, modal oppositions affect in Egyptian the temporal/aspectual category usually called "prospective."

Since these verbal categories overlap in actual strings of discourse, where they are combined with semantic references provided by the context and by the lexical choices of the speaker, it is more predictable – obviously not on the theoretical level, but rather in terms of the likelihood for a form to actually occur in spoken or written discourse[117] – for a preterite predication to be perfective, i.e. presented as completed, for a temporally unmarked form to be imperfective, i.e. not (yet) completed, and for an action expected to take place in the future to convey the attitude of the speaker to this expected predication, i.e. to exhibit modal features.

(c) A true passive voice with overt expression of the agent is relatively rare in Egyptian, and, according to a cross-linguistic tendency,[118] develops gradually out of the paradigm of perfective forms: for example, from an original **sḏm.t=f* "he has/has been heard," two forms *sḏm.t=f* "he has heard" vs. *sḏm.tw=f* "he is heard" were eventually grammaticalized (section 4.6.3.3).[119] Much more frequent is the "middle," intransitive use of transitive verbal lexemes in the perfect (*jw=f sḏm.w* "it has been heard")[120] or in the prospective (*sḏm.w=f* "it will be heard") to indicate the actual or expected result of an action in reference to its subject.

The three semantic categories of tense and aspect, mood, and voice were conveyed by morphological oppositions and superimposed on the lexical structure of the verbal lexeme, which in its turn provides a further temporal dimension, called *Aktionsart*, treated in some linguistic schools as a form of aspect.[121] This is the temporal structure inherent to the verbal lexeme; it specifies, for example, whether a verbal predication consists of a single act (*wpj* "to open," punctual *Aktionsart*), or is extended over time (*sḏr* "to sleep," durative *Aktionsart*), whether the existence of the argument(s) is affected by the predication (*qd* "to build," a *transformative* verb) or not (*sḏm* "to hear," a *non-transformative* verb), whether the predication presents the result of a process (*gmj* "to find," an *achievement*), or entails a phase preceding the goal itself (*jnj* "to fetch," an *accomplishment*), whether it conveys an action by a subject (*mšʿ* "to walk," an *activity*), or a *state* (*nḏm* "to be pleasant").[122] Rather than on the grammatical form, these temporal features depend on the ontology of the described situation, i.e. on the internal semantic structure of the lexeme, and remain constant in all its forms; they do, however, bear heavily on the spectrum of semantically acceptable combinations for each verbal root, restricting the number of choices by the speaker. Accordingly, punctual verbs will appear more frequently in the perfective aspect (*wpj.n=j* "I opened") focusing on the verbal action, whereas durative verbs will be more frequent in the imperfective (*sḏr=f* "while he sleeps") and less salient within the flow of discourse;[123] transformative verbs will be more likely than non-transformative verbs to be found in passive constructions (*jw prw qd.w* "the house was built"); verbs of achievement are unlikely candidates for imperfective uses (*gmj=j* *"I am finding"), which on the contrary are frequent with verbs of accomplishment (*zẖꜣ=j* "I am writing"); verbs of activity will display a much larger inventory of temporal or aspectual references than stative verbs, which in turn are preferably used as adjectives, etc. No verbal root, therefore, will exhibit a complete paradigm of verbal forms: rather, the morphological patterns discussed in the next sections and conventionally applied to the verb *sḏm* "to hear" and *jrj* "to do" represent a purely grammatical inventory of the Egyptian verb.

4.6.3 *Verbal morphology in earlier Egyptian*

4.6.3.1 *Tense and aspect*. The main temporal and aspectual opposition is between (a) "past" (perfect and perfective) and (b) "temporally unmarked" (imperfective and aorist) forms.

(a) The basic preterital form exhibits a suffix *.n* after the verbal stem, followed by the nominal or pronominal subject: *sḏm.n=f* "he heard." The stem was vocalized *(ca)cic- in biradical (2-rad.) and triradical roots (3-rad.), and *cac- (< *cacij-) in weak verbal classes (III-inf.):[124] *sḏm.n=f* */sa'ɟimnaf/ "he heard," *sḏm.n rmṯ* */saɟimna'raːmac/ "the man heard"; *ḏd.n=n* */'ɟidnan/ "we said," *ḏd.n ḥjm.t* */ɟidna'ḥijmat/ "the woman said"; *jrj.n=k* */'jarnak/ < */jarijnak/ "you made," *jrj.n jtj=j* */jarna'jatjaj/ < */jarijnajatjaj/ "my father made." The *sḏm.n=f* form appears in a variety of syntactic patterns: as the main predicate of a verbal sentence (Urk. I 2,8 *jnj.n=f r jsw ꜣḥ.t 200 sṯꜣ.t* "he has bought a field of 200 arouras"),[125] as topicalized VP in initial position (always with verbs of motion: Urk. I 103,7 *jj.n mšꜥ pn m ḥtp...* "this army has returned in peace..."), or in subordinate use as circumstantial VP (Urk. I 103,8 *...ẖbꜣ.n=f tꜣ ḥrj.w-šꜥ* "...after it had ravaged the sand-dwellers' land").

Originally, the temporal and aspectual reference of the *sḏm.n=f* may have been the present perfect rather than the past perfective:[126] in the early texts it does not appear as a narrative tense, but belongs to the paradigm of the present. Accordingly, the *sḏm.n=f* can also display other functions within the range of the present, especially the gnomic use, i.e. the general present in performative expressions (*ḏj.n=j n=k tꜣ.w nb* "herewith I give you all lands") or in the negative construction *nj sḏm.n=f* "he does not / cannot hear."[127]

In addition to the present perfect *sḏm.n=f*, Old Egyptian possessed two real preterites. The first one is a form in which the verbal stem is followed directly by the nominal or pronominal subject: it is called *indicative sḏm=f* and is well attested in the texts of the Old Kingdom (Urk. I 124,17 *hꜣb wj ḥm=f* "his Majesty sent me"). The stem was probably vocalized *cvc(c)i-: *hꜣb=f* */hvʀ'bif/ "he sent."[128] In classical Egyptian, this form is functionally replaced by the *sḏm.n=f* and is limited to archaic uses and bound constructions, such as the negative form *nj sḏm=f* "he did not hear."

The second form, the *stative*, originally a conjugated verbal adjective,[129] is used in Old Egyptian as first person counterpart to the indicative *sḏm=f* (Urk. I 100, 7–9 *rḏj wj ḥm=f m smr wꜥ.tj...jrj.kj r ḥzj.t (wj) ḥm=f* "His Majesty appointed me Sole Companion...I acted so that His Majesty would praise [me]"), as main predicate in the so-called pseudoverbal sentences (always with verbs of motion: Urk. I 126,2 *jw=j prj.kj m-sꜣ=f* "I went after him"), and as subordinate perfective VP following its subject as predicative complement (Urk. I 125,15–16 *gmj.n=j ḥqꜣ jꜣm šm.w rf r tꜣ-ṯmḥ* "I found that the ruler of Yam had gone off to the land of Tjemeh" < *"I found the ruler of Yam having gone off to the land of Tjemeh").[130]

The stem was *(ca)cvc- in the strong classes and *cacij- in the III-inf.:[131] first person *stp.kj* "I was chosen" (**/satvpakvj/ >) */satˈpaːkvj/,[132] second person masc. *spd.tj* "you are sharp" */saˈpidtvj/ > */səpedtə/ > Late Middle Eg. <spet>, fem. *bz.tj* "you have been introduced" */ˈbuztvj/ > Late Middle Eg. <best>;[133] third person masc. *qd.w* "it was built" */ˈquːdaw/ > **кнт** /geːt/ "to be built," *stp.w* "it was chosen" */ˈsatpaw/ > **сотп** /sotp/ "to be chosen," *msj.w* "he was born" */ˈmasjaw/ > **мосє** /mosʔ/ "to be born," fem. *jwr.tj* "she is pregnant" */jaˈwirtvj/ > */ʔaʔeʔtə/ > **єєт** /ʔeʔt/ "to be pregnant," *špj.tj* "she is ashamed" */ˈšapijtvj/ > */šəpiːtə/ > ᴮϣϥιт /špiːt/ "to be ashamed."[134]

The development from Old Egyptian past forms to the Middle Egyptian paradigm is marked by an increasing preference for textually bound oppositions between predicative forms (*sḏm.n=f* and stative) introduced by a particle or by a topicalized VP and topicalized verbal forms in initial position (only *sḏm.n=f*). The indicative *sḏm=f* and the narrative use of the first person stative become sporadic, the only licensed syntactic position of the stative being now the non-initial position, either as main predicate or as subordinate form in pseudoverbal sentences. Periphrastic constructions referring to the past, such as *ʿḥʿ.n sḏm.n=f* "then he heard" and *ʿḥʿ.n=j prj.kw* "then I came," appear already in the First Intermediate Period, superseding the indicative *sḏm=f* and the first person stative and joining as preterital forms the predicative *sḏm.n=f* introduced by a particle: Sh.S. 67 *jw wpj.n=f rꜣ=f r=j* "he opened his mouth toward me"; Sh.S. 2–3 *mk pḥ.n=n ẖnw* "look, we have reached the residence." The difference between the perfective use in the former sentence and the present perfect in the latter is an example of lexical constrictions: *wpj* "to open" indicates an accomplishment, *pḥ* "to reach" an achievement.

The perfective paradigm also exhibits a pattern with affix *.t*, the so-called *sḏm.t=f*. This form is in earlier Egyptian a linguistic remnant with a restricted range of uses: as subordinate negative perfective form after the particle *nj* (Sh.S. 97–98 *sr=sn ḏʿ nj jj.t=f* "they foretold a storm before it had come") and after prepositions implying completion, such as *r* "until" or *ḏr* "since" (Sin. B 247 *r pḥ.t=j dmj n(j) jṯw* "until I reached the town of Itju"). In spite of its occurrence only in bound constructions, this form shows a surprising stability, surviving until Coptic.

A *contingent* form *sḏm.jn=f* "then he heard," built with the particle *jn*, was used in earlier Egyptian to refer to preterital events whose occurrence was directly dependent on the situation described in the preceding context: Peas. R 1.5[135] *ḏd.jn sḫ.tj pn n ḥjm.t=f tn* "then this peasant said to his wife."[136]

(b) Unmarked forms indicate the general present or *aorist* and derive their temporal or aspectual reference from the syntactic context in which they appear. To this category belongs the basic pattern of the Egyptian conjugation system, the *sḏm=f.* This form, however, is morphologically ambiguous, consisting of at least two distinct patterns. The first one shows a reduplication of the second radical in the III-inf. (*jrr=f* from *jrj* "to do") and of II-gem. verbs (*mꜣꜣ=f* from *mꜣꜣ* "to see"), and in Old Egyptian a *j*-prefix in the 2-rad. (*j.ḏd=f* from *ḏd* "to say") and in a few weak classes;[137] it is used as topicalized VP in initial position (Sin. B 263 *jrr ḥm=k m mrj.t=f* "*your Majesty acts* according to his wish"), as nominalized VP in nominal environments (Pyr. 1223a *jr wdfj ḏꜣꜣ=ṯn mḫn.t n N pn…* "if it is delayed *that you ferry* the ferry-boat to this King…"), or in headings or titles (CT V 28c *ḥꜥꜥ jmn.t nfr.t m ḫsfw zj pn* "*this is how the Beautiful West rejoices* in welcoming this man"). Because of its formal connection to similar Afroasiatic forms (see Akk. *iparras*), this form was traditionally called "imperfective *sḏm=f*," although its use in Egyptian, rather than by aspectual features, is determined primarily by its syntactic function as topicalized or nominalized VP; hence its modern label "*emphatic* or *nominal sḏm=f*." Like its Semitic equivalent *iparras*, the nominal *sḏm=f* is based on a nominal stem and was probably vocalized *cacam-: *sḏm zꜣ=j* */saɟamˈziːʀaj/ "my son listens," *jrr=s* */jaˈraːrvs/ "she does."[138]

The second *sḏm=f* pattern is used in non-initial position, i.e. when preceded by a particle or a topicalized element. In this case, the temporally unmarked aorist form is the non-reduplicating *sḏm=f*-form, for example *jrj=f* "he does" from the verb *jrj* "to do." When following the initial particle *jw*, with or without topicalized subject, the aorist indicates a general or gnomic present (Sh.S. 17–18 *jw rꜣ n(j) zj nḥm=f sw* "a man's speech can save him"). This form was previously called "perfective *sḏm=f*," a label encompassing not only this type of *sḏm=f*, but also the indicative *sḏm=f* discussed in (a) above and the prospective (section 4.6.3.2). But the Standard theory, in its tendency to generalize the role of substitutional equivalents in similar syntactic environments, adopted the term "*circumstantial sḏm=f*," interpreting all non-initial VP as functionally adverbial. While this form, like the *sḏm.n=f* and the stative, can indeed be used adverbially as a subordinate clause when controlled by a higher syntactic node, such as the main verbal phrase (Hatnub 4,3–4[139] *jw rmṯ.w 80 ḫd.w prj=sn ḥr wꜣ.t* "Eighty men returned north, *going forth* on the road"), it functions nonetheless as true verbal predicate in many patterns, for example when it is introduced by particles (Sh.S. 18–19 *jw mdw=f ḏj=f ṯꜣm n=f ḥr* "his speech *causes* that one be clement toward him")[140] or when it functions as non-initial main clause in paratactic sequences (Sh.S. 67–69 *jw wpj.n=f rꜣ=f r=j... ḏd=f n=j* "he opened his mouth towards me... *and he said* to me"). The morphological relation between "indicative" and "aorist" *sḏm=f*, however, remains opaque.

Periphrastic constructions for the expression of the imperfective and prospective aspect emerge in the late Old Kingdom: in these pseudoverbal patterns, which follow the syntax of adverbial sentences, the prepositions *ḥr* "on" (or *m* "in" with verbs of motion) and *r* "toward" are followed by the infinitive: *jw=f ḥr sḏm* "he hears," lit. *"he is on hearing," *jw=f r sḏm* "he will hear," lit. *"he is toward hearing." These constructions indicate a "progressive present," i.e. the modally unmarked *objective future*.[141]

The stative is also used with temporally unmarked, i.e. relative present reference with adjective verbs when it follows the subject of pseudoverbal sentences: see the adjectival pattern *nfr sw* (section 4.4.1) vs. the pseudoverbal pattern with stative *jw=f nfr.w* (section 5.2), both with the meaning "he is good."

Corresponding to the *sḏm.jn=f* for past events, a *contingent* form *sḏm.ḫr=f*, built with the preposition *ḫr*, is used in explicative or diagnostic discourse to refer to general events whose occurrence depends on a condition defined in the preceding context: "if the condition X is fulfilled, the event Y occurs": pSmith 9,19–20 *jr swrj=f mw stp.ḫr=f* "if he drinks water, he chokes."[142]

Table 4.10 Tense and aspect in earlier Egyptian

		RELATION TO THE CO(N)TEXT		
TENSE	ASPECT	ABSOLUTE/ INITIAL	RELATIVE/ NON-INITIAL	CONTINGENT
PAST	PERFECT	*sḏm.n=f*		*sḏm.jn=f*
	PERFECTIVE	1 pers. Stative 3 pers. *sḏm=f*	**sḏm.t=f*	
NON-PAST	AORIST	*sḏm=f/jrr=f*	*sḏm=f/jrj=f*	*sḏm.ḫr=f*
	IMPERFECTIVE	*jw=f ḥr/m sḏm*		
	PROSPECTIVE	*jw=f r sḏm*		

Table 4.10 presents the verbal forms of earlier Egyptian according to their temporal or aspectual distribution. In Old Egyptian, the "relation to the co(n)text" depends primarily on semantic choices (*context*), whereas in the classical language it is largely dictated by the syntactic environment (*cotext*).

Also, the categories of "perfect" and "perfective" merge in Middle Egyptian into a single *sḏm.n=f*-paradigm (initial and non-initial), first person stative and third person indicative *sḏm=f* being reduced to rare historical remnants.

4.6.3.2 *Mood.* The verbal category of "mood" defines the attitude of the speaker vis-à-vis the event described in the predication and is conveyed in earlier Egyptian by three forms: (a) the imperative *sḏm*, (b) the prospective *sḏm=f*, (c) the subjunctive *sḏm=f*. Prospective and subjunctive are formally different verbal forms in Old Egyptian but merge into a unitary paradigm in the language of classical literature.[143]

(a) The *imperative* has a singular *sḏm/jrj* and a plural *sḏm(.w)/jry* with an ending *.w/.y*, mostly indicated only by the plural strokes in the hieroglyphic writing. In Old Egyptian, the weak classes display a *j*-prefix. The imperative had a stressed **i* between the prefinal and the final radical: *cv(c)cic, *ja.cic: *sḥtp* */saḥ'tip/ "pacify!" > Late Middle Egyptian <sḥtep>,[144] *j.jnj* */ja'nij/ "fetch!" > Old Coptic ⲉ/ⲁⲛⲁⲓ, *j.ḏd* */ja'ɟid/ "say!" > ⲁϫⲓ-, and probably an opposition between a masculine *-a* and a feminine *-i* form in irregular imperatives consisting of only one consonant followed by a stressed vowel: *m* "come!," masc. */(ja)maːʔ/ > ⲁⲙⲟⲩ, fem. */(ja)miːʔ/ > ⲁⲙⲏ.[145]

(b) The *prospective sḏm(.w)=f/jrj.w=f* represents originally the mood of *wish*, used as independent verbal form (Pyr. 1687a *h3j.w=k r=k m wj3 pw nj rʿw* "you will go aboard that bark of Re"), as topicalized VP in paradigmatic alternation with the "emphatic" *sḏm=f*, especially in the first and third person, when indicating events expected to occur (Pyr. 193 Nt *zj.w N pn zj=k* "this King N will perish if you perish"), in cleft sentences referring to future events (Pyr. 123d *jn ḥm nfr.t-nrw n N rḏj=s tʔ n N* "It is indeed the beautiful one who cares for the King who will give bread to the King"), in other focal environments such as questions (CT V 92f *smn.y=j sw jrf ḥr jšst* "so, to what shall I fasten it?"), in the protasis of conditional sentences after the particle *jr*,[146] or as object of verbs expressing an expectation, a wish or a desire (Pyr. 1712a^{N} *ḏd ḥrw s3ḫ.w=f jtj=f* "Horus says that he will glorify his father"). Morphologically,[147] it displays the gemination of the stem in II-gem. roots (*m33=f* "he will see" from *m33*), often a semiconsonantal suffix *.w/.y* in the infirm roots (as in *jrj.w=f/jry=f* "he will do" from *jrj*) and in the causative classes with prefix *s-* (*sfḫw=f* "he will release" from *sfḫ*), and a full stem in the anomalous verbs (for example *rḏj=f* "he will give" from *rḏj*).

The prospective was probably vocalized *cvc(c)i(w/j)-, as shown by the Greek transcription Εριευς for the demotic anthroponym *hrj=w* */hər'jew/, lit. "may-they-be-content" or by the Late Middle Egyptian form <ḥtpe> */ḥət'peʔ/

< *ḥtp=ṯ* */ḥvtˈpic/ "may you be satisfied."[148] Thus, the morphological connections between the prospective form and the indicative *sḏm=f* (section 4.6.3.1), which also displays a *i*-stem, are not yet fully understood.

(c) The *subjunctive sḏm=f/jrj=f* represents the mood of *command*, used as an independent form in sentences referring to the future (Pyr. 1619c *jw.t=k n wsjr* "you shall go to Osiris"), often – like the cohortative *'eqṭəlâh* in Hebrew or the jussive *yaqtul* in Arabic – as a first and third person counterpart of the imperative (Pyr. 1159c^{P} *j.ḥj=f m ʿbꜣ ḫrp=f m jꜣꜣ.t* "He shall strike with the lotus scepter, he shall control with the rod"), and as object of verbs of command and of the causative *rḏj* "to let" (Pyr. 1141a *jm jw.t=f* "let him come"). Its morphology exhibits the *j*-prefix in the 2-rad. (*j.nḏ=f* "he shall protect" from *nḏ*), the non-geminated form in the II-gem. (*wn=f* "he shall be" from *wnn*), no suffix in the strong roots (*sḫm=f* "he shall control" from *sḫm*), a sporadic semiconsonantal *j*-suffix in the infirm roots (*hꜣy=f* "he shall descend" from *hꜣj*), and special forms for the anomalous verbs: *ḏj=f* "he shall give" < *rḏj*, *mꜣn=f* "he shall see" < *mꜣꜣ*, *jw.t=f* "he shall come" < *jwj* and *jn.t=f* "he shall fetch" < *jnj*.[149]

The vocalization of the subjunctive displays a pattern *cac(c)a- (*ja.cca- in the classes with *j*-prefix), which appears independently or as object of the verb *rḏj* "to cause to": *ḫwj=f-(wj)* */χawˈjaf-(wvj)/ "(the God Khnum) shall protect me" > */χəʔʔof/ > Χέοψ "Cheops"; *ḏj.t hꜣj-* */ɟiːjit-haʀˈja/ "to cause him to build" > */diʔhəʔjo/ > ⲑⲓⲟ /thjo/.[150] The *a*-suffix could be connected with the old accusative or absolutive case ending inherited from Afroasiatic.[151]

In the classical language, with its preference for syntactically bound forms, prospective and subjunctive merge as a grammatical, rather than semantic mood: their use is determined primarily by the syntactic environment as main VP with future reference or as object of verbs of wish or command. The evolution from a semantic to a syntactic mood, from a verbal category whose choice depends solely on the speaker's attitude to the predication to a form only used in a set of subordinate clauses, is known from Indo-European and Afroasiatic languages[152] and represents one of the features of syntactization as a diachronic process, of "genesis of syntax ex discourse."[153] The morphology of this suppletive Middle Egyptian prospective paradigm combines features of the Old Egyptian prospective (for example the sporadic *w- > y-* suffix in the III-inf. class) and of the Old Egyptian subjunctive (for example *jw.t=f* and *jn.t=f* from *jwj* "to come" and *jnj* "to fetch" respectively).[154]

The modal contingent tense corresponding to the preterital *sḏm.jn=f* and to the general *sḏm.ḫr=f* is the form *sḏm.kꜣ=f* "then he will hear," where the particle *kꜣ* is probably connected with the root *kꜣj* "to think, devise":[155] Pyr.

1223[P] *jr wdfj ḏꜣꜣ=ṯn mẖn.t n N pn ḏd.kꜣ N pn rn=ṯn pw* "If your ferrying the ferry to this King is delayed, the King will say that name of yours."[156]

As in the case of tense and aspect, "relation to the co(n)text" is in Old Egyptian a semantic, contextual category, whereas in the classical language it depends on the syntactic, cotextual environment. Also, "prospective" and "subjunctive" have merged in Middle Egyptian into a suppletive paradigm of initial and subjunctive *sḏm=f*-forms, in which morphological features of the two earlier forms appear side by side without functional opposition. Table 4.11 summarizes the main features of the category of mood.

Table 4.11 Mood in earlier Egyptian

MOOD	RELATION TO THE CO(N)TEXT ABSOLUTE/ INITIAL	RELATIVE/ NON-INITIAL	CONTINGENT
WISH (OPTATIVE)	Prospective *sḏm=f/jrj.w=f*		*sḏm.kꜣ=f*
COMMAND (JUSSIVE)	Subjunctive *sḏm=f/jrj=f*	Subjunctive *sḏm=f/jrj=f*	*sḏm.kꜣ=f*
	Imperative *sḏm*		

4.6.3.3 *Voice.* The verbal category of "voice" defines the role of the syntactic subject in the predication conveyed by the VP.[157] In the unmarked voice (*active*), the subject is the highest argument of the verbal predication on the agentivity scale,[158] i.e. the AGENT in the case of transitive verbs (Urk. I 104,4 *ḥzj wj ḥm=f ḥr=s r jḫ.t nb* "HIS MAJESTY praised me for it more than for anything else"), or its only argument, i.e. the ENTITY, in the case of intransitive or adjectival verbs (Urk. I 103,9 *jj.n mšʿ pn m ḥtp* "THIS ARMY returned in peace"). In the *middle* voice, the agentive role, although semantically present in the underlying proposition, is not overtly conveyed by the syntactic structure of the sentence: the subject of the verbal form, therefore, indicates the PATIENT (with first-order entities) or the GOAL (with places) of the verbal predication (Urk. I 124,15 *ḥzj.t(j=j) ḥr=s ʿꜣ wr.t* "and I was praised for it very much").[159] In the *passive* voice, the role of AGENT or of CAUSE is introduced by the preposition *jn* (Sh.S. 39–41 *ʿḥʿ.n=j rḏj.kw r jw jn wꜣw n(j) wꜣḏ-wrj* "then I was brought to the island BY A WAVE OF THE SEA"). We saw in section 4.4.1 that this morpheme may have an ergative origin, since it is also used to indicate the focal subject of cleft sentences (section 4.4). In this respect, Egyptian occupies an intermediate position between a "nominative-accusative" and an "ergative-absolutive" coding: while subjects of finite suffix conjugation forms behave according to the former pattern, with an identical coding for both transitive and intransitive verbs (*sḏm=f* "*he* hears" and *prj=f* "*he* comes"), the syntax of infinitives and of adjectival sentences displays "absolutive" features: pronominal subjects are coded exactly like direct objects of transitive verbs (infinitive transitive *sḏm=f* "hearing *him*" vs. intransitive *prj.t=f* "*his* coming," transitive verbal phrase *sḏm=f sj* "he hears *her*" vs. adjectival sentence *nfr sj* "*she* is good"); moreover, logical subjects of transitive infinitives, focal subjects of cleft sentences, and overt agents of passive predicates are all introduced ergatively by *jn* (Siut I,68 *gmj.t=f jn ḥm=f* "finding him by His Majesty"; *jn nṯr mrr rmṯ.w* "*it is god* who loves people"; *jw mrj.w rmṯ.w jn nṯr* "people were loved *by god*").[160]

Middle and passive (henceforth for convenience just "passive") voice is conveyed either by synthetic stems (for example *mrj.w=f* "he will be heard"), or by means of an affix *.tj* > *.tw* between the stem (including the temporal markers) and the nominal or pronominal subject (for example *mrr.tw=f/ mrr.tw rmṯ* "he/the man is heard").

(a) The synthetic expression of the passive is conveyed in earlier Egyptian by several forms: the *stative* and the *perfect passive* *sḏm(.w)=f* as passive equivalents of the non-initial *sḏm.n=f*, the *perfective passive* *sḏm.t=f/jry.t=f* as counterparts of the active form *sḏm.t=f*, and the *prospective passive* *sḏmm=f/ jrj.w=f* corresponding to the prospective active form *sdm(.w)=f/jrj.w=f*. On the theoretical level, the passive function of verbal forms conveying the perfective or prospective aspect is predictable, since they semantically "entail," as it were, a passive feature: on the one side, perfect(ive) and prospective, unlike imperfective forms, both localize an event *outside* a reference frame, the event preceding the reference frame in the former, and following it in the latter; on the other side, the passive, privileging the patient or the goal over the agent of a verbal predication, is bound to convey the completeness of an action, shown cross-linguistically by the connections between perfective and prospective aspect on the one hand and passive voice on the other.[161]

In Old Egyptian, the perfect passive *sḏm(.w)=f* is used as independent VP with dynamic verbs (Pyr. 942a *jnj(.w) n=k bꜣ.w p dmḏ n=k bꜣ.w nḫn* "the souls of Bouto have been brought to you, the souls of Hierakonpolis have been united to you"), whereas the middle or passive stative is introduced by a topicalized subject and is preferred for the expression of a state (Pyr. 1405a[P] *tꜣ qꜣ(.w) ẖr nw.t jn ʿ.wj=ṯj tfn.t* "the earth has become high under Nut by virtue of your arms, Tefnut"). In Middle Egyptian, the use of a main VP not introduced by a particle or by the topic of the utterance is restricted to modal uses, and the difference between perfect passive *sḏm(.w)=f* and stative becomes grammatical: the pseudoverbal stative is used with pronominal subjects, the verbal passive *sḏm(.w)=f* with nominal subjects[162] – an exception being the first person, whose high position on the hierarchy of topicality allows the use of a perfect passive *sḏm(.w)=f* (CG 20518 a,1 *msy=j m rnp.t-zp 1 n(j) zꜣ-rʿw N* "I was born in the first year of the Son-of-Re the King").

(b) Aspectual and modal forms which do not semantically entail a passive feature, namely the initial *sḏm.n=f*, the *sḏm=f*'s, the subjunctive, and the contingent tenses, form their passive counterparts by means of the perfective infix **.t > .tj* (in Old Egyptian) > *.tw* (in the classical language): (1) *sḏm.n.tw=f* "he was heard," which is always used as topicalized VP, the passive *sḏm(.w)=f* functioning as its complementary form in non-topical positions (Louvre C 286,18 *gmj.n.tw ḥrw ḫrw=f mꜣʿ.w rḏj.w n=f jꜣ.t n.t jtj=f* "Horus was found justified and his father's office was bequeathed to him"),[163] (2) the form *sḏm.tw=f* "he is heard" corresponding to the various active patterns (topicalized Urk. IV 19,6 *dgg.tw=f mj rʿw wbn=f* "he is looked at like Re when he rises," circumstantial Sin. B 52 *nn twt n=f mꜣꜣ.t(w)=f* "there is no one like him when he is seen," subjunctive Pyr. 1161b[P] *j.nḏ.tj=f* "he shall be greeted"), (3) the contingent tenses *sḏm.jn.tw=f, sḏm.ḫr.tw=f, sḏm.kꜣ.tw=f.*

In table 4.12, for the sake of an immediate identification of the morphological patterns involved, the forms from irregular verbal classes have been added in certain cases. It should be remembered (see table 4.11) that the opposition between prospective passive *sḏmm=f/jrj.w=f* and subjunctive passive *sḏm.tj=f/j.ḏd.tj=f*, originally one of modality (wish vs. command), is dictated in Middle Egyptian by the syntactic position of the form within the sentence (initial vs. dependent), with a noticeable tendency for prospective passive forms to appear limited to archaic uses in religious texts.

Table 4.12 Passive voice in earlier Egyptian

TENSE	ASPECT/ MOOD	RELATION TO THE CO(N)TEXT: ABSOLUTE/ INITIAL	RELATIVE/ NON-INITIAL	CONTINGENT
PAST	PERFECT	*sḏm.n.tj=f*	Stative	*sḏm.jn.tj=f*
	PERFECTIVE	*sḏm=f/jrj.w=f*	**sḏm.t=f/jry.t=f*	
PRESENT	UNMARKED	*jrr.tj=f*	*jrj.tj=f*	*sḏm.ḫr.tj=f*
FUTURE	WISH	*sḏmm=f/jrj.w=f*		*sḏm.kꜣ.tj=f*
	COMMAND	*sḏm.tj=f/j.ḏd.tj=f*		

4.6.3.4 *Relative forms.* A feature of Egyptian verbal morphology is the presence of synthetic adjectival forms of the verb, called "relative forms," which are used as predicate of a restrictive relative clause whose subject is different from the antecedent: *rmṯ mrjw=f* "the man whom he loves." For relative forms of the verbs to be used, the antecedent must be specific; it is resumed in the relative clause by a resumptive morpheme.

Earlier Egyptian exhibits at least three relative forms: perfective *jrj.n=f* "which he made" for the past (fem. *jrj.t.n=f*, pl. *jrj.w.n=f*), aorist *jrr=f* "which he makes" for the general present (*jrr.t=f, jrr.w=f*),[164] prospective *jrjw=f* "which he will make" for the future, also sometimes used as aorist: "which he would make" (*jrj.tj=f*,[165] *jrj.w=f*). In addition, Old Egyptian may have possessed a relative equivalent of the indicative *sḏm=f* for the preterite, usually referred to in the literature as "perfective relative *sḏm=f*,"[166] again a general label which comprises both indicative and prospective base. Alternatively, one can interpret the preterital uses as examples of the prospective form in its "perfective" function.

The main morphosyntactic feature of the relative forms is their agreement in gender and number with the antecedent. The agreement is shown by the affixation of the nominal endings (masculine *.ø* or *.w* in the weak classes, fem. *.t*, pl. *.w*) to the verbal stem: CT V 321c–d *mḫꜣ.t n.t rʿw fꜣꜣ.t=f mꜣʿ.t jm=f* "the balance of Re in which he weighs Truth." Verbal classes which show a *j*-prefix in the Old Egyptian "emphatic" *sḏm=f* (section 4.6.3.1b) display the same feature in the aorist relative form: Pyr. 628e *j.ḫr ḥr nj N ḥr=f* "one on whom the King's face falls," lit. "he-who-falls the face of the King on-him."

A morphological relation between relative forms and passive participles is often assumed,[167] and in fact relative forms appear to be distinct from their indicative equivalents: (a) the vocalic pattern of the temporal affix of the relative *sḏm.n=f* may have been **nu*, rather than **na* (**ḏidnuk* "which you said" vs. **ḏidnak* "you said");[168] (b) the relative aorist *jrr=f*, which corresponds to the emphatic *sḏm=f*,[169] may have had a pattern **mara:ruf* rather than **mara:raf*; (c) the Late Middle Eg. perfective-prospective relative *sḏm=f* shows a vocalic pattern reminiscent of the relative *sḏm.n=f*. **ḏi:duf, saḏi:muf, *jari:juf.*[170]

4.6.4 Non-finite verbal forms

Non-finite verbal forms, i.e. verbal formations which do not convey the overt expression of their subject, are morphosyntactically treated as nouns derived from a verbal root. They can indicate: (a) agents or patients of a verbal action, in which case they are "participles" or *nomina agentis*; (b) the action evoked by the verbal root itself, usually referred to as "infinitive" or *nomen actionis*.

(a) The formation of participles in earlier Egyptian shows connections with Semitic.[171] There are two main participles, usually called "perfective" and "imperfective," for each of the two verbal voices; being [+N], participles display the feminine and plural agreement with the antecedent: *sḏm* "someone who hears," feminine *sḏm.t*, plural *sḏm.w*. Participial patterns, especially in the passive voice, show a considerable degree of morphological similarity to the corresponding relative forms, which are – at least in part – etymologically derived from them.[172] From a syntactic point of view, participles represent the counterpart of relative forms (section 4.6.3.4) when the subject of the relative clause is coreferential with the antecedent, the perfective participle corresponding to the perfective relative form: Sin. B 126 *nṯr ḫm šꜣ.t.n=f* "a god who ignores (participle) what he has ordained (relative form)," the imperfective participles corresponding to the aorist relative form: Louvre C 1,4 *jrr ḥzz.t=sn* "one who does (participle) what they praise (relative form)."

Perfective participles indicate the action viewed as a whole and are often found in reference to singular nouns (for example the passive *mrjw jtj=f* "beloved of his father"). The patterns for the active form are: 2-rad. and II-gem. *cic, fem. *ci:cat: *mn* */min/ "stable" > Mεμ-,[173] II-gem. also *cac: *wn* */wan/ "being" > **ⲟⲩⲟⲛ**,[174] 3-rad. and transitive III-inf. *ca:cic, fem. *caccat < **cacic-at: *nfr* */ˈna:fir/ "beautiful" > **ⲛⲟⲩϥⲉ**, *fꜣj.t* */ˈfaʀjat/ "carrying" > */faʔʔ/ (3.6.3) > **ϥⲟⲉ** "canal," lit. "that which carries (water),"[175] 4-rad. and IV-inf. *caccic, fem. *cacci:cat. Their passives are: geminated 2-rad. *$c_1vc_2v{:}c_2$iw: *ḏdw* "said," otherwise *ˈcacciw/j > *cacˈceʔ: 3-rad. *sḏdw* */ˈsaɟdiw/ "told" > */səɟˈdej/ > ᴮ**ϣϫⲏⲓ** "gossip"; III-inf. *ḥzjw* */ˈḥazjiw/ "praised" > */ḥəsˈjeʔ/ > **ϩⲁⲥⲓⲉ**,[176] fem. either *caccat/*caca:cat (< **cacac-at) or *cacci:wat: *msḏw.t* */masˈɟi:wat/ "hated" > */məsˈde:wə/ > **ⲙⲉⲥⲧⲏ**.

Imperfective participles imply a notion of repetition and often refer to plural nouns (for example the passive *mrrw nṯr.w* "beloved of the gods").[177] Since none of them has survived through Coptic, the vocalic patterns are difficult to establish: active *sḏm/jrr* "who is hearing/doing," passive *sḏm(w)/jrrw* "who is being heard/done": Khakheperreʿseneb vo 2–3 *ḏd ḥr m ḏdw n=f ḥr* "one who would give orders (active participle *ḏd* from *rḏj* "to give," lit. "a giver of orders") has become one to whom orders are given (passive participle *ḏdw*, lit. "one given to-him orders," section 7.7)." Imperfective passive participles of 2-rad. verbs do not display the gemination of the second consonant; as in the case of emphatic and relative forms, Old Egyptian imperfective active participles from 2-rad. and some weak classes are preceded by the *j*-prefix: *j.ḏd.*[178]

While earliest Egyptian had a prospective participle *sḏm/jry*, feminine *sḏm.tj/jrj.tj,*[179] this form becomes obsolete in the classical language. The future participle is conveyed by an inflected form with infix *.tj* is of general use: masc. *sḏm.tj=f*, fem. *sḏm.tj=s*, pl. *sḏm.tj=sn* "he/ she/those who will hear." This form is frequently labelled "verbal adjective" and often appears followed by an additional <j> in the singular forms (*sḏm.tj=fj, sḏm.tj=sj*). Its morphological origin is controversial: it may represent either the conjugated form of a *nisba* adjective of the type *kꜣw.tj* "worker" from *kꜣ.t* "work," or a nominalized prospective form specialized in the participial use. In fact, both its morphology and its function display prospective features, for example the rare writing of a glide *.w* in the 2-rad. and III-inf. verbs (Siut 3,1 *ḫdw.tj=sn* "who will sail downstream") or the sporadic use with passive function (Siut 1,314 *zfṯ.tj=f* "which will be slaughtered").

Table 4.13 Participles in earlier Egyptian

ASPECT AND VOICE	ACTIVE	PASSIVE
PERFECTIVE	2-rad. *mn* */min/ "stable" II-gem. *wn* */wan/ "being" 3-rad. *sḏm* */ˈsaːɟim/ "hearing" III-inf. *prj* */ˈpiːraj/ "come"	*ḏddw* */ɟvˈdvːdvw/ "said" *hnw* */ˈhiːniw/ "bent" *stp* */ˈsaːtap/ "chosen" *mrjw* */ˈmarjiw/ "beloved"
IMPERFECTIVE	2-rad. *mn* II-gem. *wnn* 3-rad. *sḏm* III-inf. *prr*	*ḏdw* *hnnw* *stp(w)* *mrrw*
PROSPECTIVE	*sḏm.tj=f/jrw.tj=f*	

(b) The Egyptian infinitive, which is the basic *nomen actionis* of the verbal root, is neutral in respect to tense, aspect, and voice: it generally implies the unmarked tense and the active voice, but it can also be found with preterital meaning in narrative discourse to mark the beginning of a paragraph: Sin. B 107 *rḏj.t=f wj m-ḥꜣ.t ẖrd.w=f* "he placed me (lit. "his placing me") in front of his children" or else with passive reference.[180] The main feature of earlier Egyptian infinitives is the morphological opposition between forms without ending and forms which display an ending *.t* affixed to the verbal stem. The most frequent patterns are 2-rad. *caːc (*mn* */maːn/ "to stay" > ⲙⲟⲩⲛ), II-gem. *caˈcac (*kmm* */kaˈmam/ "to become black" > ⲕⲙⲟⲙ), 3-rad. *caːcac (*sḏm*

*/ˈsaːɟam/ "to hear" > ⲥⲱⲧⲙ̄), 3-rad. ultimae aleph *ciˈcic (*zẖꜣ* */ziˈçiʀ/ "to write" > */sçaʔ/ > ⲥϩⲁⲓ), III-inf. *ciːcit/*ciccit (*jr.t* */ˈjiːrit/ "to do" > */ˈʔiːrə/ > ⲉⲓⲣⲉ, *mrj.t* */ˈmirjit/ "to love" > */meʔʔ/ > ⲙⲉ), caus. 2-rad. *siccit/*siciːcit (*sḏd.t* */ˈsiɟdit/ > ᴮⲥⲁϫⲓ /sacʔ/, *smn.t* */siˈmiːnit/ > ⲥⲙⲓⲛⲉ). Infinitives may be used in construct or in pronominal state followed by the subject (with intransitive verbs: *pr.t=k* */ˈpirtvk/ "your going forth") or by the object (with transitive verbs: *sḏm=f* */ˈsaɟmvf/ "to hear him"; the subject is introduced in this case by the preposition *jn*). The infinitive is a verbal noun and functions as substantive in absolute use (*pr.t m hrww* "coming forth by day"), as object of verbs (Urk. IV 57,3 *jw mꜣ.n=j šꜣd ḥr.t ḥm=f* "I saw the cutting of His Majesty's tomb") and of prepositions, especially in the pseudoverbal constructions: West. 5,3–5 *jb n(j) ḥm=k r qbb n mꜣꜣ ẖnn=sn ẖn.t m ḫdj m ḫntj* "Your Majesty's heart will be refreshed (lit. "is toward refreshing") at the sight of (lit. "for seeing") their rowing upstream and downstream."

Another verbal noun, the "complementary infinitive," is used as internal object of verbs when functioning as predicative complement in order to convey a specific connotation, as in CT I 345c *nj msj.n.tw=j js msy.t* "I was not born through regular birth," lit. "I was not born a bearing," or to provide a grammatical object for intransitive verbs when the verbal action is stressed, as in the above example *ẖnn=sn ẖn.t* "their rowing," lit. "that they row a rowing." The complementary infinitive of strong verbal classes sometimes displays the ending *.t* (for example *ʿḥʿ.t* from *ʿḥʿ* "to stand"), whereas III-inf. verbs often show the ending *yt* (for example *msy.t* from *msj* "to bear"). The complementary infinitive, therefore, represents a different verbal substantive and is not identical with the regular infinitive.

A third verbal noun, called "negatival complement," is found in earlier Egyptian under the control of a verb which conveys in its semantic value the feature [+NEGATIVE] (section 4.6.5). It is marked morphologically by the ending *.w*, which remains mostly unwritten.[181]

4.6.5 *Negative verbal forms*

Negative constructions with the particles *nj* (> Late Egyptian *bw* > Coptic ⲙ̄-) and *nn* (> Late Egyptian *bn* > Coptic ⲛ̄-) will be treated in the chapters devoted to the syntax of the sentence types. Here I would only like to discuss a peculiarity of the Egyptian negative system, i.e. the presence of verbs which convey in their semantics the feature [+NEGATIVE]. These are called "negative verbs." The most common negative verb is the 2-rad. *tm*, originally "to complete" (see Semitic **tmm*), which acquires the conjugated form of the corresponding positive pattern and is used for the negation:

(a) of all nominal or nominalized verbal forms, such as participles (*tm sḏm.w* "someone who does not hear" vs. *sḏm* "a hearer," *tmm.t ḏd.w* "that was not said" vs. *ḏdd.t* "that was said"), infinitives (CT II 131d *tm ʿq r nm.t nṯr* "Not to enter the god's place of execution"), and relative forms (Louvre C 15 *nn s.t nb.t tm.t.n=j jrj.w mn.w jm=s* "there is no place at all in which I failed to build monuments" vs. *jrj.t.n=j mn.w jm=s* "in which I built monuments").

(b) of verbal forms in syntactic dependency: topicalized "emphatic" *sḏm=f* (Peas. B1,211 *tm=k tr sḏm.w ḥr-m* "why don't you listen?," positive **sḏm=k ḥr-m*, West. 11,21–22 *tm.tw ms jnj.w hn.w ḥr-m* "why aren't vessels brought?," positive **jnn.tw hn.w ḥr-m*), also used in object clauses (Merikare E 53 *rḫ.n=k tm=sn sfn.w* "you know that they are not clement"), the subjunctive *sḏm=f* (Pyr. 675b *j.tm=k sḏm.w n=f sḏm=k ꜣb.t=f jmj.t tp=k* "should you fail to listen to him, you shall hear his *ꜣb.t* which is on your head"), the protasis of a hypothetical clause (Pyr. 277b *jr tm=k jrj.w s.t n N jrj.kꜣ N fꜣ.t m jtj=f gbb* "if you don't make a place for the King, the King will make a *fꜣ.t* on his father Geb"), the circumstantial use of modal forms (Peas. B1,244–45 *m kꜣhs ḫft wsr=k tm spr.w bw-ḏw r=k* "do not exceed when you exercise power, lest trouble befall you"), and VP introduced by conjunctions (Siut I,229 *sgr qꜣj-ḫrw r tm=f mdw.w* "to silence the vociferous, that he may cease to speak").[182]

Other negative verbs followed by the negatival complement are the III-inf. *jmj* "not to do," used in the imperative *m* and in the subjunctive *jm=f* to express a negative command (Sh.S. 111 *m snḏ(.w)* "do not fear," Peas. B1,162 *jm=k tnm.w* "you should not go astray"), and the 2-rad. *ḫm* "not to be able to," whose participle appears mostly in nominal compounds (*j.ḫm.w-skj.w* "those which cannot perish," i.e. the Circumpolar Stars). Especially in the Old Kingdom, the substantivized participle of other verbs, the most important of which is *nfr* "to be complete," is used in grammaticalized negative patterns: *nfr n X* *"it is complete to X" > "it doesn't happen that X," *nfr pw X* "X is complete" > "there is no X."[183]

4.6.6 *Verbal morphology in later Egyptian*

In this paragraph, the reader will find a general description of the historical patterns that govern the development of verbal morphology from earlier to later Egyptian. More detailed information on the functional reorganization within the linguistic system of Late Egyptian and Coptic will be provided in the discussion of verbal syntax.[184]

(a) The main evolutive tendency underlying the development of the verbal system is the well-known change from *synthetic* to *analytic* patterns of conjugation. Parallel to the loss of final vowels and to the tendency to have prefixes carry the morphological functions formerly signalled by suffixes (sections 4.1, 4.6.1), later Egyptian develops periphrastic verbal forms based on the verb *jrj* "to do" (*sḏm.n=f* "he heard" > *jr=f sdm*, lit. "he did the hearing" > Coptic ⲁ=ϥ-ⲥⲱⲧⲙ̄). The inflected form is eventually grammaticalized as a new conjugational marker and supersedes the old synthetic construction; the infinitive – and gradually the stative as well – become lexical indicators, the nucleus of the predication being represented by the conjugational base followed by the subject: earlier Egyptian prospective *wḏꜣ=f* "may he become prosperous" > Coptic ⲉϥⲉ-ⲟⲩϫⲁⲓ (conjugational base of the third person masc. Fut. III+Infinitive) "may he be safe"; earlier Egyptian stative *jw=j wḏꜣ.kw* "I am/have become prosperous" > Coptic ϯ-ⲟⲩⲟϫ (conjugational base of the first person Pres. I + Stative) "I am whole." This change from synthetic to analytic patterns in the verbal system leads to a progressive move from the earlier VSO toward a SVO word order.

(b) Later Egyptian allows the transformation (or "transposition") of the basic verbal forms into their nominalized and subordinate (adverbialized) counterparts by means of a periphrastic verbal form with *jrj* "to do" for the nominalized use and of the particle *jw* "while" – morphologically identical to the Middle Egyptian marker of initiality *jw*, but used in a new, and in a certain sense opposite function – for the adverbialized use: thus, the earlier Egyptian opposition between the initial *jrr=f* and its non-topicalized counterpart *jrj=f*, rather than by different morphological *sḏm=f*-patterns, is conveyed in later Egyptian by the use of the two distinct forms *j.jr=f-sdm*, lit. "(the fact) that he does a hearing" > ᴮⲁϥⲥⲱⲧⲉⲙ vs. *jw=f-ḥr-sdm*, lit.: "while he is on hearing" > ᴮⲉϥⲥⲱⲧⲉⲙ. These formants are eventually grammaticalized as *converters*, i.e. as free morphemes *j.jr* and *jw* prefixed to the basic form. Later Egyptian displays a whole set of such converters, for example *wn*, originally the perfective base of the verb *wnn* "to be," which ascribes to a verbal predicate a perfective value, or the relative pronoun *ntj*, which transforms it into a relative form: for example, the so-called Present I *sw ḥr sdm* "he hears" (> Coptic ϥⲥⲱⲧⲙ̄, section 4.4.2), the functional heir of the Middle Egyptian construction *jw sḏm=f*, can be converted into a nominalized *j.jr=f-sdm* "that he hears" (> Coptic ˢⲉϥⲥⲱⲧⲙ̄, ᴮⲁϥⲥⲱⲧⲉⲙ, the so-called Present II), into an adverbial form *jw=f ḥr sdm* "while he hears" (> ⲉϥⲥⲱⲧⲙ̄, ᴮⲉϥⲥⲱⲧⲉⲙ), into a preterital *wn=f ḥr sdm* "he was hearing" (> ⲛⲉϥⲥⲱⲧⲙ̄), and a relative form *ntj ḥr sdm* "who hears" (> ⲉⲧⲥⲱⲧⲙ̄).

(c) The later Egyptian verbal system displays so-called "sequential" forms; these are the narrative *jw=f ḥr sdm* "and he heard" for a sequence of events in the past – limited to Late Egyptian – and the conjunctive *mtw=f sdm* “and he will hear” for a concatenation of expected events – also shared by Demotic and Coptic (ⲛ̄ϥⲥⲱⲧⲙ̄). They are used in non-initial position in order to keep the temporal, aspectual, and modal references of the preceding section of discourse. This evolution is mirrored by a similar development in the verbal system of the Northwest Semitic languages such as Hebrew.[185]

(d) Already in Late Egyptian, and increasingly in the more recent phases of later Egyptian, verbal patterns tend to be organized within a tripartite sequence of conjugation base (often derived from a conjugated form of *jrj* “to do”), nominal or pronominal subject, and infinitive, and to acquire autonomy as main sentences or dependent clauses: for example, the earlier Egyptian construction with the negative particle *nj* followed by the past form *nj sḏm.n=f* “he cannot hear” becomes in later Egyptian the form *bw-jr=f-sdm*, in which *bw* is still recognizable as the negative morpheme but is not used productively in the language, being found only in a few bound verbal constructions, and in Coptic ⲙⲉ=ϥ-ⲥⲱⲧⲙ̄, which is not even any longer segmentable into discrete units, but rather represents a functional equivalent to the morphologically quite distinct positive form ϣⲁ=ϥ-ⲥⲱⲧⲙ̄ “he hears.”

This evolution had a profound impact at the typological level, causing Egyptian on the one hand to grammaticalize dependent clauses as paradigmatic units (for example the temporal *m-ḏr jr=f-sdm* > ⲛ̄ⲧⲉⲣⲉϥⲥⲱⲧⲙ̄ “when he heard” or the conditional Demotic *j.jr=f-ḫn-sdm* > ⲉϥϣⲁⲛⲥⲱⲧⲙ̄ “if he hears”), on the other hand to move from the fusional nature of its earlier phases (section 4.1) to the *polysynthetic* type:[186] in Coptic, sentence and clause conjugation, often followed by the verbal object, are combined into a single prosodic unit, i.e. into one word: Ps 68,22 ⲁⲩⲧⲥⲉⲓⲟⲩϩⲙ̄ϫ (*a=u-tse=i-ou-hmj*) /ʔawtsəjˈwhemc/ “they let me drink vinegar” < Late Egyptian **jr=w dj.t swr=j wʿ-ḥmḏ*, lit. “they did (*jr=w*) causing (*dj.t*) that I drink (*swr=j*) vinegar” < earlier Egyptian *(jw) ḏj.n=sn swr=j* etc.; Lk 23,35 ⲙⲁⲣⲉϥⲧⲟⲩϫⲟϥ (*mare=f-toujo=f*) /marəftəwˈɟof/ “let him save himself” < **jm jr=f-dj.t-wḏꜣ=f*, lit. “let him do (*jm jr=f*) causing (*dj.t*) that he be safe (*wḏꜣ=f*)” < earlier Egyptian *ḏj=f wḏꜣ=f* “may he cause (*ḏj=f*) that he be safe.” This change from the fusional to the polysynthetic type represents a major typological evolution in the history of Egyptian and is unparalleled in other families of the Afroasiatic phylum.

4.6.6.1 *Tense and aspect*. The *sḏm.n=f* is maintained in Late Egyptian only in formal texts, the productive form for the past being the preterital *sdm=f* (and the typologically more analytic form *jr=f-sdm* > Coptic ⲁϥⲥⲱⲧⲙ̄):[187] Urk. VI 133,20 *mšʿ=k jrm nꜣ-sbj.w* “you have gone with the rebels”; Jn 17,1 ⲁⲧⲉⲩⲛⲟⲩ ⲉⲓ "the hour (*te-ounou*) came." Its negative equivalent is *bw sdm=f*, replaced from the end of Dyn. XIX by *bw-pw=f sdm* (> *bwpw-jr=f-sdm* > ⲙ̄ⲡⲉϥⲥⲱⲧⲙ̄), a periphrastic construction derived from the grammaticalization of the verb *pꜣw* "to have done in the past":[188] RAD 80,2–3 *bw jn=f jm=w r tꜣ-šn'.t* "he didn't bring any of these to the granary"; Jn 1,10 ⲙ̄ⲡⲉⲡⲕⲟⲥⲙⲟⲥ ⲥⲟⲩⲱⲛϥ̄ "the world (*p-kosmos*) did not recognize him."

The form *sḏm.t=f*, which already in earlier Egyptian was limited to few bound constructions, is found in later Egyptian in the same perfective environments, i.e. after the negative particle *bw-sdm.t=f* "he has (or had) not yet heard" (> *bw-jr.t=f-sdm* > ⲙ̄ⲡⲁⲧϥ̄ⲥⲱⲧⲙ̄): KRI I 238,14 *ptr bw-dj.t=k jn.tw=f* "look, you have not yet caused that it be brought"; Jn 2,4 ⲙ̄ⲡⲁⲧⲉⲧⲁⲟⲩⲛⲟⲩ ⲉⲓ "my hour has not yet come," and controlled by the conjunctions *r* and *šꜣ'-r* "until" (> *šꜣ'-r jr.t=f-sdm* > ϣⲁⲛⲧ=ϥ̄-ⲥⲱⲧⲙ̄): pAnastasi IV 3,3 *r pḥ.t=k r jmꜣḫ* "until you have reached the privilege"; Mt 2,9 ϣⲁⲛⲧϥ̄ⲉⲓ "until he comes."[189]

The sequential *jw=f ḥr sdm* and its negative counterpart *jw=f ḥr tm sdm* are used in a narrative chain after an initial preterital form, a syntactic environment in which the classical language used the regular *sḏm.n=f* in "continuative" function: LRL 32,5–8 *jry=j tꜣ-š'.t jw=j (ḥr) dj.t=s n X jw=j (ḥr) ḏd n=f* "I wrote the letter and gave it to X and I said to him". The contingent tense *sḏm.jn=f* "then he said" is limited in Late Egyptian to the verb *ḏd* "to say" and to the periphrastic construction with the past converter *wn*.[190]

In the present tense, the basic paradigm is the Present I *sw ḥr sdm/sdm.w* (negative form *bn sw ḥr sdm/sdm.w*), a pseudoverbal construction in which the subject precedes the predicate, which is either the infinitive governed by the preposition *ḥr/m* or the stative: pAnastasi IV 3,5–6 *nꜣ-nḥsj.w m sḫsḫ r-ḥꜣ.t=k* "the Nubians run in front of you"; 2 Cor 5,1 ⲧⲛ̄ⲥⲟⲟⲩⲛ̄ "we know."[191] If the subject is pronominal, the Late Egyptian and Demotic third person dependent pronouns *sw* and *st* are replaced in Coptic by the old suffix pronouns *f-* and *s-* under analogical pressure: *sw ḥr sdm* > ϥⲥⲱⲧⲙ̄, whereas the new proclitic pronouns built from the particle *tj* (section 4.4.2) appear in the first and second persons (*twj/twk ḥr sdm* > ϯⲥⲱⲧⲙ̄, ⲕⲥⲱⲧⲙ̄). The Present I is negated by means of the morpheme *bn*, the heir of the classical *nn* (sections 4.7, 4.11), which in later Demotic and in Coptic is often reinforced by the adverb *jwnꜣ* > ⲁⲛ.

In addition to the Present I, which is used for the specific indication of the imperfective aspect, later Egyptian possesses a form *ḫr=f sdm* (> *ḫr-jr=f sdm* > ϣⲁϥⲥⲱⲧⲙ̄), which corresponds morphologically to the contingent present *sḏm.ḫr=f*, but functionally to the construction *jw sḏm=f* of the classical language: it acquires the function of an "aorist," i.e. of a general or gnomic present:[192] Jn 8,47 “He who is from God ϣⲁϥⲥⲱⲧⲙ̄ ⲉⲛϣⲁϫⲉ ⲙ̄ⲡⲛⲟⲩⲧⲉ listens to God’s words.” The aorist is negated by the form *bw sdm=f/bw jr=f sdm* (> ⲙⲉϥⲥⲱⲧⲙ̄): KRI II 65,1–4 *jr pḥ=j r ḥḥ jm=sn bw jr rd.wj smn ḫr w‘r=sn* “if I attack millions among them, their feet cannot stand, and they flee.”[193]

The expression of future tense and prospective aspect experiences some changes. While the pattern *jw=f r sdm* becomes grammaticalized as a bound form in Late Egyptian and represents a true temporal “objective future” (LRL 20,12 *jw=j (r) jr.t=s* “I shall do it”), its Coptic outcome, the so-called Future III ⲉ=ϥ-ⲉ-ⲥⲱⲧⲙ̄, is no longer an aspectual form, but has invaded the domain of mood, superseding the prospective *sḏm=f* (ⲉⲥⲉϣⲱⲡⲉ “amen,” lit. “may it happen”). In the presence of a nominal subject, rather than the form *jw=f r sdm*, later Egyptian shows more frequently *jr NP (r) sdm* > ⲉⲣⲉ-NP (ⲉ)-ⲥⲱⲧⲙ̄, i.e a periphrastic construction – probably of Lower Egyptian origin – with the prospective stem of the verb *jrj* “to do” which has been integrated into the paradigm of *jw=f r sdm*: KRI IV 87,1–2 *jr pꜣj=j nb r ḏd=f* “my lord will say it”; Ps 19,2 ⲉⲣⲉ-ⲡϫⲟⲉⲓⲥ ⲥⲱⲧⲙ̄ ⲉⲣⲟⲕ “may the lord listen to you.” The negative form is *bn jw=f r sdm/bn jr NP sdm* (> ⲛ̄ⲛⲉϥⲥⲱⲧⲙ̄).[194]

For the expression of the prospective aspect in the narrower sense, later Egyptian develops a Present I construction with the verb *n‘j* “to go,” which is still a free lexical construction in Late Egyptian: LRL 35,15 *twk rḫ.tw pꜣy mš‘ ntj twj m n‘y r jr=f* “you know this expedition which *I am going* to make.” In Roman Demotic and in Coptic the pseudoverbal predicate *m-n‘y* becomes a converter ⲛⲁ- and the form is grammaticalized as prospective counterpart of the Present I, called Future I: Ps 54,20 ⲡⲛⲟⲩⲧⲉ ⲛⲁ-ⲥⲱⲧⲙ̄ ⲉⲣⲟⲓ “God is going to listen to me.”[195]

Table 4.14 Tense and aspect in later Egyptian

TENSE/ASPECT		POSITIVE FORM	NEGATIVE FORM
PAST	INITIAL	*sdm=f > a=f-sôtm*	*bw-pw=f-sdm > mpe=f-sôtm*
	NON-INITIAL	*jw=f ḥr sdm*	*jw=f ḥr tm sdm*
PERF.	“UNTIL”	*šꜣ‘-r jr.t=f-sdm > šant=f-sôtm*	
	“NOT YET”		*bw-jr.t=f-sdm > mpat=f-sôtm*
PRESENT	IMPF.	*sw ḥr sdm > f-sôtm*	*bn sw ḥr sdm > n-f-sôtm an*
	AORIST	*ḫr=f sdm > ša=f-sôtm*	*bw-jr=f-sdm > me=f-sôtm*
FUTURE	PROSP.	*sw m n‘y r sdm > f-na-sôtm*	*bn sw m n‘y r sdm >n-f-na-sôtm an*
	OBJECTIVE > MODAL	*jw=f r sdm/jr NP (r) sdm > e=f-e-sôtm/ere-NP sôtm*	*bn jw=f r sdm > nne=f-sôtm*

4.6.6.2 *Mood*. The Late Egyptian imperative[196] is regularly preceded by a *j*-prefix (Coptic ⲁ-); in the later phases of the language, while the morphological imperative is kept in lexicalized remnants, the jussive function is fulfilled by the infinitive: Late Egyptian *j.ḏd, j.nw* "say, look" > Coptic ⲁϫⲓ, ⲁⲛⲁⲩ, but Late Egyptian *j.sdm* "hear" > Coptic ⲥⲱⲧⲙ̄.

Connected with the imperative is the Coptic sentence conjugation ⲙⲁⲣⲉϥⲥⲱⲧⲙ̄, derived from the paradigmatization of a construction with the imperative of *rḏj* "to cause to" followed by a periphrastic prospective *sdm=f*: *jm jr=f-sdm*, lit. "cause that he hear."[197] This form is used independently or in conjunction with the imperative when the scope of the injunction is a person other than the second: Lk 11,2 ⲙⲁⲣⲉⲡⲉⲕⲟⲩⲱϣ ϣⲱⲡⲉ "thy will (*pe=k-ouôš*) be done (*mare…šôpe*)"; Judg 14,15 ⲁⲣⲓϩⲁⲗ ⲙ̄ⲡⲟⲩϩⲁⲓ ⲁⲩⲱ ⲙⲁⲣⲉϥⲧⲁⲩⲟ ⲉⲣⲟ ⲙ̄ⲡⲉⲡⲣⲟⲃⲗⲏⲙⲁ "deceive (*ari-hal* "do a deception") your husband, that he may explain (*auô ma-re=f-tauo* "and may he explain") to you the riddle."

The basic modal form, the prospective *sdm=f* and its nominalized counterpart *j.sdm=f*,[198] was already in classical Egyptian a suppletive paradigm derived from the merging of the Old Egyptian initial prospective *jrj.w=f* and of the subjunctive *sḏm=f* (section 4.6.3.2). However, a major change can be detected in Coptic: here, the prospective *sdm=f* has disappeared and the modal function is delegated to ⲉϥⲉⲥⲱⲧⲙ̄, the old "objective future" of Middle and Late Egyptian: for example Late Egyptian KRI VI 520,10 *ḥsy twtn jmn-rʿ nsw-ntr.w* "may Amun-Re, King of the gods, praise you!," but Coptic Mt 19,19 ᴮⲉⲕⲉⲙⲉⲛⲣⲉⲡⲉⲕϣⲫⲏⲣ ⲙ̀ⲡⲉⲕⲣⲏϯ "you shall love your neighbor (*e=k-e-menre-pe=k-šphêr*) like yourself (*m-pe=k-rêti*)." In its use as main sentence, the prospective *sdm=f* is negated by the form *bn sdm=f* (< *nn sḏm=f*) and in dependent clauses by the prospective of the verb *tm* (section 4.6.5) followed by the negatival complement or by the infinitive, once the former is reduced to a mere survival in few verbs. Also, the contingent form *kꜣ sdm=f* (< *sḏm.kꜣ=f*) is still found in Late Egyptian, but disappears in the later stages.[199]

A significant change from earlier to later Egyptian is the emergence of a sequential pattern *mtw=f-sdm* > ⲛ̄ϥⲥⲱⲧⲙ̄, called "conjunctive," a non-initial form which makes a chain of events dependent on the initial form:[200] Wen. 1,44–45 "Do you not say: 'Stay one more night,' *r dj.t wḏ tꜣ-bjr j.gm=j mtw=k jj* to cause the ship that I found to depart, so that you may return?"; Pistis Sophia 121,18 ⲉϥⲧⲱⲛ ⲧⲁ-ⲛⲁⲩ ⲉⲣⲟϥ "where is he, that I may see him?"; Jn 1,39 ⲁⲙⲏⲓⲧⲛ̄ ⲛ̄ⲧⲉⲧⲛ-ⲛⲁⲩ "come and see."

The conjunctive, therefore, appears to be the modal counterpart to the temporal *jw=f ḥr sdm* (section 4.6.6.1). Its morphological origin[201] lies in an ergative pattern, known from Middle Egyptian, in which the preposition *ḥnʿ*

“with” is followed by the infinitive and a pronominal or (rarely) nominal subject, reinterpreted as consisting of a morpheme *nt-* followed by the suffix pronoun: *ḥn‘ sḏm jnk/ntf/jn NP > ḥn‘-nt=j/nt=f/ntj NP sḏm > mtw=j/mtw=f/ mtw NP sdm >* ⲧⲁⲥⲱⲧⲙ̄, ⲛ̄ϥⲥⲱⲧⲙ̄, ⲛ̄ⲧⲉ-NP ⲥⲱⲧⲙ̄.

While the syntax of these forms will be dealt with extensively in chapter 7, here we need to stress the connections between the Coptic conjunctive and the clause conjugation form (ⲛ̄)ⲧⲁⲣⲉϥⲥⲱⲧⲙ̄ < *ḏj=j jr=f sdm* “(I will cause) that he may hear.” We just saw that the morphological evolution of the conjunctive led to a form ⲧⲁⲥⲱⲧⲙ̄ in the first person singular. In later Demotic and in Coptic, however, the formant ⲧⲁ- < *ḏj=j-* “I will cause” is grammaticalized in another construction, the clause conjugation (ⲛ̄)ⲧⲁⲣⲉϥⲥⲱⲧⲙ̄,[202] in which the base ⲧⲁ- is followed by the periphrastic prospective *sdm=f* form; but the original personal reference appears neutralized, causing the expression to acquire an optative or promissive meaning: “I will cause that he hear” > “(I will cause”) may he hear” > “may he hear”: Mt 7,7 ⲁⲓⲧⲉⲓ ⲧⲁⲣ=ⲟⲩ-ϯ ⲛⲏⲧⲛ̄ ϣⲓⲛⲉ ⲧⲁⲣⲉ=ⲧⲛ̄-ϭⲓⲛⲉ ⲧⲱϩⲙ̄ ⲧⲁⲣ=ⲟⲩ-ⲟⲩⲱⲛ ⲛⲏⲧⲛ̄ “ask, and it will be given you; seek, and you will find; knock, and it will be opened to you.” Symmetrically to what happens in the case of the sentence conjugation ⲙⲁⲣⲉϥⲥⲱⲧⲙ̄, which because of its derivation from an imperative form ⲙⲁ- < *jmj* “let” is excluded from the second person use, the first person origin of the conjugational base ⲧⲁ- < *dj=j* prevents the form ⲧⲁⲣⲉϥⲥⲱⲧⲙ̄ from being used in the first person; in this case, the promissive future is replaced by the first person conjunctive (ⲛ̄)ⲧⲁ-ⲥⲱⲧⲙ̄ < *mtw=j-sdm*.

Table 4.15 Mood in later Egyptian

<table>
<tr><th>MOOD</th><th>INITIAL FORMS</th><th>NON-INITIAL FORMS</th><th>CONTINGENT</th></tr>
<tr><td>WISH
(OPTATIVE)</td><td>Prospective sdm=f
> Future III ⲉϥⲉⲥⲱⲧⲙ̄</td><td>1 pers.: mtw=j sdm
> (ⲛ̄)ⲧⲁⲥⲱⲧⲙ̄
Other persons:
dj=j-jr=f-sdm
> ⲧⲁⲣⲉϥⲥⲱⲧⲙ̄</td><td rowspan="2">k3-sdm=f</td></tr>
<tr><td>COMMAND
(JUSSIVE)</td><td>2 pers.: j.sdm > ⲥⲱⲧⲙ̄
Other persons:
jm jr=f-sdm
> ⲙⲁⲣⲉϥⲥⲱⲧⲙ̄</td><td>Conjunctive
mtw=f sdm
> ⲛ̄ϥⲥⲱⲧⲙ̄</td></tr>
</table>

4.6.6.3 *Voice.* In the preceding paragraphs, we observed many cases in which the verbal system of later Egyptian displays verbal patterns consisting of a conjugational base followed by the subject and the infinitive or the stative, resulting in the latters' tendency to function as lexical indicators rather than as grammatical forms. While this evolution did not affect heavily the morphology of the infinitive, it had a profound impact on the stative, the endings of which gradually became redundant (section 4.4.2): during Dyn. XX, the *tw*-suffix begins to be applied to the first person forms; in the Third Intermediate Period (tenth–seventh century BCE), only two forms survive, one with a *ø*- (primarily for the third persons) and one with a *t*-suffix,[203] until in Coptic each verbal root displays only one form of the stative: ϫⲟⲥⲉ /cos?/ "to be exalted" < masculine *ṯzj.w* */ˈcazjaw/ "he was exalted" vs. ⲥⲙⲟⲛⲧ "to be established" < feminine *smn.tj* */saˈmantvj/ "she was established."

Major semantic as well as morphosyntactic changes affect the expression of voice in later Egyptian. While both the simple *sdm=f* and the infixed *sdm.tw=f* forms are documented in Late Egyptian, the main innovation in the semantics of passive forms is the grammaticalization of the original perfective infix *.tw* as indefinitive pronoun "one" (French *on*, German *man*) and the ensuing tendency to interpret the infixed passive *sdm.tw NP* "NP was/is/will be heard" as an active construction with the indefinite pronoun "one heard/hears/will hear NP." In Demotic and Coptic, the indefinite pronoun *.tw* is superseded by the third person plural pronoun *=w*.

Late Egyptian keeps the perfective passive *sdm=f/jry=f* (< *sḏm=f/ jrj.w=f*): pAnastasi V 17,7–18,1 *gmy rn=w r hȝb=w m jp.t* "their name was found in order to send them on a mission," the topicalized past passive *sdm.tw=f* as the heir of the earlier Egyptian *sḏm.n.tw=f* form: KRI IV 80,12 *jṯȝ.tw=f n pȝj=f ḥm-ntr* "it is for his priest that it was stolen," the passive of the *sdm.t=f* form, documented only in the negative construction *bw sdmy.t NP*: KRI II 911,9 *bw jny.t nȝj=w ḫsf* "their answer has not yet been brought," the nominalized prospective passive *(j.)sdm.tw=f*: pAnastasi II 6,1 *j.ḏd.tw n=k sḫr n tȝ nb jw=k ḥtp.tj m ʿḥ=k* "the plan of the entire land will be reported to you when you rest in your palace," and the subjunctive passive *sdm.tw=f*: Florence 2616,10 (Khonsuemhab) *dj=j jry.tw=f n=k* "I shall cause that it be done for you."[204] Within the synchronic perspective of Late Egyptian, as we saw above, one also needs to posit a form *sdm.tw NP* belonging to the paradigm of the preterital *sdm=f* (section 4.6.6.1), in which the passive infix *.tw* is grammaticalized as indefinite subject pronoun *tw* "one": KRI VI 695,7 *jn.tw NP ntj m wsf* "one brought NP who was idle."

In Demotic and Coptic,[205] the indefinite pronoun *tw* has been replaced by constructions with the third person plural pronoun, for example in the prospective *sdm=f*: Onchsh. 4,10–11 *mj jn=w n=j w‘-gst jrm w‘-ḏm‘* "let a palette and a papyrus roll be brought to me," lit. "that they bring to me," or in the preterital ⲁϥⲥⲱⲧⲙ̄: Lk 1,13 ⲁ=ⲩ-ⲥⲱⲧⲙ̄ ⲉ-ⲡⲉ=ⲕ-ϣⲗⲏⲗ "your prayer has been heard," lit. "they heard your prayer." However, when the passive predication conveys an overt agent expression, this is rendered by a prepositional phrase with Demotic *m-dr* > Coptic ϩⲓⲧⲛ̄-/ϩⲓⲧⲟⲟⲧ=, lit. "through the hand of": pRyl. IX 5,1 *ḥwj=w stj r pꜣj=j ‘.wj – m-dr nm? m-dr nꜣj-w‘b.w* "my house has been set in fire – By whom? By these priests" (preterital *sdm=f*), 1 Cor 14,24 ⲥⲉ-ⲛⲁ-ϫⲡⲓⲟ=ϥ ϩⲓⲧⲛ̄-ⲟⲩⲟⲛ ⲛⲓⲙ "he will be blamed by everyone" (Future I). This means that the passive form, in spite of its formal identity with the third person plural, always maintained a distinct paradigmatic autonomy: the semantic structure of a sentence with a third person plural subject was different depending on whether it belonged to the active or to the passive paradigm: in the former case, the overt subject was introduced by the particle ^{S}ⲛ̄ϭⲓ/^{B}ⲛ̀ϫⲉ,[206] in the latter by a prepositional phrase with ϩⲓⲧⲛ̄-: Mt 2,16 ^{S}ⲁⲩⲥⲱⲃⲉ ⲙ̄ⲙⲟϥ ⲉⲃⲟⲗ ϩⲓⲧⲛ̄-ⲙ̄ⲙⲁⲅⲟⲥ "he was ridiculed by the magicians" (passive) vs. ^{B}ⲁⲩⲥⲱⲃⲓ ⲙⲙⲟϥ ⲛ̀ϫⲉ-ⲛⲓⲙⲁⲅⲟⲥ "the magicians ridiculed him" (active).

4.6.6.4 *Relative forms*. In later Egyptian, synthetic relative forms tend to disappear and to be replaced by analytic constructions with the relative pronoun *ntj* > ⲉⲧ-, ⲉⲧⲉ-, ⲛ̄ⲧ-. The only survivals of synthetic relative forms in Late Egyptian[207] are the relative perfective *sdm.n=f* and imperfective *jrr=f* as archaisms inherited from the classical language, and the relative past *j.sdm=f*, which – like its earlier Egyptian ancestor (section 4.6.3.4) – can only modify a specific antecedent, determined by a qualifier, a quantifier, or a determinative pronoun: Doomed Prince 6,13–14 *wn.jn pꜣ-wpw.tj ḥr šm.t ḥr smj <md.t> nb.t j.ḏd=s n pꜣj=s jtj* "then the messenger went to report everything she had said to her father," Two Brothers 1,10 *mtw=f sdm pꜣ-ḏd=sn nb* "and he would hear everything they said."

Otherwise in Late Egyptian, and regularly in Demotic and Coptic, relative forms are rendered analytically by means of the relative converter *ntj*, which converts a main predication into a relative clause: Lk 15,6 ⲡⲁ-ⲉⲥⲟⲟⲩ ⲉⲛⲧ-ⲁ=ϥ-ⲥⲱⲣⲙ̄ < Demotic **pꜣj=j-sj.w ntj jr=f-srm* "my sheep that had gone astray."[208]

4.6.6.5 *Non-finite verbal forms*. Participles, as adjectival forms of the verb (section 4.6.4), show evolutive patterns that are predictably similar to those of the relative forms: except for a few archaizing instances of the imperfective participle, the only forms in productive use in Late Egyptian are the perfective active and passive simple *j.sdm* and periphrastic *j.jr-sdm*, a remnant of which survives until Coptic ⲉⲣ-ⲥⲱⲧⲙ̄ < *j.jr-sdm* "he who did."[209] As a rule, participles are superseded in later Egyptian by verbal or pseudoverbal patterns with the relative converter *ntj*, the only trace of synthetic participles in Coptic being the so-called "conjunct participle" in construct states: ⲙⲁⲓ-ⲛⲟⲩⲧⲉ "pious" < *mrj nṯr* */ma(:)rij'na:car/ "who loves God."

In the *nomina actionis*, the negatival complement has disappeared from later Egyptian and survives only in the negative imperative of *jrj* "to do": *m jr.w* */ʔvm'ʔa:raw/ > ⲙ̄ⲡⲱⲣ. As for the infinitives,[210] the main changes from earlier to later Egyptian are phonetic: in general, they are motivated by the different forms of the infinitive in periphrastic patterns, depending on whether it was used absolutely or followed by a noun or a pronoun. This is very evident in the III-inf. verbs which, in the phonological reorganization caused in later Egyptian by a strong tonic stress (section 3.5.3), lost the ending *.t* in the absolute state (*mrj.t* */mirjit/ "to love" > Late Egyptian *mrj* */merʔə/[211] > Coptic ^{S}ⲙⲉ, ^{B}ⲙⲏⲓ /meʔ(ʔ)/) or in non-sonorant environments, such as in the nominal state, where the infinitive is followed by a noun, i.e. inevitably by a consonantal phoneme (^{S}ⲙⲉⲣⲉ-), but maintained it in a sonorant environment, for example when it was followed by the short vowel of the suffix pronoun (*mrj.t=f* */mir'ji:tvf/ "to love him" > Late Egyptian *mrj.tw=f* > ^{S}ⲙⲉⲣⲓⲧ=ϥ /mə'ri:təf/). The Late Egyptian marker <tw>, which was originally the graphic signal of this permanence of /t/ in the pronunciation before suffix pronouns, soon came to be perceived as an autonomous morpheme and was also sporadically applied to forms where it was not justified at the etymological level, such as in the infinitive of strong verbal classes (*ʿš3.tj* "to be numerous" > ⲁϣⲉⲉⲓⲧⲉ together with the regular form *ʿš3* > ⲁϣⲁⲓ), or introducing the object pronouns of the new type (*twj, twk, twf,* etc.) even when not governed by an infinitive.[212] Heirs of this new suffix pronoun are the unusual Coptic suffix pronouns used after consonants and glottal stop: first person =ⲧ (ⲕⲁⲁ=ⲧ "to place me" < **ẖ3ʿ=twj*) and second person feminine =ⲧⲉ (ⲕⲁⲁ=ⲧⲉ "to place you" < **ẖ3ʿ=twt*).

4.7 Prepositions, conjunctions, particles

Earlier Egyptian exhibits a considerable number of prepositions, whose emergence, often from the absolute use of an etymological substantive, was probably favored by the early decay of the case system in prehistoric times.[213] Prepositions can be followed by a noun or a suffix pronoun, in which case their stem shows a tonic vowel **a* (*jr=f* */ja'raf/ > ⲉⲣⲟϥ "to him"), probably the heir of the Afroasiatic absolutive case (section 4.3.1).[214] They can often function as conjunctions introducing nominalized verbal phrases.

The most important simple prepositions are: *m* "in, by, with, at," etymologically related to Sem. **b*; *r* (< *jr*) "toward, more than (comparative)," see Sem. **'l*; *n* "to, for," see Sem. **l*; *jn* "by" (with agent, section 4.4.1), etymologically connected with Arabic *'inna*; *ḥr* */ḥar/ "on, because, through," see Sem. **'al*; *ḥn'* "together with," see Ar. *'inda*, replaced in later Egyptian by *jrm*, Coptic ⲙⲛ̄ (< *r-jm* "at the side of"); *ẖr* */çur/ "under"; *ḫr*, used with the meaning "to, for" in the presence of a difference of status between the two speakers, for example *ḏd ḫr* "to speak to a superior or inferior"; *ḫft* "in front of, according to"; *mj* (< *mr*) "like, as"; *ḏr* "since"; *ḥꜣ* "behind"; *ḫnt* "in front of"; *tp* "upon" (< *tp* */tap/ "head"); *ḫt* "through"; *jmjtw* "between," from the *nisba* adjective of the preposition *m* "which is in." *Nisba* adjectives are frequently derived from simple prepositions: for example *jmj* "which is in," *jrj* "concerning," *ḫntj* "which is in front of." Compound prepositions of nominal or adverbial derivation are also frequent: *n-jb-nj* "for the sake of" (< "for the heart of"), *m-sꜣ/r-sꜣ* "in the back of, behind" *m-ẖnw* "in the interior of," *wpw-ḥr* "except" (< "separated from"), etc. Some of these are used most frequently as conjunctions: *n-mrw.t* "in order to" (< "for the love of), *n-'ꜣ.t-n.t* "inasmuch as" (< "for the greatness of"), etc.

Besides licensing the use of prepositions to introduce verbal clauses, Egyptian also possesses "true" conjunctions, the most important of which are *wnt* and *ntt* before noun clauses as object of verbs, as in English "that": Pyr. 1862a–b *ḏd=ṯn ḫr r'w wnt=f jj.w m nṯr* "you shall say to Re that he has come as god," Urk. IV 835,16 *rḫ.kw ntt ḥtp=f ḥr=s* "I knew that he would be happy with it." Etymologically, both these conjunctions are nouns: *wnt* is a feminine derivative from the root *wnn* "to be"; *ntt* is the feminine, i.e. neuter form of the relative pronoun *ntj*, according to a pattern of evolution also known in Indo-European languages: see Greek ὅτι, Latin *quod*, English *that*. Similarly, compound conjunctions built with preposition and *ntt* (*r-ntt* "so that," *ḥr-ntt* "because," *ḏr-ntt* "since") introduce adverbial clauses. In later Egyptian, *ntt* is replaced by *r-ḏd* (Coptic ϫⲉ), originally derived from the preposition *r* followed by the infinitive of the verb *ḏd* "to say" (lit. "in order to say").

Two other conjunctions introducing verbal or adverbial clauses are *jsk/sk* (> *jsṯ/sṯ*) "while" and *jr* "as for, if." The former (*sk*) is used in earlier Egyptian in clauses of circumstance, mostly following the main clause and conveying background information necessary to the understanding of the context: Urk. I 101,2–3 *jnk jr(j) m zẖꜣ wʿj.kw ḥnʿ zꜣb jrj-nḫn wʿj s̱t jꜣ.t=j m jmj-rꜣ ḫntj.w-š prw-ʿꜣ* "I alone put it in writing together only with a senior warden of Nekhen, while my office was Supervisor of the royal tenants."[215] In later Egyptian, it becomes grammaticalized in the new set of personal pronouns used as subject in an adverbial sentence: *twj, twk*, etc. (section 4.4.2). The conjunction *jr* is also used in the protasis of hypothetical verbal clauses: Pyr. 1252c–d *jr prj=f m sbꜣ pw jmn.tj n(j) p.t jn n=f sbꜣ pw rsj n(j) p.t* "if he comes out of this western gate of heaven, bring him this southern gate of heaven," or introducing topicalized adverbial clauses (section 5.3): Hatnub 22,2 *jr m wn=j m ẖrd wn=j m smr* "when I was a child, I was already a Friend," lit. "as for in my being as a child, I was already a Friend";[216] pKahun 22,8–9 *jr m-ḫt spr=sn kꜣ.tw sḏm.tw=f* (?) *m-ḥzj jry* "after they arrive, he should be confronted with this," lit. "as for after they arrive, he should be heard as concerns related matters."

As in the case of the relative pronoun (section 4.4.3), earlier Egyptian also possesses a conjunction *jwt* "that not" as negative counterpart of *ntt*. This conjunction is semantically equivalent to *ntt* followed by a negative predicate: CT I 170g–i *jw grt sḏm.n=j mdw...jwt mwt=j n=sn mwt sjn* "I have indeed heard the word...that I shall not die for them a swift death."

Apart from prepositions and conjunctions, Egyptian exhibits a certain number of morphemes, generally subsumed under the heading "particles," which may be prosodically enclitic or proclitic: the negative particles *nj* and *nn*, adverbs (for example *nḥmn* "surely" or *smwn* "probably"), interjections (*j* "oh"), and especially conjugation auxiliaries (*jw, mk, jḫ, ʿḥʿ.n*, etc.). Since the latters' behavior bears heavily on the structure of the sentence type, their patterns will be discussed in the treatment of the syntax of verbal sentences.

Further reading

Allen, J. P. *The Inflection of the Verb in the Pyramid Texts*. Bibliotheca Aegyptia II (Malibu: Undena, 1984) [A detailed morphological analysis of the earliest Egyptian corpus].

Doret, E. *The Narrative Verbal System of Old and Middle Egyptian*. Cahiers d' Orientalisme XII (Geneva: Patrick Cramer, 1986) [Verbal morphology of the stage of the language immediately following the Pyramid Texts].

Kammerzell, F. "Personalpronomina und Personalendungen im Altägyptischen," in D. Mendel and U. Claudi (eds.), *Ägypten im afro-orientalischen Kontext. Aufsätze zur Archäologie, Geschichte und Sprache eines unbegrenzten Raumes. Gedenkschrift Peter Behrens*. Afrikanistische Arbeitspapiere. Special issue 1991 (University of Cologne, 1991), 177–203 [The most thorough treatment of Egyptian pronouns, also important for comparative issues].

Loprieno, A. *Das Verbalsystem im Ägyptischen und im Semitischen. Zur Grundlegung einer Aspekttheorie.* Göttinger Orientforschungen IV/17 (Wiesbaden: Harrassowitz, 1986) [A comparative reconstruction of the Egyptian and Semitic verbal system].

Osing, J. *Der spätägyptische Papyrus BM 10808.* Ägyptologische Abhandlungen XXXIII (Wiesbaden: Harrassowitz, 1976) [Reconstruction of Egyptian nominal and verbal morphology on the basis of a Late Middle Egyptian text in a Greek-derived script].

Schenkel, W. *Aus der Arbeit an einer Konkordanz zu den altägyptischen Sargtexten. II: Zur Pluralbildung des Ägyptischen.* Göttinger Orientforschungen IV/12 (Wiesbaden: Harrassowitz, 1983), 171–230 [An analysis of plurals between graphic forms and morphological reconstruction].

Vernus, P. *Future at Issue. Tense, Mood and Aspect in Middle Egyptian: Studies in Syntax and Semantics.* Yale Egyptological Studies IV (New Haven: Yale Egyptological Seminar, 1990) [Especially important for the opposition between prospective and subjunctive in early Middle Egyptian].

Winand, J. *Etudes de néo-égyptien, I. La morphologie verbale.* Aegyptiaca Leodiensia II (Liège: CIPL, 1992) [A complete morphological analysis of the verb in Late Egyptian].

5

Nominal syntax

5.1 Introduction

Throughout its history, Egyptian displays a variety of patterns for sentences with nominal predicate.[1] The predicate of such a sentence can be a ***nominal*** (NP) or an ***adjectival*** phrase (AdjP): *rmṯ pw* "it is a man (NP)" vs. *nfr sw* "he is good (AdjP)." At the syntactic level, ***bipartite*** patterns consist only of predicate and subject, as in the above sentences, whereas ***tripartite*** patterns display a copula as carrier of the nexus (*rmṯ pw zꜣ-nht* "Sinuhe is a man"}. Finally, considering also the pragmatic dimension, the typology of Egyptian nominal sentences shows a further distinction between ***unmarked*** structures, in which third person[2] subjects follow it (*rmṯ pw, nfr sw*), whereas first and second person subjects tend to precede the predicate (*jnk rmṯ* "I am a man," *ntk nfr* "you are good"), and ***marked*** patterns, which display a generalized preference for the specific subject to occupy the first position in the sentence (*ntk ḥrw* "***you*** are Horus," *jn nṯr mrr rmṯ.t* "***it is god*** who loves mankind").

The nominal constructions to which this chapter is devoted are captured in table 5.1. We shall first consider the nominal patterns (section 5.2) and the syntactic structure in which an entire clause is embedded as predicate of a nominal sentence (section 5.3), and then move to the adjectival sentences (section 5.4). We will then devote some attention to the more complex nominal patterns such as possessive, interrogative, and existential sentences (sections 5.5–5.6) and to the impact of negation on nominal patterns (section 5.7). The last few sections will deal with the evolution of all types of nominal sentence in Late Egyptian, Demotic and Coptic (sections 5.8–5.11).

Since the part of speech ***noun*** is [+N] but [-V],[3] i.e. it has nominal but not verbal properties, patterns with substantival predicate will be insensitive to the typically verbal tense/aspect dialectics, and will always adjust to the contextual frame of reference, expressing a so-called relative present. The ***adjective***, on the other hand, is [+N] and [+V], i.e. it combines nominal and verbal properties; patterns with adjectival predicate will therefore be able to convey to a certain extent temporal or modal references.

Table 5.1 Patterns of nominal sentences in Egyptian

TYPOLOGY	MORPHOSYNTAX	
	Predicate = NP	Predicate = AdjP
UNMARKED ORDER	CLASSIFYING SENTENCE	QUALIFYING SENTENCE
Subject = 1–2 person	*jnk rmṯ* "I am a man"	*jnk nfr* "I am good"
Subject = 3 person	*rmṯ pw (zẖ3w)* "He (the scribe) is a man"	*nfr sw (rmṯ)* "He (the man) is good"
	IDENTIFYING SENTENCE (PSEUDOCLEFT)	
Subject = adjectival phrase	*rmṯ pw ḥzy.n=f* "The one whom he praised is a man"	
MARKED ORDER	SPECIFYING SENTENCE	IDENTIFYING SENTENCE (CLEFT SENTENCE)
Subject = pronoun	*ntf ḥrw* "He is Horus"	*ntf ḥzj wj* "It is he who praised me"
Subject = noun	*zẖ3w=k(pw) ḥrw* "Your scribe is Horus"	*jn rmṯ ḥzj wj* "It is the man who praised me"

5.2 Bipartite vs. tripartite patterns

5.2.1 *Classifying and identifying patterns*

The sentence *rmṯ pw* "he is a man" represents the core of an Egyptian nominal sentence, with a bare or referential predicate[4] followed in bound constructions directly by a nominal subject:

(1) Pyr. 1434b *wrrtj rn nj jtj=k* "Your father's name (*rn nj jtj=k*) is *wrrtj*"

otherwise by an enclitic pronoun, most commonly the demonstratives *pw* or less frequently *nn* (originally "this");[5] together with the predicate they build a bipartite sentence with *classifying* function:

(2) CT VI 155f B_1Bo *ḥq3=f pw* "He (*pw*) is its ruler"
(3) Sin. B 23 *dp.t mwt nn* "This (*nn*) is the taste of death"

As an enclitic, *pw* tends to move to the position after the first prosodic unit of the sentence, regardless of its position in the semantic structure, even in cases when this leftward movement breaks the surface unity of a phrase:[6]

(4) CT IV 410 (220a) *w3.t pw n.t sḫ.t j3r.w*
"This is (*pw*) the way (*w3.t*) of (*n.t* "that-of") the Fields of Rushes (*sḫ.t j3r.w*)"
(5) Sin. B 81 *t3 pw nfr* "It was (*pw*) a good land (*t3 nfr*)"

The bipartite nominal sentence consisting of predicate and subject appears expanded into a tripartite pattern when a nominal subject follows the pronoun *pw*, which in this case loses here its original deictic force and acquires the function of a semantically empty copula ("this [is]" > "is"):[7]

(6) Disp. 38 *dmj.t pw jmn.t* "The West is (*pw*) a place of residence (*dmj.t*)"
(7) Pyr. 1620a *zꜣ=k pw wsjr N* "The Osiris N is (*pw*) your son (*zꜣ=k*)"

When the subject of a nominal sentence, rather than the ***delocutive*** third person, is the ***interlocutive*** first or second person, which occupy a higher position than the third person on the hierarchy of salience,[8] the independent pronoun is used instead of the dependent pronoun. This pronoun, however, requires the more topical initial position; thus, in the first and second person, the nominal sentence displays the pattern S ⇒ [Subject pronoun+Pred]:

(8) Peas. B1,93 *ntk jtj n nmḥw* "You (*ntk*) are a father (*jtj*) to the orphan"
(9) CT III 321c *jnk wsjr* "I (*jnk*) am Osiris (*wsjr*)"

an example which also displays a version in the "delocutive" third person:

(9') CT IV 192–3b *wsjr pw* "This (*pw*) is Osiris"

In "presentative" contexts, in which a specific subject is introduced deictically, the function of predicate of a bipartite sentence S ⇒ [Pred-*pw*] is fulfilled by the independent pronoun:

(10) CT IV 24c *jnk/N pn pw* "That is me/this N"[9]
(11) Sin. B 268 *ntf pw m-mꜣꜥ.t* "This is really (*m-mꜣꜥ.t*) he (*ntf*)"

More rarely, a nominal subject can appear topicalized, i.e. dislocated to the left of the nexus "Pred-*pw*," in which case the subject is presented as the communicatively salient, pragmatically given argument within the flow of discourse,[10] followed by a regular bipartite nominal sentence pattern. In this case, the topic is resumed by the enclitic *pw* in the main sentence:

(12) Pyr. 133f *ḫnḏ šꜣsr.t ꜣw.t=f pj*
"Thigh and loaf – these are (*pj*, older form of *pw*) his meal (*ꜣw.t=f*)"

This pattern is frequent in aetiological, i.e. explicative discourse, where the subject is often topicalized and introduced by the particle *jr* "as for":

(13) CT IV 318c–d *jr zmꜣ.t-tꜣ.wj dhn.t qrs wsjr pw*
"As for the 'Unification of the Two Lands' (*zmꜣ.t-tꜣ.wj*), this means (*pw* "it is") the attribution (*dhn.t*) of Osiris' tomb (*qrs wsjr*)"

In the bipartite or tripartite nominal sentences with interlocutive "*jnk/ntk*-Pred" or delocutive "Pred-*pw*" discussed so far, the nominal predicate *classifies* the subject, i.e. it defines one or more of its semantic properties. This applies to all cases of *pw*-sentence in which the subject is a noun or a pronoun. If the subject of a nominal sentence is an adjectival phrase, i.e. a participle or a relative form (section 7.7), it agrees in gender and number with the predicate, the congruence being carried by the appropriate adjectival ending:

(14) CT VI 75g B3Bo *N tn pw mkj.t.n ḫbn.tjw*
"The one (fem.) whom the wrongdoers protected (*mkj.t.n ḫbn.tjw*) is this N (*N tn*)"
(15) Peas. B1,21 *jmj-r3 prw pw sḫ3.y=k*
"But the one (masc.) whom you mention (*sḫ3.y=k*) is the High Steward (*jmj-r3 prw*)"
(16) CT IV 228b *jnk pw ḫpr jm=ṯn*
"I am the one who has become you (*ḫpr jm=ṯn*, participle)"
(17) CT VII 250m *jnk pw šms(.w).n=sn*
"I am the one whom they followed (*šms.w.n=sn*, relative form)"
(18) Pyr. Nt 712 "Who is the one who will survive? *jnk pw zp.t(j)=f*
"I am the one who will survive (*zp.tj=f*, prospective participle)"

Although this pattern is syntactically identical to the classifying nominal sentence with nominal or pronominal subject, its semantic or pragmatic function differs from it to some extent: because of its status as object or – much less frequently – subject of a relativized VP, the head NP functions here not only as syntactic predicate of the proposition, but also as pragmatic focus of the utterance.[11] The nominal predicate, rather than classifying the subject, *identifies* it as the only specimen possessing the properties decribed by the converted verbal clause. Thus, the structure of this pattern becomes close to the English *pseudocleft* sentence: "the one whom the wrongdoers protected is this N," "the one you mention is the High Steward," "the one whom they followed is me."[12] The identifying sentence with focalized object of the relative VP occurs frequently in the construction *sḏm pw jrj.n=f* "what he did was to hear," in which the predicate is a verbal infinitive and the subject a relative form (*jry=f, jrj.n=f*) or a passive participle (*jry*) of the verb *jrj* "to do":

(19) Peas. B1,35 *prj.t pw jrj.n=f r ḥrw*
"What he did (*jrj.n=f*) is (*pw*) to go up (*prj.t*) higher (*r ḥrw*)"
(20) Sin. B 236 *jwj.t pw jry r b3k-jm*
"This servant has indeed been sent for" < "What has been done (*jry*) is (*pw*) to send for (*jwj.t r* "to come to") this servant (*b3k-jm* "the-servant-there")"

5.2.2 *Specifying patterns*

In the nominal patterns we discussed so far, the distribution of subject and predicate is readily retrievable on syntactic and semantic grounds: a set of properties which we define as the predicate – "the taste of death" in (3),

"Osiris" in (9), "his meal" in (12), "to go up" in (19), etc. – is ascribed to a subject usually more determined and semantically more specific than the features predicated of him ("this," "I," "thigh and loaf," and "what he did"). But there are Egyptian sentences of the [NP1-NP2]-type that cannot be convincingly analyzed as S ⇒ [Pred(-*pw*)-Subj], but rather as S ⇒ [Subj(-*pw*)-Pred]. This happens when the subject and the predicate are coextensive: rather than classifying the semantic sphere of the subject, the predicate *specifies* it; in a technical sense, it exhaustively characterizes its subject:[13]

(21) CT II 120g S_1C *mḥj.t=j mḥj.t wr.t*
"My flood (*mḥj.t=j*) is the Great Flood (*mḥj.t wr.t*)"[14]

(22) CT I 277c–d *zẖ3=k pw ḥrw j'w.t(j)=k pw stš*
"Your scribe (*zẖ3=k*) is (*pw*) Horus, your interpreter (*j'w.tj=k*) is Seth"

(23) CT V 59c $S_{10}C$ *bw.t=j pw 'q r nm.t-nṯr*
(23') Ibid. B_4Bo *bw.t N tn 'q r nm.t-nṯr*
"My / this N's abomination is to enter the gods' place of execution"

Similar to these from a structural point of view are instances in which a topicalized VP, i.e. a clause nominalization functioning as pragmatically "given" within the communicative flow of discourse (section 7.5), is the subject of a specifying *pw*-sentence whose predicate is an infinitive, followed in (24) by a suffix pronoun indicating its agent:

(24) Sin. B 60–61 *ršj=f pw h3j.t=f r3-pḏ.t*
"He rejoices when engaging in archery" < "that-he-rejoices (*ršj=f*) is (*pw*) his-engaging-in archery (*h3j.t=f r3-pḏ.t*)"

In the specifying sentence [Subj-*pw*-Pred], the subject and the predicate share the same extension:[15] in example (22), the subjects "your scribe" and "your interpreter" are specified by the predicates "Horus" and "Seth," subject and predicate referring to one and the same referent. When the subject is pronominal, the independent form of the personal pronouns will be used in all persons, yielding a pattern [Subj pronoun-Pred] formally similar to the one we encountered with classifying predicates in the first and second person:

(25) CT I 207c–d *ṯwt jtj=j jnk z3=k*
"You (*ṯwt*) are my father and I (*jnk*) am your son"

(26) CT IV 37f Sq_6C *ntf z3 wsjr* "He (*ntf*) is Osiris' son"

(27) CT VI 166c B_4C *nts r'w* "She is Re"

The communicative difference vis-à-vis the classifying pattern lies in the fact that the pronominal subject, rather than the *theme* of the utterance, is here its pragmatic *rheme*:[16] the identity between the subject pronoun and the predicate displays a high degree of contextual novelty. Thus, if in example (7) the subject *wsjr N* "the Osiris N" is presented as a predictable host for the predicate *z3=k* "your son," this is much less the case for the subject *ntf* "he" in (26): instead of a classifying statement "he is Oriris' son," which would be rendered by the bipartite sentence *z3 wsjr pw*, this is a sentence with rhematized subject: "*he* is Osiris' son." Pragmatic salience, i.e. the subject's role as rheme of the utterance, and semantic performance, i.e. the predicate's specifying, rather than classifying function, go hand in hand in this pattern, and it would be pointless to determine which one represents the primary strategic goal of the sentence type. The interesting point is that the linguistic hierarchies of salience, with interlocutive persons being conversationally more salient than delocutive and inanimate subjects, are kept in the distribution of the Egyptian classifying sentence, in which the first or second person is more likely to be topicalized than the third person, as in (28) vs. (28'),[17] but are neutralized in the specifying sentence, where both nominal (with copula *pw*) and pronominal subjects (without *pw*) appear topicalized, as in (29) vs. (29'):

(28) CT I 44b $S_{10}C$ *ṯwt ḥrw prj <m> šnṯ.t*
(28') Ibid. B_1Bo *ḥrw pw prj <m> šnṯ.t*
"You are (*ṯwt*)/he is (*pw*) Horus who came out (*prj*) of the battle"

(29) Pyr. $1441c^P$ *N pw w'j jm=ṯn nṯr.w*
(29') Ibid. $1441c^M$ *swt w'j jm=ṯn nṯr.w*
"N/he is the (only) one (*w'j*) among you (*jm=ṯn*), O gods (*nṯr.w*)"

Therefore, the opposition between classifying and specifying patterns, which also plays a role in the syntax of adjectival sentences,[18] was in Egyptian not only semantic, but also morphosyntactic. Coptic shows two forms which differ in their prosodic realization: the subject pronouns are unstressed when used with classifying or qualifying function: proclitic first and second person sing. **(j)anək-* > ⲁⲛⲅ̄, **(j)v̆ntək-* > ⲛ̄ⲧⲕ̄, **(j)v̆ntəc-* > ⲛ̄ⲧⲉ, pl. **(j)anən-* > ⲁⲛⲛ̄, **(j)əntacən-* > ⲛ̄ⲧⲉⲧⲛ̄ and enclitic third person **-pəw* > ⲡⲉ, **-nən*, but keep their full prosodic form when functioning as specifying or identifying elements: sing. **(j)anák* > ⲁⲛⲟⲕ, **(j)v̆nták* > ⲛ̄ⲧⲟⲕ, **(j)v̆ntác* > ⲛ̄ⲧⲟ, **(j)v̆ntáf* > ⲛ̄ⲧⲟϥ, **(j)v̆ntás* > ⲛ̄ⲧⲟⲥ, pl. **(j)anán* > ⲁⲛⲟⲛ, **(j)v̆nta:cin* > ⲛ̄ⲧⲱⲧⲛ̄, Middle Egyptian **(j)v̆nta:sin* / Late Egyptian **(j)v̆ntaw* > ⲛ̄ⲧⲟⲟⲩ.[19]

Focal pronouns provide a transition to the study of the sentence pattern with the focal particle *jn*, a morpheme which will play a central role in our discussion of adjectival sentences. The first sentence type is an archaic variant of the specifying pattern [Subj-Pred], in which the subject is introduced by the particle *jn* and functions as pragmatic focus[20] of the utterance:

(30) Pyr. 1370a *jn ppj pn z3 sm3.t jd.t wr.t*
"It is this Pepi (*ppj pn*) who is the son of the Great Wild Cow (*sm3.t jd.t wr.t*)"

Early Middle Egyptian examples of alternation between a pattern with independent pronoun in one text and with a bare nominal subject in a variant seem, if they are not the result of a mechanical change on the part of the scribe,[21] to point to the possibility of conveying the indication of focality through suprasegmental features rather than by means of the particle *jn*:

(31) CT VI 253d Sq6C *ntf ḏ.t* "*He* is Eternity"
(31') Ibid. Sq4C *N pn ḏ.t* "*This N* is Eternity"

But this pattern is already extremely rare in early Egyptian and disappears altogether in the classical language. The particle *jn* remains nonetheless the most common Egyptian marker of the function of a subject NP as focus, being also etymologically entailed in the independent pronouns of the *jnk*-series.[22]

Finally, mention should also be made of a specifying presentative pattern corresponding to the classifying *jnk pw* (section 5.2.1), in which the independent pronoun is the predicate of a first person subject expressed by a coreferential dependent pronoun:

(32) CT VII 495i *N pn wj/N wj/jnk wj zp 2*
"I am really (*zp 2* "twice," section 2.3) this N/N/myself"

or two pronouns appear in immediate juxtaposition, forming a kind of focalized "balanced sentence":[23]

(33) CT VII 157c *jnk pw s(j) stt pw wj ṯz-pẖr*
"I (*jnk*) am really it (*sj*) and it (*stt*) is really me (*wj*), and vice versa (*ṯz-pẖr*)"[24]

5.3 Entire clauses as predicate of *pw*: "thetic" statements

We saw above that any NP can act as subject or as predicate of a nominal *rmṯ pw*-sentence: not only substantives, but also infinitives and adjectival transpositions of the verb such as participles and relative forms. An interesting peculiarity of Egyptian syntax, however, is that not only nominals, but entire sentences can be nominalized and embedded as predicate of a higher classifying *pw*-sentence. This is not surprising when the clause acting as predicate of such a sentence is overtly marked as nominal, for example by means of a nominal converter such as the conjunction *ntt* "that" (originally the neuter of the relative adjective *ntj*) which merges with the enclitic *pw* to form *nt-pw*, the head of this pattern:

(34) pEbers 99,5 *nt-pw mdw=f ḫnt mt.w n.w ʿ.t nb.t*
"This means (*nt-pw*) that it speaks out of the liquids of each limb"

This pattern seems semantically to resemble the adverbial clause introduced by the conjunction *ḥr-ntt* "because"; in fact, example (35) offers the context immediately preceding (34) in the original text:

(35) pEbers 99,4 *(ḥr-ntt) mt.w=f n ʿ.t=f nb.t*
"For each of his limbs (*ʿ.t=f nb.t*) has its liquids (*mt.w=f*)"

But complications arise from the use of this construction applied not only to overt, but also to formally unmarked nominalizations of entire verbal or pseudoverbal sentences embedded as predicate of bipartite *pw*-sentences:[25]

(a) Verbal sentences:

(36) CT IV 187d *wbn=f pw m jȝb.t p.t*
"This means (*pw*) that he rises (*wbn=f*) from the Eastern part (*jȝb.t*) of the sky (*p.t*)"

(37) Sin. B 311 *jw=f pw ḥȝ.t=f r pḥ(.wj)=fj*
"This is how (*pw*) it comes from its beginning to its end"

(b) Pseudoverbal sentences (i.e. with stative or preposition + infinitive):

(38) Urk. V 53,1–2 *wnn šw pw ḥr jrj.t jmj.t-prw n gbb*
"This means (*pw*) that Shu is making (*ḥr jrj.t*) a testament (*jmj.t-prw*) in favor of Geb"

To define the semantic nature of these clauses properly, I would use the term "thetic":[26] unlike the more common "categorical" statement, in which a predicate affirms or denies a property of a well-defined and recognized subject, a thetic statement displays no clear-cut internal distribution of subject and predicate; rather, a state of affairs is presented as a whole, usually with a semantically insignificant "dummy" subject, if its presence is required by the morphosyntactic pattern: "there is water," "it rains," etc. Thetic sentences are in fact assertions containing one global message, which is not easily segmentable into discrete semantic components:

(39) Peas. R1.1 *zj pw wn.w ḫwj.n-jnpw rn=f*
"(Once upon a time) there was a man named Khuienanup" < lit. "It is that (*pw*) a man was (*zj wn.w*), Khuienanup (being) his name"

The thetic nature of these clauses is the reason for their extensive use in medical and in "aetiological" contexts which explain the development of a mythological frame: diagnoses and aetiologies present global circumstances as the result of previous statements introduced by categorical sentences:

(40) pEbers 855z "If his heart is flooded, *mhh jb=f pw mj ntj ḥr sḫȝ.t k.t md.t* this means (*pw*) that his heart is oblivious (*mhh jb=f*), like (*mj*) the one who is thinking (*ntj ḥr sḫȝ.t*) of something else"[27]

(41) CT IV 412 (162–5a) *jnk mjw pw ʿȝ nt(j) m jwnw ḏd(.w) rʿw [p]w r zȝ=f ḥrw mjw sw m nȝ n(j) bw-nfr jrj=f ḫpr rn=f pw n(j) mjw*

"'I am this great cat who is (*ntj*) in Heliopolis.' This (*pw*) is what Re says (*ḏd.w*) to his son (*r z3=f*) Horus. He is cat-like (*mjw sw*) in this goodness (*n3 nj bw-nfr*) which he does (*jrj=f*). This is how (*pw*) his name of 'cat' (*rn=f nj mjw*) comes about (*ḫpr*)"

Egyptian also displays a similar pattern which has often been associated – by the present writer as well[28] – with thetic sentences, but which in fact differs from them syntactically and semantically. Let us consider contrastively examples (41) above and (42) below:

(42) CT II 334b *r‘w pw ḏd.n=f n ḥrw*

It would be somewhat counterintuitive to argue that this clause, in which a well-defined subject (*r‘w* "Re") is not only extraposed, but also expanded by the verbal sentence following the pronoun *pw* (*ḏd.n=f n ḥrw* "he said to Horus"), conforms to the characteristic of the thetic statement, which is precisely the inadequacy of a separation between topic and comment as parts of a global judgment on a state of affairs. Yet, since this pattern can hardly be a form of tripartite nominal sentence (which would yield **he-said-to-Horus is Re*, syntactically and semantically impossible in Egyptian as much as in English), the sentence *r‘w ḏd.n=f n ḥrw* must in fact represent the predicate of *pw*. What we have here is the embedding of a verbal clause ***with topicalized subject*** as predicate of a hierarchically higher bipartite *pw*-sentence. In the case of verbal sentences, which have a VSO typological order, the fronted topic will be resumed by a coreferential pronoun in the main sentence; conversely, in the case of pseudoverbal or adverbial sentences, in which the subject precedes the predicate, there is no need for a resumptive pronoun, the noun followed by *pw* functioning both as extraposed topic (because of the "break" represented by *pw*) and as syntactic subject of the sentence. The strategies for the translation of this construction will necessarily differ from case to case, ranging from explanatory devices to the use of actualizers.

(a) Verbal sentences:

(43) CT V 110g *dp.t tn pw nj ‘pr(.w)=s m 3ḫ3ḫ.w=s*
"It is so that this ship (*dp.t tn pw*) is not equipped (*nj ‘pr.w=s*) with its spars"
S => [[[[*dp.t tn*]$_{\text{NPtopic}}$[*nj ‘pr.w=s m 3ḫ3ḫ.w=s*]$_{\text{VerbS}}$]$_{\text{VS}}$]$_{\text{NPpred}}$ [*pw*]$_{\text{subj}}$]

(44) CT II 342b *stẖ pw jrj.n=f ḫprw r=f m š3j km*
"As for Seth, it happened (*stẖ pw*) that he transformed himself (*jrj.n=f ḫprw*) into a black pig (*š3j km*) against him"

(b) Pseudoverbal sentences (i.e. with stative or preposition + infinitive):

(45) West. 6,4–6 "I asked her: 'Why don't you row?' And she answered: *nḫ3w pw nj mfk3.t m3.t ḫr.w ḥr mw*. 'Because (*pw*) a jewel of new malachite (*mfk3.t m3.t*) fell into the water' (*ḫr.w ḥr mw*)"

S ⇒ [[[*nḫꜣw nj mfkꜣ.t mꜣ.t*]$_{\text{NPtopic}}$ [~~*sw*~~ *ḫr.w ḥr mw*]$_{\text{PseudoverbS}}$]$_{\text{NPpred}}$ [*pw*]$_{\text{subj}}$]

(46) Neferti 57–58 *nzw pw r jj.t n rsj*

"But a king (*nzw pw*) will come from the South (*r jj.t n rsj*)"

(c) Adverbial sentences:

(47) Pyr. 763a–b "O King N! Let your soul stand among the gods and among the spirits, *snḏ=k pw jr ḥꜣtj.w=sn* that the fear of you (*snḏ=k*) be (*pw*) to their hearts (*jr ḥꜣtj.w=sn*)"

S ⇒ [[[*snḏ=k*]$_{\text{NPtopic}}$ [~~*sw*~~ *jr ḥꜣtj.w=sn*]$_{\text{AdvS}}$]$_{\text{NPpred}}$ [*pw*]$_{\text{subj}}$]

While we could take the AdvP "will come from the South" in (46) or "to their hearts" in (47) to be mere adverbial adjuncts of the head noun, the resulting semantic yield ("this is a king who will come from the South," "this is your fear to their hearts") does not properly satisfy the requirements of the contexts, which call for an explanation of the events described in the preceding context rather than for general statements of categorical character.

Since it lies in the nature of this pattern that the noun followed by *pw* is not only the subject of the nominalized clause, but also the topic of the nominal *pw*-sentence in which it appears embedded, it is not surprising that the well-known hierarchies of topicality (according to which the first person is a more likely topic than the second, and the second more likely than the third) favor a frequent use of this pattern with first person subjects:

(48) Sh.S. 89–91 *jnk pw hꜣj.kw r bjꜣ m wpw.t jtj*

"What happened is that I (*jnk pw*) had set out (*hꜣj.kw*) to the mines on a royal mission"

S ⇒ [[[*jnk*]$_{\text{NPtopic}}$ [(~~*wj*~~) *hꜣj.kw r bjꜣ m wpw.t jtj*]$_{\text{PseudoverbS}}$]$_{\text{NPpred}}$ [*pw*]$_{\text{subj}}$]

5.4 Sentences with adjectival predicate and cleft sentences

5.4.1 Qualifying patterns

If the general frame of the discussion of nominal sentences with substantival predicate can be directly applied to the study of adjectival sentences, this latter syntactic type displays a number of distinctive features, such as a more extensive use of focalizations and nominalizations of verbal clauses, which justify its treatment under a separate heading. In the unmarked pattern, a nominal subject regularly follows the adjectival predicate:

(49) Sin. B 155 *nfr prw=j wsḫ s.t=j*

"My house is good, my place of dwelling is large"

The subject can be any part of speech which is also [+N], including infinitives and nominalizations (substantival or adjectival) of verbal phrases:

(50) Sh.S. 182 *mk nfr sḏm n rmṯ.t*
"Look (particle *mk*), it is good for people (*n rmṯ.t*) to listen (*sḏm*, infinitive)"

(51) West. 9,22 *qsn mss=s*
"Her delivery (*mss=s* "that-she-delivers," nominalized VP) was difficult (*qsn*)"

(52) Sh.S. 124 *rš-wj sḏd dp.t.n=f*
"How (enclitic particle *wj*) happy is the one who can relate (*sḏd*, participle) what he experienced (*dp.t.n=f*)!"

(53) Pt. 629 *nfr-wj sbꜣ(.w).n jtj=f*
"How fortunate (*nfr*) is he whose father instructed him (*sbꜣw.n jtj=f* "whom his father instructed," relative form as adjectival VP)"

The main difference vis-à-vis the substantival sentence lies in the use of the dependent pronoun masculine *sw*, feminine *sj/st*, plural *sn/st* instead of the invariable demonstrative *pw* to express the pronominal subject. Moreover, since adjectival predicates are not only [+N] but also [+V] – as opposed to substantival patterns, which are [+N] but [-V] – the unmarked form of the predicate is maintained with feminine (*sj*) or plural subjects (*sn*, *st*), without agreement with the subject:

(54) Ens. Loy. 2,10 *sḥḏ-wj sw tꜣ.wj r jtn*
"How he illuminates (*sḥḏ*) the Two Lands (*tꜣ.wj*) more than the solar disk (*r jtn*)!"

(55) Sin. B 66 *ḥʿj s(j) jm=f r nṯr=sn*
"It ("the city," fem.) rejoices (*ḥʿj*) in him (*jm=f*) more than in the local god"

(56) Urk. IV 99,15 *ḏsr st r ḫpr.t m p.t*
"They were more splendid (*ḏsr*) than what happens in heaven (*ḫpr.t m p.t*)"

When the subject is thematized, a frequent construction when the subject is an entire nominal phrase rather than a single noun, the syntactic sequence is reversed to subject-predicate. In this case, however, the pattern acquires the features of the *pseudoverbal* sentence (section 6.2), the adjectival predicate being expressed not by the adjective, but by the stative, i.e. the conjugated pseudoverbal form of the root of which the adjective represents a participle:[29]

(57) Urk. IV 944,1 *(ḥr-ntt) ṯꜣw=k nj ʿnḫ nḏm.w m šr.t=j*
"Because your breath of life (*ṯꜣw=k nj ʿnḫ*) is sweet (*nḏm.w*) in my nostril (*m šr.t=j*)"

(58) Pt. 20–21 *jrr.t jꜣw n rmṯ bjn(.w) m ḫ.t nb.t*
"What old age does (*jrr.t jꜣw*) to people is bad (*bjn.w*) in every respect"

We observed in section 5.2 above that when the head noun of an AdjP is not overt, it is assumed to be a so-called *neuter*: "something" or the like. In these cases, participles and relative forms appear substantivized, i.e. treated as the predicate of nominal patterns of the *rmṯ pw*-type. Here, the overt marker of substantivization is the feminine adjectival ending *.t* of the participle (59) or the relative form (60), which in Middle Egyptian also fulfills the function of "neuter," i.e. of a semantically unspecified noun:

(59) CT VI 286a *wḏ.t n=k pw* "This is what is ordered (*wḏ.t*) to you (*n=k*)"
(60) Peas. B1,77 *mk jrr.t=sn pw* "Look (*mk*), this is what they do (*jrr.t=sn*)"

Rather than as exceptions to the rule, therefore, instances of an adjectival predicate followed by a pronominal subject *pw* should be analyzed as substantivized uses of the adjective:

(61) Peas. R7.4 *ḥns pw nj wsḫ js pw*
"It was a narrow one (*ḥns*, scil. "path"), not a broad one (*wsḫ*)"[30]

Interlocutive subjects generally behave as in the nominal pattern. The tendency of the first person is to be expressed by the independent pronoun:[31]

(62) CT VI 335b *jnk jrj ḫprw m ꜣḫ.w*
"I am someone who turned (*jrj ḫprw* "who made a transformation") into *ꜣḫ*-spirits"

whereas in the second person the use oscillates between a pattern with independent pronoun S => [pronoun-Pred] and a pattern with dependent pronouns S => [Pred-pronoun], the former being syntactically a main clause, the latter a subordinate clause:

(63) Sin. R 55 *nfr ṯw ḥn'=j* "For you (*ṯw*) are happy with me (*ḥn'=j*)"
(64) CT VII 22n *ṯwt wrj jmj msj.w*
"You are the greatest one among the children"

The tripartite pattern corresponding to the tripartite nominal sentence is also documented, though not as much as with substantival predicates, and only in exclamatory sentences with the particle *wj*:

(65) Urk. IV 1166,10 *ḥḏ-wj st nꜣ n(j) rnp.t wḏ(.t) nṯr ḫr=k*
"How bright are they (*st*) – the (*nꜣ-n*) years (*rnp.t*) which God has granted (*wḏ.t nṯr*) you!"

Examples of adjectival sentences with extraposed topicalized subject resumed by a coreferential pronoun in the body of the sentence are also rare:

(66) Pt. 25 *dp.t nb.t ꜣq sj* "All taste (*dp.t nb.t*) – it (*sj*) is lost (*ꜣq*)"

5.4.2 *Identifying (cleft) sentences*

If qualifying adjectival patterns, therefore, can be said on the whole to closely resemble classifying nominal sentences, some structural differences emerge when turning to the typologically marked types, which in Egyptological literature are usually subsumed under the headings "participial statement" and "cleft sentence."[32] We already observed that the combination of the two main features [+N] and [+V] characterizes in Egyptian a certain number of morphosyntactic structures: (a) infinitives, (b) topicalized VPs, (c) participles, (d) relative forms. While infinitives represent verbal substantives, what Arabic grammarians call the *maṣdar* of a verbal root, and thematized VPs can be generally said to acquire substantive-like *maṣdariyya* functions within the verbal clauses in which they appear, participles and relative clauses are adjectival nominalizations of a verbal sentence (section 7.7). In fact, "pure" adjectives, i.e. qualificative nouns not derived from a verbal root, are relatively rare in all Afroasiatic languages, and Egyptian is no exception to this rule. Thus, the most frequent morphosyntactic structures acting as adjectival predicates will be the participle and the relative form, the former being coreferential with the noun they modify, the latter representing the adjectival conversion of a VP whose subject is different from the antecedent. We will observe in section 7.7 that in all cases other than as object of the relative form, the antecedent of an adjectival phrase is resumed by a coreferential pronoun in the relative clause. The distinction between participles and relative forms, however, is morphologically fluid and is justified only on the basis of syntactic considerations:

(67) CT III 351c *jnk mry jtj=f mrrw jtj=f wr.t*
"I am someone beloved of his father (*mry jtj=f*, perfective passive participle) and whom his father loves (*mrrw jtj=f*, imperfective relative form) dearly (*wr.t*)"

When compared with most languages inside and outside the Afroasiatic family, Egyptian shows a considerable development of the syntactic type in which a nominal subject precedes an adjectival predicate. In discussing the nominal sentence (section 5.2.1), we saw that this typological order is semantically associated with a *specifying*, rather than classifying function of the predicate. In the case of the adjectival sentence, which displays a higher "verbality" than the nominal sentence, I prefer to call the marked type corresponding to the unmarked qualifying pattern the *identifying* sentence type:

(68) Urk. IV 895,1 *jnk sd sw* "I was the one who destroyed (*sd*) it"

From a pragmatic point of view, this sentence type carries a focalization of the subject, i.e. a higher communicative emphasis laid on it than is normally expected within the unmarked flow of discourse. The focalized subject becomes an element with contrastive function within the context in which it appears, the remainder of the utterance, including the predicative AdjP, being demoted to the rank of conversational presupposition. When the focalized subject is a noun, it appears preceded by the particle *jn* and followed by the adjectival predicate. When it is a pronoun, the independent series – which in its classical form etymologically "entails" the particle *jn* – is used:

(69) Sin. B 308 *jn ḥm=k rdj jrj.t(w)=f*
"It is Your Majesty (*jn ḥm=k*) who caused (*rdj*) that it be done (*jrj.tw=f*)"

(70) Peas. B1,116–17 *ntf dd n=f st*
"It was he (*ntf*) who would give (*dd*) it (*st*) to him (*n=f*)"

In restricted cases,[33] the independent pronoun is followed by the enclitic *pw*, thus creating not only a semantic, but also a formal identity with the identifying pseudocleft sentence (section 5.2):

(71) Peas. B1,51–52 *jnk pw mdw n=k* "I am the one who speaks (*mdw*) to you"

The marker of focality can be omitted when the focalized subject is a personal name of high contextual prominence, such as the name of the owner or a funerary text or of the author of a letter:[34]

(72) CT VII 369a *jnk/N pn/tn/jn N pn sgr mw* "It is [subj.] that pacifies the water"

Following the seminal work by Polotsky,[35] this construction has been labeled by Egyptologists "cleft sentence" on the basis of its similarities with constructions of the pattern *c'est ... qui* in French or *it is ... who* in English. In fact, its "cleft" character, i.e. the relative autonomy of the second part of the sentence vis-à-vis the first, shown for example by the lack of gender and number agreement between the subject and the cleft predicate, appears in Egyptian to result from a diachronic development: while in early Egyptian the adjectival predicate sometimes still agrees in gender and number with the nominal antecedent:

(73) CT VI 258e Sq3C *nts jtj.t ṯ3w=f* "It is she (*nts*) who took (*jtj.t*) his breath"

in the classical language the unmarked form of the adjective is regularly employed, pointing to a phenomenon of progressive grammaticalization of the clefting with the resulting "break" between focalized subject and presuppositional predicate:

(74) Adm. 12,14 *jn 'š3.t sm3 'nd.t*
"It is the majority (*'š3.t*) that kills (*sm3.ø*) the minority"

(75) pEbers 100,8–9 *ntsn dd n=s mw* "It is they (*ntsn*) that give (*dd.ø*) water to it"

The pragmatic function of the subject as focus, i.e. as promoted element dominating the communicative salience of a demoted predicate, is particularly evident in the use of the *jn*-construction in contrastive contexts such as in questions (*completive focus*):

(76) West. 9,7–8 "His Majesty asked: 'Who then will bring it to me?' And Djedi answered: *jn wrj nj p3 ḫrd.w 3 ntj m ḫ.t n(.t) rwḏ-ḏd.t jnj=f n=k sj* 'The eldest (*wrj*) of the three children (*nj p3 ḫrd.w 3*) who are in Rudjdjedet's womb will bring (*jnj=f*) it to you'"

or in order to correct an earlier contextual assumption (*replacing focus*):

(77) CT VII 464a–b "I did not order that they perpetrate evil. *jn jb.w=sn ḥḏ ḏd.t.n=j.* (Rather,) it is their hearts (*jn jb.w=sn*) that transgressed (*ḥḏ*) what I had said (*ḏd.t.n=j*)"

In the cleft sentence, which is originally an ergative construction (section 4.6.3.3), the use of relative forms or of passive participles, i.e. of adjectival conversions of the verb with a different agent from the antecedent, is not documented.[36] This restriction is due to the universal semantic hierarchy of salience whereby the subject is by far the most likely argument to be exposed to pragmatic promotion, i.e. to be topicalized or focalized.[37] In transitive verbal phrases, therefore, agents will be much more likely than patients or other arguments to become the focus of the utterance. The reader will recall that when the element assigned pragmatic focus is the patient (or less frequently any other argument), rather than the cleft sentence, Egyptian displays the pseudocleft pattern "Pred-*pw*-Subj" discussed in section 5.2. The most widespread of these constructions is the periphrastic *sḏm pw jrj.n=f/jry* "what he did (*jrj.n=f*)/what was done (*jry*) was (*pw*) to hear (*sḏm*)." The noun phrase indicating the patient of the verbal phrase is assigned in these instances the role of syntactic predicate and fronted (with or without contrastive stress) to the head position of the sentence. Examples (15) and (71) above offer good evidence for the choice of the tripartite pattern with *pw* when the pragmatically emphasized element is the patient of the verbal phrase: "Then this Nemtinakht said: 'Is this the proverb that people say: A poor man's name is pronounced on account of his master? *jnk pw mdw n=k jmj-r3 prw pw sḫ3y=k* I am the one who speaks to you, but the one whom you mention is the High Steward.'"[38]

Being [+V], adjectival predicates can also convey the expression of temporal or aspectual features, with the perfective participle in the preterite:

(78) Urk. IV 766,5 *jn ḥm=j rḏj wsr=f*
"It is My Majesty who caused (*rḏj*) that he be powerful (*wsr=f*)"

the imperfective participle in the unmarked tense (i.e. the relative present):

(79) Pt. 184 *jn nṯr jrr jqr* "It is God who brings about (*jrr*) excellence"

For the reference to the future, earlier Egyptian still shows cases of prospective participles acting as predicate of a cleft sentence,[39] but in the classical language a prospective verbal form is found as presuppositional predicate:

(80) Pyr. 537c *jn ḏr.t N wṯz=s sw* "It is N's hand that will raise (*wṯz=s*) him"

This evolution is similar to the grammaticalization of the masculine singular form of the participle for all genders and numbers in the cleft sentence: in presence of the verbal category of *modality*, the adjectival forms are replaced by a finite "*that*-form" in agreement with the antecedent.[40]

5.5 Possessive and interrogative patterns

Egyptian constructions with possessive or interrogative predicate represent a semantically specialized and syntactically regular subset of adjectival or adverbial sentences. In the case of patterns which indicate possession, the possessive indicator acts as predicate of an adjectival sentence and is followed (in the unmarked sequence Pred-Subj) or preceded (in the marked sequence Subj-Pred) by a nominal or pronominal subject. As in the basic sentence type, the distribution of marked and unmarked constructions depends on the qualifying or identifying function of the adjectival predicate.

5.5.1 Possessive constructions

In their basic form, possessive constructions[41] are normally conveyed by an adverbial sentence $S \Rightarrow [Subj_{NP}\text{-}Pred_{AP}]$ in which the predicate is introduced by the preposition *n* "to" (see section 6.2):

(81) Pyr. 2030a *ḥkꜣ=k n=k ḥkꜣ n N n=f*
"You have your magic, the King has his magic," lit. "Your magic (*ḥkꜣ=k*) is to you (*n=k*); the King's magic is to him"
(35) pEbers 99,4 *(ḥr-ntt) mt.w=f n ʿ.t=f nb.t*
"For each of his limbs (*ʿ.t=f nb.t*) has its liquids (*mt.w=f*)"

A few bound constructions, especially personal names, show an adjectival pattern[42] consisting of the determinative pronoun *nj* "that-of" as predicate (thus invariable in gender and number, see section 5.4),[43] immediately followed by a first NP indicating the argument to which the quality is ascribed and forming together with the determinative pronoun *nj* the predicative unit of the sentence, and then by a second NP as subject: the name of Amenemhat III (eighteenth century BCE) as King of Upper and Lower Egypt is

(82) *nj-mꜣʿ.t-rʿw*
"Re belongs to Maat" (< "Re is that-of-Maat," i.e. the sun god Re conforms to the principles of order, justice, etc.)[44]

Complications, however, arise from the tendency of the Egyptian writing system to have divine names graphically precede any other noun in the NP – a phenomenon which is referred to as "honorific anticipation" (section 2.3) – and from our own tendency to read as a relation of ***possession*** what is in Egyptian a predication of ***features***. The result is our perception of a semantic looseness in the mutual distribution of the NP functioning as subject and the NP acting as predicative complement, which often becomes a matter of extralinguistic, i.e. cultural interpretation: example (82) could just as well be read *nj-r'w-m3'.t* and interpreted as "Maat belongs to Re" ("Maat is that-of-Re," justice derives from the sun god Re), an alternative analysis which would also perfectly fit the religious background of the name.

This ambiguity vanishes in the more regular use of adjectival sentences with *nj* "that-of," when the subject, i.e. the entity displaying the features indicated by the predicate, is expressed by a pronoun. The pattern consists of the determinative pronoun *nj* immediately followed by the dependent pronoun indicating the subject: being an enclitic, it has to be appended to the first prosodic unit of the sentence, i.e. to the determinative pronoun itself. The dependent pronoun is followed by a NP indicating the quality ascribed to the pronominal subject and forming together with the determinative pronoun *nj* the predicative unit of the sentence: *nj- wj*-NP (< $[$**nj*-NP$]_{pred}$-$[$*wj*$]_{subj}$) "I am that-of-NP," "I belong to NP":

(83) CT III 311a T_1Be *n(j)-wj prw wsjr*
"I (*wj*) belong to the House of Osiris (**nj prw wsjr* "that-of the-House-of Osiris")"

(84) Sh.S. 62 *n(j)-sw mḥ 30*
"It (*sw*) was thirty cubits long (**nj mḥ 30* "that-of-thirty cubits")"

Syntactically, this type of adjectival sentence behaves like a qualifying pattern, allowing the subject to undergo pragmatic extraposition. In example (85), the fronted topic ("this N") is resumed by the coreferential subject pronoun in the body of the sentence (*sw*):

(85) CT IV 82p *N pn nj-sw ḫm wrj*
"As for this N, he belongs to the Great Shrine (*ḫm wrj*)"

whereas in example (86) the rhematic subject is indicated by a dependent pronoun with cataphoric function, dislocated to the end of the sentence as "tail," witness the first person variants of the same text (for the construction with *nnk* see below):

(86) CT IV 340a L_1Li *n(j)-sw N tm* "It, i.e. the Whole (*tm*), belongs to N (**nj-N*)"
(86') Ibid. B_9C *nnk tm* "To me belongs the Whole"

But when both the subject and the predicative complement are pronominal, we are confronted with the same semantic problems raised by the sequence *nj*-NP1-NP2 above, i.e. with a substantial difficulty in determining which quality is ascribed to whom, for example in (87) whether a subject "it" (in this case *jr.t ḥrw* "Horus' Eye," a feminine word) is predicated of "you" or else a subject "you" of "it":

(87) Pyr. 2033 "Formula to be recited: 'O Osiris N, take for yourself the Eye of Horus; *n(j)-ṯw s(j)* it belongs to you'"

The close syntactic tie between the adjectival head *nj* and its predicative complement makes it clear, however, that if the two arguments are conveyed by an identical morphological pattern, in this case the dependent pronoun, the original order is maintained: "it (*sj*) is that-of-you (*nj-ṯw*)."

This is confirmed by the existence of another possessive pattern. When the pronominalization affects the nominal complement of the adjectival predicate (NP1), two different constructions are preferred, corresponding to an unmarked and to a marked adjectival pattern. In the unmarked pattern, which has *qualifying* function, the possessed entity is conveyed by a nominal or pronominal subject, whereas the possessor is indicated by a predicate "belonging-to," consisting of the preposition *n* followed by the suffix pronoun of the possessor and by the *nisba jmj* from the preposition *m*:

(88) Urk. IV 96,7 *n=k-jmj ḥḏ*
"Silver (*ḥḏ*) belongs to you (*n=k-jmj* "belonging-to-you")"

(89) Sin. B 222–23 *n=k-jm(j) s(j) mj.tt ṯzm.w=k*
"It (*sj*) belongs to you (*n=k-jmj* "belonging-to-you"), like (*mj.tt*) your dogs (*ṯzm.w=k*)"

In (89), the subject is expanded by an apposition following it, but it can also be topicalized and resumed by a coreferential subject in the main sentence, as in (90):

(90) Sh.S. 151 *'ntjw n=j-jm(j) sw*
"As for myrrh (*ntjw*), it belongs to me (*n=j-jmj* "belonging-to-me")"

As the adjectival *nisba* of the preposition *m*, *n=k-jmj* can also be used non-predicatively, i.e. as an adjective following the NP it refers to and agreeing with it in gender and number; the resulting construction expresses in a prosodically stressed form the relation normally conveyed by suffix pronouns:

(91) CT III 224c *sḫm=k m pr.t-ḫrw n=k-jmj.t*
"May you control (*sḫm=k m*) the funerary offerings (*pr.t-ḫrw*, fem.) that are meant for you (*n=k-jmj.t*, feminine adj. "your")"

In the marked construction, which has an *identifying* function, the determinative pronoun *nj* is followed by the independent pronoun, and often appears combined with it into a single prosodic unit: *nj-jnk* > *nnk*, *jnk*; *nj-ntk* > *ntk*; *nj-ntf* > *ntf*.

(92) CT V 279c M_6C *nnk bꜣ nb* "Every soul belongs to me," vs.
(92') Ibid. B_1Bo *n=f-jm(j) bꜣ nb* "Every soul belongs to him"
(93) CT I 254f *jw n=k grḥ nj-ntk hrww wsjr*
"Yours is the night (*grḥ*), to you belongs the day (*hrww*), O Osiris!"
(94) Adm. 10,4 *ntf jtj bdt* "To him belong barley (*jtj*) and emmer (*bdt*)"

5.5.2 *Interrogative constructions*

The same paradigmatic identity with nominal and adjectival patterns is displayed by interrogative constructions in which the interrogative pronoun is the subject or the object of the verbal predicate.[45] As a general rule, interrogative pronouns behave like focalized subjects or objects of nominal predicates. The focalized subject pronoun *(j)n-m* "who?" (< "ergative" particle *jn* + interrogative pronoun *m* "WH") occupies the position of the independent pronoun in a specifying pattern:

(95) CT IV 243a B_9C^a *(j)n-m tr rḥ.wj*
"Who (*jn-m*) are then (*tr*) the Two Companions (*rḥ.wj*)?"

or in the cleft sentence:

(96) Sh.S. 69–70 *(j)n-m jnj ṯw nḏs*
"Who brought you, little one?" < "who (*jn-m*) the-one-who-brought (*jnj*) you (*ṯw*)?"
(97) CT V 110e M_2C *(j)n-m tr sḫm=f m tm jn(.w) n=k*
"Who then will have power over (*sḫm=f m*) that which won't bring (it) to you?"

The interrogative pronouns *m*, *zj*, or *pw* "who?" "what?" are found in the predicative position of an adjectival sentence with the usual hierarchies of topicality, i.e. preferably with a sequence "subject-predicate" in the case of interlocutive subjects, and with a clear preference for the sequence "predicate-subject" in the third person:

(98) CT III 59b *ṯwt m-tr* "Who (*m*) are you (*ṯwt*) then (particle *tr*)?"
(99) BD (Budge) 241,14 *(j)n-m tr ṯw ntk zj*
"Who (*jn-m*) are you (*ṯw*) then, who (*zj*) are you (*ntk*)?"
(100) CT IV 188b *p-tr sw ʿꜣ ḫpr ḏs=f*
"Who then (*p-tr* < *pw *tr*) is he, the great one who came into existence by himself?"
(101) Sin. B 261 *p-tr ḏd.t n=j nb=j*
"What does my lord say to me?" < "What is what-my-lord-says (*ḏd.t nb=j*) to me?"

5.6 Existential sentences and temporal-modal features

Existential sentences are those in which a nominal predicate fulfills the function of stating the existence of a subject.[46] When the existence of a nominal subject occurs absolutely – an extremely rare case in the classical language[47] – existential sentences are treated as a nominal pattern introduced by the particle *jw* (originally an auxiliary verb) as overt existential predicate:

(102) CT IV 29e *jw ø sšp ḏd N jw ø knḥ ḏd N*
"'There is light (*sšp*),' says the Deceased; 'There is darkness (*knḥ*),' says the Deceased"

(103) Disp. 123–24 *jw ø šw m ʻq-jb*
"There is a lack of close friends (*šw m ʻq-jb* "lack of one-who-enters-the-heart)"

In the much more frequent cases in which the existence of the subject is accompanied by a beneficiary or by an adverbial circumstance, the resulting sentence is adverbial. Adverbial sentences will be dealt with in the next chapter, so that just one example will suffice here:

(104) Peas. B2,65–66 *jw šd.w=k m sḫ.t jw fqꜣ=k m spꜣ.t jw ʻqw=k m šnʻ*
"Your plots of ground (*šd.w=k*) are in the field, your estate (*fqꜣ=k*) is in the nome, your income (*ʻqw=k*) is in the storehouse"

But when the existence of the subject is a function of temporal or modal features which project it to the realized past or to the potential future, the predicate of Egyptian existential sentences is a verbal form of the verb *wnn* "to be," "to exist," which is normally not used in the general present tense. In (105), the subject "my wife" and the adverb "there" are both arguments of the verbal predicate indicating existence:

(105) pKahun 12,13 *wnn tꜣj=j ḥjm.t jm*
"My wife will be there" (< "There will be my wife there")

While from a syntactic point of view the present paragraph should find its place in the treatment of adverbial and verbal sentences, the semantic kinship of the predication of "existence" with states of affairs otherwise expressed by nominal patterns justifies their presentation in this chapter. We discussed in sections 5.2 and 5.4 the basic expression of nominal (*rmṯ pw*) and adjectival (*nfr sw*) existence respectively, in section 5.3. the thetic presentation of a state of affairs by means of the demonstrative pronoun *pw* used as "dummy" subject, and in section 5.5 possession as a specialized form of adverbial or adjectival predication qualifying a subject. Rather than the absolute "being" of the subject, these patterns describe the latter's relation to the concomitant circumstances of its being. In this case, Egyptian does without any overt morphosyntactic expression of the idea of "being," choosing to shift attention to its semantic environment. But when a crucial component of the semantic environment of this "being" is represented by its temporal or modal setting, its overt expression is delegated to verbal sentences with a *sḏm=f* form of the verb *wnn* as predicate, which in classical Egyptian completely supersede the simple construction *jw* NP: they display the non-geminated form (section 4.6.3.1b) in the aorist *wn=f* "he is/was" (106) and in the subjunctive *wn=f* "that he be," which is used after verbs of wish or command (107), and the geminated form in the thematized *wnn=f* "(the fact that) he is" (108) and in the prospective *wnn=f* "he will be" with modal functions (109):

(106) West. 6,26–7,1 *jw wn nḏs ḏdj rn=f*
"There is (*jw wn*, VP *jw sḏm=f*) a well-off citizen (*nḏs*) whose name is Djedi"

(107) Pyr. 638b *rḏj.n=s wn=k m nṯr*
"She caused (*rḏj.n=s*) that you be (*wn=k*) a god (*m nṯr* "as a god")"

(108) Sin. B 43–44 *wnn jr=f tꜣ pf mj-m m-ḫmt=f*
"But how (*mj-m*) is that land (*tꜣ pf*) without him (*m-ḫmt=f*)?"

(109) Sin. B 77 *mk tw ꜥꜣ wnn=k ḥnꜥ=j*
"Now (*mk*) you are here (*tw ꜥꜣ*) and you will remain (VP *wnn=k*) with me"

We will observe in section 6.4 that in the classical language adverbial sentences such as *tw ꜥꜣ* in (109) have to be introduced by a particle of initiality when they function as initial clauses – a rule which applies to many categories of verbal sentences as well. This is the function fulfilled by *mk* in (109). Of these particles, which are syntactic complementizers and each of which represents a different proposition operator,[48] the most complex and at the same time the most germane to our discussion of existential clauses is the particle *jw*, which, if it is related to Sem. *hwy* "to be" or to Eg. *jwj* "to come,"[49] could etymologically mean something like "there exists." Whenever *jw* introduces an adverbial sentence with the preposition *m* "in" indicating a transitory, rather than an essential quality of the subject:

(110) Adm. 2,10 *jw ms jtrw m znf* "The Nile (*jtrw*) is really (*ms*) blood (*znf*)"

i.e. it has become like blood as a result of the many killings, it appears in complementary distribution with the *wnn=f* form of the type we encountered in (108)–(109). Compare the subjunctive *wn=k m nṯr* "that you be a god" in (107) with example (111), where the same message is rendered first by an unmarked adverbial present and then by the prospective tense:

(111) CT I 55b *jw=k m nṯr wnn=k m nṯr*
"You are divine (*m nṯr* "as a god") and you will be divine"

In the syntactic model of the Standard theory, these sentences have been interpreted within an adverbial understanding: both sentences are seen as adverbial, the predication of existence in the second being emphasized by the topicalized VP *wnn=k* "that-you-are." In this perspective, the second sentence would emphasize the unmarked adverbial predicate of the first: "you are divine, you are (or: will be) *divine*"; the construction with *wnn=f* is taken to be the syntactic device that converts unmarked adverbial sentences introduced by *jw* into pragmatically marked ones with promoted comment.

However – and I shall return to this point in my discussion of adverbial and verbal sentences – one of the main functions of a topicalized VP is precisely the definition of the diathetic, temporal or modal features governing the higher predication; in other words, since the thematized VP is assigned all the verbal features of the utterance, the inevitable consequence of the concentration of semantic functions on the head VP is the pragmatic emphasis on the rheme, such as the interrogative adverb *mj-m* "how?" in example (108). The complementary distribution of *jw* and *wnn* in existential clauses shows in an ideal way this interface between syntax and semantics at work: while the unmarked attribution of a quality to a subject in the general present is conveyed by nominal and adverbial predicates, the semantic complexity generated by temporal or modal features requires the resort to a verbal pattern; and symmetrically, the transformation of an adverbial sentence into a verbal clause expands the pragmatic potential of the non-verbal components of the sentence, such as what used to be the adverbial predicate in a *jw*-sentence and has now been reduced to the role of adverbial adjunct in a *wnn*-clause: "you-(are)-divine," but "you-are-X," with "X" inevitably acquiring promoted pragmatic status. In this way we can properly interpret the role of *wnn*:[50] whether the underlying morphological pattern is the emphatic *wnn=f* or the prospective *wnn=f*, the verbal character of these forms, i.e. the restriction of the predicated existence to a specific temporal or modal setting, causes the communicative emphasis of the utterance to be laid on the adverbial adjunct which modifies the predicative VP.

The later stages of the development of existential constructions in classical Egyptian, which anticipate the situation in later Egyptian (section 5.8), see a grammaticalization of *wn* and *wnn* as "converters," i.e. as free morphemes added to the sentential patterns in order to embed them into verbal clauses: in (112) and (113), the temporal converters *wn.jn*, originally the conjugational base of the contingent *sḏm.jn=f*-form, and *wnn*, originally the base of the prospective *sḏm=f*-form, assign the scope of the adjectival *nfr sw*-patterns to the past and to the future respectively:

(112) Kagemni 2,6 *wn.jn nfr st ḥr jb=sn*
"This was good in their heart" < *"It was [it is good in their heart]"

(113) pKahun 3,36 *mk wnn nḏm sj ḥr jb=f*
"Look, it will be pleasant in his heart" < *It will be [it is pleasant in his heart]"

Strategies of semantic readjustment also occur in the syntax of adjective verbs, i.e. of those verbs whose participles constitute the adjectives referred to in section 5.4: *nfr* "to be good," *ʿꜣ* "to be great," *ʿšꜣ* "to be numerous," etc. These roots express temporally unmarked situations when used in the adjectival construction *nfr sw/jnk nfr* and in the pseudoverbal construction *mk sw nfr.w* with thematized subject followed by the stative. The same applies to their substantival conversion *nfr=f* used after verbs of perception such as *mꜣꜣ* "to see" or *rḫ* "to know" (section 7.6):

(114) Urk. IV 363,6 *jw ḥm.t=j rḫ.tj nṯrr=f*
"My Majesty (*ḥm.t=j*, fem.) knows that-he-is-divine (*nṯrr=f* < *nṯrj* "to be divine")"

but not to their prospective *nfr=f*, i.e. to their verbal form appearing after verbs of volition or in main optative clauses, which displays a semantic shift in from the static to the dynamic meaning ("he will *become* good"):

(115) Pyr. 618a "O Osiris N: may your heart be raised to him, *ʿꜣj jb=k* may your heart become great, may your mouth be opened, may Horus revenge you: it cannot last that he does not revenge you"

In other words, the acquisition of true verbal features, for example the expression of tense, aspect, or mood, causes semantic readjustments that bear consequences for the syntactic environments in which a form appears.

5.7 Negative patterns

When compared with similar patterns in related Afroasiatic languages, Egyptian negative constructions display a high degree of complexity both from a syntactic and from a semantic point of view. While no separate chapter of this book is devoted to a global treatment of negation,[51] I shall discuss in each section the pertinent negative patterns and try to show how they display a surprisingly high degree of uniformity in spite of the syntactic differences among the underlying positive patterns.

Earlier Egyptian shows two main negative morphemes: the first one is indicated by a logogram of two human arms in gesture of negation and is conventionally transliterated *n* or *nj*, but from an comparative point of view it is more likely to have displayed a bilabial /m/;[52] the second one shows the same logographic sign accompanied by the phonogram *n* /n/ and is conventionally transliterated *nn*, although it probably exhibited just a single /n/;[53] in addition, there is a negative pattern in which *nj* (in the later stages of earlier Egyptian *nn*) is combined with the subordinating particle *js* (section

6.3.1) to form a continuous morpheme *nj-js* (later *nn-js*) and a discontinuous morpheme *nj...js* (later *nn...js*), depending on the construction in which they appear. In general, the functional distribution of these three negative patterns may be defined as follows:

(a) *nj* is a nexal, i.e. propositional negative particle indicating simple *contradiction,*[54] for example of a nominal *rmṯ pw*-pattern (section 5.3):

(116) Sin. B 266–68 "Then they said to His Majesty: *nj ntf pw m mꜣʿ.t* 'This (*pw*) is not (*nj*) really (*m mꜣʿ.t*) he, Sovereign my Lord!' But His Majesty said: *ntf pw m mꜣʿ.t* 'Yes, this is really he'"

The negative particle *nj* is also rarely used for the nexal contradiction of adjectival *nfr sw*-sentences, although the positive counterpart of (117) is more likely to have been a possessive **jw n=k ʿntjw wrj* "you have much myrrh" (section 5.5) than an adjectival **wrj n=k ʿntjw* "myrrh is great to you" (section 5.4):

(117) Sh.S. 150 *nj wrj n=k ʿntjw*
"You don't have much myrrh" < "Myrrh (*ʿntjw*) is not (*nj*) great (*wrj*) to you (*n=k*)"

A much higher degree of productivity is displayed by the nexal negation of sentences with verbal forms of adjectival verbs. The rules for the negation of verbal sentences apply unchanged to these sentences, with *nj nfr.n=f* negating an unmarked present state (118) and *nj nfr=f* used for the negation of a past quality (119):

(118) Siut I,280–81[55] *nj nḏm.n n=f ḫtḫt jm*
"The reverse thereof (*ḫtḫt jm*) is not pleasant (*nj nḏm.n-*) to him (*n=f*)"
(119) Urk. IV 1082,15 *nj qnd=j [ḥr ṯz n(j) sprw]*
"I did not become angry (*nj qnd=j*) at the appeal of a petitioner"

Older texts show cases of contradictory negations of existential patterns (section 5.6) corresponding to positive constructions with *jw (wn)* (120), of adverbial sentences (121), or of *wnn=f* in prospective verbal sentences (122):

(120) Pyr. 1322c *nj pq=f nj mnqb=f*
"There is no (*nj*) bread of his (*pq=f*), there is no fan of his (*mnqb=f*)"
(121) Pyr. 2293b[N] *nj jtj=k m rmṯ* "You father (*jtj=k*) is not (*nj*) a man (*m rmṯ*)"
(122) BH I 25,98–99 *nj wnn zꜣ=f ḥr ns.t=f*
"His son will not be (*nj wnn zꜣ=f*) on his seat (*ḥr ns.t=f*)"

But as a general trend, *nj*-patterns are diachronically recessive in nominal sentences, tending gradually to disappear and their function to be assumed by existential patterns with *nn* – see under (b) – or by focalized patterns with *nj-js* – see under (c) below.

(b) *nn* is a predicative negative particle, denying the existence of a subject:

(123) Disp. 121–22 "To whom shall I speak today? *nn m3ʿ.tjw* There are no righteous people"

(124) Sin. B 309 *nn šw3w jry n=f mj.tt*
"There is no commoner for whom the same has been done (*jry* "who-was-done," *mj.tt* "the same," *n=f* "for him," relative clause modifying the subject *šw3w* "commoner," see section 7.7.2)"

From an etymological point of view, *nn* is presumably the result of the addition of an intensifier to the nexal *nj*, much in the same way in which similar predicate denial operators developed in Indo-European languages: Latin *non* < **ne-oenum* "not-one," English *not*, German *nicht* < **ne-wicht* "not-something," etc.[56] And in accordance with the complex interface displayed by existential statements (section 5.6) between nominal or adverbial sentences on the one hand and verbal sentences with the verb *wnn* "to be" on the other hand, *nn* can also appear combined in a construction with the perfective participle of *wnn* to form a new predicative form *nn-wn* "there is not," which in later historical phases of the language will become the regular operator for the negation of existence: *nn-wn*-Subj "there is no Subj":

(125) Disp. 130 *nn-wn pḥ.wj=fj*
"There is no end to it" < "Its end (*pḥ.wj=fj*) does not exist"

Once "intensified" morphemes of the kind of Latin *non* or Egyptian *nn* are created, the basic original marker of contradiction tends to fall under its pressure and either to disappear altogether, as in many Indo-European languages, or to become restricted to *bound* constructions, which is the case in Egyptian: in an evolution beginning in early Egyptian, then investing gradually different spheres of the classical language, and finally concluding its development in Late Egyptian, *nn* (and its later Egyptian heir conventionally transcribed *bn*) will emerge as the only *unbound* negative morpheme of the language and take over many domains originally covered by *nj*, such as adverbial or existential sentences:

(126) Pyr. 638b *nn ḫftj=k m rn=k n(j) nṯr*
"You have no enemy (*nn ḫftj=k*) in your name of 'God'"

(127) Sh.S. 100–101 *nn wḫ3 m-ḥr-jb=sn*
"There was no idiot (*nn wḫ3*) among them (*m-ḥr-jb=sn*)"

(c) *nj-js* and *nj...js* represent focal negations indicating *contrariety*; *nj-js* immediately precedes the negated syntagm, which is often an adverbial adjunct or an adverbial clause (128), more rarely the focalized nominal subject of a cleft sentence (129):[57]

(128) Pt. 74–75 "If you find a disputant in action *m ḥwrw nj-js mj.tw=k* who is poor (*m ḥwrw* "as a poor"), and not (*nj-js*) your equal (*mj.tw=k*)"

(129) CT III 336f–i *nj-js jtj=j rḏj n=j nj-js mʔw.t=j rḏj n=j jn jwʿ pw {pw} ʿꜣ knz.t swt rḏj n=j s(j)*
"Not my father (*jtj=j*) gave (it) to me; not my mother (*mʔw.t=j*) gave (it) to me, but this heir (*jwʿ pw*), the great one (*ʿꜣ*) of Kenzet – he (*swt*) is the one who gave it to me"

The discontinuous *nj...js*, on the other hand, wraps the first prosodic unit of the sentence:

(130) CT VI 332k–n *jrw=k pw nj jrw=j js pw ʿšm=k pw nj ʿšm=j js pw*
"This (*pw*) is your form (*jrw=k*), it is not (*nj...js*) *my* form; this is your image (*ʿšm=k*), it is not *my* image"

Rather than the nexus between the subject *pw* and the predicate *jrw=k* or *ʿšm=k*, which remains unaffected by the insertion of the negative marker, the scope of the negation in these examples is represented by the *focus* of the utterance, which is the predicative complement in (128), the subject in (129), and the suffix pronoun in (130). The scope of this negative pattern is *internal* to the proposition in that the truth of the predicative nexus of existence (*pw*) of a certain *jrw* "form" or of a certain *ʿšm* "image" is shown by the preceding positive sentences to be upheld and not modified by the insertion of the negative operator. What the focal negation performs is the creation of a polarity, of a pragmatic contrast to its explicit or implicit positive counterpart; rather than its contradictory, it represents its marked contrary.[58] It appears in nominal and adjectival patterns to negate one of the semantic or syntactic components of the predicate, such as its intensional meaning:

(131) Disp. 31–32 "This is what my soul said to me: *nj ntk js zj jw=k tr [...] ʿnḫ.tj*
You are not (*nj ntk js*) a real man (*zj*), although you are indeed [...] alive"

the indication of possession in the patterns *nj-sw* and *nj-jnk*:

(132) CT III 390e *nj nj-wj js zpꜣ.t* "I do not belong to the district (*zpꜣ.t*)"

(133) BD (Naville) II,40/8 *nj nj-jnk js rꜣ=k* "Your spell (*rꜣ=k*) is not mine"[59]

or an adverbial modifier, for example a "virtual" relative clause (section 6.3.3, 7.3):

(134) CT II 160b–c *nj jnk js wꜣḏ swꜣj=f jnk wꜣḏ prj m nb.t*
"I am not a passing-by (*swꜣj=f* "which passes by") *wꜣḏ*-amulet; (rather,) I am a *wꜣḏ*-amulet coming forth from mankind (*prj m nb.t*)"

The construction *nj...js* supplies the negative counterpart to all patterns involving focality, such as the subject of a specifying sentence S => [Subj-*pw*-Pred] in (135) or of a cleft sentence S => [*jn*-Subj-Pred] in (136):

(135) Pyr. 1233b *N pw ḏḥwtj nḏ ṯn nj N js pw stš jṯ(j) s(j)*
"N is Thoth who protects (*nḏ*) you, N is not Seth who takes (*jṯj*) it ("Horus' Eye")"

(136) Pyr. 1324a–b *nj jn js N pn ḏd nn jn ḥkꜣ ḏd nn*
"It is not N (*nj jn js N*) who says this; (rather,) it is a magician (*ḥkꜣ*) who says this"

In accordance with the so-called **O > E** drift,[60] which is the general trend of "weak" contradictory negations to move to the "strong" contrary pole of semantic oppositions, the pattern *nj...js* will tend on the one hand to be historically replaced by *nn...js* (*nj* > *nn*), on the other hand to assume functions originally fulfilled by the simple *nj* (*nj* > *nj...js*); examples from a non-literary text of the First Intermediate Period (137), a post-cassical literary text (138) and from a later copy (Dyn. XVIII) of a literary text of the Middle Kingdom (139) are:

(137) Nag' ed-Dêr 84, A6–7[61] "I am a successful citizen who lives out of his own wealth, *nn-js m gmj.t.n=j m-ʿ jtj=j* and not out of (*m*) what was bequeathed to me by (*gmj.t.n=j m-ʿ* "what I found from") my father"

(138) West. 9,6 *mk nn jnk js jnn n=k sj*
"Look, it is not I (*jnk*) who bring (*jnn*) it to you"

(139) Pt. 213–14 (L_2) *nn zꜣ=k js pw nn msj.n.tw=f js n=k*
"He is not *your* son; he wasn't born (*nn msj.n.tw=f js*) to *you*"[62]

One may then compare the typologically innovative *nn-js* in (137) with the classical *nj-js* in (128) above, the function of *nn...js* in (138) with the *nj...js* in (131)-(132), and *nn...js* in (139) with the older *nj...js* in a similar semantic environment in a monumental text of the classical period (140):

(140) Berlin 1157,18–20 "As for any son of mine who will keep this border which My Majesty made, *zꜣ=j pw* he is my son, born to My Majesty...But as for him who abandons it, who will not fight for it, *nj zꜣ=j js* he is not my son, he was not born to me"[63]

Negative patterns with the basic morpheme *nj* will therefore be exposed to two types of diachronic pressure: morphosyntactically, to the tendency for the simple negative to be replaced by a "intensified" version (*nj* > *nn*) more likely to acquire predicative status and to function as negative existential operator; semantically, to the tendency for propositional contradictories to be reinforced into focal contraries (*nj* > *nj...js*, *nn...js*); the original morpheme will be maintained preferably in bound, especially verbal constructions.

A last observation pertains to a semantically interesting peculiarity of the verb *nfr*, whose basic meaning is "to be complete" and which is mostly in the positive sense of "to be good," but which is also integrated into the negative system of Egyptian because of the opposite connotation "to be finished" it can acquire in specific contexts. This appropriation of the lexical potential of a verb into the morphosyntactic system of negations occurs rather often in verbal patterns, the most paradigmatic example being the verb *tm* "to be complete," from which the negative counterparts of nominal transpositions of the verb (topicalized forms, participles and relative clauses, infinitives) are formed and which will be discussed in chapter 7. But a tripartite pattern with a substantivized participle of the verb *nfr* as predicate of a S => [Pred-*pw*-Subj] should find its mention here:

(141) Adm. 4,11–12 *nfr pw pẖr.wt jrj*
"There are no appropriate (*jrj*) remedies (*pẖr.wt*)"

That this pattern is grammatically treated exactly like a positive sentence is proved by its possibility to be integrated into the system of converters (section 5.6) in less formal Middle Egyptian texts:

(142) pKahun 22,7 *jr wnn nfr pw ḏdd.t nb.t (j)r=s*
"If (*jr*) there should be (*wnn*) nothing that has been said (*ḏdd.t*) about it..."

From what we have seen so far in this paragraph, we can obtain the Egyptian version (β) of the traditional square of semantic oppositions (α)[64] applied to the negation of nominal patterns:

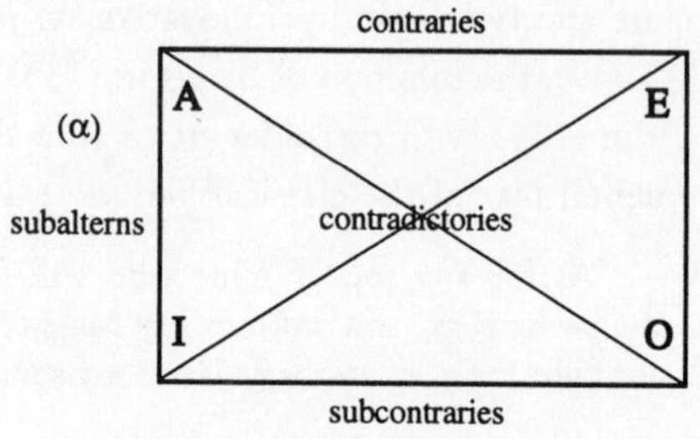

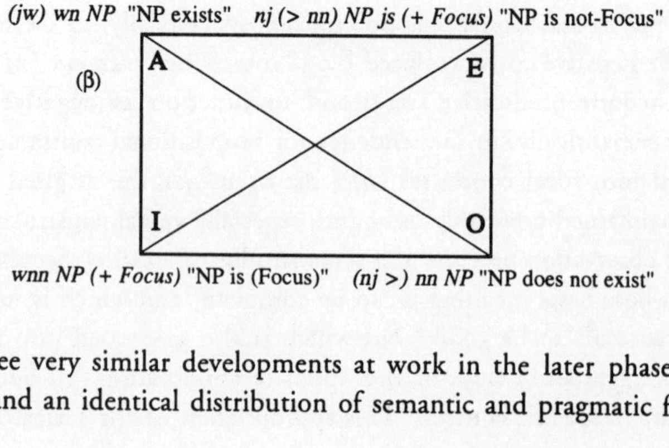

We shall see very similar developments at work in the later phases of the language, and an identical distribution of semantic and pragmatic functions of negative morphemes and patterns applied to the other syntactic types as well – verbal, pseudoverbal and adverbial.

5.8 Nominal sentences in later Egyptian

While semantic principles and macrosyntactic structures of the nominal sentence in later Egyptian[65] still follow the models of the classical language:

(143) pChester Beatty I vo C 1,4 *ḫsbd mꜣʿ šnj=s*
"Her hair (*šnj=s*) is true lapislazuli (*ḫsbd mꜣʿ*)"

(144) Two Brothers 1,10 *nfr pꜣ-smw n s.t ḥmn.t*
"The grass (*pꜣ-smw*) of such-and-such a place (*n s.t ḥmn.t*) is good (*nfr*)"

both of which are examples of the well-known pattern "Pred-Subj," distribution and frequency of the morphosyntactic patterns undergo a higher degree of change. In general, following a trend we already observed in the less classical forms of Middle Egyptian, movements of topicalization and focalization tend to play a more crucial role in the later phases of the language – which probably finds its justification both in the cross-linguistic tendency towards the grammaticalization of pragmatic phenomena[66] and in the different cultural setting of the texts in Late Egyptian, Demotic, and Coptic. Late Egyptian and Demotic are less bound than the classical language to the religious and monumental sphere, which remained the domain of the postclassical form of Middle Egyptian often referred to as "Late Middle Egyptian"[67] or *égyptien de tradition*;[68] Coptic is the vehicle of a different religious world altogether. Thus, later Egyptian as a whole is scholastically less fixed and therefore more open to the communicative needs of contemporary speech. For example, while both the nominal patterns *rmṯ pw/jnk rmṯ* and the adjectival sentence *nfr sw/jnk nfr* are indeed maintained:

(145) Doomed Prince 4,9 *ṯsm pꜣj* "It (*pꜣj*) is a dog"

(146) Onchsh. 16,23 *jnk pꜣj=k sn* "I (*jnk*) am your brother (*pꜣj=k sn*)"

(147) Ps 5,5 ⲛ̄ⲧⲕ̄ ⲟⲩⲛⲟⲩⲧⲉ "You (*ntk*) are a god (*ou-noute*)"

(148) Heb 11,4 ⲟⲩⲇⲓⲕⲁⲓⲟⲥ ⲡⲉ "He (*pe*) is just (*ou*-δίκαιος "a just man")"

the closer ties exhibited by later Egyptian to the spoken registers of discourse are evident in its preference for patterns with topicalized subject, including its frequent recourse to dislocated pronominal subjects, i.e. to topicalized arguments placed outside the body of the sentence:

(149) Wen. 2,8 *ntk jḫ pꜣ-jn=k n=j gr jnk*
"But (*gr*) *you*, what (*jḫ*) have *you* brought me?"

(150) Cant 1,5–6 ⲁⲛⲟⲕ ⲇⲉ ⲁⲛⲅ̄ ⲟⲩⲕⲁⲙⲏ...ϫⲉ ⲁⲛⲅ̄ ⲟⲩⲕⲁⲙⲏ ⲁⲛⲟⲕ
"But as for me (*anok* δέ), I am (*ang*) black (*ou-kamê*)...that (*je*) I am black"

In these examples, the subject is fronted as pragmatic topic (*ntk*, *anok*) and resumed by a coreferential pronoun in the relative clause "that which you have brought" in (149) and in the nominal sentence "I am black" in (150) Both examples also exhibit a rear extraposition of the indirect object in (149) and of the subject in (150) respectively, resumed as rhematic "tail"[69] (*jnk*, *anok*) and cataphorically anticipated by the suffix pronoun of the prepositional phrase *n=j* "to me" in (149) and again by the subject of the nominal sentence *ang ou-kamê* "I am black" in (150).

It is therefore surprising that, although the topicalized bipartite pattern with extraposed subject resumed by the demonstrative pronoun or copula *pw* > *pꜣj*[70] after the predicate is indeed maintained in Late Egyptian:

(151) oDeM 437,2–3 *pꜣ-hꜣ.t j.jr=k bꜣkw pꜣj*
"Your coming down was work-related" < "The coming down which you did (*pꜣ-hꜣ.t j.jr=k*) – it was work (*bꜣkw pꜣj*)"

it is not as frequent in this phase of the language as the later Egyptian propensity for the use of topicalizations would lead one to assume; that it did, however, remain a productive pattern in the language is shown by its vitality in Demotic,[71] where S =› [Subj-Pred-copula] has become the most common form of nominal sentence, and in Coptic, especially in Bohairic:[72]

(152) Onchsh. 27,13 *rmt jw=f mḫj jrm nꜣ-pꜣj=f tmj ꜥbjn ḏ.t pꜣj*
"A man (*rmt*) who vilifies (*jw=f mḫj*) his fellow-citizens (*nꜣ-pꜣj=f tmj* "those of his city" Coptic *na-pe=f-time*) is (*pꜣj*) is despicable (*ꜥbjn*) forever (*ḏ.t*)"

(153) Cant 1,15 ⲛⲟⲩⲃⲁⲗ ϩⲉⲛⲃⲁⲗ ⲛ̄ϭⲣⲟⲟⲙⲡⲉ ⲛⲉ
"Your eyes (*nou-bal*) are (*ne*) eyes of a dove (*hen-bal n-croompe*)"

Turning to the specifying patterns, the balanced sentence [Subj-Pred] documented in examples (21)–(23) in section 5.2 is alive and well in Late Egyptian and Demotic:

(154) pBM 10052, 5,8–9 "I didn't see anything else: *pꜣ-ptr=j pꜣ-ḏd=j* what I saw (*pꜣ-ptr=j*) is what I said (*pꜣ-ḏd=j*)"

(155) pRyl. IX 3,7–8 *pꜣ-hp j.jr=w n=w dj.t šp=w sḫ n šw 50*
"The judgment (*pꜣ-hp*) that they will get (*j.jr=w n=w* "that they will do to them") is to have them receive (*dj.t šp=w*) fifty blows of whip"[73]

(156) Onchsh. 13,7 *jrj rmt-swg rmt-swg*
"The friend (*jrj*) of an idiot is an idiot (himself)"

(157) pWien KM 3877 I,x+3 *nꜣ-j.jr=f nb n ḥs ḫsf*
"All he has done (*nꜣ j.jr=f nb*) as singer (*n ḥs < m ḥs*) is vice (*ḫsf*)"[74]

The tripartite specifying sentence [Subj-*pw*-Pred], on the other hand, is not productive in Late Egyptian,[75] a stage in the history of the language in which tripartite patterns generally appear to be under pressure (section 5.9).

But this sentence pattern displays renewed vitality in Coptic,[76] where the construction [Subj-*pe*-Pred] maintains the specifying functions it had in the older phases of the language:

(158) 1 Cor 15,56 пієів де м̄пмоу пе пнове тбом де м̄пнове пе пномос
"But (δέ) the sting (*p-ieib*) of death (*m-p-mou*) is (*pe*) the sin (*p-nobe*), and the power (*t-com*) of sin is the law (νόμος)"

As in the corresponding patterns of the classical language, the subject of a later Egyptian nominal sentence can also be an adjectival form of the verb, coreferential with the antecedent (participle)[77] as in (159) and (160) or controlled by a different subject (relative form) as in (161) or (162):

(159) Two Brothers 15,4 *bjꜣj.t ʿꜣ.t tꜣj-ḫpr.t*
"What happened (*ḫpr.t*) is (*tꜣj*) a great wonder (*bjꜣj.t ʿꜣ.t*)"

(160) 1 Thess 5,24 оупістос пе пентаqтаϩмн̄
"He who has summoned us (*p-ent-a=f-tahm=n*) is (*pe*) trustworthy (*ou-πίστος*)"

(161) pBM 10052, 14,7 *ʿḏꜣ pꜣj-ḏd=f nb*
"Everything he said (*ḏd=f nb*) is (*pꜣj*) wrong (*ʿḏꜣ*)"

(162) Ex 35,10 ϩенϣпнре не нетнаааү нак
"What I shall do (*n-et=i-na-aa=u*) for you (*na=k*) are (*ne*) wonders (*hen-špêre*)"

One should pay attention here to the change in the syntax of the copula *pw* > *pꜣj* > пє. Unlike the Middle Egyptian *pw*, which is invariable both in classifying and in specifying patterns, in later Egyptian the situation is more complex. While the Coptic specifying sentence [Subj-*pe*-Pred] maintains the invariable copula, later Egyptian classifying and qualifying sentences display gender and number agreement of the copula with its antecedent: masc. *pꜣj* (пє), fem. *tꜣj* (тє) pl. *nꜣj* (нє). In this way, an original [Pred-*pꜣj*-Subj] is reinterpreted as a bipartite pattern in which an adjectival form, introduced by the so-called prosthetic *yod*, i.e. by the initial *j* which in Late Egyptian regularly precedes participles and relative forms, functions as the subject preceded by the newly created definite article *pꜣ* (п-), *tꜣ* (т-), *nꜣ* (н̄-): what used to be typologically a tripartite [*bjꜣj.t ʿꜣ.t*] [*tꜣj*] [*ḫpr.t*] "what happened is a great wonder" is therefore treated in Late Egyptian as a bipartite [*bjꜣj.t ʿꜣ.t*] [*tꜣ-j.ḫpr.t*] "a great wonder is (that)-which-happened." We will see in the next section that this reinterpretation of the structure of the tripartite nominal sentence has important consequences for the overall distribution of nominal patterns in later Egyptian.

5.9 Old and new cleft sentences

Quite expectedly, Late Egyptian maintains in full productivity the Middle Egyptian cleft sentence, the pattern in which the subject of the adjectival predicate is the focus of the utterance and is introduced by the particle *jn* (written *m* in less formal texts) – sometimes omitted in specific pragmatic environments[78] – or by the independent pronouns:

(163) Horus and Seth 6,14–7,1 *jn r3=k j.ḏd sw ḏs=k jn šs3 ḥr=k wp tw ḏs=k*
"It is your own mouth (*r3=k...ḏs=k*) that said (*j.ḏd*) it, your own intelligence (*šs3 ḥr=k*) that judged (*wp*) you (*tw*)"

(164) LRL 70,14–15 *ḫr ntk j.jr=k ʿn-smy n ṯ3.tj ḥr=w*
"Now (*ḫr*), it is you who will report (*ntk j.jr=k ʿn-smy*) to the vizier about them (*ḥr=w*)"

But this pattern survives through Coptic only in functional remnants (table 5.2).[79] The parentheses in the last row symbolize the vestigial status of the construction ⲁⲛⲟⲕ (ⲡ)ⲉⲣ-ⲥⲱⲧⲙ̄ in Coptic.

Table 5.2 The evolution of the cleft sentence *jn*-NP_1-NP_2

PHASE	TENSE		
	PRETERITE	AORIST	PROSPECTIVE
EARLIER EGYPTIAN	*jn NP sḏm* (perf.) "It is NP who heard"	*jn NP sḏm* (imperf.) "It is NP who hears"	*jn NP sḏm=f* (prosp.) "It is NP who will hear"
LATE EG. 1	*m NP j.sdm* "It is NP who heard"	*m NP j.jr sdm* "It is NP who hears"	*m NP j.jr=f sdm* "It is NP who will hear"
LATE EG. 2 – DEM.1	*NP j.jr sdm* "It is NP who heard"	*NP ntj ḥr sdm* "It is NP who hears"	*NP ntj-jw=f r sdm* "It is NP who will hear"
DEM.2 – COPTIC	(*anok p-er-sôtm* "It is I who heard")	*anok p-et-sôtm* "It is I who hear"	*anok p-et-na-sôtm* "It is I who shall hear"

The reason for the decay of this pattern in the later stages of the language lies in the threat represented by the emergence of a new syntactic pattern in Late Egyptian. This new construction is a second type of cleft sentence, occurring in Late Egyptian when the focalized argument is not the subject, but rather the object or one of the adverbial adjuncts of the verbal predicate, and gradually expanding in Demotic and Coptic to subjects as well. One will recall that in Middle Egyptian nominal sentences, the pragmatic prominence of an argument different from the agent was not conveyed by the cleft sentence S ⇒ [*jn*-Focus-Pred], but rather by the pseudocleft pattern S ⇒ [Pred-*pw*-Subj]. In this construction, the dislocated patient occupies the role of pragmatically promoted predicate of the sentence. The new later Egyptian cleft sentence type is in fact nothing else than the heir of this earlier Egyptian tripartite pattern; but while in the Middle Egyptian pseudocleft construction the contrastive stress was simply an additional, optional feature of the predicate, in later Egyptian the pattern is completely reinterpreted as a bipartite cleft sentence, in which focalization was the primary function of the pattern: S => [Focus-*pɜ*-Presupposition]. The originally predicative head noun has now become the focus of the utterance; the old copula *pw* is reinterpreted as a definite article *pɜ* defining the second nominal phrase, which is now a presuppositional predicate conveyed by a participle (165) or a relative VP (166), which in the later stages are replaced by a relative clause introduced by the converter *ntj* (167):

(165) pBM 10052, 13,7–8 *N pɜj=f sn pɜ-jy n=j*
"It was his brother N (*N pɜj=f sn*) who came (*pɜ-jy*) to me (*n=j*)"

(166) Cod. Herm. 7,7[80] *jn.t=f r-ḥrj n pɜ jʔr pɜ-j.jr=j*
"To bring it (*jn.t=f*) out of the river (*r-ḥrj n pɜ jʔr*) is what I did (*pɜ-j.jr=j*)"

(167) Rom 9,1 ^{S}ⲟⲩⲙⲉ ⲧⲉϯϫⲱ ⲙ̄ⲙⲟⲥ, ^{B}ⲟⲩⲙⲏⲓ ⲡⲉϯϫⲱ ⲙ̄ⲙⲟⲥ
"It is the truth (^{S}*ou-me*, ^{B}*ou-mêi*, "(a) truth") that I say (^{S}*te-t=i-jô*, ^{B}*pe-t=i-jô*)"[81]

Any argument of the cleft sentence can appear topicalized and resumed by a coreferential pronoun:

(168) 2 Khaemwaset 4,21–22 *nɜj-sḏy zɜ-wsjr pɜ-ntj jr n-jm=w*
"As for these sayings (*nɜj-sḏy*), it is Siosiri who is doing (*pɜ-ntj jr*) them (*n-jm=w*)."

But here, of course, a question arises: how can we discern whether later Egyptian did in fact maintain a functional difference between the new form of cleft sentence shown in examples (165)–(168) and a formally identical heir of the tripartite nominal pattern [Pred-*pw*-Subj] displayed by examples (159)–(162)? How can one confidently state that the first position in (165)–(168) is occupied by the focalized subject or object, whereas the same slot in (159)–(162) is taken by the predicate, pragmatically promoted as it may be? How should we decide whether

(169) Horus and Seth 14,5–6 *mɜʿ.t(j) m ḥḥ n sp pɜ(j)-ḏd ḏḥwtj n tɜ-psḏ.t*

is an adjectival sentence "What Thoth said to the Ennead is absolutely true," or rather a cleft sentence "It is the absolute truth that Thoth said to the Ennead"?

The answer to this question represents one of the thorniest issues of later Egyptian grammar and must be sought in the diachronic observation of the morphological form and the syntactic behavior of the copula *pɜ(j)*, *tɜ(j)*, *nɜ(j)* and, at least to a certain extent, in the study of the corresponding negative patterns (section 5.11). As one will recall, the cleft sentence with *jn* was reserved in earlier Egyptian to the focalization of the agent, whereas the pseudocleft pattern S => [Pred-*pw*-Subj] was used when the focalized element was the patient of the VP: the emphasized element became the syntactic predicate, whereas the VP underwent adjectival conversion as the subject of the sentence. In fact, Late Egyptian itself exhibits no formal differences between the vestiges of this tripartite pattern and the new bipartite cleft sentence, and we can only infer that, if there was any difference between the two constructions, suprasegmental features must have played a role in conveying it. The history of the language shows that in Late Egyptian the linguistically more productive construction was clearly felt to be the cleft sentence: in Roman Demotic and especially in Coptic, only the cleft sentence pattern is kept and a *new* tripartite nominal pattern with congruing copula ⲡⲉ, ⲧⲉ, ⲛⲉ is added to the syntactic inventory of the language:[82] in this new pattern, the first position is taken by the predicate followed by the copula, the original determinative pronoun having completed its functional evolution and become the definite or possessive article of the subject:

(170) Prov 12,1 ⲟⲩⲁⲑⲏⲧ ⲇⲉ ⲡⲉ ⲡⲉⲧⲙⲟⲥⲧⲉ ⲛ̄ⲛⲉϫⲡⲓⲟ
"The one who hates (*p-et-moste* < **pꜣ-ntj ḥr msḏj.t*) the reproaches (*ne-jpio*) is (*pe*) senseless (*at-hêt* "without mind")"

whereas Bohairic shows a marked preference for the topicalized pattern:

(170') Ibid. ᴮⲫⲏ ⲉⲧⲙⲟⲥϯ ⲛⲟⲩⲥⲟϩⲓ ⲟⲩⲁⲧϩⲏⲧ ⲡⲉ
"The one (*phê*) who hates (*et-mosti*) a reproof (*n-ou-sohi*) is (*pe*) senseless"

Now again, as in earlier Egyptian, the language exhibits a clear opposition between a bipartite cleft sentence with only one pronoun of the *p*-series (in Sahidic ⲡⲉⲧ-, ⲧⲉⲧ-, ⲛⲉⲧ- congruing with the focalized antecedent,[83] in Bohairic ⲡⲉⲧ-/ⲡⲉ ⲉⲧ- invariable in gender and number), morphologically undistinguishable from the definite article of the following noun but syntactically serving as nexal copula preceding a NP without determinative morpheme,[84] and a tripartite nominal pattern with two pronouns of the same series (in Sahidic ⲡⲉ ⲡⲉⲧ-, ⲧⲉ ⲧⲉⲧ-, ⲛⲉ ⲛⲉⲧ-, in Bohairic ⲡⲉ ⲫⲏ ⲉⲧ-, ⲧⲉ ⲑⲏ ⲉⲧ-, ⲛⲉ ⲛⲏ ⲉⲧ-), the first of which is a true copula and the second of which precedes the subject as demonstrative pronoun (ⲡⲁⲓ, ⲧⲁⲓ, ⲛⲁⲓ), as definite article (if the subject is a simple noun phrase), or as determinative pronoun (if the subject is a relative clause).

The evolution from the earlier Egyptian tripartite pattern S => [Pred-*pw*-Subj] to the situation in Coptic is summarized in table 5.3. Parentheses indicate that the pattern is not formally distinguishable; its paradigmatic existence, therefore, cannot be established with certitude. In Demotic and Coptic, the use of the new cleft sentence pattern observed in table 5.2 is extended to the construction with focalized subjects,[85] leading to the decay of the old cleft sentence.

Table 5.3 The evolution of the pattern NP_1-*pw*-NP_2

PHASE	PATTERN	
	PSEUDOCLEFT SENTENCE (WITH OPTIONAL FOCUS)	CLEFT SENTENCE (WITH REGULAR FOCUS)
EARLIER EG.	*ḥjm.t pw sḏm.t.n=f* "The one whom he heard is a woman"	
LATE EG. 1	(*w'.t-ḥm.t tȝj-sdm=f* "The one whom he heard is a woman")	*w'.t-ḥm.t tȝ-j.sdm=f* "It is a woman that he heard"
LATE EG. 2 – DEM. 1		*w'.t-ḥm.t tȝ-j.jr=f sdm* "It is a woman that he heard"
DEM. 2 – COPTIC	^{S}*ou-shime te t-ent-a=f-sotm=s* ^{B}*thê et-a=f-sothm=es ou-shimi te* "The one whom he heard is a woman"	^{S}*ou-shime te-nt-a=f-sotm=s* ^{B}*ou-shimi pe-et-a=f-sothm=es* "It is a woman that he heard"

5.10 Interrogative, possessive, and existential patterns

In later Egyptian, one of the frequent uses of specifying (with substantival predicate) or identifying (with adjectival predicate) bipartite sentences occurs with interrogative pronouns such as *nm* (< *jn-m*) "who?" (Coptic ⲛⲓⲙ) or *jḫ* "what?" (Coptic ⲁϣ, ⲟⲩ) or with the interrogative adjective *jṯ* "which?"[86] as predicates, occupying the first or the second position in the pattern, depending on whether the subject is delocutive, i.e. third person, or interlocutive, in which case it complies with the hierarchies of salience discussed in sections 5.2–5.4:

(171) Truth and Falsehood 5,3 *ntk šrj nm* "Whose son (*šrj nm*) are you?"

(172) Horus and Seth 2,13 *jḫ pȝ-ntj-jw=n r jr=f*
"What shall we do?" < "What (is) the(-thing)-which-(*pȝ-ntj*) we-shall-do-it (*jw=n r jr=f*)?"

(173) pBM 10052, 13,7 *jṯ šms n N pȝ-jy n=k*
"Which one of N's messengers came to you?" < "Which messenger (*jṯ šms*) of N's is the one who came (*pȝ-jy*) to you?"

In the possessive patterns, later Egyptian follows rather closely the constructions of the classical language. While the frequent fusion of the head NP *nj-sw*/ *nj-st* "he/she is one-of" into *ns-*, which is a frequent formative for personal names (*ns-mnw* "He-belongs-to-Min"), is primarily a phonetic and graphic phenomenon,[87] the most relevant evolution concerns the identifying pattern with pronominal predicate: in Late Egyptian, independent pronouns are used in this function without the introductory determinative pronoun *nj*, keeping until the end of the second millennium BCE the old form of the second and third person pronouns (*ntk sw*, *twt sw* "it belongs to you"; *ntf sw*, *swt sw* "it belongs to him"). A good example of Late Egyptian possessive patterns at work is:

(174) Wen. 1,20–21 *jꜣ jr pꜣ-jṯꜣj j.ṯꜣj tw ntk sw ns-tꜣj=k br*
"But the thief who robbed you– he is *yours*, he belongs to *your* ship!,"

where the subject of the sentence is topicalized and resumed by the dependent pronoun *sw* and where the indication of possession is conveyed by the identifying independent pronoun *ntk* ("belonging to you") in the first sentence, and by the qualifying adjectival morpheme *ns-* in the second.

In the more recent stages of later Egyptian, the situation changes. While Demotic still maintains the use of stressed pronouns in adjectival sentences to indicate possession:

(175) Siut 8,26[88] *ntk st nꜣj=k nk.t ntj-ḥrj*
"Your property (*nꜣj=k nk.t*) above (*ntj-ḥrj* "which is above") is yours (*ntk*)"

in Coptic the older indicators of possession of type *nj-sw* and *nj-ntf* have disappeared and been superseded by a new set of possessive pronouns deriving from the independent use of the determinative pronoun ⲡⲁ- < *pꜣ n-* "that-of" (with nominal referent) and of the possessive article (with pronominal referent); these have replaced in later Egyptian the older synthetic indication by means of the suffix pronoun, still kept in a few lexical items referring most frequently to the sphere of the human body: earlier Egyptian *sn=f* "his brother" > later Egyptian *pꜣj=f sn* (Coptic ⲡⲉϥⲥⲟⲛ), in pronominal use *pꜣw=f* (Coptic ⲡⲱϥ) "his, of his":

(176) Ex 19,5 ⲡⲱⲓ ⲅⲁⲣ ⲡⲉ ⲡⲕⲁϩ ⲧⲏⲣϥ̄
"For (γάρ) the entire world (*p-kah têr=f* "the earth [to] its entirety") belongs to me (*pô=i pe* "is mine")"

As for existential clauses, we have already discussed the diachronic tendency exhibited by Egyptian to move away from the expression of existence conveyed by simple adverbial or adjectival sentences towards an increasing use of constructions with forms of the verb *wnn* "to be," originally limited to the expression of temporal, aspectual, or modal features of the predicated existence, but soon regularly used in negative patterns and gradually extended to the indication of absolute existence. This historical trend appears concluded in Late Egyptian, where the existential predicates *wn* "there is" and *mn* (< *nn-wn*) "there is not," often combined with the preposition *m-dj* "by, with" (< *m-'w* "in the hand of")[89] precede the indefinite subject, adverbial constructions being maintained for specific subjects (pattern *pꜣ-rmt m pr* "the scribe is in the house," section 6.6):

(177) Two Brothers 3,5–6 *wn pḥ.tj 'ꜣ jm=k*
"There is great strength (*pḥ.tj 'ꜣ*) in you (*jm=k*)!"
(178) LRL 10,8–9 *yꜣ wn hrw dy r-ḥꜣ.t=tn*
"But you still have time" < "But there is day (*wn hrw*) here (*dy*) before you (*r-ḥꜣ.t=tn*)"
(179) LRL 3,6 *mn m-dj=w btꜣ*
"They have no damage (*btꜣ*)" < "There is no damage with-them (*m-dj=w*)"
(180) RAD 53,16–54,1 *mn ḥbs.w mn sqn mn rm.w mn sjm*
"There are no clothes, no ointment, no fish, no vegetables"

The later developments[90] see a combination of two phenomena: (a) first, a permanence of the opposition between the predication of existence for definite subjects by means of an adverbial sentence introduced by the prepositions ⲛ̄ⲧⲟⲟⲧ= < *m-ḏr.t=* "in the hand of," ⲛ̄ⲧⲁ= < *m-dj=* "by," ⲙ̄ⲙⲟ= < *jm=* "in," ⲉⲣⲟ= "to" indicating the locative, the beneficiary or any other adjunct and the verbal or adjectival predication with ⲟⲩⲛ̄- and ⲙⲛ̄- in the case of indefinite subjects:

(181) Ps 134,17 ⲛⲉⲩⲟⲩⲉⲣⲏⲧⲉ ⲙ̄ⲙⲟⲟⲩ
"They have feet" < "(There are) their feet (*ne=u-ouerête*) in them (*mmo=ou*)"
(182) Lk 14,22 ⲁⲩⲱ ⲟⲛ ⲟⲩⲛ̄ ⲙⲁ "And (*auô*) there is (*oun*) still (*on*) a place"

(b) second, a grammaticalization of the possessive patterns *wn m-dj* and *mn m-dj* as ⲟⲩⲛ̄ⲧⲉ-, ⲟⲩⲛ̄ⲧⲁ= and ⲙⲛ̄ⲧⲉ-, ⲙⲛ̄ⲧⲁ= respectively. Conforming to the cross-linguistic tendency for prepositional compounds indicating possession followed by their subject to be semantically (and eventually also syntactically) reinterpreted as predicative phrases controlling a *direct object*,[91] these constructions are treated in Coptic (regularly in Sahidic, less so in Bohairic, where the original construction is maintained together with the reinterpreted pattern) as VPs with the meaning "to have" followed by their original morphosyntactic subject, now treated as a direct object; the latter is often accompanied by a localistic[92] indicator, namely the adverb ⲙ̄ⲙⲁⲩ "there," and introduced by the preposition ⲛ̄-, ⲙ̄ⲙⲟ= when the pronominal beneficiary is prosodically stressed (ⲟⲩⲛ̄ⲧⲁ=, ⲙⲛ̄ⲧⲁ=):

(183) Jn 4,44 ⲙ̄ⲙⲛ̄ⲧⲉ ⲡⲣⲟⲫⲏⲧⲏⲥ ⲧⲁⲉⲓⲟ ϩⲙ̄ ⲡⲉϥϯⲙⲉ ⲙ̄ⲙⲓⲛ ⲙ̄ⲙⲟϥ
"A prophet receives no honor in his own village" < "There-is-not-by (*mmnte-*) a prophet (προφήτης) honor (*taeio*) in his village (*hm pe=f-time*) his own (*mmin mmo=f*)"

(184) 2 Cor 4,7 ⲟⲩⲛ̄ⲧⲁⲛ ⲇⲉ ⲙ̄ⲙⲁⲩ ⲙ̄ⲡⲉⲓⲁϩⲟ
"But we have this treasure" < "But (δέ) there-is-by-us (*ounta=n*) there (*mmau*) this treasure (*m-pei-aho*, object)"

5.11 Negation in later Egyptian

Nominal negative patterns regularly display the morpheme  *bn* (Coptic ⲛ̄) as the heir of Middle Egyptian *nn*, which is still used in the literary register and with which *bn* was also phonetically identical,[93] the grapheme <b> serving presumably only as a semantic indicator of negation, much like the sign of the open arms conventionally transliterated *nj* in Middle Egyptian:

(185) Wen. 2,11–13 *nn fꜣy-mlk pꜣ-wn=w jr.t=f n pꜣj=j jt jr jnk gr jnk nn jnk pꜣj=k bꜣk*
"What they did for my father (*n pꜣj=j jt*) was not a royal gift (*nn fꜣy-mlk*), and as for myself (*jr jnk gr jnk*), I am not your servant either (*nn jnk pꜣj=k bꜣk*)"

One will recall that in the presence of pragmatic focality, such as in a cleft sentence, the negation tends to become one of contrariety rather than one of nexal contradiction. In this case, the later Egyptian negative pattern is the discontinuous *bn...jwnꜣ* (Demotic *bn...jn*, Coptic ⲛ̄...ⲁⲛ), which corresponds functionally to the Middle Egyptian *nj...js* (> *nn...js*):

(186) Wen. 2,23 *bn mšꜥ swgꜣ jwnꜣ nꜣ-ntj twj jm=w*
"It is not foolish travels (*mšꜥ swgꜣ*) that I am engaged in!" < "Not foolish travels (are) the(-ones)-that-(*nꜣ-ntj*) I-am in-them"

The pervasive **O > E** drift discussed in section 5.7 above, however, caused not only the negative morpheme *bn* to invade further than the postclassical Middle Egyptian *nn* domains previously covered by the simple propositional negation *nj* (> Late Egyptian *bw*, limited to bound verbal patterns), but also the originally focal negative marker to be used in non-focal constructions, such as in nominal and adjectival patterns:

(187) oBerlin 10627,6 *bn ntk rmt jwnꜣ*
(187') pRyl. IX 1,18 *bn ntk rmt jn* "You are not a (real) man"[94]

(188) LRL 2,1 *ḫr jnk pꜣj=tn nfr bn jnk pꜣj=tn bjn jwnꜣ*
"For I am (to) your benefit (*pꜣj=tn nfr*), and not (to) your disadvantage (*pꜣj=tn bjn*)"

(189) pBM 10052, 11,21 *bn mꜣꜥ jwnꜣ nꜣ* "This (*nꜣ*) is not true (*mꜣꜥ*)"

We observed in section 5.7 that this phenomenon corresponds to the cross-linguistic tendency for focal negations of contrariety to progressively invade semantic spheres and syntactic patterns previously negated by "weak" contradiction: in fact, more formal or literary Late Egyptian texts show instances, such as example (185) above, in which nominal patterns are negated by the simple morpheme without the focal reinforcer. Comparing (189) with the same adjectival pattern in (190), one will observe a number of signals of a higher linguistic register:[95] the absence of *jwnꜣ*, the use of older *nn* for *bn*, and the topicalization of the subject resulting in the tripartite pattern [Topic-Pred-copula$_{\text{Subj}}$], otherwise rare in Late Egyptian:

(190) pAnastasi I 18,2 *pꜣ-jn.t=k r sḫt=n nn nfr pꜣw*
"The fact of bringing you (*pꜣ-jn.t=k*) to punish us (*r sḫt=n*) is not good"

This gradual invasion of *bn...jwnꜣ* into the semantic domain of the simple *nn* > *bn* can be observed in the side-by-side coexistence, sometimes as variants of the same text, as is the case in (193)–(193'), of identical constructions with and without *jwnꜣ*, showing that it would be artificial always to ascribe to the negative pattern with *jwnꜣ* a higher degree of focality:

(191) LRL 6,8 *bn nfr pꜣj-j.jr=k* "What you have done (*pꜣj-j.jr=k*) is not good"

(192) Ani 8,11 *bn nfr jwnꜣ nꜣ-šm.w m ḥrj=f*
"The behavior (*nꜣ-šm.w*) as his superior (*m ḥrj=f*) is not good"

(193) KRI II 53,4 *bn rmṯ pw pꜣ-ntj m-ẖnw=n*
"The one who is among us (*pꜣ-ntj m-ẖnw=n*) is not (just) a man (*bn rmṯ pw*)"

(193') KRI II 53,5 *bn rmṯ.w jwnꜣ nꜣw pꜣ-ntj m-ẖnw=sn*
"Those who are among them are (*nꜣw*) not (real) men (*bn rmṯ.w jwnꜣ*)"

Although the version displayed by (193') probably represents an error in the scribal transmission, since the text is concerned here with King Ramses II's military bravery rather than with the enemies' cowardice, the correspondence of a nominal *rmṯ pw*-sentence built according to the classical pattern with a rare example of the later Egyptian tripartite pattern negated by *bn... jwnꜣ* shows that, if originally the cleft sentence exhibited *jwnꜣ* whereas the unmarked nominal sentence did not, the **O** > **E** drift led to a progressive merging of the two negative patterns.[96] The later evidence confirms these evolutive lines: Demotic *bn...jn* and Coptic ⲛ̄...ⲁⲛ are the *only* morphemes used in the negation of nominal patterns, with a tendency in Coptic, shared once more by similar patterns in other languages,[97] to drop the actual negative marker (*n*) and to keep only the reinforcer (*an*):

(194) pKrall 23,11[98] *bn-jw ꜣẖj jn pꜣj pꜣ-rmt*
"The man is (*pꜣj*) not a reed (*bn-jw ꜣẖj jn*)"

(195) Siut 23,11 *bn-jw nts jn tȝj* "This is (*tȝj*) not hers (*bn-jw nts jn*)"[99]

(196) Gal 4,31 ⲚⲀⲚⲞⲚ ⲚϢⲎⲢⲈ ⲚⲦϨⲘϨⲀⲖ ⲀⲚ ⲀⲖⲖⲀ ⲀⲚⲞⲚ ⲚⲀ ⲦⲢⲘϨⲎ

"We (*anon*) are not (*n...an*) the children (*n-šêre*) of the slave woman (*n-t-hmhal*), but (ἀλλά) we are those of (*na*, see 5.10) the free woman (*t-rmhê*)"

(197) 1 Jn 4,10 ⲀⲚⲞⲚ ⲀⲚ ⲠⲈⲚⲦⲀⲚⲘⲈⲢⲈ ⲠⲚⲞⲨⲦⲈ ⲀⲖⲖⲀ ⲚⲦⲞϤ ⲠⲈⲚⲦⲀϤⲘⲈⲢⲒⲦⲚ

"It is not we (*anon an pe-*) who loved (*nt-a=n-mere-*) God (*p-noute*), but rather (ἀλλά) he (*ntof*) who loved us (*pe-nt-a=f-merit=n*)"

And according to the later Egyptian preference for topicalized patterns, the negation *bn...jwnȝ* is also regularly applied to the predicate of a tripartite sentence [Topic-Pred-copula$_{Subj}$], in which it follows the extraposed subject:

(198) Dem. Krug A 11[100] *pȝ-ẖl (n) rn=f bn-jw pȝj=j šrj jn pȝj*

"The said young man (*pȝ-ẖl n rn=f*) is not (*bn...jn pȝj*) my son (*pȝj=j šrj*)"

(199) Jn 8,13 ⲦⲈⲔⲘⲚⲦⲘⲚⲦⲢⲈ ⲚⲞⲨⲘⲈ ⲀⲚ ⲦⲈ

"Your testimony (*te=k-mnt-mntre*) is not (*n...an te*) genuine (*ou-me* "a truth")"

Finally, the passage below from the "Tale of Wenamun," the last known literary text of the New Kingdom (around 1070 BCE) should offer a short summary of some of the main points treated in the last sections (sections 5.8–5.11):

(200) Wen. 2,23–24 *mn jmw nb ḥr-tp j(t)r jw bn ns-jmn ntf pȝ-jm ḥr ntf pȝ-lbln ntj-twk (ḥr) ḏd jnk sw*

"There is no ship (*mn jmw*) on the waters (*ḥr-tp jtr*) which does not (*jw bn*) belong to Amun (*ns-jmn*). To him belong the sea (*ntf pȝ-jm*) and also Lebanon, of which you say: 'It belongs to me (*jnk sw*)'"

Further reading

Callender, J. B. *Studies in the Nominal Sentence in Egyptian and Coptic.* Near Eastern Studies XXIV (Berkeley–Los Angeles: University of California Press, 1984).

Doret, E. "Phrase nominale, identité et substitution dans les Textes des Sarcophages," *Revue d'Egyptologie* 40 (1989), 49–63; 41 (1990), 39–56; 43 (1992), 49–73.

Johnson, J. H. "Demotic nominal sentences," in *Studies Presented to Hans Jakob Polotsky*, ed. by D.W. Young (Beacon Hill: Pirtle & Polson, 1981), 414–30.

Junge, F. "Nominalsatz und Cleft Sentence im Ägyptischen," in *Studies Presented to Hans Jakob Polotsky*, ed. by D. W. Young (Beacon Hill: Pirtle & Polson, 1981), 431–62.

Loprieno, A. "Der ägyptische Satz zwischen Semantik und Pragmatik: die Rolle von *jn*," *Studien zur Altägyptischen Kultur. Beihefte III* (1988), 77–98.

Polotsky, H.J. *Grundlagen des koptischen Satzbaus.* American Studies in Papyrology XXVII–XXIX (Atlanta: Scholars' Press, 1987–90), 9–140.

Satzinger, H. "Nominalsatz und Cleft Sentence im Neuägyptischen," in *Studies Presented to Hans Jakob Polotsky*, ed. by D. W. Young (Beacon Hill: Pirtle & Polson, 1981), 480–505.

Shisha-Halevy, A. *Coptic Grammatical Categories*. Analecta Orientalia LIII (Rome: Pontifical Biblical Institute, 1986).

Vernus, P. "Observations sur la prédication d'identité ("Nominal predicate")," in *Crossroads III Preprints*.

Westendorf, W. *Beiträge zum ägyptischen Nominalsatz*. Nachrichten der Akademie der Wissenschaften in Göttingen, Phil.-Hist. Klasse, vol. 3, Göttingen 1981.

6

Adverbial and pseudoverbal syntax

6.1 Introduction

The adverbial sentence represents one of the most frequent patterns from Old Egyptian to Coptic.[1] In this syntactic type, a nominal or pronominal subject (NP), which can be bare or preceded by a particle, is followed by an adverbial phrase (AP) as predicate:[2]

$$S \Rightarrow [(\text{Particle-})NP_{subj}\text{-}AP_{pred}].$$

The adverbial predicate can be an adverb proper, as in (1), or a prepositional phrase, as in (2):

(1) Sin. B 77 *mk tw ꜥꜣ* "Look (particle *mk*), you (*tw*) are here (*ꜥꜣ*)"

(2) Sin. B 156 *sḫꜣ.y=j m ꜥḥ* "The memory of me (*sḫꜣ.y=j*) is in the palace (*m ꜥḥ*)"

Similarly to what we observed in the treatment of nominal sentences (section 5.4), any type of NP, for example a relative verbal form in (3), can be found in a prepositional phrase functioning as the predicate of an adverbial sentence:

(3) Pt. 216 *wdj r=k m ḫbd.n=sn*
"He who acts (*wdj*) against you (*r=k*) is one whom they have rejected (*ḫbd.n=sn*, relative *sḏm.n=f*)"

In rare cases, all of them belonging to the earliest phase of the language and mostly in interrogative environments, the AP appears dislocated to the left of the NP:

(4) Pyr. 681a *ṯnj ḥrw prj m šnṯ*
"Where (*ṯnj*) is Horus who came forth from the serpent?"

but this pattern disappears from the syntax of the classical language.[3]

Since the part of speech "adverb" is [-N] and [-V],[4] i.e. it has neither nominal nor verbal properties, patterns with adverbial predicate will draw their temporal reference from their context: the time setting of adverbial sentences is determined by the contextual tense.[5] Some prepositions, however, naturally evoke a time reference associated with their semantic scope; this is the case with *m* "in, as," which expresses a simultaneous situation of the subject, as in (3) and in (5), or *r* "toward, bound to," which often implies a prospective reference, as in (6):

(5) Neferti 54 *sꜣ-ʿ m nb-ʿ*
"The former weak-of-arm (*sꜣ-ʿ*) is now (*m* "is as") a strong-of-arm (*nb-ʿ*)," lit. *"the broken-of-arm (is) as lord-of-arm"[6]

(6) Sin. B 280–81 *jw=f r smr m-m srj.w*
"He (*jw=f*) will be (*r*) a Friend (*smr*) among the officials (*srj.w*)," lit. *"truly he (is) toward a Friend among the officials"

Adverbial sentences of the type represented in (5)–(6) represent a bridge to the common syntactic pattern in which the predicate is not an AP in the narrower sense, i.e. an adverb or a prepositional phrase, but rather a form of the verbal paradigm used in a syntactically adverbial environment. Such an environment can either be a prepositional phrase with *ḥr*, *m* (mostly with verbs of motion), or *r* followed by the infinitive:[7]

(7) Khakheperreʿseneb 12 *nhpw ḥr ḫpr rʿw-nb*
"Dawn (*nhpw*) comes (*ḥr ḫpr* "happens") every day (*rʿw-nb*)"

(8) Peas. R1.2–3 *mṯ wj m hꜣj.t r km.t*
"Look, I am going down (*wj m hꜣj.t*) to Egypt (*r km.t*)," lit. *"I am in going-down"

(9) Sh.S. 117–18 *mk tw r jrj.t ꜣbd ḥr ꜣbd*
"Look, you will spend (*tw r jrj.t*) month after month (*ꜣbd ḥr ꜣbd*)" lit. "you are toward making"

or a non-initial stative following its nominal or pronominal subject:

(10) Peas. B1,101 *mk wj ꜣtp.kw* "Look, I am burdened (*ꜣtp.kw*)"

While sentences (1)–(6) are usually called *adverbial*, patterns of the type (7)–(10), in which the predicate is morphologically and semantically a form of the verbal paradigm, are ascribed by Egyptologists the label *pseudoverbal sentences*. We saw in section 4.6.4 that the infinitive combines nominal and verbal properties ([+N] and [+V]); the same holds true for the stative, originally a conjugated verbal adjective (section 4.4.1). This feature [+V] displayed by their predicate allows pseudoverbal sentences, in spite of their syntactic likeness to adverbial sentences, to be more sensitive to tense, aspect, or mood:

(11) Merikare E 93 *jw=f ḥr ʿḥꜣ ḏr rk nṯr*
"*He has been fighting* (lit. "he is on fighting) since god's time (*ḏr rk nṯr*)"

(12) pKahun 11,16–18 "Testament made by the Controller of *phyle* Intef-meri, called Kebi, for his son Meri-intef, called Iu-seneb: *jw=j ḥr rḏj.t pꜣj=j mtj-n(j)-sꜣ n zꜣ=j mry-jntf* 'Herewith I give my (*pꜣj=j*) office of controller of *phyle* (*mtj-nj-sꜣ*) to my son Meri-intef'"

(13) West. 5,3–15 *jb n(j) ḥm=k r qbb n m33 ẖnn=sn ẖn.t m ḫdj m ḫntj* "'Your Majesty's heart will be refreshed (*r qbb*) at seeing (*n m33*, section 4.6.4b) how they row up and down, *jw=k ḥr m33 zš.w nfr.w n(w) š=k* as you watch (*jw=k ḥr m33*, section 6.4.2a) the beautiful thickets of your lake *jw=k ḥr m33 sḫ.wt=f ḫf33.wt=f nfr.w* and as you watch its fine fields and banks; *jw jb=k r qbb ẖr=s* truly (*jw*, section 6.4.2), your heart will be refreshed (*r qbb*) by these things!' – *jw=j ḥm r jrj.t ẖnj.t* 'Indeed (*ḥm*), I shall go boating! Let there be brought to me twenty oars of ebony plated with gold, with handles of *sqb*-wood plated with electrum. Let there be brought to me twenty women with the prettiest body, breasts, and braids, who haven't yet given birth. And let there be brought to me twenty nets and let them be given to these women instead of their clothes.' So everything was done according to His Majesty's order. And they rowed up and down, *wn.jn* (section 5.6) *jb n(j) ḥm=f nfr.w n m33 ẖnn=sn* and His Majesty's heart became happy (*nfr.w*) at seeing how they rowed (*ẖnn=sn*)"

Whenever possible, adverbial and pseudoverbal sentences will be treated here as a syntactic unit: in the history of Egyptian, the original morphological and semantic differences between them – which will be pointed out when they emerge in the course of our discussion – tend to be neutralized, and in the more recent phases of later Egyptian pseudoverbal patterns lose their syntactic autonomy vis-à-vis adverbial sentences.

6.2 Adverbial and pseudoverbal patterns

We observed in chapter 4 that Egyptian displays great flexibility in the morphosyntactic variety of the subject of a nominal sentence, which can be any NP, including a nominalized VP (section 5.2). The same flexibility applies to the subject of adverbial or pseudoverbal sentences. It can range from a bare noun:

(14) Peas. B1,332 *jw ʿqw=k m šnʿ* "Your income (*ʿqw=k*) is in the storehouse (*šnʿ*)"

(15) Sh.S. 42 *jb=j m sn.nw=j*
"My heart (*jb=j*) was my (only) companion (*sn.nw=j*)"

to a suffix, a dependent, or (only in archaic texts) independent pronoun:

(16) Peas. B1,249 *jw=f m jmj-ḥ3.t n jrr*
"He is (*jw=f*) a model (*jmj-ḥ3.t* "one who is in the front") for the evildoer (*jrr* "doer")"

(17) Peas. B1,208 *mk tw m mnjw* "Look (*mk*), you (*tw*) are a shepherd (*mnjw*)"

(18) Pyr. 1114b^{P} *jnk jr p.t* "I (*jnk*) am toward (*jr*) heaven (*p.t*)"

to a participle, a relative form, or rarely an infinitive:

(19) Adm. 8,3 *wn m wpw.tj ḥr h3b ky*
"He who used to be (*wn*) a messenger (*wpw.tj*) now sends (*ḥr h3b*) someone else (*ky*)"

(20) Pt. 20–21 *jrr.t j3w n rmṯ bjn(.w) m ḫ.t nb.t*
"What old age does (*jrr.t j3w*) to people is bad (*bjn.w*, stative) in every respect"

(21) Pyr. 1730a *jws šm.t=k tn jtj N mj šm ḥrw n jtj=f wsjr*

"Behold (*jws*, particle), this going of yours (*šm.t=k tn*), O father the King, is like (*mj*) Horus going (*šm ḥrw*, nominalized VP) to his father Osiris"

The subject position of an adverbial sentence can also be filled by a complex syntagm in which the subject slot of an adverbial clause (S^1) is converted into a verbal phrase introduced by *wnn*, a grammaticalized form of the verb "to be" (S^2):

$$S^1 \Rightarrow [(\text{Particle})\text{-}NP_{subj}\text{-}AP_{pred}] > S^2 \Rightarrow [[\textit{wnn}\text{-}NP_{subj}]_{VP}\text{-}AP]$$

This conversion, which was already discussed in the treatment of nominal syntax (section 5.6), allows the originally unmarked adverbial clause to acquire modal features, conveyed by the prospective *wnn=f* in (22), or to confer pragmatic prominence to an adverbial adjunct such as an interrogative adverb, as signalled by the emphatic *wnn=f* in (23):

(22) pKahun 12,13 *wnn tꜣj=j ḥjm.t jm*
"My wife will be (*wnn tꜣj=j ḥjm.t*) there (*jm*)"

$S^1 \Rightarrow$ [(*jw*$_{part}$) [*tꜣj=j ḥjm.t*]$_{NPsubj}$ [*jm*]$_{APpred}$] "my wife is there"

> $S^2 \Rightarrow$ [[*wnn tꜣj=j ḥjm.t*]$_{VP}$ [*jm*]$_{AP}$] "my wife will be there"

(23) Sin. B 43–44 *wnn jr=f tꜣ pf mj-m m-ḫmt=f*
"But (*jr=f*) how (*mj-m*) is that land (*wnn tꜣ pf*) without him (*m-ḫmt=f*)?"

$S^1 \Rightarrow$ [(*jw*) [*tꜣ pf*]$_{NPsubj}$ [*m-ḫmt=f*]$_{APpred}$] "that land is without him"

> $S^2 \Rightarrow$ [[[*wnn tꜣ pf*]$_{VP}$ [*m-ḫmt=f*]$_{AP}$] [*mj-m*]$_{AP}$] "how is that land without him?"

The functional yield of the transformation of an adverbial into a verbal sentence by means of the converter *wnn* is particularly evident when the adverbial sentence is contextually juxtaposed to its converted verbal counterpart. In (24), an adverbial sentence indicating the general present is followed by a verbal sentence with a prospective *wnn*-form conveying modal features:

(24) CT I 55b *jw=k m nṯr wnn=k m nṯr*
"You are divine (*m nṯr* "as a god") and you will be divine"

At this juncture, a short digression is in order. We just saw that any NP, including nominal forms of the verb and VP resulting from the use of a form of the verb *wnn* "to be" as converter, can be found as head of an adverbial sentence. Generalizing the scope of the paradigmatic flexibility displayed by the head syntagm of an adverbial sentence, the Standard theory, i.e. the approach to Egyptian grammar which developed in the footsteps of H. J. Polotsky (section 1.3), came to interpret *all* cases of an initial verbal form accompanied by an AP:

(25) Adm. 1,5 *mꜣꜣ zj zꜣ=f m ḫrwy=f* "a man now regards his son as his enemy"

as complex adverbial sentences in which the adverbial phrase, in this case the predicative complement *m ḫrwy=f* "as his enemy," functions as predicate of a sentence whose subject is the nominalized VP, in this case *mꜣꜣ zj zꜣ=f* "a man regards (*mꜣꜣ zj*) his son (*zꜣ=f*)." The underlying structure of (25), therefore, would be *that-a-man-regards-his-son (is) as-his-enemy."[8] This analysis seems to be confirmed by the study of the negative patterns: in fact, these initial verbal forms are negated by the corresponding form of the negative verb *tm* followed by the negatival complement (section 7.8.5):

(26) West. 6,5 *tm=ṯ ẖnj(.w) ḥr-m* "Why (*ḥr-m*) don't you (*tm=ṯ*) row (*ẖnj.w*)?"

which is the negative counterpart of **ẖnn=ṯ ḥr-m* "why do you row?"

A predictable, but problematic effect of this strictly substitutional analysis, however, was the extension of its scope to non-initial verbal forms, which – because of their paradigmatic similarity to adverbial phrases – came to be interpreted as "circumstantial" (section 4.6.3.1) predicates of an adverbial sentence:

(27) Sin. R 21–22 *bjk ꜥẖ=f ḥnꜥ šms.w=f* "the Falcon (*bjk*) flies with his followers"

Here, the VP *ꜥẖ=f* "he flies" is perceived by the Standard theory to be functionally equivalent to (or "transposed" into) the predicate of an adverbial sentence, syntactically identical to the adverb or the prepositional phrase in (1)–(3). Following this model, the underlying structure of (27) would be *"the-Falcon (is) while-he-flies." The ultimate consequence of this approach was the drastic reduction in the inventory of verbal sentences posited for classical Egyptian and the dramatic growth of the category "Adverbial Phrase," which was believed to encompass the vast majority of predicative structures.[9]

In recent years, the limits of this approach have become evident. First of all, the restricted inventory of sentence patterns licensed in Middle Egyptian seems to be at odds with the variety of stylistic forms and devices documented in the classical literature; examples are the semantics of tense and aspect and pragmatic topicalization or focalization phenomena – two areas which are not adequately addressed in the Standard theory. Secondly, while relevant in the assessment of syntactic properties, paradigmatic substitution does not justify by itself a homogeneous treatment of such different morphological and semantic realities as adverbs (which are [-N], [-V]) and nouns ([+N], [-V]) on the one hand vs. verbal forms ([-N], [+V]) on the other. In particular one should be careful not to confuse the pragmatic notion of *topic*, such as *mꜣꜣ zj zꜣ=f* "a man regards his son" in (25), *tm=ṯ ẖnj.w* "the fact that you don't row" in (26), or *bjk* "the Falcon" in (27), with the syntactic and semantic concept of *subject*, as is the noun *zj* "a man" in (25), the second person feminine pronoun in (26), and the third person pronoun in (27). Also, a circumstantial VP behaves like any other independent sentence[10] in that it can build a main clause when introduced by a proclitic particle (section 7.3):

(28) Sh.S. 2–3 *mk pḥ.n=n ẖnw*
"Look (*mk*), we have reached (*pḥ.n=n*) the residence (*ẖnw*)"

whereas this is not the case with a bare adverb (**mk* ꜥꜣ "look here"), with a prepositional AP (**mk m prw* "look in the house"), or with an adverbial clause of the type discussed in section 6.3 (**mk ḥr-ntt*... "look, because..."').[11] There does exist a sentence pattern in which an AP follows an initial particle:

(29) Sin. B 225 *jw-ø mj sšm rsw.t* "It was like (*mj*) the situation of a dream"

But these are instances in which the underlying non-specific nominal subject ("it," i.e. the entire event described in the preceding context) has been omitted under relevance (section 6.3.3).[12] Thirdly, although very powerful from the point of view of the internal *description* of grammatical structures, the Standard theory is more vulnerable at the level of an adequate *explanation* of linguistic phenomena,[13] creating a model of Egyptian syntax where a great variety of verbal patterns is idiosyncratically balanced by a marginal role assigned to verbal predication as opposed to its nominal and especially adverbial conversions. It seems appropriate, therefore, to stick to a verbalistic approach to Egyptian syntax and to treat patterns with verbal predicate as verbal sentences. Attempts aimed at expanding the inventory of sentence types licensed within the Standard theory by means of adjustments of the theory itself will be discussed in the next chapter (sections 7.4–7.5).

From a purely syntactic point of view, what we call a "pseudoverbal" sentence is in fact nothing other than an adverbial sentence in which the NP of the prepositional predicate is an infinitive, the stative being – as it were – the surface structure acquired by an underlying prepositional phrase "in the state of." But on the other hand, the choice of a verbal root allows pseudoverbal patterns to become much more sensitive than adverbial sentences to semantic features, such as the expression of tense, aspect, or mood. In fact, pseudoverbal sentences are best understood as grammaticalized constructions in which the preposition has lost its original semantic scope and has acquired a new status: the locative function of *ḥr*, *m* or *r* is reinterpreted as indicating the "position" of the actor within the predication expressed by the verbal infinitive.[14] This "position" of the subject is in fact the main feature of verbal aspect as defined in section 4.6.2 above: while prepositions like *ḥr* "on" or *m* "in" will express different nuances of imperfectivity depending on the

Aktionsart of the verb, the former being preferred for *accomplishments* and *achievements*, the latter for *activities*, the stative being confined to *states*, *r* "toward" will tend to be grammaticalized as a marker of prospectivity. Contrast example (30), in which the preposition *ḥr* keeps its original locative meaning, with (31), a sentence drawn from the same literary text, where *ḥr* is grammaticalized in the pseudoverbal pattern "*ḥr* + infinitive":

(30) Adm. 7,10 *mṯn šps.wt ḥr šd.w* "Look, noble ladies are on rafts (*ḥr šd.w*)"

(31) Adm. 8,13 *mṯn šps.wt ḥr sḫs* "Look, noble ladies are fleeing (*ḥr sḫs*)"

The situational meaning of *ḥr* in (30), i.e. "on rafts," is applied in (31) to the location of the subject *šps.wt* "noble ladies" within the action evoked by the verb *sḫs* "to flee"; the result is a viewing of the verbal action as "imperfective," i.e. as not(-yet)-complete(d).

Finally, topicalization can be applied to any argument of an adverbial or pseudoverbal sentence when different from the subject, which functions in fact as the "default" topic of these patterns. When topicalized, the element is dislocated to the left of the entire construction and resumed by a coreferential pronoun in the main clause:

(32) Adm. 7,7 *qn ẖzy ḥr nḥm [ḫ.t]=f*
"As for the brave man (*qn*), the coward steals (*ḥr nḥm*) his property"

This construction occurs with particular frequency when the topicalized element controls an adverbial or pseudoverbal sentence the subject of which is a body part:[15]

(33) CT III 370b *jw ḥrj.w-p.t jb=sn nḏm.w*
"The heart of those who are in heaven is happy," lit. "those who are in heaven (*ḥrj.w-p.t*) – their heart is happy (*jb=sn nḏm.w*)"

6.3 Adverbial conversions

6.3.1 Adverbial clauses

Any type of Egyptian sentence – nominal, adverbial, or verbal – can be converted into an adverbial clause by means of a subordinating conjunction. This conjunction is often the pronominal morpheme *ntt* "that" (see Greek ὅτι, Latin *quod*), already referred to in section 5.3, introduced by a preposition, for example *ḥr-ntt* "because" followed by a nominal sentence in (34), *r-ntt* "to the effect that" with a pseudoverbal sentence in (35), and *ḏr-ntt* "since" with a verbal sentence in (36):

(34) Siut I,288 *ḥr-ntt jnk zꜣ wʿb mj wʿj jm=ṯn nb*
"because I (*jnk*) am the son of a priest (*zꜣ wʿb*) like (*mj*) anyone among you"

(35) pKahun 27,8–9 "This is a letter to my lord (may he be alive, prosperous, and healthy) *r-ntt h3w nb n(j) nb=j ʿnḫ.w wḏ3.w snb.w ʿḏ.w wḏ3.w m s.wt=sn nb* to the effect that all the affairs (*h3w nb*) of my lord (may he be alive, prosperous, and healthy) are safe (*ʿḏ.w*, stative) and well (*wḏ3.w*, stative) in all their places (*s.wt=sn nb*)"

(36) Berlin 1157,11 *ḏr-ntt sḏm nḥsj r ḫr n(j) r3*
"since the Nubian (*nḥsj*) listens to a verbal attack (*ḫr nj r3*, lit. "a fall of mouth")"

A certain number of prepositions can also function as conjunctions, for example *n* "for" > "because," *m* "in" > "when," *n-mrw.t* "for the sake of" > "in order to," *r* "toward" > "so that," and control an embedded verbal sentence converted into an adverbial clause. A particular perfective verb form, the *sḏm.t=f* (section 4.6.3.1), is used only after prepositions implying completion, such as *r* "until" or *ḏr* "since" and as subordinate negative perfective form after the particle *nj* (section 7.8):

(37) Urk. I 101,4–7 "Never before had one like me heard the secret of the King's harem; but His Majesty made me hear it *n jqr(=j) ḥr jb n(j) ḥm=f r srjw=f nb r sʿḥ=f nb r b3k=f nb* because I was worthy (*jqr=j*) in His Majesty's heart more than (*r*) any official of his, more than any noble of his, more than any servant of his"

(38) Urk. IV 897,11–13 *rḫ.n(=j) qd=k twj m zšj m wn=k m šms.wt jtj=j*
"I knew your character while I was still (*tw=j*, section 6.6) in the nest (*m zšj*), when you were (*m wn=k* "in you-are") in my father's following"

(39) Sin. B 247 *r pḥ.t=j dmj n(j) jtw* "until I reached (*r pḥ.t=j*) the town of Itju"

Under the control of a conjunction one also finds adverbial or pseudoverbal sentences that have been converted into verbal sentences by means of a verb form from the root *wnn* "to be"; from a pseudoverbal sentence **jw rn.w=sn mn.w* "their names are established," we obtain:

(40) Meir III,11 *jrj.n=j nw n-mrw.t wnn rn.w=sn mn(.w) n ḏ.t*
"I did this so that their names (*rn.w=sn*) be established (*mn.w*, stative) forever"

In some cases, especially with the prepositions *m* "in" and *m-ḫt* "after," the adverbial clause is topicalized (section 5.4) and dislocated to the left of the main sentence, with or rarely without the introductory particle *jr* "as for":

(41) Hatnub 22,2 *jr m wn=j m ḫrd wn=j m smr*
"When I was a child (lit.: "as-for in my-being as a child"), I was (already) a Friend"

(42) West. 8,22–23 *ḫr m-ḫt spr=f wʿj r wʿj ʿḥʿ.n p3 smn ʿḥʿ.w ḥr g3g3*
"And so (*ḫr*), after the one had reached the other (lit. *"after it reached the one to the one"), the goose stood (*ʿḥʿ.n p3 smn ʿḥʿ.w*) cackling (*ḥr g3g3*)"

The main function of *jr* "as for," however, is to introduce hypothetical verbal clauses. In Egyptian as well as in many other languages,[16] the protasis of a conditional sentence is treated as an adverbial topicalization of a verbal sentence. Depending on the semantic message conveyed by the hypothetical sentence,[17] the verbal predicate of the converted protasis can be a preterital *sḏm.n=f* implying an unfulfilled condition (43), an aorist *sḏm=f* conveying the idea of possibility (44), a subjunctive (45) for deontic modality, or a prospective (46) in temporal contexts ("when"):[18]

(43) Adm. 12,6 *jr znm.n.tw=n nj gmj.n=j tw*
"If we had been fed (passive *sḏm.n=f*), I would not have found you"
(44) Peas. B1,85–87 *jr h3j=k r šj n(j) m3ʿ.t sqdj=k jm=f m m3ʿ.w nn kfj nby.t ḥt3=k*
"If you go down (*h3j=k*) to the sea of righteousness (*m3ʿ.t*) and sail on it (*sqdj=k jm=f*) with the right wind (*m3ʿ.w*), no storm (*nby.t*) will strip away (*kfj*) your sail"
(45) pKahun 6,24 *jr grt m3n=k ḫ.t ḥr jr.wj=sj nn msj=s r nḥḥ*
"If indeed you see (*m3n=k*, 4.6.3.2c) something on her eyes, she will never (*r nḥḥ*) give birth"
(46) Pyr. 1252e–f *jr prj=f m sb3 pw j3b.tj n(j) p.t jn n=f sb3 pw mḥ.t(j) n(j) p.t*
"If/when he comes out (*prj=f*) of this eastern gate of heaven, bring (*jn*) to him this northern gate of heaven"

Adverbial sentences can be converted into hypothetical clauses by transforming them into verbal sentences governed by a grammaticalized form of the verb *wnn* "to be," mostly the "emphatic" *sḏm=f*. For example, the adverbial sentence **jw=k m sšmy* "you are a leader" is converted into the verbal sentence **wnn=k m sšmy* and introduced by *jr* when functioning as adverbial protasis in hypothetical discourse:

(47) Pt. 264–65 *jr wnn=k m sšmy hr sḏm=k mdw sprw*
"If you are a leader, be pleasing (*hr*) when you hear (*sḏm=k*) the word of the petitioner"

In other cases, the element indicating the semantic tie to the main sentence, rather than a preposition or a prepositionally derived conjunction, is a "particle," i.e. a morpheme which functions as complementizer outside the sentence boundary.[19] In these cases, one does not deal with syntactic subordination, but rather with a linkage between two main clauses; the clause introduced by the particle provides contextual background information, and is in this respect semantically dependent upon the main clause, but remains syntactically a nominal, adverbial, or verbal main clause. The most important particles indicating contextual dependence are *jsk/sk* (> *jsṯ/sṯ* > *jst/st*),[20] which often follow the foreground segment of discourse, and *jḫr/ḫr*, which usually precede it. Both of them have a temporal or circumstantial meaning:

(48) Sin. R 22–24 *bjk ʿḫ=f ḥnʿ šms.w=f* – see example (27) – *nn rḏj.t rḫ st mšʿ=f jst h3b.Ø r msj.w-nzw wn.w m-ḫt=f m mšʿ pn*
"The Falcon flies with his followers, without letting (*nn rḏj.t*, section 6.5.2) his army (*mšʿ=f*) know it. Meanwhile (*jst*), the royal children who were (*wn.w*) with him (*m-*

ḫt=f, lit. "after him") in this army had been informed (*h3b.ø r msj.w-nzw*, lit. "ø had been sent to the royal children," perfect passive *sḏm.w=f* with omission of the subject pronoun under relevance)"

(49) Urk. I 101,2–3 *jnk jrj m zẖ3 w'.k(j) ḥn' z3b jrj-nḫn w'(.w) sṯ j3.t=j m jmj-r3 ḫntj.w-š prw-'3*

"I acted (participial statement, section 5.4.2) as scribe (*m zẖ3*) alone (*w'.kj*), with a senior (*z3b*) warden of Nekhen (*jrj-nḫn*) alone, my rank (*j3.t=j*) being that of overseer (*jmj-r3*) of the royal tenants"

(50) Urk. I 83,13–14 *jḫr ḥzj wj ḥm=f rdj ḥm=f 'q=j r ẖnw-'*

"Since His Majesty (*ḥm=f*) praised me, His Majesty caused me to enter (lit. "caused that I enter") the Privy Chamber (*ẖnw-'*)"

and can appear sometimes combined in the same clause:

(51) Urk. I 41,12–13 *jḫr sk ḥm=f ḥzj=f sw ḥr=s m3 sw ḥm=f j.sn[=f t3]*

"While His Majesty was praising him (*ḥzj=f sw*) for it, His majesty saw him as he was kissing (*j.sn=f*, section 6.3.2) the ground"

The interface between embedded adverbial clauses and non-initial main clauses, for which Egyptian uses identical sentence patterns, becomes especially clear if we turn our attention to the function of the enclitic particle *js*. Etymologically, this morpheme is the basic constituent of the particle *jsk/jsṯ* referred to above (*jsk* < **js=k*), and possibly derives from the ending of a proto-Egyptian locative case (section 4.3.1).[21] Its function can be best assessed if we discriminate between three levels of linguistic analysis:

(a) At the semantic level, *js* transforms a "categorical" into a "thetic" sentence (section 5.3),[22] i.e. into a statement in which a state of affairs is presented globally as a simple assertion, and not, as in the case of the ordinary categorical statement, as the compound of a subject qualified by a predicate or a topic followed by a comment. When accompanying an entire sentence, therefore, *js* embeds it as a whole informational unit into the preceding segment of discourse. This is why this particle is used *inter alia* as a meta-linguistic operator[23] in explanatory clauses representing the object of verbs of perception such as *ḏd* "to say," *sḏm* "to hear," *rḫ* "to know" or the like, whether or not introduced by the conjunction *ntt/wnt*:

(52) CT I 28c–29a B3Bo *sḏm=sn ḏd.t=s nb.t nfr m hrww [p]n ntt ṯwt js šw.t tw wbn.t m t3-nṯr*

"May they hear all the good things she says (*ḏd.t=s nb.t nfr*) on this day, namely (*js*) that you are (or "yours is") this feather which appears (*wbn.t*) in god's land"

(53) Urk. IV 363,6–7 *jw ḥm.t=j rḫ.tj nṯrr=f jrj.n=j js (s)t ḫr wḏ=f*

"My Majesty (*ḥm.t=j*, fem.) knows (*rḫ.tj*) that he is divine and that I did this according to his order"

In these sentences, *js* presents the explanatory sentence as a "thetic," i.e. global object of the verbal predication, as the metalinguistic content – as it were – of "saying" or "knowing": "My Majesty knows: *jrj.n=j st ẖr wḏ=f* 'I-did-this-according-to-his-order,'" parallel to the use of a nominal *sḏm=f* (section 4.6.3.1b) in the first explanatory clause: "My Majesty knows: *nṯrr=f* 'that-he-is-divine'."

(b) At the discourse level, *js* represents a symmetrical counterpart to *jḫr* or *jsk*, in that it grants pragmatic prominence, rather than backgrounding function, to the sentence in which it appears. The utterance marked by *js* does not convey the discourse *topic*, i.e. the background against which the new information is presented as relevant, but rather a contrastive *focus*, i.e. a contextually unexpected argument or state of affairs:

(54) Sh.S. 149–54 "Then he laughed at me for what I had said as something he deemed foolish, and he said to me: 'You don't have much myrrh, although you now own incense. *jnk js ḥqꜣ pwn.t ꜥntjw n=j-jmj sw ḥknw pf ḏd.n=k jn.t=f bw pw wr n jw pn ḫpr js jwd=k ṯw r s.t tn nj zp mꜣ=k jw pn ḫpr(.w) m nwy* I, on the other hand (*js*), am the ruler of Punt! Myrrh – it belongs to me (*n=j-jmj sw*); this oil which you mentioned (*ḏd.n=k*) you were going to send (*jn.t=f*, lit. "to send it") – there's plenty on this island! And (*js*) when it happens (*ḫpr*) that you depart from this place, you'll never see (*nj zp mꜣ=k*) this island again, since it will have turned (*ḫpr.w*, stative) into water"

(55) Adm. 12,1 *mnjw pw n(j) bw-nb nn bjn m jb=f ꜥnd jdr=f jrj.n=f js hrww r nw(j.t)=st* "He is the shepherd (*mnjw*) of everyone (*bw-nb*); there is no evil in his heart. His herds (*jdr=f*) are few, but (*js*) he spends the day (*jrj.n=f hrww*) taking care of them (*r nwj.t=st*, lit. "to take care of them")"

The clauses with *js* convey contextually unexpected information: in (54), the first *js* allows the speaker to emphasize the contrast between the interlocutor's powerlessness and his own prominence, whereas the second instance of *js* creates a pragmatic opposition between the present and the future situation; in (55), it is assumed that, if herds are few, the shepherd would not be expected to spend the day herding them – a contrast which attracts the attentional focus of discourse.

(c) At the syntactic level, *js* is a marker of dependency (section 6.4). In early texts, any sentence type (nominal, adverbial, or verbal) accompanied by this particle is converted into a dependent clause, either nominal (in the case of the object clause of verbs of saying, hearing, or knowing) or adverbial (in the other constructions). What follows are examples of nominal (56), adverbial (57)–(58), pseudoverbal (59), and verbal sentences (60) converted into dependent clauses by means of *js*. In the case of adverbial embedding, the clause is often introduced by an explicit marker of subordination, such as a conjunction (*n*, *ḥr-ntt*, etc.).[24] The translation techniques may vary, but they should aim to render the interplay of semantic theticity, discourse focality, and syntactic dependency that constitute the functional array of this particle.

(56) Pyr. 543c *nḏr.n n=f N sd=k n N js pw nṯr z3 nṯr*
"The King has seized (*nḏr.n*) for himself your tail, for the King is a god (*nṯr*), son of a god"

The subordinate clause is an embedded nominal sentence introduced by the conjunction *n* "since, for" (= preposition *n* "to, for").

(57) Pyr. 884 *rḏj(.w) n=k ‘.wj h3j n=k rwj.t rḏj(.w) n=k ḫf3.t sbḥ n=k mnj.t wr.t wsjr js m s.t ‘.wj=f(j)*
"Arms (*‘.wj*) have been given to you, ritual dances (*rwj.t*) have come down to you, food (*ḫf3.t*) has been given to you; the Great Reviver (*mnj.t wr.t*) has cried (*sbḥ*) for you – Osiris being in the place of his arms!"[25]

Following the pattern observed in section 6.2, when a main adverbial sentence is transformed into a dependent clause accompanied by *js*, it undergoes the usual conversion into a verbal sentence introduced by a topicalized form of *wnn* "to be"; from an underlying adverbial sentence **jw N pn m-‘b=sn* "the King is among them," we obtain:

(58) Pyr. 1489b–90a *ḏd=k wnn js N <p>n m-‘b=sn nṯr.w jmj.w p.t*
"You will say (*ḏd=k*) that this King is among them (*m-‘b=sn*), namely the gods who are (*jmj.w*) in heaven"

In pseudoverbal sentences, however, the conversion does not take place:

(59) CT VII 475i–j *ḏd.n=sn jw=j js rḫ.k(w) sn m sšm.w=sn*
"They said that I know them in their behavior"

Finally, example (60) shows the particle *js* converting a verbal sentence into a dependent clause. In this case, the contrast between main and dependent clause evoked by *js* is probably best rendered in English by breaking the discourse continuity:

(60) Pyr. 777c *jw.n=ṯ sdẖ=ṯ z3=ṯ jw.n=ṯ js ẖnm=ṯ wrj pn*
"You have come (*jw.n=ṯ*, fem.) that you may hide (*sdẖ=ṯ*) your son – you have come that you may join (*ẖnm=ṯ*) this Great One."

6.3.2 Adverbial phrases

As a rule, Egyptian adverbial phrases – whether they represent a pragmatic focus of the utterance or a mere predicative adjunct – follow the main predication. We saw in sections 5.2.1 and 6.3.1, however, that the particle *jr* "as for," etymologically the full form of the preposition *r* "toward," is used for the topicalization of a phrase (*jr* "as for") or of a clause (*jr* "if"); the resulting AP is dislocated to the left of the main clause. In rare instances, bare adverbial phrases can also be extraposed to the left of the main clause:

(61) Adm. 14,14 *mj-m jrf zj nb ḥr smꜣ sn=f*
"How can any man (*zj nb*) kill (*smꜣ*) his fellow?"

In specific semantic environments, a bare noun phrase can be used as adverbial adjunct, as if introduced by a preposition.[26] This pattern is rather frequent with indications of time:

(62) Pt. 186 *šms jb=k tr n(j) wnn=k*
"Follow (*šms*) your heart as long as you live (*tr nj wnn=k*, lit. "time-of-your-being")"

and in the colophon formula of a literary text:

(63) Sin. B 311 *jw=f pw ḥꜣ.t=f r pḥ(.wj)=fj mj gm.yt m zẖꜣ*
"This is how it comes (*jw=f pw*, section 5.3) from its beginning (*ḥꜣ.t=f*, lit. "its beginning") to its end (*r pḥ.wj=fj*) as found (*gm.yt*) in writing"

Nominal phrases are not the only syntactic formations capable of acquiring adverbial function. Verbal and pseudoverbal sentences can also appear embedded as AP without overt markers of adverbialization:

(64) Sin. B 233–34 *mw m jtrw zwr.tw=f mrj=k*
"The water in the river (*mw m jtrw*) is drunk (*zwr.tw=f*) *when you wish* (*mrj=k*)"

While the semantic meaning of this type of adverbialization (whether temporal "when you wish," causal "because you wish," hypothetical "if you wish," etc.) remains vaguer than in the cases in which the embedding of a sentence into an adverbial clause is explicitly signalled by a conjunction, its adverbial character is shown by its treatment as adjunct under the control of another phrase,[27] for example the verbal phrase *zwr.tw=f* "it is drunk" in (64). In this environment, the adverbialized VP belongs to the same substitutional category of a simple AP, as shown by a comparison of (64) above and (27) below, an example we already considered in the preceding section:

(27) Sin. R 21–22 *bjk ʿẖ=f ḥnʿ šms.w=f* "The Falcon flies *with his followers*"

The treatment of a VP as adverbial adjunct occurs frequently, but not exclusively, as oblique complement of verbs of perception such as *mꜣꜣ* "to see" or *gmj* "to find." In the case of a verbal form, for example the circumstantial *sḏm=f* in (65)–(66), the controlling element, usually the logical object of the main predication, is resumed by the suffix pronoun of the subordinate adverbial VP;[28] in the case of a pseudoverbal sentence, for example *ḥr* + infinitive in (67), the subject is omitted under agreement if coindexed with the subject of the main predication:

(65) Sin. B 52–53 *prj-ʿ nn twt n=f mꜣꜣ.tw=f hꜣj=f rꜣ-pḏ.tjw ẖʿm=f rꜣ-ḏꜣj.w*
"He is a fighter (*prj-ʿ* "one whose arm is stretched") without peer (*nn twt n=f* "without likeness to him") when he is seen (*mꜣꜣ.tw=f*) *charging down upon* (*hꜣj=f*) *the Bowmen* and *approaching* (*ẖʿm=f*) *the opponents*"

(66) pKahun 30,30 *gmj.n=j nb=j ʿnḫ.w wḏꜣ.w snb.w ḫntj=f*
"I found (*gmj.n=j*) my Lord (may he be alive, prosperous and healthy) *travelling southward* (*ḫntj=f*)"

(67) Adm. 8,5–6 *mṯn nfr zj ḥr wnm kꜣ.w=f*
"Look, a man is happy (*nfr zj*) *when he eats* (*ḥr wnm*) his food (*kꜣ.w=f*)"

This last example shows that the coreferential subject of a subordinate pseudoverbal clause is omitted when it is not governed by a verb of perception. But when the subject of the adverbial clause is different from the controlling NP, it remains overt, as is demonstrated by the different treatment of the two adverbial phrases in (68); the coreferential second person subject is omitted before the stative *ḏj.tj*, whereas the non-coreferential *jḥ.w*, i.e. the subject of *ḥr* + infinitive, is overt:

(68) Sin. B 193–9 *p.t ḥr=k ḏj.tj m mstp.t jḥ.w ḥr jtḥ=k*
"The heaven (*p.t*) is above you (*ḥr=k*), while you are placed in the hearse (*ḏj.tj m mstp.t*) and (while) oxen (*jḥ.w*) pull you (*ḥr jtḥ=k*)"

The transformation of a verbal or pseudoverbal sentence into a controlled AP is, therefore, a different phenomenon from the use of a VP in a main clause following a noun, a topicalized verbal form, or an introductory particle (section 6.2):[29] the former is a truly adverbial conversion, the scope of the VP being restricted to the *adverbial phrase*, whereas the latter is a pattern in which the VP functions as the main predicate of a *verbal clause*. This difference is not recognized by the Standard theory.

Instead of an entire clause (section 6.3.2), the particle *js* can also control a lower adverbial node, i.e. a simple adverbial phrase. In (69), the predicative complement introduced by *m* is further expanded in the two APs controlled by *js*, with the preposition *m* omitted under relevance; in (70), the two adverbial adjuncts introduced by *js* convey the emphasized goal of the state of affairs expressed in the main nominal sentence:

(69) Pyr. 727b–c *hꜣj n=k m zꜣb šmʿw jnpw js ḥr ẖ.t=f wpjw js ḫnt jwnw*
"Go down for yourself (*n=k*) as Jackal of Upper Egypt (*šmʿw*) – as Anubis on his belly (*ḥr ẖ.t=f*), as Opener (*wpjw*) in front of Heliopolis (*jwnw*)"

(70) Urk. I 222,18–223,2 *jnk wpj wʿr.t tn js r sbj.t ḥr jmj ẖr.t-nṯr js r jrj.t mrr.t(=j)*
"I was the one who opened (*wpj*) this area – on the one hand, in order to react against (*r sbj.t ḥr*) whoever was in the Necropolis, on the other hand, in order to do (*r jrj.t*) what I cherish (*mrr.t=j*)"[30]

6.3.3 *Converted vs. unconverted relative clauses*

Relative clauses are embedded subordinate clauses used to modify a nominal antecedent.[31] Egyptian syntax exhibits two types of relative clause.[32] The more common one, the "true" relative clause, represents the conversion of a main sentence into a subordinate clause. In the case of a verbal sentence, this syntactic transformation is performed by adjectival forms of the verb, i.e. participles and relative forms; the corresponding patterns will be dealt with in section 7.5. In the case of adverbial (71) or pseudoverbal sentences (72), and only very rarely of verbal sentences,[33] the subordinating morpheme is the relative adjective *ntj* or an adjectival conversion of the verb *wnn* "to be":

(71) Sin. B 33–34 *mtr.n wj rmṯ.w km.t ntj.w jm ḥn'=f*
"The Egyptians (*rmṯ.w km.t*) who (*ntj.w*) were there (*jm*) with him (*ḥn'=f*) having borne witness for me"

(72) Urk. IV 386,4–10 *ḥw.t-nṯr nb.t qsj wn.t wꜣ.tj r fḫ... sḏsr.n=j sj*
"The temple of the lady of Cusae (*nb.t qsj*) which had fallen (*wn.t wꜣ.tj* *"which was having-fallen," participle + stative) into ruin... – I rededicated (*sḏsr.n=j*) it"

In these sentences, when the subject of the relative clause is coreferential with the antecedent, it is omitted under agreement and replaced by the relative converter (73); if it differs from it, it is resumed by a pronoun in the relative clause (74):

(73) Peas. B1,287 *nj rḫ.n.tw wnn.t m jb*
"That which is in the heart (*wnn.t m jb*) cannot be known"

(74) West. 11,10–11 *pty nꜣ ntt n jj.wn r=s*
"What (*pty*) is the reason (*nꜣ*, lit. "this") for which (*ntt...r=s*) we (*n*) have come (*jj.wn*, stative)?"

The use of these converted relative clauses, however, is limited to *specific* antecedents: non-specific NPs are modified in Egyptian by adverbial clauses. The adverbial pattern which modifies a non-specific antecedent is called *virtual* or *unconverted* relative clause. Any sentence type (verbal, pseudoverbal, adverbial, or nominal) can be embedded into the main clause as an adverbial phrase modifying a non-specific antecedent; syntactically, these clauses behave exactly like the ordinary adjuncts we discussed in section 6.3.2, as is shown by the identical treatment of the pseudoverbal relative clause *jw=f m jj.t* which modifies *ḥfꜣw* "a serpent" in (75) and the similar pattern *jw=f ḥr md.t* controlled by the main verbal clause *sḏm.n=j ḫrw=f* "I heard his voice" in (76):

(75) Sh.S. 61–62 *gmj.n=j ḥfꜣw pw jw=f m jj.t*
"I found that it was a serpent *which was coming*"

(76) Sin. B 1–2 *sḏm.n=j [ḫr]w=f jw=f ḥr md.t*
"I heard his voice *while he was speaking*"

Thus, any unconverted main sentence can be embedded as adverbial adjunct into a higher syntactic node. When the controlling element is a noun, the AP functions as unconverted relative clause modifying the noun; when the controlling node is an entire clause, it functions as adverbial adjunct modifying the predication. That a virtual relative clause is in fact a sentence embedded as AP modifying a noun clause, is shown by the different possible interpretations and translations which can often be given to a sentence in which this pattern appears, depending on whether one takes the embedded AP to modify the noun, in which case it is a "virtual" relative clause, as in (a) in examples (77)–(80), or the entire predication, in which case it functions as ordinary adjunct, as in (b) in the same passages.

(A) Embedding of a *verbal* sentence:

(77) pEbers 91,3 *kt n.t msḏr ḏj=f mw*
lit. "Another (remedy) of an ear it-gives water"
(a) S^a =› [*kt n.t* [*msḏr ḏj=f mw*]$_{\text{NP}}$]$_{\text{Pred}}$ ⌊~~*pw*~~]$_{\text{Subj}}$
"(This is) another remedy for an ear that gives off water"
(b) S^b =› [*kt n.t msḏr* ⌊*ḏj=f mw*]$_{\text{VP}}$]$_{\text{Pred}}$ ⌊~~*pw*~~]$_{\text{Subj}}$
"(This is) another remedy for an ear if it gives off water"

(B) Embedding of a *pseudoverbal* sentence:

(78) Merikare E 51 *m smꜣ(.w) zj jw=k rḫ.tj ꜣḫ.w=f*
lit. "Do-not kill a-man you-know his-worth"
(a) S^a =› [*m smꜣ.w* [*zj jw=k rḫ.tj ꜣḫ.w=f*]$_{\text{NP}}$]
"Do not kill a man whose worth you know"
(b) S^b =› [*m smꜣ.w zj* ⌊*jw=k rḫ.tj ꜣḫ.w=f*]$_{\text{PseudoverbalP}}$]
"Do not kill a man if you know his worth"

(C) Embedding of an *adverbial* sentence:

(79) Sh.S. 119–21 *jw dp.t r jj.t m ẖnw sqd.w jm=s rḫ.n=k ø*
lit. "A boat is toward-coming from-the-residence sailors in-it you-know"
(a) S^a =› ⌊*jw* [*dp.t sqd.w jm=s rḫ.n=k*]$_{\text{NP}}$ *r jj.t m ẖnw*]
"A boat in which there are sailors whom you know will come from the residence"
(b) S^b =› ⌊*jw dp.t r jj.t m ẖnw* [*sqd.w jm=s rḫ.n=k*]$_{\text{AP}}$]
"A boat will come from the residence, with sailors in it whom you know"

This last sentence offers an example of a "virtual" relative clause (i.e. the unconverted verbal predicate *rḫ.n=k* "you know" with the omission of the resumptive object pronoun **st* "them," see below) embedded into a higher pattern of the same type (*sqd.w jm=s*).

(D) Embedding of a *nominal* sentence:

(80) Peas. R 1.1 *zj pw wn(.w) ḫwj.n-jnpw rn=f*
lit. "It is that a man was – Khuienanup his-name"

(a) S^a => [[*zj ḫwj.n-jnpw rn=f*]$_{NP}$ *wn.w*]$_{Pred}$ [*pw*]$_{Subj}$
"There was a man whose name was Khuienanup"

(b) S^b => [*zj wn.w* [*ḫwj.n-jnpw rn=f*]$_{NP}$]$_{Pred}$ [*pw*]$_{Subj}$
"There was a man named Khuienanup"

In converted, i.e. true relative clauses, resumptive pronouns are omitted under agreement when they immediately follow the agreement-carrier.[34] This is most often the case when the resumptive element is the *subject* of the relative clause, whether verbal, in which case the agreement is carried by a participle:

(81) Disp. 78–79 *mḫj=j ḥr msj.w=s sd.w ø m swḥ.t*
"I shall grieve (*mḫj=j*) for her children who have been broken (*sd.w*) in the egg"

or adverbial, in which case one finds a relative converter:

(82) Sh.S. 170–71 *'ḥ'.n=j ḥr jꜣš n mš' ntj ø m dp.t tn*
"Then I called out to the crew (*mš'*) which was in this boat"

Omission of the resumptive pronoun can also take place, however, when it indicates the *object* of the verbal action, provided it immediately follows the agreement-carrier, as in (79) above as opposed to (83) below, where the resumptive object pronoun (*st*) is overt:

(83) Sin. B 144–45 *kꜣ.t.n=f jrj.t=s r=j jrj.n=j st r=f*
"That which he had planned (*kꜣ.t.n=f*) to do (*jrj.t=s* "to do it") to me, I did it to him"

"Virtual" relative clauses, on the other hand, are unconverted; they do not display any adjectival element, whether participle, relative form, or converter, as carrier of the agreement. This explains why their subject always needs to be overt: in the abovementioned example (75), the non-specific *ḥfꜣw* "a serpent," which is the predicate of a *pw*-sentence functioning as object of the VP, is resumed by the subject pronoun in the virtual relative clause *jw=f m jj.t* "which was coming":

(75) Sh.S. 61–62 *gmj.n=j ḥfꜣw pw jw=f m jj.t*
"I found that it was a serpent which was coming"

S => [*gmj.n=j* [[*ḥfꜣw jw=f m jj.t*][*pw*]]]
*[I found [[serpent it-is-coming] (is) [this]]]

as opposed to the omission of the subject under agreement in (84), where the object of the verbal predication is a specific noun phrase immediately followed by the stative, i.e. by the pseudoverbal predicate:

(84) Urk. I 125,15–16 *gmj.n=j ḥqꜣ jꜣm šm(.w) r=f r tꜣ-ṯmḥ*
"I found that the ruler of Yam had himself gone to the land of Libya"
S => [*gmj.n=j ḥqꜣ jꜣm* [~~*sw*~~ *šm.w r=f r tꜣ-ṯmḥ*]]
*[I found the ruler of Yam [~~he~~ had gone to the land of Libya]]

Being unconverted, virtual relative clauses display no morphological signal of subordination. The only link to the main sentence is represented by the resumptive element; in addition to pronouns, words capable of conveying resumption are the so-called "prepositional adverbs," which are prepositions inflected by means of an invariable adverbializing element *-y* or *-w*, possibly the same morpheme found in the circumstantial forms of the stative.[35] An example is offered by *jry* "thereof, thereto" in (85):

(85) Sin. R 11–12 *jst rf zbj.n ḥm=f mšꜥ r tꜣ-tmḥj.w zꜣ=f smsw m ḥrj jry*
"Meanwhile (*jst rf*, section 6.3.1), His Majesty had sent off (*zbj.n ḥm=f*) to the land of the Libyans an army (*mšꜥ*) whose leader was his elder son," lit. "his elder son as a leader (*m ḥrj*) thereof"

Thus, both converted and unconverted relative clauses exhibit resumptive elements which point back to the noun phrase they modify. When omission of the resumptive element occurs, it is not caused by grammatical *agreement*, but by semantic *relevance*.[36] Unlike mandatory omission under agreement, omission under relevance is an optional device sensitive to the hierarchies of animacy and salience, with subjects that are low on either of these hierarchies more likely to be deleted. An example of optional subject omission under relevance in "true" relative clauses is provided by contrasting (86), where the omitted subject is inanimate, with (87), where it is animate and overt:

(86) Neferti 26 *nj zr.n=j ntt nj jj=ø*
"I cannot foretell (*nj zr.n=j*) that which (*ntt*) has not yet come about (*nj jj=ø*)"
(87) Peas. B2,80 *m pḥ(.w) ntj nj pḥ=f tw*
"Do not attack (*m pḥ.w*) one who (*ntj*) has not attacked you"

The same distribution characterizes the subject omission under relevance in virtual relative clauses; while in both cases the subject is non-specific, which justifies the use of an unconverted relative clause, it is omitted under relevance in (88), where it is inanimate, but maintained in (89), where it is human:

(88) Adm. 7,1 *mṯn js jrj(.w) ḫ.t nj pꜣ=ø ḫpr*
"Look now, things have been done (*jrj.w ḫt*) which did not use (*nj pꜣ=ø*) to happen"
(89) Peas. B1,204–5 *mk tw m ḥrj-šnꜥw nj rḏj.n=f swꜣ šw ḥr-ꜥ*
"Look, you are (like) a storehouse supervisor (*ḥrj-šnꜥw*) who does not let (*nj rḏj.n=f*) a poor man (*šw*) pass in (*swꜣ*) at once (*ḥr-ꜥ*)"

6.4 Initial vs. non-initial clauses

6.4.1 General features

In our discussion thus far, we have considered examples of adverbial sentences regardless of the function of the proclitic particle by which they are sometimes introduced. The presence or absence of this morpheme, however, is an important feature in the syntax of adverbial sentences, and its function has been the subject of intense discussion among students of Egyptian.

The general rule is that adverbial and pseudoverbal patterns of the type:

$$S \Rightarrow \text{Particle}^{37} + NP + AP$$

are *initial* main sentences, whereas bare patterns of the type:

$$S \Rightarrow NP + AP$$

are *non-initial* clauses, either paratactically juxtaposed to the initial predication as non-initial main clauses or controlled as subordinate clauses by another phrase, according to the patterns described in section 6.3 above. This flexibility displayed by sentence patterns, which can appear both as independent main sentence or as subordinate clause, depending on the syntactic environment, is a common feature of Egyptian syntax, being shared by nearly all patterns, whether nominal, adverbial, or verbal.

The dialectics between the initial (main) sentence introduced by a particle and the non-initial (coordinate or subordinate) bare adverbial clause is captured in the following passage:

(90) Sin. R 8–11 *jw ẖnw m sgr jb.w m gmw rw.tj-wr.tj ḫtm.w [šny.]t m [tp]-ḥr-mꜣs.t p'.t m jmw*
"The residence was in silence (*sgr*), the hearts in mourning (*gmw*), the Two Great Portals were shut (*ḫtm.w*), the courtiers head-on-knee (*tp-ḥr-mꜣs.t*), the nobles in grief (*jmw*)"

Here, the past reference is obviously not an inherent quality of the adverbial or pseudoverbal sentence, but rather a feature derived from the preceding context, which in this case is determined by a narrative infinitive (section 4.6.4b), followed by a series of main verbal or pseudoverbal clauses:

(91) Sin. R 5–8 *rnp.t-zp 30 ꜣbd 3 ꜣḫ.t sw 7 'r nṯr r ꜣḫ.t=f nzw-bjt sḥtp-jb-r'w sḥr=f r p.t ẖnm(.w) m jtn ḥ'.w-nṯr ꜣbḫ(.w) m jrj sw*
"Regnal year 30, third month of the Inundation, day 7: Ascending (*'r*) of the god to his horizon (*r ꜣḫ.t=f*); the King of Upper and Lower Egypt (*nzw-bjt*) Sehetepibre' flew (*sḥr=f*) to heaven, having become united (*ẖnm.w*) with the sun-disk; the god's body (*ḥ'.w-nṯr*) merged (*ꜣbḫ.w*) with the one who created (*jrj*) him"

It is important to appreciate the difference between "initiality" as a property of *discourse* and "independence" vs. "subordination" as syntactic features of the *clause*. In (90), all adverbial and pseudoverbal clauses are main clauses, in the sense that – if taken individually – they all represent well-formed Egyptian sentences paratactically organized within a chain of discourse. Only the first sentence, however, is introduced by a particle of initiality (*jw*), which indicates that the corresponding adverbial sentence (*ẖnw m sgr*) opens a new segment of discourse. In (91), the discourse setting is provided by the date and the narrative infinitive. The following sentences depend on it from the point of view of the narrative sequence; within this context, the verbal sentence with topicalized subject "the King flew to heaven" and the pseudoverbal sentence "the god's body merged with the one who created him" are both non-initial main clauses paratactically linked to the initial form; the pseudoverbal adjunct "having become united with the sun-disk," on the other hand, is controlled by the preceding VP *sḥr=f r p.t* "he flew to heaven"; not only is it non-initial, but it is also syntactically subordinate.

The difference between the linguistic levels of clause vs. discourse has not played any tangible role in the Standard theory, which – as one will recall – was primarily interested in the sentence level. Thus, scholars working within that frame have oscillated between three positions: (a) considering adverbial and pseudoverbal clauses not introduced by a particle to be subordinate clauses, the initial sentence introduced by the particle being the only main sentence;[38] (b) as a variant thereof, taking the proclitic particle to apply to all subsequent sentences, but to be – as it were – omitted under relevance;[39] (c) taking bare adverbial and pseudoverbal sentences not introduced by an initial particle to be main clauses which in a chain of discourse become hypotactically linked to the initial sentence; in this case, the particle is thought to convey the syntactic/pragmatic "theme" (or "subject," or "figure") of the entire macrosentence and to function, therefore, essentially as a nominal element, similar to the initial verbal forms *sḏm=f* and *sḏm.n=f* in emphatic function (section 4.6.3.1).[40]

None of these analyses, however, is entirely satisfactory. If option (a) were true, Egyptian discourse would display a strikingly low number of main clauses and an equally surprisingly high number of subordinate clauses, which is linguistically rather unlikely. The difficulty with option (b) is that all forms of omission, including omission under relevance, seem to require in Egyptian specific environments or conditions, whereas in this case the scope of the introductory particle would lack clear boundaries; option (c) requires the assumption of a thematic function for a particle, i.e. for the lowest syntactic element in the hierarchy of animacy and salience.[41] This assumption is equally not convincing.

The analysis presented here draws a distinction between the level of *clause* and the level of *discourse*, and thus provides a satisfactory account of adverbial and pseudoverbal syntax. Adverbial and pseudoverbal sentences introduced by a particle are always main clauses; non-initial patterns may be paratactically linked *main* clauses or embedded *subordinate* clauses. The difference between forms with and without introductory particle lies on the discourse level, in that the sentence introduced by an initial proclitic particle opens a segment of *text*.[42] This discourse opening function need not be filled by a particle; it can also be assumed by a temporal setting, as in example (91) above, by an initial noun phrase, as in (92), or by a verbal sentence, as in (93):

(92) Pt. 7–19 *jty nb=j tnj ḫpr(.w) jꜣw hꜣj.w wgg jw.w jḥw ḥr mꜣw sḏr n=f ḫdr(.w) r'w-nb jr.tj nḏs.w 'nḫ.wj jmr.w pḥ.tj ḥr ꜣq n wrḏ-jb rꜣ gr(.w) nj mdw.n=f jb tm.w nj sḫꜣ.n=f sf qs mn(.w) n=f n-ꜣww bw-nfr ḫpr(.w) m bw-bjn dp.t nb.t šm.t(j)*
"Sovereign (*jty*), my lord! Age (*tnj*) has showed up, old age (*jꜣw*) has arrived; weakness (*wgg*) has come, feebleness (*jḥw*) grows; if one tries to sleep, one is in discomfort (lit. "the one who sleeps is discomforted") all day; eyes (*jr.tj*) are dim, ears (*'nḫ.wj*) deaf, strength (*pḥ.tj*) is declining because of exhaustion (*wrḏ-jb*); the mouth is silent and cannot speak (*nj mdw.n=f*), the heart (*jb*) is finished and cannot recall (*nj sḫꜣ.n=f*) the past (*sf* "yesterday"); bones ache (lit. "the bone has been aching") completely (*n-ꜣww*); good has turned (*ḫpr.w*) into evil; all taste is gone (*šm.tj*)"

(93) Peas. B1,135–37 *ḏd.jn sḫ.tj pn ḫꜣw n(j) 'ḥ'.w ḥr sjꜣ.t n=f mḥ n(j) ky ḥr hqs hꜣ.w=f sšm r hp.w ḥr wḏ 'wꜣ.t*
"Then the peasant said: 'He who measures (*ḫꜣw*) the corn-heaps cheats (*ḥr sjꜣ.t*) for his own interest (*n=f*); he who fills (*mḥ*) for another steals (*ḥr hqs*) the other's property; he who should rule (*sšm*) according to the laws (*r hp.w*) orders theft (*ḥr wḏ 'wꜣ.t*)"

The initial vocative phrase "Sovereign my lord" in (92) and the narrative tense "then the peasant said" in (93) both display the feature [+INITIAL]; they open a discourse unit which is expanded by means of main adverbial or pseudoverbal clauses which lack the initiality feature of the first discourse nucleus,[43] but are paratactically annexed to the initial NP or VP. We also saw that in contexts of syntactic dependency, the same bare patterns can appear embedded as subordinate clauses – a flexibility shared by nearly all Egyptian sentence patterns. Example (94) provides a sequence of two statives, the first of which is the predicate of a non-initial main clause paratactically linked to the initial verbal sentence introduced by the particle *mk* "look," whereas the second functions as subordinate adverbial phrase controlled by the first form, which immediately precedes it:

(94) Sh.S. 2–7 *mk pḥ.n=n ḫnw...jz.wt=n jj.tj ʿḏ.tj*
"Look, we have reached (*pḥ.n=n*) the residence (*ḫnw*)...and our crew (*jz.wt=n*) has arrived (*jj.tj*) safely (*ʿḏ.tj* "it being safe")"

Since they provide the discourse setting by opening a new textual unit, initial particles offer an ideal insight into the interface of syntax, pragmatics, and semantics. Most of them can also introduce verbal sentences, following a pattern of syntactic distribution similar to the one we just discussed: sentences introduced by an initial particle are initial main clauses, bare verbal sentences function either as non-initial main clauses or as embedded subordinate clauses.

Thus, all particles, not only markers of initiality such as *jw* or *mk*, but also the hypotactic *jsk*, *jḫr* or *js* referred to in section 6.3.1, are ideal examples of what contemporary X-bar theory calls "complementizers," i.e. constituents added to a bare sentence in order to generate a specific clausal unit.[44] In this respect, rather than operating with the traditional two levels of clausal linkage (parataxis vs. hypotaxis or coordination vs. subordination), it seems particularly suitable to analyze Egyptian syntactic phenomena positing three "cluster points," representing three different stages of grammaticalization:[45]

(a) *Parataxis*, i.e. the linkage between main clauses. This linkage remains usually unexpressed in Egyptian syntax, as in the case of bare adverbial, pseudoverbal or verbal sentences which follow an initial main clause within a chain of discourse. A specimen of paratactic chain was provided in (90):

(90) Sin. R 8–11 *jw ḫnw m sgr jb.w m gmw rw.tj-wr.tj ḫtm.w [šny.]t m [tp]-ḥr-mꜣs.t pʿ.t m jmw*
"The residence was in silence, the hearts in mourning, the Two Great Portals were shut, the courtiers head-on-knee, the nobles in grief"

(b) *Hypotaxis*, i.e. a semantic, rather than syntactic dependency of a sentence on the discourse nucleus. Hypotactically linked clauses are usually introduced by particles such as *jsk*, *jḫr* or *js*; their semantic scope and their pragmatic setting can be properly understood only in reference to the message conveyed in the textual nucleus, as in (85), the passage which in Sinuhe's text immediately follows (90):

(85) Sin. R 11–12 *jst rf zbj.n ḥm=f mšʿ r tꜣ-tmḥj.w zꜣ=f smsw m ḥrj jry*
"Meanwhile, His Majesty had sent off to the land of the Libyans an army whose leader was his elder son"

(c) *Subordination*, i.e. the syntactic dependency of a clause on a higher node, which itself can be a main or a subordinate clause. Subordination is usually signalled by morphological markers such as prepositions (for example *m* "in" > "when") governing nominalized verbal phrases, conjunctions (such as *ḥr-ntt* "because"), or particles (*jr* "if"):

(38) Urk. IV 897,11–13 *rḫ.n(=j) qd=k twj m zšj m wn=k m šms.wt jtj=j*
"I knew your character while still in the nest, when you were in my father's following"

In the absence of an overt marker of dependency, subordination can also be determined by syntactic control. In this case, one speaks of "embedding," as in the case of adverbial or verbal sentences functioning as virtual relative clauses or controlled by a verb of perception:

(66) pKahun 30,30 *gmj.n=j nb=j ʿnḫ.w wḏ3.w snb.w ḫntj=f*
"I found my Lord (may he be alive, prosperous and healthy) travelling southward"

In fact, it is well-known that more explicit devices of clause linkage, such as conjunctions, signal a lower degree of syntactic, pragmatic, or semantic integration than less explicit markers, or no markers at all.[46]

I think that this tridimensional approach can account for most of the uncertainties faced by students of Egyptian in dealing with issues of parataxis vs. hypotaxis.[47] The historical development in later Egyptian is for markers of adverbial hypotaxis to become grammaticalized as introductory particles of a main clause pattern or as signals of syntactic subordination.[48] An example of the former is provided by the evolution of the Present I pattern (section 6.6.1), and of the latter by the grammaticalization of conjugational forms of the verb *wnn* "to be" as converters (past *wn*, prospective *wnn*, nominal *wnn*, and relative *wnn*, *wnn.t*, *wnn.w*, section 7.9) or as conjunction (*wnt* "that").

6.4.2 The proclitic particles jw *and* mk

The most important and complex proclitic particle is *jw*, examples of which we already encountered throughout this chapter.[49] Its semantic scope can be defined as an overt assertion of truth ("truly," "indeed," and the like), i.e. as the explicit positive counterpart to a negative statement (section 6.5); pragmatically, it relates the event described in the verbal or adverbial sentence to the speaker's situation or personal experience – without necessarily implying his direct involvement:

(95) Sin. B 81–84 [Sinuhe describes the beginnings of his stay in Asia and the generosity displayed by the chief of Upper Retjenu. He is allowed to choose for himself the best available land, a place named Yaa]
jw d3b.w jm=f ḥnʿ j3rr.t...jw jtj jm ḥnʿ bd.t
"In it (*m=f*), there were figs (*d3b.w*) together with grapes (*j3rr.t*)...and there was barley (*jtj*) together with emmer (*bd.t*)"

(96) Sin. B 246 [Sinuhe describes his trip back to Egypt, where he and the Asiatics who accompany him are welcomed with gifts which he distributes to his servants]
dm.n=j wʿw jm nb m rn=f jw wdp.w nb ḥr jrj.t=f
"I called (*dm.n=j*) each and everyone there (*wʿw jm nb*) by name (*m rn=f*): every servant (*wdp.w*) was performing his task (*ḥr jrj.t=f* "on his task")"

When compared with other initial particles, however, the complexity of *jw* becomes apparent when we consider its two other uses, which will play a key role in conditioning its functional development in later Egyptian (section 6.6). Unlike other particles, *jw* can also function as mere morphological carrier of the subject pronoun in a bare sentence S => Pronoun + AP, i.e. as semantically and syntactically neutral morpheme which only serves to support the subject of a subordinate adverbial clause. Morphologically, such a sentence will look exactly like an initial main clause introduced by the particle *jw*; syntactically, however, it will appear embedded into the sentential nucleus. We have already encountered this use in examples (75), where *jw* functions as carrier of the third person subject in an unconverted relative clause ("who was coming") – since an interpretation as initial main clause would yield no convincing meaning – and (76), where it introduces the subject of an embedded circumstantial clause ("while he was speaking"). Here are two further examples in which the pronominal subject of an embedded clause (in the first case as a free adverbial adjunct, in the second as object of a verb of perception) is carried by what we might call the "void" *jw*:

(97) Sh.S. 32–33 *ḏʿ prj(.w) jw=n m w3ḏ-wrj*
"A storm (*ḏʿ*) came (*prj.w*) while we were at sea (*w3ḏ-wrj* "the Great Green")"

(98) Sh.S. 72–73 *rḏj=j rḫ=k tw jw=k m ss ḫpr.tj m ntj nj m3.t(w)=f*
"I shall cause (*rḏj=j*) that you find yourself (*rḫ=k tw*) in ashes (*jw=k m ss* "you being in ashes"), having turned into (*ḫpr.tj m*) someone who (*ntj*) cannot be seen"

It will be argued in section 6.6 that this particular function of *jw* is at the root of the functional change this particle experiences in later Egyptian.

We saw in section 5.6 that, in extremely rare cases,[50] *jw* can introduce the subject of an absolute existential sentence[51] consisting only of one element:

(99) CT IV 29e *jw ø sšp ḏd N jw ø knḥ ḏd N*
"'There is light (*sšp*),' says the Deceased. 'There is darkness (*knḥ*),' says the Deceased"

This seems to prove that, at least historically, the origin of *jw* has to be sought in a verbal lexeme indicating existence: "there is," "it happens that," and the like. This lexeme was grammaticalized as a complementizer already in the formative period of the language, leaving only sporadic instances of its earlier, semantically fuller use.

The other frequent initial particle is *mk* "look, behold," which we have already met in many passages above. It too can introduce adverbial, pseudoverbal, or verbal sentences, conveying a "presentative" function (see Hebrew *hinneh*),[52] i.e. relating the event described in the predication not, like *jw*, to the speaker's sphere, but rather to the moment or the situation in which the speech act is performed:

(100) Sh.S. 106–8 "Then the boat fell apart, and of those who were in it no one was left except me *mk wj r-gs=k* and look, I am now by you"

Etymologically, *mk* and its variants fem. *mṯ*, pl. *mṯn* are grammaticalized prospective forms of a verb meaning "to see" followed by a second person suffix pronoun: "may you see."

6.5 Negation in adverbial and pseudoverbal patterns

6.5.1 Negation of adverbial and pseudoverbal sentences

Negative patterns for adverbial and pseudoverbal sentences follow rather closely the syntactic paradigms and the semantic evolution we observed in dealing with nominal sentences (section 5.7). In early periods, the negation of an adverbial sentence was obtained by placing the basic negative particle *nj* before the sentence:

(101) Pyr. 890b *nj sw jr tꜣ jw N jr p.t*
"He is not towards the earth (*tꜣ*): the King is towards heaven (*p.t*)"

In this earliest stage of the language, the scope of the negative particle can also be a sentence introduced by *jw*:

(102) Harhotep 67–68 *nj jw=k m p.t nj jw=k m tꜣ*
"You are not in heaven, you are not on earth"

or the converted counterpart of the adverbial sentence, which we observed in examples (22)–(24) above:

(103) BH I 25,98–99 *nj wnn zꜣ=f ḥr ns.t=f*
"His son will not be (*nj wnn zꜣ=f*) on his seat (*ḥr ns.t=f*)"

But the situation changes in classical Egyptian. While the pattern with the particle *nj* is kept alive in the Middle Kingdom for the negation of adverbial sentences with a topicalized subject resumed by a coreferential independent pronoun in the comment:

(104) Sin. B 185 *sḫr pn jnj n=f jb=k nj ntf m jb(=j) r=k*
"This plan (*sḫr*) which took away to itself (*jnj n=f*) your heart – it was not in my heart against you (*r=k*)"

(105) Sin. B 255 *ḥ3.tj=j nj ntf m ẖ.t=j*
"And my heart (*ḥ3.tj=j*) – it was no longer part of myself (*m ẖ.t=j* "in my body")"

the basic morpheme for the negation of adverbial sentences becomes now the operator of denial *nn*, etymologically the result of the addition of an intensifier to the basic particle *nj* (section 5.7). Rather than simply negate the propositional nexus, the predicative operator *nn* affects the "verifiability" of the state of affairs described in the sentence, which is the reason for the use of this particle in the negation of prospective verbal forms as well (section 6.4). Thus, together with the replacement of the contradictory *nj* by the existential *nn*, classical Egyptian documents the exclusion from the scope of negative adverbial and pseudoverbal sentences of the particle *jw*, i.e. the morpheme which conveys an explicit assertion of truth:

(106) Sh.S. 100–1 *nn wḫ3 m-ḥr-jb=sn* "There was no fool among them"

the negative counterpart of **jw (wn) wḫ3 m-ḥr-jb=sn* "there was a fool among them," or

(107) Sh.S. 131 *nn wj m-ḥr-jb=sn* "I was not among them"

the negative equivalent of a sentence **jw=j m-ḥr-jb=sn* "I was among them."

Similarly, pseudoverbal patterns are also negated by *nn*:

(108) Sh.S. 73–75 *jw mdw=k n=j nn wj ḥr sḏm=s*
"You talk to me (*jw mdw=k*) to me, but I am not hearing it"

(109) Merikare E 48 *m sqr(.w) nn st 3ḫ(.w) n=k*
"Do not kill: it is not useful (*nn st 3ḫ.w*) to you"[53]

These constructions, however, are rare in classical Middle Egyptian, the usual form for the negation of a pseudoverbal construction being a negative verbal form:

(110) Peas. B2,113–14 *mk wj ḥr spr n=k nj sḏm.n=k st*
"Look, I petition you, but you do not hear it"

Only by the end of the classical period, with the syntactic reorganization of the function of *jw*, the pseudoverbal patterns develop full-fledged negative paradigms corresponding to the positive forms *jw=f ḥr sḏm* and *jw=f r sḏm*: *nn sw ḥr sḏm* > *nn jw=f ḥr sḏm* "he is not hearing," *nn sw r sḏm* > *nn jw=f r sḏm* "he will not hear."[54]

(111) Paheri 7 *mt nn jw=j r w3ḥ=t* "Look (*mt*), I am not going to leave you"

6.5.2 Negation of adverbial phrases

Rather than an entire adverbial sentence, however, negation can also invest an adverbial phrase as one of the syntactic constituents of a sentence. As we observed in section 6.3.2, an adverbial phrase can function in Egyptian either as pragmatic focus, enjoying informational prominence within the utterance, or as adverbial adjunct, providing background information for the understanding of the main predication.

(A) If the adverbial phrase represents the pragmatic *focus* of the utterance, negation is conveyed – as in the case of nominal phrases, see section 5.7c – by the morpheme  *nj-js*, which immediately precedes the phrase it refers to, or by its discontinuous counterpart *nj...js*, which wraps the first prosodic unit of the sentence. Rather than the predicative "contradiction" conveyed by the simple *nj*, negative patterns involving *js* indicate "contrariety": the negation does not affect the predicative nexus of the sentence, but is internal to the proposition, the scope of the negation being limited to a *phrase*. The continuous *nj-js* is used with true adverbial phrases involving sharp contrast and is immediately prefixed to the scope of the negation:

(112) Peas. B1,291–92 *jw=k sbꜣ.t(j) jw=k ḥmw.t(j) jw=k t(w)t(.tj) nj-js n ʿwn*
"You are educated, you are skilled, you are accomplished, but not (*nj-js*) for the purpose of (*n*) robbing!"

(113) West. 8,12–17 "Then His Majesty said: 'Is the rumor true that you can join a severed head?' And Djedi answered: 'Yes, I can, O sovereign my Lord.' Then His Majesty said: 'Have a prisoner brought to me from the prison, that he may be executed!' And Djedi said: *nj-js n rmṯ.w* 'Not to people, O sovereign my Lord! Look, it is forbidden to do such a thing to the Noble Cattle'"

Unlike its continuous form *nj-js*, the discontinuous *nj…js* does not follow the positive portion of the sentence, but rather surrounds it, with the particle *js* located before the scope of the negation. Besides being of regular use in the negation of a nominal focus (section 5.7), *nj…js* can refer to simple adverbial phrases:

(114) Pyr. 475b–c *zẖꜣ N m ḏbʿ wrj nj zẖꜣ=f js m ḏbʿ šrr*
"The King writes (*zẖꜣ N*) with a big finger; it is not with a little finger (*m ḏbʿ šrr*) that he writes"

(115) Pyr. 333a–c *mk N prj.w mk N jwj=f nj jw.n=f js ḏs=f jn jpw.wt =ṯn jnj.t sw*
"Look, the King has arrived! Look, the King is coming! But he has not come (*jw.n=f*) by himself (*ḏs=f*): it is your messages (*jpw.wt =ṯn*) that have fetched (*jnj.t*) him!"

or to pseudoverbal and verbal phrases embedded according to the patterns discussed in section 6.3.2: as predicative complement, such as the *sḏm=f* or the stative in (116)–(116'), and of the complementary infinitive in (117):

(116) Pyr. 833a *šm.n=k ʿnḫ=k nj šm.n=k js m(w)t=k*
(116') CT I 187e *šm.n=k ʿnḫ.t(j) nj šm.n=k js m(w)t(.tj)*
"You have gone away alive (*ʿnḫ=k/ʿnḫ.tj*), you haven't gone away dead (*mwt=k/mwt.tj*)"
(117) Pyr. *1947 Nt[b] *nj m(w)t.n=k js m(w)t.t ʿnḫ.n=k ʿnḫ.t m-ʿb=sn j.ḫm.w-sk(j.w)*
"You haven't really (*mwt.t*, section 4.6.4b) died; you have become alive (*ʿnḫ.n=k ʿnḫ.t*) with them – the Imperishable Stars"

or as "virtual" relative clause with circumstantial *sḏm=f*:

(118) CT II 160b–c *nj jnk js wꜣḏ swꜣj=f jnk wꜣḏ prj m nb.t*
"I am not a *wꜣḏ*-amulet which passes by (*swꜣj=f*); I am the *wꜣḏ*-amulet which came forth (*prj*) from mankind"

We observed in section 5.7 the impact of the so-called **O > E** drift,[55] i.e. the tendency for "weak" *contradictory* negations to move toward the "strong" *contrary* pole of semantic oppositions. The same trend is documented in adverbial and pseudoverbal patterns as well: just as the simple *nj* is functionally superseded by its intensified counterpart *nn* in the language of classical literature (section 6.5.1), in non-literary or more recent Middle Egyptian the patterns *nj-js/nj...js* tend to be replaced by *nn-js/nn...js*. Examples of *nn-js* are already found in non-literary texts of the First Intermediate Period (119), and the discontinuous *nn...js* is documented in a Dyn. XVIII copy of a literary text of the Middle Kingdom (120):

(119) Nagʿ ed-Dêr 84, A6–7 "I am successful citizen who lives out of his own wealth *nn-js m gmj.t.n=j m-ʿ jtj=j* and ***not*** out of (*m*) what was bequeathed me by (*gmj.t.n=j m-ʿ* "what I found from") my father (*jtj=j*)"
(120) Pt. 213–14 (L_2) *nn zꜣ=k js pw nn msj.n.tw=f js n=k*
"He is not ***your*** son; he wasn't born (*nn msj.n.tw=f js*) to ***you***"

This evolution leads in later Egyptian (section 6.6.1) to a generalized use of *nn...js* > *bn...jwnꜣ* > ⲛ̄...ⲁⲛ for the negation of all adverbial patterns.

(B) If the negation affects an adverbial adjunct deprived of pragmatic prominence, functioning as background information for the understanding of the main predication, the older phases of earlier Egyptian make use of a negative circumstantial operator *ny*[56] before the embedded verbal phrase:

(121) Pyr. 244b–c *ḫnd.n N ḥr zbn ḥrw ny rḫ=f*
"The King trod (*ḫnd.n N*) unknowingly (*ny rḫ=f*) on the glideway of Horus (*ḥr zbn ḥrw*)."
(122) Urk. I 232,10–11 *sk ḏd.n ḥm=f mry n(j) ḥm(=j) wḏꜣ=f wr.t ny sqr.n=f*
"Meanwhile (*sk*), His Majesty said: 'It is My Majesty's wish (*mry nj ḥm=j* "the-desired-one of My Majesty"[57]) that he be very prosperous (*wḏꜣ=f wr.t*), without having conducted military actions (*ny sqr.n=f* "while-not he-made-warfare")'"

The morpheme *ny* stems from the addition of the morpheme *.y*, i.e. the same element we encountered in the prepositional adverbs and possibly in the ending of the circumstantial forms of the stative, to the negative particle *nj* (sections 4.6.3.1, 5.3.3). In classical Middle Egyptian, the tendency for contradictory negations to acquire contrary functions leads to the obsolescence of *ny* and to its replacement by "strong" constructions with *nn* + Infinitive (when the subject of the embedded AP is coindexed with the subject of the main predication) or with *nj-js* (when the subject of the embedded AP is different):

(123) Sh.S. 16–17 *wšb=k nn njtjt* "You shall answer without hesitating (*nn njtjt*)"

(124) BD 125γ,28 *nn ḏj=n 'q=k ḥr=n j.n bnš.w n(.w) sbꜣ pn nj-js ḏd.n=k rn=n*
"'We shall not let you enter (*nn ḏj=n 'q=k*) through us' – said the jambs of this gate 'unless (*nj-js*) you have pronounced our name'"

In the history of Egyptian, therefore, negative patterns built with the basic morpheme *nj* are exposed to two types of diachronic pressure: morphosyntactically, to the tendency for the simple negative to be replaced by a "reinforced" version (*nj* > *nn*) more likely to acquire predicative status and to function as negative existential operator; semantically, to the tendency for simple propositional contradictories to become focal contraries (*nj* > *nj...js* > *nn...js*). The original negative morpheme *nj* > *bw* will be maintained only in bound verbal constructions.

6.6 Adverbial sentences in later Egyptian

The evolution of adverbial patterns in later Egyptian exhibits three major changes vis-à-vis the classical stage of the language:

6.6.1 *The Present I and its conversions*

The old hypotactic clause controlled by the conjunction *jsk/sk* > *jsṯ/sṯ* > *jst/st* (section 6.4) develops into an initial main sentence introduced by a bare nominal subject or a new series of pronouns resulting from the grammaticalization of the conjunction *sṯ* > *st* > *tj* (section 4.4.2) followed by the adverbial predicate. While its hypotactic origin is evident in the classical language and in its use as circumstantial clause in the Middle Egyptian of Dyn. XVIII:

(125) Sin. R 11–14 "Meanwhile, His Majesty had sent off to the land of the Libyans an army whose leader was his elder son, the good god Sesostris. *tj-sw hꜣb(.w) r ḥwj.t ḫꜣz.wt r sqr jmj.w ṯḥn.w* Now, he had been sent (*tj-sw hꜣb.w*) in order to smite (*r ḥwj.t*) the foreign countries and to punish (*r sqr*) those who are in Tjehenu"

(126) Urk. IV 890, 10–12 *šms.n(=j) nb=j r nmt.wt=f ḥr ḫꜣs.t mḥt.t rsj.t mrj=f jw=j m jrj rd.wj=f(j) tj-sw ḥr prj nḫt.w=f*

"I followed my lord (*šms.n=j nb=j*) in his footsteps in northern (*mḥt.t*) and southern (*rsj.t*) foreign countries, because he wanted (*mrj=f*) me to be following him closely (*jw=j m jrj rd.wj=fj*) while he was (*tj-sw*) in the battlefields of his victories"

(127) Urk. IV 1823, 17–18 *[mꜣ.n]=j kf'=f ḥr p{t}rj jst sw mj mnw rnp.t mḏd-'*
"I saw that he made captures (*kf'=f*) on the battlefield (*prj*), being (*jst sw*) like Min in a year (*rnp.t*, section 6.3.2) of distress (*mḏd-'* "stroke of hand")"

this construction has become in Late Egyptian the paradigmatic pattern for the expression of the main adverbial or pseudoverbal clause, conventionally called the *Present I*.[58] In the construction *ḥr* or *m* + Infinitive, the preposition is kept in Late Egyptian during early Dyn. XIX,[59] but disappears in recent phases. This phenomenon is the result of the final grammaticalization of the pseudoverbal pattern: the preposition has lost its original semantic value completely, and the bare infinitive has now come to build a paradigmatic class with the stative and the "true" adverbial sentence:

(128) Dem. Mag. Pap. 16,26 *twj nw r pꜣ-wyn ẖn tꜣ-st.t n pꜣ-ẖbs*
"I see (*twj nw r*) the light (*pꜣ-wyn*) in (*ẖn*) the flame of the lamp"

(129) 2 Cor 5,1 ⲧⲛ̄ⲥⲟⲟⲩⲛ̄ "We know"

One will recall that the conjunction *sk/sṯ* was followed in classical Egyptian by the nominal subject or by a *dependent* pronoun. Its grammaticalized later Egyptian successor, however, displays the *suffix* pronoun in the first and second persons: **tj-wj* > Late Egyptian *twj* > Coptic ϯ-; masc. **tj-ṯw*, fem. **tj-ṯn* > Late Egyptian *twk*, *twt* > Coptic ⲕ- (see below), ⲧⲉ-; **tj-n* > Late Egyptian *twn* > Coptic ⲧⲛ̄-; **tj-ṯn* > Late Egyptian *twtn* > Coptic ⲧⲉⲧⲛ̄-:

(130) LRL 12,5–6 *twj m šs twj snb.kw* "I am in order, I am healthy"

(131) Horus and Seth 16,2 *twk m nsw nfr* "You are a good king"

In the third person, the Late Egyptian Present I shows a bare specific noun or a bare dependent pronoun (sing. *sw/st*, pl. *st* > ⲥⲉ-), thus appearing to be the morphological heir of the *non-initial* main clause of earlier times:

(132) pAnastasi IV 3,5–6 *nꜣ-nḥsj.w m sẖsẖ r-ḥꜣ.t=k*
"The Nubians (*nꜣ-nḥsj.w*) run (*m sẖsẖ*) in front of you"

(133) pAnastasi II 1,2 *sw r-jwd ḏꜣhꜣ r tꜣ-mrj*
"It (*sw*) lies between (*r-jwd...r*) Palestine and the Beloved Land"

In more recent later Egyptian, i.e. in Demotic and Coptic, the syntax of nominal subjects remains unchanged, but analogical pressures lead in the second person masc. and in the third person sing. forms to the use of the *suffix*, and not the dependent pronoun: *e=k* > ⲕ-, *e=f* > ϥ-, *e=s* > ⲥ-:[60]

(134) Onchsh. 18,11 *nꜣ-ẖrt.w n pꜣ-lḫ mš' n pꜣ-ẖyr*
"The children (*nꜣ-ẖrt.w*) of the fool walk in (*n* < *m*) the street"
(135) Ps 104,7 ⲡⲉϥϩⲁⲡ ϩⲙ̄ ⲡⲕⲁϩ ⲧⲏⲣϥ̄
"His judgment (*pe=f-hap*) is in (*hm*) the entire world (*p-kah têr=f* "the world [in] its entirety")"
(136) 1 Jn 2,8 ϥⲣ̄ ⲟⲩⲟⲉⲓⲛ "He (*f-*) shines (*r ouein* "to make light")"

This concept of "analogical pressures" requires a word of explanation. The later Egyptian morpheme *jw* > Demotic *e* > Coptic *ø* that controls the suffix pronouns is already sporadically found in Late Egyptian texts of the first millennium BCE[61] and represents, together with the introductory morpheme of the so-called Future III (see section 6.6.2), the outcome of the initial particle *jw* discussed in section 6.4.2. This means that this *jw* is *formally*, but not *functionally* identical to the subordinating later Egyptian *jw* > ⲉ- which we will address in section 6.6.3. With the gradual obsolescence of the dependent pronouns and their replacement as indicators of the object of a verbal phrase by morphemes of the *tw*-series (section 4.6.6.5), the use of the classical third person pronouns *sw/st* was progressively restricted: while in Demotic the morphological marker *e=* is still spelled out, in Coptic the suffix pronoun is used, as it were, "absolutely."

The morphological suppletion exhibited in the later Egyptian paradigm of the Present I between the first and second persons, which make use of a pronominal subject derived from the grammaticalization of the particle *tj* followed by a pronoun (*twj/twk ḥr sḏm* > ϯ-ⲥⲱⲧⲙ̄), and the third persons (both nominal and pronominal), which still maintain the bare sentence pattern (*pꜣ-rmt/sw ḥr sḏm* > ⲡⲣⲱⲙⲉ-/ϥ-ⲥⲱⲧⲙ̄), finds an easy historical explanation in our discussion in section 6.4 above. The later Egyptian adverbial sentence, i.e. the Present I, combines in fact the syntactic features of *three* earlier Egyptian patterns (delegating to the lexicon, i.e. mainly to additional particles, the expression of nuances). These three patterns are:

(a) the initial main sentence, introduced in Middle Egyptian by *jw* or *mk*:

(137) Doomed Prince 7,2–3 *ptr twk m-dj=j m šrj*
"Look, you are for me (*m-dj=j* "by me") like a son"

(b) the bare, i.e. "paratactically" annexed non-initial main clause:

(138) pBM 10052, 4,12–14 *ḏd=f... sw wḥm m smtj m ꜣbd 4 šmw sw 10 sw gmy w'b (m) nꜣj-jṯꜣ.w*
"He said: [...] He was questioned again (*sw wḥm m smtj* *"he was repeated in questioning") in the month 4 of the Summer, day 10 and was found (*sw gmy*) innocent (*w'b*, stative controlled by the preceding stative *gmy*, see example 94) of these thefts"

(c) the "hypotactic" adverbial clause:[62]

(139) pMayer A 6,21–23 *ḫr-jr twj m jy r-ḫrj jw=j gm(.t) A B*
"While (*ḫr-jr*) I was going (*twj m jy*) down (*r-ḫrj*), I found (*jw=j gm*, sequential past form) A and B"

In other words, later Egyptian syntax neutralizes the opposition between paratactic and hypotactic linkage in adverbial[63] main clauses: while the morphosyntactic successor of the initial, the non-initial, and the "hypotactic" adverbial clause, the Present I is used in later Egyptian as the *only* adverbial and pseudoverbal main clause pattern.

Relative clauses. This evolution finds an interesting parallel in the morphology of later Egyptian relativization of adverbial sentences. The syntactic behavior of relative clauses does not experience any change in the transition from earlier to later Egyptian: "virtual" relative clauses are still treated as subordinate adverbial clauses (section 6.6.3), while "true" relative clauses are introduced by the relative converter *ntj* (section 6.3.3). By the end of the New Kingdom (eleventh century BCE), however, the morphological patterns of the true relative clause begin to show a very intriguing feature: when introducing a pronominal subject, the converter *ntj* is followed – interestingly enough, at first in the second person masculine and in the third person forms, from Demotic onward in all persons – not by the series *twj, twk, sw,* etc., but by a suffix pronoun supported by *jw*: *ntj twj* > *ntj-jw=j* > ⲉϯ-, *ntj twk* > *ntj-jw=k* > ⲉⲧⲕ̄-, *ntj twt* > *ntj-jw(=t)* > ⲉⲧⲉ-, *ntj sw* > *ntj-jw=f* > ⲉⲧϥ̄-, *ntj st* > *ntj-jw=s* > ⲉⲧⲥ̄-, *ntj twn* > *ntj-jw=n* > ⲉⲧⲛ̄-, *ntj twtn* > *ntj-jw=tn* > ⲉⲧⲉⲧⲛ̄-, *ntj st* > *ntj-jw=w* > ⲉⲧⲟⲩ-.[64] Here again, although this element *jw* is formally identical to the indicator of subordination and has often been taken to be the same morpheme, it represents in fact nothing other than the outcome of the old initial particle further reduced to the role of mere indicator of a vocalic *schwa*, as documented in the transition from Late Egyptian *sw ḥr sḏm* to Demotic *e=f stm* and Coptic ϥⲥⲱⲧⲙ̄ and their relative counterparts *ntj sw ḥr sḏm* > *ntj-e=f stm* > ⲉⲧϥ̄ⲥⲱⲧⲙ̄.

Existential and past converters. In the treatment of nominal sentences, we observed that Egyptian shows a tendency to delegate the expression of the existence of indefinite subjects to verbal sentences in which the predicate is a form of the verb *wnn* "to be" (section 5.6). In later Egyptian, non-specific subjects of adverbial predicates are introduced by the existential predicates *wn* > ⲟⲩⲛ̄- "there is" and *mn* (< *nn-wn-*) > ⲙⲛ̄- "there is not," often combined with the preposition *m-dj* "by, with" (< *m-ʿw* "in the hand of") > ⲟⲩⲛ̄ⲧⲁ= (section 5.10), the use of the Present I being limited to specific subjects:

(140) Wen. 1,58 *jn wn m-dj=f js.t ḫ3rw*
"Does he have (*jn wn m-dj=f* "is there with him") a Syrian crew?"

This morpheme represents the grammaticalization of the aorist *sḏm=f* of the verb *wnn*; it is therefore etymologically related to, but functionally different from the past converter *wn* > ⲛⲉ=/ⲛⲉⲣⲉ-, which turns any adverbial or pseudoverbal (or verbal, see section 7.3) sentence into its preterital counterpart, often called in Coptic grammar "Imperfect":

(141) pBM 10052, 14,18 *wn n3j=w ḫn.w (ḥr) nḥb.t=w*
"Their (*n3j=w*) things (*ḫn.w*) were on their backs (*nḥb.t=w*)"
(142) LRL 2,8 *y3 wn=j mr.kw* "Indeed (*y3*) I was ill"
(143) Jn 2,1 ⲛⲉⲣⲉⲧⲙⲁⲁⲩ ⲛ̄ⲓ̅ⲥ̅ ⲙ̄ⲙⲁⲩ
"The mother (*t-maau*) of Jesus (*n-IS*) was (*nere-*) there (*mmau*)"

The Future I. From Dyn. XX (twelfth century BCE) onward, later Egyptian exhibits a Present I construction in which the preposition *m* is followed by the infinitive of the verb of movement *nʿj* "to go," controlling for its part an infinitival phrase with *r*:

(144) LRL 35,15 *twk rḫ.tj p3j-mšʿ ntj twj m nʿj r jr=f*
"You know this expedition which I am going to do"

This construction is the antecedent of a Demotic and Coptic paradigm, the "Future I" (also called *progressive* or *Instans*),[65] in which a morpheme -ⲛⲁ- is placed between the subject of a Present I construction and the predicate, which can be an infinitive or a stative. In Coptic, this form supersedes the Late Egyptian and Demotic prospective *sḏm=f* for the expression of the temporal (i.e. non-modal) future:

(145) Job 13,17 ϯⲛⲁϣⲁϫⲉ ⲅⲁⲣ ⲉⲧⲉⲧⲛ̄ⲥⲱⲧⲙ̄
"For (γάρ) I shall speak (*ti-na-šaje*) while you listen (*e=tetn-sôtm*)"

6.6.2 The fate of pseudoverbal patterns

The second major evolution in later Egyptian is brought about by the disappearance of the pseudoverbal sentence as an autonomous syntactic category. We observed in the preceding paragraph that the distinction between the true adverbial phrase, the stative, and the prepositional construction *ḥr/m* + infinitive is neutralized in later Egyptian, with all patterns merging in the Present I and in its converted forms. The other pseudoverbal construction of

Middle Egyptian, namely the objective future *jw=f r sdm* (section 4.6.3.1), is integrated into the verbal conjugation, where it bears the label *Future III*:[66]

(146) KRI I 238,14 *jw=j r dj.t jn.tw=f* "I shall cause that it be brought (*jn.tw=f*)"

In spite of its pseudoverbal origin, this form is synchronically treated as a grammaticalized bound pattern: while the preposition *r* is frequently omitted in Late Egyptian, it is usually expressed in Demotic[67] and is mandatory in the parallel Coptic conjugation pattern with pronominal subjects: ⲉ=ϥ-ⲉ-ⲥⲱⲧⲙ̄. This unexpected revival of the preposition begins with increased frequency during Dyn. XXV (around 700 BCE), and is probably due to the need to distinguish between the Future III and the Present I, once the second and third persons of the latter paradigm became expressed by suffix pronouns supported by *jw* (section 6.6.1).

In the presence of nominal subjects, the introductory particle of the Future III is not *jw*, as in its Middle Egyptian ancestor:

(147) Sh.S. 119–20 *jw dp.t r jj.t m ẖnw* "A ship will come from the Residence"

but rather *jr* > Coptic ⲉⲣⲉ-,[68] which is originally a grammaticalized prospective form of the verb *jrj* "to do," reanalyzed as converter and suppletively integrated into the paradigm of the Future III: *jrj pꜣ rmt sḏm* > *jr pꜣ rmt (r) sḏm* "the man will hear":

(148) KRI II 229,4 *jr pꜣ-wr ꜥꜣ n ḫtꜣ dj.t jn.tw=w n N*
"The Great Chief of Hatti (*ḫtꜣ*) will let (*dj.t*) them be brought (*jn.tw=w*) to the King"

Interestingly enough, in the corresponding Coptic pattern ⲉⲣⲉ-ⲡⲣⲱⲙⲉ ⲥⲱⲧⲙ̄ the preposition remains unexpressed:[69]

(149) Ps 19,2 ⲉⲣⲉⲡⲛⲟⲩⲧⲉ ⲥⲱⲧⲙ̄ ⲉⲣⲟⲕ "God (*p-noute*) will listen to you"

One wonders, therefore, whether the rare Late Egyptian writings of the preposition are not in fact hypercorrections due to the merging of two originally different patterns, i.e. the pseudoverbal *jw=f r sḏm* with pronominal subjects and the verbal *jrj pꜣ-rmt sḏm* with nominal subjects, into the suppletive paradigm of the Future III.

On the semantic level, with the progressive obsolescence of the prospective verbal form and its functional replacement through the Future I in later Demotic (section 6.6.1), the Future III acquired in Coptic – where it is also known as "energetic future"[70] – modal features:[71]

(150) Ex 23,7 ⲉⲕⲉⲥⲁϩⲱⲕ ⲉⲃⲟⲗ ⲛ̄ϩⲁⲡ ⲛⲓⲙ ⲛ̄ϫⲓⲛϭⲟⲛⲥ
"You shall distance yourself (*e=k-e-sahô=k*) from (*ebol n-*) any iniquitous judgment (*hap nim n-jincons* "any judgment of doing-evil")"

Following a general trend in Egyptian, the Future III can be preceded by syntactic converters such as the subordinating *jw* (section 6.6.3), the past converter *wn*, and the relative adjective *ntj* (section 6.6.1).

6.6.3 Main vs. subordinate clauses

Thus, from being a marker of discourse *initiality*, the unbound morpheme *jw* has become in later Egyptian a signal of syntactic *dependency*, following a readily retrievable grammaticalization path the origin of which must be sought in the use of *jw* as mere morphological carrier of the pronominal subject of an embedded adverbial clause in classical Egyptian. As we saw above, the direct functional successor of the Middle Egyptian *jw* still survives in the more recent stages of the language, but only in *bound*, i.e. unsegmentable constructions: (a) in the second masculine and third person singular forms of the Demotic and Coptic Present I (section 6.6.1); (b) in the Future III (section 6.6.2); (c) in the so-called "sequential" narrative *jw=f ḥr sdm* "and he heard" (section 4.6.6), which we will consider more closely in section 7.9.3. In these three constructions, *jw* is an integral component of the adverbial or verbal phrase. But as a *free* morpheme, capable of being prefixed to any sentence type, *jw* has become in later Egyptian the indicator of adverbial subordination. When prefixed to an adverbial sentence, the pattern is known as "circumstantial present":

(151) KRI IV 388,4 *ȝbd 2 ȝḫ.t sw 17 jw jpy jw ḫn[sw] ḥr bȝk n pȝ-nb*
"Second month of the Inundation (*ȝbd 2 ȝḫ.t*), day 17, with Ipi and Khonsu working ("while Ipi and Khonsu are working") for the lord"

(152) Two Brothers 15,10–16,1 *ptr twj ʿnḫ.kw m r-ʿ jw=j m kȝ*
"Look (*ptr*), I am still (*m r-ʿ*) alive as a bull (*jw=j m kȝ* "I being as a bull")"

(153) Tob 3,11 ⲁⲩⲱ ⲁⲥⲧⲱⲃϩ ⲉⲥϩⲁϩⲧⲙ̄ ⲡϣⲟⲩϣⲧ
"And (*auô*) she prayed (*a=s-tôbh*) while being (*e=s*) beside (*ha-ht-m*, lit. "under the heart of") the window"

As a subordinate pattern, the circumstantial form competes with its main sentence equivalent, the Present I, in the protasis of hypothetical sentences: initial particles such as *jr*, the more classical morpheme, or *jnn*, the more colloquial one, for "if" control either a Present I (154) or a subordinate clause with *jw* (155), thus offering an example of the decay of the "hypotactic "linkage in later Egyptian (section 6.6.1) and its replacement by main or subordinate clauses:

(154) LRL 69,15–16 *jnn nȝj=k sḥn.w ʿšȝ r=k bn jw=k (r) rḫ šm(.t) m pȝj-sḥn n pr-ʿȝ ʿnḫ wḏȝ snb*

"Even if your orders are too numerous (*'š3*, stative) for you, you will not be able (*bn jw=k r rḫ*, negative Future III, section 6.7) to go away (*šm.t*) from this order of Pharaoh (may he be alive, prosperous and healthy)"

(155) LRL 68, 9–10 *jr jw=k m ṯ3.tj bn jw=j (r) h3j r n3j=k sk.tjw*
"Even if you become vizier (*jw=k m ṯ3.tj* "you are as a vizier"), I will not go down (*bn jw=j r h3j*) to your ships"

Much like the subordinate adverbial sentence of classical Egyptian, the later Egyptian circumstantial present can also be embedded into a syntactic pattern, for example as oblique complement of verbs of perception:

(156) Wen. 2,66 *ptr st jw=w (m) n'j r qbḥ*
"Look at (*ptr*) them as they go (*jw=w m n'j*) toward the coolness (*qbḥ*)"

or as virtual relative clause (section 6.3.3):

(157) Doomed Prince 4,6–8 "Now, after the youth had grown, he went up to his roof, *jw=f ḥr gmḥ w'-ṯsm jw=f m-s3 w'-n sj-'3 jw=f ḥr šm.t ḥr t3-mj.t* and he saw (*jw=f ḥr gmḥ*, sequential past form) a dog which was after (*jw=f m-s3*) an adult (*sj-'3* "big man") who was walking (*jw=f ḥr šm.t*) on the road"

As suggested above, this later Egyptian use of *jw* as indicator of circumstantiality derives from the twofold function of this particle in the classical language (section 6.4.2), namely on the one hand its main function as marker of initiality, and on the other hand its role as syntactically neutral morphological carrier of the pronominal subject in embedded adverbial clauses. It can be argued that this Middle Egyptian use of *jw* was itself the result of a weakening of its original semantic or pragmatic function as an overt signal of the truth value of the predication.[72]

With the reorganization of syntactic patterns leading to the neutralization of the classical opposition between initial and non-initial patterns and the emergence of the Present I and of new unconverted verbal forms (section 7.9.2), this morphological *jw*, the use of which was restricted in Middle Egyptian to subordinate adverbial clauses, was reinterpreted[73] in Late Egyptian as the syntactic marker of the adverbial nature of the sentence. In this way, the morpheme *jw* experienced a transition from its original semantic function ("indeed"), which was predominant in classical Egyptian but was neutralized in subordinate adverbial clauses, where *jw* acted as mere morphological support, to its later Egyptian nature as marker of adverbial subordination: "while." Reanalyzed, therefore, as carrier of subordination, *jw* > ϵ- is freed from its narrow scope in the adverbial clause and extended to all sentence patterns, including nominal sentences, as in (158–159), and verbal sentences, as in (160–161):

(158) pAbbott 6,1–2 "You have rejoiced at the entrance of my house. *yꜣ jḫ jw jnk pꜣ ḥꜣ.tj-ʿ ḏd smj n pꜣ ḥqꜣ ʿnḫ wḏꜣ snb* Why so (*yꜣ jḫ*), since (*jw*) I am the mayor who reports (*ḏd smj* "who says reports") to the Ruler (may he be alive, prosperous and healthy)?"

(159) 2 Cor 8,9 ⲁϥⲣ̄ϩⲏⲕⲉ ⲉⲧⲃⲉ ⲧⲏⲩⲧⲛ̄ ⲉⲩⲣⲙ̄ⲙⲁⲟ ⲡⲉ

"Although (*e-*) he was rich (*ou-rmmao pe*), he became poor (*a=f-r hêke*) for you (*etbe têutn*)"

(160) KRI VI 243,7 *jw=j r dj.t n=f ḫꜣr 2 (jp.t) 3 jw jw=f (r) dj.t ʿnḫ n nb ʿnḫ wḏꜣ snb*

"I shall give him 2 *khar* and 3 *oipe* when (*jw*) he gives (*jw=f r dj.t*) an oath by the lord (may he be alive, prosperous and healthy)"

(161) Mk 16,2 ⲁⲩⲉⲓ ⲉϩⲣⲁⲓ ⲉⲡⲉⲙϩⲁⲟⲩ ⲉⲁⲡⲣⲏ ϣⲁ

"They went up (*a=u-ei ehrai*) to the tomb (*pe-mhaou*) after (*e-*) the sun had risen (*a-p-rê ša*)"

6.7 Later Egyptian negative patterns

We observed in section 6.5 the effects of the so-called **O > E** drift on the development of negative patterns in adverbial sentences: on the one hand, the simple particle *nj* displays the early tendency to be superseded by its reinforced counterpart *nn*; on the other hand, propositional contradictory negations move toward the focal contrary pole, with *nj > nj…js > nn…js*.

The Late Egyptian negative adverbial and pseudoverbal patterns follow this historical model. The Middle Egyptian morphemes *nj* and *nn* are now written <bw> (a morpheme limited to bound verbal phrases, section 7.9.2) and <bn> (the only free negative morpheme in this stage of the language). Adverbial and pseudoverbal sentences, which used to be negated by *nn*, now display the pattern *bn* + Present I:

(162) pDeM 8, 3[74] *bn nꜣj=k jrj jm r-ḏr=w*

"Your colleagues (*nꜣj=k jrj*) are not all of them (*r-ḏr=w*) there (*jm*)"

(163) LRL 34,10–11 "I carried out all my lord's missions and orders which were assigned to me. *bn twj (ḥr) nnj* I am not negligent"

The negative Present I is syntactically analogous to the positive pattern: it too can appear in relative (*ntj*) and adverbial conversions (*jw*):

(164) Doomed Prince 7,8 *jw=s ḥr ḫpr ḥr sꜣw pꜣj=s hꜣj r-jqr sp 2 jw bn sj ḥr dj.t pr=f r-bnr*

"And she began (*ḫpr* "happen") to watch (*sꜣw*) her husband very closely (*r-jqr sp 2* "twice excellently"), without allowing him to go out (*pr=f r-bnr* "that he go out"),"

or in the protasis of a hypothetical sentence (section 6.6.3):

(165) oWien NB, H9[75] *ḫr jr jw bn sw ḥr dj.t=f n=k jw=k ḥr jnj n=j pꜣj=f ḫnk*

"And (*ḫr*) if he does not give it (*dj.t=f*) to you, you bring me (*n=j*) his *ḫnk*"

Negation by means of *bn* is also typical for the Future III. It should be remembered that in Middle Egyptian (section 6.5.1) pseudoverbal patterns do not usually exhibit a specific negative counterpart, but rather use instead the corresponding negative verbal form, which in the case of *jw=f r sḏm* is the prospective *sḏm=f* preceded by *nn*:[76]

(166) pKahun 6,24 *jr grt mꜣn=k ḫ.t ḥr jr.tj=sj nn msj=s r nḥḥ*
"If you detect (*mꜣn=k*, subjunctive) something on her eyes (*jr.tj=sj*), she will never (*r nḥḥ*) bear"

With the syntactic reorganization of the function of *jw* at the end of the classical period, the pseudoverbal patterns develop negative paradigms modeled upon the positive forms:[77] the rare negative pseudoverbal construction *nn sw r sḏm* "he will not hear" is now grammaticalized as *nn jw=f r sḏm*, which supersedes *nn sḏm=f* as the negation of the Future III and represents the direct ancestor of Late Egyptian *bn jw=f/jr pꜣ-rmt (r) sḏm* and of Coptic ⲛ̄ⲛⲉϥⲥⲱⲧⲙ̄:

(167) pBerlin 3038,195 *jr tm.t(w) r=s nn jw=s r msj.t*[78]
"If it doesn't happen to her (*r=s*), she will not bear (*msj.t*)"
(168) pBM 10052, 6,10 *bn jr pꜣj=j sn (r) dj.t mdw.tw m-dj=j*
"My brother will not allow that one interfere (*mdw.tw* "that one talk") with me"
(169) Ex 23,7 ⲛ̄ⲛⲉⲕⲙⲟⲩⲟⲩⲧ ⲛ̄ⲟⲩⲁⲧⲛⲟⲃⲉ ⲙⲛ̄ ⲟⲩⲇⲓⲕⲁⲓⲟⲥ
"You shall not kill (*nne=k-mouout*) an innocent (*at-nobe* "without sin") and (*mn*) a righteous"

A focal adverbial phrase is negated by the operator of contrariety *bn... jwnꜣ*, which is the functional heir of classical Middle Egyptian *nj...js* (> post-classical *nn...js*). The only syntactic difference between the two patterns is that, unlike its Middle Egyptian ancestor *js*, the Late Egyptian reinforcer *jwnꜣ* usually follows the negated focal element:

(170) pMayer A 3,25 *bn wn=f jrm=j jwnꜣ* "He was not *with me*"
(171) LRL 49,1 *rmt ø jw bn ꜥꜣ=f m-dj=f jwnꜣ*
"He is a man without any experience at all," lit. "who does not have (*jw bn... m-dj=f*, virtual relative clause) his maturity (*ꜥꜣ=f*) at all (*jwnꜣ*)"

The later development follows predictable lines: the contrary negation with *bn...jwnꜣ* will progressively invade the domain of the simple particle *bn* and will become in Coptic (ⲛ̄...ⲁⲛ) the paradigmatic negative form of all adverbial and pseudoverbal patterns, i.e. of the Present and Future I and their conversions, which supersede all adverbial negations of earlier times:[79]

(172) Jn 9,21 ⲛ̄ⲧⲛ̄ⲥⲟⲟⲩⲛ̄ ⲁⲛ "We (*tn-*) do not (*n...an*) know (*sooun*)"

(173) 1 Cor 9,20 ⲁⲓϣⲱⲡⲉ ⲛ̄ⲛⲉⲧϩⲁ ⲡⲛⲟⲙⲟⲥ ϩⲱⲥ ⲉⲓϩⲁ ⲡⲛⲟⲙⲟⲥ ⲉⲛϯϣⲟⲟⲡ ⲁⲛ ⲁⲛⲟⲕ ϩⲁ ⲡⲛⲟⲙⲟⲥ
"To those who (*nnet-*) are under the Law (νόμος), I have become (*a=i-šôpe*) like (*hôs*) one who is (*e=i-*, lit. "in that I am") under the Law, although I (*ti-*) myself (*anok*) am not (*e-n... an*) under to the Law"

Finally, the negative particle ⲛ̄- is often omitted and the reinforcing ⲁⲛ is kept as the only carrier of negative value (section 5.11):[80]

(174) Job 27,6 ϯⲥⲟⲟⲩⲛ̄ ⲅⲁⲣ ⲁⲛ ⲙ̄ⲙⲟⲓ ⲉⲁⲓⲣ̄ ϩⲱⲃ ⲉⲙⲉϣϣⲉ
"For I am not aware that I did improper things," lit. "I do not know (*t=i-sooun an*) myself (*mmoi*) having done (*e-a=i-r*) improper things (*e-me-šše*)"

Further reading

Collier, M. "Predication and the circumstantial *sḏm(.f)/sḏm.n(.f)*," *Lingua Aegyptia* 2 (1992), 17–65.

Graefe, E. *Mittelägyptische Grammatik für Anfänger* (Wiesbaden: Harrassowitz, fourth edn 1994), 47–53.

Loprieno, A. "On the typological order of constituents in Egyptian," *Journal of Afroasiatic Languages* 1 (1988), 26–57.

Polotsky, H. J. *Grundlagen des koptischen Satzbaus.* American Studies in Papyrology XXVII–XXIX (Atlanta: Scholars' Press, 1987–90), 203–60.

Vernus, P. "Le rhème marqué: typologie des emplois et effets de sens en Moyen Egyptien," *Lingua Aegyptia* 1 (1991), 333–55.

7

Verbal syntax

7.1 Introduction

The treatment of verbal phrases has experienced an ironical dichotomy in contemporary Egyptological linguistics: on the one hand, the variety of morphological forms and semantic functions has been analyzed in detail for all the phases of the language;[1] on the other hand, the dominant approach to the study of Egyptian syntax, the so-called "Standard theory," has downplayed the role of the "verbal phrase" (VP) as a syntactic category, viewing most of the instances in which a verbal form appears in an Egyptian text as *conversions* of the verb into the syntactic functions of a noun phrase (NP), an adjective phrase (AdjP), or an adverbial phrase (AP).[2] The study of verbal phrases as predicate of the sentence, therefore, has played a relatively minor role in Egyptological linguistics from the late sixties onward, being rather superseded by a syntax of verbal forms in non-verbal functions.

This approach, however, has been challenged in recent years and is now being replaced by more verbalistic accounts of Egyptian syntax (section 6.2). The fundamental contribution of the Standard theory to our understanding of Egyptian syntax remains the recognition of the extreme functional versatility of Egyptian VPs when compared with their equivalents in European languages: while in most syntactic environments verbal forms do keep their function as clausal predicate, they also exhibit a proclivity to be embedded into syntactically higher units. We have already considered the use of a participial VP in the focalized cleft sentence in section 5.4 and the conversion of a VP into an adverbial phrase in section 6.3.2. Egyptian verbal phrases can also be embedded via topicalization (section 7.5) or relativization (section 7.7). Here, the subordinate character of the VP is signalled by the use of morphologically distinct patterns, namely the so-called "emphatic" and "relative" forms respectively. Verbal phrases can also appear embedded as noun phrases when governed by a verb of perception (for example *mꜣꜣ* "to see"), of wish (*mrj* "to desire"), or of command (*wḏ* "to order") (section 7.6). Egyptian verbal phrases, therefore, can appear in the following syntactic environments:

(a) the independent verbal sentence (section 7.2);
(b) the initial and the non-initial main clause (section 7.3);
(c) the embedded adverbial clause and the virtual relative clause (section 7.4);
(d) the sentence with topicalized predicate (section 7.5);
(e) the object clause of a verb of perception, wish, or command (section 7.6);
(f) the "true" relative clause (section 7.7).

Finally, we shall consider the impact of negation on verbal patterns (section 7.8) as well as the evolution of verbal syntax in later Egyptian (section 7.9).

My analysis offers no separate treatment of interrogative sentences.[3] The reason is that any nominal, adverbial, pseudoverbal, or verbal sentence type can be converted without any syntactic change into a YES-NO interrogative sentence by prefixation of the particle *jn*, i.e. the same "ergative" morpheme found in the structure of independent pronouns (section 4.4.1), as marker of the agent of a passive predicate (section 4.6.3.3), and in the cleft sentence (section 5.4.2).[4]

7.2 The independent verbal sentence

We saw above (section 4.6.3) that classical Egyptian possesses a verbal system of the VSO-type which conveys through infixes oppositions of tense, aspect, mood, and voice. A basic syntactic environment of a verbal form is the independent verbal sentence, in which a VP predicate can function alone as nucleus of the sentence (section 6.4), without being necessarily accompanied by adverbial adjuncts. Independent verbal sentences tend to become rarer in the history of Egyptian: while in Old Egyptian this pattern still displays a variety of forms, ranging from the indicative *sḏm=f* in the third person and the stative in the first person in the preterite tense (1–2) to the subjunctive *sḏm=f* and the prospective *sḏm(.w)=f* in the future tense (3–4), its use in the classical language appears confined, except for a few literary remnants (5), to the modal forms imperative and prospective (6–7), the narrative use of the infinitive (8), and the contingent tenses (9–11):

(1) Urk. I 221,10 *r[ḏj] n(=j) ḥm=f nbw.w ʿnḫ.w t? ḥnq.t*
"His Majesty (*ḥm=f*) gave (*rḏj*) me gold objects, life amulets, bread and beer"

(2) Urk. I 140,8 *qrs.k(j) zj pn m jz=f mḥj nḫb*
"I buried (*qrs.kj*) this man in his tomb (*jz=f*) to the north of Nekheb"

(3) Pyr. 1161b^{P} *j.nḏ.tj=f* "Let him be greeted"

(4) Urk. I 39,17–40,1 *jn mrj=ṯn rʿw dwꜣ=ṯn nṯr nb n N*
"Will you love (*jn mrj=ṯn*) the Sun God? (Then) you should worship (*dwꜣ=ṯn*), every god (*nṯr nb*) for the King"

(5) Sin. B 114 *ḏd.k(w) nj rḫ=j sw*
"I said (*ḏd.kw*): I do not (*nj*) know him"

(6) Pyr. 259b *N pj sḏm N pj wn jm*
"O King (*N pj*), listen! O King, be (*wn*) there (*jm*)!"

(7) CT I 81a–b *j.gr.w zp 2 rmṯ.w sḏm zp 2 rmṯ.w*
"Be silent (*j.gr.w*, imperative plural), be silent (section 2.3), O men! Listen, listen, O men!"

(8) Sin. B 4–5 *rdj.t wj jmj.t(w) bꜣ.tj r jrj.t wꜣ.t šmw=s*
"I put myself (*rdj.t wj* "putting me," narrative infinitive, section 4.6.4) between two bushes (*bꜣ.tj*), in order to make road (*jrj.t wꜣ.t*) for someone to travel (*šmw=s* "its [the road's] goer")"

(9) Peas. B1,33–34 *ḏd.jn sḫ.tj pn jry=j hzj.t=k*
"Then the peasant (*sḫ.tj pn*) said (*ḏd.jn*, contingent tense *sḏm.jn=f*): I shall do (*jry=j*, prospective *sḏm=f*) what you wish (*hzj.t=k*, prospective relative form, section 7.7)"

In colloquial and post-classical Middle Egyptian, the contingent form is replaced by a converted construction with the *sḏm.jn=f* of the verb *wnn* followed by a verbal (10) or pseudoverbal clause (11) as grammatical subject of the contingent tense:[5]

(10) Peas. Bt 35 *wn.jn ḫnn sdb=f ḥr mw npnp.t=f ḥr jtj-šmʿw*
"And so its fringe touched (*ḫnn sdb=f ḥr*) the water, its hem the upper Egyptian barley"

(11) West. 6,1 *wn.jn jb n(j) ḥm=f qb(.w)*
"Then His Majesty's heart (*jb nj ḥm=f*) became refreshed (*qb.w*, stative, section 6.1)."

In these sentences, the VP exhaustively contains a segment of discourse: as in the case of nominal or adjectival sentences, initiality is here an inherent feature of the verbal pattern without recourse to an introductory particle. Therefore, when an initial particle such as *mk* appears, for example before a prospective *sḏm=f*, it does not represent a required syntactic complementizer, but fulfills a merely lexical function:

(12) Heqanakhte 2,29 *mṯn jry=j šmw ʿꜣ*
"Look (*mṯn*), I will spend (*jry=j*) the summer here"

Like all initial patterns, the independent verbal sentence may be followed by a paratactic non-initial main clause, for example the subjunctive in (13), or control an embedded subordinate clause, as in (14):

(13) Sin. B 199 *mḥ ḥr ḫꜣ.t jw.t=k*
"Think (*mḥ*) of the corpse, and come back (*jw.t=k* "you will come back")!"

(14) Sin. B 45–46 *ḏd.k(w) r=j n=f wšb=j n=f*
"As for me (*r=j*), I replied him (*ḏd.kw n=f wšb=j n=f* "I said to him in-that-I-answer him")"

7.3 Initial vs. non-initial main clauses

In treating the adverbial sentence, we observed that the presence or absence of an introductory particle such as *jw* "truly" or *mk* "look" is the syntactic feature which discriminates between initial and non-initial main clauses: while the sentence *jw ẖnw m sgr* "the residence was in silence" occupies the first position in a chain of discourse, the clause *jb.w m gmw* is paratactically linked to the preceding context: "(and) the hearts were in mourning" (section 6.4).

A similar distinction applies to verbal sentences.[6] The modal *sḏm=f* can be used indiscriminately as an initial and a non-initial form,[7] but when the predicate of a verbal sentence is an aorist *sḏm=f* (active)/ *sḏm.tw=f* (passive) or a past *sḏm.n=f* (active)/ *sḏm(.w)=f* (passive), the distribution is identical to that of adverbial and pseudoverbal patterns:

A. The sentence pattern "Particle + VP" is an initial main clause:

(15) Sh.S. 73–75 *jw mdw=k n=j nn wj ḥr sḏm st*
"You speak (*mdw=k*) to me, but I am not hearing it (section 6.5.1)"

(16) Sin. B 181 *mk jnj.t(w) n=k wḏ pn n(j) nzw*
"Look, this royal order is being brought (*jnj.tw*) to you (*n=k*)"

(17) Sh.S. 81–82 *jw wpj.n=f r3=f r=j jw=j ḥr ẖ.t=j m-b3ḥ=f*
"He opened (*wpj.n=f*) his mouth towards me while I was (*jw=j*, section 6.4.2) on my belly (*ḥr ẖ.t=j*) in front of him (*m-b3ḥ=f*)"

(18) CT II 201a B₁₇C *jw rḏj.w n=k ṯ3w jw wḏ(.w) ø n 3b.t=k tn*
"Breath has been given (*rḏj.w ṯ3w*) to you, an order has been issued (*wḏ.w ø* "it has been ordered")[8] to this family of yours (*3b.t=k tn*)"

Besides *jw* and *mk*, Middle Egyptian initial verbal clauses can be introduced by particles derived from the grammaticalization of the *sḏm=f* or, more frequently, the *sḏm.n=f* of particular verbs.[9] The most important of these particles is *ʿḥʿ.n(=f)* "then," originally the grammaticalized preterite of the verb *ʿḥʿ* "to stand."[10] The third person pronominal subject is usually omitted under relevance (section 6.3.3):

(19) Sh.S. 76–77 *ʿḥʿ.n rḏj=f wj m r3=f*
"Then he placed (*rḏj=f*) me in his mouth"

(20) Peas. R8.1 *ʿḥʿ.n zš.n=f sw ḥr zm3-t3 n(j) r3-w3.t*
"Then he spread it out (*zš.n=f sw*) on the interment (*zm3-t3*) at the edge of the road"

(21) West. 5,13 *ʿḥʿ.n jrj(.w) ø mj wḏ.t nb.t ḥm=f*
"Then it was done (*jrj.w ø*, passive *sḏm.w=f* with omission of the subject under relevance, sections 6.2, 6.3.3) according to (*mj*) everything his Majesty had commanded (*wḏ.t nb.t ḥm=f*, relative form, section 7.7)"

While not used with adverbial patterns, the particle *ʿḥʿ.n* is frequently found in pseudoverbal sentences with the stative (22) or with *ḥr* + Infinitive

(23), which in post-classical Middle Egyptian[11] tends to periphrastically replace the synthetic *sḏm.n=f*:

(22) Sh.S. 39–41 *'ḥ'.n=j rdj.kw r jw jn wꜣw n(j) wꜣḏ-wrj*
"Then I was brought (*'ḥ'.n=j rdj.kw*) to the island by (*jn*, section 4.6.3.3) a wave of the sea"

(23) Urk. IV 2,12 *'ḥ'.n=j ḥr jrj.t w'w r-ḏbꜣ=f m pꜣ jmw n pꜣ smꜣ m hꜣw nb-tꜣ.wj nb-pḥtj-r'w mꜣ'-ḫrw*
"Then I became a soldier (*'ḥ'.n=j ḥr jrj.t w'w*) in his stead on the ship (*jmw*) 'The Raging Bull (*pꜣ smꜣ*)' in the time of the Lord of the Two Lands (*nb-tꜣ.wj*) Nebpehtire, justified (*mꜣ'-ḫrw*)"

B. When not introduced by an initial particle, the bare verbal sentence – i.e. the bare active *sḏm=f/sḏm.n=f* and their passive counterparts *sḏm.tw=f* and *sḏm(.w)=f* – functions as non-initial main clause, paratactically linked to the preceding section of discourse. This pattern is very common in past contexts, where the bare *sḏm.n=f* sets forth the rhythm of narration, as in example (24), but is much less frequent with the aorist *sḏm=f*, such as *psj=f* in (25).

(24) Sin. B 5–9 *jrj.t=j šm.t m ḫnt.yt nj kꜣ(=j) spr r ẖnw pn ḫmt.n=j ḫpr hꜣ'.yt nj ḏd=j 'nḫ(=j) r-sꜣ=f nmj.n=j mꜣ'.tj m hꜣ.w nh.t zmꜣ.n=j m jw-snfrw*
"I made a journey (*jrj.t=j šm.t*, narrative infinitive) southward (*m ḫnt.yt* "against the river flow"), and I did not plan (*nj kꜣ=j*, section 7.8) to reach (*spr r*) the residence; I thought (*ḫmt.n=j*, non-initial main verbal clause) that there would be (*ḫpr*) turmoil and I did not expect to survive (*nj ḏd=j 'nḫ=j* "I did not say that I would live") after it; I crossed (*nmj.n=j*, non-initial main verbal clause) the lake Maaty in the Sycamore neighborhood, and I arrived (*zmꜣ.n=j*, non-initial main verbal clause) at Snefru Island"

(25) Sin. B 26–27 *'ḥ'.n rdj.n=f n=j mw psj=f n=j jrṯ.t*
"Then he gave me water (*mw*) and boiled (*psj=f*) for me milk (*jrṯ.t*)"

Rather, the aorist *sḏm=f* is used when the subject of the sentence is topicalized and resumed by a coreferential pronoun in the verbal phrase; in this case too we observe a contrast between the initial construction "*jw*-Topic+VP" on the one hand (26) and the non-initial main clause "Topic+VP" (27) or the hypotactic clause "particle-Topic+VP" (28) on the other:

(26) Sh.S. 17–19 *jw rꜣ n(j) zj nḥm=f sw jw mdw=f ḏj=f ṯꜣm n=f ḥr*
"A man's mouth (*rꜣ nj zj*) saves (*nḥm=f*) him, his speech (*mdw=f*) causes (*ḏj=f*) him to be forgiven (*ṯꜣm n=f ḥr*, lit. "that the face be veiled for him")"

(27) Sin. B 109–14 "Then, a hero of Retjenu came, and he challenged me in my tent. He was a winner without peer, who had subdued it all. He said that he would duel me, and he thought that he would ransack me: he meant to plunder my cattle under the counsel of his tribe. *ḥqꜣ pf nḏnḏ=f ḥn'=j* But the ruler (*ḥqꜣ pf*) conferred (*nḏnḏ=f*) with me"

(28) Sin. R 11–16 "Meanwhile, His Majesty had sent off to the land of the Libyans an army whose leader was his elder son, the good god Sesostris. Now, he had been sent in order to smite the foreign countries and to punish those of Tjehenu, *tj-sw ḥm jj=f jnj.n=f sqr.w-ʿnḫ n(.w) ṯḥn.w mnmn.t nb.t nn ḏrw=s smr.w n.w stp-sꜣ hꜣb=sn r gs jmn.tj r rḏj.t rḫ zꜣ-nzw sšm ḫpr m ʿḫnw.tj* and now he (*tj-sw*, hypotactic particle + topicalized subject) was returning (*jj=f*, non-initial verbal clause) having brought (*jnj.n=f*, verbal phrase embedded as AP) prisoners of the Tjehenu and all kinds of cattle beyond number (*nn ḏrw=s* "[which] there was not its limit"). The officials of the palace (*smr.w n.w stp-sꜣ*, topicalized subject) sent (*hꜣb=sn*, non-initial verbal clause) to the western border in order to inform the King's son (*rḏj.t rḫ zꜣ-nzw* "to let the King's son know") about the event that had occurred at court"

The constructions "Topic+*sḏm=f*" and "Topic+stative" represent common patterns for the topicalization of any argument of a verbal or pseudoverbal predicate. While the subject is obviously the most likely argument to undergo such a pragmatic movement, because of its higher discourse predictability and relevance,[12] instances of topicalization of the object (29) or of an adjunct (30) do occur; in all these instances, the topic is resumed by a coreferential pronoun in the main clause:

(29) Sh.S. 10–11 *mk rf n jj.(wj)n m ḥtp tꜣ=n pḥ=n sw*
"Look (*mk*), we have arrived (*n jj.wjn*, pseudoverbal sentence) in peace; our land (*tꜣ=n*) – we have reached it"

(30) Adm. 7,4 *mṯn sštꜣ n(j) tꜣ ḫmm ḏr.w=f sḥꜣ.w*
"Look, the unknown (*ḫmm*) secret of the land – its limits (*ḏr.w=f*) have been revealed (*sḥꜣ.w*)"

In this respect, the structure of the pattern "(Particle-)Topic+*sḏm=f*," rather than to the simple adverbial or pseudoverbal sentence of the type S => (Particle-)Subj+Pred as held by the Standard theory,[13] is to be equated to the *topicalized* adverbial sentence with extraposition of an argument different from the subject (section 6.2)[14] – the initial subject being the "default" topic of a sentence – and the *topicalized* nominal sentence often introduced by *jr* (section 5.2.1):[15] in all these three patterns, the topicalized argument is dislocated to the left of a main clause (verbal, adverbial, or nominal) and resumed by a coreferential element.

It should be observed that in the classical language, subject topicalization is not licensed with the preterital forms *sḏm.n=f* (active) and *sḏm(.w)=f* (passive). While in the case of the latter the restriction is due to the fact that, when the subject of a passive preterital form is topicalized, the pseudoverbal "perfect" with the stative is used instead:

(31) Sin. B 307–8 *jw twt=j sḫr(.w) m nbw* "My statue was overlaid with gold"

rare examples of *jw=f sḏm.n=f* are still documented in the Old Egyptian and in the Coffin Texts:

(32) CT I 74i *jw wp-wꜣ.wt wpj.n=f n=f wꜣ.wt nfr.(w)t*
"Wepwawet has opened (*wpj.n=f*) for him the good ways"

The obsolescence of this pattern in standard Middle Egyptian may have been caused by the universal tendency of preterites to organize the flow of discourse around the *action*, or better the nexus between the action itself and its agent, rather than around the subject, which for its part tends to acquire pragmatic prominence with predicates conveying a *state*.[16] Thus, if in a preterital frame the discourse attention is directed towards the subject, the result is not a topicalization, but rather a *focalization*, which is achieved by "cleaving" the subject and demoting the predicate to the role of presupposition (section 5.4.2). In Old Egyptian, the predicate of a cleft sentence can still be a finite verbal form:[17]

(33) Pyr. 1428d–e[M] *nj rḫ N mꜢw.t=f tpj.t rḫ.t.n=f jn nw.t msj.n=s N ḥnꜥ wsjr*
"The King does not know (*nj rḫ N mꜢw.t=f*) his initial mother (*mꜢw.t=f tpj.t*) whom he used to know: it is Nut (*jn nw.t*) who has given birth (*msj.n=s*) to the King together with Osiris"

whereas Middle Egyptian generalizes the use of the participial statement as the only cleft sentence pattern. The passage above from the "Pyramid Texts" as transmitted in King Pepi's pyramid already exhibits the participial cleft sentence (*jn nw.t msj.t*):

(33') Pyr. 1428d–e[P] *nj rḫ N pn mꜢw.t=f tpj.t rḫ.t.n=f jn nw.t msj.t N pn ḥnꜥ wsjr*

We will discuss in sections 7.5.1–3 the devices displayed by Egyptian verbal syntax for the pragmatic focalization of arguments other than the subject.

7.4 Verbal clauses embedded as adverbial phrases

In section 6.4, we established a tripartite distribution of linkage patterns: *parataxis* as a linkage between juxtaposed main clauses, *hypotaxis* as a textual, rather than syntactic dependency of a clause on the main discourse unit, and *subordination* as the syntactic dependency of a clause on the main sentence, whereby *embedding* represents a form of subordination not signalled by morphological markers. As we observed in the two preceding chapters, Egyptian syntax makes abundant use of embedding: nominal, adverbial and pseudoverbal sentences which otherwise function as main clauses, can also appear "embedded," i.e. controlled by a higher syntactic node.

Predictably, this possibility of being syntactically embedded into a higher syntactic unit also applies to verbal sentences. Let us consider the following narrative sequence from the tale of Sinuhe, which immediately follows the passage given in example (25) above:

(34) Sin. B 9–11 *wrš.n=j m ʿḏ n(j) sḫ.t ḥḏ.n=j wn hrww ḫpj.n=j zj ʿḥʿ m r3-w3.t tr.n=f wj snḏ.n=f*
"I spent the day (*wrš.n=j*) at the border of the field. I set forth at dawn (*ḥḏ.n=j* *"I dawned") when it was day (*wn hrww*), and I encountered (*ḫpj.n=j*) a man standing at the edge of the road: he greeted (*tr.n=f*) me in fear (*snḏ.n=f* "he feared")"

While the forms *wrš.n=j, ḥḏ.n=j, ḫpj.n=j*, and *tr.n=f* are non-initial main clauses paratactically linked to the independent verbal sentence *jrj.t=j šm.t m ḫnt.yt* "I made a journey southward" which opens the narrative sequence in Sin. B 5, the two verbal forms *wn hrww* "when it was day" (aorist *sḏm=f*) and *snḏ.n=f* "he feared" (*sḏm.n=f*), although morphologically identical to their main clause equivalents, do not provide narrative foreground information; rather, they supply additional background information to the predicate and function, therefore, as adverbialized VP. In Egyptological literature, the use of VP embedded as AP is usually called "circumstantial" *sḏm=f, sḏm.n=f*, or passive *sḏm(.w)=f*. As suggested in section 6.3.2, the Standard theory did not fully recognize the opposition between non-initial *main* clauses and embedded *subordinate* clauses, considering all non-initial *sḏm=f* and *sḏm.n=f* forms circumstantial, i.e. functionally adverbial. But the difference between paratactically linked main clause and subordinate dependent clause lies in their temporal and aspectual setting: the predicate of the former is a foreground main tense ("I set forth at dawn," "he greeted," etc.), whereas the latter exhibits a background dependent tense which does not modify the flow of events, but only the predicative node it refers to ("when it was day," "since he was afraid," etc.).

One of the functions of an embedded adverbial clause in Egyptian is that of modifying a non-specific noun, i.e. of serving as "virtual" relative clause (section 6.3.3), "true," i.e. converted relative clauses being limited to specific antecedents. It is not surprising, therefore, that a verbal sentence with bare *sḏm=f* or *sḏm.n=f* can be embedded in such an environment:

(35) Peas. B1,262–63 *m ʿwn(.w) ḥwrw ḥr ḫ.t=f fn rḫ.n=k sw*
"Do not rob (*ʿwn*) a pauper (*ḥwrw*) of his things, a weakling (*fn*) whom you know"

In the following example, different types of embedded sentences share the function of unconverted relative clause:

(36) West. 6,26–7,2 *jw wn nḏs ḏdj rn=f ḥmsj=f m ḏd snfrw mꜣʿ-ḫrw jw=f m nḏs n(j) rnp.t 110*
"There is (*jw wn*, section 5.6) a well-off citizen (*nḏs*) whose name is Djedi, who lives in Djed-Snefru-the-Justified and whose age is 110 years"

The three sentences "whose name is Djedi," "who lives in Djed-Snefru-the-Justified," and "whose age is 110 years," modify the non-specific antecedent *nḏs* and are, therefore, unconverted relative clauses controlled by the NP "a well-off citizen." In spite of the fact that the first sentence is nominal (*ḏdj rn=f* "his name is Djedi"), the second verbal (*ḥmsj=f m*... "he lives in..."), and the third adverbial (*jw=f m nḏs*... *"he is as a citizen..."), they all function as "virtual" relative clauses modifying their respective nominal antecedents.

Embedded relative clauses frequently occur in the pattern *jnk* + [NP]/ø + $[VP]_{AP}$ "I am a NP/someone who [VP]":[18]

(37) CT VI 162q *jnk nb mꜣʿ.t mrj=f nfr.t*
"I am a truthful one (*nb mꜣʿ.t* "possessor of truth") who loves (*mrj=f*) goodness"

(38) CT VII 479k–l *jnk spd=f p.t jnk sḫm=f m kkw*
"I am someone who restores (*spd=f*) heaven, I am someone who has power (*sḫm=f*) over darkness"

In these sentences, the aorist *sḏm=f* is circumstantially embedded as virtual relative clause modifying the antecedent, which is overt in example (37) (*nb mꜣʿ.t* "a truthful one"), but omitted under relevance in (39) (ø "someone"). Since it refers to a non-specific antecedent, whether overt or omitted, the resumptive pronoun is always in the third person (*spd=f, sḫm=f*). This pattern, therefore, is different both from a similar construction in which the entire verbal (39) or adverbial clause (40) is nominalized as the predicate of a specifying nominal sentence (section 5.2.2), since in this case the verbal or adverbial clause does not modify a nominal antecedent, but rather constitutes by itself the nominal predicate of the sentence:

(39) CT III 386b S_1C^a *jnk mrr=f-jrr=f jtj nṯr.w*
"I am He-who-acts-when-he likes (balanced sentence *mrr=f-jrr=f* "he-likes-he-acts," section 7.5), the gods' father"

(40) CT V 259c *jnk rd=f-r-p.t ʿ=f-r-tꜣ*
"I am He-whose-foot-is to-heaven (*rd=f r p.t* "his foot is towards heaven"), He-whose-arm-is to-earth (*ʿ=f r tꜣ* "his arm is towards earth")"

and from the prospective cleft sentence (section 5.4.2), in which the focalized independent pronoun is extraposed and resumed by a *coreferential* suffix pronoun in the main clause. In this latter construction, the pronoun does not resume a non-specific antecedent, but rather it refers back to the extraposed specific focus:

(41) pKahun 28,27 *jnk rḏj=j jrj.tw=f n=k*
"It is I (*jnk*) who will cause (*rḏj=j*) that it be done (*jrj.tw=f*) for you (*n=k*)"

7.5 The verbal sentence with topicalized predicate

7.5.1 General characteristics

One of the most striking features of the Egyptian verbal system, first discovered by H. J. Polotsky[19] and eventually raised to the role of keystone of the "Standard theory"[20] which is derived from Polotsky's work, is the possibility for verbal phrases to be topicalized so as to occupy the clause initial position. This phenomenon of topicalization of an entire predicative phrase consisting of the verbal form accompanied by its arguments occurs in three syntactic environments:

(a) Most frequently when the topicalized predicate is the *theme* of a focalized adverbial adjunct:[21]

(42) West. 12,21 *ḥnw.t=j jrr=ṯ pꜣ jb ḥr-m*
"O my mistress (*ḥnw.t=j*), why (*ḥr-m* "on what") are you in this mood (*jrr=ṯ pꜣ jb* "you make this heart")?"

(43) Peas. B1,298–99 *ntk ḥmw n(j) tꜣ r-ḏr=f sqdd tꜣ ḫft wḏ=k*
"You (*ntk*, section 5.2.2) are the rudder (*ḥmw*) of the entire world; it is by your command (*ḫft wḏ=k*) that the land sails (*sqdd tꜣ*)"

(b) When the topicalized predicate provides a clausal *topic* dislocated to the left of the main sentence, creating a semantically correlative pattern.[22] The main sentence acting as *comment* of the topicalized VP can be verbal (44), adverbial (45), or nominal (46):

(44) CT III 24a–25b B_2Bo *hꜣꜣ=sn r tꜣ m ḥfꜣw.w hꜣy=j m qꜣb.w=sn prr=sn r p.t m bjk.w pr(y)=j ḥr ḏnḥ.w=sn*
"If they go down (*hꜣꜣ=sn*) to the earth as snakes, I shall go down (*hꜣy=j*, prospective) in their coils; if they go up to heaven as falcons, I shall go up on their wings"

(45) CT III 100h–101b *prr=sn r p.t m bjk.w jw=j ḥr ḏnḥ.w=sn hꜣꜣ=sn r tꜣ m ḥfꜣw.w jw=j ḥr qꜣb.w=sn*
"If they go up to heaven as falcons, I am on their wings (*jw=j ḥr ḏnḥ.w=sn*); if they go down to the earth as snakes, I am on their coils"

(46) CT VI 295s–96c B_1Bo *pꜣ.n N pn m bjk sbk pw N pn ngg.n N pn m bjk sbk pw N pn spꜣ.n N pn m gbgꜣ jnpw pw N pn nb qrs.t*
"Since the deceased (*N pn*) flew up (*pꜣ.n*) as a falcon, the Deceased is Sobek; since the deceased screeched (*ngg.n*) as a falcon, the deceased is Sobek; since the deceased flew (*spꜣ.n*) as a vulture, the deceased is Anubis, lord of the tomb"

(c) In headings of chapters, where the entire text of the spell functions in fact as comment of the topicalized predicate:[23]

(47) CT III 204a *jrr zj mrr.t=f m ḫr.t-nṯr*
"[This spell describes] how a man does (*jrr zj*) what he wishes (*mrr.t=f*) in the necropolis."

In these three syntactic environments, conversion into a topicalized VP can affect the following verbal forms:

(1) In the aorist tense, the unmarked *sḏm=f* is converted into the so-called *nominal* or *emphatic* form, characterized by the reduplication or gemination of the second consonant in the infirm and geminated classes (section 4.6.3.1). Its passive counterpart displays the *tw*-suffix:

(48) Urk. IV 1111,6–7 *jnn.tw n=f jmj.t-prw nb ntf ḫtm st*
"It is to him that all testaments (*jmj.t-prw nb*) are brought; he is the one (*ntf*) who seals them"

(2) In the past tense, the "emphatic" *sḏm.n=f* (section 4.6.3.1) and its passive form *sḏm.n.tw=f* (section 4.6.3.3) are used. While the emphatic *sḏm.n=f* is morphologically undistinguishable from the non-topicalized form we encountered in the preceding sections,[24] it is the only *sḏm.n=f*-pattern licensed with verbs of movement, which use the stative for the main clause function (*jw=f jj.w* "he has come"). The passive *sḏm.n.tw=f* is also limited to the topicalized function, since the passive *sḏm(.w)=f* and the stative are the forms used as passive equivalents to the *sḏm.n=f* in non-initial uses (sections 7.3–4):

(49) Sin. B 148–49 *thj.n=f r k.t ḫ3s.t jw mjn jb=f j'j(.w)*
"While he previously erred (*thj.n=f*) to another country, today (*mjn*) his heart is appeased"

(50) Urk. IV 365,11 *jrj.n.tw nn ḥr-m*
"Why (*ḥr-m*) has this been done (*jrj.n.tw nn*)?"

Sporadic examples of topicalized uses of the stative with morphological gemination in post-classical Middle Egyptian must be understood as hypercorrections resulting from the gradual obsolescence of the first person independent use of this form (section 7.2) and its subsequent inclusion into the regular paradigm of initial nominalized forms:[25]

(51) Urk. IV 119,10 *ḏḏ.kw ḥr mḫ3.t* "I have been placed (*ḏḏ.kw*) on the balance"

(3) In modal contexts, the prospective form is used (section 4.6.3.2). In Old Egyptian, this form exhibits both an active *sḏm(.w)=f/jrj.w=f* and a passive *sḏmm=f/jrj.w=f.* In the classical language, prospective and subjunctive have merged into a single paradigm: the passive form of the Middle Egyptian suppletive prospective *sḏm=f* displays the analytic pattern with *tw*-suffix, which is originally the form of the subjunctive:

(52) CT V 93c–d *wd(j.w)=j sw jrf ṯn(w) ḏd=k sw m wzš.wt=s*
"'Where shall I put (*wdj.w=j*) it?' – 'You should put (*ḏd=k*, emphatic)[26] it in her bilge-water'"

(53) Pyr. *1960b–c *jw N r gs jꜣb.t(j) n(j) nw.t jwrr N jm msj.w N jm*
"The King is directed toward the eastern side of Nut: it is there (*jm*) that the King shall be conceived (*jwrr N*), it is there that the King shall be born (*msj.w N*)"

(54) Sin. B 202 *jrj.tw nn mj-m n bꜣk thj.n jb=f r ḫꜣs.wt ḏrḏr.yt*
"How (*mj-m* "like what?") can this be done (*jrj.tw nn*) for a servant (*bꜣk*) whose heart lured him to foreign countries (*ḫꜣs.wt ḏrḏr.yt*)?"

(4) One will recall that when the expression of the subject of an adverbial or pseudoverbal sentence is accompanied by temporal or modal features projecting it into the realized past or to the potential future, the predicate of these sentences is a verbal form of *wnn* "to be," for example the unmarked aorist *wn=f* and its topicalized equivalent *wnn=f* "he is," the prospective *wnn=f* "he will be," or the subjunctive *wn=f* "that he be" (sections 5.6, 6.2). The same conversion into a verbal sentence predicated by *wnn* applies to adverbial and pseudoverbal sentences in the same environments in which verbal clauses undergo topicalization by means of "emphatic" forms:

(a) when an adverbial adjunct enjoys pragmatic salience:

(55) CT V 54c–55a B9C *jn jj.n=k r jṯj<.t> ḥꜣ.tj=j pn n(j) ‘nḫ.w*
"Have you come (*jn jj.n=k*) in order to take away (*r jṯj.t*) this heart of mine (*ḥꜣ.tj=j pn*) that belongs to the Living Ones (*‘nḫ.w*)?"

(b) when the topicalized clause predicated by *wnn* is extraposed as topic of a correlative main sentence:

(56) Sin. B 252–54 *wn.k(w) r=f dwn.kw ḥr ẖ.t=j ḫm.n(=j) wj m-bꜣḥ=f*
"Although indeed stretched out on my belly (topicalized form of **jw r=f wn=j dwn.kw* "I was streched out"), still I did not recognize myself before him (non-initial main clause)"

(c) in headings or titles:

(57) CT VI 333a *wnn zj m-m ‘nḫ.w*
"[This spell describes] how a man will be (*wnn zj*) among (*m-m*) the living (*‘nḫ.w*)"

Initial clauses predicated by *wnn*, therefore, are the topicalized equivalent of adverbial sentences introduced by an indicator of syntactic initiality such as *jw* (*jw=f m prw* "he is at home" vs. *wnn=f mj-m* "how is he?," *jw=k ḥr rḏj.t* "you give" vs. *wnn=k ḥr rḏj.t nn rḫ* "it is without knowledge that you give"), according to a syntactic pattern similar to the conversion of otherwise unmarked verbal sentences into a sentence with topicalized predicate (*jw mdw=f n=j* "he speaks to me" vs. *jrr=f m mrj.t=f* "he acts *according to his wish*").

7.5.2 Topicalized vs. adverbialized verbal forms

A frequent pattern with a topicalized verbal form is one in which the pragmatically emphasized adverbial slot is occupied by a verbal phrase embedded as "circumstantial" form, indicating an action simultaneous (aorist *sḏm=f* "in that he hears/heard"), anterior (active past *sḏm.n=f* "after he has/had heard," passive *sḏm(.w)=f* "after he has/had been heard") or subsequent (prospective *sḏm=f* "that he may hear") to the one conveyed by the initial verbal form. In these sentences, which are labeled in Egyptological literature "complex adverbial sentences," two concomitant conversions take place: the topicalization of the main predicate of the sentence, and the adverbial embedding of the verbal phrase which occupies rhematic position:

(58) Pt. 366 *mdw.y=k rḫ.n=k wḥ'=k*
"You should talk (*mdw.y=k*, prospective) only when you know (*rḫ.n=k*) that you understand (*wḥ'=k*, section 7.6)"

(59) Manchester 3306,8[27] *jrj.n=j n=j mjḥ'.t tw s3ḫ.tj smnḫ s.t=s r rwḏ nṯr '3*
"I made for myself this magnificent tomb (*mjḥ'.t tw s3ḫ.tj* "this tomb, it being beautified, stative), after its location had been perfectly set (*smnḫ s.t=s*) at the terrace of the Great God"

At this point, however, a question may be raised: since the *sḏm.n=f*, unlike the aorist *sḏm=f*, does not exhibit, with the exception of the verb *rḏj* "to give," a morphological opposition between its topicalized and its main clause uses, how is it possible to discriminate between a non-initial main clause in a narrative sequence of the type we discussed in section 7.3 on the one hand and a topicalized *sḏm.n=f*-predicate on the other?

The following is a frequently discussed passage from "Sinuhe":

(60) Sin. B 26–34 "Then he gave me water and boiled milk for me. I went with him to his tribe: what they did was good. Land passed me to land: I set out to Byblos and reached Qedem. *jrj.n=j rnp.t-gs jm jnj wj 'mmwnnšj ḥq3 pw n(j) (r)ṯnw-ḥrj.t ḏd=f n=j nfr ṯw ḥn'=j sḏm=k r3 n(j) km.t ḏd.n=f nn rḫ.n=f qd=j sḏm.n=f šs3=j mtr.n wj rmṯ.w-km.t ntj.w jm ḥn'=f* I spent (*jrj.n=j*) a year and a half (*rnp.t-gs*) there; Ammunenshi, the ruler of Upper Retjenu, took me (*jnj wj 'mmwnnšj*) and said to me (*ḏd=f n=j*): 'You will be happy (*nfr ṯw* "you are good") with me, and you will hear (*sḏm=k*) the language of Egypt.' He said this (*ḏd.n=f nn*) because he knew my character (*rḫ.n=f qd=j*) and had heard of my skills (*sḏm.n=f šs3=j*), the Egyptians (*rmṯ.w-km.t*) who were (*ntj.w*) there with him having witnessed for me (*mtr.n wj*)"

Since the first verbal form of the Egyptian text sets forth the narrative sequence ("I spent a year and a half there"), it is clearly a non-initial main clause paratactically annexed to the preceding segment of discourse, which is opened by the initial construction "then he gave me water," already discussed in example (24). The two subsequent *sḏm=f*-forms *jnj wj 'mmwnnšj* "Ammunenshi took me" and *ḏd=f n=j* "he said to me" provide background information for the understanding of Sinuhe's stay, and are therefore embedded as AP into the main clause predicated by *jrj.n=j*. The form *ḏd.n=f* "he said this," on the other hand, which opens a new narrative segment after a direct speech, offers a paradigmatic example of topicalized VP: it thematizes Ammunenshi's words, and its use is syntactically justified by the presence of the three following embedded *sḏm.n=f*s which explain the background of Ammunenshi's speech. Rather than by a simple past, these adverbial *sḏm.n=f*s should be rendered in European languages by a perfective past form: since they represent a past background to a preterital main VP, they acquire the function of pluperfect forms in English: "because he knew (= had learnt)," "and had heard," "having witnessed."

Thus, the opposition between topicalized and adverbialized *sḏm.n=f* in Egyptian discourse is not a feature of morphosyntax, since the same verbal form can be used as paratactic main clause, as initial topicalized form, or as embedded adverbialized VP, but a matter of tense-aspect dialectics, of ***sequence of tenses***,[28] of organization of temporal and aspectual features in discourse. In fact, the interplay between the main clause verbal predicate, the foreground topicalized VP, and the embedded verbal forms in adverbial function is a frequent device of Egyptian literary style. The main difference between the non-initial main clause and the so-called complex adverbial sentence lies in the syntactic and pragmatic status of the verbal phrase: in the former case, the VP is a paratactically linked verbal clause which carries the discourse sequence (foreground); in the latter, the topicalized VP (theme) controls a subordinate VP embedded as adverbial adjunct (background):

(61) Urk. I 103,7–104,4 *jj.n mšʿ pn m ḥtp ḫbꜣ.n=f tꜣ ḥrj.w-šʿj... jj.n mšʿ pn m ḥtp [jnj.n=f ṯz.wt] jm=f ʿšꜣ.t wrj.t m sqr.w-ʿnḫ ḥzj w(j) ḥm=f ḥr=s r ḫ.t nb*
"This army returned (*jj.n mšʿ pn*, topicalized VP) in peace after having ravaged (*ḫbꜣ.n=f* "it ravaged," verbal phrase embedded as AP) the land of the Sand-dwellers ... This army returned (*jj.n mšʿ pn*, topicalized VP) in peace having brought (*jnj.n=f* "it brought," verbal phrase embedded as AP) from there very many troops as captives (*sqr.w-ʿnḫ* "bound for life"): His Majesty praised (*ḥzj*, indicative *sḏm=f*, section 7.2) me for it beyond measure (*r ḫ.t nb* "more than anything")"

7.5.3 The "balanced" sentence

We should now consider a sentence pattern with topicalized VP that has often attracted the attention of students of Egyptian.[29] This construction, called "balanced sentence" (German *Wechselsatz*), consists of two topicalized *sḏm=f* or (more rarely) *sḏm.n=f* forms, often, but not exclusively, from the same verbal root, juxtaposed to each other. The effect is the "autofocality"[30] of the predicative nexus in each of the two portions of the sentence, with a direct temporal or logical dependence of the second predicate upon the first, i.e. "if...then," or "as soon as...then":

(62)　Pyr. 798a　　　*j.šm=k j.šm ḥrw mdw=k mdw stš*
"If you go, Horus goes – if you speak, Seth speaks"

(63)　Berlin 1157,12　　*ꜣd.tw r=f ḏḏ=f sꜣ=f*
"No sooner is he attacked (*ꜣd.tw r=f* "one attacks him"), he turns (*ḏḏ=f* "he gives") his back"

(64)　Urk. IV 348,9　　*wnn p.t wnn=ṯ ḥr=j*
"As long as heaven exists, you (fem.) shall be with me (*ḥr=j*)"

(65)　pTurin 54065[31]　　*ḫpr.n(=j) ḫpr.n ḫpr.t ḫpr.n ḫpr.t [nb.t m]-ḫt ḫpr=j*
"As soon as I came into existence, Being (*ḫpr.t*) came into existence; each being (*ḫpr.t nb.t*) came into existence after (*m-ḫt*) my coming into existence"

While different from both the pattern in which a topicalized VP is dislocated to the left of a main sentence with unconverted verbal predicate (section 7.5.1b) and the "complex adverbial sentence" in which the thematized VP signals the pragmatic focality of an embedded "circumstantial" VP (section 7.5.2), the balanced sentence nonetheless shares with both of them a semantic correlation between the two verbal phrases.[32] Let us consider the following textual variant of (44) in which the topicalized VP is not extraposed to the main sentence, but rather correlates with another "emphatic" form:

(44')　CT III 24a–25b S₂C　*hꜣꜣ=sn r tꜣ m ḥfꜣw.w hꜣy=j ḥr qꜣb.w=sn prr=sn r p.t m bjk.w prr=j r ḏnḥ.w=sn*
"If they go down to the earth as snakes, I shall go down on their coils; they go up (*prr=sn*) to heaven as falcons – I go up (*prr=j*) to their wings"

In the first of the two sentences, the topicalized VP *hꜣꜣ=sn* is extraposed, and the predicate of the main sentence functioning as its comment is an independent verbal form, namely a prospective *hꜣy=j*; the second is a balanced sentence with two "autofocal" VPs (*prr=sn – prr=j*). In the balanced sentence, both correlated VPs are integral constituents of the sentence; the topicalized VP dislocated to the left of a main clause, on the contrary, is an extraposed subordinate clause and entertains a paradigmatic relation with extraposed nominal topics (section 7.3) and with *adverbial* phrases in topical extraposition, which also appear in similar patterns:

(44")　CT III 24a–25b B₁Be　*hꜣꜣ=sn r tꜣ m ḥfꜣw.w hꜣy=j m qꜣb.w=sn (j)r prj.t=sn r p.t m bjk.w pry=j ḥr ḏnḥ.w=sn*
"If they go down to the earth as snakes, I shall go down in their coils; as for their going up (*prj.t=sn*, infinitive) to heaven as falcons, I shall go up on their wings"

Also in the so-called "complex adverbial sentence" the topicalized (or better *thematized*, since no real extraposition occurs) VP is a mandatory component of the sentence pattern; rather than a contingent event, however ("if they go down, *I shall go down*"), the scope of the emphasis it conveys is here a circumstance determining, accompanying, or resulting from it ("you should talk *only when you know* that you understand").

7.5.4 Other focalizing uses of the topicalized VP

Thus, the use of topicalized verbal forms allows the pragmatic stress to be laid on a phrasal or clausal *comment*. The pattern "Emphatic form+AP" is in fact the most common device for the focalization of an argument other than the *subject* of a verbal clause, which, as one will recall (sections 5.4.2, 7.3), is focalized by becoming the subject of a participial statement (or cleft sentence). When the focalized element is the patient, i.e. the *object* of a verbal predicate (section 5.2.1), Egyptian has recourse to the conversion of the verbal clause into an identifying (pseudocleft) sentence in which the object of the VP becomes the pragmatically focalized predicate of a tripartite nominal construction "Pred-*pw*-relative form," for example *NP pw ḥzy.n=sn* "[The one whom they praised] is NP."

There exists, however, a rare, but linguistically sophisticated focalization pattern for the object of a VP, in which the object is converted into a prepositional phrase introduced by *m* "as":[33]

(66) Peas. B1,166 *jn ḫm=k ø m hꜣ.w=j*
"Are you ignorant (*jn ḫm=k*) only of *my* problems (*hꜣ.w=j*)?"

The verb *ḫm* "not to know, to be ignorant of" is transitive; it should, therefore, display a direct object. But in order to emphasize the pronominal referent ("only of *my* problems"), here the syntactic slot of the direct object is left empty (ø) and a prepositional phrase with *m* "as" used instead, lit. *"are you ignorant (of it) as my problems?" The syntactic structure of these sentences, the most common of which is the formula "The King N *jrj.n=f ø m mnw=f n jtj=f...*" frequently inscribed on royal monuments,[34] involves a form of omission under relevance (section 6.3.3) of the object of the verbal predicate and its resumption, as it were, by the prepositional phrase introduced by *m*: "As for King N, it is as his monument that he made this for his father..." Interestingly enough, this focalizing pattern with the raising to AP of an object NP is not limited to *grammatical* objects, but can be applied to *logical* objects of a VP, for example the subject of a passive verbal predicate (see also section 7.5):

(67) Adm. 12,13–14 *jr šm zj 3 ḥr w3.t gmm.tw=ø m zj 2*
"If (*jr*) three people leave (*šm zj 3*) on a road, only two are found"

In order to mark the contrast between the active subject of the protasis ("three people leave") and the passive subject of the apodosis ("only two are found," one of them having been the victim of the other two's violence), the latter's slot is left empty under relevance in the main clause *gmm.tw=ø* "(it) is found" and resumed in the prepositional phrase *m zj 2* "(only) two people." In a similar vein, one observe the following example:

(68) Urk. IV 897,11–16 *rḫ.n(=j) qd=k twj m zšj m wn=k m šmsw jtj=j ḏj=j ø m ḥr=k m j3.t ṯ.t jdn=k n mšʿ mj ḏd.tj(=j) srsj=k qn.yt nzw*
"I knew your character (*qd=k*) while I was still in the nest (*tw=j m zšj*, section 6.3.1), when you were (*m wn=k* "in you-are") in my father's following. I shall indeed give you the office of the Royal Table (*j3.t ṯ.t*), so that you become for me lieutenant of the Army (*jdn=k n=j mšʿ*) under my command (*mj ḏd.tj=j* "according to what I will say"), and supervise (*srsj=k*) the Royal Guard"

Here, the predicate of the clause *ḏj=j ø m ḥr=k m j3.t ṯ.t* is an objectless prospective form of the verb *rḏj* "to give," modified by the prepositional phrase *m ḥr=k* "in your face" to yield *"I shall give ø in your face as the office of the Royal Table" > "I shall indeed give you the office of the Royal Table." The omitted object is resumed by the prepositional phrase *m j3.t ṯ.t* "(as) the office of the Royal Table," which is the focalized element of the utterance. The English translation "I shall *indeed* give you the office of the Royal Table" attempts to identify the prepositional adjunct as discourse focus.

7.6 Verbal clauses embedded as noun phrases

In the topicalized verbal sentence which we considered in the preceding section, the initial VP serves as the "theme" or "topic" of the sentence, i.e. it assumes a function which is usually performed by a noun phrase. In other syntactic environments, however, these converted forms, i.e. the emphatic past *sḏm.n=f*, the aorist *sḏm=f*, the prospective *sḏm(.w)=f*, and the conversion of an adverbial or pseudoverbal pattern by means of *wnn* do not appear dislocated as pragmatic topic of a complex sentence, but rather embedded as noun phrase into a higher syntactic node. These environments are: (A) the use of a topicalized form embedded into a higher nominal or verbal sentence, and (B) its syntactic control by a verb, by a preposition, or by the genitive marker, i.e. the determinative pronoun *nj* "that of."

(A) The topicalized verbal form functions as the predicate of the embedded clause in "thetic" statements (section 5.3), i.e. in bipartite nominal sentences in which an entire verbal clause appears embedded as predicate of a higher *pw*-sentence:

(69) pEbers 855z *mhh jb=f pw*
"This means (*pw*) that his heart is oblivious (*mhh jb=f*)"

(70) Urk. V 53,1–2 *wnn šw pw ḥr jrj.t jmj.t-prw n gbb*
"This means that Shu is making (*šw ḥr jrj.t*) a testament (*jmj.t-prw*) in favor of Geb"

The nominalized VP can be also converted into the subject of a higher nominal or verbal clause, for example a qualifying adjectival clause (section 5.4.1) or a subordinate verbal clause (section 6.3.1):

(71) CT VI 194c B_1P^a *štȝ-w(j) dgg=k*
"How secret (*štȝ*) is the way you look (*dgg=k* "that you look")!"

(72) Pyr. 1223a^P *jr wdfj ḏȝȝ=ṯn mḫn.t n N pn ḏd.kȝ N pn rn=ṯn pw n rmṯ.w rḫ(.w).n=f*
"If it is delayed (*wdfj*) that you ferry (*ḏȝȝ=ṯn*) the ferry-boat to this King, this King will say (*ḏd.kȝ N pn*) your name to the people whom he knows"

In these sentences, the entire clause predicated by the reduplicated *sḏm=f*, whether consisting only of the verbal form as in (71) "the way you look," or of a more complex predicate as in (72) "that you ferry the ferry-boat to this King," is the subject of the adjectival or verbal predicate.

(B) A clause predicated by an "emphatic" form or construction can appear embedded as the noun phrase object of a verb of perception such as *rḫ* "to know" or *ḏd* "to say":

(73) Urk. IV 363,6–7 *jw ḥm.t=j rḫ.tj nṯrr=f jrj.n=j js (s)t ḥr wḏ=f*
"My Majesty (*ḥm.t=j*, fem.) knows (*rḫ.tj*) that he is divine (*nṯrr=f*, aorist of *nṯrj* "to be divine") and that I did this (*jrj.n=j st*, emphatic *sḏm.n=f*) according to his order"

(74) Urk. I 62,12 *rḫ.n(=j) ḥm mrr w(j) rʿw ḥr rdj.t=f n(=j) ṯw*
"I know for sure (*ḥm*) that Reʿ loves me, because he has given (*ḥr rdj.t=f* "on his having given") you to me"

(75) Pyr. 1490a *ḏd=k wnn js N <p>n m ʿb=sn nṯr.w jmj.w p.t*
"You will say that this King exists among them, namely the gods who are in heaven"

(76) Pyr. 1862a–n^N *ḏd=ṯn ḫr rʿw wnt=f jj(.w) m nṯr*
"You shall say to Re that he has come as god"

Unlike in (73) and (74), where syntactic dependency is conveyed only by the use of a nominal VP (*nṯrr=f* and *mrr wj rʿw*),[35] in the last two examples the object clause controlled by the verb *ḏd* "to say" is identified by explicit markers of subordination, namely the particle *js* in (75) and the conjunction *wnt* in (76). As we observed in sections 6.3.1 and 6.4, the difference between the two patterns is that the presence of *js* evokes not only syntactic *dependency* but also pragmatic *focality*, whereas the latter feature is absent from the unmarked sentence introduced by the conjunction *ntt* or *wnt* (section 4.7).

The pattern in which a clause predicated by a nominalized VP represents the embedded object of a verbal predicate is particularly frequent under the control of verbs of wish or command such as *mrj* "to wish," *rḏj* ("to give" >) "to cause," or *wḏ* "to order." The predicate of these clauses is usually the subjunctive *sḏm=f*:[36]

(77) Pyr. 1295a *wḏ.n jnpw ḫntj zḥ-nṯr h3y=k m sb3 m nṯr dw3(j)*
"Anubis, who presides over the god's booth (*zḥ-nṯr*), has ordered that you descend (*h3y=k*) as star (*sb3*), as the Morning Star (*nṯr dw3j* "the morning god")"

(78) Urk. IV 132,16–17 *rḏj.n=f wn=j m jb.w rmṯ.w mrj.t(w)=j ḫr nṯr=j*
"He caused that I be (*wn=j*) in the people's heart and that I be loved (*mrj.tw=j*) by my god"

There are instances, however, in which an entire complex adverbial sentence predicated by the "emphatic" *sḏm=f* can appear embedded as object of a verb of wish or command or controlled by a preposition:

(79) Urk. I 301,3–5 *jw wḏ.n ḥm(=j) srr=f jrr=f qd m sp3.wt (j)ptn ḫft wḏ=k jrr=f m wḥm(w)=k*
"My Majesty commanded that he become an official (*srr=f*) and acquire a good reputation (*jrr=f qd*) in these districts according to (*ḫft*) your command that he become (*jrr=f*) your herold"

(80) pKahun 1,7 "(Hail to you, Kha'kaure'...) *stj šsr mj jrr sḫm.t sḫr=f ḫ3.w m ḫm.w b3.w=f*
who shoots the arrow as does Sakhmet (*mj jrr sḫm.t*), killing (*sḫr=f* "as he kills") thousands as people who ignore (*ḫm.w*) his might"

(81) Peas. B1,109–10 *m mrr=k m3=j snb.kw swdf=k sw '3 nn wšb r ḏd.t(j)=f nb.t*
"If you wish (*m mrr=k* "in that-you-wish," section 6.3.2) to see me (*m3=j*, infinitive + suffix pronoun) happy (*snb.kw*, stative), you should keep (*swdf=k*) him here without answering (*nn wšb*) to anything he may say (*ḏd.tj=f*, section 7.7)"

But since Egyptian prepositions can often function as conjunctions (see section 4.7), it is difficult to draw a morphological distinction between a VP embedded as NP under the control of a preposition and a VP which keeps its verbal features in a subordinate clause introduced by a conjunction. This is notably the case with the verbal pattern used only in the negative form (section 7.8) or as an adverbial clause introduced by the prepositions or conjunctions *r* "until" and *ḏr* "since," namely the *sḏm.t=f* (section 6.3.1). In this form, the morpheme *.t* can be taken as nominal marker related to the feminine ending of the substantivized relative form, in which case the form would be an embedded NP (*r sḏm.t=f* "to that-he-has heard"), or, more probably, as marker of perfectivity (*r sḏm.t=f* "until he-has-heard"):[37]

(82) Pt. 126 *m mdw(.w) n=f r j3š.t=f*
"Do not talk to him until he has invited you to (*r j3š.t=f*)"

Finally, the "emphatic" form is also used as NP after the determinative pronoun *nj*, i.e. as the *nomen rectum* of a genitival construction:

(83) Pt. 186 *šms jb=k tr n(j) wnn=k*
"Follow your heart as long as you live (*tr nj wnn=k* "time of that-you-are")"

(84) Urk. IV 132,9–10 *sk3=j m ḥtr.w=j n.w nfr.t m sḫw.t n.t jrr=j ḏs=j r jsj=j n(j) ḫr.t-nṯr*
"And I ploughed (*sk3=j*) with my handsome yoke of oxen (*ḥtr.w=j n.w nfr.t* "my yoke of beauty") in the fields that I myself had selected (*sḫ.wt n.t jrr=j ḏs=j* "the fields of that-I-do-myself") to be my tomb (*jsj=j*) of the Necropolis"

This construction has to be contrasted with the more regular pattern with the converted relative forms, which will be considered in the next section: although there is no apparent difference in meaning, the construction with *nj* followed by the "emphatic" *sḏm=f* seems to be limited to nuclear verbal clauses consisting only of the verbal form and two arguments at the most, i.e. the subject and rarely the object:

(85) Pt. 641–42 *jṯj.n=j rnp.t 110 m ʿnḫ n(j) ḏḏ nzw*
"I spent 110 years of life given to me by the king (*nj ḏḏ nzw* "those-of that-the-king-gives")"

Instead of only a verbal predicate, an entire sentence can also be embedded as *nomen rectum* of a genitival construction; in this case, exactly as in the embedding of an adverbial clause (section 6.3.1), the verbal form is the one which would occur in the underlying non-embedded sentence, i.e. no morphological conversion takes place:

(86) Urk. IV 520,1 *wnm=k tʔ=k r mrr=k mj sḫr=k n(j) wn=k tp t3*
"You shall eat your bread according to your wish (*r mrr=k*, see (c) above), as when you were on earth ("according to your custom of you-were-on-earth")"

7.7 Converted relative clauses

7.7.1 General features

Egyptian possesses two types of relative clauses, depending on whether the antecedent is non-specific or specific (section 6.3.3): in the former case, it is modified by a "virtual" relative clause, i.e. an unconverted verbal clause embedded as adverbial adjunct; in the latter case, it is modified by a relative converter or by adjectival conversions of the verb. When the subject of the relative clause is coreferential with the antecedent it modifies, the active or passive participle is used:

(87) Urk. IV 74,9–11 *dj-nzw-ḥtp (n) nḫb.t ḥḏ.t nḫn dj=s ḫ.t nb.t nfr.t wʿb.t prr.t ḫr wḏḥ=s m tp-trj nb n(j) p.t n k3 n(j)...*
"May the king give an offering (to) Nekhbet, the White One of Hierakonpolis, that she may give (*dj=s*) all good and pure things which go up (*prr.t*, imperfective active

participle of *prj*) on her altar (*wdḥ=s*) during each festival of Beginning of Heaven to the *ka* of..."

(88) pKahun 35,31 *sḏm.n b3k jm md.t m zẖ3 pn jny n b3k jm*
"Your servant (*b3k jm* "the servant there") has heard the matter in the letter (*zẖ3 pn* "this letter"[38]) which was brought (*jny*, past passive participle of *jnj*) to your servant"

In the Old Kingdom, there are cases in which a relative verbal clause is introduced by the relative adjective *ntj*.[39] This type of conversion is more frequent in negative sentences (section 7.8.6), since in these patterns the predicate does not immediately follow the antecedent, but is separated from it by the negative morpheme. Positive examples are rare:

(89) Siut I,295 *p3 t? ḥ(n)q.t...ntj rḏj.n=j n=ṯn sw*
"the bread and beer...which I gave to you"

But the most frequent relative conversion of a verbal clause whose subject is different from the modified antecedent is fulfilled in earlier Egyptian by special forms of the verbal conjugation, usually called *relative forms*.[40] Etymologically, these forms are probably connected with participles (section 4.6.3.4) and display the usual nominal endings (masc. *.j* > *.w*, almost never expressed, fem. *.t*, pl. *.w*) in agreement with the specific antecedent they modify; they appear, however, fully integrated into the finite conjugational system of the *sḏm.n=f* for the past (90), of the geminated or reduplicated *sḏm=f* for the aorist (91),[41] and of the prospective *sḏm(.w)=f* for modal uses (92). The link to the specific antecedent in the main clause is established by a coreferential element; in the case of the object pronoun, the resumptive element may be omitted under relevance, if local to the agreement-carrying predicate:[42]

(90) Sin. B 101–2 *ḫ3s.t nb.t rwj.t.n=j r=s jw jrj.n=j hd=j jm=s dr.t(j) ḥr smw ẖnm.wt=s*
"Every foreign country (*ḫ3s.t nb.t*) against which I advanced (*rwj.t.n=j r=s*, fem. relative past "which (fem.)-I-advanced against-it") – I made my attack (*hd=j*) against it, it being driven (*dr.tj*, stative) from the pastures of its wells (*ẖnm.wt=s*)"

(91) Pyr. 36a–b *wsjr N mj n=k jr.t ḥrw hp.t m-ʿ stš jṯj.t=k ø jr r3=k wpp.t=k r3=k jm=s*
"Osiris the King! Take to yourself the Eye of Horus which escaped from Seth (*hp.t*, fem. participle coreferential with the antecedent *jr.t ḥrw*), which you should take (*jṯj.t=k*, fem. relative prospective) to your mouth and with which you keep opening your mouth (*wpp.t=k r3=k jm=s*, fem. relative aorist "which (fem.)-you-open your-mouth with-it")"

(92) pKahun 12,9–10 *nts rḏj=s n mry=s nb m n3y=s ẖrd.w msj(.w)=s n=j ø*
"And she shall give (it) to anyone she likes (*mry=s*, headless masc. relative prospective, i.e. without antecedent)[43] among her children whom she may bear (*msj.w=s*, pl. relative prospective "whom-she-may-bear") to me"

The link to the antecedent in the main clause can also be carried by a resumptive pronoun in an embedded subordinate clause:

(93) Urk. IV 341,7–8 (Queen Hatshepsut) *tj.t [ḏsr.t] n.t jmnw mrj.t.n=f wn=s ḥr ns.t=f*
"noble image of Amun, whom he has wished (*mrj.t.n=f*) that she be (*wn=s*, subjunctive form with resumptive pronoun referring back to the feminine antecedent) on his throne"

When used without explicit antecedent, the feminine form of a relative verbal form is often substantivized in the "neuter" meaning ("that which"). It mostly appears as object of a verbal phrase or under the control of a preposition:

(94) Sin. B 213 *w'f.n=k šnn.t jtn*
"You have subdued that which the sun-disk encircles (*šnn.t jtn*)"
(95) BD (Budge) 261,1 *jw sḥtp.n=j nṯr m mrr.t=f*
"I satisfied (*sḥtp.n=j*) the god with that which he likes (*mrr.t=f*)"

and also as subject or as predicate of a nominal sentence, in the syntactic environments we analyzed in section 5.2.

Thus, the relativization of a verbal clause involves the entire clause, and is morphologically marked by the conversion of the predicate into an adjectival form of the verb, i.e the participle when its subject is coreferential with the antecedent:

(96) Sin. B 304–5 *ḫ'w nb dd.w r rwd jrj(.w) ḫr.t=f jm*
"All the equipment (*ḫ'w nb*) that is to be put (*dd.w* "which is given") into a shaft – its management was then (*jm* "there") taken care of (*jrj.w ḫr.t=f*)"

and the relative form when it differs from it:

(97) Urk. I 9,14–16 *jrj.n(=j) nw n jtj=j sk sw ḫpj(.w) r jmn.t ḥr wꜣ.wt nfr.wt ḫpp.wt jmꜣḫw.w ḥr=sn*
"I did this (*nw*) for my father when he went (*sw ḫpj.w*, stative) to the West on the beautiful ways on which the deceased go (*ḫpp.wt jmꜣḫw.w ḥr=sn* "which (fem.pl.) the deceased go on them")"

7.7.2 *Relative conversion of agentless sentences*

In the examples of relative verbal forms we discussed so far, the converted predicate, whether transitive or intransitive, is always in the *active* voice and displays an *overt* subject. On the basis of these constructions, conjugated relative forms might be viewed as semantically equivalent to passive participles of transitive (*jr.t jṯj.t=k* "the eye which you should take" = *"the eye taken-by-you") or intransitive verbs (*ḫꜣs.t rwj.t.n=j r=s* "the country against which I advanced" = *"the country advanced-by-me against it"), and in fact one of the most adhered-to theories about their origin viewed them, exactly like the indicative forms of the suffix conjugation *sḏm=f*, *sḏm.n=f*, etc., as derived from passive participles followed by their subject, later grammaticalized as finite verbal forms.[44] This functional correspondence between passive participles and relative forms is particularly explicit when the substantivized passive participle of verbs such as *mrj* "to love" or *ḥzj* "to praise" is used instead of the relative form (*mry* "beloved one," *ḥzy/ḥzz.y* "praised one"):

(98) Pt. 137 *jw=f r rdj.t n ḥzz.y=f*
"He will give to the one whom he praises (*ḥzz.y=f* "his praised one")"

Let us now turn, however, to the relative conversion of two semantically more complex sentence types, namely (a) the *subjectless* intransitive predicate whose subject is omitted under relevance, and (b) the *passive* constructions with or without explicit subject. In these clauses, the adjectival agreement is not carried by a relative form, but by a passive participle, although their overt or omitted subject differs from the antecedent it modifies. Let us consider example (99):

(99) Urk. IV 269,7–8 (King Thutmosis I) *ḫsr šn.w m-qꜣb km.t ḥ''.w m jrj.t.n=f nb.t*
"who drives (*ḫsr*) troubles away from (*m-qꜣb* "from within") Egypt, over all whose deeds one rejoices"

In the first portion of this verse, the underlying verbal sentence which has undergone relative conversion is **ḫsr=f šn.w m-qꜣb km.t* "he drives troubles away from Egypt"; its subject (*=f*) being coreferential with the antecedent (the King), the adjectival agreement is carried by the active participle. In the second part, however, the subject of the underlying clause is not the King, but rather an indefinite pronoun "one," which has been omitted under relevance:[45] **ḥ''.tw m jrj.t.n=f nb.t* "one rejoices (*ḥ''.tw*) over all that which he has done (*jrj.t.n=f*, substantivized headless relative form)." Here, the indefinite subject is omitted from the relative clause and the adjectival agreement with the antecedent is carried by the passive participle *ḥ''.w* *"rejoiced": Egyptian uses the passive participle in spite of the fact that the logical subject of the relative clause is different from the antecedent.

Similar to these constructions are the examples in which the subjectless predicate, rather than an intransitive verbal form, is an objectless transitive verbal phrase:

(100) Urk. I 184,1 *šms(=j) tp mꜣ.w n.w wjꜣ 'ꜣ r bw ḏd(.w) ø jm [r tꜣ]*
"And I followed the sterns (*mꜣ.w*) of the great bark to the place (*bw*) where one lands"

where the underlying main clause which has undergone relative conversion is **ḏd.tw ø jm r tꜣ* "it is there (*jm*) that one lands (*ḏd.tw ø r tꜣ* "one gives ø to land")."

The same type of agreement applies to the relative conversion of a passive predicate with overt subject in the aorist *jrr.tw=f* – when topicalized – or *jw jrj.tw=f* – when functioning as main clause – and in the prospective *jrj.tw=f*. In these constructions, the converted relative clause is headed by a perfective or imperfective passive participle rather than by a relative form, although the overt subject is different from the modified antecedent. The semantic reason for this syntactic behavior is the divorce, typical for passive predications, between *grammatical* and *logical* subject: while the overt grammatical subject is usually the object of the verbal action, the logical subject (i.e. the agent) remains in most cases unexpressed.[46] In view of this semantic weakness of the grammatical subject of a passive predicate, which, being a "patient," scores lower than the antecedent on the hierarchy of case-roles,[47] it is the antecedent, whether implicit, as in (101), or explicit, as in (102), which takes over the subject function in the relative clause as well, creating a bifrontal pattern in which the participle in congruence with the antecedent is followed by the grammatical subject (and logical patient) of the relative clause, i.e. a pattern structurally similar to the syntax of the relative verbal forms:

(101) pEbers 247 *jr jrr.w n=f nb pẖr.t tn...*
"As for everyone for whom this remedy is made (*jrr.w n=f pẖr.t tn* "made [masc. passive participle] to-him this remedy)..."

which represents the relative conversion of **jw jrj.tw n=f pẖr.t tn* "this remedy is made for him," or

(102) CT I 70d *nj rḏj(.w)=k m ḫb.t ḏd.t sbj.w jm=s*
"You shall not be put (section 7.8) in the place of execution (*ḫb.t*) in which the rebels are put (*ḏd.t sbj.w jm=s* "put (fem. passive participle)-the rebels in-it")"

from a main clause **ḏd.tw sbj.w jm=s* "the rebels are put in it."[48] It is interesting to observe that in the presence of a pronominal subject, the suffix pronoun in the underlying verbal clause ([+V], [-N]) becomes a dependent pronoun in the converted adjectival relative clause ([+V], [+N]):

(103) Urk. IV 1116,7–8 *ntf š3j 'ḥ'.w r š3j.w nb n=f sw ntf zbb wpw.tjw nb n(.w) prw-nzw r [zbb.w nb n=f st]*
"It is he (*ntf*) who assigns boats (*'ḥ'.w*) to everyone to whom it should be assigned, it is he who sends all royal messengers (*wpw.tjw nb*) to everyone to whom they are sent"

In a cleft sentence, the verbal predicate is converted into a participial predicate which represents the presupposition of the focalized subject (section 5.4.2). In the two cleft sentences in (103), the verbal clauses undergoing conversion are the prospective **š3j.tw=f n=f* "it (i.e. a boat) should be assigned to him" and the aorist **jw zbj.tw=sn n=f* "they are sent to him."[49] Since the predicates resulting from the relative conversion are the perfective passive participle *š3j.w* "assigned" for the prospective[50] and the imperfective passive participle *zbb.w* "sent" for the aorist, a second morphological conversion takes place: the dependent pronoun, which conveys the subject of adjectival sentences, is used instead of the suffix pronoun characteristic of verbal sentences: *š3j.w nb n=f sw* "everyone (*nb*) to whom (*n=f* "to him") it (*sw*, i.e. the boat, subject of the converted clause) is assigned (*š3j.w*, predicate of the converted clause)," *zbb.w nb n=f st* "everyone to whom they (*st*, subject) are sent (*zbb.w*, singular "bifrontal" predicate of the relative clause).

Finally, let us consider the relative conversion of the perfective passive *jw sḏm(.w)=f* (verbal form) and *jw=f sḏm(.w)* (stative).[51] Even in cases when their grammatical subject is overt, sentences predicated by this verbal form share with the other patterns discussed in this section the agentless feature: their grammatical subject is the patient of the verbal action, the logical subject, i.e. the agent role, remaining mostly unexpressed, but if necessary conveyed by the "ergative" marker *jn* (section 4.4.1). We would, therefore, expect the relative conversion of these sentences to be conveyed by the same pattern, i.e. by an adjectival clause predicated by a past passive participle in congruence with the antecedent. This is indeed the case both in headless (104) and in regularly headed (105) relative clauses derived from an underlying perfective passive *jw sḏm(.w)=f/jw=f sḏm(.w)*:

(104) Pyr. 1699a *jj n=n jry mr.t r=f jn sn=f stš j.n=sn(j) psḏ.tj*
"'He to whom (*r=f*) pain (*mr.t*) was inflicted (*jry* "made") by his brother Seth comes to us,' say the Two Enneads (*j.n=snj psḏ.tj* "they say – the Two Enneads")"

from a main sentence **jw jrj.w r=f mr.t jn sn=f stš* "pain was inflicted to him by his brother Seth," or

(105) Pyr. 276c *j nṯr ʿ3 ḫmm rn=f*
"O Great God whose name (*rn=f*) is unknown"

from a main sentence **jw rn=f ḫm.w* "his name is unknown." The predicates of the converted clauses are the passive participles *jry* "made" and *ḫmm* "unknown,"[52] their subjects *mr.t* "pain" and *rn=f* "his name" respectively. The latter case is an example of the so-called *bahuvrīhi*-construction, typical for the expression of physical or moral qualities, in which an asyndetic adjectival or pseudoverbal sentence modifies an animate antecedent.[53]

With pronominal subjects, however, rather than the expected dependent pronoun, this pattern displays the suffix pronoun, making it appear a relative verbal form *sḏm(.y)=f* in all respects similar to the relative conversions of the active *sḏm.n=f* for the past, of the geminated or reduplicated *sḏm=f* for the aorist, and of the prospective *sḏm(.w)=f* for the future:

(106) Pyr. 27d *rꜣ=k rꜣ n(j) bḥz jrṯ.t hrww ms(y)=f jm*
"Your mouth (*rꜣ=k*) is the mouth of a suckling calf (*bḥz jrṯ.t* "a calf of milk") on the day in which it was born"

(107) CT I 248e B4C *jtj=ṯ pw msy=ṯ n=f*
"He is your father (*jtj=ṯ*) to whom you (fem.) were born"

The underlying sentences before relative conversion are assumed to be **jw msj.w bḥz m hrww* (passive *sḏm(.w)=f* with following nominal subject) "a calf was born on a certain day" > **jw=f msj.w jm* (stative with preceding pronominal subject) "it was born then" and *jw=ṯ msj.tj n=f* "you were born to him." Morphologically, one could posit the existence of a finite relative passive *sḏm(.y)=f jm* "in which he was heard," corresponding to the active *sḏm(.w).n=f* "which he heard." In this case, a parallel could be drawn to the passive equivalent of the active *sḏm.t=f* after negative particle *nj* or prepositions (section 4.6.3.1), itself etymologically a perfective (or prospective) relative form,[54] which looks like a perfective passive participle followed by its nominal subject, but of which rare examples with pronominal suffix are also documented:

(108) Pyr. 779b *sḫm.n=ṯ m ẖ.t mꜣw.t=ṯ tfnt nj ms(y).t=ṯ*
"You have acquired power (*sḫm.n=ṯ*) in the body (*ẖ.t*) of your mother Tefnut, before you were born"

(109) CT V 124a–b M3C *mk rk s(j) ḥr wḫr.t nj šdy.t=s*
"Look, she is at the wharf (*wḫr.t*), without having been cut out yet"

Alternatively, instead of positing the presence of a special verb form, and in order to keep the symmetry with the other cases of agentless or passive relative conversion, one can analyze the predicates in these sentences as conjugated participles (*msy=f* "born-he," *msy=ṯ* "born-you"), in which the use of the suffix pronoun instead of the dependent series is a signal of the progressive assimilation of passive relative clauses to their active equivalents, before the global reorganization of relative patterns which takes place in later Egyptian and which will be discussed in section 7.9.4.

Thus, the general rule of relativization of Egyptian verbal clauses can be formulated in the following way: verbal clauses in which the overt agent of the verbal predicate is different from the modified antecedent are converted into relative clauses by means of a finite adjectival form of the verbal conjugation, i.e. a relative VP; verbal clauses in which the agent of the predication is either coreferential with the modified antecedent or remains unexpressed are converted into relative clauses by means of a non-finite adjectival form, i.e. a participle.

7.8 Negation in verbal clauses

The nature and the structure of Egyptian negative particles and constructions have already been presented in section 4.6.5; also, their behavior in nominal and adverbial sentences was analyzed in sections 5.7 and 6.5. We shall now observe that the negation of verbal sentences basically involves the same morphemes and displays a similar distribution of semantic and pragmatic functions.

7.8.1 Contradictory negation in main verbal clauses

Initial and non-initial verbal clauses are negated by means of the contradictory particle *nj* preceding the verbal predicate in the perfective *nj sḏm.t=f* (110), in the preterite *nj sḏm=f* (111) or in the aorist *nj sḏm.n=f* (112). The main semantic peculiarity of these sentences is the phenomenon of polarity called in Egyptological literature "Gunn's rule":[55] while the negation of the aorist *(jw) sḏm=f* "he hears" shows the past form *nj sḏm.n=f* "he cannot/does not hear," the negative counterpart of the preterite exhibits the indicative form *nj sḏm=f* "he did not hear":

(110) Pyr. 1466b–c *msj(.w) N pn jn jtj=f tm nj ḫpr.t p.t nj ḫpr.t tꜣ*
"This King has been generated by (*msj.w N pn jn*) his father Atum before heaven had come into existence (*nj ḫpr.t p.t* "and heaven had not yet become"), before earth (*tꜣ*) had come into existence"

(111) Manchester 3306,4 *nj rḏj=j sꜣ=j n ꜥꜣmw*
"I did not turn (*nj rḏj=j* "I did not give") my back to the Asiatic"

(112) Pt. 13–14 *rꜣ gr(.w) nj mdw.n=f jb tm.w nj sḫꜣ.n=f sf*
"The mouth (*rꜣ*) is silent, and cannot speak (*nj mdw.n=f*); the heart is dumb, and cannot remember (*sḫꜣ.n=f*) the past (*sf* "yesterday")"

This polarity in the behavior of the negative main clause patterns has been variously explained.[56] The crucial typological point is that the negative patterns of natural languages are not always the result of a simple juxtaposition of a negative morpheme to the positive statement; rather, they often appear grammaticalized as *bound* constructions, and their evolution runs independent of the historical changes experienced by their positive counterpart.[57] In this respect, it is likely that the structure of the negative aorist *nj sḏm.n=f* "he cannot/does not hear" goes back to an early use of the *sḏm.n=f* as present perfect "he has heard" (section 4.6.3.1):

(113) Pyr. 18c *wsjr N ḏj.n(=j) n=k jr.t ḥrw*
"Osiris the King! I give you herewith (*ḏj.n=j n=k* "I have just given you") the Eye of Horus"

The corresponding contradictory pattern, therefore, was originally something like "he has not heard," from which the meaning as negative aorist "(and thus:) he cannot/does not hear" is easily derivable on semantic grounds. Similarly, the *sḏm=f*-form negated by the morpheme *nj* in the negative past "he did not hear" is in fact nothing other than the Old Egyptian indicative *sḏm=f*, which is the usual preterital form "he heard" in the early stages of the history of the language (section 4.6.3.1). That the *sḏm=f*-form used in the negative pattern is in fact the indicative is shown by the full writing of the verbal form as *rḏj=j* (rather than as aorist *ḏj=j*)[58] in examples (112) and (114):

(114) Urk. I 83,13–14 *jḫr ḥzj w(j) ḥm=f rḏj ḥm=f ʿq(=j) r ẖnw-ʿ*
"Since His Majesty praised me (section 6.3.1), His Majesty caused (*rḏj ḥm=f*) that I enter (*ʿq=j r*) the Privy Chamber"

In this case, the negative patterns outlived their positive equivalents: the *sḏm.n=f* maintained in the negative construction the "gnomic" function in which it was gradually replaced by the aorist *sḏm=f* for positive statements, and the indicative *sḏm=f* was still used in the negative past form even after it had been superseded by the *sḏm.n=f* for the expression of the preterite tense in positive sentences.

7.8.2 Modal negation

One will recall that the history of Egyptian morphology displays the trend to reduce the inventory of *sḏm=f*-forms (section 4.6.3) – probably concomitant with the development of a strong word stress and the progressive decay of unstressed vowels (section 3.4.3) – to the advantage of a more rigid syntax and of infixed, and later periphrastic verbal forms. This tendency is particularly evident in the negative patterns for future or prospective main verbal clauses. In Old Egyptian and in the religious texts of the Middle Kingdom (Coffin Texts), both the prospective *sḏm(.w)=f/jrj.w=f* and the subjunctive *sḏm=f/jrj=f* appear negated in main clauses by the particle *nj*:[59]

(115) CT II 225c–e *nj jj.n=j n=ṯn nj jwj=j n=ṯn r jrj.t=j jꜣꜣw*
"I do not come (*nj jj.n=j*) to you, I will not come (*nj jwj=j*, prospective) to you until I have become (*r jrj.t=j*, section 6.3.1) a fighter (?)"

(116) Pyr. 1753 *jnk ḥrw wsjr N nj ḏj(=j) z(w)nw=k prj rsj jr(=j) j.nḏ(=j) kw*
"I am Horus, Osiris the King: I shall not cause (*nj ḏj=j*, subjunctive) you to suffer (*zwnw=k*)! Come, awake to me: I shall protect (*j.nḏ=j*, subjunctive) you"

The same applies to the corresponding passives *sḏmm=f/jrj.w=f* (117) and *sḏm.tw=f* (118):

(117) Pyr. 1323 *nj j'j=f sw m ḫ3w nj sn=f ḫpš nj ḏ3j=f jw' nj ḫbss n=f t3 nj sqy n=f wdn.t pry r=f šwy r=f N pn jr p.t*
"He will not wash (*nj j'j=f*) himself in a bowl, he will not smell (*nj sn=f*) a foreleg, he will not pass (*nj ḏ3j=f*) a piece of meat, the earth will not be hacked up (*nj ḫbss t3*) for him, offerings will not be laid down (*nj sqy wdn.t*) for him; this King will go forth (*pry*) and ascend (*šwy*) himself (*r=f*) to heaven!"

(118) Pyr. 243 *prj ḥḏ.t 'm.n=s wrj.t 'm.n ns ḥḏ.t wrj.t nj m3.tj ns*
"The White Crown will come forth (*prj ḥḏ.t*) after it has swallowed (*'m.n=s*, section 7.5.2) the Great One (*wrj.t*), after the tongue of the White Crown (*ns ḥḏ.t*) has swallowed the Great One; but the tongue will not be seen (*nj m3.tj ns*)"

Although the functional opposition between prospective and subjunctive in the negative patterns is probably even thinner than in the corresponding positive constructions, it is the subjunctive, the originally more deontic form, that already in Old Egyptian displays a sporadic tendency to be negated by the "intensified" form of the negative particle (section 5.7) written with the overt indication of the phoneme /n/:

(119) Pyr. 444c^{W} *šnṯ n šnṯ=j*
"O *šnṯ*-snake, I shall not be opposed!"

This evolution is completed in the Middle Egyptian suppletive paradigm (section 4.6.3.2), whose negative equivalent is *nn sḏm=f*.[60] In the preceding chapters, we already observed that weak contradictory operators in verbless sentences exhibit the tendency to be gradually superseded by stronger, contrary negations. In the case of the classical Egyptian subjunctive, the choice of the operator of denial *nn* appears motivated by the *lack of verifiability* (or of "*jw*-hood") inherent to the semantics of modal predicates:

(120) Siut IV,79 *nn wn rn=f tp t3 nn qrs.tw=f*
"His name shall not be on earth; he shall not be buried," i.e. *it is not verifiable (*nn*) that his name be on earth (*wn rn=f tp t3*) and that he be buried (*qrs.tw=f*)

(121) Sin. B 279 *nn snḏ jr.t dgj.t n=k*
"The eye which sees you will not be afraid," i.e. *it is not verifiable (*nn*) that the eye (*jr.t*) looking at you (*dgj.t n=k*) be afraid (*snḏ*)

The subjunctive *sḏm=f* is also used to negate the very possibility of the occurrence of an event in the construction *nj-zp sḏm=f* "never did he hear," in which *zp* is a grammaticalized form of the verb *zp* "to happen."[61] This form is usually the indicative *sḏm=f* for the expression of the negative past (section 7.8.1), lit. "it did not happen (indicative) that he would hear (subjunctive)":

(122) Urk. I 106,3 *nj zp jrj.t(j) j3.t tn (j)n b3k nb ḏr b3ḥ*
"Never (*nj zp*) since the beginning (*ḏr b3ḥ*) had this office been held (*jrj.tj j3.t tn*) by any servant (*jn b3k nb*)"

but also the aorist after the negative relative converter *jwtj* "one who not" (section 7.8.6) or the subjunctive for the future, lit. "it will not happen (subj.) that he hear (subj.)":

(123) Urk. I 47,5 *jwtj zp jrj=f šnn.t rmṯ.w nb*
"One who never did what people would suffer from (*šnn.t rmṯ.w nb*)"

(124) Herdsman 6 *nn zp jry=j ḏd.t.n=s*
"I will never do what she said (*ḏd.t.n=s*)"

However, the use of the negative prospective or subjunctive in clauses of wish or expectation, where it is sometimes accompanied by intensifiers such as *ḥꜣ* "would that"[62] or *w/ꜣ*,[63] does not exhaust the domain of negative modality in earlier Egyptian. Sentences conveying a command in the imperative or in the subjunctive form are negated by means of the corresponding imperative or subjunctive form of the negative verb *jmj* "not to do" (section 4.6.5), i.e. *m* and *jm=f* respectively, followed by the negatival complement of the negated verb:

(125) Pt. 476 *m wšb(.w) m zp n(j) shꜣ*
"Do not answer (*m wšb.w*) with an attitude (*zp*) of hostility (*shꜣ*)"

(126) Peas. B1,162 *ʿqꜣ ns=k jm=k tnm.w*
"Straighten (*ʿqꜣ*) your tongue and do not (*jm=k*) go astray (*tnm.w*)"

When the subject of the negative clause is a noun, it appears affixed to the negatival complement, rather than to the conjugated negative verb; this pattern is particularly frequent in the so-called *bahuvrīhi*-construction, i.e. the pattern in which a physical or moral quality is predicated of an animate antecedent:

(127) Sh.S. 111–12 *m snḏ(.w) zp 2 nḏs m ꜣ(j)t.w jb=k*
"Do not fear, do not fear, little one (*nḏs*), do not be coward (lit. "do-not be-pale your-heart")"

This type of negative construction must have experienced a much wider use in earlier times, because one still finds cases in which not only nominal, but also pronominal subjects appear controlled by the negatival complement rather than by the negative verb:

(128) Pyr. 1267a–b *jm jw(.w) wsjr m jw.t=f tw ḏw.t m wn(.w)=k ʿ.wj=k(j) n=f*
"Let not Osiris come in that evil coming of his (*jw.t=f tw ḏw.t*); do not open your arms to him"

In the first of these two sentences, the subject of the subjunctive form *jm* is the noun "Osiris" placed after the negatival complement: *jm=f jw.w* "let him not come" vs. *jm jw.w wsjr* "let not Osiris come." In the second sentence, however, the impicit subject of the negative imperative *m wn.w* "do not open" appears resumed, as it were, by the overt second person suffix pronoun *=k* under the control of the negatival complement.

In post-classical Middle Egyptian and in later Egyptian, the synthetic negative imperative *m* is replaced by its periphrastic expansion *m jrj.w* > *m-jr* "do not do" > "don't," discussed more closely in section 7.9.2 below.

7.8.3 Contrary negation in verbal clauses

In our treatment of verbal syntax, we noticed that Egyptian makes abundant use of topicalized and adverbialized verbal phrases, embedding them into a higher sentence node. The most common of these environments is the clause in which the verbal predicate is converted into the "emphatic" form in order to isolate an adverbial adjunct in pragmatic prominence (section 7.5). These sentences differ from unmarked clauses ("I came here") in that the attentional flow of the utterance shifts from the verbal predicate to an adverbial modifier ("I came here from London"). The negation of these patterns, therefore, will not involve contradiction of the predicative nexus ("I didn't come here"), but rather *contrariety*, i.e. a restriction of the negative scope to the focalized element: "I didn't come here *from London,*" implying "but from somewhere else"; the nexus remains unaffected by the negative operator: "I did come here, but not from London."

In Egyptian, the operator of contrariety is  *nj-js* with its discontinuous form *nj...js*. This negation, although used in verbal clauses, actually affects an adverbial element rather than the verbal predicate, and was discussed at some length in section 6.5.2. Two examples will suffice here. In the first one (129), the adverbial adjunct given pragmatic focus is an adverbial phrase consisting of preposition + noun; in the second (130–130'), the focalized element is an adverbialized VP (or a stative), i.e. an unconverted verbal or pseudoverbal form embedded as adverbial phrase into the verbal main clause:

(129) Pyr. 475b–c *zẖ3 N m ḏbʿ wrj nj zẖ3=f js m ḏbʿ šrr*
"The King writes (*zẖ3 N*) with a big finger (*m ḏbʿ wrj*); it is not (*nj...js*) with a little finger (*m ḏbʿ šrr*) that he writes"

(130) Pyr. 833a *šm.n=k ʿnḫ=k nj šm.n=k js m(w)t=k*
(130') CT I 187e *šm.n=k ʿnḫ.t(j) nj šm.n=k js m(w)t(.tj)*
"You have gone away (*šm.n=k*) alive (*ʿnḫ=k*, aorist *sdm=f*/*ʿnḫ.tj*, stative), you haven't gone away dead (*mwt=k/mwt.tj*)"

The language, therefore, makes a distinction between contrary negation by means of *nj...js*, in which the scope of the negation is limited to the adverbial focus, and simple contradiction of a predicative nexus by means of *nj*. In (131), an example of contradictory negation of the type analyzed in section 7.8.1, the discourse interface between the initial cleft sentence, which focalizes the third person subject (section 5.4.2), and the following negative verbal clause shows that what is being denied in the latter is obviously the entire predicative nexus "the King goes against him," rather than the prepositional phrase alone:

(131) Pyr. 232a *swt jj r N nj šm N r=f*
"He is the one (*swt*) who came (*jj*) against the King – the King did not go (*nj šm N*) against him"

7.8.4 *Negation of verbal predicates embedded as AP*

The discussion of negative patterns in nominal, adverbial, and verbal clauses has shown us that the distribution of negative forms is dictated in Egyptian primarily by semantic or pragmatic, rather than syntactic factors. Further evidence of this tendency is provided by the study of the negation of verbal forms embedded as adverbial phrases into a higher sentence. These are regularly negated by *nj...js* when functioning as focus, as in (132), where the scope of the negation is the "virtual" relative clause modifying a non-specific antecedent as predicate of a classifying sentence ("a *wꜣḏ*-amulet"):

(132) CT II 160b–c *nj jnk js wꜣḏ swꜣj=f jnk wꜣḏ prj m nb.t*
"I am not a *wꜣḏ*-amulet which passes by (*swꜣj=f*); I am the *wꜣḏ*-amulet which came forth (*prj*, participle) from mankind (*nb.t*)"

However, a non-focalized embedded VP is negated in Old Egyptian by the "circumstantial" negative *ny* (section 6.5.2) followed by the aorist verbal form:

(133) Urk. I 16,15–17 *zꜣ-nzw nj-kꜣ.w-rꜥw[...] jrj=f wḏ.t-mdw.w ꜥnḫ(.w) ḥr rd.wj=f(j) ny mn=f jḫ.t*
"As for the royal son Nikaureʿ [...], he made a testament (*wḏ.t-mdw.w* "a command of words") being alive (*ꜥnḫ.w*) on his feet, while not suffering (*ny mn=f*) in anything"

(134) Urk. I 43,5 *(...) hbn(j) ḫtm ny zp [jrj.t(j) mjt.t n bꜣk] nb ḏr pꜣw.t tꜣ*
"(...) sealed ebony, no similar thing having ever been done (*ny zp jrj.tj mj.tt*, section 7.8.2) for any servant since the beginning of the world (*ḏr pꜣw.t tꜣ*)"

We also observed that the **O** > **E** drift, i.e. the tendency for contradictory negations to acquire contrary functions, led in classical Egyptian to the obsolescence of *ny* and its replacement by "strong" constructions with *nn* + infinitive, when the subject of the embedded AP is coindexed with the subject of the main predication, or with *nj-js* followed by a finite verbal form, when the subject of the embedded AP is different:

(135) Siut I,293 *ḥ'.n rdj.n=f n=sn st r tꜣ nn šdj.t st m-'=sn*
"Then he released it for them (*rdj.n=f n=sn st r tꜣ* "he put it to the earth for them"), without taking (*nn šdj.t*) it away from them"

(136) BD 125γ,28 *nn dj=n 'q=k ḥr=n j.n bnš.w n(.w) sbꜣ pn nj-js ḏd.n=k rn=n*
"'We shall not let you enter (*nn dj=n 'q=k*) through us,' said the jambs of this gate, 'unless (*nj-js*) you have pronounced our name'"

7.8.5 Negation of verbal predicates embedded as NP

Topicalized verbal forms. Let us return for a moment to the analysis of negations in the sentence with topicalized predicate. Since in this utterance the pragmatic focus shifts from the verbal predicate to an adverbialized or adverbial element, the scope of its negative counterpart with *nj...js* is the focalized element itself: rather than a contradictory negation of the predicative nexus, these sentences display a contrary negation of the focus.

This redistribution of the pragmatic focuses is achieved by means of a conversion of the verbal predicate into a "topicalized" form: while it is only in the aorist that this conversion results in a *morphologically* different form from the parallel main verbal pattern (*jrr=f* vs. *jrj=f*), the *syntactic* transformation equally applies to the *sḏm.n=f* and the prospective *sḏm=f*. When the scope of the negation does not invest the pragmatic focus of a sentence with topicalized predicate, but rather the presuppositional predicate itself – a frequent environment in the case when the focalized element is an interrogative adverb – Egyptian has recourse to a construction with the verb *tm* "to complete" > "not to do" as a finite verbal form followed by the negatival complement (section 4.6.4) of the negated verb:

(137) Peas. B1,211 *sḏm.w nj ꜣ sḏm.n=k tm=k tr sḏm(.w) ḥr-m*
"Hearer (*sḏm.w*), you don't really (*ꜣ*) hear! So (*tr*), why (*ḥr-m*) don't you hear (*tm=k sḏm.w*)?"

(138) West. 6,5 *tm=ṯ ḫnj(.w) ḥr-m* "Why (*ḥr-m*) don't you (*tm=ṯ*) row (*ḫnj.w*)?"

In these two examples, the negative verbal patterns correspond to the positive sentences **sḏm=k ḥr-m* "why do you hear?" or **ḫnn=ṯ ḥr-m* "why do you row?" The construction with *tm* is also used to negate a contingent tense (139) or in headings or titles, with the nominal subject placed after the negatival complement, as in the case of *jmj* (140):

(139) Pyr. 696f–g *m jnj(.w) sṯj hdn=ṯ r N tm.ḫr.ṯ jnj(.w) sṯj hdn=ṯ r N*
"'Do not bring the smell of the *hdn*-plant to the King!' Therefore, you do not bring the smell of the *hdn*-plant to the King"

(140) CT VI 384h *tm ḥwꜣ.w zj m ḫr.t nṯr*
"[This spell describes] how a man does not putrefy (*tm ḥwꜣ.w zj*) in the Necropolis"

Nominal conversions. The use of a conjugated verbal form of *tm* followed by the negatival complement (and in later times by the infinitive)[64] represents the common syntactic device for generating the negative equivalent of any nominal or adjectival conversion of the verb, whether finite or non-finite. Accordingly, this construction is found in all the patterns we considered in sections 7.5–6. Let us consider first the "balanced sentence" with two topicalized VPs (section 7.5.4) and its interface with the protasis of a conditional clause:

(141) CT V 326g–h *jwj=k r=j ḏd=j r=k tmm=k jw(.w) r=j tm=j ḏd(.w) r=k*
"You come to me, I'll speak to you; you don't come to me, I won't speak to you"[65]
(142) CT V 323h–i *jwj=k r=j ḏd=j r=k tm=k jw(.w) r=j nn ḏd=j r=k*
"You come to me, I'll speak to you; if you don't come (*tm=k jw.w*) to me, I won't speak (*nn ḏd=j*) to you"

A contrastive analysis of (141) and (142) provides interesting insights into the historical syntax of the balanced sentence. While in the former example both the positive and the negative statement are treated as balanced sentences, in the latter the use of different negative patterns shows that these are clauses with a topicalized VP (*jwj=k – tm=k jw.w*) extraposed to the left of a main sentence with prospective *sḏm=f* (*ḏd=j – nn ḏd=j*).[66]

In the more usual form of conditional clause in classical Egyptian, in which the protasis is introduced by the conjunction *jr* (section 6.3.1), a negative condition is expressed by the conjugated form of *tm*:

(143) pKahun 7,53–56 *jr tm=f snb(.w) wdn=f ẖr ḏbʿ.w=k tm tm(.w) jr.tj=fj šnj.ḫr=k jr.tj=fj m p3q.t st3.t(j) m ḫ.t r dr ḥ3.tj*
"If it (i.e. the bull) does not recover (*tm=f snb.w*), it is heavy (*wdn=f*) under your fingers, and his eyes do not close (*tm*), you shall surround (*šnj.ḫr=k*) his eyes with a potsherd (*p3q.t*) heated with fire, in order to remove (*dr*) the *ḥ3.tj*-disease"

or treated as an adverbial clause under the control of a noun clause:

(144) pEbers 49,8 *kt sm3ʿ mwy.t tm=s m3ʿ.w*
"This (is) another (remedy) for putting right (*sm3ʿ*) the water (*mwy.t*) if it is not right"

Furthermore, the negative verb *tm* is commonly found in "thetic" statements for the negation of the verbal clause embedded as nominal predicate of a classifying *pw*-pattern:

(145) pSmith 4,2–3 *jr r3=f mr(.w)... tm=f wn.w r3=f pw mdw=f*
"If his mouth (*r3=f*) is tied..., this means (*pw*) that he cannot open (*tm=f wn.w*) his mouth to speak (*mdw=f* "that he may speak")"

or as the object of a verb of perception in the aorist (146) and of verbs of wish or command in the subjunctive (147):

(146) Pyr. 998 *mṯn nw ḏd(w).n=ṯn nṯr.w tm N wnn(.w) m ḫnt=ṯn mṯn N mn(.w) m ḫnt=ṯn m jmnw*
"Look at what you said, gods, (namely) that the King is not (*tm N wnn.w*) before you: look, the King is now established (*N mn.w*) before you as a victorious bull (*jmnw*)"

(147) Harhotep 396–97 *jw wḏ.n gbb jtj wsjr tm=j wnm(.w) ḥs tm=j zwr(.w) wsš.t*
"Geb, Osiris' father, has commanded (*wḏ*) that I not eat (*tm=j wnm.w*) excrements and that I not drink (*tm=j zwr.w*) urine"

Like its positive counterpart (section 7.2), the negative subjunctive with *tm* is also used as a non-embedded subordinate clause (corresponding to English "lest") after the imperative:

(148) Peas. B1,245 *m kꜣhs.w ḫft wsr=k tm spr(.w) bw-ḏw r=k*
"Do not be ruthless (*kꜣhs*) as a result of (*ḫft* "according to") your power, lest misfortune (*bw-ḏw*) befall you"

Finally, the negative nominal conversion by means of *tm* is also used after prepositions or conjunctions, in the *sḏm.t=f*-form, and in the negation of the infinitive:

(149) Siut I,229 *sgr qꜣj-ḫrw r tm=f mdw.w*
"To silence (*sgr*) the loud-voiced so that he may not speak"

(150) Pt. 465–66 *jrj zp ḥnꜥ=f wꜥw r tm.t=k mn(.w) ḫr.t=f*
"Solve the problem (*jrj zp* "do the matter") with him alone (*wꜥw*, stative), until you don't suffer (*tm=k mn.w*, transitive) any more because of his situation (*ḫr.t=f*)"

(151) CT VI 303r *tm šm(.w) sḫd(.w)*
"Not to walk (*tm šm.w*) while being upside down (*sḫd.w*, stative)"

7.8.6 Negation of adjectival conversions

Adjectival conversions of the verb are treated like nominal VPs: participles and relative forms are negated by the corresponding form of *tm* followed by the negatival complement:

(152) Urk. IV 780,10–13 *tꜣ.w nb štꜣ(.w) n.w pḥw.w stt... tmm.w ḫnd(.w) st jn ky.w bjtj.w wp-ḥr ḥm=f*
"All the secret lands (*tꜣ.w nb štꜣ.w*) of the limits of Nubia...which were not trodden upon by any other kings except His Majesty"

(153) Urk. IV 1074,4–5 *ḏḥwtj pw m ḫt nb nn md.t tm.t.n=f ꜥrq(.w) [sj]*
"He is Thoth (*ḏḥwtj*) in everything: there is nothing which he does not understand"

In (152), the participial form of *tm* is the one displayed by the negated verb in the positive pattern, i.e. in this case the perfective passive **ḫnd.w* "those which were trodden upon" vs. *tmm.w ḫnd.w* "those which were not trodden upon"; the form *tmm.w* shows the gemination of the second consonant typical for the 2-rad. roots (section 4.6.4). In (153), the past relative form *tm.t.n=f ʿrq.w* "which he does not understand" is the negative equivalent of a relative clause **ʿrq.t.n=f* "which he understands" and modifies the feminine antecedent *md.t* "a thing," i.e. the subject of a nominal sentence predicated by *nn* (section 5.7), resumed by the object pronoun *sj* "it."

One will recall (section 6.3.3) that in Egyptian the use of *adjectival* relative clauses introduced by a converter of the series *ntj* is restricted to specific antecedents, non-specific nouns being modified by unconverted *adverbial* clauses. The same opposition is present in their negative counterparts: in (154), the specific noun *zj* "the man" is modified by a "true" negative relative clause introduced by *ntj*, whereas in (155) the non-specific participle *wnm* "an eater" is modified by a "virtual relative clause," i.e. by an unconverted negative verbal sentence embedded as adverbial phrase:

(154) pEbers 12,15 *zj ntj nj fgn.n=f* "the man who cannot defecate"
(155) Siut I,272 *wnm nj sb(j)n.n=f*
"a beneficiary (*wnm* "an eater") who cannot withdraw from the principal (*nj sbjn.n=f* "he cannot cut down")"

A different set of negative relative clauses, however, displays an interesting feature: the presence of a negative converter *jwtj* (fem. *jwtt*, pl. *jwtj.w*) "which not," paired by a rare negative conjunction *jwt(t)* "that not." These morphemes represent a semantic fusion of relative element (*ntj*) plus negative operator (*nj* for verbal sentences, *nn* for nominal and adverbial sentences):

(156) Pt. 234–37 *kf3-jb jwt(j) pẖr=f ḏd(.w) m ẖ.t=f ḫpr=f m ṯzw ḏs=f*
"The trustworthy man (*pḥ-jb* "he whose heart is clear") who does not vent (*pẖr*) what is said in his belly (*ẖ.t=f*) – he will himself (*ḏs=f*) become a leader (*ṯzw*)"
(157) Urk. I 122,6–8 *jw rdj.n(=j) t? n ḥqr ḥbs n ḥ3y zm3.n(=j) t3 m jwt(j) mẖn.t=f*
"I gave bread (*t?*) to the hungry (*ḥqr*), clothes to the naked (*ḥ3y*), I ferried across (*zm3.n=j t3*) with (*m*) the boatless (*jwtj mẖn.t=f* = *ntj nn mẖn.t=f* "he whose boat does not exist")"
(158) Urk. IV 68,3 *jwtj wn=f ḫr rmṯ.w*
"One whom people do not blame," lit. one-who-is-not (*jwtj*) his blame (*wn=f*) by the people (*ḫr rmṯ.w*)

Historically, verbal and adverbial clauses controlled by *jwtj* tend to be superseded by analytic equivalents with *ntj*+negative form (159);[67] this trend was probably inaugurated in cases in which the nominal antecedent modified by the negative relative clause is the object, rather than the subject of the main clause (160):

(159) Sh.S. 72–73 *rdj=j rḫ=k tw jw=k m ss ḫpr.t(j) m ntj nj mꜣ.t(w)=f*
"I shall cause that you see yourself in ashes (*ss*), having turned into someone who cannot be seen," instead of a typologically more archaic *...*m jwtj mꜣ.tw=f*, or
(160) Peas. B1,347 *m pḥ(.w) ntj nj pḥ.n=f*
"Do not attack him who (*ntj*) cannot attack (*nj pḥ.n=f*)."

It needs to be stressed that negative verbal clauses controlled by *jwtj* (or by its more analytic version *ntj nj*) are proportionally more frequent than positive verbal clauses introduced by *ntj*. The reason is obvious: while in the positive relative clauses the predicate, whether participle or relative form, immediately follows the antecedent it modifies, in the negative equivalents the presence of the negative morpheme breaks this contiguity between modified NP and VP. In terms of their semantic performance, constructions with *jwtj* and negative forms of adjectival conversions are, therefore, quite similar to each other. However, they differ syntactically: while participles or relative forms negated by *tm* are conversions of a relative clause, i.e. S => NEG[AdjP], constructions with *jwtj* or *ntj*+negative form represent the conversion of a nominal, adverbial, or verbal negative clause, i.e. S' => ADJ [Neg S]. One may compare the functional equivalence vs. the syntactic variety in the two examples below, where the same quality is rendered by a negated participle (*tm bꜣg.w*) in (161) and by the relative conversion of a negative sentence (*jwtj qdd=f*) in (162), or the sequence of attributes in (161) is alternatively conveyed by a negative conversion of an adjectival phrase (*tm bꜣg.w* => NEG[*bꜣgj*]) and by a relative conversion of a negative sentence (*jwtj qdd=f* => ADJ [*nj qdj.n=f*]):

(161) Urk. IV 959,15 *tm bꜣg(.w) ḥr rḏy.t m ḥr=f jwtj qdd=f m grḥ ḫrp rsj-tp*
"One who is not fatigued in (performing) what has been entrusted to him (*rḏy.t m ḥr=f* "what has been put to his face"), one who does not sleep at night (*grḥ*), a vigilant leader"
(162) Urk. IV 410,5–6 *jwtj b(ꜣ)gg=f ḥr mn.w n nb nṯr.w*
"One who is not fatigued in (building) the monuments (*mn.w*) of the Lord of the gods"

A proof of this variance in the hierarchy of conversions affecting negative equivalents of relative clauses is provided by the behavior of verbal predicates: while in the constructions with *tm* and *ntj nj* the morphosyntactic idiosyncrasies of the forms before conversion are always kept – for example the morphological features of a perfective passive participle *ḫnd.w* are transferred to *tmm.w* in (152), those of a past relative form *ʿrq.t.n=f* to *tm.t.n=f* in (153), and the bound negative aorist pattern *nj pḥ.n=f* follows Gunn's rule (section 7.8.1) even when controlled by the relative adjective *ntj* in example (160) – relativization by means of *jwtj* provokes a global reorganization of the syntactic structure of the sentence: the verbal form controlled by *jwtj* is always a converted nominal VP, i.e. the aorist *jrr=f* for the general present and the *sḏm.n=f* for the past: in (161), *jwtj qdd=f* represents the adjectival conversion of an underlying negative verbal sentence **nj qdj.n=f m grḥ* "he does not sleep at night." This usage, however, is probably itself the result of an evolution from a more synthetic stage, still documented in the Pyramid Texts, in which Gunn's rule also applies to *jwtj* followed by a *sḏm.n=f* with aorist function:

(163) Pyr. 2057–58 *N pw wʿw m (j)fdw jpw wnn.w msj.w tm msj.w nw.t jwtj.w ḥwꜣ.n=sn nj ḥwꜣ N jwtj.w jmk.n=sn n jmk N jwtj.w ḫr.n=sn jr tꜣ m p.t nj ḫr N jr tꜣ m p.t*
"The King is one of these four beings (*jfdw jpw wnn.w*) whom Atum bore (*msj.w tm*) and whom Nut bore, who cannot putrefy (*jwtj.w ḥwꜣ.n=sn = ntj.w nj ḥwꜣ.n=sn*) – the King shall not putrefy! – who cannot decay (*jwtj.w jmk.n=sn = ntj.w nj jmk.n=sn*) – the King shall not decay! – who cannot fall (*jwtj.w ḫr.n=sn = ntj.w nj ḫr.n=sn*) to the earth from heaven – the King shall not fall to the earth from heaven!"

7.9 Verbal syntax in later Egyptian

7.9.1 General features

When compared to the classical language, the verbal system of later Egyptian is characterized both by a great richness of morphological forms and by a simplification of syntactic patterns (section 4.6.6). From a typological point of view, earlier Egyptian *synthetic* forms in which a predicative base consisting of verbal stem plus affixes is followed by the subject (V-S) are replaced by periphrastic equivalents with the verb *jrj* "to do": *sḏm.n=f* > *sdm=f* > *jr=f-sdm* "he heard." These forms are reanalyzed as *analytic* pattterns with a predicative base consisting of verbal prefix plus subject followed by the infinitive, i.e. the verbal lexeme: *jr=f-sdm* *"he did the hearing" > **ⲁ=ϥ-ⲥⲱⲧⲙ̄** "he heard." This evolution, favored by the expiratory stress which reduced the functional yield of unstressed vowels, eventually led the *flectional* earlier Egyptian type to acquire *polysynthetic* features: an entire sentence with subject, predicate, and peripheral components, can appear in Coptic as one prosodic unit: classical *jw-sḏm.n=f*$_1$ *rmṯ*$_2$ */jawsaˈɟimnaf ˈraːmac/ > Late Egyptian *jr=f-sdm*$_1$ *wʿ-rm(t)*$_2$ */ʔarəfˈsoːdəm waʕˈroːmə/ > Coptic **ⲁϥⲥⲉⲧⲙⲟⲩⲣⲱⲙⲉ** /ʔafsətmˈwroːmə/ "he heard a man."

From a syntactic point of view, the transition from the earlier to the later Egyptian stage is accompanied by numerous adjustments in the structure of main and subordinate clauses on the one hand and of embedded constructions on the other, with an increased presence of pseudoverbal constructions with preposition+infinitive and stative replacing simple verbal patterns, for example *wn.jn=f ḥr sdm*, *ʿḥʿ.n=f ḥr sdm* "then he heard."[68] The following sections presuppose a familiarity with the formal evolution of verbal patterns in later Egyptian as described in section 4.6.6.

7.9.2 Initial verbal clauses and parataxis

In the transition to the later Egyptian main clause patterns, the initial particle of the classical language has ceased to be a functionally relevant component of the sentence: positive and negative verbal forms are now autonomous patterns often labeled *sentence conjugations*,[69] which can also appear paratactically linked to the preceding segment of discourse. For example, the Late Egyptian form *sdm=f* > Demotic *jr=f-sdm* > Coptic Perfect I ⲁ=ϥ-ⲥⲱⲧⲙ̄ is the successor of the Middle Egyptian preterital pattern *jw sḏm.n=f*:[70]

(164) LRL 57,7 *sdm=j md.wt nb* "I heard all matters"

(165) Dem. Mag. Pap. V20,2–3 *jr=f šk3=f r ḏ3ḏ3=f n 3 r n md.t-jkš*
"He hit him (*jr=f šk3=f* *"he did the beating of him") on his head with three spells (*r*) in the Cushite language (*md.t-jkš* "the thing of Kush")"

(166) 1 Jn 2,11 ⲁⲡⲕⲁⲕⲉ ⲧⲱⲙ ⲛ̄ⲛⲉϥⲃⲁⲗ
"Darkness (*p-kake*) closed (*a... tôm*) his eyes (*n-ne=f-bal*)"

The indicative *sḏm=f* in the earlier Egyptian negative past *nj sḏm=f* (section 7.8.1) is now replaced by a periphrastic construction with the verb *p3w* "to have done in the past":[71] *nj sḏm=f* > *n p3w=f sdm* > *bw-pw=f-sdm* > ⲙ̄ⲡⲉ=ϥ-ⲥⲱⲧⲙ̄. One will remember that the use of the negative morpheme *bw* > ⲙ̄-, the heir of the Middle Egyptian particle *nj*, is now restricted to bound verbal phrases, i.e. to sentence conjugations:

(167) Deut 1,43 ⲁⲓϣⲁϫⲉ ⲇⲉ ⲛⲙ̄ⲙⲏⲧⲛ̄ ⲁⲩⲱ ⲙ̄ⲡⲉⲧⲛ̄ⲥⲱⲧⲙ̄ ⲛⲁⲓ
"I spoke (*a=i-šaje*) to you (*nmmê=tn*) but (*auô*) you did not listen (*mpe=tn-sôtm*) to me"

A similar periphrastic evolution is characteristic for the perfective negative form *nj sḏm.t=f* (section 7.8.1) "he has/had/will have not yet heard," which develops into the Late Egyptian *bw sdm.t=f* > *bw jr.t=f sdm* and the Coptic sentence conjugation ⲙ̄ⲡⲁⲧϥ̄ⲥⲱⲧⲙ̄:

(168) KRI III 160,14 *bw jr.t st-ḥr spr r=j* "Sathor has not yet reached (*spr r*) me"

(169) Jn 2,4 ⲙ̄ⲡⲁⲧⲉⲧⲁⲟⲩⲛⲟⲩ ⲉⲓ
"My hour (*ta-ounou*) has not yet come (*mpate... ei*)"

For the general present *jw(=f) sḏm=f*, Late Egyptian originally uses the adverbial construction known as Present I (section 6.6.1), but later develops a new verbal aorist *ḫr sḏm=f* "he hears" from the contingent pattern *sḏm.ḫr=f* "then he hears."[72] In Demotic and Coptic, ϣⲁ=ϥ-ⲥⲱⲧⲙ̄, i.e. the sentence conjugation derived from it, is used with "gnomic" meaning:[73]

(170) KRI II 88,1–5 *jr pꜣ-ntj nb ḫr šm r ẖ'm=f ḫr jw hh=s n ḫ.t r wḏb ḥ'.w=f*
"As to anyone who sets out (*šm*) to approach him (*ẖ'm=f*), its blast of fire (*hh=s n ḫ.t*) comes (*jw*) to consume (*wḏb*) his body"

(171) Myth 3,29–30 *ḫr ḥl[=f] r tꜣ-p.t jrm nꜣ-ꜣpd.w ḫr hrw ḫr ḫpr=f ẖn pꜣ-mw jrm nꜣ-rym.w n-mnꜣj*
"He flies (*ḫr ḥl=f*) to heaven with (*jrm*) the birds everyday (*ḫr hrw*); he is (*ḫr ḫpr=f*) in the water with the fish daily (*n-mnꜣj*)"

(172) Lk 4,6 ϯϯ ⲛⲁⲕ ⲛ̄ⲧⲉⲓⲉⲍⲟⲩⲥⲓⲁ ⲧⲏⲣⲥ̄ ⲙⲛ̄ ⲡⲉⲩⲉⲟⲟⲩ...ⲁⲩⲱ ϣⲁⲓⲧⲁⲁⲥ ⲙ̄ⲡⲉϯⲟⲩⲁϣϥ̄
"I give (*t=i-ti*) you all this power (ἐξουσία) and (*mn*) their glory (*pe=u-eoou*)...and (*auô*) I give it (*ša=i-taa=s*, aorist) to whomever I want (*p-et=i-ouaš=f* "the one whom I want him)"

The negative sentence conjugation pattern corresponding to ϣⲁϥⲥⲱⲧⲙ̄ is Middle Egyptian *nj sḏm.n=f > bw sḏm(.n)=f > bw jr=f sdm >* ⲙⲉ=ϥ-ⲥⲱⲧⲙ̄:[74]

(173) KRI II 65,1–4 *jr pḥ=j r ḥḥ jm=sn bw jr rd.wj smn ḫr w'r=sn*
"If I attack (*pḥ=j*) thousands of them, their feet cannot (*bw jr rd.wj*) remain stable (*smn*), and they run away (*ḫr w'r=sn*)"

(174) Jn 4,9 ⲙⲉⲣⲉⲓⲟⲩⲇⲁⲓ ⲧⲱϩ ⲙⲛ̄ ⲥⲁⲙⲁⲣⲓⲧⲏⲥ
"Jews do not mix (*mere... tôh*) with Samaritans"

In the future tense or prospective aspect, the situation is in some respects similar to the aorist. As we saw in chapter 6, the objective future is expressed in Late Egyptian and early Demotic by the adverbial pattern *jw=f r sdm*, and in later Demotic and Coptic by the "progressive" form of the Present I, i.e. by the Future I ϥⲛⲁⲥⲱⲧⲙ̄ (section 6.6.1). The modal future, on the other hand, is conveyed in Late Egyptian by the prospective *sdm=f*, the heir of the classical prospective *sḏm=f*:[75]

(175) Horus and Seth 5,3–4 *ḏꜣy=tn r pꜣ-jw ḥrj-jb*
"May you cross (*ḏꜣy=tn*) to the island in the middle"

Although the bare *sdm=f* is still found in Demotic in modal contexts,[76] the more recent phases of later Egyptian show the emergence of two patterns conveying epistemic or deontic connotations. The first one is the old objective future *jw=f r sdm/j.jr pꜣ-rmt (r) sdm*, which – together with its negative equivalent *bn jw=f r sdm* > ⲛ̄ⲛⲉ=ϥ-ⲥⲱⲧⲙ̄ – is now the Future III, completely integrated into the paradigm of verbal sentence conjugations:[77]

(176) Gen 3,16 ⲉⲣⲉϫⲡⲟ ⲛ̄ⲛⲟⲩϣⲏⲣⲉ ϩⲛ̄ ⲟⲩⲁϣⲁϩⲟⲙ
"You shall bear (*er=e-jpo*) your children (*n-nou-šêre*) in (*hn*) sorrow (*ašahom*)"

(177) Ex 23,7 ⲉⲕⲉⲥⲁϩⲱⲕ ⲉⲃⲟⲗ ⲛ̄ϩⲁⲡ ⲛⲓⲙ ⲛ̄ϫⲓⲛϭⲟⲛⲥ ⲛ̄ⲛⲉⲕⲙⲟⲩⲟⲩⲧ ⲛ̄ⲟⲩⲁⲧⲛⲟⲃⲉ ⲙⲛ̄ ⲟⲩⲇⲓⲕⲁⲓⲟⲥ ⲁⲩⲱ ⲛ̄ⲛⲉⲕⲧⲙⲁⲉⲓⲟ ⲛ̄ⲟⲩⲁⲥⲉⲃⲏⲥ ⲉⲧⲃⲉ ⲇⲱⲣⲟⲛ

"You shall distance yourself (*e=k-e-sahô=k*) from any word of falsity (*jincons*); you shall not kill (*nne=k-mouout*) an innocent (*n-ou-at-nobe*) and a just, and you shall not justify (*nne=k-tmaeio*) a culprit (ἀσεβής) because of (*etbe*) a gift (δῶρον)"

The second modal pattern of Demotic and Coptic is etymologically a causative construction in which *mj*, the imperative of the verb *rḏj* "to give, to cause to," is followed by a prospective verbal form periphrastically built with the verb *jrj* "to do": *mj jr=f sdm* > ⲙⲁ-ⲣⲉ=ϥ-ⲥⲱⲧⲙ̄, lit. "cause that-he-do hearing" > "let him hear." This form is labeled "optative" and is used in complementary distribution with the imperative:[78]

(178) Dem. Mag. Pap. 2,26 *my jrj qmj mḥ pꜣ-tꜣ n wyn*
"Let creation (*qmj*) fill the earth with light (*wyn*)"

(179) Mt 6,9 ⲙⲁⲣⲉⲡⲉⲕⲣⲁⲛ ⲟⲩⲟⲡ
"May your name (*pe=k-ran*) be hallowed (*mare... ouop*)"

The imperative itself undergoes some changes: in Late Egyptian, one can observe the early tendency towards the grammaticalization of *jmj* > *mj*, i.e. the imperative of *rḏj*, as verbal prefixes in lexicalized units;[79] in Demotic and Coptic, the imperative is replaced by the infinitive in the majority of verbs, its existence as an autonomous morphological category being gradually limited to the 2-rad. (*j.ḏd* from *ḏd* "to say") and the III-inf. roots (*j.jr* from *jrj* "to do"),[80] until in Coptic it only survives in a few remnants (*mj* > ⲙⲁ "give!," *jmj* > ⲁⲙⲟⲩ "come!," *j.wn* > ⲁⲟⲩⲱⲛ "open!," etc.).[81]

In the negative, both imperative and optative display a periphrastic form of causative origin, with the imperative of the verb *jmj* followed by the negatival complement of the verb *jrj* (*m jr.w* > ⲙ̄ⲡⲣ̄-) and by the simple infinitive in the case of the imperative (*sḏm* > ⲥⲱⲧⲙ̄), or by the causative infinitive[82] in the case of the optative (*dj.t jr=f sḏm* > ⲧⲣⲉ=ϥ-ⲥⲱⲧⲙ):

(180) Lk 23,28 ⲙ̄ⲡⲣ̄ⲣⲓⲙⲉ "Do not (*mpr-*) cry!," vs. ⲣⲓⲙⲉ "cry!"

(181) Jon 1,14 ⲙ̄ⲡⲣ̄ⲧⲣⲉⲛⲙⲟⲩ
"Let us not (*mpr-tre=n*) die!," vs. ⲙⲁⲣⲉⲛⲙⲟⲩ "let us die"

The causative infinitive is a productive form of the Coptic conjugation system, being used not only in the negative optative, but also as a counterpart of the simple infinitive in prospective clauses controlled by the preposition ⲉ-, when the subject is different from that of the main clause:

(182) Lk 7,6–7 ⲛ̄ϯⲙ̄ⲡϣⲁ ⲅⲁⲣ ⲁⲛ ⲉⲧⲣⲉⲕⲉⲓ ⲉϩⲟⲩⲛ ϩⲁ ⲧⲁⲟⲩⲉϩⲥⲟⲓ ⲉⲧⲃⲉ ⲡⲁⲓ ⲣⲱ ⲙ̄ⲡⲓⲁⲁⲧ ⲛⲙ̄ⲡϣⲁ ⲉⲉⲓ ϣⲁⲣⲟⲕ
"For (γάρ) I am not worthy (*t=i-mpša*, lit. *"I am in-worthiness") that you should enter (*e-tre=k-ei*, causative inf.) under my roof (*t=a-ouehsoi* "my addition-of-beams"); for this reason (*etbe pai*) I too (*rô*) did not consider myself worthy (*mp=i-aa=t n-mpša* "I did not make myself in worthiness") of coming (*e-ei*, simple inf.) to you (*šaro=k*)"

and in sentence conjugations in order to convey causative meaning. This infinitive form represents the grammaticalized equivalent of the infinitives of the type *dj.t sꜣw=* > ⲧⲥⲓⲟ "to make sated" or *dj.t ꜥnḫ=* > ⲧⲁⲛϩⲟ "to keep alive," in which the final vowel *ó* derives from the stressed **á* of the Middle Egyptian subjunctive stem (section 4.6.3.2). In the verse "he made the hungry sated with good things," the causative preterite is rendered in Sahidic by the Perfect I of the causative verb ⲧⲥⲓⲟ "to make sated," in Bohairic by the Perfect I of the causative infinitive ⲑⲣ=ⲟⲩ-ⲥⲓ "to cause that they be sated":

(183) Lk 1,53 ˢⲁϥⲧⲥⲓⲉⲛⲉⲧϩⲕⲁⲉⲓⲧ ⲛ̄ⲁⲅⲁⲑⲟⲛ
"He-made-sated-those-who-are-hungry (*a=f-tsie n-et-hkaeit*) good-things (ἀγαθόν)"
(183') Ibid. ᴮⲛⲏ ⲉⲧϩⲟⲕⲉⲣ ⲁϥⲑⲣⲟⲩⲥⲓ ⲛ̀ⲁⲅⲁⲑⲟⲛ
"Those who were (*nê et-*) hungry, he-caused-that-they-be-sated (*a=f-thr=ou-si*) good-things"

We saw in section 4.6.6.3 that a common form of topicalization in the latest phase of Egyptian consists in resuming the subject of a conjugation pattern by means of the particle ˢⲛ̄ϭⲓ/ᴮⲛ̀ϫⲉ. In this respect, the use of the causative infinitive generates ambiguity, since the topicalized element can be the subject of the sentence conjugation, as in (184), or the subject of the causative infinitive, i.e. the object of the conjugation pattern, as in (185):

(184) Ps 83,12 ᴮⲛ̀ⲛⲉϥⲑⲣⲟⲩⲉⲣ ϧⲁⲉ ⲛ̀ⲛⲓⲁⲅⲁⲑⲟⲛ ⲛ̀ϫⲉ ⲡϭ̅ⲥ̅
"The Lord (*p-c(ôi)s*) will not let the good things be in want (*nne=f-thr=ou-er xae* "he-will-not-cause-that-they do-end")"
(185) Ps 102,12 ᴮⲁϥⲑⲣⲟⲩⲟⲩⲉⲓ ⲙ̀ⲙⲟⲛ ⲛ̀ϫⲉ ⲛⲉⲛⲁⲛⲟⲙⲓⲁ
"He let our wrongdoings (ἀνομία) be far (*a=f-thr=ou-ouei*) from us (*mmo=n*)"

This ambiguity is solved in the case of passive constructions. While Late Egyptian maintains the synthetic passives of the classical language (past *sḏm(.w)=f*, aorist and prospective *sḏm.tw=f*),[83] with the *tw*-infix as indefinite pronoun, in Demotic and Coptic passive forms are superseded by analytic constructions with the third person plural (section 4.6.6.3).[84] When topicalized, the logical subject, i.e. the grammatical agent, of a passive construction is introduced by the preposition (*ḥr-ḏr.t n* >) ϩⲓⲧⲛ̄- "by means of, through" rather than by ⲛ̄ϭⲓ. Contrast example (185) above, where the third person plural pronoun refers to a specific noun ("our wrongdoings") and is topicalized by ⲛ̀ϫⲉ, with (186), where it conveys the grammatical subject of a passive construction (*"they become stronger than you" => "you are overcome"), whereas the agent ("evil") is topicalized by means of ϩⲓⲧⲛ̄-:

(186) Rom 12,21 ⲙ̄ⲡⲣ̄ⲧⲣⲉⲩϫⲣⲟ ⲉⲣⲟⲕ ϩⲓⲧⲙ̄ ⲡⲡⲉⲧϩⲟⲟⲩ
"Do not be overcome by evil," lit. *"do-not-cause-that-they-become-strong (*mpr-tre=u-jro*) upon-you (*ero=k*) through that-which-is evil (*p-pet-hoou*)"

Table 7.1 From initial verbal clauses to sentence conjugation patterns

	MIDDLE EGYPTIAN	LATE EGYPTIAN I	LATE EG. II – DEMOTIC I	DEMOTIC II – COPTIC
PERFECTIVE	*(sḏm.n=f)* *nj sḏm.t=f*	*(sdm=f)* *bw sdm.t=f >* *bw-jr.t=f sdm*	*(jr=f sdm >)* *wꜣḥ=f sdm* *bw-jr.t=f sdm*	(ϩⲁϥⲥⲱⲧⲙ̄) ⲙ̄ⲡⲁⲧ̄ϥⲥⲱⲧⲙ̄
PRETERITE	*jw sḏm.n=f* *nj sḏm=f*	*sdm.n=f* *bw sdm=f >* *bw-pw=f sdm*	*sdm=f > jr=f sdm* *bn-pw=f sdm*	ⲁϥⲥⲱⲧⲙ̄ ⲙ̄ⲡⲉϥⲥⲱⲧⲙ̄
AORIST	*jw(=f) sḏm=f* *nj sḏm.n=f*	*(twj ḥr sdm)* *bw sdm=f*	*ḫr jr=f sdm* *bw jr=f sdm*	ϣⲁϥⲥⲱⲧⲙ̄ ⲙⲉϥⲥⲱⲧⲙ̄
OBJECTIVE FUTURE	*jw=f r sḏm* *nn sḏm=f*	*jw=f r sdm* *bn jw=f r sdm*	*twj m nꜥj r sdm*	ϯⲛⲁⲥⲱⲧⲙ̄
MODAL FUTURE	*sḏm(.w)=f* *nn sḏm=f*	*sdm=f* *bn sdm=f*	*jw=f r sdm/* *mj sdm=f* *bn jw=f r sdm/* *m-jr dj sdm=f*	ⲉϥⲉⲥⲱⲧⲙ̄/ ⲙⲁⲣⲉϥⲥⲱⲧⲙ̄ ⲛ̄ⲛⲉϥⲥⲱⲧⲙ̄/ ⲙ̄ⲡⲣ̄ⲧⲣⲉϥⲥⲱⲧⲙ̄
PASSIVE VOICE	*sḏm(.w)=f* *sḏm.tw=f*	*sdm(.w)=f* *sdm.tw=f*	*jr=w sdm=f* *dj.t jr=w sdm=f*	ⲁⲩⲥⲟⲧⲙϥ̄ ⲧⲣⲉⲩⲥⲟⲧⲙϥ̄

7.9.3 Non-initial verbal clauses and hypotaxis

In sections 6.4 and 7.4, we analyzed the types of linkage between Egyptian sentences according to a tripartite distribution: *parataxis* as the linkage between main clauses, *hypotaxis* as the textual dependency of a main clause on a discourse nucleus, and *subordination* as the syntactic dependency of a converted (i.e. morphologically marked) or embedded (i.e. morphologically unmarked) clause on a higher node. This tripartite model proves very useful in trying to understand the syntactic evolution faced by non-initial patterns: while in Middle Egyptian non-initial main clauses are *paratactically* linked to the initial sentence, Late Egyptian develops two *hypotactic* "sequential" forms,[85] which follow an initial main clause or sentence conjugation. The first one is the narrative form *jw=f ḥr sdm* "and he heard" (section 4.6.6.1) with its negative counterpart *jw=f ḥr tm sdm*, which sets forth a sequence of events in the past (187) and fulfills the function of a non-initial main clause *sḏm(.n)=f* in Middle Egyptian (section 7.3). The second form is the non-narrative conjunctive *mtw=f sdm* "and he hears/will hear" (section 4.6.6.2), negative *mtw=f tm sdm*, which describes a mostly modal concatenation of events subsequent to the one conveyed by the initial main clause (188), and is therefore the functional heir of the Middle Egyptian subjunctive *sḏm=f*, see section 7.2 and example (13) above:

(187) Two Brothers 4,6–9 *wn.jn=s ḥr jnj(.t) ʿd pdr jw=s ḥr ḫpr mj ntj qnqn.tj n-ʿḏꜣ n ꜣbw ḏd n pꜣy=s hꜣy m pꜣy=k sn šrj j.jr-qnqn(=j) jw pꜣy=s hꜣy ḥr wḥʿ m rwhꜣ m pꜣy=f sḫr ntj rʿ-nb jw=f ḥr spr r pꜣy=f pr jw=f ḥr gmj(.t) tꜣy=f ḥm.t sḏr.tj mr.tj n-ʿḏꜣ jw=s ḥr tm dj.t mw ḥr ḏr.t=f m pꜣy=s sḫr...*
"Then she took (*wn.jn=s ḥr jnj.t*) fat and grease and she became (*jw=s ḥr ḫpr*) as if she had been beaten (lit. "like she who has been beaten falsely"), wishing (*n ꜣbw*) to say to her husband: 'It was your younger brother who beat me (*j.jr-qnqn=j*).' Her husband returned (*jw pꜣy=s hꜣy ḥr wḥʿ* "and her husband returned") in the evening according to his daily habit; he reached his house (*jw=f ḥr spr r pꜣy=f pr* "and he reached his house") and found (*jw=f ḥr gmj.t*) his wife lying down (*sḏr.tj*) as if she was ill (*mr.tj n-ʿḏꜣ* "being ill falsely"); she didn't pour water (*jw=s ḥr tm dj.t mw* "and she didn't pour water") on his hands according to her habit..."

(188) RAD 54,8–12 *j.šm r-ḥrj mtw=tn nwy nꜣy=tn ḫʿ.w mtw=tn ḫtm nꜣy=tn sbꜣ.w mtw=tn jnj nꜣy=tn ḥm.wt nꜣy=tn ẖrd.w mtw=j šm r-ḥꜣ.t=tn r tꜣ-ḥw.t A mtw=j dj.t ḥms=tn jm m-dwꜣw*
"Go up (*j.šm r-ḥrj*), gather (*mtw=tn nwy*) your tools, seal (*mtw=tn ḫtm*) your doors, take (*mtw=tn jnj*) your wives and children, and I will go (*mtw=j šm*) before you to the temple of A and cause you to settle (*mtw=j dj.t ḥms=tn*) there tomorrow"

While these two forms are only used after an initial syntagm ("then she took" and "go up" in the two passages above), they are not *syntactically* subordinate to, but rather *semantically* dependent on it. For the past sequential, the hypotactic nature of the linkage to the initial pattern is shown by the fact that the latter need not be a main verbal clause, but can also be a simple adverbial phrase:

(189) Two Brothers 10,4 *ḫr-jr m-ḫt hrw.w qn.w ḥr-sꜣ nn jw bꜣtꜣ ḥr šm.t r bḥs m pꜣy=f sḫr ntj rʿ-nb*
"Many days thereafter, Bata went hunting (*jw bꜣtꜣ ḥr šm.t r bḥs* "and Bata went to hunt") according to (*m*) his daily habit"

or even a subordinate clause, such as the temporal (i.e. adverbial) clause in (190) or the relative (i.e. adjectival) clause in (191): because of their topicalized position in discourse, these subordinate clauses perform the function of the semantic nucleus of the sequential form, which in this case is the only *main* clause:

(190) Doomed Prince 4,6–7 *ḫr-jr m-ḫt pꜣ-ẖrd ʿꜣ.y jw=f ḥr ṯzy r tꜣy=f tp-ḥw.t*
"When the youth had grown, he went up (*jw=f ḥr ṯzy* "and he went up") to his roof (*tp-ḥw.t* "head of the house")"

(191) pTurin jud. 4,7 *jnj.tw=f ḥr nꜣ-md.wt j.sdm=f jw=f (ḥr) ḥꜣp=w*
"He was brought in (*jnj.tw=f*) because of the things (*nꜣ-md.wt*) which he had heard (*j.sdm=f*) and hidden (*jw=f ḥr ḥꜣp=w* "and he hid them")"

It is this close connection between the past *jw=f ḥr sdm* and the preceding clause which allows one to understand its later functional development: in Demotic and Coptic, the hypotactic sequential form is replaced by the asyndetic juxtaposition of preterital sentence conjugation patterns (Perfect I);[86] the language has lost the hypotactic pattern for the expression of the sequential past and replaced it with a paratactic form of linkage:

(192) NHC VI,4, 44:26–29[87] ⲧⲟⲧⲉ ⲁϥⲃⲱⲗⲕ̄ ⲁϥⲟⲩⲱⲛϩ̄ ⲉⲃⲟⲗ ⲁϥⲟⲩⲱϣⲉ ⲉⲧⲁⲗⲟ ⲛϥ̄ⲟⲩⲱⲧⲃ̄ ⲉϩⲣⲁⲓ ⲉⲡⲧⲟⲡⲟⲥ ⲉⲧⲙ̄ⲙⲁⲩ
"Then he became angry (*a=f-bôlk*), he revealed himself (*a=f-ouônh ebol*), and he desired (*a=f-ouôše*) to go up (*e-talo*, prepostion + infinitive) and to pass (*n=f-ouôtb*, conjunctive) beyond that place (τόπος)"

On the other hand, as shown by this last example, the non-narrative conjunctive not only survives down to Coptic, but even extends its array of use in the most recent phase of Egyptian.[88] The hypotactic, rather than subordinate character of this form is shown by the observation of some of its semantic and syntactic properties. Semantically, the conjunctive refers to events whose occurrence is so intimately linked to the main nucleus that they represent in fact a necessary constituent of the entire message, rather than an independent action. The nucleus itself is not properly speaking an *independent* clause, since its meaning is as closely connected with the concatenated event expressed by the conjunctive as the latter is with it.[89] The distribution of negations[90] in the following two examples helps elucidate this point:

(193) NHC VI 15, 5–7[91] ⲙⲡⲣ̄ⲛⲁⲩ ⲉⲣⲟⲉⲓ ϩⲓ ⲧⲕⲟⲡⲣⲓⲁ ⲛ̄ⲧⲉⲧⲛ̄ⲃⲱⲕ ⲛ̄ⲧⲉⲧⲛ̄ⲕⲁⲁⲧ ⲉⲉⲓⲛⲏϫ ⲉⲃⲟⲗ
"Do not see me (*mpr-nau ero=ei*) on the dungheap, and then go (*n=tetn-bôk*) and leave me (*n=tetn-kaa=t*) cast aside (*e=ei-nêj ebol*, section 7.9.5)"

(194) RAD 57,9–10 *bn sdm=j md.t bn ptr=j ṯꜣy m nꜣ s.wt ‘ꜣy.w(t) mḏ.wt mtw=j ḥꜣp=f*
"I will not hear (*bn sdm=j*) anything or see (*bn ptr=j* "I will not see") any wrongdoing in the great deep places and then hide it (*mtw=j ḥꜣp=f*)"

Taken individually, the initial pattern in both examples appears to be an independent sentence conjugation, i.e. the negative imperative in example (193) ("do not see me on the dungheap") and the negative modal future in (194) ("I will not hear anything," "I will not see any wrongdoing"). Semantically, however, both initial sentences are opaque, since the actions they evoke do not yield by themselves any satisfactory sense: the action of "seeing" in (193) seems unlikely to fall under the jurisdiction of a negative imperative, and the denial of "hearing" and "seeing" in (194) is hardly what the speaker is promising *per se*: rather, the scope of the negation invests in both cases the predicate of the initial as well as the non-initial verbal form: "do not do the following: [you see me on the dungheap and then you go away and leave me cast aside]," "I will not do the following: [I hear something or see a wrongdoing in the great deep places and then hide it]."

Thus, it would be more appropriate to argue that, in presence of the conjunctive, the only independent clause is in fact the entire macrosentence encompassing both the conjunctive and the form by which it is controlled: both are main clauses hypotactically organized within a chain of *predicted* or *predictable* events. Even in the rare instances in which the conjunctive seems to display narrative function,[92] it actually follows a relative present, i.e. aorist tense, the past temporal reference being in this case a feature of the *context* in which the forms are embedded rather than of the *form* itself.[93] In example (195), the younger brother's "loading himself" and "driving the cattle" are not presented as a narrative sequence, but as a concatenation of events that together constitute the concept of "being after the cattle," conveyed here by the circumstantial conversion (section 7.9.5) of an adverbial sentence:

(195) Two Brothers 4,3–5 *ḫr-jr {m-ḫt} ḥr trj n rwhꜣ wn.jn pꜣy=f sn ʿꜣ wḥʿ r pꜣy=f pr jw pꜣy=f sn šrj m-sꜣ nꜣy=f jꜣw.t m[tw=f] ꜣtp tw=f m ḫ.t nb n sḫ.t mtw=f jnj nꜣy=s jꜣw.t r-ḥꜣ.t=f r dj.t sḏr=w <m> pꜣy=sn jhꜣy.t ntj m pꜣ-dmj*
"Now in the evening (*ḥr trj n rwhꜣ*), the elder brother returned (*wḥʿ*) to his house, while (*jw*) the younger brother tended his cattle (*nꜣy=f jꜣw.t*), loaded (*mtw=f ꜣtp*) himself (*tw=f*)[94] with all things of the field, and drove (*mtw=f jnj*) his cattle before him, in order to let them sleep (*r dj.t sḏr=w*) in their stable in the village (*pꜣ-dmj*)"

To its hypotactic linkage the conjunctive also owes the possibility of being embedded into a sentence with topicalized predicate (section 7.5) or into the protasis of a hypothetical clause introduced by *jr* (section 6.3.1), and thus share with the VP by which it is controlled a focalized adverbial adjunct or a main clause apodosis respectively.[95] Once more, while the conjunctive does not function *per se* as topicalized VP, it adopts the syntactic environment of the nucleus to which it is joined:

(196) pLeiden I 361,4–5 *j.jr=j nḏ ḫr.t=k mtw=k hꜣb n=j ḥr ʿ=k snb=k*
"It is about your condition (*ʿ=k*) and your health (*snb=k*) that I am inquiring (*j.jr=j nḏ*) and that you should write (*mtw=k hꜣb*) to me"

(197) pBM 10052, 8,21–22 *jr jw ky ḥr jj.t mtw=f sʿḥʿ=k jry=j*
"If another comes (*jw ky ḥr jj.t*) and accuses you (*mtw=f sʿḥʿ=k*), I shall act (*jry=j*)"

But it is perhaps in its rare independent uses that the conjunctive shows most clearly its *contextual* form of dependency. The conjunctive can be used absolutely, i.e. without being joined to any preceding form, in formulae of prayer and oath, even if the initial text of the prayer or the oath itself is omitted, i.e. it is taken to be contextually "given":

(198) LRL 51,15–52,2 [The author of the letter says that he prays daily the gods to grant the addressee life and old age, saying:] *mtw=t ptr nꜣ ꜥḏd-šrj.w m-jr jrj.t btꜣ jr=w* "I expect you to take care of the small children. Do not do them any harm"

Table 7.2 Initial vs. non-initial main clauses

CLAUSE	DISCOURSE	EARLIER EGYPTIAN	LATE EGYPTIAN	DEMOTIC – COPTIC
INITIAL MAIN CLAUSE	NARRATIVE	*jw sḏm.n=f*	*sdm=f*	ⲁϥⲥⲱⲧⲙ̄
	MODAL	prospective *sḏm(.w)=f*	*sdm=f*	ⲉϥⲉⲥⲱⲧⲙ̄
NON-INITIAL MAIN CLAUSE	NARRATIVE	*sḏm.n=f*	*jw=f ḥr sdm*	ⲁϥⲥⲱⲧⲙ̄
	MODAL	subjunctive *sḏm=f*	*mtw=f sdm*	ⲛ̄ϥⲥⲱⲧⲙ̄

7.9.4 Dependent clauses and subordination

The evolution of subordinate clauses in later Egyptian shows similarities with the historical development of initial and non-initial main clauses discussed in sections 7.9.2–3. The main distinction to be drawn is between Middle Egyptian dependent clauses introduced by an explicit marker of subordination on the one hand and "embedded" clauses on the other. As a rule, subordinate clauses originating in a pattern "preposition (or conjunction) + periphrastic verbal form" become in Coptic bound patterns, which – because of their subordinate character – are called *clause conjugations* and are negated by ⲧⲙ̄ < *tm*. From the Middle Egyptian protasis of a hypothetical clause introduced by *jr* (section 6.3.1), later Egyptian first derives a variety of patterns in which the particle *jr* or *jnn* controls a verbal predicate (199), a Present I (200), a Future III (201), or a subordinate circumstantial form (202),[96] then reduces all these options to a clause conjugation pattern in which the circumstantial prefix is frequently followed in the positive form by the morpheme ϣⲁⲛ (203–204):[97]

(199) LRL 1,11 *jr jry=j ḥḥ n btꜣ bw jrj=j wꜥ-nfr*
"If I have done millions of mistakes, can I not do (*bw jrj=j*) one good thing (*wꜥ-nfr*)?"

(200) LRL 68,2 *ḫr jnn tw=k (ḥr) ḏd ꜥrw nꜣw jw=j m nmḥw*
"Now if you say (*twk ḥr ḏd*) 'Out of here!,' I am an orphan (*nmḥw*)"

(201) pBM 10052, 12,17–18 *jnn jw=k (r) ḏd j.gꜣ gꜣy=j*
"If you say 'Lie! (*j.gꜣ*),' I shall lie (*gꜣy=j*)"

(202) pBM 10052, 3,16–17 *jr jw=k ẖdb.tj jw=k ḫꜣꜥ.tj r mw jw njm (r) wḫꜣ=k*
"If you are killed (*ẖdb*) and thrown (*ḫꜣꜥ*) into the water, who (*njm*) will look for you?

(203) Jn 11,40 ⲉⲣϣⲁⲛⲡⲓⲥⲧⲉⲩⲉ ⲧⲉⲛⲁⲛⲁⲩ
"If you (*er=ø-šan-*, fem.) believe (πιστεύειν), you shall see (*te=ø-na-nau*)"

(204) Lk 13,3 ⲉⲧⲉⲧⲛ̄ⲧⲙ̄ⲙⲉⲧⲁⲛⲟⲓ ⲧⲉⲧⲛ̄ⲁⲧⲁⲕⲟ
"If you do not (*e-te=tn-tm-*, pl.) repent (μετανοεῖν), you shall perish (*te=tn-(n)a-tako*)"

Likewise, the construction *r sḏm.t=f* (section 6.3.1) is gradually replaced in Late Egyptian by the periphrastic *j.jr.t=f sdm*, where the preposition is written as a prothetic *yod*, and in the more recent phases of later Egyptian by a similar construction in which the grammaticalization of *j.jr.t=f sdm* causes the original *r* to be reinforced by the preposition *šꜣʿ* "until," leading to the Coptic clause conjugation ϣⲁⲛⲧϥ̄ⲥⲱⲧⲙ̄ "until he hears":[98]

(205) Wen. 2,36 *jmj jn.tw=f šꜣʿ-j.jr.t=j šj r rsj*
"Let him be brought (*jmj jn.tw=f* "cause that he be brought") until I have gone (*šj* < *šm.t*) to the South"

(206) NHC VI 40,16–20 ⲁⲩⲱ ϥⲛⲁϣⲱⲡⲉ ⲛ̄ⲁⲥⲱⲙⲁⲧⲟⲛ ⲛ̄ⲛⲁⲧⲥⲱⲙⲁ ⲛϥ̄ⲣⲱⲕϩ̄ ⲛ̄ⲑⲩⲗⲏ ϣⲁⲛⲧⲉϥⲣ̄ ⲕⲁⲑⲁⲣⲓⲍⲉ ⲙ̄ⲡⲧⲏⲣϥ̄ ⲁⲩⲱ ⲧⲕⲁϭⲓⲁ ⲧⲏⲣⲥ̄
"And it will become (*f-na-šôpe*) incorporeal (ἀσώματον) and bodiless (*at*-σῶμα) and burn (*n=f-rôkh*, conjunctive) the matter (ὕλη), until it purifies (*šant=ef-r*-καθαρίζειν) the universe (*p-têr=f* "the its-entirety") and all the evil (*kacia* <= κακία)"

The other clause conjugation with a somewhat symmetrical temporal meaning, ⲛ̄ⲧⲉⲣⲉϥⲥⲱⲧⲙ̄ "when he heard," derives from the prospective *sḏm=f* following the conjunction *ḏr* > Late Egyptian *m-dr* "when, since." This subordinate clause can precede the main sentence, in which case it appears introduced in Late Egyptian by the topicalizing particle *jr* and followed by a hypotactic sequential past as main clause, or follow it:

(207) Two Brothers 5,1 *jr m-dr jw.t=f [r] jṯꜣ n=k pr.t jw=f (ḥr) gmj(.t)=j ḥms.kw* <*m*> *wʿ.t*
"When he came (*jw.t=f*) to fetch (*jṯꜣ*) for you seed, he found me (*jw=f ḥr gmj.t=j*) sitting (*ḥms.kw*) alone"

(208) Khaemwaset 5,35 *stnj jw r mn-nfr ḥlg=f r nꜣy=f ẖrd.w n-drt gmj=f st ʿnḫ*
"Setne came (*jw*, stative) to Memphis and embraced (*ḥlg=f r*) his children when he found (*gmj=f*) them alive (*ʿnḫ*, stative)"

(209) Mt 14,23 ⲛ̄ⲧⲉⲣⲉϥⲕⲱ ⲇⲉ ⲉⲃⲟⲗ ⲙ̄ⲡⲙⲏⲏϣⲉ ⲁϥⲁⲗⲉ ⲉϩⲣⲁⲓ ⲉϫⲙ̄ ⲡⲧⲟⲟⲩ
"But (δέ) when he released (*kô ebol*) the crowd (*mêêše*), he went up (*a=f-ale ehrai*) to the mountain (*ejm p-toou* *"to the head of the mountain")"

Finally, mention should be made of the clause conjugation ⲧⲁⲣⲉϥⲥⲱⲧⲙ̄ "so that he will hear," which is the subordinate equivalent of the sentence conjugation ⲙⲁⲣⲉϥⲥⲱⲧⲙ̄ "let him hear" and of the hypotactic conjunctive ⲛϥ̄ⲥⲱⲧⲙ̄ "and he shall hear." This pattern, often called *promissive future* or *conjunctive future*,[99] is mostly used in Sahidic and consists of an invariable grammaticalized form of the first person subjunctive *ḏj=j* "so that I shall cause" > ⲧⲁ- followed, as in the case of the sentence conjugation, by a periphrastic prospective *jr=f sdm*;[100] it conveys the speaker's commitment that the event expressed in the clause conjugation will result from a fulfillment of the main predicate from which it is syntactically controlled:

(210) Mt 7,7 ⲁⲓⲧⲉⲓ ⲧⲁⲣⲟⲩϯ ⲛⲏⲧⲛ̄ ϣⲓⲛⲉ ⲧⲁⲣⲉⲧⲛ̄ϭⲓⲛⲉ ⲧⲱϩⲙ̄ ⲧⲁⲣⲟⲩⲟⲩⲱⲛ ⲛⲏⲧⲛ̄
"Ask (αἰτεῖν), and it will be given to you (*tar=ou-ti nê=tn* "and they will give to you"). Seek, and you will find (*tare=tn-cine*). Knock, and it will be opened to you (*tar=ou-ouôn* "and they will open") to you"

The difference between conjunctive and promissive[101] is twofold: at the syntactic level, the former is a *hypotactic* non-initial main clause, whereas the latter is a *subordinate* pattern; at the semantic level, the control exerted by the preceding verbal form is *objective* in the case of the subjunctive, which serves to join two actions intimately linked to each other, and *subjective* in the case of the promissive, where it is the speaker who assures the semantic dependency of the second event on the first. But there are indications that the opposition between the two forms was perceived to be weak and tended to be neutralized. On the one hand, the promissive, which predictably lacked an etymological first person **dj=j jr=j sdm* *"so that I cause that I hear," borrowed into its paradigm the first person conjunctive (ⲛ̄)ⲧⲁⲥⲱⲧⲙ̄, causing the pattern to grammaticalize the promissive meaning regardless of the etymological origin of the introductory morpheme: "and I will cause that he hear" > "(and I will cause:) may he hear" > "that he may hear" (section 4.6.6.2). On the other hand, promissive and conjunctive tend to gradually merge into one functional paradigm: examples of this tendency are the promissive function of the conjunctive prenominal conjugation base (ⲛ̄)ⲧⲉ in post-classical Sahidic and the sporadic use of the Bohairic conjunctive for the Sahidic promissive (211–211'):

(211) Lk 6,37 ˢⲕⲱ ⲉⲃⲟⲗ ⲧⲁⲣⲟⲩⲕⲱ ⲛⲏⲧⲛ̄ ⲉⲃⲟⲗ
(211') Ibid. ᴮⲭⲱ ⲉⲃⲟⲗ ⲟⲩⲟϩ ⲛ̀ⲧⲟⲩⲭⲱ ⲛⲱⲧⲉⲛ ⲉⲃⲟⲗ
"Forgive, and (ᴮ*ouoh*) you will be forgiven (ˢ*tar=ou-kô nê=tn ebol*, promissive vs. ᴮ*nt=ou-khô nô=ten ebol*, subjunctive)"

7.9.5 From embedding to conversion

But the most substantial evolution from earlier to later Egyptian is surely the one that concerns *embedding*, i.e. clausal subordination not signalled by an explicit marker of syntactic dependency. In the preceding chapters and sections, we devoted some attention to the syntactic behavior of nominal, adverbial, and verbal main clauses converted in specific syntactic environments into subordinate clauses controlled by a higher sentence node. In classical Egyptian, this conversion usually follows a synthetic or fusional type: for example, nominal conversion into a topicalized VP is carried by specific verbal forms in the aorist or by the unconverted form in the past and the prospective (section 7.5), adjectival conversion into a relative VP is signalled by the adjectival endings of the verbal form (section 7.7), while adverbial conversion into a circumstantial VP is realized by the unconverted form of the basic VP controlled by the main predicate (section 7.4).

In later Egyptian, earlier synthetic constructions are replaced by analytic patterns in which the nature of the syntactic dependency is specified by an initial morpheme usually called *converter*. While converters are already found in earlier Egyptian, where they are mostly applied to nominal and adverbial sentences – for example the converters from the verb *wnn* "to be," which allow a nominal or adverbial sentence to acquire the temporal, modal, or pragmatic features of a verbal sentence (sections 5.6, 6.2), or the relative converter *ntj* used for the relativization of adverbial clauses with specific antecedent (section 6.3.3) – their number and uses increase dramatically in later Egyptian. As a general rule, the embedded constructions of the classical language, whether verbal (A), substantival (B), adjectival (C), or adverbial (D), have been replaced in later Egyptian by explicit patterns of subordination marked by syntactic converters.

(A) *Past converter.* In the treatment of nominal and adverbial sentences (sections 5.6, 6.6.1), we observed the historical tendency of Egyptian to delegate the expression of the existence of indefinite subjects to verbal sentences in which the predicate is a form of the verb *wnn* "to be," grammaticalized in Late Egyptian as converter *wn*,[102] as well as the ties between this morpheme and the past converter *wn* > ⲛⲉ=/ⲛⲉⲣⲉ-, which turns any adverbial or pseudoverbal sentence into its preterital counterpart, called in Coptic "Imperfect." As a converter of *verbal* sentences, the morpheme *wn* is relatively rare in Late Egyptian, but becomes quite frequent in Demotic and Coptic (ⲛⲉ), where it converts any verbal form into a background preterite:[103]

(212) Mt 27,15 ⲛⲉϣⲁⲣⲉⲡϩⲏⲅⲉⲙⲱⲛ ⲕⲁⲟⲩⲁ ⲉⲃⲟⲗ
"The governor (ἡγεμών) used to (*ne-šare...*) release (*kô ebol*) one (*oua*)"

(B) *Topicalized verbal forms.* Late Egyptian, apart from archaic uses of the classical forms, possesses two topicalized verbal patterns:[104] the general *j.jr=f sdm* "that he does/did the hearing" > "that he hears/heard," etymologically the topicalized form of the periphrastic *jr=f sdm* "he hears," which had replaced the topicalized aorist *sḏm=f* and *sḏm.n=f*, and the prospective-modal *j.sdm=f* "that he will hear" as the heir of the emphatic prospective *sḏm=f* of Middle Egyptian.[105] Coptic, where topicalized VPs are usually referred to as "second tenses,"[106] has returned to a tripartite division, with a Perfect II ⲛ̄ⲧⲁϥⲥⲱⲧⲙ̄ (213), etymologically derived from the relative conversion *ntj jr=f sdm*, a Present II ^{S}ⲉϥⲥⲱⲧⲙ̄/^{B}ⲁϥⲥⲱⲧⲉⲙ (214) from *j.jr=f sdm*, and a Future II ⲉϥⲛⲁⲥⲱⲧⲙ̄ (215) from *j.jr=f-n'j-sdm*, i.e. from the analogical use of the converter *j.jr* applied to an original pseudoverbal pattern (section 6.6.1). The syntax of these converted sentences follows the classical Egyptian model:

(213) Ps 117,23 ⲛ̄ⲧⲁⲡⲁⲓ ϣⲱⲡⲉ ⲉⲃⲟⲗ ϩⲓⲧⲙ̄ ⲡϫⲟⲉⲓⲥ
"It is through (*ebol hitm-*) the Lord (*p-joeis*) that this happened (*nta-pai šôpe*)"

(214) Jas 1,13 ⲉⲩⲡⲉⲓⲣⲁⲍⲉ ⲙ̄ⲙⲟⲓ ⲉⲃⲟⲗ ϩⲓⲧⲙ̄ ⲡⲛⲟⲩⲧⲉ
"It is by God (*ebol hitm p-noute* "through the god") that I am being tempted (*e=u-πειράζειν mmoi* "that-they-tempt me")"

(215) Judg 6,15 ⲡⲓⲥⲣⲁⲏⲗ ⲉⲓⲛⲁⲛⲁϩⲙⲉϥ ϩⲛ̄ ⲟⲩ
"How shall I save Israel?," lit. "Israel – that-I-shall-save-him (*e=i-na-nahm=ef*) (is) through-what (*hn-ou*)"

Second tenses are negated in later Egyptian by the functional heir of classical *nj...js* (section 6.7), i.e. Late Egyptian *bn...jwnꜣ* > Coptic (ⲛ̄)...ⲁⲛ:

(216) Acts 26,26 ⲛ̄ⲧⲁⲡⲉⲓϩⲱⲃ ϣⲱⲡⲉ ⲁⲛ ϩⲙ̄ ⲡϩⲱⲡ
"This matter (*pei-hôb*) didn't happen (*nta... šôpe an*) secretly (*hm p-hôp* "in the secret")!"

(C) *Relativization.* Synthetic *adjectival* conversions, i.e. relative forms, experience in Late Egyptian a progressive functional decay: only the perfective relative forms *sdm.n=f* as a Middle Egyptian archaism and *j.sdm=f* as the more recent pattern are regularly used:

(217) Doomed Prince 6,13–14 *wn.jn pꜣ-wpw.t(j) ḥr šm.t ḥr smj <md.wt> nb.t j.ḏd=s n pꜣy=s jtj*
"Then the messenger (*pꜣ-wpw.tj*) went to report (*smj*) to her father (*pꜣy=s jtj*) all the things (*md.wt nb.t*) she had said (*j.ḏd=s*)"

whereas the relative aorist (apart from archaisms)[107] and the prospective relative form have already been replaced by analytic constructions with *ntj* followed by a pseudoverbal pattern *sw ḥr sdm=f* (Coptic ⲉⲧϥ̄ⲥⲱⲧⲙ̄ ⲙ̄ⲙⲟϥ, ⲉⲧⲉⲣⲉ ⲡⲣⲱⲙⲉ ⲥⲱⲧⲙ̄ ⲙ̄ⲙⲟϥ) and *jw=f r sdm=f* (Coptic ⲉⲧϥ̄ⲛⲁⲥⲱⲧⲙ̄ ⲙ̄ⲙⲟϥ, ⲉⲧⲉⲣⲉ ⲡⲣⲱⲙⲉ ⲛⲁⲥⲱⲧⲙ̄ ⲙ̄ⲙⲟϥ, section 7.9.2) respectively:

(218) pBologna 1094, 6,4 *mtw=k smj n ṯꜣ.tj ḥr pꜣ-ḥḏ 'šꜣ ntj šmsw jꜣy ḥr ḏd jmj tw=f*
"And you shall make a report (*mtw=k smj*) to the vizier (*ṯꜣ.tj*) concerning the quantity of silver (*pꜣ-ḥḏ 'šꜣ* *"the many silver") which the servant Iay says: 'Give it! (*jmj tw=f*, see 4.6.6.5)'"

(219) Jn 6,42 ⲙⲏ ⲙ̄ⲡⲁⲓ ⲁⲛ ⲡⲉ ⲓ̅ⲥ̅ ⲡϣⲏⲣⲉ ⲛ̄ⲓⲱⲥⲏⲫ ⲡⲁⲓ ⲁⲛⲟⲛ ⲉⲧⲛ̄ⲥⲟⲟⲩⲛ̄ ⲙ̄ⲡⲉϥⲉⲓⲱⲧ ⲙⲛ̄ ⲧⲉϥⲙⲁⲁⲩ
"Isn't this (*m-pai an pe*) Jesus, the son of Joseph, the one (*pai*) whose father and mother we ourselves (*anon*) know (*et=n-sooun m-pe=f-eiôt mn te=f-maau* "that we know his father and his mother")"[108]

(220) RAD 56,15–16 *jw=j (r) dj.t ʿḏɜ=ṯn m qnb.t nb ntj jw=ṯn (r) šm(.t) r=s*
"I shall cause that you be found guilty (*ʿḏɜ=ṯn*) in any tribunal (*qnb.t*) to which you go ("that you will go to it")"

(221) Rom 4,6 ⲕⲁⲧⲁ ⲑⲉ ⲟⲛ ⲉϣⲁⲣⲉⲇⲁⲩⲉⲓⲇ ϫⲱ ⲙ̄ⲡⲙⲁⲕⲁⲣⲓⲥⲙⲟⲥ ⲙ̄ⲡⲣⲱⲙⲉ ⲡⲁⲓ ⲉⲧⲉⲣⲉ ⲡⲛⲟⲩⲧⲉ ⲛⲁⲱⲡ ⲉⲣⲟϥ ⲛ̄ⲟⲩⲇⲓⲕⲁⲓⲟⲥⲩⲛⲏ ⲁϫⲛ̄ ⲛⲉϩⲃⲏⲩⲉ
"In the manner (κατά *t-he*) in which (*e-*) David too (*on*) proclaims blessed (*šare…jô m-p*-μακαρισμός *m-* "says the proclamation of blessedness to") the man (*p-rôme*) to whom God (*p-noute*) will count (*ôp*) justice (δικαιοσύνη) without the works (*ajn-ne-hbêue*)"

In Demotic and Coptic, the perfective relative form too gives way to the analytic pattern *(pɜ-) ntj jr=f sdm=f* > (ⲡ)ⲉⲛⲧⲁϥⲥⲟⲧⲙϥ̄ "whom he heard." One will recall that an identical analytic evolution also affects the participial relative clauses, i.e. those clauses whose subject is identical to the antecedent they modify (section 5.9):[109] only the perfective participle keeps in Late Egyptian a synthetic structure *j.sdm*, but it too is replaced during Dyn. XXV (eighth–seventh century BCE) by the periphrastic *j.jr sdm* and eventually by the verbal clause introduced by the relative converter *(pɜ-) ntj sdm=f* > (ⲡ)ⲉⲛⲧ-ⲁ=ϥ-ⲥⲱⲧⲙ̄ "who heard."[110] The imperfective participle acquired very soon in Late Egyptian the periphrastic form *j.jr sdm*, which in Dyn. XXV is replaced by a relative pseudoverbal clause with *(pɜ-) ntj*: *j.jr sdm* > *(pɜ-) ntj ḥr sdm* > (ⲡ)ⲉⲧ-ⲥⲱⲧⲙ̄ "who hears"; the prospective participle *sḏm.tj=f* is rare in Late Egyptian and is progressively replaced by the converted relative Future III *ntj-jw=f r sdm*, and in later Demotic and Coptic by the Future I *(pɜ-) ntj m nʿj r sdm* > (ⲡ)ⲉⲧ-ⲛⲁ-ⲥⲱⲧⲙ̄ "who will hear."

(D) *Adverbial conversion.* We saw in the preceding chapter that the morpheme *jw*, from being a marker of discourse initiality in earlier Egyptian, became in later Egyptian a signal of syntactic dependency, following a grammaticalization path which finds its origin in the use of *jw* as mere morphological carrier of the pronominal subject of an embedded adverbial clause in classical Egyptian (section 6.6.3). We also observed that the direct functional successor of the Middle Egyptian *jw* survives in the more recent stages of the language only in bound, i.e. unsegmentable constructions, such as the Future III (section 7.9.2) or the sequential past form (section 7.9.3). But as a free morpheme, capable of being prefixed to any sentence type, *jw* functions in later Egyptian as the indicator of adverbial subordination.

We already discussed in section 6.6.3 the impact of this functional change on the syntax not only of adverbial clauses, but also of nominal and verbal clauses. Here, I shall only stress that the later Egyptian converter *jw* can control the entire functional spectrum of subordinate verbal clauses, from those functioning as backgrounding adverbial adjunct (section 7.4):

(222) LRL 45,10–11 *tw=n jj.tj m pꜣy=n nb j.rdj jw=n r pꜣ ntj tw=tn jm jw dj=f jnj=n wʿ-šʿ.t*
"We have arrived (Present I); it is our lord who caused (*j.rdj*, perfective participle) that we come (*jw=n*, prospective *sdm=f*) to the (place) where you are (*pꜣ ntj tw=tn jm* "the one that you are there"), having let (*jw dj=f* "while he caused") us bring a letter"

to the emphasized AP of a sentence whose main VP is topicalized (section 7.5.2):

(223) LRL 56,12–13 *j.jr=k spr dj.t jw=j m pꜣ tꜣ rsj jw grḥ=k jm=f*
"Only after you are finished (*jw grḥ=k*) with it will you succeed in (*j.jr=k spr*) causing me to come back (*dj.t jw=j*) from the Southland (*m pꜣ tꜣ rsj*)"
(224) Job 1,21 ⲛ̄ⲧⲁⲓⲉⲓ ⲉⲃⲟⲗ ϩⲛ̄ ϩⲏⲧⲥ̄ ⲛ̄ⲧⲁⲙⲁⲁⲩ ⲉⲓⲕⲏⲕ ⲁϩⲏⲩ ⲉⲓⲛⲁⲃⲱⲕ ⲟⲛ ⲉⲓⲕⲏⲕ ⲁϩⲏⲩ
"Naked (*e=i-kêk-ahêu* *"while I am stripped naked," stative) I came out of (*nta=i-ei ebol hn-*) my mother's womb (*hêt=s n-t=a-maau* "her-womb of-my-mother"), and naked shall I go (*e=i-na-bôk*) back (there) (*on*)"

to its function as "virtual" relative clause modifying a non-specific noun:

(225) Two Brothers 8,2 *jst jr sḫꜣy=k wʿ n bjn jst bw jr=k sḫꜣy wʿ n nfr m-rꜣ pw wʿ n nkt jw jry=j sw n=k*
"Now, if you remember a bad thing (*wʿ n bjn* "one of evil"), can't you remember a good thing (*wʿ n nfr* "one of good") or anything at all (*wʿ n nkt* "one of thing") that I have done (*jw jry=j sw*) for you?"
(226) Lk 10,39 ⲛⲉⲟⲩⲛ̄ⲧⲥ̄ ⲟⲩⲥⲱⲛⲉ ⲇⲉ ⲡⲉ ⲉϣⲁⲩⲙⲟⲩⲧⲉ ⲉⲣⲟⲥ ϫⲉ ⲙⲁⲣⲓⲁ
"And she had (*ne-ount=s pe*, preterital possessive construction, see sections 5.10 and 7.9.5A) a sister (*ou-sône*) who was called (*e-ša=u-moute ero=s* *"while they call to her") Mary"

In Sahidic Coptic, one also finds the "virtual" relative clause introduced by ⲉ- instead of the expected *ntj* > ⲉⲧ(ⲉ) documented by *pꜣ-ntj* > ⲡⲉⲧ(ⲉ) after specific nouns or demonstrative pronouns used appositionally:[111]

(227) Ps 32,12 ⲡϩⲉⲑⲛⲟⲥ ⲉⲡϫⲟⲉⲓⲥ ⲡⲉ ⲡⲉϥⲛⲟⲩⲧⲉ
"The people (ἔθνος) whose god is the Lord (*e-p-joeis pe pe=f-noute* "its god being the Lord," section 5.9)"
(228) Lk 19,30 ⲧⲉⲧⲛⲁϩⲉ ⲉⲩⲥⲏϭ ⲉϥⲙⲏⲣ ⲡⲁⲓ ⲉⲙⲡⲉⲗⲁⲁⲩ ⲛ̄ⲣⲱⲙⲉ ⲁⲗⲉ ⲉⲣⲟϥ ⲉⲛⲉϩ
"You will find (*he e-*) a tied colt (*ou-sêc e=f-mêr*), one on which no man ever (*eneh*) sat (*e-mpe-laau n-rôme ale ero=f* "while any man didn't sit on it")"

The use of the adverbial conversion by means of *jw* > ⲉ- is also found in a variety of other patterns, for example *t-he e-* in (221),[112] and especially under the control of verbs of perception such as *gmj* "to find" or *nw* "to see," which in classical Egyptian were followed by a pseudoverbal or adverbial construction (section 6.3.2),

(228) LRL 7,11–12 *yꜣ j.jr=j gmj(.t) jw dj=f jw wꜥ tsm r ṯꜣy=j*
"Indeed (*yꜣ*) I found out (*j.jr=j gmj.t*, topicalized VP, see example (223)) that he had caused a boat to come (*dj=f jw wꜥ tsm*) to take me (*ṯꜣy=j*)"

(229) Rev 9,1 ⲁⲓⲛⲁⲩ ⲉⲩⲥⲓⲟⲩ ⲉⲁϥϩⲉ ⲉⲃⲟⲗ ϩⲛ̄ ⲧⲡⲉ ⲉϩⲣⲁⲓ ⲉϫⲙ̄ ⲡⲕⲁϩ
"I saw that a star had fallen (*a=i-nau e-u-siou e-a=f-he* *"I saw a star while it had fallen") down from heaven (*pe*) to earth (*kah*)"

and as predicative complement of the verb ϣⲱⲡⲉ "to be, become":

(230) 1 Tim 3,12 ⲛ̄ⲇⲓⲁⲕⲟⲛⲟⲥ ⲙⲁⲣⲟⲩϣⲱⲡⲉ ⲉⲁⲩϩⲙⲟⲟⲥ ⲙⲛ̄ ⲟⲩⲥϩⲓⲙⲉ ⲛ̄ⲟⲩⲱⲧ
"The deacons should marry (*mar=ou-šôpe e-a=u-hmoos* "may-they-be having-married") only one woman (*ou-shime n-ouôt*)"

Further reading

Allen, J. P. *The Inflection of the Verb in the Pyramid Texts.* Bibliotheca Aegyptia II (Malibu: Undena, 1984).

Collier, M. "The circumstantial *sḏm(.f)/sḏm.n(.f)* as verbal verb-forms in Middle Egyptian," *Journal of Egyptian Archaeology* 76 (1990), 73–85.

Collier, M. "The relative clause and the verb in Middle Egyptian," *Journal of Egyptian Archaeology* 77 (1991), 23–42.

Doret, E. *The Narrative Verbal System of Old and Middle Egyptian.* Cahiers d' Orientalisme XII (Geneva: Patrick Cramer, 1986).

Johnson, J. H. *The Demotic Verbal System.* Studies in Ancient Oriental Civilization XXXVIII (Chicago: The Oriental Institute, 1976).

Junge, F. *"Emphasis" and Sentential Meaning in Middle Egyptian.* Göttinger Orientforschungen IV/20 (Wiesbaden: Harrassowitz, 1989).

Polotsky, H. J. "The Coptic conjugation system," *Orientalia* 29 (1960), 392–422.

Polotsky, H. J. "Les transpositions du verbe en égyptien classique," *Israel Oriental Studies* 6 (1976), 1–50.

Shisha-Halevy, A. *Coptic Grammatical Categories.* Analecta Orientalia LIII (Rome: Pontifical Biblical Institute, 1986).

Vernus, P. *Future at Issue. Tense, Mood and Aspect in Middle Egyptian: Studies in Syntax and semantics.* Yale Egyptological Studies IV (New Haven: Yale Egyptological Seminar, 1990).

Winand, J. *Etudes de néo-égyptien, I. La morphologie verbale.* Aegyptiaca Leodiensia II (Liège: CIPL, 1992).

Epilogue

Throughout this book, we have observed the extraordinary vitality of a dead language. Although one of the latest languages to have been deciphered and analyzed from a linguistic perspective, Ancient Egyptian proves to be an ideal field for linguistic investigation. Its visually most appealing feature, the hieroglyphic script in which the language was mainly expressed, is a complex but flexible pictographic system suited to convey the phonological, morphological, and lexical oppositions of the language as perceived by its users. By the same token, the history of the system and of its manual varieties (Hieratic and Demotic) offers the opportunity to observe the various functional pressures to which it was exposed: while preserving a certain degree of immutability during three millennia, the hieroglyphic script expanded or restricted its phonological and semantic potential depending both on the social composition of the scribal élite and on the cultural nature of the texts. Finally, the interface between changes in the religious *Weltanschauung* from the emergence of Hellenism to the rise of Christianity on the one hand and the "alphabetic revolution" which caused Egyptian to be rendered in a Greek-derived script (Coptic) provides a comprehensive basis for the study of the relationship between language, writing system, and cultural ideology: firstly, in Egypt and elsewhere, it is the script, rather than the language, that becomes a symbol of "heathendom," of the old religious order which a new revealed religion aims to overcome; secondly, the alphabetic system is not an inevitable outcome of a writing system which privileges the phonological level: although it possessed from the beginning a set of monoconsonantal signs, the hieroglyphic system never departed from its complex fusion of semagrams and phonograms, but on the contrary expanded in its final stages the number and the functional role of its iconic elements.

Egyptian phonology also proves to be a revealing area of linguistic research. In spite of certain limits, such as the lack of indication of vowels, some irregularities in the correspondences with other Afroasiatic languages, the ambiguities in the graphic rendition, which prevent a thorough assessment of the underlying phonetic reality, one can nonetheless observe at work a broad spectrum of phonological oppositions and evolutions from the Afroasiatic prehistory of the language down to Coptic: the vocalic sound shifts, the fate of the emphatic series, the tendency to move the point of articulation of velar and palatal consonants to the apical region, and the devoicing of voiced phonemes provoke, as we saw, wide-ranging effects of structural as well as comparative relevance.

On the morphological side, Ancient Egyptian exhibits a high number of features common to other Afroasiatic, and particularly Semitic languages, especially in the domain of nominal morphology: feminine and plural patterns, pronouns, some numerals. But it also shows a substantial degree of autonomy in the area of verbal forms, which are not easily interpretable within a traditional genealogical model. How should the language historian deal with this variety of forms and patterns? Is Egyptian more archaic or more innovative than the related languages? How related to each other are Afroasiatic languages after all? It is not surprising, therefore, that Egyptological linguists have rediscovered morphology, which had been somewhat neglected in the second part of this century in the wake of the "Polotskyan revolution" that prompted an increased attention to the structurally more promising domain of syntax.

To the modern linguist, syntax and its extensions, such as typology or pragmatics, still represent in fact the most challenging aspect of Ancient Egyptian. On the one hand, the language displays a rigid sentence structure with a rather limited number of basic nominal, adverbial, and verbal patterns; on the other hand, it also licenses, as we saw, an extremely wide array of syntactic conversion (or "transformation," depending on the linguistic obedience) or embedding (or "subordination") and a frequent recourse to pragmatic movements of topicalization (or thematization) or focalization (or rhematization). Even in the absence of a complete reconstruction of the morphological patterns involved, this interplay between syntactic rigidity and pragmatic flexibility provides an ideal documentary basis for the student of Egyptian philology and of general linguistics alike: the former will benefit from a more thorough understanding of the discourse structures of the language by applying it to the textual diversity of more than 4000 years of written history—from literary to religious texts, from private to administrative *corpora*, from the registers of the pyramid towns in the third millennium BCE to the liturgy of the mediaeval Christian church; the latter will observe the synchronic reality vs. the diachronic evolution of syntactic survivals and innovations drawn from the "spoken language" – an unknown entity, yet in constant dialectics with the codified forms of written Egyptian – elementary verbless patterns vs. multi-tier embeddings of verbal predicates, the idiolect of a specific author vs. the impact of the linguistic policies enforced by the Egyptian state in a linguistic domain whose historical and typological variety can be compared to Latin and the Romance languages or to Classical Arabic and its present-day dialects.

If after reading this book, therefore, linguists will decide to have frequent recourse to Ancient Egyptian, and Egyptologists will discover that the study of the linguistic structures of their language of expertise provides useful insights into the overall understanding of Egypt as a cultural entity, the book will have fulfilled part of its original goal.

Notes

1 The language of Ancient Egypt

1. C. T. Hodge (ed.), *Afroasiatic. A Survey*. Janua Linguarum Series Practica CLXIII (The Hague–Paris: Mouton, 1971); *Die Sprachen Afrikas*, vol. II *Afro-Asiatisch*, ed. by B. Heine, Th. C. Schadeberg, and E. Wolff. (Hamburg: Helmut Buske, 1981).
2. For example S. Moscati (ed.), *An Introduction to the Comparative Grammar of the Semitic Languages*. Porta Linguarum Orientalium VI (Wiesbaden: Harrassowitz, second edn 1969), 16 ff.
3. I. M. Diakonoff, *Semito-Hamitic Languages. An Essay in Classification* (Moscow: Akademia Nauk, 1965).
4. A. Zaborski, "Afro-asiatic languages," in W. Bright (ed.), *International Encyclopedia of Linguistics*, vol. I (Oxford University Press, 1992), 36–37.
5. B. Comrie, *Language Universals and Linguistic Typology* (Chicago University Press, second edn 1989), 42–51.
6. R. Hetzron, "Semitic languages," in *International Encyclopedia of Linguistics*, vol. III, 412–17.
7. Id., "Two principles of genetic reconstruction," *Lingua* 38 (1976), 89–108.
8. For example A. Willms, *Die dialektale Differenzierung des Berberischen*. Afrika und Übersee XXXI (Berlin: Reimer, 1980).
9. H. J. Sasse, "Cushitic languages," in *International Encyclopedia of Linguistics*, vol. I, 326–30.
10. See the lexical list by A. Zaborski, "Der Wortschatz der Bedscha-Sprache. Eine vergleichende Analyse," in *ZDMG. Supplement VII* (Stuttgart: Franz Steiner Verlag, 1989), 573–91.
11. P. Newman, "Chadic," in *International Encyclopedia of Linguistics*, vol. I, 253–54.
12. H. C. Fleming, "Cushitic and Omotic," in M. L. Bender et al. (eds.), *Language in Ethiopia* (Oxford University Press, 1976), 34–53.
13. W. Schenkel, *Einführung in die altägyptische Sprachwissenschaft*. Orientalistische Einführungen (Darmstadt: Wissenschaftliche Buchgesellschaft, 1990), 7–10; the most recent treatment of the history of Egyptian is F. Junge, "Sprachstufen und Sprachgeschichte," in *ZDMG. Supplement VI* (Stuttgart: Franz Steiner, 1985), 17–34.
14. For the nature of the different registers of Late Egyptian see the discussion in J. Winand, *Etudes de néo-égyptien, I. La morphologie verbale*. Aegyptiaca Leodiensia II (Liège: CIPL, 1992), 3–30.

15. The term "Coptic" probably derives from the Arabic rendition of the Greek adjective Αἰγύπτιος "Egyptian," although a similar form of the word (Hebr. *giftit*) is known from two Talmudic passages (Shabbat 115a, Megilla 18a) from no later than the third century CE: M. Jastrow, *A Dictionary of the Targumim, Talmud Babli, Yerushalmi, and the Midrashic Literature* (New York: Judaica Press, 1971), 241.
16. For indications of Demotic dialects see E. Lüddeckens, "Demotisch," in *LÄ* I, 1054.
17. W. Schenkel, "Zu den Verschluß- und Reibelauten im Ägyptischen und (Hamito-)Semitischen. Ein Versuch zur Synthese der Lehrmeinungen," *LingAeg* 3 (1993), 148.
18. J. B. Callender, "Grammatical models in Egyptology," *Orientalia* 42 (1973), 47–77; a description of the development of Egyptological linguistics is offered by Schenkel, *Altägyptische Sprachwissenschaft*, 17–23.
19. See his *Ägyptische Grammatik* (Berlin, 1894; fourth edn 1928) and *Neuägyptische Grammatik* (Leipzig, 1880; second edn 1933).
20. *Egyptian Grammar, Being an Introduction to the Study of Hieroglyphs* (Oxford University Press, 1927; third edn 1957)
21. *Studies in Egyptian Syntax* (Paris: Paul Geuthner, 1924).
22. See for example Gardiner, *Egyptian Grammar*, 4.
23. *Collected Papers* (Jerusalem: Magnes Press, 1971).
24. "Les transpositions du verbe en égyptien classique," *Israel Oriental Studies* 6 (1976), 1–50; *Grundlagen des koptischen Satzbaus*, 2 vols. American Studies in Papyrology XXVII–XXIX (Atlanta: Scholars' Press, 1987–90).
25. For its history and description see L. Depuydt, "The Standard theory of the 'emphatic' forms in Classical (Middle) Egyptian," *OLP* 14 (1983), 13–54.
26. If not *all* of them, as in the most extreme form of the theory, favored by F. Junge, *Syntax der mittelägyptischen Literatursprache. Grundlagen einer Strukturtheorie* (Mainz am Rhein: Philipp von Zabern, 1978).
27. The copula ("is") is not expressed in Egyptian.
28. See the conferences in which this evolution has been debated: *Crossroad. Chaos or the Beginning of a New Paradigm.* Papers from the Conference on Egyptian Grammar (Helsingør, 28–30 May 1986), ed. by G. Englund and P. J. Frandsen. CNI Publications I (Copenhagen: Carsten Niebuhr Institute, 1986); *Crossroads II.* Proceedings of the Second International Conference on Egyptian Grammar (Los Angeles, 17–20 October 1990), ed. by A. Loprieno, *Lingua Aegyptia* 1 (1991); *Crossroads III Preprints* (Yale University, 1994).
29. M. Collier, "The circumstantial *sḏm(.f)/sḏm.n(.f)* as verbal verb-forms in Middle Egyptian," *JEA* 76 (1990), 73–85; a modern handbook whose expanded version in English is going to replace Gardiner's *Egyptian Grammar* as a standard reference work is J. F. Borghouts, *Egyptisch. Een inleiding in taal en schrift van het Middenrijk*, 2 vols. Mededelingen en Verhandelingen van het Vooraziatisch-Egyptisch Genootschap "Ex Oriente Lux" XXX (Leuven: Peters, 1993).
30. For the former see for example F. Junge, *"Emphasis" and Sentential Meaning in Middle Egyptian*. Göttinger Orientforschungen IV/20 (Wiesbaden: Harrassowitz, 1989), reviewed in a verbalistic sense by M. Collier, "Predication and the circumstantial *sḏm(.f)/sḏm.n(.f)*," *LingAeg* 2 (1992), 17–65.

2 Egyptian graphemics

1. See H. G. Fischer, "Hieroglyphen," in *LÄ* II, 1189–99 with an extensive bibliography.
2. Because of the formal similarities with Egyptian hieroglyphs, the term "hieroglyphs" has also been applied to the writing system of Luwian, an Anatolian language related to cuneiform Hittite spoken and written during the Late Bronze and Iron Ages (between ca. 1500–700 BCE) in southern and southwestern Anatolia and northern Syria: hence the misleading definition "Hittite hieroglyphs" with which they are often referred to: see the discussion in I. J. Gelb, *A Study of Writing* (Chicago University Press, revised edn 1963), 81–84.
3. W. F. Albright, *The Protosinaitic Inscriptions and Their Decipherment* (Cambridge, Mass.: Harvard University Press, 1966); R. Giveon, "Protosinaitische Inschriften," in *LÄ* IV, 1156–59.
4. See St. Wenig, "Meroe, Schrift und Sprache," in *LÄ* IV, 104–7.
5. For the most complete treatment of the principles underlying the Egyptian writing system, their history, and their recovery see W. Schenkel, "Schrift," in *LÄ* V, 713–35.
6. We shall see in section 3.3 that the phoneme conventionally transcribed "glottal stop" by Egyptologists (ꜣ) was originally a uvular trill /ʀ/, which already in earlier Egyptian evolved into a glottal pronunciation and was assimilated to etymological /ʔ/. A parallel evolution to /ʔ/ affected the original initial /j/.
7. See the comments by F. Coulmas, "Writing systems," in *International Encyclopedia of Linguistics*, vol. IV, 253–57.
8. I borrow this term from S. Sauneron, *L'écriture figurative dans les textes d'Esna*. Esna VIII (Cairo: IFAO, 1982), 47–80 ("La philosophie d'une écriture").
9. L. Depuydt, "On Coptic sounds," *Orientalia* 62 (1993), 359.
10. W. Schenkel, "Syllabische Schreibung," in *LÄ* VI, 114–22. In recent years, studies have become more numerous: Th. Schneider, *Asiatische Personennamen in ägyptischen Quellen des Neuen Reiches*. Orbis Biblicus et Orientalis CXIV (Freiburg–Göttingen: Vandenhoeck & Ruprecht, 1992); J. Zeidler, "A new approach to the Late Egyptian 'syllabic orthography'," in *Sesto Congresso Internazionale di Egittologia. Atti*, vol. II (Turin: Italgas, 1993), 579–90; J. E. Hoch, *Semitic Words in Egyptian Texts of the New Kingdom and Third Intermediate Period* (Princeton University Press, 1994), 487–504.
11. For a list of examples and table see ibid., 492–501.
12. A. Loprieno, "Zahlwort," in *LÄ* VI, 1306–19.
13. Adapted from Gardiner, *EG*, 25.
14. Table 2.2 is drawn from ibid., pl. 2.
15. F. Kammerzell, "Zeichenverstümmelung," in *LÄ* VI, 1359–61.
16. Fischer, in *LÄ* II, 1196.
17. A major contribution to this problem can be expected from the excavations in the predynastic and early dynastic cemeteries at Abydos: G. Dreyer et al., "Umm el-Qaab. Nachuntersuchungen im frühzeitlichen Königsfriedhof. 5./6. Vorbericht," *MDAIK* 49 (1993), 51–56 and table 7.

18. P. Kaplony, *Die Inschriften der ägyptischen Frühzeit*, 2 vols. and supplements. Ägyptologische Abhandlungen VIII–IX (Wiesbaden: Harrassowitz, 1963–64) and J. Kahl, *Das System der ägyptischen Hieroglyphenschrift in der 0.–3. Dynastie*. Göttinger Orientforschungen IV/29 (Wiesbaden: Harrassowitz, 1994).
19. B. J. Kemp, *Ancient Egypt. Anatomy of a Civilization* (London: Routledge, 1989), 111.
20. The fundamental list of hieroglyphic signs and their values is provided by Gardiner, *EG*, 438–548.
21. K. J. Seyfried, *Das Grab des Amonmose (TT 373)* (Mainz: Philipp von Zabern, 1990), 42.
22. P. W. Pestman, *Chronologie égyptienne d'après les textes démotiques*. Papyrologica Lugduno-Batava XV (Leiden: E. J. Brill, 1967), 127.
23. S. Sauneron, "L'écriture ptolémaïque," in *Textes et langages de l'Egypte pharaonique. Hommages à Jean-François Champollion*. Bibliothèque d'Etude LXIV/1 (Cairo: IFAO, 1972), 45–56.
24. A list of Ptolemaic signs and their readings can be found in *Valeurs phonétiques des signes hiéroglyphiques d'époque gréco-romaine*, 3 vols. (Montpellier: University of Montpellier, 1988–90).
25. E. Iversen, *The Myth of Egypt and its Hieroglyphs in European Tradition* (Princeton University Press, 1961), 57–123.
26. H. W. Fairman, "Notes on the alphabetic signs employed in the hieroglyphic inscriptions of the temple of Edfu," *ASAE* 43 (1943), 193–310; id., "Introduction to the study of Ptolemaic signs and their values," *BIFAO* 43 (1945), 51–138.
27. Such as in the litanies in the temple of Esna: Sauneron, *Esna VIII*, 47–217.
28. E. Drioton, "Les principes de la cryptographie égyptienne," *Comptes-rendus des séances de l'Académie des Inscriptions et Belles Lettres* (Paris, 1953), 355–64.
29. Fairman, *ASAE* 43 (1943), 301.
30. A similar sign is perhaps the one used as a semagram or determinative of the god Nehebkau in some variants from the Coffin Texts, such as CT VI 133k or 392h. I thank Wolfgang Schenkel for this suggestion.
31. Fischer, in *LÄ* II, 1196; Schenkel, in *LÄ* V, 716–17.
32. Such as pSalt 825, a contemporary Hieratic text written in Ptolemaic Egyptian: see Ph. Derchain, *Le papyrus Salt 825 (BM 10051). Rituel pour la conservation de la vie en Egypte*. Mémoires de l'Académie Royale de Belgique, Classe des Lettres LVIII/1a (Brussels, 1965).
33. J. Osing, *Der spätägyptische Papyrus BM 10808*. Ägyptologische Abhandlungen XXXIII (Wiesbaden: Harrassowitz, 1976). For the Old Coptic material see ibid., 1–2.
34. See E. Winter, "Philae," in *LÄ* IV, 1023.
35. R. S. Bagnall, *Egypt in Late Antiquity* (Princeton University Press, 1993), 235 ff.
36. Graphemes which are present only in Bohairic or Akhmimic or whose phonological features in these dialects differ from Sahidic are indicated in parentheses.
37. *The Hieroglyphics of Horapollo*, translated by G. Boas with a new foreword by A. Grafton (Princeton University Press, 1993).
38. For this cultural milieu see G. Fowden, *The Egyptian Hermes. A Historical Approach to the Late Pagan Mind* (Princeton University Press, 1986), 13–74.

39. For a presentation of the decipherment in its cultural milieu see Iversen, *The Myth of Egypt*, 124–45.
40. "Lettre à M. le Professeur H. Rosellini…sur l'alphabet hiéroglyphique," *Annali dell'Istituto di corrispondenza archeologica* 9, Rome 1837, 5–100.

3 Egyptian phonology

1. For the reconstruction of the phonological evolution from Afroasiatic to Egyptian see Schenkel, *Altägyptische Sprachwissenschaft*, 48–57; F. Kammerzell, review of *Les langues dans le monde ancien et moderne*, *LingAeg* 2 (1992), 157–75; J. Zeidler, review of Petráček, *Vergleichende Studien*, *LingAeg* 2 (1992), 189–222.
2. Hoch, *Semitic Words in Egyptian Texts*, 399–437.
3. The most complete description of these rules and of the patterns of Egyptian vocalization is found in J. Osing, *Die Nominalbildung des Ägyptischen*, 2 vols. (Mainz am Rhein: Philipp von Zabern, 1976), 10–30.
4. Schenkel, *Altägyptische Sprachwissenschaft*, 23–28. This book presents an up-to-date picture of Egyptian phonology (pp. 24–93).
5. A. Faber, "Interpretation of orthographic forms," in Ph. Baldi (ed.), *Linguistic Change and Reconstruction Methodology*. Trends in Linguistics, Studies and Monographs 45 (Berlin–New York: Mouton de Gruyter, 1990), 627 ff.; id., "Second Harvest: *šibbōleθ* revisited (yet again)," *JSS* 37 (1992), 1–10. For dialectal differences in the case of Akk. *š* see W. von Soden, *Grundriss der akkadischen Grammatik*. Analecta Orientalia XXXIII–XLVII (Roma: Pontificium Institutum Biblicum, 1969), § 30.
6. Faber, in *Linguistic Change and Reconstruction Methodology*, 627; id., *JSS* 37 (1992), 1–10; Hoch, *Semitic Words in Egyptian Texts*, 407–8.
7. What is often referred to as "rules of decorum": see Chr. Eyre and J. Baines, "Interactions between Orality and Literacy in Ancient Egypt," in K. Schousboe and M. T. Larsen (eds.), *Literacy and Society* (Copenhagen: Akademisk Forlag, 1989), 91–119.
8. "Afroasiatic" is here used as a conventional term to indicate the set of linguistic features which Egyptian shares with a certain number of other language families (Semitic, Berber, Cushitic, Chadic), without implying the belief in the existence of an actual proto-language ancestral to these families. The different theoretical models are discussed in A. Loprieno, *Das Verbalsystem im Ägyptischen und im Semitischen. Zur Grundlegung einer Aspekttheorie*. Göttinger Orientforschungen IV/17 (Wiesbaden: Harrassowitz, 1986), 1–12, 187–90.
9. O. Rössler, "Das Ägyptische als semitische Sprache," in F. Altheim and R. Stiehl (eds.), *Christentum am Roten Meer I* (Berlin–New York: Walter de Gruyter, 1971), 275–77. Later evidence for the original dental articulation of Eg. <ʿ> will be discussed in section 3.6.
10. See the comparable evolution from Proto-Sem. **ḍ* to Aram. <q>, later <ʿ>: **'rḍ* > <'arqā> > <'arʿā> "earth": C. Brockelmann, *Grundriß der vergleichenden Grammatik der semitischen Sprachen*, vol. I (Berlin: Reuther & Reichard, 1908), 134.

11. A possible remnant of the early pronunciation of this phoneme is perhaps its outcome as Coptic /r/ in specific phonetic surroundings: ^{B}ⲭⲣⲟⲃⲓ "sickle" < *ẖ3b.t* */ça'ʀabjvt/ (?), with [çʀ] > [kʰr]. See the references in W. Westendorf, *Koptisches Handwörterbuch* (Heidelberg: Carl Winter Universitätsverlag, 1965), 67. An etymological glottal stop /ʔ/, however, was probably present in the original phonological inventory of Egyptian, as shown by words such as *nʔ.t* */'nu:ʔat/ "city" (> Hebr. *nō'* /roʔ/ > Akk. transcription *né-e'/ ni-i'* "Thebes") or *mʔw.t* */'meʔwat/ "mother" (> Coptic ⲙⲁⲁⲩ /maʔw/).
12. F. Kammerzell, "Personalpronomina und Personalendungen im Altägyptischen," in D. Mendel and U. Claudi (eds.), *Ägypten im afro-orientalischen Kontext. Gedenkschrift Peter Behrens*. Afrikanistische Arbeitspapiere, special issue 1991 (University of Cologne, 1991), 201.
13. Osing, *Nominalbildung*, 857.
14. Ibid., 316.
15. See also the observations by Kammerzell, in *Gedenkschrift Peter Behrens*, 198 ff.
16. Rössler, "Das Ägyptische als semitische Sprache," 263–326; among Egyptologists see primarily Schenkel, *Altägyptische Sprachwissenschaft*, 24–57; see also Kammerzell, *LingAeg* 2 (1992), 169–71; Zeidler, *LingAeg* 2 (1992), 206–10.
17. A discussion of adequacy and advantages of this simpler solution is offered by Hoch, *Semitic Words in Egyptian Texts*, 425 ff.
18. Schenkel, *Altägyptische Sprachwissenschaft*, 33–41. In loanwords from Egyptian to Semitic, Eg. *d* is always rendered by Sem. *ṭ*: Eg. *jdmj* */jv'du:mvj/ [jv't'u:m(vj)] > Hebr. *'ēṭûn* "red linen." The same holds true for Babylonian transcriptions of Eg. words: *jfdw* */jaf'daw/ [jvf't'aw] "four" = Middle Bab. *ipṭau*: Th.O. Lambdin, *Egyptian Loanwords and Transcriptions in the Ancient Semitic Languages* (Baltimore: Johns Hopkins University Press, 1952), 136–37; Sem. *ṭ*, on the other hand, is rendered both by Eg. *d* (with which it shared "markedness," in spite of the phonetic difference between Eg. glottalization and Sem. pharyngealization) and by Eg. *t* (with which it shared "voicelessness," in spite of the difference between Eg. glottalization and Sem. aspiration). Also, Eg. /g/ and /q/ were probably articulated as ejectives [k'] and [q'] respectively, which explains why Eg. *g* = [k'] is always rendered by Sem. *q* = [q]: Eg. *gstj* */'gastvj/ ['k'ast(vj)] "palette" > Hebr. *qešet* (< **qašt*) "bow": ibid., 148, whereas both Sem. *q* = /q/ (because of its voicelessness) and Sem. *g* = /g/ (because of its velarity) are rendered by Eg. *g* = [k']. As for the Eg. palatal ejective *ḏ*, it regularly corresponds to Sem. "emphatic" *ṣ*: *ḏ'n.t* */'ɟuʕnat/ ['c'uʕn(at)] "(the city of) Tanis" > Hebr. *ṣō'an* (< **ṣuʕn*). See Hoch, *Semitic Words in Egyptian Texts*, 429–30.
19. See the consistency of the evolutions Eg. /d/ > Coptic ⲧ, Eg. /ɟ/ > Coptic ϫ, Eg. /g/ > Coptic ⲕ or ϭ: W. H. Worrell, *Coptic Sounds*. University of Michigan Studies. Humanistic Series XXVI (Ann Arbor: University of Michigan Press, 1934), 17–30.
20. For the discussion of similar "glottalic" approaches to the phonology of Indo-European and of the proximity of voiced phonemes to ejectives see and J. H. Greenberg, "Some generalizations concerning glottalic consonants, especially implosives," *IJAL* 36 (1970), 123–45 and W. R. Schmalstieg, "A few issues of contemporary Indo-European linguistics," in *Linguistic Change and Reconstruction Methodology*, 362–65. An exception is represented by /b/, most probably [b],

in which the feature [+VOICED] was presumably kept because of the difficulty of maintaining in a linguistic system a glottalized [p'], due to the distance between glottis and lips: see the discussion by Schmalstieg ibid., 363–64. For a discussion of the relationship between voicing and types of phonation in general see J. Durand, *Generative and Non-linear Phonology*. Longman Linguistics Library (London–New York: Longman, 1990), 55.

21. This pattern of devoicing represents a form of "initial strengthening": H. H. Hock, *Principles of Historical Linguistics* (Berlin–New York: Walter de Gruyter, second edn 1991), 162–64.
22. An excellent analysis of the relation between three different types of stops (voiced-unaspirated, voiceless-aspirated, and voiceless-unaspirated) is provided by Worrell, *Coptic Sounds*, 17 ff.: while Egyptian "voiceless" plosives are aspirated, their "voiced" counterparts, which were probably articulated as ejectives, correspond rather to Worrell's "half-voiced" (i.e. voiceless-unaspirated) stops.
23. Kammerzell, in *Gedenkschrift Peter Behrens*, 190 ff.
24. Osing, *Nominalbildung*, 870 f.
25. Ibid., 454.
26. W. Schenkel, "Das Wort für 'König (von Oberägypten)'," *GM* 94 (1986), 57–73 suggests the interpretation of *z* as affricate [t͡s], among other reasons because it stands for /t/ + /s/ in the word *nzw* "king," whose more traditional writing is *ntsw*. Whether an affricate (as suggested by Schenkel and by the equation with Afroas. **s*) or an ejective (as suggested here on the basis of the historical evolution to a voiceless counterpart which it shares with voiced plosives), it is not surprising that this phoneme should be used to indicate a sibilant immediately following a nasal, a phonetic surrounding which often tends to generate affrication: /ns/ < <nts> or <nz> = [vnt͡s] (Schenkel) or else <nz> = [vns'] > <nts> = /ns/ [vnt͡s] (as suggested here): for "consonantal epenthesis" (as in the case of [vns] > [vnt͡s]) see Hock, *Principles of Historical Linguistics*, 117 ff.
27. See J. A. Goldsmith, *Autosegmental and Metrical Phonology* (Oxford: Blackwell, 1990), 107–8.
28. W. Schenkel, *Aus der Arbeit an einer Konkordanz zu den altägyptischen Sargtexten. II: Zur Pluralbildung des Ägyptischen*. Göttinger Orientforschungen IV/12 (Wiesbaden: Harrassowitz, 1983), 171–230; id., *Einführung*, 63–78.
29. F. Kammerzell, "Augment, Stamm und Endung. Zur morphologischen Entwicklung der Stativkonjugation," *LingAeg* 1 (1991), 189–92; id., in *Gedenkschrift Peter Behrens*, 198 ff. The fall of final vowels is usually seen in connection with the transition from the *Dreisilbengesetz* to the *Zweisilbengesetz* in the prehistory of Egyptian: see G. Fecht, *Wortakzent und Silbenstruktur*. Ägyptologische Forschungen XXI (Glückstadt: J. J. Augustin, 1960), §§ 392–406; Schenkel, *Altägyptische Sprachwissenschaft*, 78–86.
30. See Zeidler, *LingAeg* 2 (1992), 216.
31. In the following examples, the reconstruction of the phonological structure of a specific word in early Egyptian is accompanied by the later evidence (Akkadian transcriptions from the New Kingdom, Meroitic borrowings, or the Coptic form of the word) on which this reconstruction is based.
32. Osing, *Nominalbildung*, 558 ff.
33. Ibid., 532–33. For Meroitic see sections 1.1. and 2.1.

34. Fecht, *Wortakzent und Silbenstruktur*, §§ 325–347.
35. G. Fecht, "Prosodie," in *LÄ* IV, 1127–54; for the general issues Durand, *Generative and Non-linear Phonology*, 219–24.
36. Osing, *Nominalbildung*, 420, 619–20.
37. Ibid., 463.
38. This process of lenition may appear surprising if one sticks to the phonetic classification of /ʔ/ as a "glottal stop," but becomes quite understandable within a generative phonological frame, in which /ʔ/ is classified as "laryngeal glide," sharing the same features [-CONS, +SON] as the bilabial glide /w/ or the palatal glide /j/: Durand, *Generative and Non-linear Phonology*, 42, 102.
39. Osing, *Nominalbildung*, 463, 809–10.
40. Hoch, *Semitic Words in Egyptian Texts*, 492–93.
41. Ibid., 499–500.
42. Fecht, *Wortakzent und Silbenstruktur*, § 172.
43. Ibid., § 172; Osing, *Nominalbildung*, 148.
44. Schenkel, *Altägyptische Sprachwissenschaft*, 87–88; Osing, *Nominalbildung*, 377.
45. Ibid., 20, 605–6, 149.
46. Ibid., 20–21. This is probably a case of phonetically motivated suspension of the contrast between /iː/ and /eː/: see Durand, *Generative and Non-linear Phonology*, 57.
47. Ibid., 730, 476.
48. Ibid., 477.
49. Ibid., 463.
50. For recent accounts and literature on Coptic dialectology see the corresponding entries in Aziz S. Atiya (ed.), *The Coptic Encyclopedia*, vol. VIII (New York: Macmillan Publishing Company, 1991) on Akhmimic (pp. 19–27, by P. Nagel), Bohairic (pp. 53–60, by A. Shisha-Halevy), Fayyumic (pp. 124–31, by R. Kasser), Lycopolitan (pp. 151–59, by P. Nagel) and Sahidic (pp. 194–202, by A. Shisha-Halevy).
51. A. Loprieno, "Methodologische Anmerkungen zur Rolle der Dialekte in der ägyptischen Sprachentwicklung," *GM* 53 (1981), 55–75.
52. Voiceless stops were articulated with aspiration in specific phonetic environments. This feature was probably common to the entire Coptic domain: while most dialects do not indicate this feature in their graphic conventions, Bohairic uses the corresponding Greek *aspiratae* ⲫ, ⲑ, ⲭ (for ⲡ, ⲧ, ⲕ) and the Coptic sign ϭ (for ϫ). The voiced phonemes (plosives ⲇ /d/ and ⲅ /g/ and fricative ⲍ /z/) are limited to Greek borrowings and are realized as voiced stops. "Ejective" phonemes, on the contrary, are characteristic for the vocabulary of Egyptian stock and are realized as ejective stops. They are written with the corresponding Greek *tenuis*.
53. In Sahidic and in most other dialects, the phoneme /ʔ/ is rendered by <ø> in initial and final position, and by the reduplication of the vocalic grapheme (<vv> = <vʔ>) when immediately following the stressed vowel of a word. In Akhmimic and Lycopolitan, /ʔ/ in final position of monosyllabic words is rendered by <ⲉ>. In Bohairic, /ʔ/ is expressed by <ø> in any nonfinal position; at the end of a monosyllabic word, etymological /ʔ/ (primary or secondary) has evolved into <ⲓ> (this feature being shared by Fayyumic).

54. The phoneme /x/ is rendered by an independent grapheme in Akhmimic (ⳉ) and in Bohairic (ϧ), but not in Sahidic; however, its presence in the underlying phonological inventory left traces in internal vocalic oppositions of the type ^{S}ⲥⲉϩⲧ < */seḥɟvw/ "leprosy" vs. ^{S}ⲥⲁϩⲧ < */seχtvj/ "weaver."
55. The existence of a phoneme /ʕ/, which I subsume here under the heading "glottal" because of its historical merger with /ʔ/, is doubtful; however, its presence in the underlying phonological inventory left traces in final vocalic oppositions of the type ϩⲕⲁ "wool" < */çqaʕ/ < *ẖʿq* */ça'ʕaq/ vs. ϩⲕⲟ "to be hungry" < */ḥqoʔ/ < *ḥqr* */ḥa'qar/.
56. Fayyumic is known for its "lambdacism": <ⲗ> appears in many words in which the other dialects display <ⲣ>. The ratio between the two phonemes in all other Coptic dialects is 70% to 30% in favor of <ⲣ>, whereas Fayyumic has a proportion of 80% to 20% in favor of <ⲗ>: R. Kasser, "Fayyumic," in *Coptic Encyclopedia* VIII, 125.
57. The most up-to-date account of Coptic phonology is by F. Hintze, "Zur koptischen Phonologie," *Enchoria* 10 (1980), 23–91, to which the reader is referred for a generative treatment of an underlying phonological system of Coptic shared by the dialects independent of their different graphic conventions.
58. See its frequent alternation with <ϥ> /f/ and <ⲟⲩ> /w/: ^{SF}ⲛⲟⲩⲃ ~ ⲛⲟⲩϥ < *nbw* /na:baw/ "gold," ^{S}ⲃⲟⲓⲛⲉ ~ ^{B}ⲟⲩⲱⲓⲛⲓ < *bjn.t* /'bajnvt/ "harp."
59. However, final /ʔ/ is expressed by <ⲉ> in Sahidic and <ⲓ> in Bohairic in doubly-closed syllables, see below.
60. See H. J. Polotsky, review of Till, *Koptische Dialektgrammatik*, *Göttingische Gelehrte Anzeigen* 196 (1934), 60; Hintze, *Enchoria* 10 (1980), 40–41.
61. See the discussion of these phonetic properties in Worrell, *Coptic Sounds*, 17–23.
62. The reason for rendering aspirated stops in the majority of dialects with the corresponding Greek *tenuis* would be that Greek *aspiratae* generally represent in Coptic the combination of the corresponding voiceless phoneme followed by the glottal fricative: ⲫ = /ph/ (rather than $/p^h/$), ⲑ = /th/ (rather than $/t^h/$), ⲭ = /kh/ (rather than $/k^h/$).
63. As generally assumed by scholars (see R. Kasser, "Phonology," in *Coptic Encyclopedia* VIII, 184–86), except for Bohairic ϭ, which some linguists consider phonemically distinct from ϫ: see A. Shisha-Halevy, "Bohairic," ibid., 54.
64. Hintze, *Enchoria* 10 (1980), 50.
65. H. Satzinger, "Zur Phonetik des Bohairischen und des Ägyptisch-Arabischen im Mittelalter," *WZKM* 63–64 (1971), 40–65; id., "Pronunciation of Late Bohairic," in *Coptic Encyclopedia* VIII, 60–65.
66. Hock, *Principles of Historical Linguistics*, 121.
67. For the older assumption that Coptic displays an exact correspondence between graphemic appearance and phonological structure see R. Kasser, "Syllabication," in *Coptic Encyclopedia* VIII, 207 ff.
68. This is a general context for the development of aspiration, called "delayed voicing onset," also present in Modern English and German: Hock, *Principles of Historical Linguistics*, 121.
69. Background information, discussion and examples in Osing, *Nominalbildung*, 15–17, 403–48.
70. Osing, *Nominalbildung*, 11; Hintze, *Enchoria* 10 (1980), 49.

71. This phonological law is discussed by Th. Vennemann, *Preference Laws for Syllable Structure and the Explanation of Sound Change* (Berlin–New York–Amsterdam: Mouton de Gruyter, 1988), 40–41.
72. Goldsmith, *Autosegmental and Metrical Phonology*, 108–12.
73. A very plausible case has been made by F. Kammerzell, "Ueber die Verschiedenheit von geschriebener und gesprochener Sprache," paper read at the Sixth International Congress of Egyptology (Turin, 1–8 September 1991) and by Zeidler, *LingAeg* 2 (1992), 207–10 for the interpretation of a few lexical doublets which display /ʕ/ in their Old and Middle Eg. and /d/ in their Late Eg. form as two dialectal variants of a common Afroas. ancestor with etymological */d/.
74. W. Crum, *A Coptic Dictionary* (Oxford: Clarendon Press, 1939), 207 *s.v.* ⲙⲟⲩϣⲧ̄.
75. Osing, *Nominalbildung*, 754; Schenkel, *Pluralbildung*, 197 ff.; Zeidler, *LingAeg* 2 (1992), 195, and section 3.3.3 below.
76. Bibliographic information in R. Kasser, "Ayin," in *Coptic Encyclopedia* VIII, 45–47.
77. For other possible signals of a preservation of the phoneme /ʕ/ in final position see the discussion on the glottal stop /ʔ/ in section 3.4.3 below.
78. As we saw above, /e/ = <ø> in Sahidic, Akhmimic and Lycopolitan, <ⲉ> in Bohairic, and <ⲏ> or <ⲩ> in Fayyumic before sonorant phonemes (including ⲃ).
79. The presence of a short vowel [ə] is indicated in most dialects by a supralinear stroke (called in German *Vokalstrich*) over the following consonant.
80. This is yet another case of phonetically motivated neutralization of a phonological opposition.
81. Osing, *Nominalbildung*, 27–30, 475–500.
82. If the stressed syllable of earlier Egyptian was of the type cv:$ and the first consonant of the posttonic syllable /w/, /j/, or /ʔ/, Egyptian posttonic vowels in syllables of the type $cvw, $cvj, and $cvʔ have left different traces in the final long vowels or diphthongs of Coptic: Schenkel, *Altägyptische Sprachwissenschaft*, 91 f.
83. For a recent presentation of the state of the art see L. Depuydt, "On Coptic sounds," *Orientalia* 62 (1993), 338–75.
84. Within a generative approach see Hintze, *Enchoria* 10 (1980), 32–35, 48–54; within a traditional historical model see also the phonemes /x/, /x̠/ und /X/ as suggested by H. Satzinger, "Phonologie des koptischen Verbs (saʿidischer Dialekt)," in M. Görg (ed.), *Festschrift Elmar Edel*. Ägypten und Altes Testament I (Bamberg: Urlaub, 1979), 348.
85. See Goldsmith, *Autosegmental and Metrical Phonology*, 92, 107–8. Needless to say, the phonetic realization of these phonological strings may very well have been [ˈšaɟə], [ˈjopə], or [ˈsotəp], but in this instance the phonetic dimension is both impossible to reconstruct and irrelevant within the context of our discussion.
86. Many scholars would interpret the syllabic structure of these words somewhat differently, namely as ^{S}ⲉⲓⲟⲧⲉ, ^{B}ⲓⲟϯ = /ˈjotə/. From the point of view of the economy of a linguistic system, however, this phonological analysis presents the drawback of positing the existence of a stressed open syllable /ˈcv-/ in a plurisyllabic word, which is not documented throughout the history of the Egyptian language and is unnecessary at the purely synchronic level as well: see section 3.4.3

87. Hintze, *Enchoria* 10 (1980), 49.
88. See the discussion in Osing, *Nominalbildung*, 440.

4 Elements of historical morphology

1. Comrie, *Language Universals and Linguistic Typology*, 42–51.
2. See Schenkel, *Altägyptische Sprachwissenschaft*, 13–17 and references.
3. For the different methodological approaches to the study of Afroasiatic see Loprieno, *Verbalsystem*, 1–12.
4. This is the approach adopted by a majority of scholars working within the "semitocentric" genetic model: for example O. Rössler, "Verbalbau und Verbalflexion in den semitohamitischen Sprachen. Vorstudien zu einer vergleichenden semitohamitischen Grammatik," *ZDMG* 100 (1950), 461–514.
5. This is the so-called "allogenetic" theory of G. W. Tsereteli, "Zur Frage der Beziehung zwischen den semitischen und hamitischen Sprachen," *MIO* 16 (1970), 271–80.
6. For representatives of two forms of this theoretical model see Loprieno, *Verbalsystem* and K. Petráček, *Altägyptisch, Hamitosemitisch und ihre Beziehungen zu einigen Sprachfamilien in Afrika und Asien. Vergleichende Studien.* Acta Universitatis Carolinae Philologica Monographia XC (Prague: Charles University, 1988).
7. See especially T. Givón's work, for example *Syntax. A Functional-Typological Introduction*, vol. I (Amsterdam: Benjamins, 1984), 360–72.
8. A good example of an extreme triradical approach to Arabic verbal morphology is offered by R. M. Voigt, *Die infirmen Verbaltypen des Arabischen und das Biradikalismus Problem.* Veröffentlichungen der Orientalischen Kommission XXXIX (Stuttgart: Franz Steiner, 1988).
9. In more recent times, attention is being paid to the witnesses of prehistoric contact between Egyptian and Indo-European; see for example J. Ray, "Are Egyptian and Hittite related?," in A. B. Lloyd (ed.), *Studies in Pharaonic Religion and Society in Honour of J. Gwyn Griffiths* (London: Egypt Exploration Society, 1992), 124–36 and F. Kammerzell, "Zur Etymologie des ägyptischen Zahlworts '4'," in *Crossroads III Preprints.*
10. See F. Hintze, "Die Haupttendenzen der ägyptischen Sprachentwicklung," *Zeitschrift für Phonetik und allgemeine Sprachwissenschaft* 1 (1947), 85–108; W. Schenkel, "Die Konversion, ein Epiphänomen der kemischen (ägyptisch-koptischen) Sprachgeschichte," *MDAIK* 21 (1966), 123–32.
11. For a formal analysis of morphological derivation in Egyptian see Ch. Reintges, "Formal and functional aspects of the Egyptian root lexicon," in *Crossroads III Preprints.*
12. From the root *mr* "to tie" see *mr(w)* */ˈmu:raw/ > ⲙⲏⲣ "river bank" vs. *jmr.wt* */jaˈmirwat/ > [B]ⲁⲙⲏⲓⲣⲓ "inundation": Osing, *Nominalbildung*, 196.
13. From *wḫꜣ* "to blow" see *ḫꜣw* */ˈχu:ʀuw/ > ϩⲏ "blow (of the wind)": Osing, *Nominalbildung*, 97.
14. See *mn* */ma:n/ "to be stable" > ⲙⲟⲩⲛ vs. *smn.t* */ˈsimnit/ "to establish" > [B]ⲥⲉⲙⲛⲓ, *smn.t* */siˈmi:nit/ > [S]ⲥⲙⲓⲛⲉ: Osing, *Nominalbildung*, 54 ff.

15. See the masculine *nkt* */nu'kut/ > ⲛ̄ⲕⲁ /nkaʔ/ "thing" from the root *ktt* "(to be) small" or the feminine *nḥḏ.t* */nuḥɟat/ > ⲛⲁϫϩⲉ /nachə/ "tooth" from *ḥḏ* "(to be) white": Osing, *Nominalbildung*, 211–12; M.Th. Derchain-Urtel, "Das *n*-Präfix im Ägyptischen," *GM* 6 (1973), 39–54.
16. H. Grapow, *Die Wortbildungen mit einem Präfix* m- *im Ägyptischen*. APAW, Phil.–Hist. Kl., V, Berlin 1914. This formation is much rarer in Egyptian than in other Afroasiatic languages, see Osing, *Nominalbildung*, 119.
17. In the following table, conventional Egyptological transcriptions are maintained for the sake of accessibility. For the underlying phonological reality see chapter 2 on phonology. Also, vocalized forms are always preceded by an asterisk to indicate their reconstructed, rather than documented nature.
18. P. J. Hopper and E. C. Traugott, *Grammaticalization*. Cambridge Textbooks in Linguistics (Cambridge University Press, 1993), 32–62.
19. See the excellent study by Zeidler, *LingAeg* 2 (1992), 210–21.
20. Stems in **-i* or **-u* show in very rare cases the semivocalic ending <jj> =: **ij* or <w> =: **uw* instead of <–ø> respectively: Schenkel, *Pluralbildung*, 202.
21. Osing, *Nominalbildung*, 25, 891.
22. Ibid., 312.
23. For an analysis of this syntactic phenomenon see A. Loprieno, "Osservazioni sullo sviluppo dell' articolo prepositivo in egiziano e nelle lingue semitiche," *Oriens Antiquus* 19 (1980), 1–27.
24. See Fecht, *Wortakzent und Silbenstruktur*, §§ 78 ff.; a modern treatment of this issue is Schenkel, *Altägyptische Sprachwissenschaft*, 81–86.
25. Osing, *Nominalbildung*, 604.
26. Ibid., 532–33. For Meroitic see sections 1.1 and 2.1.
27. A different explanation is offered by W. Schenkel, *Frühmittelägyptische Studien*. Bonner Orientalistische Studien, N.S. XIII (University of Bonn, 1962), 58: *dp.t* */dvppvt/ < **/dvpwvt/ vs. *dp.wt=f* */dvpwv:tvf/.
28. Ibid., 408 ff.
29. Moscati, *Comparative Grammar of the Semitic Languages*, 87.
30. Schenkel, *Pluralbildung*, 202–4.
31. See discussion and bibliography in Zeidler, *LingAeg* 2 (1992), 194–95.
32. The two forms of the plural coexist sometimes in the same lexeme, for example in **ʒabád* > ⲉⲃⲟⲧ /ʔə'bot/ "month," **nāṯar* > ⲛⲟⲩⲧⲉ /nu:tə/ "god"; (a) *w*-plural **ʒabúd-w* > ⲉⲃⲁⲧⲉ /ʔə'batʔ/, **naṯúrw* > ⲛ̄ⲧⲉⲉⲣ(ⲉ) /nteʔr/; (b) *aw*-plural **ʒabūd-aw* > ⲉⲃⲏⲧ, **naṯūr-aw* > ⲛ̄ⲧⲏⲣ /nte:r/. See the discussion in Osing, *Nominalbildung*, 751 ff.; Schenkel, *Pluralbildung*, 197 ff. For the metathesis -urw > -ewr > -eʔr see section 3.6.1.
33. See Zeidler, *LingAeg* 2 (1992), 191–97.
34. For the metathesis -χw- > -wš- see section 3.6.1.
35. Fecht, *Wortakzent und Silbenstruktur*, § 206.
36. For the metathesis -irw- > -ejr- > -eʔr- see 3.6.1.
37. For the evolution of posttonic diphthongs see Osing, *Nominalbildung*, 28–30; Schenkel, *Altägyptische Sprachwissenschaft*, 91–92.
38. That in words of the *i*-stem the pattern with *aw*–plural (ⲧⲉϣⲉ vs. ⲧⲉϣⲉⲉⲩ) is probably not identical to the simple *w*-plural (see ⲉϩⲉ vs. ⲉϩⲉⲩ above) is shown by the presence vs. absence of a glottal stop in Coptic: while the simple *w*-plural

-iww results in ^{SB}–ⲉⲩ /-ew/ (ⲉϩⲉⲩ < **jaḥiww*), the plural **ijwaw* (particularly frequent in adjectives and participles) exhibits the outcome ^{S}–ⲉⲉⲩ(ⲉ), ^{B}–ⲉⲩ /-eʔw(ə)/; for the presence of a glottal stop in Bohairic in spite of the graphic rendering as <ø> see section 3.6.1. It should be stressed that this Coptic outcome of Egyptian **eʔwv(w)* characterizes only this plural pattern; in other cases, the outcome is ^{S}–ⲁⲁⲩ, ^{B}–ⲁⲩ /-aʔw/: Osing, *Nominalbildung*, 426–37.

39. Zeidler, *LingAeg* 2 (1992), 216 interprets plural patterns of the type cacuw- in biradical nouns (for example ⲥⲟⲛ vs. ⲥⲛⲏⲩ "brother"), which I see as the product of a survival of the old case ending **-u* in a new functional environment, resulting in the emergence of a *w*-glide, as a lengthening device for the analogic modelling of biradical nouns upon triradical patterns of the type cacuc-. In fact, the two phenomena, i.e. the diachronic memory of the old case ending and the synchronic analogy with triradical patterns may have both contributed to the grammaticalization of these patterns. In general, the vocalic stem cacuc- seems to have originally characterized collective nouns and to have been later extended to the plural: Schenkel, *Pluralbildung*, 205–7.
40. Ibid., 208–9.
41. That here the phonological sequence is /-owwə/ and not */-oʔwə/ is shown by the Bohairic treatment of the tonic vowel as <ω> (as is always the case in diphthongs) rather than as <o>, which indicates /oʔ/ before a semiconsonantal /w/, as in ^{SB}ϩⲟⲟⲩ /hoʔw/ "day"; see section 3.6.1.
42. See Osing, *Nominalbildung*, 290–94.
43. See Schenkel, *Pluralbildung*, 209.
44. Osing, *Nominalbildung*, 871.
45. Ibid., 634.
46. W. C. Till, *Koptische Grammatik (Saïdischer Dialekt)*. Lehrbücher für das Studium der orientalischen und afrikanischen Sprachen I (Leipzig: Verlag Enzyklopädie, fourth edn 1970), § 81.
47. Osing, *Papyrus BM 10808*, 254.
48. For the discussion of this issue see W. F. Edgerton, "Stress, vowel quantity, and syllable division in Egyptian," *JNES* 6 (1947), 1–17; Schenkel, *Pluralbildung*, xi–xiii.
49. For a modern presentation of this dichotomy within Coseriu's approach, including its historical antecedents (especially Hjelmslev's distinction between *system*, *norm* and *usage*) see K. Ezawa, *Sprachsystem und Sprechnorm* (Tübingen: Max Niemeyer, 1985).
50. These conventions are governed by the "rules of decorum": Chr. Eyre and J. Baines, "Interactions between orality and literacy in Ancient Egypt," in K. Schousboe and M.T. Larsen (eds.), *Literacy and Society* (Copenhagen: Akademisk Forlag, 1989), 91–119.
51. The presence of a posttonic syllabic pattern -cv# in earlier Egyptian is posited by the present writer (see section 3.4.3) but usually rejected in scholarship on Egyptian phonology in the footsteps of Fecht, *Wortakzent und Silbenstruktur*, including Osing, *Nominalbildung* and Schenkel, *Altägyptische Sprachwissenschaft*.
52. See Schenkel, *Pluralbildung*, 217, 228.
53. See Osing, *Nominalbildung*, 488.
54. As in the analysis by Schenkel, *Pluralbildung*, 198.

55. For the CT see ibid., 228; the writing <ḥfꜣjjw> in the Book of the Dead (mentioned by Osing, *Nominalbildung*, 488) is more easily interpreted as a hybrid form which combines at the graphic level the old (*w-*) and the new (*j-*) plural morpheme.
56. For a phonological, rather than morphological interpretation of the reason for the frequent presence of semiconsonantal endings in Egyptian words (*contingent extrasyllabicity*) see section 3.4.3.
57. Osing, *Nominalbildung*, 554.
58. Ibid., 558 ff.
59. From the *nisba* adjective *tpj* "relative to the head."
60. A treatment of personal pronouns in earlier Egyptian which takes into account the Afroasiatic perspective is Kammerzell, in *Gedenkschrift Behrens*, 177–203.
61. Ibid., 189–91, 198–99.
62. A similar phenomenon is known from Japanese, where /hu/ = [ɸu] and /hi/ = [çi]: Ezawa, *Sprachsystem und Sprechnorm*, 103–12. The Egyptian phoneme /s/ was probably characterized by a phonetic feature of palatality.
63. J. Wackernagel, "Über ein Gesetz der indogermanischen Wortstellung," *IF* 1 (1892), 333–436.
64. Early texts show examples of preterital cleft sentences *jn*+NP+*sḏm.n=f* see B. Gunn, *Studies in Egyptian Syntax* (Paris: Paul Geuthner, 1924), 59–60; J. P. Allen, *The Inflection of the Verb in the Pyramid Texts*. Bibliotheca Aegyptia 2 (Malibu: Undena, 1984), § 408. A rare example of cleft adverbial sentence is Heqaib 10,20, see P. Vernus, "Le rhème marqué: typologie des emplois et effets de sens en Moyen Egyptien," *LingAeg* 1 (1991), 337: *jn jm.wj n(.wj) ẖr.t-jb jn jmj-rꜣ ‘ḫnw.tj n(j) ḥm=f m-sꜣ jrj* "It was two precious ships (*jm.wj n.wj ẖr.t-jb* "two ships of desire") and His Majesty's Chamberlain (*jmj-rꜣ ‘ḫnw.tj nj ḥm=f*) that were delegated to that (*m-sꜣ jrj* "[who were] thereafter")."
65. The first person independent pronoun is also used in adverbial and pseudoverbal clauses embedded into a higher nominal sentence, see section 4.3.
66. See Kammerzell, in *Gedenkschrift Behrens*, 192 ff.
67. Within an "ergative" understanding of the focus marker *jn* one may think of examples such as CT V 27d–e Sq6C *smn ṯb.wt n.t N pn ḥr ꜣkr jn ꜣs.t smn=s N pn jn ꜣs.t ḥr ꜣkr m nṯr ‘nḫ* "The sandals of this N will be established (*smn*) on Earth by Isis (*jn ꜣs.t*); it is Isis (*jn ꜣs.t*) who will establish (*smn=s*) this N on Earth as a living god," where in the first instance the particle *jn* introduces the agent of a passive verbal form, in the second it marks as focus the subject of an active verbal form cataphorically anticipated by the suffix pronoun in the verbal predicate. A similar syntactic type is shown in the frequent quotation formula in Late Egyptian letters: *j.n=f m pꜣj=n nb* "so said our lord," where the subject is extraposed to the right and introduced by the focal particle *m* (< *jn*), lit. "so he said, indeed our lord." See Gardiner, *EG*, § 227.5.
68. See the insightful and prudent discussion by Zeidler, *LingAeg* 2 (1992), 210–21.
69. The variant with ending *j* documented in the Old Kingdom and frequently in the Coffin Texts (Kammerzell, in *Gedenkschrift Behrens*, 192) is probably just a writing of *jnk* followed by a reinterpreted first person determinative "<j> + MAN."
70. See Schenkel, *Altägyptische Sprachwissenschaft*, 105–8.

71. The semiconsonantal suffix *.w* > *.j* is adverbial in origin: see for example the negative marker of circumstantiality *ny*: G. Moers, "Freie Varianten oder funktional gebundene Morpheme? Zu den Graphien der altägyptischen Negation *n*," *LingAeg* 3 (1993), 33–58, § 2.1. It is mostly found in the earliest texts when the stative is used adverbially, especially as predicative complement: F. Kammerzell, "Funktion und Form. Zur Opposition von Perfekt und Pseudopartizip im Alt- und Mittelägyptischen," *GM* 117/18 (1990), 181–202.
72. See now K. Jansen-Winkeln, "Das ägyptische Pseudopartizip," *OLP* 24 (1993), 5–28.
73. The Akkadian "permansive" is originally not a form of the verbal paradigm, but rather a nominal sentence pattern with a conjugated verbal adjective: see G. Buccellati, "An interpretation of the Akkadian stative as a nominal sentence," *JNES* 27 (1968), 1–12; J. Huehnergard, "'Stative', predicative form, pseudo-verb," *JNES* 46 (1987), 215–32.
74. See Loprieno, *Verbalsystem*, 38–50.
75. Ibid., 160–78.
76. An exception is the survival of the third person plural -ⲥⲟⲩ, -ⲥⲉ in Coptic constructions after a certain number of infinitives (for example *zẖꜣ st* > ⲥϩⲁⲓⲥⲟⲩ "to write them"), of imperatives (*jrj st* > ⲁⲣⲓⲥⲟⲩ "do it"), and in patterns indicating possession (*wn m-dj=f st* > ⲟⲩⲛ̄ⲧⲁϥⲥⲉ "he has them"): Till, *Koptische Grammatik*, § 200, 292–93; Polotsky, *Grundlagen*, 76–78.
77. J. Borghouts, "Object pronouns of the *tw*–type in Late Egyptian," *OLP* 11 (1980), 99–109.
78. For a similar typological phenomenon see the use of the Spanish preposition *a* to introduce specified human objects: J. N. Green, "Spanish," in *International Encyclopedia of Linguistics*, vol. IV, 58–64.
79. In Demotic and Coptic, analogic pressures will lead to the adoption of the third person suffix pronoun in this pattern (masculine ϥ-, feminine ⲥ-).
80. This diachronic process is analyzed by Winand, *Etudes de néo-égyptien*, 103–49.
81. A few Demotic verbs have kept the first, rather than the third person singular form of the stative, for example *ḥmsy.k* "to sit"; only one of them (ⲛ̄ⲕⲟⲧⲕ̄ "to sleep" < *jn.qdyt.k*) survived down to Coptic. See Winand, *Etudes de néo-égyptien*, 139.
82. Gardiner, *EG*, § 511,3.
83. See Kammerzell, *LingAeg* 2 (1992), 165.
84. Loprieno, *Oriens Antiquus* 19 (1980), 1–27.
85. F. Kammerzell, "Ueber die Verschiedenheit von geschriebener und gesprochener Sprache," paper read at the Sixth International Congress of Egyptology (Turin, 1–8 September 1991) and Zeidler, *LingAeg* 2 (1992), 207–10 argue convincingly for the interpretation of a few lexical doublets which display /ʕ/ in their earlier Egyptian and /d/ in their later Egyptian form as two dialectal variants of a common Afroasiatic ancestor with etymological */d/.
86. Z. Žába, *Les Maximes de Ptaḥḥotep* (Prague: Czechoslovakian Academy of Sciences, 1956).
87. The use of the past form *sḏm.n=f* after the particle *nj* to negate the general tense is a phenomenon known in Egyptological literature as "Gunn's rule" (section 7.8).

88. The earlier and later Egyptian forms are in fact etymologically identical; the opposition between *d* and *ʿ* is based on the "Upper Egyptian" (*d*) vs. "Lower Egyptian" (ʿ) outcome of thr Afroasiatic **d*, see section 3.6.1.
89. See for example for Indo-European the observations by O. Szemerényi, *Einführung in die vergleichende Sprachwissenschaft* (Darmstadt: Wissenschaftliche Buchgesellschaft, 1980), 204–5; see now J. Gvozdanovic (ed.), *Indo-European Numerals*. Trends in Linguistics, Studies and Monographs LVII (Berlin–New York: Mouton de Gruyter, 1992). In Afroasiatic, however, numerals display a much wider degree of innovativeness than in Indo-European: see P. de Wolf, "Erläuterungen zu den Zählwesen im Osthamitischen," in *ZDMG. Supplement VII* (Stuttgart: Franz Steiner Verlag, 1989), 560–73.
90. For a more thorough treatment of numerals see A. Loprieno, "Zahlwort," in *LÄ* VI, 1306–19 and Schenkel, *Altägyptische Sprachwissenschaft*, 53–57.
91. T. G. Penchoen, *Tamazight of the Ayt Ndhir*. Afroasiatic Dialects I (Malibu: Undena, 1973), 24.
92. From an underlying root *šnj* "to be round" > "the round number."
93. See *sn* "brother."
94. The word is not documented in hieroglyphic Egyptian, but can be reconstructed on the basis of puns. It represents the dual of *mḏw* "10" (**/muɟawa:taj/), see the same derivational process in Semitic (for example Arabic *ʿišrūna* "20" vs. *ʿašar* "10") and in Indo-European **wīkm̥tī* "20" < **(d)wī (de)km̥ti* "two tens": O. Szemerényi, *Studies in the Indoeuropean System of Numerals*. Indogermanische Bibliothek (Heidelberg: Carl Winter, 1960), 129.
95. Probably a dual form of "100."
96. From the root *ʿbꜣ* "to be complete."
97. Coptic shows that the numerals "300"–"900" were built with a genitival construction of the corresponding unit and the word for "100."
98. The word is not documented in hieroglyphic Egyptian, but can be reconstructed on the basis of puns; it is possibly connected with the root *ḥmw* "to be skilled."
99. Probably derived from an Afroasiatic word for "hand," see Sem. **yad* (**/jadi:jaw/ "hand-like"). See the etymology of Indo-European **dekm̥* "10" < "two hands": Szemerényi, *Studies*, 69. However, the etymology of Egyptian "5" from an older word for "hand" presents phonological difficulties: J. Zeidler, "Nochmals zur Etymologie der Handhieroglyphe," *GM* 72 (1984), 39–47; Schenkel, *LingAeg* 3 (1993), 137–49.
100. The numerals "50"–"90" are not documented in full writing, but can be reconstructed on the basis of the Coptic forms as derived from the corresponding units with the addition of a *w*– (plural?) suffix.
101. This numeral is written as a rebus with the sign for *ḏbʿ* "finger" (see Sem. *ṣbʿ*). The etymology is unclear.
102. Rather than "one million" in the numerical sense, this word refers to a generally "limitless" quantity.
103. The root *psḏ* is probably tied to the semantic realm of "new," see *psḏ* "sunrise" and *psḏn.tjw* "new moon," IE **newn̥* "9" and **newos* "new": Szemerényi, *Studies*, 173.

104. This new interest has been especially spurred by two major studies: Allen, *Inflection of the Verb* and E. Doret, *The Narrative Verbal System of Old and Middle Egyptian*. Cahiers d'Orientalisme 12 (Geneva: Patrick Cramer, 1986). See in both cases the reviews by W. Schenkel, "Zur Verbalflexion der Pyramidentexte," *BiOr* 42 (1985), 481–94 and id., *Archiv für Orientforschung* 35 (1988), 237–45.
105. For a general overview see Schenkel, *Altägyptische Sprachwissenschaft*, 109–15.
106. Ibid., 115–21.
107. For diathetic oppositions in the infinitive L. Depuydt, "Zum Passiv im Ägyptischen," *Orientalia* 56 (1987), 129–35.
108. Schenkel, *Altägyptische Sprachwissenschaft*, 105–108.
109. Loprieno, *Verbalsystem*, 27–55; id., "Focus, mood, and negative forms: Middle Egyptian syntactic paradigms and diachrony," *LingAeg* 1 (1991), 201–26.
110. For the general linguistic problem see B. Comrie, *Aspect*. Cambridge Textbooks in Linguistics (Cambridge University Press, 1976).
111. B. Comrie, *Tense*. Cambridge Textbooks in Linguistics (Cambridge University Press, 1985).
112. In fact, the earlier tendency to consider the Semitic verbal system as tenseless has itself been challenged: R I. Binnick, *Time and the Verb. A Guide to Tense & Aspect* (Oxford University Press, 1991), 434–44.
113. An excellent study of the interface between these two categories is provided by Binnick, *Time and the Verb*; see the summary 452–61.
114. Ibid., 44.
115. See F. Palmer, *Mood and Modality*. Cambridge Textbooks in Linguistics (Cambridge University Press, 1986).
116. Binnick, *Time and the Verb*, 51–125.
117. Ibid., 339 ff.
118. See Comrie, *Aspect*, 84–86; Hock, *Principles of Historical Linguistics*, 344–50.
119. Loprieno, *Verbalsystem*, 38–50.
120. Binnick, *Time and the Verb*, 383 ff.
121. Ibid., 139–49.
122. These oppositions are similar to the Aristotelian concept of "aspect"; here, I basically follow Z. Vendler, "Verbs and times," in *Linguistics in Philosophy* (Ithaca: Cornell University Press, 1967), 97–121. See Binnick, *Time and the Verb*, 170–214.
123. Ibid., 371–434.
124. See Osing, *Papyrus BM 10808*, 30–31; Zeidler, *LingAeg* 2 (1992), 214–16.
125. Already in Old Egyptian and increasingly in the classical language, the form *sḏm.n=f* is introduced in the indicative use by an initial particle such as *jw*, *mk*, etc. See chapter 6 for a detailed analysis.
126. The difference between "perfect" and "perfective" aspect is that in the former the event time (E) *precedes* the reference frame (R), in the latter E is *included* in R: see Binnick, *Time and the Verb*, 207–14, 295–300.
127. Ibid., 247 ff.
128. See ^{S}ⲙⲉϣⲁⲓ "I don't know," ^{F}ⲉⲙⲉϣⲏⲓ "except" < *(jw) nj rḫ=j* (*/rvʹχij/): see Schenkel, *Altägyptische Sprachwissenschaft*, 112–14; Osing, *Papyrus BM 10808*, 36, 174–78.
129. Jansen-Winkeln, *OLP* 24 (1993), 18.

130. W. Schenkel, "*sčm.t*-Perfekt und *sčm.ti*-Stativ: die beiden Pseudopartizipien des Ägyptischen nach dem Zeugnis der Sargtexte," in H. Behlmer (ed.), *...Quaerentes Scientiam. Festgabe für Wolfhart Westendorf zu seinem 70. Geburtstag überreicht von seinen Schülern* (Göttingen: Seminar für Ägyptologie und Koptologie, 1994), 157–82 suggests that the preterital ("Perfekt") and the subordinate ("Stativ") use of the stative are in fact two distinct morphological forms, the former corresponding to the Northwest Semitic suffix conjugation, the latter to the Akkadian stative.
131. Kammerzell, *LingAeg* 1 (1991), 165–99. See the vocalization patterns with *u* and *i* in the formation of the Semitic passive: Loprieno, *Verbalsystem*, 152–78. For the vocalization of the Egyptian forms see Fecht, *Wortakzent und Silbenstruktur*, §§ 348–59; Osing, *Nominalbildung*, 468–75; J. Osing, "Die Partizipien im Ägyptischen und in den semitischen Sprachen," in J. Osing and G. Dreyer (eds.), *Form und Maß. Beiträge zur Literatur, Sprache und Kunst des alten Ägypten. Festschrift für Gerhard Fecht*. Ägypten und Altes Testament XII (Harrassowitz: Wiesbaden, 1987), 351–55. The difference between *(ca)cuc- and *(ca)cic- may have been originally one of *Aktionsart*, with the former used preferably with transitive, the latter with intransitive verbs.
132. The reconstruction of the first person stative pattern is based solely on comparative evidence: see Kammerzell, in *Gedenkschrift Behrens*, 191–92; Schenkel, in *Festgabe Westendorf* has */sv'tepkaw/ (perfect) vs. */svt'pa:kaw/ (stative). For the syncope of the posttonic short vowel due to the change from the *Dreisilbengesetz* to the *Zweisilbengesetz* see Fecht, *Wortakzent und Silbenstruktur*, §§ 348–59 and section 3.4.3 above.
133. Osing, *Papyrus BM 10808*, 28–29, 153–60; Schenkel, in *Festgabe Westendorf* suggests */sv'tepta/ (perfect) vs. */svt'pa:taj/ (stative) for the masculine, */sv'tepti/ (perfect) vs. */svt'pa:tij/ (stative) for the feminine form.
134. For the third person feminine, Coptic survivals allow a reconstruction of the two patterns *cacac-tvj vs. *cacic-tvj in the earlier Egyptian form: transitive *smn.tj* */sa'mantvj/ "she is established" > ⲥⲙⲟⲛⲧ "to be stable" vs. intransitive *ḥqr.tj* */ḥa'qirtvj/ "she is hungry" > ϩⲕⲁⲉⲓⲧ "to be hungry." Schenkel, in *Festgabe Westendorf* pleas for a vocalization */'satpaw/ (perfect) vs. */sv'te:paw/ (stative) for the masculine, */sv'tepti/ (perfect) vs. */svt'pa:tij/ (stative) for the feminine form.
135. The passages of the "Eloquent Peasant" are quoted according to the text edition by R. B. Parkinson, *The Tale of the Eloquent Peasant* (Oxford: Griffith Institute, 1991).
136. For the "contingent" tenses see L. Depuydt, "The contingent tenses of Egyptian," *Orientalia* 58 (1989), 1–27 and his monograph *Conjunction, Contiguity, Contingency* (Oxford University Press, 1993).
137. See Allen, *Inflection of the Verb*, §§ 141, 259, 395.
138. On the basis of later evidence, J. F. Quack, "Über die mit *'nḫ* gebildeten Namenstypen und die Vokalisation einiger Verbalformen," *GM* 123 (1991), 91–100 suggests a pattern with final stress */jarra'ras/.
139. R. Anthes, *Die Felseninschriften von Hatnub*. Untersuchungen zur Geschichte und Altertumskunde Ägyptens IX (Leipzig: J. C. Hinrichs'sche Buchhandlung, 1928).

140. Collier, *JEA* 76 (1990), 73–85; id., "Circumstantially adverbial? The circumstantial *sḏm(.f)/sḏm.n(.f)* reconsidered," in S. Quirke (ed.), *Middle Kingdom Studies* (New Malden: SIA Publishing, 1991), 21–50.
141. P. Vernus, *Future at Issue. Tense, Mood and Aspect in Middle Egyptian: Studies in Syntax and Semantics.* Yale Egyptological Studies IV (New Haven: Yale Egyptological Seminar, 1990), 163–93; for the latter ibid., 9–15.
142. Depuydt, *Conjunction, Contiguity, Contingency*, 208–33.
143. See the discussion in Loprieno, *LingAeg* 1 (1991), 210–17.
144. Osing, *Papyrus BM 10808*, 40–41.
145. C. Peust, "Zur Herkunft des koptischen н," *LingAeg* 2 (1992), 120.
146. Discussion and references in Doret, *Narrative Verbal System*, 23.
147. Allen, *Inflection of the Verb*, §§ 213–399 and Schenkel, *BiOr* 42 (1985), 481–94.
148. Osing, *Papyrus BM 10808*, 36, 174–78.
149. Allen, *Inflection of the Verb*, §§ 265–67.
150. Osing, *Papyrus BM 10808*, 33–36, 167–70.
151. J. B. Callender, "Afroasiatic cases and the formation of Ancient Egyptian constructions with possessive suffixes," *Afroasiatic Linguistics* II/6 (Malibu: Undena, 1975); J. D. Ray, "An approach to the *sḏm.f*: forms and purposes," *LingAeg* 1 (1991), 243–58..
152. See Loprieno, *Verbalsystem*, 118–23; Palmer, *Mood and Modality*, 126 ff.
153. T. Givón, *On Understanding Grammar.* Perspectives in Neurolinguistics and Psycholinguistics (New York: Academic Press, 1979), 207 ff.; id., "From discourse to syntax: Grammar as a processing strategy," in T. Givón (ed.), *Syntax and Semantics*, vol. XII: *Discourse and Syntax* (New York: Academic Press, 1979), 81–112.
154. See J. Allen, "Synthetic and analytic tenses in Old Egyptian," in *L'Egyptologie en 1979. Axes prioritaires de recherches*, vol. I. Colloques internationaux du CNRS 595 (Paris: CNRS, 1982), 25; W. Schenkel, "*sḏm=f* und *sḏm.w=f* als Prospektivformen," in D. W. Young (ed.), *Studies Presented to Hans Jacob Polotsky* (Beacon Hill: Pirtle & Polson, 1981), 506–27.
155. See R. Hannig, "The particle *kꜣ*," *GM* 95 (1987), 9–19.
156. Depuydt, *Conjunction, Contiguity, Contingency*, 234–46.
157. See the discussion on valency and participant-roles in J. Lyons, *Semantics*, vol. *II* (Cambridge University Press, 1977), §§ 12.3–12.6.
158. The "agentivity scale" is closely connected with the hierarchies of "animacy" and of "salience" which play a major role in the syntactic organization of participant roles within the sentence and in the distribution of pragmatic relevance: see Givón, *Syntax*, vol. I, 85–185; in the case of Egyptian, see A. Loprieno, "On the typological order of constituents in Egyptian," *Journal of Afroasiatic Languages* 1 (1988), 26–57.
159. Egyptian does not know the advancement to subject of the role of "beneficiary," or recipient of the action (as in the English construction *I was given a book*), which is always introduced by the preposition *n* "to." The closest Egyptian pattern to the advancement to subject of the beneficiary is a form of asyndetic relative clause without resumptive element, in which a physical or psychological characteristic of a specific antecedent is modified by an adjectival sentence: *rmṯ*

nfr ḥr "the man whose face is beautiful" < *"the man – the face is beautiful." This pattern is similar to the so-called *bahuvrīhi* constructions in Indo-European languages and to Semitic patterns such as the Arabic adjectival phrase *'ar-rağulu 'l-ḥasanu 'l-wağhi* "the man whose face is beautiful," lit. "the man – the one beautiful of the face" (K. Jansen-Winkeln, "Exozentrische Komposita als Relativphrasen im älteren Ägyptisch," *ZÄS* 121 [1994], 51–75), and in part also to the Indo-European and Semitic "relational accusative" of the *tamyīz*-type: see W. Wright, *A Grammar of the Arabic Language*, third edition revised by W. Robertson Smith and M.J. de Goeje, vol. II (Cambridge University Press, 1898), § 44. In Egyptian, the relational accusative is found in lexicalized constructions consisting of a verbal root followed by its object, for example in the participial eulogy *ḏj-ʿnḫ* "who is given life," from *rḏj-ʿnḫ* "to give life"; see W. Schenkel, *Tübinger Einführung in die klassisch-ägyptische Sprache und Schrift* (Tübingen, 1991), § 7.5.5.

160. For a general assessment of this problem of the Egyptian verb see P. Grandet and B. Mathieu, "La construction ergative de l'accompli égyptien," in *Sesto Congresso Internazionale di Egittologia. Atti*, vol. II (Turin: Italgas, 1993), 145–51.
161. Binnick, *Time and the Verb*, 297, 389 ff.; Loprieno, *Verbalsystem*, 38–50.
162. W. Westendorf, *Der Gebrauch des Passivs in der klassichen Literatur der Ägypter*. Veröffentlichungen des Instituts für Orientforschung XVIII (Berlin: Deutsche Akademie der Wissenschaften, 1953).
163. H. J. Polotsky, "The 'emphatic' *sḏm.n.f* form," *RdE* 11 (1957), 109–17. For the text see A. Moret, "La légende d'Osiris à l'époque thébaine d'après l'hymne à Osiris du Louvre," *BIFAO* 30 (1931), 725–50.
164. In Old Egyptian, this form displays a *j*-prefix in the 2–rad. and in a few weak classes: *j.ḏd=f* "which he says": Allen, *Inflection of the Verb*, §§ 631–36.
165. For the ending *.tj* in the feminine prospective relative form see Gunn, *Studies*, 1–25.
166. Gardiner, *EG*, §§ 380–89.
167. Discussion and references in W. Schenkel, *Die altägyptische Suffixkonjugation*. Ägyptologische Abhandlungen XXXII (Wiesbaden: Harrassowitz, 1975) and Osing, in *Festschrift Fecht*, 356–60.
168. See the form *zinnuk* as Akkadian transcription of the relative form *ḏd.n=k* "which you said": Zeidler, *LingAeg* 2 (1992), 214–16.
169. J. P. Allen, "Form, function, and meaning in the Early Egyptian verb," *LingAeg* 1 (1991), 4. In Coptic, emphatic forms are marked by morphemes of relative origin, such as the relative pronoun *nt-* in *ntafsôtm* "the fact that he heard."
170. Osing, *Papyrus BM 10808*, 38–40, 179–86. If the reconstruction of a vocalization **nu* for the temporal affix of the relative form *sḏm.n=f* is correct, one would be tempted to posit **u* (rather than **i*, as assumed by Osing) for the relative *sḏm=f* as well.
171. For a full account see Osing, in *Festschrift Fecht*, 337–50.
172. Ibid., 358–60.
173. See the toponym *mn-nfr* */minnvfvr/ > Μεμφις, ⲙⲛ̄ϥⲉ and the Akkadian transcription of *mn-mꜣʿ.t-rʿw* "Re is stable of truth" (the royal name of King Sethi I) as *mi-in-mu-a-ri-a*, corresponding to a later Eg. form */min̦muʔʕəˈriʕə/: Osing, in *Festschrift Fecht*, 341.

174. This pattern is frequent when the participle is substantivized, as in **ⲟⲩⲟⲛ** "someone."
175. III-inf. verbs of movement show the pattern *ci:caj (*prj* */pi:raj/ "one who has come out"), adjective verbs the patterns 2-rad. *cac (*ꜥꜣ* */ʕaʀ/ "big"), 3-rad., II-gem. and III-inf. *ca:cic (*gꜣw* */ga:ʀiw/ "narrow"), *ci:cac (*šrr* */ši:rar/ "small") and *cu:cic (*wrj* */wu:rij/ "great") as well: Schenkel, *Altägyptische Sprachwissenschaft*, 86–92.
176. Substantivized participles belonging to this pattern also display the forms 3–rad. *ca:cac, II-gem., III- and IV-inf. *caccij (rather than *cacciw): see Osing, in *Festschrift Fecht*, 348–50.
177. For the tendency of unmarked participles to be associated with singular nouns and of marked participles to refer rather to plural referents see W. Schenkel, "'Singularisches' und 'pluralisches' Partizip," *MDAIK* 20 (1965), 110–14.
178. See Allen, *Inflection of the Verb*, §§ 600–43.
179. Gunn, *Studies*, 26–39.
180. Ibid., 65–68.
181. The only indication of the original vocalization of the negatival complement is provided by the Coptic negative imperative **ⲙ̄ⲡⲱⲣ** < *m jrj.w* "do not do," in which -**ⲱⲣ** < *jrj.w* */ja:rvw/.
182. These VPs could also be seen as nominalized forms controlled by prepositions (section 6.3.1).
183. See Gardiner, *EG*, §§ 351–52.
184. The best and most complete account of the verbal morphology of Late Egyptian is provided by Winand, *Etudes de néo-égyptien*; for Demotic one will refer to J.H. Johnson, *The Demotic Verbal System*. Studies in Ancient Oriental Civilization 38 (Chicago: Oriental Institute, 1976); for Coptic H. J. Polotsky, "The Coptic conjugation system," *Orientalia* 29 (1960), 392–422 and id., *Grundlagen*. Incidentally, the phonological shape of the verb *sḏm* in Coptic (*sôtm*) shows that in this word the palatal sound had been dentalized (see section 3.5.1). This is why, for later Egyptian, I adopt the transcription *sdm*.
185. A. Loprieno, "The sequential forms in Late Egyptian and Biblical Hebrew: a parallel development of verbal systems," *Afroasiatic Linguistics* VII/5 (Malibu: Undena, 1980), 1–19.
186. Comrie, *Language Universals and Linguistic Typology*, 45–51.
187. Winand, *Etudes de néo-égyptien*, 179–98.
188. Ibid., 198–208.
189. Ibid., 289–97.
190. Ibid., 441–57, 190–91.
191. Ibid., 401–39.
192. Ibid., 231–41.
193. Polotsky, *Grundlagen*, 194–97; Depuydt, *Conjunction, Contiguity, Contingency*, 208 ff.
194. Winand, *Etudes de néo-égyptien*, 481–517.
195. Polotsky, *Grundlagen*, 213–16.
196. Winand, *Etudes de néo-égyptien*, 151–78.
197. Polotsky, *Grundlagen*, 165–68.

198. Winand, *Etudes de néo-égyptien,* 209–58, 265–79; P. Cassonnet, "Modalités énonciatives et temps seconds *i.sḏm.f* en néo-égyptien," in *Crossroads III. Preprints.*
199. For the Coptic functional heir ϥⲛⲁⲥⲱⲧⲙ̄ ⲡⲉ (as opposed to the prospective simple ϥⲛⲁⲥⲱⲧⲙ̄) see Depuydt, *Conjunction, Contiguity, Contingency,* 244–46.
200. Ibid., 1–116, also J. Borghouts, "A new approach to the Late Egyptian conjunctive," *ZÄS* 196 (1979), 14–24. While the conjunctive can indeed join events in the past, specifically when a focalization is at play and the events themselves are framed within a general present, its primary function is *modal*: see the use of the English verb *would* in narrative discourse, when the consecutive "unwinding of events" rather than their past reference is stressed.
201. Winand, *Etudes de néo-égyptien,* 457–65.
202. This form is variously called "Final," "Future conjunctive," or "Promissive future": Polotsky, *Grundlagen,* 163–65; Depuydt, *Conjunction, Contiguity, Contingency,* 75–93. The sporadic initial *n-* is not justified at the etymological level and probably represents the result of analogic pressure from the conjunctive.
203. Winand, *Etudes de néo-égyptien,* 103–49.
204. Ibid., 299–341.
205. Discussion and references in Polotsky, *Grundlagen,* 181–84.
206. Ibid., 179.
207. Winand, *Etudes de néo-égyptien,* 375–98.
208. Polotsky, *Grundlagen,* 45–62.
209. Ibid., *Grundlagen,* 59–60; Winand, *Etudes de néo-égyptien,* 343–73.
210. Ibid., *Etudes de néo-égyptien,* 41–101.
211. In Late Egyptian, the ending of the infinitive of the III-inf. verbs is still written <t>, but frequently also <jj>, which is probably a writing of the vowel /ə/: ibid., 56–60, 100–101.
212. Ibid., 95–100; Osing, *Nominalbildung,* 333–38; Borghouts, *OLP* 11 (1980), 99–109.
213. For the tendency of linguistic functions originally conveyed by morphological case oppositions to be gradually replaced by syntactic devices such as a more rigid word order or a development of adverbial constructions see Hock, *Principles of Historical Linguistics,* 309–79.
214. Zeidler, *LingAeg* 2 (1992), 219–21.
215. See the treatment of this particle in Doret, *Narrative Verbal System,* 25, *passim.*
216. Ibid., 155 *passim.*

5 Nominal syntax

1. The most complete treatment for the classical language is provided by E. Doret, "Phrase nominale, identité et substitution dans les Textes des Sarcophages," *RdE* 40 (1989), 49–63; 41 (1990), 39–56; 43 (1992), 49–73, who also gives a detailed philological analysis of the examples and a complete bibliography of secondary literature. For the general linguistic issue see K. Hengeveld, *Non-verbal Predication. Theory, Typology, Diachrony.* Functional Grammar Series XV (Berlin: Mouton de Gruyter, 1992).

2. For the difference between "interlocutive" first and second persons and "delocutive" third person see Polotsky, *Grundlagen*, 19–20.
3. G. Gazdar, E. Klein, G.K. Pullum, and I. A. Sag, *Generalized Phrase Structure Grammar* (Oxford University Press, 1985), 20–21; Hengeveld, *Non-verbal Predication*, 26–30. In the following discussion, I use the term "substantive" to indicate the "noun" in the narrower sense, i.e. to the exclusion of the adjective.
4. Ibid., 75–77.
5. In early Egyptian there are still traces of gender and person congruence between nominal predicate and pronominal subject, *tw* being used with feminine and *nw* with plural nouns: Doret, *RdE* 40 (1989), 50.
6. See Wackernagel, *IF* 1 (1892), 333–436.
7. Hengeveld, *Non-verbal Predication*, 32 ff.
8. Comrie, *Language Universals and Linguistic Typology*, 185–200; for Egyptian see Loprieno, *JAAL* 1 (1988), 26–57.
9. As a general remark to the many parallel variants in the CT here and in many of the examples quoted in this chapter, one should reckon in many cases with "mechanical," i.e. not always grammatically correct alternations between pronominal and nominal subjects. See Schenkel, *Tübinger Einführung*, § 6.1.1.1.
10. W. Chafe, "Givenness, contrastiveness, definiteness, subjects, topics, and point of view," in Ch. N. Li (ed.), *Subject and Topic* (New York: Academic Press, 1976), 25–55; E. F. Prince, "Toward a taxonomy of given-new information," in P. Cole (ed.), *Radical Pragmatics* (New York: Academic Press, 1984), 223–55.
11. See P. Schachter, "Focus and relativization," *Language* 49 (1973), 19–46.
12. Other than the cleft sentence (section 5.4.2), which always displays a contrastive stress on the fronted noun, the pseudocleft sentence shows only an optional focalization of this NP: T. Givón, *Syntax. A Functional-Typological Introduction*, vol. II (Amsterdam: John Benjamins, 1990), 704–5.
13. P. J. Frandsen, "On the relevance of logical analysis," in *Crossroad*, 145–59; W. Schenkel, "Zur Struktur des dreigliedrigen Nominalsatzes mit der Satzteilfolge Subjekt-Prädikat im Ägyptischen," *SAK* 14 (1987), 265–82; in general Hengeveld, *Non-verbal Predication*, 82–88.
14. Because of its similarity to a verbal sentence with two topicalized forms (section 7.5), nominal patterns with lexically identical subject and predicate are labeled "balanced sentences."
15. J. Lyons, *Semantics*, vol. I (Cambridge University Press, 1977), §§ 7.1.–4.
16. M. A. K. Halliday, "Language structure and language function," in J. Lyons (ed.), *New Horizons in Linguistics* (Harmondsworth: Penguin Books, 1970), 140–65.
17. See the opposition perceived by Arabic grammarians between *al-mutakallim* "the one who speaks" (first person) and *al-muḫâṭab* "the interlocutor" (second person) on the one hand vs. *al-ɣâ'ib* "the absent one" (third person) on the other hand.
18. For adjectival sentences, I adopt a slightly different terminology, i.e. "qualifying" for the unmarked type (corresponding to the classifying pattern in nominal sentences) and "identifying" for the cleft (and the pseudocleft, see above) sentence. See the discussion in Doret, *RdE* 40 (1989), 50 ft. 16. See also F. Junge, "Nominalsatz und Cleft sentence im Ägyptischen," in *Studies Polotsky*, 431–62; W. Schenkel, "Fokussierung. Über die Reihenfolge von Subjekt und Prädikat im

klassisch-ägyptischen Nominalsatz," in *Studien zu Sprache und Religion Ägyptens zu Ehren von Wolfhart Westendorf*, vol. I (Göttingen: Seminar für Ägyptologie und Koptologie, 1984), 157–74.

19. A rare evidence of the presence of this difference in tonic patterns for older Egyptian could be conveyed by the writing of the first person independent pronoun as *jn* instead of *jnk* before a word beginning with /k/ in CT IV 21c BH2C *jn(k) kɜ mɜ'.t* "I am the bull of Maat": J. Borghouts, "Prominence constructions and pragmatic functions," in *Crossroad*, 62.
20. S. C. Dik et al., "On the typology of focus phenomena," in T. Hoekstra, H. van der Hulst, and M. Moortgat (eds.), *Perspectives on Functional Grammar* (Dordrecht: Foris, 1980), 41–74.
21. As suggested by Schenkel, *Tübinger Einführung*, § 6.1.1.1.
22. H. Satzinger, "Structural analysis of the Egyptian independent personal pronoun," in H. G. Mukarovsky (ed.), *Proceedings of the Fifth International Hamito-Semitic Congress 1987*, vol. 2. Beiträge zur Afrikanistik XLI (Vienna: Institut für Afrikanistik, 1991), 121–35; Kammerzell, in *Gedenkschrift Behrens*, 192 ff. See also section 4.4.1.
23. For these constructions M. Gilula, "An unusual nominal pattern in Middle Egyptian," *JEA* 62 (1976), 160–75.
24. See similar formulae in later texts: BD 64,5 *ntf pw jnk jnk pw ntf* "He is really I and I am really he" or BD (Lepsius) 162,8 *ntf ntk* "He is you" quoted by Gilula, *JEA* 62 (1976), 173 and corresponding to the Coptic pattern with double thematic pronoun ⲁⲛⲟⲕ ⲡⲉ ⲛ̄ⲧⲟⲟⲩ ⲁⲩⲱ ⲛ̄ⲧⲟⲟⲩ ⲡⲉ ⲁⲛⲟⲕ, see Polotsky, *Grundlagen*, 33–34 and sections 5.8–5.9 below.
25. Loprieno, *JAAL* 1 (1988), 37–38.
26. The best treatment of this issue is H. J. Sasse, "The thetic/categorical distinction revisited," *Linguistics* 25.3 (1987), 511–80 who offers a theoretical analysis as well as many examples from a variety of languages.
27. It might be useful here to point out that *any* verbal form can appear in these sentences, irrespective of its temporal or modal features: we have a so-called "emphatic" form in example (40), which may be contrasted for example with a "prospective" form in pRam. IV C 18: If he vomits it, *mwt=f pw* "this means (*pw*) that he will die (*mwt=f*)."
28. Loprieno, *LingAeg* 1 (1991), 202–4.
29. The stative is also used to express the adjectival predicate in the so-called *bahuvrīhi* construction, an asyndetic clause modifying a specific antecedent and predicating a physical or moral quality of his: CT III 370b *jw ḥrj.w-p.t jb=sn nḏm.w* "the heart of those who are in heaven is happy," lit. "those who are in heaven (*ḥrj.w-p.t*) – their heart is happy (*jb=sn nḏm.w*)." See Jansen-Winkeln, *ZÄS* 121 (1994), 67 ff. and section 6.2 below.
30. The existence of a construction NP + *sw* is advocated by E. Doret, "Cleft sentence, substitutions et contraintes sémantiques en égyptien de la première phase (V–XVIIII Dynastie)," *LingAeg* 1 (1991), 59; the pattern may be documented in the CT – see example (41): CT IV 412 (164a) *mjw sw* "he is cat-*like*" – and could be the symmetrical counterpart of AdjP + *pw*, being used in marked contexts in which NP, rather than a noun, represents the set of *qualities* associated with it. It is more probable, however, that *mjw* is here in fact a *nisba* adjective

mjwj "cat-like," a frequent pattern with nouns of animals in the CT. If this is the case, the construction NP + *sw* does not exist. I thank Wolfgang Schenkel for calling my attention to this point.

31. For the very rare cases of AdjP-*wj* see A. H. Gardiner, *The Admonitions of an Egyptian Sage from a Hieratic Papyrus in Leiden (Pap. Leiden 344 recto)* (Leipzig: J. C. Hinrichs'sche Buchhandlung, 1909), 104, and *EG*, 425; the example is Khakheperre'seneb 13 *znn wj ḥr jb=j* "and I am sad (*znn*) in my heart." Rather than an initial main clause, the adjectival sentence functions here as a dependent clause.
32. See A. Loprieno, "Der ägyptische Satz zwischen Semantik und Pragmatik: die Rolle von *jn*," *SAK Beihefte* III (1988), 77–98; Doret, *LingAeg* 1 (1991), 57–96; Vernus, *LingAeg* 1 (1991), 333–55.
33. See Doret, *RdE* 40 (1989), 62; 41 (1990), 58; 43 (1992), 64–66.
34. P. Vernus, "Etudes de philologie et de linguistique (VI)," *RdE* 38 (1987), 175–81; Doret, *RdE* 41 (1990), 42 ff.
35. H. J. Polotsky, *Etudes de syntaxe copte* (Cairo: Société d'Archéologie Copte, 1944), 21–98.
36. Vernus, *LingAeg* 1 (1991), 338. See also Gunn, *Studies*, 59. A possible, but doubtful example of a relative form as predicate of a cleft sentence is Pt. 173–74 *jn w'j sḫpr.w nṯr jrj nb wḥj.t nḥj=s šms=f* "It is the lonely one whom God causes to become the head of a family who wishes to follow him": see G. Fecht, "Cruces Interpretum in der Lehre des Ptahhotep (Maximen 7, 9, 13, 14) und das Alter der Lehre," in *Hommages à François Daumas*, 2 vols. (University of Montpellier, 1986), 233–35. But the morphosyntactic segmentation of this passage is far from established.
37. S. C. Dik, *Functional Grammar*. Publications in Language Sciences VII (Dordrecht: Foris, 1981), 87; Comrie, *Language Universals and Linguistic Typology*, 62–65.
38. We saw above that, because of their pragmatic salience, in the pattern "Independent pronoun-*pw*-NP" they combine, as it were, the role of syntactic predicate of the proposition (belonging formally to the tripartite pattern Pred-*pw*-Subj) and that of pragmatic focus of the utterance (alternating functionally with the cleft sentence S => Focus-AdjP). In this passage from the "Eloquent Peasant," moreover, the choice of the pattern *jnk-pw*–AdjP is also motivated by stylistic requirements, such as the need to create a contrastive parallelism between the two sentences.
39. The archaic cases of *jn*+NP+*sḏm.tj=f* and *jn*+NP+*sḏm.tj* are discussed by Doret, *RdE* 40 (1989), 61–62.
40. Some authorities posit the existence of a cleft sentence pattern in which the prospective form does not agree in person with the antecedent: see BM 614,8 *jnk mrj=f nfr.t msḏj=f ḏw.t* "There is only me (*jnk*) who will always cherish (*mrj=f*) good and hate (*msḏj=f*) evil." This is, however, a different pattern with an adverbialized VP modifying as virtual relative clause an indefinite antecedent omitted under relevance. For a discussion see Gunn, *Studies*, 60–61; A. Shisha-Halevy, "The narrative verbal system of Old and Middle Egyptian," *Orientalia* 58 (1989), 253; J. Borghouts, "*jnk mr(i)=f*: an elusive pattern in Middle Egyptian," in *Crossroads III Preprints*. This pattern will be analyzed in more detail in section 7.4.

41. For a discussion of expressions of possession see M. Gilula, "An adjectival predicative expression of possession in Middle Egyptian," *RdE* 20 (1968), 55–61; H. Satzinger, "Syntax der Präpositionsadjektive ('Präpositionsnisben')," *ZÄS* 113 (1986), 141–53; in general see Hengeveld, *Non-verbal Predication*, 126–29.
42. W. Westendorf, "Beiträge zum ägyptischen Nominalsatz." *NAWG, Phil.-Hist. Kl.*, III, Göttingen 1981, 83–86.
43. The same determinative pronoun in apposition to the head noun, and therefore agreeing with it in gender, number, and person (fem. *n.t*, pl. *n.w*), is in fact the usual marker of the indirect genitive.
44. "Maat" is the most fundamental concept of the Egyptian encyclopaedia, involving cosmological order, moral truth, administrative justice, and social cohesion between the members of Egyptian society. See J. Assmann, *Ma'at. Gerechtigkeit und Unsterblichkeit im Alten Ägypten* (Munich: C.H. Beck, 1990).
45. For interrogative patterns in which the scope of the question invests an adverbial adjunct see sections 6.1–2; for so-called "YES-NO" interrogative sentences, in which the scope of the question is the predicative nexus itself see sections 7.1–2, 7.5.1.
46. Hengeveld, *Non-verbal Predication*, 103–29.
47. Schenkel, *Tübinger Einführung*, § 6.4.2.1.
48. Th. Ritter, "On particles in Middle Egyptian," *LingAeg* 2 (1992), 127–37.
49. Gardiner, *EG*, § 461.
50. For a thorough discussion see Vernus, *Future at Issue*, 46–51. See also the alternation between "subjunctive" *wn* in its older functions as "mood of command" (Loprieno, *LingAeg* 1 [1991], 210–17) and "prospective" *wnn* in its use as "mood of wish" as in example (111)): CT III 300b–d "May your (fem.) head be raised, your forehead be revived, may you speak to your own self: *wn=ṯ m nṯr wnn=ṯ m nṯr* you shall be a god, you will be a god."
51. For a general treatment see A. Loprieno, "Topics in Egyptian negations," in *Gedenkschrift Behrens*, 213–35.
52. See the distribution *m/n* in Old Egyptian occurrences of the negative particle: E. Edel, *Altägyptische Grammatik*. Analecta Orientalia XXXIV–XXXIX (Rome: Pontifical Biblical Institute, 1955–64), §§ 1104–5; for the comparative evidence see V. L. Davis, *Syntax of the Negative Particles* bw *and* bn *in Late Egyptian*. Münchner Ägyptologische Studien XXIX (Berlin: Deutscher Kunstverlag, 1973), 168–202.
53. W. Westendorf, "Zur Lesung der mittelägyptischen (prädikativen) Negation ," *GM* 36 (1979), 61–67; *GM* 45 (1981), 71–80.
54. L. R. Horn, *A Natural History of Negation* (Chicago University Press, 1989).
55. F. Ll. Griffith, *The Inscriptions of Siût and Dêr Rîfeh* (London: Egypt Exploration Society, 1889).
56. Horn, *Negation*, 452 ff.; see A. Meillet and J. Vendryès, *Traité de grammaire comparée des langues classiques* (Paris: Maisonneuve, fourth edn 1968), § 180.
57. This happens when the presuppositional predicate is demoted to the level of a textually recurring theme: Loprieno, in *Gedenkschrift Behrens*, 219.
58. Horn, *Negation*, 6–14 *passim*.
59. Gunn, *Studies*, 170; Gilula, *RdE* 20 (1968), 61.

60. Loprieno, in *Gedenkschrift Behrens*, 226–31. See below for the square of semantic oppositions as applied to negative constructions in verbal clauses. The abbreviations are derived from the characteristic vowels of the two Latin words ***AffIrmo*** (I declare) and ***nEgO*** (I deny).
61. D. Dunham, *Naga-ed-Dêr Stelae of the First Intermediate Period* (London: Oxford University Press, 1937).
62. See also the typologically later *nn...js* for the negation of the imperfective participle in a cleft sentence in West. 9,6 *nn jnk js jnn n=k sj* "Not I am the one who brings it to you." Papyrus Westcar (pBerlin 3033) belongs to the later classical texts, probably composed during Dyn. XV: W. K. Simpson, "Pap. Westcar," in *LÄ* IV, 744–46.
63. C. J. Eyre, "The Semna Stelae: quotation, genre, and functions of literature," in S. I. Groll (ed.), *Studies in Egyptology Presented to Miriam Lichtheim*, vol. I (Jerusalem: Magnes Press, 1990), 134–65.
64. Horn, *Negation*, 10 and *passim*, to whom I refer for a detailed explanation of the properties of the four corners ***AffIrmo*** and ***nEgO***.
65. H. Satzinger, "Nominalsatz und Cleft Sentence im Neuägyptischen," in *Studies Polotsky*, 480–505; J. Černý and S. I. Groll, *A Late Egyptian Grammar*. Studia Pohl, Series Maior IV (Rome: Pontifical Biblical Institute, third edn 1984), 517–37.
66. See Hock, *Principles of Historical Linguistics*, 314–19, 670 for the bibliography. This general problem has been studied repeatedly by T. Givón; see for example his *On Understanding Grammar*. Perspectives in Neurolinguistics and Psycholinguistics (New York: Academic Press, 1979), esp. 207 ff. or "From discourse to syntax: Grammar as a processing strategy," in T. Givón (ed.), *Syntax and Semantics*, vol. XII: *Discourse and Syntax* (New York: Academic Press, 1979), 81–112.
67. Junge, in *ZDMG Supplement VI*, 17–34.
68. For example P. Vernus, "Deux particularités de l'égyptien de tradition: *ntj iw* + Présent I; *wnn.f ḥr sḏm* narratif," in *L'Egyptologie en 1979. Axes prioritaires de recherches*, vol. I. Colloques internationaux du CNRS (Paris: CNRS, 1982), 81–89.
69. Dik, *Functional Grammar*, 153–56.
70. This morpheme is kept as *pw* only after the interrogative *jḫ*: *jḫ-pw* "what?"
71. J. H. Johnson, "Demotic nominal sentences," in *Studies Polotsky*, 414–30. For examples drawn from the "Instructions of Onchsheshonqy" (pBM 10508) see id., *Thus Wrote 'Onchsheshonqy. An Introductory Grammar of Demotic*. Studies in Ancient Oriental Civilization XLV (Chicago: Oriental Institute, second edn 1991).
72. Polotsky, *Grundlagen*, 29–36.
73. L. Depuydt, "*Onchsheshonqy* 2,13 and 4,1–2; a philological note," in *Studies Lichtheim*, vol. I, 116–21.
74. H. J. Thissen, "Bemerkungen zum demotischen Harfner-Gedicht," in *Studies Lichtheim*, vol. II, 992. See the regular pattern Onchsh. 8,23*rnn.t rmt-rḫ rꜣ=f* "The wealth (*rnn.t*) of a wise man (*rmt-rḫ*) is his speech (*rꜣ=f*)."

75. Theoretically, sentences such as example (154) could indeed be analyzed as a tripartite pattern in which the determinative pronoun preceding the second relative form is taken to be the old copula *pw* > *p3j*. This typological problem has diachronic implications as well (section 5.9).
76. Polotsky, *Grundlagen*, 36–43. This construction is much more frequent in Sahidic than in Bohairic, where it appears to be replaced by the tripartite sentence with topicalized subject resumed by the pronominal copula after the predicate, as in example (153) above: the Bohairic version of example (158) is [*t-souri* ("the sting") *gar m-ph-mou*] [*ph-nobi*] [*pe*] [*t-jom de m-ph-nobi*] [*ph-nomos*] [*pe*].
77. From the point of view of its morphosyntactic structure, the Coptic "participle" in example (160) and the "relative form" in (162) both contain in fact complete adjectival transpositions of a VP, regardless of the coreferentiality with the predicative NP: coreferential (*rectus*) "the one (*p-*) who (*-ent-*) did (*-a=f-*) summon (*-tahm=n*)" vs. not coreferential (*obliquus*) "the (things) (*n–*) which I (*et=i-*) shall (*-na-*) do them (*-aa=u*)." For a full treatment see Polotsky, *Grundlagen*, 45–127.
78. Although one will remember that in Middle Egyptian too the indicator of focality can be deleted when the subject is the author of a letter or the owner in the frame of a funerary text, Late Egyptian shows an expansion of the pattern S => NPfocus + AdjPpred: Truth and Falsehood 6,6 *p3j=j sn šrj j.kmn (w)j* "It was my younger brother who blinded me," particularly frequent in circumstantial clauses: Vernus, *RdE* 38 (1987), 175 ff. The reason for the higher frequency of the pattern without introductory particle in Late Egyptian when compared to the preceding stages of the language is most probably to be sought in the contemporary emergence of the new type of cleft sentence, for which see below.
79. Polotsky, *Grundlagen*, 59–61 (for ϵp– as remnant of the perfective participle *j.jr* "who did"), 121 (for *et-* < *ntj ḥr*); A. Shisha-Halevy, "Bohairic-Late Egyptian Diaglosses: a Contribution to the Typology of Egyptian," in *Studies Polotsky*, 314–38, especially 322–23 sees the higher frequency of this pattern in Bohairic, where it is used not only, as in Sahidic, with personal pronouns, but also with proper names, interrogative pronouns, demonstratives, and numerals as one of the typological features linking Bohairic to Late Egyptian as opposed to Middle Egyptian.
80. G. Mattha and G. R. Hughes, *The Demotic Legal Code of Hermopolis West*. Bibliothèque d'Etude XLV (Cairo: IFAO, 1975). A thorough study of the cleft sentence pattern with focalized infinitive is J. F. Quack, "Die Konstruktion des Infinitivs in der Cleft Sentence," *RdE* 42 (1991), 189–207.
81. *pe-t=i-jô* < *p3-ntj=j ḥr ḏd*.
82. H. J. Polotsky, "Nominalsatz und Cleft Sentence im Koptischen," *Orientalia* 31 (1962), 413–30.
83. There are, however, cases in which Sahidic and other dialects also show an invariable *pe* as copula of the cleft sentence: see Polotsky, *Grundlagen*, 119–21 and example (197).
84. That this is actually the function of the *p*–pronoun is shown by the congruence in gender and number displayed by any resumptive pronoun in the presupposition with the focalized *antecedent*, with which it still builds a tight syntactic unit even beyond the copula itself ([S]*ou-me te-t=i-jô mmo=s*, [B]*ou-mêi pe-t=i-jô mmo=s*), as opposed to the agreement of a resumptive pronoun with the *new*

copula in the case of the nominal sentence, the NP_{subj} representing actually a mere semantic expansion of the copula itself: see Polotsky, *Orientalia* 31 (1962), 419 *ou-me pe p-et=i-jô mmo=f* "what I say is true" < "Truth (fem.) is (*pe*) that-which-I-say-it (masc.)." See Polotsky, *Grundlagen*, 109–14. As concerns the gender and number of the copula in tripartite patterns of this latter type, the general rule is that in the presence of agreement between the NP_{pred} and NP_{subj}, the copula will follow them; if there is a difference, the copula will be uniformly the masculine *pe*: see Polotsky, *Grundlagen*, 42–43.

85. Onchsh. 14,4 *nts tɜ-ntj ṯɜ.t=f* (< *ḥr ṯɜj.t=f*) "*This* is what seizes him," Ps 22,1 ⲡϫⲟⲉⲓⲥ ⲡⲉⲧⲙⲟⲟⲛⲉ ⲙ̄ⲙⲟⲓ "It is the Lord who tends (*p-et-moone* < **pɜ-ntj ḥr mjnj*) me."
86. Of Semitic origin: see Hebrew *'ê-ze(h)* "which?".
87. A similar contraction can be observed in the case of the Middle Egyptian enclitic particle of admiration *wj*, which in Late Egyptian appears to have merged with the dependent third person pronoun into the new particle *wsj* "how...!": Amenemope 2,6 *dns-wsj pɜ-šmw m ḥɜtj=f* "how concerned is the heated man in his heart!" < **dns-wj sw pɜ-šmw* "how concerned is he, (namely) the heated man (*pɜ-šmw*)!"
88. Sir H. Thompson, *A Family Archive from Siut from Papyri in the British Museum* (Oxford University Press, 1934).
89. Rather than a true phonetic change, this is a case of lexical doublets in which Middle Egyptian shows the regular Eg. outcome of Afroas. */d/, whereas Late Egyptian keeps a variant with the ejective dental plosive inherited from its Afroas. prehistory: see Zeidler, *LingAeg* 2 (1992), 208 and the discussion in section 3.6.
90. Polotsky, *Grundlagen*, 68–78.
91. Compare the fate of the construction *yeš l-X* in Modern Hebrew: originally meaning an impersonal existential "there is to X," it is now frequently followed by the preposition *et* indicating a definite direct object: see for example H. Rosén, *Good Hebrew. Meditations on the Syntax of the "Proper" Language* (in Hebrew) (Jerusalem: Kiryat Sepher, 1966), 34–35; T. Givón, "Topic, pronoun and grammatical agreement," in *Subject and Topic*, § 9.2.
92. See the discussion on localism in Lyons, *Semantics*, vol. 2, § 15.7; S. C. Dik, *The Theory of Functional Grammar. Part I: the Structure of the Clause.* Functional Grammar Studies 9 (Dordrecht: Foris, 1989), 176 ff.; for the relationship between existential predicates and locative constructions see Hengeveld, *Non-verbal Predication*, 96–100.
93. See J. Osing, "Zur Lesung der neuägyptischen-demotischen Negation 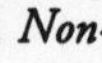," *Enchoria* 10 (1980), 93–104.
94. Compare this sentence with *nj ntk js zj* in example (131).
95. For the different registers in this text see O. Goldwasser, "On the choice of registers. Studies on the grammar of Papyrus Anastasi I," in *Studies Lichtheim*, vol. I, 200–40.
96. Satzinger, in *Studies Polotsky*, 489 suggests that while the unmarked nominal sentence was negated by a pattern in which *bn...jwnɜ* isolates the NPpred, in the cleft sentence the same discontinuous morpheme wraps the entire sentence. While this would indeed make perfect sense from a linguistic point of view, since

the cleft sentence represents a tighter unit than the unmarked nominal sentence, his example pBM 10052, 5,20 *(jw) bn pꜣ-jnr ‘ꜣ j.psš=n jm=f jwnꜣ* "(and) it was not the big stone with which we had divided" is not conclusive: here the context proves that this is not an example of a negated cleft sentence, but rather of negation of a NP followed by a relative clause functioning as its modifier: the expression "with which we divided" is not the presuppositional predicate of the sentence, but an apposition to "the big stone," which is the actual scope of the focal negation.

97. See in French the frequent colloquial use of the bare original reinforcer *pas* instead of the whole discontinuous morpheme *ne..pas*: *Je t'ai pas vu* < *Je ne t'ai pas vu* "I haven't seen you."
98. E. Bresciani, *Der Kampf um den Panzer des Inaros (Papyrus Krall)*. Mitteilungen aus der Papyrussammlung der Österreichischen Nationalbibliothek, N.S. VIII (Vienna: Georg Prachner Verlag, 1964).
99. We observed that after Late Egyptian had displayed the tendency to reduce original tripartite patterns to bipartite sentences, Demotic and Coptic reintroduced the tripartite structure by "recreating" a copula immediately following the predicate, both in the topicalized pattern [Subj-Pred-*pꜣj*] and in the more "classical," but rarer [Pred-*pꜣj*-Subj]: Johnson, in *Studies Polotsky*, 414 ff.
100. For the text see W. Spiegelberg, *Demotische Texte auf Krügen*. Demotische Studien V (Leipzig: J. C. Hinrichs'sche Buchhandlung, 1912), 14.

6 Adverbial and pseudoverbal syntax

1. A basic treatment of the adverbial sentence in classical Egyptian can be found in Gardiner, *EG*, §§ 116–124; for later Egyptian, the substitutional "Standard theory" of adverbial forms is presented in Polotsky, *Grundlagen*, 203–60.
2. For the general linguistic perspective see Hengeveld, *Non-verbal Predication*, 237–56.
3. See the discussion in Loprieno, *LingAeg* 1 (1991), 205–8.
4. Gazdar et al., *Generalized Phrase Structure Grammar*, 20–21; Hengeveld, *Non-verbal Predication*, 26–30.
5. Binnick, *Time and the Verb*, 405–15.
6. This type of adverbial sentence, in which a nominal subject expressing a former (positive) situation is contrasted to an adverbial predicate conveying a later (negative) state of affairs, is a frequent stylistic device in the classical literary genre of "Lamentations"; in Egyptological literature, it is known as the "Then-Now-Scheme," see W. Schenkel, "Sonst-Jetzt. Variationen eines literarischen Formelements," *Welt des Orients* 15 (1984), 51–61.
7. See the discussion in Vernus, *Future at Issue*, 5–15, 143–93.
8. The first systematic treatment is H.J. Polotsky, "Egyptian Tenses," *Israel Academy of Sciences and Humanities. Proceedings*, II/5 (Jerusalem 1965). The theory was expanded in id., "Les transpositions du verbe en égyptien classique," *Israel Oriental Studies* 6 (1976), 1–50, and finalized in its application to Coptic in id., *Grundlagen*.

9. This particular form of the Standard theory is defended by Junge, *Syntax der mittelägyptischen Literatursprache* and id., *"Emphasis" and Sentential Meaning.*
10. See Collier, in *Middle Kingdom Studies*, 26–29.
11. Id., *LingAeg* 2 (1992), 50–60.
12. The "omission under relevance" is studied by M. Collier, "The relative clause and the verb in Middle Egyptian," *JEA* 77 (1991), 23–42.
13. For the difference in the analysis of a scientific hypothesis between the criteria of the "lack of internal contradiction" vs. the "adequate explanation of the phenomenon" see W. Schenkel, *Zur Rekonstruktion der deverbalen Nominalbildung des Ägyptischen.* Göttinger Orientforschungen IV/13 (Wiesbaden: Harrassowitz, 1983), 2–4.
14. For a general treatment see Hopper and Traugott, *Grammaticalization*; for the reanalysis of grammatical features leading to grammaticalization phenomena see ibid., 40–62.
15. Jansen-Winkeln, *ZÄS* 121 (1994), 67 ff. and section 5.4.1.
16. For a general linguistic treatment of this issue see J. Haiman, "Conditionals are topics," *Language* 54 (1978), 564–89.
17. See M. Malaise, "La conjugaison suffixale dans les propositions conditionelles introduites par *ir* en ancien et moyen égyptien," *CdE* 60 (1985), 152–67.
18. Prospective and subjunctive merge in classical Middle Egyptian, see section 4.6.3.2.
19. See A. Radford, *Transformational Grammar. A First Course.* Cambridge Textbooks in Linguistics (Cambridge University Press, 1988), 134.
20. Doret, *Narrative Verbal System*, 22–24, 96 *passim*. See now also L. Depuydt, "Zur Bedeutung der Partikeln *jsk* und *js*," *GM* 136 (1993), 11–25.
21. See the locative origin of subordinating conjunctions in Indo-European languages, for example Greek εἰ and Latin *si* ("if") from the locative of the demonstrative pronoun **so-*, thus meaning originally "in case," "in that": L. R. Palmer, *The Latin Language* (London: Faber and Faber, 1961), 331; id., *The Greek Language* (Atlantic Highlands: Humanities Press, 1980), 285.
22. Sasse, *Linguistics* 25.3 (1987), 511–80.
23. Horn, *Negation*, 379–82.
24. Depuydt, *GM* 136 (1993), 22–23.
25. This cryptic passage refers to the fact that the deceased king, who is the addressee of the funerary cult (evoked by the offering "arms"), is mythically equated to the god Osiris, revived by his sister-wife Isis.
26. See the use of the accusative with adverbial function in Arabic, for example *yawman* "one day, once": Wright, *A Grammar of the Arabic Language*, vol. I, § 364.
27. Collier, in *Middle Kingdom Studies*, 48–49.
28. There are, however, sporadic cases of omission of the resumptive pronoun under relevance: see Adm. 7,1 in example (87) below.
29. See examples (22)–(23) and the discussion in 6.2.
30. A translation of *js* with German "und zwar," although within a slightly different understanding of the passage, is given by Depuydt, *GM* 136 (1993), 22.
31. See the treatment by Givón, *Syntax*, 645–98.
32. Collier, *JEA* 77 (1991), 23–42.

33. Gardiner, *EG*, § 201.
34. Collier, *JEA* 77 (1991), 37 ff.
35. E. Edel, "Die Herkunft des neuägyptisch-koptischen Personalsuffixes der 3. Person Plural *-w*," *ZÄS* 84 (1959), 17–38; Kammerzell, *GM* 117/118 (1990), 181–202, esp. 188–89. See section 4.6.3.1 above.
36. For a treatment of omission under relevance see Collier, *JEA* 77 (1991), 36 ff.
37. See Ritter, *LingAeg* 2 (1992), 127–37.
38. This is the most common approach among scholars working within the Polotskyan frame: see the presentation by E. Graefe, *Mittelägyptische Grammatik für Anfänger* (Wiesbaden: Harrassowitz, fourth edn 1994), 47–51.
39. Schenkel, *Tübinger Einführung*, 152–55.
40. This is the position defended by Junge, *"Emphasis" and Sentential Meaning*, 42–68.
41. Ritter, *LingAeg* 2 (1992), 127 ff.
42. "Discourse" features are in fact textual features linking linguistic units beyond the level of sentential syntax. For an introduction see G. Brown and G. Yule, *Discourse Analysis* (Cambridge University Press, 1983).
43. With Hopper and Traugott, *Grammaticalization*, 169 I understand "nucleus," which is usually a main clause, as a syntactic unit capable of conveying an autonomous message, as opposed to its "margins," usually coordinate or subordinate clauses, which semantically and pragmatically rely on the nucleus.
44. Discussion and bibliography in Ritter, *LingAeg* 2 (1992). 129 ff.
45. Hopper and Traugott, *Grammaticalization*, 167–203.
46. Ibid., 171.
47. See for example F. Junge, "How to study Egyptian grammar and to what purpose. A summary of sorts," *LingAeg* 1 (1991), 389–426.
48. Hopper and Traugott, *Grammaticalization*, 177–84.
49. The bibliography on *jw* is very extensive, since this particle has been traditionally viewed as the most typical initial morpheme and has, therefore, played a substantial role in the development of the Standard theory; for an introduction see Schenkel, *Altägyptische Sprachwissenschaft*, 186–94; id., *Tübinger Einführung*, 152–55.
50. Schenkel, *Tübinger Einführung*, § 6.4.2.1.
51. Hengeveld, *Non-verbal Predication*, 103–29.
52. R. Hannig, "Zum mittelägyptischen Tempussystem," *GM* 56 (1982), 41–42.
53. Or "if it is not useful to you." See the discussion in J. F. Quack, *Studien zur Lehre für Merikare*. Göttinger Orientforschungen IV/23 (Wiesbaden: Harrassowitz, 1992), 33.
54. See Gardiner, *EG*, § 468,4; Vernus, *Future at Issue*, 130–31.
55. Loprieno, in *Gedenkschrift Behrens*, 226–31.
56. B. Gunn, "A negative word in Old Egyptian," *JEA* 34 (1948), 27–30; Allen, *Inflection of the Verb*, § 340; Doret, *Narrative Verbal System*, 36; Moers, *LingAeg* 3 (1993), 34–38.
57. Allen, *Inflection of the Verb*, § 63; Doret, *Narrative Verbal System*, 84.
58. Winand, *Etudes de néo-égyptien*, 401–39.
59. Erman, *Neuägyptische Grammatik*, § 477; Winand, *Etudes de néo-égyptien*, 413–23.

60. See Johnson, *Demotic Verbal System*, 32–48.
61. Winand, *Etudes de néo-égyptien*, 438.
62. Ibid., 408–9.
63. But not verbal, see the sequential forms in chapter 7.
64. See the discussion by Winand, *Etudes de néo-égyptien*, 427–39. In Coptic there are still remnants of the linguistic situation which preceded the adoption of the *jw*-paradigm, as shown by the third person plural prefix ετcε- (vs. Sahidic ετοʏ-) in the so-called "Middle Egyptian" dialect: ibid., 437 with bibliography.
65. Johnson, *Demotic Verbal System*, 94–99; Polotsky, *Grundlagen*, 213–16.
66. Winand, *Etudes de néo-égyptien*, 481–517. There are rare Late Egyptian examples of a stative or a prepositional phrase as predicate of a Future III-like construction (513 ff.); these sentences indicate a state in the future, and are probably the remnants of the linguistic stage which immediately preceded the grammaticalization of the Future III as a bound verbal pattern.
67. Johnson, *Demotic Verbal System*, 153 ff.
68. Examples of the construction with *jw* followed by a nominal subject, however, do exist in Late Egyptian, and become more numerous in the Theban texts of the Third Intermediate Period (roughly from 1000 to 700 BCE). Since a Future III with nominal subjects preceded by *jw* > ⲁ- is also exhibited by Akhmimic (ⲁ-ⲡⲣⲱⲙⲉ ⲁ-ⲥⲱⲧⲙⲉ), Winand, *Etudes de néo-égyptien*, 502–4 suggests that the opposition between the patterns *jr NP (r) sḏm* and *jw NP r sḏm* was originally dialectal, the former being of Lower Egyptian, the latter of Upper Egyptian origin.
69. The form ⲉⲣⲉ-ⲡⲣⲱⲙⲉ ⲉ-ⲥⲱⲧⲙ̄ is documented in the Middle Egyptian dialect of Coptic, see A. Shisha-Halevy, "'Middle Egyptian' gleanings: grammatical notes on the 'Middle Egyptian' text of Matthew," *CdE* 58 (1983), 314.
70. Polotsky, *Grundlagen*, 193–94.
71. This reanalysis of modally unmarked verbal forms as syntactically distinct modal verbs is a well-known linguistic phenomenon documented, for example, in the history of English (in Old English, and partially in Middle English, *may*, *shall*, *can*, etc. were still regularly conjugated verbs: Hopper and Traugott, *Grammaticalization*, 45–48) or in the Romance development of the future (fr. *aimerai*) and conditional (fr. *aimerais*) from modally neutral periphrastic constructions in Vulgar Latin (**amare habeo* vs. **amare habui*): see E. Coseriu, *Synchronie, Diachronie und Geschichte*. Internationale Bibliothek für allgemeine Linguistik III (Munich: Wilhelm Fink, 1974), 132–51.
72. For similar phenomena Hopper and Traugott, *Grammaticalization*, 177–84.
73. Hock, *Principles of Historical Linguistics*, 329–57.
74. After Černý and Groll, *Late Egyptian Grammar*, 307.
75. After P. J. Frandsen, *An Outline of the Late Egyptian Verbal System* (Copenhagen: Akademisk Forlag, 1974), 101–102.
76. W. Westendorf, *Grammatik der medizinischen Texte.* Grundriß der Medizin der Alten Ägypter 8 (Berlin: Akademie Verlag, 1962), § 201.
77. Gardiner, *EG*, § 468,4; Vernus, *Future at Issue*, 130–31.
78. Corresponding to a positive form *jw=s r msj.t*: Westendorf, *Grammatik der medizinischen Texte*, § 399 bb.

79. Including the construction *nn* + infinitive, now analytically replaced by a negative circumstantial form: see the forms ⲉⲛ̄ϥⲥⲟⲟⲩⲛ̄ ⲁⲛ "without his knowledge" or ⲉϥϣⲁϫⲉ ⲁⲛ "without speaking" in Till, *Koptische Grammatik*, § 404.
80. See in French the frequent colloquial use of the bare original reinforcer *pas* instead of the whole discontinuous morpheme *ne..pas*: *J'ai pas mangé* < *Je n'ai pas mangé* "I haven't eaten."

7 Verbal syntax

1. For Old Egyptian see for example Allen, *Inflection of the Verb*; for the language of the First Intermediate Period see Doret, *Narrative Verbal System*. For later Egyptian, detailed studies on verbal syntax are provided by Frandsen, *Late Egyptian Verbal System*, Winand, *Etudes de néo-égyptien*, and Johnson, *Demotic Verbal System*; for Coptic see Polotsky, *Orientalia* 29 (1960), 392–422 and A. Shisha-Halevy, *Coptic Grammatical Categories*. Analecta Orientalia LIII (Rome: Pontifical Biblical Institute, 1986).
2. For a historical presentation of the foundations of the Standard theory see Depuydt, *OLP* 14 (1983), 13–54. The systematic account of the theory of "conversions" (or "transpositions") is presented in Polotsky, *IOS* 6 (1976), 1–50.
3. For nominal and adverbial arguments as scope of the question see sections 5.5.2 and 6.1–2.
4. In general see D. P. Silverman, *Interrogative Constructions with JN and JN-JW in Old and Middle Egyptian*. Bibliotheca Aegyptia I (Malibu: Undena, 1980). For semantic and pragmatic treatments of interrogative sentences see F. Junge, "Form und Funktion ägyptischer Satzfragen," *BiOr* 40 (1983), 545–59, and especially D. Sweeney, "What's a rhetorical question?," *LingAeg* 1 (1991), 315–31.
5. In Late Egyptian, this construction is replaced by its periphrastic variant *wn.jn=f ḥr sḏm* *"then he was on hearing" > "then he heard." See discussion and examples in section 7.9.
6. Collier, in *Middle Kingdom Studies*, 21–45.
7. See example (13) for a non-initial use of the subjunctive following the imperative.
8. Omission of the subject under relevance occurs fairly frequently with the passive *sḏm(.w)=f*, see Gardiner, *EG*, § 422. The reason for this frequency is to be sought in the low relevance of impersonal subjects ("it") in establishing the context of a passive predication; see Collier, *JEA* 77 (1991), 36–37.
9. See Gardiner, *EG*, §§ 469–83.
10. A similar phenomenon of grammaticalization led in Biblical Hebrew to the use of the preterite of the verb *qûm* "to stand up," i.e. *wayyāqom*, lit. "and he stood up," to express the beginning of an action in a narrative sequence, with a gradual neutralization of the original meaning of the verbal form indicated by *qûm*: 2 Sam 19,9 *wayyāqom hammelek wayyēšeb baššaʿar* *"and the king stood up and sat at the door" > "then the king sat at the door."
11. And then in Late Egyptian: see discussion and examples in section 7.9.
12. Chafe, in *Subject and Topic*, 25–55; Prince, in *Radical Pragmatics*, 223–55.

13. For the most cogent arguments see Junge, *Syntax der mittelägyptischen Literatursprache*, 38 ff. and the discussion in Loprieno, *JAAL* 1 (1988), 41–46.
14. For example Adm. 7,7 *qn ḫzy ḥr nḥm [ḫ.t]=f* "As for the brave man, the coward steals his property."
15. For example CT IV 318c–d *jr zmꜣ.t-tꜣ.wj dḥn.t qrs wsjr pw* "As for the 'Unification of the Two Lands,' this means the attribution of Osiris' tomb."
16. See the discussion by Loprieno, in *Crossroad*, 265–68 and id., *JAAL* 1 (1988), 33–35. Passives and perfects, i.e. states, reduce the number of arguments involved in discourse, privileging the grammatical subject as semantic "goal" of the predicate, see B. Comrie, "Aspect and voice: some reflections on perfect and passive," in *Syntax and Semantics*, vol. XIV: *Tense and Aspect*, ed. by Ph. J. Tedeschi and A. Zaenen (New York: Academic Press, 1981), 65–78. Thus, the subject acquires in this case the role of "emerger" out of a "ground": see Borghouts, in *Crossroad*, 46.
17. See Gunn, *Studies*, 59–60 and Allen, *Inflection of the Verb*, § 408.
18. See now the thorough analysis by J. Borghouts, "*jnk mr(i)=f*: an elusive pattern in Middle Egyptian," in *Crossroads III Preprints*, from whom I have drawn the following examples.
19. Polotsky, *Etudes de syntaxe copte*.
20. See Depuydt, *OLP* 14 (1983), 13–54.
21. Polotsky, "Egyptian Tenses," §§ 16–21.
22. A. Niccacci, "Su una formula dei 'Testi dei Sarcofagi'," *Liber Annuus* 30 (1980), 197–224.
23. Polotsky, *IOS* 6 (1976), 14–15.
24. An exception is the verb *rdj* "to give," which displays the form *rdj.n=f* when topicalized and *dj.n=f* in the non-topicalized uses: see Polotsky, *IOS* 1 (1976), 18–23.
25. For an example in which the stative is extraposed as topic of a main sentence see example (56) below.
26. For the suppletive relationship between the first person prospective and the second person emphatic in focal environments see Loprieno, *LingAeg* 1 (1991), 210–17.
27. Stela of Khuisobek, see J. Baines, "The Stela of Khusobek: private and royal military narrative and values," in *Festschrift Fecht*, 43–62.
28. See Junge, *"Emphasis" and Sentential Meaning*, 56–60.
29. See for a general treatment Schenkel, *Altägyptische Sprachwissenschaft*, 177–79; id., *Tübinger Einführung*, 249–50.
30. For this term see Shisha-Halevy, *Coptic Grammatical Categories*, 72–74.
31. This passage was first quoted by A. Roccati, see P. Vernus, "Formes 'emphatiques' en fonction non 'emphatique' dans la protase d'un système corrélatif," *GM* 43 (1981), 73–88 and since then has often been the object of grammatical analysis, see the latest discussion in Junge, *"Emphasis" and Sentential Meaning*, 17, 54.
32. The explanation of this contingency between two *sḏm.n=f* the second of which does not indicate an event *preceding*, but rather *following* the first, has been a traditional problem of the "Standard theory," which tended to view any verbal form preceded by an emphatic VP as adverbial in function. Solutions have been offered by Vernus, *GM* 43 (1981), 73–88 with the suggestion of a "second

scheme" in which the event indicated by the first (subordinate) VP conditions the event indicated by the second (main) VP, and Depuydt, *Conjunction, Contiguity, Contingency*, 117–200, who posits a correlation between the "emphatic" and the "adverbial" VP similar to the one existing in English between events correlated by the expression "no sooner... than." This contingency between the two verbal events is not a problem, however, for the approach presented here, since the first of the two VPs is viewed as an extraposed topicalized VP, and the second as a main clause verbal pattern. See Sin. B 200 *šdj.n.t(w)=f n=j dj.n(=j) wj ḥr ẖ.t=j* "When it was read to me (extraposed topicalized VP), I fell on my belly (main clause)."

33. D. P. Silverman, "An emphasized object of a nominal verb in Middle Egyptian," *Orientalia* 49 (1980), 199–203.
34. K. Jansen-Winkeln, "Vermerke. Zum Verständnis kurzer und formelhafter Inschriften auf ägyptischen Denkmälern," *MDAIK* 46 (1990), 146–50 and bibliography. This author interprets the *sḏm.n=f* in this case as a relative form referring to the monument itself as antecedent omitted under relevance.
35. For a discussion of this type of embedding see J. P. Allen, "Form, function, and meaning in the early Egyptian verb," *LingAeg* 1 (1991), 3–10.
36. In Old Egyptian, verbs of wish (such as *mrj*) controlled the prospective, whereas verbs of command (such as *rḏj*) were followed by the subjunctive, see Loprieno, *LingAeg* 1 (1991), 210–17. In the classical language, however, prospective and subjunctive merged into one suppletive paradigm, see section 4.6.3.2.
37. See Loprieno, *Verbalsystem*, 38–50.
38. The use of the demonstrative adjective *pn* is here a sign of its gradual loss of deictic reference and its drift towards a function as definite article. The same evolution affected the pronouns of the *pꜣ*–series, which eventually developed into the definite article of later Egyptian, see section 4.4.3.
39. See Edel, *Altägyptische Grammatik*, § 1058.
40. For a discussion of the variety of possible relative patterns see Polotsky, *IOS* 6 (1976), 7–13 and H. Satzinger, "Attribut und Relativsatz im älteren Ägyptisch," in *Festschrift Westendorf*, vol. I, 125–56.
41. In fact, the emphatic aorist *jrr=f* could be etymologically identical to the relative form, see Allen, *LingAeg* 1 (1991), 3–10. This would imply that the sentence with topicalized predicate (section 7.5) is a form of preposed REL/topic sentence, see Givón, *Syntax*, 222–23.
42. Collier, *JEA* 77 (1991), 36–42.
43. See Givón, *Syntax*, 683–86.
44. This is the so-called "passive theory" of Gardiner, *EG*, § 386 and Westendorf, *Der Gebrauch des Passivs*, according to whom the difference between indicative and relative forms lies in the fact that in the former the subject of the passive participle would be explicit, resulting in the object of the verbal predicate (*mrj=f wj* *"I am a beloved-of-him" > "he loves me"), whereas in the latter it would remain unexpressed (*mrj.w=f* *"beloved of him" > "whom he loves"). Other theories about the origin of the indicative and relative forms of the suffix conjugation are (a) the "active–passive theory," according to which the indicative forms would be derived from active participles (*mrj=f* "a lover is he" > "he loves"), and the relative forms from passive participles (*mrj.w=f* *"beloved of

him" > "whom he loves"), and the "noun of action–active participles" theory, which sees the origin of indicative forms in substantival constructions (*mrj=f* "the fact that he loves") and of relative forms in active participles (*mrj.w=f* "loving-of-him" > "whom he loves"). For a methodological assessment see Schenkel, *Suffixkonjugation.*

45. One will recall that omission under relevance is sensitive to the hierarchies of animacy and salience, indefinite subjects being more likely to undergo this deletion: see section 6.3.3.
46. When expressed, the logical subject of a passive construction is introduced by the "ergative" preposition *jn*, see section 4.4.1.
47. See for example Comrie, *Language Universals and Linguistic Typology*, 124–37; Givón, *Syntax*, 126–34.
48. Properly speaking, the underlying verbal clauses in these examples should not display the resumptive pronouns *=f* and *=s* respectively, but rather the referent nouns "someone" and *ḫb.t* "place of execution," but I disregard this feature for the sake of simplicity, i.e. in order to avoid the discussion of yet another syntactic conversion.
49. Here again, the underlying verbal clauses without resumptive pronoun are **š3j.tw n=f ʿḥʿ* "a boat is assigned to him" and **jw zbj n=f wpw.tjw* "messengers are sent to him."
50. The prospective participle *sḏm.tj=f* is used mostly – although not solely, see section 4.6.4 – in the active voice. In the passive voice, the early prospective participle is gradually replaced by the perfective passive participle, pointing once more to the semantic connections between perfective aspect and prospective mood in Egyptian: Loprieno, *Verbalsystem*, 38–50.
51. For the distributional relation between these two forms in the expression of the past passive see section 4.6.3.3.
52. The gemination of the second consonant is characteristic only of perfective participles of 2-rad. roots, see section 4.6.4.
53. See chapter 4 n. 159, chapter 5 n. 29, chapter 6 n. 15.
54. Discussion in A. Loprieno, "The form *sḏmt.f*: verbal predicate or 'transposition'?," *GM* 37 (1980), 17–29.
55. See Gunn, *Studies*, 93–118.
56. For some of the Egyptological explanations see Polotsky, *IOS* 6 (1976), 44–46; R. Hannig, "Die neue Gunn'sche Regel," in *Festschrift Westendorf*, 63–70; Schenkel, *Tübinger Einführung*, § 7.3.1.1.1–2.
57. See Loprieno, *LingAeg* 1 (1991), 201–202.
58. For the morphology of this verb see Allen, *Inflection of the Verb*, § 391.
59. Ibid., §§ 360–63.
60. See Vernus, *Future at Issue*, 121–30.
61. Moers, *LingAeg* 3 (1993), 49–51.
62. M. Collier, "Constructions with *ḥ3* revisited," *GM* 120 (1991), 13–32.
63. See the excellent discussion by F. Kammerzell, "Die altägyptische Negation *w*: Versuch einer Annäherung," *LingAeg* 3 (1993), 17–32. The negative particle *w/3* is used to mark the prospective *sḏm=f* as "pertinent" or "contingent" prohibitive form.
64. Gardiner, *EG*, § 344.

65. The irregular gemination of the 2-rad. stem in the form *tmm=k* is probably the result of analogic pressures coming from the "emphatic" aorist of III-inf. verbs (*jrr=f*), gemination being perceived as the most typical feature of a topicalized VP. We saw in section 7.5.1 that similar cases of irregular reduplication are documented for the stative as well.
66. Niccacci, *Liber Annuus* 30 (1980), 211–13.
67. The relative converter *jwtj* survives through Coptic only as a lexicalized element in nouns meaning "without the quality expressed by the controlled word," for example ⲁⲧ-ⲛⲟⲃⲉ "without sin" or ⲁⲧ-ⲙⲟⲩ "immortal."
68. Winand, *Etudes de néo-égyptien*, 474–80.
69. Polotsky, *Orientalia* 29 (1960), 399–422. See also id., *Grundlagen*, 169–202; Frandsen, *Late Egyptian Verbal System*, 1–78.
70. Winand, *Etudes de néo-égyptien*, 192–98; Johnson, *Demotic Verbal System*, 178–203. Later Demotic and some Coptic dialects (Fayyumic and Lycopolitan) document a periphrastic pattern *wꜣḥ=f sdm* > ϩⲁϥⲥⲱⲧⲙ̄ *"he laid hearing" > "he heard." This pattern originally indicated a past background (ibid., 203–14), and thus represented the positive equivalent of ⲙ̄ⲡⲁⲧϥ̄ⲥⲱⲧⲙ̄ (s. below), but became in Coptic a mere dialectal variant of ⲁϥⲥⲱⲧⲙ̄.
71. Gardiner, *EG*, § 484.
72. Winand, *Etudes de néo-égyptien*, 231–36.
73. Johnson, *Demotic Verbal System*, 132–53; Polotsky, *Grundlagen*, 194–97.
74. Winand, *Etudes de néo-égyptien*, 236–41.
75. Ibid., 209–58.
76. Johnson, *Demotic Verbal System*, 218–22.
77. Polotsky, *Grundlagen*, 193–94.
78. Ibid., 160–63.
79. Winand, *Etudes de néo-égyptien*, 172–76.
80. Johnson, *Demotic Verbal System*, 27–29.
81. Till, *Koptische Grammatik*, § 298.
82. See Polotsky, *Grundlagen*, 141–59.
83. Winand, *Etudes de néo-égyptien*, 299–331.
84. Polotsky, *Grundlagen*, 181–84.
85. Loprieno, *Afroasiatic Linguistics* VII/5, 1–19.
86. Depuydt, *Conjunction, Contiguity, Contingency*, 26–34.
87. For this text see P. Cherix, *Le concept de Notre Grande Puissance (CG VI,4)*. Orbis Biblicus et Orientalis XLVII (Fribourg–Göttingen: Vandenhoeck & Ruprecht, 1982).
88. Depuydt, *Conjunction, Contiguity, Contingency*, 13.
89. The syntactic behavior of the later Egyptian subjunctive is similar to the Arabic pattern in which the particle *fa-* introduces a "hypotactic," rather than subordinate clause in which the subjunctive conveys an action as result of a preceding event ("nucleus"): *iɣfir lī yā rabbi fa-'adḫulu 'l-ǧannata* "Pardon me, O Lord, that I may enter Paradise." See Wright, *A Grammar of the Arabic Language*, vol. II, § 15.
90. See the insightful discussion by Depuydt, *ibid.*, 45–66, to whom I owe the examples.

91. For this text see G. MacRae, "Thunder: Perfect Mind," in D. M. Parrott (ed.), *Nag Hammadi Codices V,2–5 and VI with Papyrus Berolinensis 8502,1 and 4*. Nag Hammadi Studies 11 (Leiden: E. J. Brill, 1979), 231–55.
92. E. F. Wente, "The Late Egyptian conjunctive as a past continuative," *JNES* 21 (1969), 304–11.
93. See the use of the conditional *would* in English to refer to actions expected to take place after the past event which is being referred to: "he promised that he *would* come."
94. See Borghouts, *OLP* 11 (1980), 99–109.
95. Id., *ZÄS* 196 (1979), 14–24.
96. See Frandsen, *Late Egyptian Verbal System*, 100–102, 227–32.
97. See Polotsky, *Grundlagen*, 258–60. In Coptic, the protasis of a hypothetical clause can also be introduced by the conjunction ⲉϣⲱⲡⲉ "if," which derives from the grammaticalization of a circumstantial clause *jw=s ḫpr* "if it happens." See Till, *Koptische Grammatik*, §§ 447–60.
98. See Winand, *Etudes de néo-égyptien*, 292–97. In this Coptic conjugation pattern, the /n/ is a purely phonetic phenomenon, probably originating in a nasal pronunciation of /ʕ/; for a similar phenomenon in some traditions of Hebrew reading see A. Loprieno, "Observations on the traditional pronunciation of Hebrew among Italian Jews," in A. Kaye (ed.), *Semitic Studies in Honor of Wolf Leslau*, vol. II (Wiesbaden: Harrassowitz, 1991), 931–48. The /n/ is absent from some dialects such as Bohairic or Akhmimic, which display the form ϣⲁⲧⲉϥⲥⲱⲧⲉⲙ.
99. Polotsky, *Grundlagen*, 163–65; Depuydt, *Conjunction, Contiguity, Contingency*, 75–93.
100. M. Gilula, "A Middle Egyptian example for the Coptic *tarefsōtm*," *JNES* 34 (1975), 135–36.
101. Depuydt, *Conjunction, Contiguity, Contingency*, 80–82.
102. Winand, *Etudes de néo-égyptien*, 409–13, 494–95.
103. Polotsky, *Orientalia* 29 (1960), 397.
104. See Winand, *Etudes de néo-égyptien*, 259–87.
105. Cassonnet, in *Crossroads III Preprints*. Being shared by Old and Late Egyptian, the prothetic *yod* could be a dialectal feature of the "Upper Egyptian" dialect, not shared by Middle Egyptian, a "Lower Egyptian" dialect: on the geographic origin of Middle vs. Late Egyptian see Schenkel, *LingAeg* 3 (1993), 148.
106. The distinction between "first" and "second tenses" is traditional in Coptic grammar, but it is only with the emergence of Polotsky's model in the *Etudes de syntaxe copte* that the term "second tense" has been associated to the nominal, or topicalized function of the VP and that second tenses have been seen as the heirs of the Middle Egyptian geminating *sḏm=f*.
107. On the relative form *mrr=f* in Late Egyptian see Winand, *Etudes de néo-égyptien*, 387–88.
108. For this use of ⲡⲁⲓ see Polotsky, *Grundlagen*, 245–47.
109. Ibid., 343–73.
110. For vestigial remnants of the perfective participle *j.jr sdm* > ⲉⲣⲥⲱⲧⲙ̄ in Coptic see section 5.9 and Polotsky, *Grundlagen*, 59–60.
111. Ibid., 62–68, 245–47.
112. Ibid., 237–60.

References

Albright, W. F. *The Protosinaitic Inscriptions and Their Decipherment* (Cambridge, Mass.: Harvard University Press, 1966).

Allen, J. P. "Synthetic and analytic tenses in Old Egyptian," in *L'Egyptologie en 1979. Axes prioritaires de recherches*, vol. I. Colloques internationaux du CNRS 595 (Paris: Centre National de la Recherche Scientifique, 1982), 19–27.

Allen, J. P. *The Inflection of the Verb in the Pyramid Texts.* Bibliotheca Aegyptia II (Malibu: Undena, 1984).

Allen, J. P. "Form, function, and meaning in the Early Egyptian verb," *Lingua Aegyptia* 1 (1991), 1–32.

Anthes, R. *Die Felseninschriften von Hatnub.* Untersuchungen zur Geschichte und Altertumskunde Ägyptens IX (Leipzig: J. C. Hinrichs'sche Buchhandlung, 1928).

Assmann, J. *Ma'at. Gerechtigkeit und Unsterblichkeit im Alten Ägypten* (Munich: C. H. Beck, 1990).

Bagnall, R. S., *Egypt in Late Antiquity* (Princeton University Press, 1993).

Baines, J. "The Stela of Khusobek: private and royal military narrative and values," in J. Osing and G. Dreyer (eds.), *Form und Maß. Beiträge zur Literatur, Sprache und Kunst des Alten Ägypten. Festschrift für Gerhard Fecht.* Ägypten und Altes Testament XII (Wiesbaden: Harrassowitz, 1987), 43–62.

Binnick, R. I. *Time and the Verb. A Guide to Tense & Aspect* (Oxford University Press, 1991).

Boas, G. *The Hieroglyphics of Horapollo*, translated by G. Boas with a new foreword by A. Grafton (Princeton University Press, 1993).

Borghouts, J. "A new approach to the Late Egyptian conjunctive," *Zeitschrift für Ägyptische Sprache und Altertumskunde* 196 (1979), 14–24.

Borghouts, J. "Object pronouns of the *tw*-type in Late Egyptian," *Orientalia Lovaniensia Periodica* 11 (1980), 99–109.

Borghouts, J. "Prominence constructions and pragmatic functions," in *Crossroad*, 45–70.

Borghouts, J. *Egyptisch. Een inleiding in taal en schrift van het Middenrijk*, 2 vols. Mededelingen en Verhandelingen van het Vooraziatisch-Egyptisch Genootschap "Ex Oriente Lux" XXX (Leuven: Peters, 1993).

Borghouts, J. "*jnk mr(i)=f*: an elusive pattern in Middle Egyptian," in *Crossroads III Preprints.*

Bresciani, E. *Der Kampf um den Panzer des Inaros (Papyrus Krall).* Mitteilungen aus der Papyrussammlung der Österreichischen Nationalbibliothek, N.S. VIII (Vienna: Georg Prachner Verlag, 1964).

Brockelmann, C. *Grundriß der vergleichenden Grammatik der semitischen Sprachen*, vol. I (Berlin: Reuther & Reichard, 1908).

Brown, G. and G. Yule, *Discourse Analysis* (Cambridge University Press, 1983).
Buccellati, G. "An interpretation of the Akkadian stative as a nominal sentence," *Journal of Near Eastern Studies* 27 (1968), 1–12.
Callender, J. B. "Grammatical models in Egyptology," *Orientalia* 42 (1973), 47–77.
Callender, J. B. *Studies in the Nominal Sentence in Egyptian and Coptic*. Near Eastern Studies XXIV (Berkeley–Los Angeles: University of California Press, 1984).
Callender, J. B. "Afroasiatic cases and the formation of Ancient Egyptian constructions with possessive suffixes," *Afroasiatic Linguistics* II/6 (Malibu: Undena, 1975).
Cassonnet, P. "Modalités énonciatives et temps seconds *i.sḏm.f* en néo-égyptien," in *Crossroads III Preprints*.
Černý, J. and S. I. Groll. *A Late Egyptian Grammar*. Studia Pohl, Series Maior IV (Rome: Pontifical Biblical Institute, third edition 1984).
Chafe, W. "Givenness, contrastiveness, definiteness, subjects, topics, and point of view," in Ch. N. Li (ed.), *Subject and Topic* (New York: Academic Press, 1976), 25–55.
Cherix, P. *Le concept de Notre Grande Puissance (CG VI,4)*. Orbis Biblicus et Orientalis XLVII (Fribourg–Göttingen: Vandenhoeck & Ruprecht, 1982).
Collier, M. "The circumstantial *sḏm(.f)/sḏm.n(.f)* as verbal verb-forms in Middle Egyptian," *Journal of Egyptian Archaeology* 76 (1990), 73–85.
Collier, M. "Circumstantially adverbial? The circumstantial *sḏm(.f)/sḏm.n(.f)* reconsidered," in S. Quirke (ed.), *Middle Kingdom Studies* (New Malden: SIA Publishing, 1991), 21–50.
Collier, M. "Constructions with *ḥꜣ* revisited," *Göttinger Miszellen* 120 (1991), 13–32.
Collier, M. "The relative clause and the verb in Middle Egyptian," *Journal of Egyptian Archaeology* 77 (1991), 23–42.
Collier, M. "Predication and the circumstantial *sḏm(.f)/sḏm.n(.f)*," *Lingua Aegyptia* 2 (1992), 17–65.
Comrie, B. *Aspect*. Cambridge Textbooks in Linguistics (Cambridge University Press, 1976).
Comrie, B. "Aspect and voice: some reflections on perfect and passive," in *Syntax and Semantics*, vol. XIV: *Tense and Aspect*, ed. by Ph. J. Tedeschi and A. Zaenen (New York: Academic Press, 1981), 65–78.
Comrie, B. *Language Universals and Linguistic Typology*. (Chicago University Press, second edition 1989).
Comrie, B. *Tense*. Cambridge Textbooks in Linguistics (Cambridge University Press, 1985).
Coptic Encyclopedia, ed. by Aziz S. Atiya, vol. VIII, Appendix: Linguistics (New York: Macmillan Publishing Company, 1991).
Coseriu, E. *Synchronie, Diachronie und Geschichte*. Internationale Bibliothek für allgemeine Linguistik 3 (Munich: Wilhelm Fink, 1974).
Coulmas, F. "Writing systems," in W. Bright (ed.), *International Encyclopedia of Linguistics*, vol. IV (Oxford University Press, 1992), 253–57.
Crossroad. Chaos or the Beginning of a New Paradigm. Papers from the Conference on Egyptian Grammar (Helsingør, 28–30 May 1986), ed. by G. Englund and P. J. Frandsen. CNI Publications 1 (Copenhagen: Carsten Niebuhr Institute, 1986).

Crossroads II. Proceedings of the Second International Conference on Egyptian Grammar (Los Angeles, 17–20 October 1990), ed. by A. Loprieno, *Lingua Aegyptia* 1 (1991).

Crossroads III Preprints (Yale University, 1994), to be published in *Lingua Aegyptia* 4 (1994).

Crum, W. E. *A Coptic Dictionary* (Oxford: Clarendon Press, 1939).

Davies, W. V. *Egyptian Hieroglyphs* (London: British Museum, 1987).

Davis, V. L. *Syntax of the Negative Particles* bw *and* bn *in Late Egyptian*. Münchner Ägyptologische Studien XXIX (Berlin: Deutscher Kunstverlag, 1973).

de Wolf, P. "Erläuterungen zu den Zählwesen im Osthamitischen," in *Zeitschrift der Deutschen Morgenländischen Gesellschaft. Supplement VII* (Stuttgart: Franz Steiner Verlag, 1989), 560–73.

Depuydt, L. "The Standard theory of the 'emphatic' forms in Classical (Middle) Egyptian: a historical survey," *Orientalia Lovaniensia Periodica* 14 (1983), 13–54.

Depuydt, L. "Zum Passiv im Ägyptischen," *Orientalia* 56 (1987), 129–35.

Depuydt, L. "The contingent tenses of Egyptian," *Orientalia* 58 (1989), 1–27.

Depuydt, L. "*Onchsheshonqy* 2,13 and 4,1–2; a philological note," in S. Israelit-Groll (ed.), *Studies in Egyptology Presented to Miriam Lichtheim*, vol. I (Jerusalem: Magnes Press), 116–21.

Depuydt, L. "On Coptic sounds," *Orientalia* 62 (1993), 338–75.

Depuydt, L. "Zur Bedeutung der Partikeln *jsk* und *js*," *Göttinger Miszellen* 136 (1993), 11–25.

Depuydt, L. *Conjunction, Contiguity, Contingency* (Oxford University Press, 1993).

Derchain, Ph. *Le papyrus Salt 825 (BM 10051). Rituel pour la conservation de la vie en Egypte*. Mémoires de l'Académie Royale de Belgique, Classe des Lettres LVIII, 1a (Brussels, 1965).

Derchain-Urtel, M.Th. "Das *n*-Präfix im Ägyptischen," *Göttinger Miszellen* 6 (1973), 39–54.

Diakonoff, I. M. *Semito-Hamitic Languages. An Essay in Classification* (Moscow: Akademia Nauk, 1965).

Dik, S. C. *Functional Grammar*. Publications in Language Sciences VII (Dordrecht: Foris, 1981).

Dik, S. C. *The Theory of Functional Grammar. Part I: the Structure of the Clause*. Functional Grammar Studies IX (Dordrecht: Foris, 1989).

Dik, S. C. et al., "On the typology of focus phenomena," in T. Hoekstra, H. van der Hulst, and M. Moortgat (eds.), *Perspectives on Functional Grammar* (Dordrecht: Foris, 1980), 41–74.

Doret, E. *The Narrative Verbal System of Old and Middle Egyptian*. Cahiers d'Orientalisme XII (Geneva: Patrick Cramer, 1986).

Doret, E. "Phrase nominale, identité et substitution dans les Textes des Sarcophages," *Revue d'Egyptologie* 40 (1989), 49–63; 41 (1990), 39–56; 43 (1992), 49–73.

Dreyer, G. et al., "Umm el-Qaab. Nachuntersuchungen im frühzeitlichen Königsfriedhof. 5./6. Vorbericht," *Mitteilungen des Deutschen Archäologischen Instituts. Abteilung Kairo* 49 (1993), 51–56.

Drioton, E. "Les principes de la cryptographie égyptienne," *Comptes-rendus des séances de l'Académie des Inscriptions et Belles Lettres* (Paris, 1953), 355–64.

Dunham, D. *Naga-ed-Dêr Stelae of the First Intermediate Period* (London: Oxford University Press, 1937).

Durand, J. *Generative and Non-linear Phonology*. Longman Linguistics Library (London–New York: Longman, 1990), 55.

Edel, E. *Altägyptische Grammatik*. Analecta Orientalia XXXIV–XXXIX (Rome: Pontifical Biblical Institute, 1955–1964).

Edel, E. "Die Herkunft des neuägyptisch-koptischen Personalsuffixes der 3.Person Plural *-w*," *Zeitschrift für Ägyptische Sprache und Altertumskunde* 84 (1959), 17–38.

Edgerton, W. F. "Stress, vowel quantity, and syllable division in Egyptian," *Journal of Near Eastern Studies* 6 (1947), 1–17.

Erman, A. *Ägyptische Grammatik* (Berlin, 1894; fourth edition 1928).

Erman, A. *Neuägyptische Grammatik* (Leipzig: Wilhelm Engelmann, second edition 1933).

Erman, A. and H. Grapow. *Wörterbuch der ägyptischen Sprache* (Berlin: Akademie-Verlag, 1926–53).

Eyre, C. J. "The Semna Stelae: quotation, genre, and functions of literature," in S. I. Groll (ed.), *Studies in Egyptology Presented to Miriam Lichtheim*, vol. I (Jerusalem: Magnes Press, 1990), 134–65.

Eyre, C. J. and J. Baines, "Interactions between orality and literacy in Ancient Egypt," in K. Schousboe and M.T. Larsen (eds.), *Literacy and Society* (Copenhagen: Akademisk Forlag, 1989), 91–119.

Ezawa, K. *Sprachsystem und Sprechnorm* (Tübingen: Max Niemeyer Verlag, 1985).

Faber, A. "Interpretation of orthographic forms," in Ph. Baldi (ed.), *Linguistic Change and Reconstruction Methodology*. Trends in Linguistics, Studies and Monographs 45 (Berlin–New York: Mouton de Gruyter, 1990), 619–37.

Faber, A. "Second Harvest: šibbōleθ revisited (yet again)," *Journal of Semitic Studies* 37 (1992), 1–10.

Fairman, H. W. "Notes on the alphabetic signs employed in the hieroglyphic inscriptions of the Temple of Edfu," *Annales du Service des Antiquités de l'Egypte* 43 (1943), 193–310.

Fairman, H. W. "Introduction to the study of Ptolemaic signs and their values," *Bulletin de l'Institut Français d'Archéologie Orientale* 43 (1945), 51–138.

Faulkner, R. O. *A Concise Dictionary of Middle Egyptian* (Oxford University Press, 1962).

Fecht, G. *Wortakzent und Silbenstruktur*. Ägyptologische Forschungen XXI (Glückstadt: Verlag J. J. Augustin, 1960).

Fecht, G. "Prosodie," *LÄ* IV, 1127–54.

Fecht, G. "Cruces Interpretum in der Lehre des Ptahhotep (Maximen 7, 9, 13, 14) und das Alter der Lehre," in *Hommages à François Daumas*, 2 vols. (University of Montpellier, 1986), 233–35.

Fischer, H. G. "Hieroglyphen," in *LÄ* II, 1189–99.

Fleming, H. C. "Cushitic and Omotic," in M. L. Bender et al. (eds.), *Language in Ethiopia* (Oxford University Press, 1976), 34–53.

Fowden, G. *The Egyptian Hermes. A Historical Approach to the Late Pagan Mind* (Princeton University Press, 1986).

Frandsen, P. J. *An Outline of the Late Egyptian Verbal System* (Copenhagen: Akademisk Forlag, 1974).
Frandsen, P. J. "On the relevance of logical analysis," in *Crossroad*, 145–59.
Gardiner, A.. H. *The Admonitions of an Egyptian Sage from a Hieratic Papyrus in Leiden (P. Leiden 344 recto)* (Leipzig: J. C. Hinrichs'sche Buchhandlung, 1909).
Gardiner, A. H. *Egyptian Grammar, Being an Introduction to the Study of Hieroglyphs* (Oxford University Press, 1927; third edition 1957)
Gazdar, G., E. Klein, G. K. Pullum, and I. A. Sag, *Generalized Phrase Structure Grammar* (Oxford University Press, 1985).
Gelb, I. J. *A Study of Writing* (Chicago University Press, revised edition 1963).
Gilula, M. "An adjectival predicative expression of possession in Middle Egyptian," *Revue d'Egyptologie* 20 (1968), 55–61.
Gilula, M. "A Middle Egyptian example for the Coptic *tarefsōtm*," *Journal of Near Eastern Studies* 34 (1975), 135–36.
Gilula, M. "An unusual nominal pattern in Middle Egyptian," *Journal of Egyptian Archeology* 62 (1976), 160–75.
Giveon, R. "Protosinaitische Inschriften," in *LÄ* IV, 1156–59.
Givón, T. "Topic, pronoun and grammatical agreement," in Ch. N. Li (ed.), *Subject and Topic* (New York: Academic Press, 1976), 149–88.
Givón, T. *On Understanding Grammar.* Perspectives in Neurolinguistics and Psycholinguistics (New York: Academic Press, 1979).
Givón, T. "From discourse to syntax: Grammar as a processing strategy," in T. Givón (ed.), *Syntax and Semantics*, vol. XII: *Discourse and Syntax* (New York: Academic Press,1979), 81–112.
Givón, T. *Syntax. A Functional-Typological Introduction*, 2 vols. (Amsterdam: Benjamins, 1984–1990).
Goldsmith, J. A. *Autosegmental and Metrical Phonology* (Oxford: Blackwell, 1990).
Goldwasser, O. "On the choice of registers. Studies on the grammar of Papyrus Anastasi I," in S. I. Groll (ed.), *Studies in Egyptology Presented to Miriam Lichtheim*, vol. I (Jerusalem: Magnes Press, 1990), 200–40.
Graefe, E. *Mittelägyptische Grammatik für Anfänger* (Wiesbaden: Harrassowitz, fourth edition 1994).
Grandet, P. and B. Mathieu. "La construction ergative de l'accompli égyptien," in *Sesto Congresso Internazionale di Egittologia. Atti*, vol. II (Turin: Italgas, 1993), 145–51.
Grapow, H. *Die Wortbildungen mit einem Präfix* m- *im Ägyptischen.* Abhandlungen der Preußischen Akademie der Wissenschaften, Phil.-Hist. Klasse, V, Berlin 1914.
Green, J. N. "Spanish," in W. Bright (ed.), *International Encyclopedia of Linguistics*, vol. IV (Oxford University Press, 1992), 58–64.
Greenberg, J. H. "Some generalizations concerning glottalic consonants, especially implosives," *International Journal of American Linguistics* 36 (1970), 123–45.
Griffith, F. Ll. *The Inscriptions of Siût and Dêr Rîfeh* (London: Egypt Exploration Society, 1889).
Gunn, B. *Studies in Egyptian Syntax* (Paris: Paul Geuthner, 1924).
Gunn, B. "A negative word in Old Egyptian," *Journal of Egyptian Archaeology* 34 (1948), 27–30.
Gvozdanovic, J. (ed.), *Indo-European Numerals.* Trends in Linguistics, Studies and Monographs LVII (Berlin–New York: Mouton de Gruyter, 1992).

Haiman, J. "Conditionals are topics," *Language* 54 (1978), 564–89.

Halliday, M. A. K. "Language Structure and Language Function," in J. Lyons (ed.), *New Horizons in Linguistics* (Harmondsworth: Penguin Books, 1970), 140–65.

Hannig, R. "Zum mittelägyptischen Tempussystem," *Göttinger Miszellen* 56 (1982), 41–42.

Hannig, R. "Die neue Gunn'sche Regel," in *Studien zu Sprache und Religion Ägyptens zu Ehren von Wolfhart Westendorf*, ed. by F. Junge, vol. 1: Sprache (Göttingen: Hubert & Co, 1984), 63–70.

Hannig, R. "The Particle *kꜣ*," *Göttinger Miszellen* 95 (1987), 9–19.

Hengeveld, K. *Non-verbal Predication. Theory, Typology, Diachrony.* Functional Grammar Series XV (Berlin: Mouton de Gruyter, 1992).

Hetzron, R. "Two principles of genetic reconstruction," *Lingua* 38 (1976), 89–108.

Hetzron, R. "Semitic languages," in W. Bright (ed.), *International Encyclopedia of Linguistics*, vol. III (Oxford University Press, 1992), 412–17.

Hintze, F. "Die Haupttendenzen der ägyptischen Sprachentwicklung," *Zeitschrift für Phonetik und allgemeine Sprachwissenschaft* 1 (1947), 85–108.

Hintze, F. "Zur koptischen Phonologie," *Enchoria* 10 (1980), 23–91.

Hoch, J. E. *Semitic Words in Egyptian Texts of the New Kingdom and Third Intermediate Period* (Princeton University Press, 1994).

Hock, H. H. *Principles of Historical Linguistics* (Berlin–New York: Walter de Gruyter, second edition 1991).

Hodge, C. T. (ed.), *Afroasiatic. A Survey.* Janua Linguarum Series Practica CLXIII (The Hague–Paris: Mouton, 1971).

Hopper, P. J and E. C. Traugott, *Grammaticalization.* Cambridge Textbooks in Linguistics (Cambridge University Press, 1993).

Horn, L. H. *A Natural History of Negation* (Chicago University Press, 1989).

Huehnergard, J. "'Stative', predicative form, pseudo-verb," *Journal of Near Eastern Studies* 46 (1987), 215–32.

Iversen, E. *The Myth of Egypt and its Hieroglyphs in European Tradition* (Princeton University Press, 1961).

Jansen-Winkeln, K. "Vermerke. Zum Verständnis kurzer und formelhafter Inschriften auf ägyptischen Denkmälern," *Mitteilungen des Deutschen Archäologischen Instituts. Abteilung Kairo* 46 (1990), 127–56.

Jansen-Winkeln, K. "Das ägyptische Pseudopartizip," *Orientalia Lovaniensia Periodica* 24 (1993), 5–28.

Jansen-Winkeln, K. "Exozentrische Komposita als Relativphrasen im älteren Ägyptisch," *Zeitschrift für Ägyptische Sprache und Altertumskunde* 121 (1994), 51–75.

Jastrow, M. *A Dictionary of the Targumim, Talmud Babli, Yerushalmi, and the Midrashic Literature* (New York: Judaica Press, 1971).

Johnson, J. H. *The Demotic Verbal System.* Studies in Ancient Oriental Civilization XXXVIII (Chicago: The Oriental Institute, 1976).

Johnson, J. H. "Demotic nominal sentences," in *Studies Presented to Hans Jakob Polotsky*, ed. by D. W. Young (Beacon Hill: Pirtle & Polson, 1981), 414–30.

Johnson, J. H. *Thus Wrote 'Onchsheshonqy. An Introductory Grammar of Demotic.* Studies in Ancient Oriental Civilization XLV (Chicago: Oriental Institute, second edition 1991).

Junge, F. *Syntax der mittelägyptischen Literatursprache. Grundlagen einer Strukturtheorie* (Mainz: Philipp von Zabern, 1978).

Junge, F. "Nominalsatz und Cleft Sentence im Ägyptischen," in *Studies Presented to Hans Jakob Polotsky*, ed. by D. W. Young (Beacon Hill: Pirtle & Polson, 1981), 431–62.

Junge, F. "Form und Funktion ägyptischer Satzfragen," *Bibliotheca Orientalis* 40 (1983), 545–59.

Junge, F. "Sprachstufen und Sprachgeschichte," in *Zeitschrift der Deutschen Morgenländischen Gesellschaft. Supplement VI* (Stuttgart: Franz Steiner, 1985), 17–34.

Junge, F. *"Emphasis" and Sentential Meaning in Middle Egyptian*. Göttinger Orientforschungen IV/20 (Wiesbaden: Harrassowitz, 1989).

Junge, F. "How to study Egyptian grammar and to what purpose. A summary of sorts," *Lingua Aegyptia* 1 (1991), 389–426.

Kahl, J. *Das System der ägyptischen Hieroglyphenschrift in der 0.–3. Dynastie*. Göttinger Orientforschungen IV/29 (Wiesbaden: Harrassowitz, 1994).

Kammerzell, F. "Zeichenverstümmelung," in *LÄ* VI, 1359–61.

Kammerzell, F. "Funktion und Form. Zur Opposition von Perfekt und Pseudopartizip im Alt- und Mittelägyptischen," *Göttinger Miszellen* 117/18 (1990), 181–202.

Kammerzell, F. "Augment, Stamm und Endung. Zur morphologischen Entwicklung der Stativkonjugation,"*Lingua Aegyptia* 1 (1991), 165–99.

Kammerzell, F. "Ueber die Verschiedenheit von geschriebener und gesprochener Sprache," paper read at the Sixth International Congress of Egyptology (Turin, 1–8 September 1991).

Kammerzell, F. "Personalpronomina und Personalendungen im Altägyptischen," in D. Mendel and U. Claudi (eds.), *Ägypten im afro-orientalischen Kontext. Aufsätze zur Archäologie, Geschichte und Sprache eines unbegrenzten Raumes. Gedenkschrift Peter Behrens*. Afrikanistische Arbeitspapiere, special issue 1991 (University of Cologne, 1991), 177–203.

Kammerzell, F. Review of *Les langues dans le monde ancien et moderne, Lingua Aegyptia* 2 (1992), 157–75.

Kammerzell, F. "Die altägyptische Negation *w*: Versuch einer Annäherung," *Lingua Aegyptia* 3 (1993), 17–32.

Kammerzell, F. "Zur Etymologie des ägyptischen Zahlworts '4'," in *Crossroads III Preprints*.

Kaplony, P. *Die Inschriften der ägyptischen Frühzeit*, 2 vols. and supplements. Ägyptologische Abhandlungen VIII–IX (Wiesbaden: Harrassowitz, 1963–64).

Kasser, R. "'Ayin," in *Coptic Encyclopedia* VIII, 45–47.

Kasser, R. "Fayyumic," in *Coptic Encyclopedia* VIII, 124–31.

Kasser, R. "Syllabication," in *Coptic Encyclopedia* VIII, 207–14.

Kemp, B. J. *Ancient Egypt. Anatomy of a Civilization* (London: Routledge, 1989).

Lambdin, Th.O. *Egyptian Loanwords and Transcriptions in the Ancient Semitic Languages* (Baltimore: Johns Hopkins University Press, 1952).

Lepsius, R. "Lettre à M. le Professeur H. Rosellini...sur l'alphabet hiéroglyphique," *Annali dell'Istituto di corrispondenza archeologica* 9, Rome 1837, 5–100.

Lexikon der Ägyptologie (*LÄ*), ed. by W. Helck, E. Otto and W. Westendorf, 6 vols. (Wiesbaden: Harrassowitz, 1975–1986).

Loprieno, A. "Osservazioni sullo sviluppo dell'articolo prepositivo in egiziano e nelle lingue semitiche," *Oriens Antiquus* 19 (1980), 1–27.

Loprieno, A. "The form *sdmt.f*: verbal predicate or 'transposition'?," *Göttinger Miszellen* 37 (1980), 17–29.

Loprieno, A. "The sequential forms in Late Egyptian and Biblical Hebrew: a parallel development of verbal systems," *Afroasiatic Linguistics* VII/5 (Malibu: Undena, 1980), 1–19.

Loprieno, A. "Methodologische Anmerkungen zur Rolle der Dialekte in der ägyptischen Sprachentwicklung," *Göttinger Miszellen* 53 (1981), 55–75.

Loprieno, A. "Zahlwort," in *LÄ* VI, 1306–19.

Loprieno, A. *Das Verbalsystem im Ägyptischen und im Semitischen. Zur Grundlegung einer Aspekttheorie*. Göttinger Orientforschungen IV/17 (Wiesbaden: Harrassowitz, 1986).

Loprieno, A. "On the typological order of constituents in Egyptian," *Journal of Afroasiatic Languages* 1 (1988), 26–57.

Loprieno, A. "Der ägyptische Satz zwischen Semantik und Pragmatik: die Rolle von *jn*," *Studien zur Altägyptischen Kultur. Beihefte III* (1988), 77–98.

Loprieno, A. "Focus, mood, and negative forms: Middle Egyptian syntactic paradigms and diachrony," *Lingua Aegyptia* 1 (1991), 201–26.

Loprieno, A. "Observations on the traditional pronunciation of Hebrew among Italian Jews," in A. Kaye (ed.), *Semitic Studies in Honor of Wolf Leslau*, vol. II (Wiesbaden: Harrassowitz, 1991), 931–48.

Loprieno, A. "Topics in Egyptian negations," in D. Mendel and U. Claudi (eds.), *Ägypten im afro-orientalischen Kontext. Aufsätze zur Archäologie, Geschichte und Sprache eines unbegrenzten Raumes. Gedenkschrift Peter Behrens*. Afrikanistische Arbeitspapiere, special issue 1991 (University of Cologne, 1991), 213–35.

Lüddeckens, E. "Demotisch," in *LÄ* I, 1052–56.

Lyons, J. *Semantics*, 2 vols. (Cambridge University Press, 1977).

MacRae, G. "Thunder: Perfect Mind," in D.M. Parrott (ed.), *Nag Hammadi Codices V,2–5 and VI with Papyrus Berolinensis 8502,1 and 4*. Nag Hammadi Studies XI (Leiden: E. J. Brill, 1979), 231–55.

Malaise, M. "La conjugaison suffixale dans les propositions conditionelles introduites par *ir* en ancien et moyen égyptien," *Chronique d'Egypte* 60 (1985), 152–67.

Mattha, G. and G. R. Hughes, *The Demotic Legal Code of Hermopolis West*. Bibliothèque d'Etude XLV (Cairo: Institut Français d'Archéologie Orientale, 1975).

Meillet, A. and J. Vendryès, *Traité de grammaire comparée des langues classiques* (Paris: Maisonneuve, fourth edition 1968).

Moers, G. "Freie Varianten oder funktional gebundene Morpheme? Zu den Graphien der altägyptischen Negation *n*," *Lingua Aegyptia* 3 (1993), 33–58.

Moret, A. "La légende d'Osiris à l'époque thébaine d'après l'hymne à Osiris du Louvre," *Bulletin de l'Institut Français d'Archéologie Orientale* 30 (1931), 725–50.

Moscati, S. (ed.), *An Introduction to the Comparative Grammar of the Semitic Languages*. Porta Linguarum Orientalium VI (Wiesbaden: Harrassowitz, second edition 1969).

Nagel, P. "Akhmimic," in *Coptic Encyclopedia* VIII, 19–27.

Nagel, P. "Lycopolitan," in *Coptic Encyclopedia* VIII, 151–59.

Newman, P. "Chadic," in W. Bright (ed.), *International Encyclopedia of Linguistics*, vol. I (Oxford University Press, 1992), 253–54.

Niccacci, A. "Su una formula dei 'Testi dei Sarcofagi'," *Studium biblicum franciscanum. Liber Annuus* 30 (1980), 197–224.

Osing, J. *Der spätägyptische Papyrus BM 10808*. Ägyptologische Abhandlungen XXXIII (Wiesbaden: Harrassowitz, 1976).

Osing, J. *Die Nominalbildung des Ägyptischen*, 2 vols. (Mainz: Philipp von Zabern, 1976).

Osing, J. "Zur Lesung der neuägyptischen-demotischen Negation ," *Enchoria* 10 (1980), 93–104.

Osing, J. "Die Partizipien im Ägyptischen und in den semitischen Sprachen," in J. Osing and G. Dreyer (eds.), *Form und Mass. Beiträge zur Literatur, Sprache und Kunst des Alten Ägypten. Festschrift für Gerhard Fecht*. Ägypten und Altes Testament XII (Wiesbaden: Harrassowitz, 1987), 337–60.

Palmer, F. *Mood and Modality*. Cambridge Textbooks in Linguistics (Cambridge University Press, 1986).

Palmer, L. R. *The Latin Language* (London: Faber and Faber, 1961).

Palmer, L. R. *The Greek Language* (Atlantic Highlands: Humanities Press, 1980).

Parkinson, R. B. *The Tale of the Eloquent Peasant* (Oxford: Griffith Institute, 1991).

Penchoen, T. G. *Tamazight of the Ayt Ndhir*. Afroasiatic Dialects I (Malibu: Undena, 1973).

Pestman, P. W. *Chronologie égyptienne d'après les textes démotiques*. Papyrologica Lugduno-Batava XV (Leiden: E. J. Brill, 1967).

Petráček, K. *Altägyptisch, Hamitosemitisch und ihre Beziehungen zu einigen Sprachfamilien in Afrika und Asien. Vergleichende Studien*. Acta Universitatis Corolinae Philologica Monographia XC (Prague: Charles University, 1988).

Peust, C. "Zur Herkunft des koptischen ⲏ," *Lingua Aegyptia* 2 (1992), 117–25.

Polotsky, H. J. Review of Till, *Koptische Dialektgrammatik*, *Göttingische Gelehrte Anzeigen* 196 (1934).

Polotsky, H. J. *Etudes de syntaxe copte* (Le Caire: Société d'Archéologie Copte, 1944).

Polotsky, H. J. "The 'emphatic' *sḏm.n.f* form," *Revue d'Egyptologie* 11 (1957), 109–17.

Polotsky, H. J. "The Coptic conjugation system," *Orientalia* 29 (1960), 392–422.

Polotsky, H. J. "Nominalsatz und Cleft Sentence im Koptischen," *Orientalia* 31 (1962), 413–30.

Polotsky, H. J. "Egyptian Tenses," *Israel Academy of Sciences and Humanities. Proceedings*, II/5 (Jerusalem 1965).

Polotsky, H. J. *Collected Papers* (Jerusalem: Magnes Press, 1971).

Polotsky, H. J. "Les transpositions du verbe en égyptien classique," *Israel Oriental Studies* 6 (1976), 1–50.

Polotsky, H. J. *Grundlagen des koptischen Satzbaus*. American Studies in Papyrology XXVII–XXIX (Atlanta: Scholars' Press, 1987–90).

Prince, E. F. "Toward a taxonomy of given-new information," in P. Cole (ed.), *Radical Pragmatics* (New York: Academic Press, 1984), 223–55.

Quack, J. F. "Die Konstruktion des Infinitivs in der Cleft Sentence," *Revue d'Egyptologie* 42 (1991), 189–207.

Quack, J. F. "Über die mit *'nḫ* gebildeten Namenstypen und die Vokalisation einiger Verbalformen," *Göttinger Miszellen* 123 (1991), 91–100.

Quack, J. F. *Studien zur Lehre für Merikare*. Göttinger Orientforschungen IV/23 (Wiesbaden: Harrassowitz, 1992).

Radford, A. *Transformational Grammar. A First Course*. Cambridge Textbooks in Linguistics (Cambridge University Press, 1988).

Ray, J. "Are Egyptian and Hittite Related?," in A. B. Lloyd (ed.), *Studies in Pharaonic Religion and Society in Honour of J. Gwyn Griffiths* (London: Egypt Exploration Society, 1992), 124–36.

Ray, J. "An approach to the *sḏm.f*: forms and purposes," *Lingua Aegyptia* 1 (1991), 243–58.

Reintges, Ch. "Formal and functional aspects of the Egyptian root lexicon," in *Crossroads III Preprints*.

Ritter, Th. "On particles in Middle Egyptian," *Lingua Aegyptia* 2 (1992), 127–37.

Rosén, H. *Good Hebrew. Meditations on the Syntax of the "Proper" Language* (in Hebrew) (Jerusalem: Kiryat Sepher, 1966).

Rössler, O. "Verbalbau und Verbalflexion in den semitohamitischen Sprachen. Vorstudien zu einer vergleichenden semitohamitischen Grammatik," *Zeitschrift der Deutschen Morgenländischen Gesellschaft* 100 (1950), 461–514.

Rössler, O. "Das Ägyptische als semitische Sprache," in F. Altheim and R. Stiehl (eds.), *Christentum am Roten Meer I* (Berlin–New York: Walter de Gruyter, 1971), 275–77.

Sasse, H. J. "Cushitic languages," in W. Bright (ed.), *International Encyclopedia of Linguistics*, vol. I (Oxford University Press, 1992), 326–30.

Sasse, H. J. "The thetic/categorical distinction revisited," *Linguistics* 25.3 (1987), 511–80.

Satzinger, H. "Zur Phonetik des Bohairischen und des Ägyptisch-Arabischen im Mittelalter," *Wiener Zeitschrift für die Kunde des Morgenlandes* 63–64 (1971), 40–65.

Satzinger, H. "Phonologie des koptischen Verbs (saʿidischer Dialekt)," in M. Görg (ed.), *Festschrift Elmar Edel*. Ägypten und Altes Testament I (Bamberg: Urlaub, 1979), 343–68.

Satzinger, H. "Nominalsatz und Cleft Sentence im Neuägyptischen," in *Studies Presented to Hans Jakob Polotsky*, ed. by D. W. Young (Beacon Hill: Pirtle & Polson, 1981), 480–505.

Satzinger, H. "Attribut und Relativsatz im älteren Ägyptisch," in *Studien zu Sprache und Religion Ägyptens zu Ehren von Wolfhart Westendorf*, ed. by F. Junge, vol. I: Sprache (Göttingen: Hubert & Co, 1984), 125–56.

Satzinger, H. "Syntax der Präpositionsadjektive ('Präpositionsnisben')," *Zeitschrift für Ägyptische Srache und Altertumskunde* 113 (1986), 141–53.

Satzinger, H. "Structural analysis of the Egyptian independent personal pronoun," in H. G. Mukarovsky (ed.), *Proceedings of the Fifth International Hamito-Semitic Congress 1987*, vol. 2. Beiträge zur Afrikanistik XLI (Vienna: Institut für Afrikanistik, 1991), 121–35.

Satzinger, H. "Pronunciation of Late Bohairic," in *Coptic Encyclopedia* VIII, 60–65.

Sauneron, S. "L'écriture ptolémaïque," in *Textes et langages de l'Egypte pharaonique. Hommages à Jean-François Champollion*. Bibliothèque d'Etude LXIV/1 (Cairo: Institut Français d'Archéologie Orientale, 1972), 45–56.

Sauneron, S. *L'écriture figurative dans les textes d'Esna*. Esna VIII (Cairo: Institut Français d'Archéologie Orientale, 1982).

Schachter, P. "Focus and relativization," *Language* 49 (1973), 19–46.

Schenkel, W. *Frühmittelägyptische Studien*. Bonner Orientalistische Studien, N.S. XIII (University of Bonn, 1962).

Schenkel, W. "'Singularisches' und 'pluralisches' Partizip," *Mitteilungen des Deutschen Archäologischen Instituts. Abteilung Kairo* 20 (1965), 110–14.

Schenkel, W. "Die Konversion, ein Epiphänomen der kemischen (ägyptisch-koptischen) Sprachgeschichte," *Mitteilungen des Deutschen Archäologischen Instituts. Abteilung Kairo* 21 (1966), 123–32.

Schenkel, W. *Die altägyptische Suffixkonjugation*. Ägyptologische Abhandlungen XXXII (Wiesbaden: Harrassowitz, 1975).

Schenkel, W. "*sḏm=f* und *sḏm.w=f* als Prospektivformen," in *Studies Presented to Hans Jakob Polotsky*, ed. by D.W. Young (Beacon Hill: Pirtle & Polson, 1981), 506–27.

Schenkel, W. *Aus der Arbeit an einer Konkordanz zu den altägyptischen Sargtexten. II: Zur Pluralbildung des Ägyptischen*. Göttinger Orientforschungen IV/12 (Wiesbaden: Harrassowitz, 1983), 171–230.

Schenkel, W. *Zur Rekonstruktion der deverbalen Nominalbildung des Ägyptischen*. Göttinger Orientforschungen IV/13 (Wiesbaden: Harrassowitz, 1983).

Schenkel, W. "Fokussierung. Über die Reihenfolge von Subjekt und Prädikat im klassisch-ägyptischen Nominalsatz," in *Studien zu Sprache und Religion Ägyptens zu Ehren von Wolfhart Westendorf*, herausgegeben von F. Junge. Band I: Sprache (Göttingen: Hubert & Co, 1984), 157–74.

Schenkel, W. "Sonst–Jetzt. Variationen eines literarischen Formelements," *Die Welt des Orients* 15 (1984), 51–61.

Schenkel, W. "Schrift," in *LÄ* V, 713–35.

Schenkel, W. "Zur Verbalflexion der Pyramidentexte," *Bibliotheca Orientalis* 42 (1985), 481–94.

Schenkel, W. "Syllabische Schreibung," in *LÄ* VI, 114–22.

Schenkel, W. "Das Wort für 'König (von Oberägypten)'," *Göttinger Miszellen* 94 (1986), 57–73.

Schenkel, W. "Zur Struktur des dreigliedrigen Nominalsatzes mit der Satzteilfolge Subjekt-Prädikat im Ägyptischen," *Studien zur Altägyptischen Kultur* 14 (1987), 265-82.

Schenkel, W. Review of Doret, *Narrative Verbal System*, *Archiv für Orientforschung* 35 (1988), 237–45.

Schenkel, W. *Einführung in die altägyptische Sprachwissenschaft*. Orientalistische Einführungen (Darmstadt: Wissenschaftliche Buchgesellschaft, 1990).

Schenkel, W. *Tübinger Einführung in die klassisch-ägyptische Sprache und Schrift* (Tübingen, 1991).

Schenkel, W. "Zu den Verschluß- und Reibelauten im Ägyptischen und (Hamito)-Semitischen. Ein Versuch zur Synthese der Lehrmeinungen," *Lingua Aegyptia* 3 (1993), 137–49.

Schenkel, W. "*sčm.t*-Perfekt und *sčm.ti*-Stativ: die beiden Pseudopartizipien des Ägyptischen nach dem Zeugnis der Sargtexte," in H. Behlmer (ed.), *... Quaerentes Scientiam. Festgabe für Wolfhart Westendorf zu seinem 70. Geburtstag überreicht von seinen Schülern* (Göttingen: Seminar für Ägyptologie und Koptologie, 1994), 157–82.

Schmalstieg, W. R. "A few issues of contemporary Indo-European linguistics," in Ph. Baldi (ed.), *Linguistic Change and Reconstruction Methodology*. Trends in Linguistics, Studies and Monographs 45 (Berlin–New York: Mouton de Gruyter, 1990), 359–74.

Schneider, Th. *Asiatische Personennamen in ägyptischen Quellen des Neuen Reiches*. Orbis Biblicus et Orientalis CXIV (Freiburg–Göttingen: Vandenhoeck & Ruprecht, 1992).

Seyfried, K. J. *Das Grab des Amonmose (TT 373)* (Mainz: Philipp von Zabern, 1990).

Shisha-Halevy, A. "'Middle Egyptian' gleanings: grammatical notes on the 'Middle Egyptian' text of Matthew," *Chronique d'Egypte* 58 (1983), 311–29.

Shisha-Halevy, A. "Bohairic," in *Coptic Encyclopedia* VIII, 53–60.

Shisha-Halevy, A. "Bohairic-Late Egyptian diaglosses: a contribution to the typology of Egyptian," in *Studies Presented to Hans Jakob Polotsky*, ed. by D. W. Young (Beacon Hill: Pirtle & Polson, 1981), 314–38.

Shisha-Halevy, A. "Sahidic," in *Coptic Encyclopedia* VIII, 194–202.

Shisha-Halevy, A. "The narrative verbal system of Old and Middle Egyptian," *Orientalia* 58 (1989), 247–54.

Shisha-Halevy, A. *Coptic Grammatical Categories*. Analecta Orientalia LIII (Rome: Pontifical Biblical Institute, 1986).

Silverman, D. P. *Interrogative Constructions with JN and JN-JW in Old and Middle Egyptian*. Bibliotheca Aegyptia I (Malibu: Undena, 1980).

Silverman, D. P. "An emphasized object of a nominal verb in Middle Egyptian," *Orientalia* 49 (1980), 199–203.

Simpson, W. K. "Pap. Westcar," in *LÄ IV*, 744–46.

Spiegelberg, W. *Demotische Texte auf Krügen*. Demotische Studien V (Leipzig: J. C. Hinrichs'sche Buchhandlung, 1912).

Die Sprachen Afrikas, vol. II *Afroasiatisch*, ed. by B. Heine, Th. C. Schadeberg, and E. Wolff (Hamburg: Helmut Buske, 1981).

Sweeney, D. "What's a rhetorical question?," *Lingua Aegyptia* 1 (1991), 315–31.

Szemerényi, O. *Studies in the Indoeuropean System of Numerals*. Indogermanische Bibliothek (Heidelberg: Carl Winter, 1960).

Szemerényi, O. *Einführung in die vergleichende Sprachwissenschaft* (Darmstadt: Wissenschaftliche Buchgesellschaft, 1980).

Thissen, H. J. "Bemerkungen zum demotischen Harfner-Gedicht," in S. I. Groll (ed.), *Studies in Egyptology Presented to Miriam Lichtheim*, vol. II (Jerusalem: Magnes Press, 1990), 980–93.

Thompson, Sir H. *A Family Archive from Siut from Papyri in the British Museum* (Oxford University Press, 1934).

Till, W.C. *Koptische Grammatik (Saïdischer Dialekt)*. Lehrbücher für das Studium der orientalischen und afrikanischen Sprachen I (Leipzig: Verlag Enzyklopädie, fourth edition 1970).

Tsereteli, G. W. "Zur Frage der Beziehung zwischen den semitischen und hamitischen Sprachen," *Mitteilungen des Instituts für Orientforschung* 16 (1970), 271–80.

Valeurs phonétiques des signes hiéroglyphiques d' époque gréco-romaine, 3 vols. (University of Montpellier, 1988–90).

Vendler, Z. *Linguistics in Philosophy* (Ithaca: Cornell University Press, 1967).

Vennemann, Th. *Preference Laws for Syllable Structure and the Explanation of Sound Change* (Berlin–New York–Amsterdam: Mouton de Gruyter, 1988).
Vernus, P. "Formes 'emphatiques' en fonction non 'emphatique' dans la protase d'un système corrélatif," *Göttinger Miszellen* 43 (1981), 73–88.
Vernus, P. "Deux particularités de l'égyptien de tradition: *ntj iw* + Présent I; *wnn.f ḥr sḏm* narratif," in *L'Egyptologie en 1979. Axes prioritaires de recherches*, vol. I. Colloques internationaux du CNRS, 595 (Paris: Centre National de la Recherche Scientifique, 1982), 81–89.
Vernus, P. "Etudes de philologie et de linguistique (VI)," *Revue d'Egyptologie* 38 (1987), 175–81.
Vernus, P. *Future at Issue. Tense, Mood and Aspect in Middle Egyptian: Studies in Syntax and Semantics*. Yale Egyptological Studies IV (New Haven: Yale Egyptological Seminar, 1990).
Vernus, P. "Le rhème marqué: typologie des emplois et effets de sens en Moyen Egyptien," *Lingua Aegyptia* 1 (1991), 333–55.
Vernus, P. "Observations sur la prédication d'identité ("Nominal predicate")," in *Crossroads III Preprints*.
Voigt, R. M. *Die infirmen Verbaltypen des Arabischen und das Biradikalismus-Problem*. Veröffentlichungen der Orientalischen Kommission XXXIX (Stuttgart: Franz Steiner, 1988).
von Soden, W. *Grundriss der akkadischen Grammatik*. Analecta Orientalia XXXIII–XLVIII (Rome: Pontifical Biblical Institute, 1969).
Wackernagel, J. "Über ein Gesetz der indogermanischen Wortstellung," *Indogermanische Forschungen* 1 (1892), 333–436.
Wenig, St. "Meroe, Schrift und Sprache," in *LÄ* IV, 104–107.
Wente, E. F. "The Late Egyptian conjunctive as a past continuative," *Journal of Near Eastern Studies* 21 (1969), 304–11.
Westendorf, W. *Der Gebrauch des Passivs in der klassischen Literatur der Ägypter*. Veröffentlichungen des Instituts für Orientforschung XVIII (Berlin: Deutsche Akademie der Wissenschaften, 1953).
Westendorf, W. *Grammatik der medizinischen Texte*. Grundriß der Medizin der Alten Ägypter VIII (Berlin: Akademie Verlag, 1962).
Westendorf, W. *Koptisches Handwörterbuch* (Heidelberg: Carl Winter, 1965).
Westendorf, W. "Zur Lesung der mittelägyptischen (prädikativen) Negation ," *Göttinger Miszellen* 36 (1979), 61–67; *Göttinger Miszellen* 45 (1981), 71–80.
Westendorf, W. *Beiträge zum ägyptischen Nominalsatz*. Nachrichten der Akademie der Wissenschaften in Göttingen, Phil.-Hist. Klasse, vol. III, Göttingen 1981.
Willms, A. *Die dialektale Differenzierung des Berberischen*. Afrika und Übersee XXXI (Berlin: Reimer, 1980).
Winand, J. *Etudes de néo-égyptien, I. La morphologie verbale*. Aegyptiaca Leodiensia II (Liège: CIPL, 1992).
Winter, E. "Philae," in *LÄ* IV, 1023.
Worrell, W.H. *Coptic Sounds*. University of Michigan Studies. Humanistic Series 26 (Ann Arbor: University of Michigan Press, 1934).
Wright, W. *A Grammar of the Arabic Language*. Third edition revised by W. Robertson Smith and M. J. de Goeje, 2 vols. (Cambridge University Press, 1896–98).

Zaborski, A. "Afro-asiatic languages," in W. Bright (ed.), *International Encyclopedia of Linguistics*, vol. I (Oxford University Press, 1992), 36–37.

Zaborski, A. "Der Wortschatz der Bedscha-Sprache. Eine vergleichende Analyse," in *Zeitschrift der Deutschen Morgenländischen Gesellschaft. Supplement VII* (Stuttgart: Franz Steiner Verlag, 1989), 573–91.

Zeidler, J. "Nochmals zur Etymologie der Handhieroglyphe," *Göttinger Miszellen* 72 (1984), 39–47.

Zeidler, J. Review of Petráček, *Vergleichende Studien*, *Lingua Aegyptia* 2 (1992), 189–222.

Zeidler, J. "A New Approach to the Late Egyptian 'Syllabic Orthography'," in *Sesto Congresso Internazionale di Egittologia. Atti*, vol. II (Torino: Italgas, 1993), 579–90.

Žába, Z. *Les Maximes de Ptaḥḥotep* (Prague: Czechoslovakian Academy of Sciences, 1956).

INDEX OF PASSAGES

EGYPTIAN

Admonitions 1,5 147
2,10 123
4,11–12 130
7,1 161, 270
7,4 188
7,7 150, 274
7,10 150
8,3 146
8,5–6 157
8,13 150
10,4 121
12,1 154
12,6 152
12,13–14 199
12,14 116
14,14 156
Amenemope 2,6 268
Ani 8,11 141
Beni Hassan I 25,98–99 126, 168
Berlin 1157,11 151
12 197
18–20 129
Book of the Dead 64,5 262
125γ,28 172, 215
(Budge) 241,14 121
(Budge) 261,1 204
(Lepsius) 162,8 263
(Naville) II,40/8 128
British Museum 614,8 264
Cairo CG 20518 a,1 85
Codex Hermopolis 7,7 135
CT I 28c–29a 153
44b 108
55b 123, 147
70d 206
74i 189
81a–b 185
170g–i 101
187e 171, 213
207c–d 107
248e 208
254f 121
277c–d 107
345c 89
CT II 120g 107
131d 90
160b–c 128, 171, 214
201a 186
225c–e 210
334b 111
342b 111
CT III 24a–25b 192, 197
59b 121
100h–101b 192
204a 193
224c 120
300b–d 265
311a 119
321c 105
336f–i 128
351c 115
370b 150, 263
386b 191
390e 128
CT IV 21c 263
24c 105
29e 122, 167
37f 107
82p 119
187d 110
188b 121
192–93b 105
228b 106
243a 121
318c–d 105, 274
340a 119
410 (220a) 104
412 (162–5a) 110
412 (164a) 263
CT V 27d–e 253
28c 79
54c–55a 194

59c 107
92f 81
93c–d 194
110e 121
110g 111
124a–b 208
259c 191
279c 121
321c–d 85
323h–i 216
326g–h 216
CT VI 75g 106
76c 66
133k 243
155f 104
162q 191
166c 107
194c 200
253d 109
258e 116
286a 114
295s–96c 192
303r 217
314b 70
332k–n 128
333a 194
335b 114
384h 215
392h 243
CT VII 22n 114
157c 109
250m 106
369a 116
464a–b 117
475i–j 155
479k–l 191
495i 109
Dem. Krug A 11 142
Dem. Magical Papyrus of London and Leiden 2,26 223
16,26 173
V20,2–3 221
Dispute between a Man and his Ba 31–32 128
38 105
78–79 160
121–22 127
123–24 122
130 127
Doomed Prince 4,6–7 226
4,6–8 179
4,9 131
6,13–14 98, 233
7,2–3 174
7,8 180
Ens. Loyaliste 2,10 113
Harhotep 67–68 168
396–97 217
Hatnub 4,3–4 79
22,2 101, 151
Heqaib 10,20 253
Heqanakhte 2,29 185
Herdsman 6 212
Horus and Seth 2,13 137
5,3–4 222
6,14–7,1 134
14,5–6 135
16,2 173
Kagemni 2,6 124
Khaemwaset 5,35 230
2 Khaemwaset 4,21–22 135
Khakheperre'seneb 12 145
13 264
vo 2–3 87
Khonsuemhab (Florence 2616), 10 97
K*RI* I 238,14 93, 177
II 53,4 141
II 53,5 141
II 65,1–4 94, 222
II 88,1–5 222
II 229,4 177
II 911,9 97
III 160,14 221
IV 80,12 97
IV 87,1–2 94
IV 388,4 178
VI 243,7 180
VI 520,10 95
VI 695,7 97
Louvre C 1,4 87
C 15 90
C 286,18 85
LRL 1,11 229
2,1 140
2,8 176
3,6 139
6,8 141
7,11–12 236
10,8–9 139
12,5–6 173
20,12 94

32,5–8 93
34,10–11 180
35,15 94, 176
45,10–11 235
49,1 181
51,15–52,2 229
56,12–13 235
57,7 221
68,2 229
68,9–10 179
69,15–16 178
70,14–15 134
Khuisobek
(Manchester 3306),4 209
8 195
Meir III,11 151
Merikare E 48 169
E 51 159
E 53 90
E 93 145
Myth of the Sun's Eye
(Leiden I 384 recto) 3,29–30 222
Nag' ed-Dêr 84, A6–7 129, 171
Neferti 26 161
54 145
57–58 112
Onchsheshonqi 4,10–11 98
8,23 266
13,7 132
14,4 268
16,23 131
18,11 174
27,13 132
oBerlin 10627,6 140
oDeM 437,2–3 132
oWien NB, H9 180
Paheri 7 169
pAbbott 6,1–2 180
pAnastasi I 18,2 141
22,1 22
pAnastasi II 1,2 173
6,1 97
pAnastasi IV 3,3 93
3,5–6 93, 173
pAnastasi V 17,7–18,1 97
pBerlin 3038,195 181
pBM 10052, 3,16–17 229
4,12–14 174
5,8–9 132
5,20 269
6,10 181
8,21–22 228
11,21 140
12,17–18 229
13,7 137
13,7–8 135
14,7 133
14,18 176
pBologna 1094, 6,4 233
pChester Beatty I vo C 1,4 131
pDeM 8, 3 180
pEbers 12,15 218
49,8 216
91,3 159
99,4 110, 118
99,5 109
100,8–9 116
247 206
855z 110, 200
pKahun 1,7 201
3,36 125
6,24 152, 181
7,53–56 216
11,16–18 145
12,9–10 203
12,13 122, 147
22,7 130
22,8–9 101
27,8–9 151
28,27 192
30,30 157, 166
35,31 203
pKrall 23,11 141
pLeiden I 361,4–5 228
pMayer A 3,25 181
6,21–23 175
pRamesseum IV C 18 263
pRylands IX 1,18 140
3,7–8 132
5,1 98
pSmith 4,2–3 216
9,19–20 79
pTurin 54065 197
pTurin jud.4,7 226
pWien KM 3877 I,x+3 132
Peasant B1,21 106
B1,33–34 185
B1,35 106
B1,51–52 116
B1,77 114
B1,85–87 152
B1,93 105

B1,101 145
B1,109–10 201
B1,116–17 116
B1,135–37 164
B1,162 90, 212
B1,166 198
B1,204–205 161
B1,208 146
B1,211 90, 215
B1,244–45 90
B1,245 217
B1,249 146
B1,262–63 190
B1,287 158
B1,291–92 170
B1,298–99 192
B1,332 146
B1,347 219
B2,65–66 122
B2,80 161
B2,113–14 169
Bt 35 185
R1.1 110, 160
R1.2–3 145
R1.5 79
R7.4 114
R8.1 186
Ptahhotep 7–19 164
13–14 209
20–21 113, 146
25 114
74–75 128
126 201
137 205
173–74 264
184 117
186 156, 202
213–14 (L2) 129, 171
216 144
234–37 218
235 70
264–65 152
366 195
465–66 217
476 212
629 113
641–42 202
Pyr. 18c 209
27d 208
36a–b 203
123d 81
133f 105
193 81
232a 214
243 211
244b–c 171
259b 185
276c 207
277b 90
333a–c 170
444c 211
475b–c 170, 213
537c 118
543c 155
618a 125
628e 86
638b 123, 127
675b 90
681a 144
696f–g 215
727b–c 157
763a–b 112
777c 155
779b 208
798a 197
833a 171, 213
884 155
890b 168
942a 84
998 217
1114b 64, 146
1141a 82
1159c 82
1161b 85, 184
1223 83
1223a 79, 200
1233b 129
1252c–d 101
1252e–f 152
1267a–b 212
1295a 201
1322c 126
1323 211
1324a–b 129
1370a 108
1405a 84
1428d–e 189
1434b 104
1441c 108
1466b–c 209
1489b–90a 155
1490a 200

1619c	82
1620a	105
1687a	81
1699a	207
1712a	81
1730a	146
1753	210
1862a–b	100
1862a–n	200
2030a	118
2033	120
2057–58	220
2293b	126
Nt 712	106
*1947 Nt[b]	171
*1960b–c	194
RAD 53,16–54,1	139
54,8–12	226
56,15–16	234
57,9–10	227
80,2–3	93
Shipwrecked Sailor 2–3	78, 149
2–7	165
10–11	188
16–17	172
17–18	79
17–19	187
18–19	79
32–33	167
39–41	83, 187
42	146
61–62	158, 160
62	119
67	78
67–69	80
69	70
69–70	121
72–73	167, 219
73–75	169, 186
76–77	186
81–82	186
89–91	112
97–98	78
100–101	127, 169
106–108	168
111	90
111–12	212
117–18	145
119–20	177
119–21	159
124	113
131	169
149–54	154
150	126
151	120
170–71	160
182	113
Sinuhe B 1–2	158
B 4–5	185
B 5–9	187
B 9–11	190
B 23	104
B 26–27	187
B 26–34	195
B 33–34	158
B 43–44	123, 147
B 45–46	185
B 52	85
B 52–53	157
B 60–61	107
B 66	113
B 77	123, 144
B 81	104
B 81–84	166
B 101–102	203
B 107	88
B 109–14	187
B 114	185
B 126	87
B 144–45	160
B 148–49	193
B 155	112
B 156	144
B 181	186
B 185	169
B 193–9	157
B 199	185
B 200	275
B 202	194
B 213	204
B 222–23	120
B 225	149
B 233–34	156
B 236	106
B 246	167
B 247	78, 151
B 252–54	194
B 255	169
B 261	121
B 263	79
B 266–68	126
B 268	105

B 279 211
B 280–81 145
B 304–305 204
B 307–308 188
B 308 116
B 309 127
B 311 110, 156
R 5–8 162
R 8–11 162, 165
R 11–12 161, 165
R 11–14 172
R 11–16 188
R 21–22 148, 156
R 22–24 152
R 55 114
Siut (Dem. Pap.) 1,314 88
3,1 88
8,26 138
23,11 142
Siut (Hier. Inscr.) I,68 84
I,229 90, 217
I,272 218
I,280–81 126
I,288 150
I,293 215
I,295 203
IV,79 211
Truth and Falsehood 5,3 137
6,6 267
Two Brothers 1,10 98, 131
3,5–6 139
4,3–5 228
4,6–9 226
5,1 230
8,2 235
10,4 226
15,4 133
15,10–16,1 178
Urk. I 2,8 77
9,14–16 204
16,15–17 214
39,17–40,1 184
41,12–13 153
43,5 214
47,5 212
62,12 200
83,13–14 153, 210
100, 7–9 77
101,2–3 101, 153
101,4–7 151
103,7 77
103,7–104,4 196
103,8 77
103,9 83
104,4 83
106,3 211
122,6–8 218
124,15 83
124,17 77
125,15–16 78, 161
126,2 77
140,8 184
184,1 205
192,14 70
221,10 184
222,18–223,2 157
232,10–11 171
301,3–5 201
Urk. IV 2,12 187
19,6 85
57,3 89
68,3 218
74,9–11 202
96,7 120
99,15 113
119,10 193
132,9–10 202
132,16–17 201
269,7–8 205
341,7–8 204
348,9 197
363,6 125
363,6–7 153, 200
365,11 193
386,4–10 158
410,5–6 219
520,1 202
766,5 117
780,10–13 217
835,16 100
890,10–12 172
895,1 115
897,11–13 151, 166
897,11–16 199
944,1 113
959,15 219
1074,4–5 217
1082,15 126
1111,6–7 193
1116,7–8 206
1166,10 114
1823,17–18 173

Urk. V 53,1–2 110, 200
Urk. VI 133,20 92
Wenamun 1,20–21 138
1,44–45 95
1,58 176
2,8 131
2,11–13 140
2,23 140
2,23–24 142
2,36 230
2,66 179
Westcar 5,3–5 89
5,3–15 146
5,13 186
6,1 185
6,4–6 111
6,5 148, 215
6,26–7,1 123
6,26–7,2 191
8,12–17 170
8,22–23 151
9,6 129, 266
9,7–8 117
9,22 113
11,10–11 158
11,21–22 90
12,21 192

COPTIC

Acts 26,26 233
Cant 1,5–6 131
1,15 132
1 Cor 9,20 182
14,24 98
15,56 133
2 Cor 4,7 140
5,1 93, 173
8,9 180
Deut 1,43 221
Ex 19,5 138
23,7 177, 181, 222
35,10 133
Gal 4,31 142
Gen 3,16 222
Heb 11,4 131
Jas 1,13 233
Jn 1,10 93
1,39 95
2,1 176
2,4 93, 221
4,9 222
4,44 140
6,42 233
8,13 142
8,47 94
9,21 181
11,40 229
17,1 92
1 Jn 2,11 221
2,8 174
4,10 142
Job 1,21 235
13,17 176
27,6 182
Jon 1,14 223
Judg 6,15 233
14,15 95
Lk 1,13 98
1,53 224
4,6 222
6,37 231
7,6–7 223
10,39 235
11,2 95
13,3 229
14,22 139
15,6 98
19,30 235
23,28 223
23,35 92
Mk 16,2 180
Mt 2,9 93
2,16 98
6,9 223
7,7 96, 231
14,23 230
19,19 95
27,15 232
NHC VI 4, 44:26–29 227
5, 5–7 227
40,16–20 230
Pistis Sophia 121,1 95
Prov 12,1 136
Ps 5,5 131
19,2 94, 177
22,1 268
32,12 235
54,20 94
68,22 92
83,12 224

102,12	224
104,7	174
117,23	233
134,17	139
Rev 9,1	236
Rom 4,6	234
9,1	135
12,21	224
1 Thess 5,24	133
1 Tim 3,12	236
Tob 3,11	178

Index of morphemes

Egyptian

j-prefix (Old and Late Egyptian) 79, 81-82, 86, 88, 95-99, 232–33, 259
j.jr (later Egyptian converter) 91–92, 98, 134, 137, 222, 232–34, 267, 278
jw (earlier Egyptian) 74, 79, 101, 122–24, 126, 163, 165–69, 174–75, 194, 234, 271
jw (later Egyptian converter) 91, 174, 177–80, 234–35
jw + VP/stative (earlier Egyptian) 75–80, 91, 93, 123, 186–87, 207, 209, 221, 229
jw=f r sḏm 80, 94, 169, 177, 181, 222, 225, 233, 272
jw=f ḥr sḏm (earlier Egyptian progressive) 80, 158, 169
jw=f ḥr sḏm (later Egyptian sequential) 91, 93–95, 178, 225, 227, 229
jwnꜣ (negative reinforcer) 93, 140–41, 171, 181, 233, 268
jwt(t) (negative conjunction "that not") 101, 218
jwtj (negative relative converter) 70, 212, 218–20
jmj (negative verb) 90, 212–13, 215, 223
jm (imperative of *rḏj*) 92, 95–96, 223, 225
jn (focal, "ergative" morpheme) 64–65, 70, 83–84, 89, 100, 103, 108–9, 115–16, 121, 134, 136–37, 207, 253
jn (interrogative particle) 184
jnn (later Egyptian conjunction) 178, 229
jr (preposition/conjunction) 100, 151–52, 155, 166, 178, 188, 216, 228–30
jrj "to do" as auxiliary verb 91–96, 99, 177, 220–25, 230
jḫ (optative particle) 101
jḫr (particle) 15, 154, 165
js (dependency particle) 153–55, 157, 165, 181, 200
jsk/sk, jsṯ/sṯ (particle) 100, 152–54, 165, 172

ʿḥʿ.n + verbal form 101, 186–87, 220

wʿ (indefinite article) 56, 60
wn (verbal form > converter) 91, 93, 123–27, 166, 175–76, 178, 194, 232, 265
wnn (verbal form > converter) 123–27, 147, 150, 152, 155, 158, 166, 194, 199, 232, 265
wnt (conjunction "that") 100, 153, 166, 200
wn.jn (verbal form > converter) 185, 220, 273

bw (negative particle) 89, 92–94, 97, 140, 172, 221–22, 225
bw-pw (negative particle) 92, 94, 221, 225
bn (negative particle) 89, 93–95, 140–42, 180–82, 222, 225, 268–69

pꜣ, tꜣ, nꜣ (definite article) 7, 60, 68–69
pw > pꜣj (copula) 68–70, 103–14, 117, 131–37, 263–64, 266–67, 269

m (interrogative pronoun) 70, 121
m jr(j.w) (negative imperative) 99, 213, 223, 225, 260
mḥ (ordinal morpheme) 72

mk, mṯ, mṯn (particle) 75, 101, 125, 149, 165–68, 185–86
mtw=f sḏm (later Egyptian conjunctive) 92, 95–96, 225–29

nj (determinative pronoun) 68, 70, 118–21, 138, 199, 265
nj (negative particle) 89, 92, 125–30, 140, 168–72, 180, 209–13, 219–20, 254
ny ("circumstantial" negative particle) 171–72, 214, 254
nj...js (negative particle) 127–30, 170–72, 180–81, 213–214, 233
nj-zp (negative particle) 211–12
-nw (ordinal morpheme) 72
nfr (negative verb) 90, 129–30
nn (negative particle) 89, 125–30, 140, 169, 171–72, 180–81, 211, 214, 218, 225, 273
nn-wn > *mn* (negative predicate) 127, 139
ntj (relative converter) 70, 91, 98–99, 109, 135, 160, 175, 178, 203, 218–19, 234–35
ntt (conjunction "that") 100, 109–10, 149–50, 153, 200

rḏj "to give, cause" as auxiliary verb 82, 95–96, 223–25, 230–31

sḏm, j.sḏm (imperative "hear") 81, 83, 95, 184, 223
sḏm (infinitive "to hear") 73, 76, 84, 88–90, 223
sḏm, j.sḏm (participle "hearer") 73, 87–88, 90, 99, 202–4, 207, 217–19
sḏm pw jrj.n=f (pseudocleft sentence) 104, 106, 198
sḏm(.w) (negatival complement) 73, 89, 212–13, 215–17
sḏm(.w) (stative) 74–77, 80, 84–85, 97, 184, 188, 193, 207, 257
sḏm=f (Old and later Egyptian indicative "he heard") 77–80, 92, 94, 184, 210, 221, 225, 229
sḏm=f/jrr=f (initial "emphatic" aorist "he hears") 73–74, 79–80, 84–85, 90, 124, 152, 163, 193, 195–202, 215–17, 232–33, 274, 277
sḏm=f/jrj=f (non-initial "circumstantial" aorist "he hears") 73–76, 79–80, 84–85, 152, 185–90, 195, 215
sḏm=f/jrj.w=f (perfective passive "he was heard") 84–85, 97, 186–90, 193, 195, 199, 207–8, 224
sḏm=f/jrj.w=f (modal prospective "may he hear") 81–85, 91, 94–96, 124, 152, 184, 193–99, 203, 210, 215–16, 225, 229–30, 232, 274–76
sḏm=f (relative "which he hears, will hear") 86, 90, 98, 106, 203, 207, 233, 259
sḏm=f/jrj=f (subjunctive "that he may hear") 81–85, 90, 95, 152, 184–85, 210, 224, 226, 229, 275
sḏm.jn=f (contingent "then he heard") 78, 80, 85, 124, 185
sḏm.n=f (past "he heard") 54, 77–80, 84, 91, 152, 186–90, 193, 195–96, 198–99, 203, 209–10, 215, 225, 229, 253–54, 256, 274–75
sḏm.n=f (relative "which he heard") 86–87, 90, 98, 106, 203, 218, 233, 259
sḏm.ḫr=f (contingent "then he hears") 80, 85, 93, 221
sḏm.kꜣ=f (contingent "then he will hear") 82, 85, 96
sḏm.t=f (perfective "he has [been] heard") 76, 78, 80, 84–85, 93, 97, 151, 201, 208, 217, 225, 230
sḏm.tj=f (prospective participle "who will hear") 88, 276
sḏm.tw=f, sḏm.n.tw=f, etc. *see tw*
sḏmm=f/jrj.w=f (prospective passive "may he be heard") 7, 54, 76, 84–85, 193, 210

tw (passive morpheme in verbal forms) 76, 85, 97, 186–87, 193, 205–6, 224
tw (indefinite pronoun) 97–98, 205, 224
twj ḥr sḏm (later Egyptian Present I) 67, 91, 172–75, 180–81, 221
tm (negative verb) 89–90, 215–20, 225, 229, 277

Coptic

ⲁ- (imperative prefix) 81, 95, 223
ⲁ=, ⲁ- (Perfect I) 54, 91–92, 94, 221, 225, 229, 277
ⲁⲛ (negative particle) 94, 140–41, 171, 181, 233, 273
ⲁⲛⲟⲕ vs. ⲁⲛⲧ̄ 108, 263
ⲁⲧ- (negative morpheme) 277
ⲉ=, ⲉⲣⲉ- (circumstantial) 91, 174, 179
ⲉ=, ⲉⲣⲉ- (Present II) 91, 232
ⲉ-, ⲉⲧ-, ⲉⲧⲉ, ⲛ̄ⲧ- (relative converter) 91, 98, 134–35, 234–35, 259, 267
ⲉⲣ- (vestigial participle of ⲉⲓⲣⲉ) 99, 134, 267, 278
ⲉⲧ=, ⲉⲧⲉⲣⲉ- (relative Present I) 175, 233, 272
ⲉ=ϥ-ⲉ-, ⲉⲣⲉ- (Future III) 91, 94–96, 177–79, 222, 225, 229, 272
ⲉϣⲱⲡⲉ (conditional conjunction) 278
ⲙ̄ (negative particle) 89, 221, 256
ⲙⲁ- (imperative of ϯ) 96, 223
ⲙⲁⲣⲉ=, ⲙⲁⲣⲉ- (optative) 7, 54, 92, 95–96, 223, 225, 230
ⲙⲉ=, ⲙⲉⲣⲉ- (negative aorist) 92, 94, 222, 225
ⲙⲉϩ- (ordinal morpheme) 72
ⲙⲛ̄- (negative existential morpheme) 139, 175
ⲙⲛ̄ⲧⲁ=, ⲙⲛ̄ⲧⲉ- "not to have" 140
ⲙ̄ⲡⲁⲧ=, ⲙ̄ⲡⲁⲧⲉ- "not yet" 93–94, 221, 225, 277
ⲙ̄ⲡⲉ=, ⲙ̄ⲡⲉ- (negative Perfect I) 93–94, 221, 225
ⲙ̄ⲡⲱⲣ, ⲙ̄ⲡⲣ̄- (negative imperative) 99, 223, 225, 260
ⲛ̄ (determinative morpheme) 56, 72
ⲛ̄ (negative particle) 89, 140, 171, 181, 233
-ⲛⲁ- (future morpheme) 94, 176, 222, 225, 233, 261
ⲛⲉ=, ⲛⲉⲣⲉ- (imperfect) 91, 176, 232
ⲛⲉ- (preterite morpheme) 232
ⲛ̄ⲛⲉ=, ⲛ̄ⲛⲉ- (negative Future III) 94, 181, 222, 225
ⲛ̄(ⲧ)=, ⲛ̄ⲧⲉ- (conjunctive) 92, 95–96, 229–231
ⲛ̄ⲧⲁ- "by" 139
ⲛ̄ⲧⲁ=, ⲛ̄ⲧⲁ- (Perfect II) 232, 259
ⲛ̄ⲧⲁ=, ⲛ̄ⲧⲉ- (genitival morpheme) 71, 139
ⲛ̄ⲧⲉⲣⲉ=, ⲛ̄ⲧⲉⲣⲉ- (temporal) 92, 230
ⲛ̄ⲧⲟⲟⲧ=, ⲛ̄ⲧⲛ̄- "by, through" 139
ⲛ̄ϭⲓ, ^{B}ⲛ̀ϫⲉ (topicalizing particle) 98, 224
ⲡ(ⲉ)-, ⲧ(ⲉ)-, ⲛ(ⲉ)- (definite article) 7, 54, 56, 60, 68–69, 133
ⲡⲉ, ⲧⲉ, ⲛⲉ (copula) 68–69, 131–37, 263, 267–68
ⲡⲉ=, ⲧⲉ=, ⲛⲉ= (possessive adjective) 69, 138
ⲡ(ⲉ)ⲓ-, ⲧ(ⲉ)ⲓ-, ⲛ(ⲉ)ⲓ- (demonstrative adjective) 69
ⲡⲱ=, ⲧⲱ=, ⲛⲟⲩ=/ⲡⲁ-, ⲧⲁ-, ⲛⲁ- 69, 138
ⲡⲁⲓ/ⲡⲏ, ⲧⲁⲓ/ⲧⲏ, ⲛⲁⲓ/ⲛⲏ (demonstrative pronoun) 69, 136, 278
ⲧ- (causative prefix) 223–25
ϯ-, NP- (Present I) 67, 91, 93–94, 173–75, 221
ⲧⲁⲣⲉ=, ⲧⲁⲣⲉ- (promissive future) 96, 230
ⲧⲣⲉ=, ⲧⲣⲉ- (causative infinitive) 223–26
ⲟⲩ- (indefinite article) 7, 54, 56, 60
ⲟⲩⲛ̄- (existential morpheme) 139, 175
ⲟⲩⲛ̄ⲧⲁ=, ⲟⲩⲛ̄ⲧⲉ- "to have" 139–40, 176
ϣⲁ=, ϣⲁⲣⲉ- (general present) 92–94, 221, 225
-ϣⲁⲛ- (conditional morpheme) 92, 229
ϣⲁⲛⲧ=, ϣⲁⲛⲧⲉ- "until" 93, 230, 278
^{LF}ϩⲁ= (perfective) 225, 277
ϩⲓⲧⲟⲟⲧ=, ϩⲓⲧⲛ̄- (preposition) 98, 224
ϫⲉ (conjunction) 100

INDEX OF LEXEMES

This index contains references to the lexical entries mentioned or discussed in the main text and in the notes, but not to those which only occur in the Egyptian and Coptic examples.

EGYPTIAN

ꜣ'' "to speak in a foreign language" 31
ꜣbd "month" 53, 61–62

j interjection "oh" 101
j "to say" 52
jꜣq "vegetables" 32
jjjꜣmt Sem. toponym *yarmuta* 38
jwj "to come" 82, 123
jwn "color" 31, 35
jb "heart" 31, 100
jfdw "four" 37, 71, 245
jmꜣḫ "veneration" 57
jmj "which is in" 100, 120
jmj "not to do" 90, 212, 215
jmjtw "between" 100
jmn "right side" > "West" 34, 56
jmn.tj "West" 56
jmn.tt "West" 57
jmr.wt "inundation" 250
(j)n-m "who?" 69, 137
jnj "to fetch" 76, 81–82
jnn "we" 36, 65, 67
jnk "I" 31, 41, 64, 67
jn.qdyt (Dem.) "to sleep" 254
jr "as for, if" 100, 151, 155, 166, 178, 188, 216, 228–29
jrj "concerning, thereof" 100, 161
jrj "to do" 76, 79, 91, 94, 106 *passim*
jrm (Late Eg.) "with" 100
jḥj "ox" 58
jḫ "what?" 69, 137
jḫ-pw "what?" 266
jzr "tamarisk" 31, 34
jswt "price" 50
jšst "what?" 69
jtj "father" 33, 36, 59
jtrw "river" 47
j̱t "which?" 69, 137
jdmj "red linen" 245

ʿ.t n.t sbꜣ.w "school" 41
ʿꜣ "great, big" 56–57, 125, 260
ʿꜣ "here" 68
ʿjqj "consecration" 47
ʿbꜣ "to be complete" 255
ʿf.tj "the one there" 68–69
ʿffj "fly" 31
ʿn.tj "the one here" 68–69
ʿnḫ "oath" 58
ʿr.t "door" 31
ʿḥʿ "to stand" 53, 89
ʿšꜣ "numerous" 46, 48, 99, 125
ʿq "to enter" 53
ʿkꜣm Sem. toponym *ʿakram* 38

wꜣḏ "green" 31-32
wʿw "one" 56, 71–72
wʿw "soldier" 39
wʿb "to be pure" 30
wʿr.tj "legs" 60
wbḫ "to become white" 37
wpj "to open" 76, 78
wpw.t "occupation" 49, 57
wpw.tj "messenger" 37, 57
wpw-ḥr "except" 100
wn "being" 87
wnn "to be" 91, 100
wrj "great" 260

wḫ3 "to blow" 250
wsḫ "broad, wide" 35, 53
wsḫ.t "breadth" 47
wdpw "servant" 32
wdḥ "fruit" 50
wḏ "to order" 183, 201
wḏ3 "to be whole" 67

b3k-n-rn=f "Bocchoris" 34
bjn "bad" 33
bjn.t "harp" 248
bz "to introduce" 78

p.t "heaven" 49, 57, 59
p3 (*t3, n3*) "the said" 36, 68–69
p3j (*t3j, n3j*) (later Eg.) "this" 68–70
pw (*tw, jpw, jptw*) "this" 68
pw "who, what?" 69, 121
p(w)-tr "who?" 69
pf (*tf, jpf, jptf*) "that" 68
pn (*tn, jpn, jptn*) "this" 68
prj "to come out" 260
pr.t "seed" 57
pḥ "to reach" 78
pḥ.wj "buttocks" 60
psḏ "sunrise" 255
**psḏ.jw* "90" 71
psḏw "nine" 37–38, 71
psḏn.tjw "new moon" 255
pšs.t "half" 47
ptḥ "the god Ptah" 34
pḏ.t "bow" 38, 57

f3j.t "carrying" 87

m "who, what?" 69
m "in, with" 66, 80, 100, 145, 149, 151, 166
m "come!" 81
m-ʿw "by" 71
m-ẖnw "in, within" 100
m-s3 "behind" 100
m-dj "by" 71, 139, 176
m-ḏr.t "through" 139
mʔw.t "mother" 245
m33 "to see" 52, 54, 79, 82, 125, 156, 183
m3ʿ.t "truth" 39
mʿb3 "30" 71
mj "as, like" 100
mj-m "how?" 69
mn "to be stable" 36, 53, 87–88, 250
mn-nfr "Memphis" 57, 259
mnj "Menes" 38
mr "to tie" 250
mrj "to desire, love" 52, 54, 89, 98, 183, 201, 205
mrj.w "beloved" 38
mrw "river bank" 250
mḥ "to fill" 72
mḥj.t "the goddess Mehit" 39
mḥj.t "northwind" 39
mšʿ(j) "to walk" 45, 76
mšd (Dem.) "to wander" 45
md.t "matter, thing" 57
mdw "word" 36–37, 58
mḏw "ten" 71, 25

n "to, for" 100, 151, 155, 258
n-jb-nj "for the sake of" 100
n-ʿ3.t-n.t "inasmuch as" 100
n-mrw.t "in order to" 100, 151
nʔ.t "city" 245
n3, see p3
n(j) "that-of" 70
nʿj "to go" 94
nw "these" 68
nb "lord, possessor" 36, 57
nbw "gold" 248
nf "those" 68
nfr "good, perfect" 39, 54, 56, 87, 90, 125–26
nn "these" 68, 104
nḥmn "surely" 101
nḥḏ.t "tooth" 251
ns "tongue" 31
nkt "thing" 251
ngmgm "to be gathered" 54
ntw (later Eg.) "they" 66–67
ntf "he" 65, 67
nts "she" 65, 67
ntsn "they" 65, 67
ntk "thou (masc.)" 65, 67
nṯ "thou (fem.)" 65, 67
nṯn "ye" 65, 67
nṯr "god" 35, 45, 48, 53–54, 56
nṯr.t "goddess" 35
nṯrj "divine" 54
nḏm "pleasant, sweet" 32, 76

r "until, to, more than" 78, 80, 100, 145, 149, 151, 201

r-ntt "so that" 100, 150
r-sꜣ "behind" 100
r-ḏd "that is" 100
rꜣ "mouth" 58
rʿw "the god Re" 39, 62
rmṯ "man" 36, 46, 52, 56–57
rn "name" 46
rnp.t "year" 59
rḫ "to know" 125, 153, 200
rdw "plant" 58–60
rd.wt "flora" 60
rdj "to give, cause" 82, 87, 95–96, 195, 201, 223–225, 230, 274

hꜣb "to send" 77
hꜣbw "event" 59
h(j)bw "ibis" 48
hnw "jar" 38
hrww "day" 36, 56, 58–59, 62

ḥꜣ "would that" 212
ḥꜣ "behind" 100
ḥꜣ.t "front, beginning" 41, 72
ḥꜣ.tj "first" 72
ḥjm.t "woman" 59
ḥpjw "the god Apis" 35
ḥfꜣw "snake" 55–56, 62, 253
ḥfn "10,000" 71
ḥm-nṯr "priest" 57
ḥmw "to be skilled" 255
**ḥmw* "40" 71
ḥmsj "to sit" 52, 254
ḥnʿ "with" 95–96, 100
ḥnw "jar" 47
ḥr "face" 56
ḥr "on, because" 32, 80, 100, 145, 149
ḥr-m "why?" 69
ḥr-ntt "because" 100, 110, 150, 166
ḥrj "upper part" 56
ḥrj-pḏ.t "overseer of the archery" 39
ḥrw "the god Horus" 38, 56
ḥḥ "million" 71
ḥzj "to praise" 87, 205
ḥqr "to be hungry" 67, 248, 257
ḥtp "pleasing" 36
ḥṯṯ.t "armpit" 57
ḥḏ "to be white" 251

ḫꜣ "1000" 41, 71
ḫprw "form, transformation" 37, 41, 55, 58

ḫft "in front of" 100
ḫm "not to know" 90
**ḫmn.w* "80" 71
ḫmnw "eight" 39, 71
ḫmtw "three" 71
ḫnt "in front of" 100
ḫntj "which is in front of" 100
ḫr "to, for" 80, 100
ḫrw "voice" 41
ḫrw "Hurrian" > "servant" 46
ḫrp "to lead" 72
ḫt "through" 100

ẖ(w).t "body" 41
ẖꜣb.t "sickle" 245
ẖʿq "wool" 248
ẖmm "to become hot" 34
ẖnw "interior" 48
ẖnmw "the god Khnum" 35
ẖnn "to approach" 48
ẖr "under, beneath" 58, 100
ẖr.t "food offerings" 58
ẖrj "which is beneath" 58

zꜣ "son" 56
zꜣ-tꜣ "snake" 57
zꜣjw.tj "Asyut" 39, 43
zj "to go away" 52
zj "who, what?" 69
zjnw "physician" 47
zp "time" 72
zp "to happen" 211
znḥmw "locust" 34–35, 52
zẖꜣ "to write" 46, 76, 89
zẖꜣw "scribe" 58

**sjs.w* "60" 71
sjsw "six" 71
swt (Old Eg.) "he" 65, 67
sbꜣ "star" 60
sbꜣ.wt "constellations" 60
sp.t "lip" 34, 60
spd "to be sharp" 78
sfḫ "to release" 81
**sfḫ.w* "70" 71
sfḫw "seven" 32, 71
smwn "probably" 101
smn "to make stable" 89, 250, 257
sn "brother" 46, 53–54, 59, 255
sn.t "sister" 53–54
sn.wj, fem. *sn.tj* "two" 47, 60, 71

snb "to be healthy" 54, 66
snbb "to greet" 54
snsn "to befriend" 54
sḥtp "to pacify" 81
sšꜣꜣ "to land" 52
stp "to choose" 36–37
stp.n-rꜥw "Satepnariʿa" 29
stt (Old Eg.) "she" 65, 67
sḏm "to hear" 53–54, 73–76, 78, 88, 153
sḏr "to sleep" 76
sḏd "to tell" 49, 87, 89

šmm, see ẖmm
šmsj "to worship" 47
šnj "to be round" 255
šnj "tree" 38
**š(n).t* "100" 71
**š(n).tj* "200" 71
šrr "small" 260

qꜣb "inner part" 29, 32
qbb "to become cool" 42
qnj "to become fat" 47
qrf "ambush" 46
qs "bone" 42
qd "to build" 76, 78

kꜣ particle 82
kꜣj "to think" 82
kꜣ.t "work" 88
kꜣw.tj "worker" 88
kꜣm "vineyard" 31
kꜣmw "gardener" 56
km.t "Egypt" 42, 56–57
kmm "to become black" 88
ktt "to be small" 251

gꜣw "narrow" 260
gmj "to find" 42, 46, 54, 76, 156, 235
grg.t "dowry" 42
gstj "palette" 245

tꜣ, see pꜣ
tꜣ "land" 49
tꜣ.wj "the two lands" > "Egypt" 38
tꜣš "border" 56, 59
tꜣšj "neighbor" 56, 58
tp "head" 72, 100
tpj "first" 36, 72, 253

tf "spittle" 42
tm "to be complete" 89–90, 130

**dj.w* "50" 71
djw "five" 71
dwn "to stretch" 32
db "horn" 42
dbn "weight measure" 38
dp.t "boat" 58
dnj.t "part" 50

ṯꜣj "to take" 42
ṯwt (Old Eg.) "thou (masc.)" 65, 67
ṯpr Sem. borrowing *sôper* "scribe" 29
ṯb-nṯr "Sebennytos" 34
ṯmt (Old Eg.) "thou (fem.)" 65, 67
ṯr.t "willow" 42–43

ḏꜣ.t "dish" 43
ḏʿn.t "tanis" 39, 245
**ḏw.tj* "20" 71
ḏbʿ "to seal" 44
ḏbʿ "10,000" 42, 46–47, 71
ḏbʿ "finger" 255
ḏnb "to turn" 32
ḏr "since" (prep.) 78–79, 100, 151, 201
ḏr-ntt "since" (conj.) 100, 150
ḏr.t "hand" 42–43
ḏrj "to be strong" 44–45
ḏd "to say" 37, 42–44, 79–80, 93, 100, 153, 200

COPTIC

SLⲁⲉⲓⲕ, Bⲁⲓⲕ "consecration" 47
ⲁⲙⲟⲩ, fem. ⲁⲙⲏ "come!" 81, 223
ⲁⲙⲛ̄ⲧⲉ "afterlife" 57
Bⲁⲙⲏⲓⲣⲓ "inundation" 250
ⲁⲙⲣⲏϩⲉ "asphalt" 48
ⲁⲛⲓ- "fetch!" 81
ⲁⲛⲁⲩ "look!" 95
SBⲁⲛⲟⲕ, ALFⲁⲛⲁⲕ "I" 41, 44, 67
SBⲁⲛⲟⲛ, ALFⲁⲛⲁⲛ "we" 67
ⲁⲛⲥⲏⲃⲉ/ⲁⲛϫⲏⲃⲉ "school" 41
ⲁⲛⲁϣ, pl. ⲁⲛⲁⲩϣ "oath" 58, 61
ⲁⲥⲟⲩ "price" 50
ⲁϣ "what" 70, 137
ⲁϣⲁⲓ, ⲁϣⲉⲉⲓⲧⲉ "to become many" 46, 48, 99

ⲁϥ "fly" 31
ⲁϫⲓ- "say!" 81, 95. *See also* ϫⲱ
[B]ⲁϭⲟ "armpit" 57

[BF]ⲃⲱⲕ "servant" 41
[S]ⲃⲱⲱⲛ(ⲉ), fem. ⲃⲟⲟⲛⲉ, [A]ⲃⲟⲩⲟⲩⲛⲉ, [B]ⲃⲱⲛ "bad" 46, 60
[S]ⲃⲟⲓⲛⲉ, [B]ⲟⲩⲱⲓⲛⲓ "harp" 248

ⲉ-, [SB]ⲉⲣⲟ=, [AL]ⲁⲣⲁ=, [F]ⲉⲗⲁ= "to, toward" 47, 100
ⲉⲃⲣⲁ "seed" 57
ⲉⲃⲟⲧ, pl. ⲉⲃⲏⲧ, ⲉⲃⲁⲧⲉ "month" 61–62, 251
ⲉⲙⲛ̄ⲧ "West" 56
[F]ⲉⲙⲉϣⲏⲓ "except" 256. *See also* ⲙⲉϣⲁ=
ⲉϩⲉ, pl. ⲉϩⲉⲩ "ox" 58

ⲉⲓⲟⲡⲉ "occupation" 49–50, 57
[S]ⲉⲓⲟⲟⲣ(ⲉ), [B]ⲓⲟⲣ, [A]ⲓⲟⲟⲣⲉ/ⲓⲱⲱⲣⲉ, [F]ⲓⲁⲁⲗ/ⲓⲁⲁⲣ "river" 47
ⲉⲓⲣⲉ "to do" 89
ⲉⲓⲱⲧ, [B]ⲓⲱⲧ, pl. [S]ⲉⲓⲟⲧⲉ, [B]ⲓⲟϯ, [AL]ⲉⲓⲁⲧⲉ, [F]ⲉⲓⲁϯ "father" 49, 57–59, 249

[S]ⲕⲱ, [B]ⲭⲱ, [L]ⲕⲱ(ⲉ), [AL]ⲕⲟⲩ "to lay" 49
[S]ⲕⲃⲟ, [B]ⲭⲃⲟⲃ "to become cool" 42
[S]ⲕⲏⲙⲉ, [B]ⲭⲏⲙⲓ "Egypt" 42
ⲕⲙⲟⲙ "to become black" 88
[S]ⲕⲛ̄ⲛⲉ, [B]ⲕⲉⲛⲓ, [A]ⲕⲛ̄ⲛⲓⲉ, [F]ⲕⲏⲛⲛⲓ "to become fat" 47
[B]ⲭⲣⲟⲃⲓ "sickle" 245
ⲕⲣⲟϥ "ambush" 46
ⲕⲁⲥ, pl. ⲕⲉⲉⲥ "bone" 42, 61
ⲕⲱⲧⲉ "to turn" 60

ⲗⲁⲥ "tongue" 31

ⲙⲁ "give!" 96, 223
ⲙⲁⲓ- "lover-of" 99. *See also* ⲙⲉ "to love"
ⲙⲉ, [B]ⲙⲏⲓ, ⲙⲉⲣⲉ-, ⲙⲉⲣⲓⲧ= "to love" 89, 99
[S]ⲙⲉ/ⲙⲉⲉ, [B]ⲙⲉⲓ/ⲙⲏⲓ, [SAL]ⲙⲏⲉ, [A]ⲙⲓⲉ, [F]ⲙⲉⲓ/ⲙⲉⲉⲓ/ⲙⲏⲓ "truth" 47, 49
ⲙⲁⲁⲃ "30" 71
ⲙⲛ̄ "with" 100
ⲙⲟⲩⲛ "to stay, be stable" 88, 250
ⲙⲛ̄ⲧⲣⲱⲙⲉ "mankind" 57. *See also* ⲣⲱⲙⲉ
ⲙⲛ̄ϥⲉ "Memphis" 57, 259
ⲙⲏⲣ "river bank" 250
ⲙⲉⲥⲧⲏ "hated" 87
ⲙⲏⲧ "ten" 71
[B]-ⲙⲧⲁⲩ "words" > "magic" 37, 58
ⲙ̄ⲙⲁⲩ "there" 139
ⲙⲁⲁⲩ "mother" 245
[S]ⲙⲟⲟⲩ, [B]ⲙⲱⲟⲩ, [A]ⲙⲁⲏ "water" 44
ⲙⲉϣⲉ-, ⲙⲉϣⲁ= "not to know" 256. *See also* [F]ⲉⲙⲉϣⲏⲓ
ⲙⲏⲏϣⲉ, [B]ⲙⲏϣ "crowd" 45
ⲙⲟⲟϣⲉ, [B]ⲙⲟϣⲓ "to walk" 44–45
ⲙⲟⲩϣⲧ̄ "to examine" 45

ⲛ̄-, ⲛⲁ= "to" 47
[B]ⲛⲏⲃ, [L]ⲛⲉⲡ "lord" 55
ⲛⲟⲩⲃ, ⲛⲟⲩϥ "gold" 41, 248
ⲛ̄ⲕⲁ "thing" 251
ⲛ̄ⲕⲟⲧⲕ̄ "to sleep" 254
ⲛⲓⲙ "who?" 69
ⲛ̄ⲧⲁ=, ⲛ̄ⲧⲉ- "by, of" 71, 139
[SAL]ⲛ̄ⲧⲟ, [B]ⲛ̀ⲑⲟ, [F]ⲛ̄ⲧⲁ "thou (fem.)" 49, 67
ⲛⲟⲩⲧⲉ, pl. ⲛ̄ⲧⲉⲉⲣⲉ/ⲛ̄ⲧⲏⲣ/ⲛ̄ⲇⲉⲉⲣⲉ/ⲛ̄ⲧⲁⲓⲣ "god" 35, 45, 48, 56, 251
[S]ⲛ̄ⲧⲟⲕ, [B]ⲛ̀ⲑⲟⲕ, [ALF]ⲛ̄ⲧⲁⲕ "thou (masc.)" 67
-ⲛⲧⲱⲣⲉ "goddess" 35
[S]ⲛ̄ⲧⲟⲥ, [B]ⲛ̀ⲑⲟⲥ, [ALF]ⲛ̄ⲧⲁⲥ "she" 67
[SL]ⲛ̄ⲧⲱⲧⲛ̄, [B]ⲛ̀ⲑⲱⲧⲉⲛ, [A]ⲛ̄ⲧⲱⲧⲛⲉ, [F]ⲛ̄ⲧⲁⲧⲉⲛ "ye" 67
ⲛ̄ⲧⲟⲟⲧ=, ⲛ̄ⲧⲛ̄- "by, through" 139. *See also* ⲧⲱⲣⲉ
[S]ⲛ̄ⲧⲟⲟⲩ, [B]ⲛ̀ⲑⲱⲟⲩ, [ALF]ⲛ̄ⲧⲁⲩ "they" 67
[S]ⲛ̄ⲧⲟϥ, [B]ⲛ̀ⲑⲟϥ, [ALF]ⲛ̄ⲧⲁϥ "he" 67
ⲛⲟⲩϥⲉ "beautiful" 87
ⲛⲁϫϩⲉ "tooth" 251
ⲛⲟϭ "great, big" 56

ⲡ(ⲉ)-, ⲧ(ⲉ)-, ⲛ(ⲉ)- "the" 7, 54, 56, 69, 133
ⲡⲉ, ⲧⲉ, ⲛⲉ (copula) 69, 131–33, 136, 267
ⲡⲉ=, ⲧⲉ=, ⲛⲉ= (possessive adjective) 69, 138
ⲡ(ⲉ)ⲓ-, ⲧ(ⲉ)ⲓ-, ⲛ(ⲉ)ⲓ- "this" (adj.) 69

ⲡⲱ=, ⲧⲱ=, ⲛⲟⲩ=/ⲡⲁ-, ⲧⲁ-, ⲛⲁ- (possessive pronoun) 69–70, 138
ⲡⲁⲓ/ⲡⲏ, ⲧⲁⲓ/ⲧⲏ, ⲛⲁⲓ/ⲛⲏ "this" (pron.) 69, 136, 278
ⲡⲉ, pl. ⲡⲏⲩⲉ "heaven" 49, 57, 59
ⲯⲓⲧ "nine" 37, 71
ⲡⲉⲥⲧⲁⲓⲟⲩ "90" 71
ⲡⲓⲧⲉ "bow" 57
ⲡⲁϣⲉ/ⲡⲓϣⲉ "half" 47
ⲡⲁϩⲟⲩ "buttocks" 60

ⲣⲏ "sun" 42
ⲣⲟ, pl. ⲣⲱⲟⲩ "mouth" 58
ⲣⲱⲙⲉ, [B]ⲣⲱⲙⲓ "man" 45–46, 56, 60
ⲣⲙ̄ⲛ̄ⲕⲏⲙⲉ "Egyptian man" 56
ⲣⲙ̄ⲙⲁⲟ "rich" 57
ⲣⲟⲙⲡⲉ, pl. ⲣⲙ̄ⲡⲟⲟⲩⲉ "year" 59
[SB]ⲣⲁⲛ, [AL]ⲣⲉⲛ, [F]ⲗⲉⲛ "name" 46, 49
ⲣⲱⲧ, pl. [B]ⲣⲟϯ "plant" 58

ⲥⲉ "60" 71
ⲥⲁⲃⲉ, fem. ⲥⲁⲃⲏ "wise" 60
[S]ⲥⲁⲉⲓⲛ, [A]ⲥⲉ(ⲉ)ⲓⲛⲉ, [BF]ⲥⲏⲓⲛⲓ "physician" 47
ⲥⲓⲟⲟⲩⲧ "Asyut" 43
[S]ⲥⲙⲓⲛⲉ, [B]ⲥⲉⲙⲛⲓ "to establish" 89, 97, 250, 257
[SB]ⲥⲟⲛ, [ALF]ⲥⲁⲛ, pl. ⲥⲛⲏⲩ "brother" 46, 59–60, 252
ⲥⲱⲛⲉ "sister" 60
ⲥⲛⲁⲩ/ⲥⲛⲟⲩ, [A]ⲥⲛⲟ, fem. ⲥⲛ̄ⲧⲉ "two" 47, 60, 71–72
ⲥⲡⲟⲧⲟⲩ "lips" 60
ⲥⲓⲧⲉ "basilisk" 57
ⲥⲱⲧⲙ̄ "to hear" 89 *passim*
ⲥⲱⲧⲡ̄ "to choose" 37, 49
ⲥⲟⲟⲩ "six" 71
ⲥⲁϣϥ̄ "seven" 71
[B]ⲥⲁϧ, pl. ⲥϧⲟⲩⲓ "scribe" 58
ⲥϩⲁⲓ "to write" 46, 89
ⲥϩⲓⲙⲉ, pl. [S]ϩⲓⲟⲙⲉ, [B]ϩⲓⲟⲙⲓ, [AL]ϩⲓⲁⲙⲉ, [F]ϩⲓⲁⲙⲓ "woman" 49, 59
ⲥⲁϩⲧ "weaver" 248
ⲥⲉϩⲧ "leprosy" 248

ⲧⲟ "land" 41, 49
ⲧⲟⲉ/ⲧⲟⲓⲉ/ⲧⲁ(ⲉ)/ⲧⲟ "part" 50
[SAL]ⲧⲃⲁ, [B]ⲑⲃⲁ, [F]ⲧⲃⲉ "10000" 41–42, 46–47, 71
ⲧⲏⲏⲃⲉ, [A]ϯⲉⲓⲃⲉ "finger" 48
ⲧⲱⲱⲃⲉ, [B]ⲧⲱⲃ/ⲧⲱⲡ "to seal" 44
ⲧⲁⲓ, [B]ⲑⲁⲓ "this (fem.)" 42, 69
ⲧⲁⲓⲟⲩ "50" 71
ϯⲙⲉ, pl. ⲧⲙⲉ "town" 61
ⲧⲉⲛⲧⲱⲣⲉ "Dendera" 43
ⲧⲁⲡ "horn" 41–42
[SA]ⲧⲱⲣⲉ, [B]ⲧⲱⲣⲓ, st. pron. [SAL]ⲧⲟⲟⲧ=, [F]ⲧⲁⲁⲧ=, [B]ⲧⲟⲧ= "hand" 42–44, 49, 66
ⲧⲱⲣⲉ, [B]ⲑⲱⲣⲓ "willow" 42–43
ⲧⲥⲓⲟ "to make sated" 224
ϯⲟⲩ "five" 71
ⲧⲟϣ, pl. ⲧⲟⲟϣ "border, province" 56, 59
ⲧⲉϣⲉ, pl. ⲧⲉϣⲉⲉⲩ "neighbor" 56, 59, 251
ⲧⲁϥ, [B]ⲑⲁϥ "spittle" 42

ⲟⲩⲁ "one" 56, 71–72
ⲟⲩⲁⲁⲃ "holy" 30
ⲟⲩⲏⲏⲃ "priest" 30, 44
ⲟⲩⲟⲡ "to be pure" 30, 41
ⲟⲩⲃⲁϣ "to become white" 37
ⲟⲩⲟⲛ "someone, human being" 87, 260
ⲟⲩⲱⲛ "to open" 223
ⲟⲩⲉⲣⲏⲧⲉ "foot" 60
ⲟⲩⲧⲁϩ "fruit" 50
[S]ⲟⲩⲉϣⲥⲉ/ⲟⲩⲟϣⲥⲉ, [B]ⲟⲩⲉϣⲥⲓ/ⲟⲩⲏϣⲥⲓ "breadth" 47
ⲟⲩⲟϫ "to be whole" 67

ⲱⲡ "account" 43

ϣⲉ "100" 71
ϣⲟ "1000" 41, 71
ϣⲙⲟⲩⲛ "eight" 71
ϣⲟⲙⲛ̄ⲧ "three" 71
[SAL]ϣⲙ̄ϣⲉ, [B]ϣⲉⲙϣⲓ, [F]ϣⲏⲙϣⲓ "to worship" 47
ϣⲛⲉ "net" 47
ϣⲱⲡⲉ, stat. [SL]ϣⲟⲟⲡ, [B]ϣⲟⲡ "to become" 41, 236
ϣⲏⲣⲉ "son" 60
ϣⲉⲉⲣⲉ "daughter" 60
ϣⲟⲣⲡ "first" 72
ϣⲏⲧ "200" 71
ϣϥⲉ "70" 71
[S]ϣⲁϫⲉ, [B]ⲥⲁϫⲓ "to tell" 49, 89
[B]ϣϫⲏⲓ "gossip" 87

ϥⲟⲉ "canal" 87
ϥⲧⲟⲟⲩ "four" 37, 71

ϩⲏ "beginning" 41
ϩⲏ "body" 41
ϩⲏ "blow (of the wind)" 250
ϩⲟ, st. pron. ϩⲣⲁ= "face" 56
ϩⲱⲃ, ϩⲃⲏⲩⲉ "thing, event" 59
ϩⲓⲃⲱⲓ, ^{B}ϩⲓⲡ "ibis" 41, 48
ϩⲃⲟⲩⲓ "snake" 62
ϩⲕⲁ "wool" 248
ϩⲕⲟ, stat. ϩⲕⲁⲉⲓⲧ "to be hungry" 67, 248, 257
^{SL}ϩⲁⲗ, ^{A}ϩⲉⲗ, ^{F}ϩⲉⲗ ("Hurrian ">) "servant" 46
ϩⲙⲉ "40" 71
ϩⲙⲉⲛⲉ "80" 71
ϩⲟⲩⲛ "inside" 48
ϩⲱⲛ "to approach" 48
ϩⲟⲛⲧ "priest" 57
ϩⲛⲁⲩ/ϩⲛⲟⲩ "jar" 47
ϩⲣⲉ "food" 58
^{SL}ϩⲓⲣ, ^{B}ϧⲓⲣ, ^{A}ϩⲓⲣ, ^{F}ϩⲓⲗ "street" 48
ϩⲣⲁⲓ "upper part" 56
ϩⲣⲁⲓ "lower part" 58
^{S}ϩⲣⲟⲟⲩ, ^{B}ϧⲣⲱⲟⲩ, ^{A}ϩⲣⲁⲩ "voice" 41
ϩⲁⲥⲓⲉ "praised" 87
ϩⲟⲟⲩ, pl. ^{A}ϩⲣⲉⲩ "day" 44, 56, 58–59, 62, 252
ϩⲟϥ, fem. ϩϥⲟ, pl. ϩⲃⲟⲩⲓ "snake" 56, 60, 62

ϫⲉ "(so) that" 100
^{SB}ϫⲏ "dish" 43
^{S}ϫⲓ, ^{B}ϭⲓ "to take" 42
ϫⲱ "to say" 37
^{S}ϫⲟⲉⲓⲥ, ^{B}ϭⲱⲓⲥ "lord" 42
^{S}ϫⲱⲱⲙⲉ, ^{B}ϫⲱⲙ, ^{A}ϫⲟⲩⲟⲩⲙⲉ "book" 44, 46, 48–49
ϫⲙ̄ⲡⲉϩ "apple" 48
^{S}ϫⲟⲟⲣ, ^{B}ϫⲟⲣ "to be strong" 44
ϫⲓⲥⲉ, ϫⲟⲥⲉ "to be exalted" 97
ϫⲟⲩⲱⲧ "20" 71

^{B}ϭⲏ "quince" 43
ϭⲙⲉ "gardener" 56
^{S}ϭⲓⲛⲉ, ^{B}ϫⲓⲙⲓ "to find" 42
^{B}ϭⲣⲏϫⲓ "dowry" 42

AFROASIATIC

*ðupp "fly" 31
*wsɣ "wide" 35
*wrḳ "green" 32
*xanam "ram" 35
*x̣al "on" 32
*lib "heart" 31
*lwn "color" 31
*lis "tongue" 31
*nx̣m "sweet" 32
*sulx̣am "locust" 34–35
*sṗɣ "seven" 32
*ḳrb/ḳlb "interior" 32
*śapat "lip" 34
*šu: "he" 34

PROTO-SEMITIC

*'l "toward" 100
*'lp "1,000" 71
*'anāku "I" 31
*'rḍ "earth" 244
*'aṯl "tamarisk" 31, 34
*b "in, by, with, at" 100
*dalt "door" 31
*ḏbb "fly" 31
*hwy "to be" 123
*wḥd "one" 71
*warq "leaf" 32
*ḥmm "to become hot" 34
*ṭwl "to be long" 32
*yad "hand" 255
*ymn "right side" > "South" 34
*yarmuta (toponym) 38
*karm "vineyard" 31
*l "to" 100
*libb "heart" 31
*lawn "color" 31, 35
*lɣz "to speak foreign languages" 31
*lišān "tongue" 31
*n'm "sweet" 32
*'akram (toponym) 38
*'al "on, up" 32, 100
*ṣb' "finger" 255
*qrb "interior" 29
*śapat "lip" 34
*šb' "seven" 32, 71
*šdš "six" 71

**šuwa* "he" 34
**tmm* "to complete" 89
**tš'* "nine" 71
**ṯmny* "eight" 71
**ṯny* "two" 71

AKKADIAN (including transcriptions of Egyptian words)

(a)ḫ-pe/i-e/ir "transformations" 37, 58
a/i/uḫ-ri-píta "overseer of the troops" 39
'anāku "I" 65
dubbum "fly" 31
ḫa-ma-an "eight" 39
ḫi-na "jar" 38
-ḫuru "(the god) Horus" 38
ḫu-u'-ru "form" 58
ipṭau "four" 245
ma-a'-ia-, ma-a-i- "beloved" 38
-ma-ḫe-e "Northwind" 39
-ma-ḫu-u "(the goddess) Mehit" 39
ma-né-e "Menes" 38–39
-mu-a "truth" 39
-na-a-pa "good" 39
né-e'/ni-i' "Thebes" 245
pi/e-ši-iṭ "nine" 38
-pí-ta "bow" 38, 57
qerbum "interior" 32
-ri-ia/-re-e "(the god) Re" 39
šá-te-ep-na-ri/e-a "Satepnari'a" 29
ṣe-e'-nu/ṣa-a'-nu "Tanis" 39
ši-ia-a-u-tu "Asyut" 39
-sini "tree" 38
-ta-a-wa "the Two Lands" 38
ti-ba-an "*dbn*-weight" 32
ú-i-ú/ú-e-eḫ/ú-e-e "soldier" 39
ú-pu-ti/ú-pu-ut "messengers" 37
zinnuk "which you said" 259

ARABIC

'asyūṭ "(the city of) Asyut" 43
'inna particle 100
dandara "Dendera" 43
ḏubāb "fly" 31
'ašar "ten" 255
'išrūna "twenty" 255
'inda "by" 100
ɣanam "sheep" 35
fa "and" 277
qlb "to turn around" 32
qalb, pl. *qulūb* "heart" 58
laɣaza "to speak enigmatically" 31
mā "what?" 69
man "who?" 69
ws' "wide" 35
waṣīf "servant" 32

ARAMAIC

'ar'ā "earth" 244

HEBREW

'ê-ze(h) "which?" 268
'ēṭûn "red linen" 245
'ānōkî "I" 65
gifṭit "Egyptian, Coptic" 241
hinne(h) "behold" 168
zəbûb "fly" 31
yarmût toponym 38
l'z "to speak in a foreign language" 31
nō' "Thebes" 245
sol'ām "locust" 34–35
sôpēr "scribe" 29
'okrān toponym 38
ṣō'an "Tanis" 39, 245
qešet "bow" 245
qûm "to stand" 273

INDO-EUROPEAN

**dekm̥* "ten" 255
**newn̥* "nine" 255
**newos* "new" 255
**wīkm̥tī* "twenty" 255

GREEK (including transcriptions of Egyptian words)

Βογχοριϛ/Βοκχοριϛ/Βοχορινιϛ "Bocchoris" 34
εἰ conj. "if" 270
Κλεοπάτρα 27
Μέμφις "Memphis" 57, 87, 259

-μχης "(the goddess) Mehit" 39
-νηφις "his lord" 55
ὅτι conj. "that" 100, 150
Πτολεμαῖος 27
Σεβεννύτος "(the city of) Sebennytos" 34
Φθά "(the god) Ptah" 34
Χέοψ "Cheops" 82

LATIN

non "not" 127
quod conj. "that" 100, 150
si conj. "if" 270

BERBER

mraw "ten" 71

HAUSA

fuɗu "four" 71

MEROITIC

apote "messenger" 37, 57

Index of topics

"abnormal Hieratic" 22
absolutive 55, 82, 84, 100
accent, *see* stress
accomplishment 76, 150
accusative 55, 65, 82–83, 259, 270
achievement 76, 150
active 63, 72, 83–88, 97–99, 186–88, 193, 199, 202, 204, 208, 253, 275–76
activity (verb of) 76, 150
adjective 54, 56–58, 68–70, 72, 76–77, 88, 100, 103, 109, 113–16, 120, 125, 137, 145, 158, 178, 203, 219, 241, 252–54, 260, 262–63, 275
adjective (or adjectival) verb 65, 80, 83, 125–26, 260
adjectival clause, pattern, sentence 64, 80, 83–84, 103, 108, 112–22, 124–26, 128, 131, 135, 138, 140–41, 185, 200, 206–7, 218, 226, 232, 258, 262, 264
adjectival construction, form, phrase 54, 57, 68, 86, 99, 103, 106, 113, 115, 118, 133, 158, 160, 204, 208, 219, 259
adjectival conversion, transposition 109, 112, 115, 117, 120, 136, 158, 202, 216–17, 219–20, 231, 233, 267
adjectival predicate 103, 112–18, 120, 122, 134, 137, 139, 200, 263
adverb 68–69, 93, 101–1, 122–24, 139, 144–45, 147–49, 161, 215
adverbial adjunct, modifier, phrase 9, 112, 122, 124, 127–28, 134, 144–48, 155–59, 164, 167, 170–71, 176, 178, 181–84, 189, 192, 194–97, 202, 213–14, 218, 226, 228, 234, 265
adverbial clause, pattern, sentence 64–67, 70, 80, 100–1, 110–12, 118, 122–27, 131, 138–39, 144–82, 184, 186, 188–92, 194, 196–202, 209, 214, 216, 218–22, 226, 228, 231–34, 253, 261, 269
adverbial conversion, subordination, transposition (adverbialization) 9, 79, 91, 149–51, 154–57, 161, 178–80, 190, 195–96, 213, 215, 232–35, 264, 274–75
adverbial predicate 122, 124, 144, 172, 176, 269
Afroasiatic 1, 4–5, 12, 28–35, 37, 45, 51–58, 61, 63, 69, 71, 73, 79, 82, 92, 99, 115, 125, 244, 246, 249–55, 268
agent 54, 63–64, 75, 83–84, 86, 97, 99, 107, 117, 134, 136, 184, 189, 206–8, 224, 253
agentivity 83, 258
agentless 204, 207–8
agreement 86–87, 113, 116, 118, 133, 156, 158, 160–61, 203, 205–6, 267–68
Akhmimic 14, 25, 41, 47–50, 243, 247–49, 272, 278
Akkadian 2, 29, 31–32, 37–39, 51, 57–58, 63–66, 73, 79, 244–46, 254, 257, 259
Aktionsart
    durative 76
    punctual 76
allogenetic 250
alphabet, alphabetic system 3, 7, 11–16, 23–26, 28, 40, 42, 73
analytic (vs. synthetic) 5, 7, 51–57, 69, 90–92, 98, 193, 218–20, 224, 232–34, 273
anaphoric 68

antecedent 69–70, 85–87, 98, 115–18, 133, 136, 158, 190–92, 202–8, 212, 214, 218–19, 232, 234, 257, 263–64, 267, 275
aorist 76–80, 86–87, 93–94, 123, 134, 152, 176, 186–87, 190–95, 199–200, 203, 206–25, 228, 231–33, 275, 277
apposition 566, 72, 120, 235, 265, 269
Arabic 1–3, 7, 11, 15, 31–32, 35, 43, 51, 56–58, 70, 73, 82, 100, 115, 241, 250, 255, 259, 262, 270, 277
archaism, archaic 20, 51, 77, 85, 98–99, 108, 146, 219, 232–33, 264
article (definite, indefinite) 6–7, 43, 52, 56, 60, 68–69, 133–38, 275
aspect, aspectual 3, 53, 66, 73–80, 82–85, 88, 91–94, 103, 117, 139, 145, 148–50, 184, 190, 196, 222, 256, 276
"autofocality," "autofocal" 196–97
Åkerblad, Johan David 26

background 100, 152, 154, 170–71, 190, 196, 232, 235, 277
bahuvrīhi 207, 212, 259, 263
"balanced sentence" 109, 132, 191, 196–97, 216, 262
Barthélemy, Jean 26
beneficiary 122, 139–40, 258
Berber 3, 5, 71, 244
biconsonantal, biradical 1, 12, 14, 20, 36, 48, 52, 54, 77, 252
bisyllabic 36, 44, 55
Bohairic 14, 25, 34, 40–49, 69, 132, 16, 139, 224, 231, 243, 247–49, 252, 267, 278
bound (construction, pattern) 69–70, 77–78, 82, 84, 92–94, 104, 118, 127, 129, 131, 140, 209, 219, 221, 229, 234, 272
broken plural 58

cardinal number 71–72
cartouche 27
case 1, 4, 36, 51, 55, 59, 65, 82, 100, 153, 252, 261
categorical (vs. thetic) 110, 112, 153
causative 53–54, 81–82, 223–24
Chadic 4–5, 244
Champollion, Jean-François 26
circumstance, circumstantial 9, 73, 77, 79, 85, 90, 100, 122, 148–49, 152, 156, 161, 167, 171–72, 178–79, 190–91, 195–98, 214, 228–29, 232, 254, 267, 272, 278
clause conjugation 92, 95–96, 229–30
cleft sentence 64, 69–70, 81–84, 104, 112–18, 121, 127–28, 133–37, 140–41, 183–84, 189, 191, 198, 207, 214, 253, 262, 264, 266–69
Cleopatra 27
clitic 52
collective noun 60
command 82–85, 90, 96, 123, 183–84, 201, 212, 217, 265, 275. *See also* mood
comment 111, 124, 153, 168, 192–93, 197–98
comparative degree 100
comparative evidence, method, reconstruction 1, 29, 34, 50, 61, 71, 101, 125, 257, 265
complementary infinitive 170
completive focus 116
"complex adverbial sentence" 148, 195–98, 201
compound noun 18
conditional 81, 92, 152, 216, 272, 278. *See also* hypothetical
conjunct participle 99
conjunction 4, 66, 90, 93, 99–101, 109–10, 150–56, 166, 172–73, 200–1, 216–18, 229–30, 270, 278
conjunctive 91, 95–96, 225, 227–31, 261
conjunctive future 230, 261
consonant, consonantal 1, 3–5, 12–16, 19, 24, 28, 30, 32–50, 52, 54–56, 59, 64–65, 81, 87, 99, 193, 218, 249, 276
consonantal epenthesis 246
context, contextual 48, 75, 78–80, 82, 100, 103, 105, 108, 110, 112, 115–17, 129, 144, 147, 149, 152, 154, 162–64, 186–87, 193, 222, 228, 248–49, 263, 269, 273
contingent tense 78, 80, 82–83, 85, 93, 95–96, 124, 184–85, 198, 215, 221

contradiction, contradictory 126–29, 140–41, 169–72, 180–81, 209–11, 213–15
contrariety, contrary 127–29, 140–41, 170–72, 180–81, 211, 213–15
control 69–70, 79, 89, 93, 133, 139, 150–51, 156–59, 162–64, 166, 172, 174, 176, 178, 185, 189, 191, 196, 199–201, 204, 212–13, 216, 218–20, 223, 228–29, 231–35, 260, 275, 277
converter 91–94, 98, 109, 124, 130, 135, 147, 158, 160, 166, 175–78, 202, 212, 218, 232–34, 277
copula 68–69, 103, 105, 108, 132–36, 141–42, 241, 267–69
cotext, cotextual 80, 83
Cushitic 4–5, 244

de Sacy, Silvestre 26
decipherment 8, 26–27
default consonant 49
deictic 52–53, 65, 67, 70, 105
delocutive 105, 108, 137, 262
demonstrative 7, 68–69, 104, 113, 122, 132, 136, 235, 267, 270, 275
Demotic (language phase, writing) 7, 10–14, 17–20, 22–26, 28, 31
dental, *see* consonant, phoneme
deontic modality 75, 152, 211, 222. *See also* mood
dependent clause 85, 92, 95, 152–55, 190, 264. *See also* subordinate clause
dependent pronoun 64, 93, 105, 109, 113–14, 119–20, 138, 146, 173–74, 206–8, 229, 268
determinative grapheme 13, 16, 19, 21–23, 28
determinative pronoun 56–57, 68, 70, 98, 118–19, 121, 136, 138, 199, 202
dialect 2–4, 7–8, 14, 29, 31, 34, 40–42–49, 69, 241, 243–44, 247–49, 254, 267, 272, 277–78
diathesis, diathetic 124, 256. *See also* voice
discontinuous morpheme 126, 128, 140, 170–71, 213, 268–69, 273
distributive number 72
dual 58, 60, 64–65, 67, 72, 74

"dummy" morpheme 110, 122
durative, *see Aktionsart*
dynamic verb 84

ejective, *see* consonant, phoneme
embedding, embedded phrase 103, 109–12, 151, 153–60, 164–67, 170–72, 178–79, 183–85, 188–202, 204, 213–18, 220, 225, 228–29, 231–32, 234, 253, 275
emphasis, emphasized phrase 79, 81, 86–89, 115, 117, 124, 136, 147, 152, 154, 157, 163, 183, 193–202, 213, 232, 235, 259, 263, 274–75, 277
emphatic consonants 1, 3, 5, 32, 34, 245
enclitic 64–67, 101, 104–5, 108–9, 116, 119, 153, 268
energetic future 176
epistemic modality 75, 222. *See also* mood
ergative-absolutive coding 84
ergativity, ergative 65, 70, 83–84, 95, 117, 121, 184, 207, 253, 276
Erman, Adolf 8
exclamatory 114
existential 103, 121–29, 137–39, 167, 169, 172, 175, 268
extraposition 111, 114, 119, 132, 142, 156, 188, 191, 194, 197–98, 216, 253, 274–75
extrasyllabicity 36, 55, 253

Fayyumic 41, 47–49, 247–49, 277
feminine (vs. masculine) 1, 3–4, 35, 54, 57–61, 63–69, 81, 87, 97, 99–100, 113, 120, 149, 201, 204, 218, 251, 254, 257, 259, 262
flectional 1, 51, 220
focus, focality, focalization 4, 64, 70, 81, 83–84, 106–9, 112, 115–17, 121, 126–29, 131–32, 134–37, 140–41, 148, 154–55, 170, 172, 180–81, 183, 189, 191–92, 197–200, 207, 213–15, 228, 253, 261–64, 267, 269, 274
foreground 152, 190, 196
fricative, *see* consonant, phoneme
fusional 1, 51, 92, 231

future 75, 80–82, 85–87, 94–96, 118, 122, 124, 154, 176–77, 184, 194, 208, 210, 212, 222, 225, 227, 272
Future I 94, 98, 176–77, 181, 222, 225, 234
Future II 232
Future III 94, 96, 174, 177–78, 181, 222, 225, 229, 234, 272

Gardiner, Sir Alan H. 8, 10
gemination 52, 54, 81–82, 87, 123, 193, 203, 208, 218, 276–78
gender 4–6, 52–53, 60, 68–69, 72–74, 86, 106, 116, 118, 120, 133, 136, 262, 265, 267–68
genetic 1, 51, 250
genitive 55–57, 199, 265
glide, *see* semiconsonant, semivowel
grammatical (vs.logical) 82, 161, 185, 198, 206–7, 224, 274
grammaticalization, grammaticalized 4, 51, 55, 66–67, 75, 90–97, 100, 116, 118, 124, 130–31, 139, 147, 149–50, 152, 165–68, 172–78, 181, 186, 205, 209, 211, 223–24, 230–34, 252, 270, 272–73, 278
Gunn, Battiscombe 8
"Gunn's rule" 209, 219–20, 254

Hamito-Semitic 1
Hausa 5, 71
Hebrew 2–3, 31, 34–35, 38–39, 56–57, 65, 82, 92, 168, 241, 245, 268, 273
hierarchy (of animacy, salience, topicality) 84, 105, 108, 112, 117, 121, 137, 161, 164, 206, 219, 258, 276
Hieratic 11, 17–18, 21–22, 28, 36, 62, 243
hieroglyphs, hieroglyphic 6, 11–27, 36, 59, 61–62, 71–72, 81, 242–43
"hieroglyphic Egyptian" 30, 62, 255
Hittite hieroglyphs 242
honorific anticipation 18
hypotaxis, hypotactic 163, 165–66, 172, 175, 178, 187, 189, 225–31, 277
hypothetical 90, 101, 151–52, 156, 181, 278. *See also* conditional

ideogram, ideographic writing 12–13, 18, 22, 61, 72
imperative 75, 81–83, 90, 95–96, 99, 184, 212–13, 217, 223, 227, 254, 260, 273
Imperfect 176, 232
imperfectivity, imperfective 75–77, 79–80, 84, 87–88, 93, 98–99, 117, 150, 206–7, 234, 266
impersonal 268, 273
indefinite article, *see* article
indefinite (subject, pronoun) 70, 97, 139, 176, 205, 224, 232, 264, 276
independent clause, sentence 81–82, 84, 95, 148, 162, 184–85, 190, 193, 197, 227–228
independent pronoun 64–66, 105, 107, 109, 114–16, 121, 134, 138, 146, 168, 184, 191, 253, 263–64
indicative 75, 77–82, 86, 184, 205, 209–11, 221, 256, 275–76
Indo-European 51, 82, 100, 127, 245, 250, 255, 259, 270
infinitive 53, 60, 63, 65–67, 72, 73–74, 80, 84, 87–93, 95–97, 99–100, 106–7, 109–12, 115, 130, 145–46, 149–50, 156, 170, 172–73, 176–77, 184, 186, 214–17, 220, 223–24, 254, 256, 261, 267, 273
initiality, initial (morphology and syntax) 9, 64, 75, 77–80, 83, 85, 91, 93–96, 105, 123, 147–49, 162–68, 172, 174–75, 178–79, 184–89, 192–96, 199, 209, 214, 221, 225–29, 231–32, 234, 256, 264, 271
initiality, initial (phonology) 34–35, 41, 44, 50, 242, 246–47
interdental, *see* consonant, phoneme
interjection 101
interlocutive 105, 108, 114, 121, 137, 262
interrogative 64, 67, 70, 103, 118, 121, 124, 137, 144, 147, 184, 215, 265–67, 273
intransitive 65–66, 76, 83–84, 88–89, 204–5, 257

Kircher, Athanasius 26

labial, *see* consonant, phoneme
Lepsius, Richard 27
lexicalization, lexicalized 52, 54, 57, 95, 223, 259, 277
lexicon, lexicographical 8, 10–11, 21, 30, 174
linkage 152, 165–66, 175, 178, 189, 225–28
literature, literary 2, 5–7, 14, 23, 31, 40, 81, 129, 140–42, 148, 150, 156, 171, 184, 196, 269
liquid, *see* consonant, phoneme
loanword 48, 245
locative 55, 139, 149–50, 153, 268, 270
logical (vs. grammatical) 64, 84, 156, 198, 205–7, 224, 276
logogram 13, 16, 18, 20–22, 125
Lycopolitan 41, 47, 49, 247, 249, 277

main (clause, sentence, predicate) 77–79, 82, 84, 92, 95, 98, 100, 105, 111, 114, 120, 125, 149–53, 155–59, 161–67, 170–75, 178–79, 184–99, 203–4, 206–7, 209–10, 213, 215–16, 218, 220–21, 223, 225–31, 235, 264, 271, 274–75
masculine, *see* feminine
maṣdar 115
Meroitic 4, 11, 37, 57, 246, 251
"middle" voice 66, 76, 83–84
monoconsonantal 12–15, 20
monoradical 52
monosyllabic 41, 247
mood 74–76, 81–83, 85, 94–96, 125, 145, 149, 184, 265, 276. *See also* command, modality, wish
modality, modal 75, 80, 82, 84–85, 90–92, 94–95, 103, 118, 121–24, 139, 147, 152, 176, 178, 184, 186, 193–94, 203, 210–11, 222–23, 225, 227, 229, 232, 261, 263, 272

narrative (verbal forms, tenses) 66, 77–78, 88, 91, 93, 162–64, 178, 184, 190, 195–96, 225, 228–29, 261, 273
nasal, *see* consonant, phoneme
negation 89, 125–31, 140–42, 168–72, 180–82, 209–20, 227–28, 266, 269
negatival complement 73, 89–90, 95, 99, 148, 212–13, 215–17, 223, 260
negative aorist 209–10, 219
negative circumstantial 171, 214, 254, 273
negative condition 216
negative conjunction 101, 218
negative conjunctive 225
negative converter, morpheme, particle 70, 92–93, 101, 125–31, 140–42, 168–72, 180–82, 203, 208–21, 265, 276
negative counterpart, equivalent 77, 92–94, 97, 101, 128, 130, 148, 169–70, 181, 209, 211, 215–16, 218–19, 222, 225
negative existential 129, 172
negative Future III 181, 222
negative imperative 90, 99, 213, 223, 227, 260
negative modality 212, 223, 227
negative past 210–11, 221
negative perfective 78, 151
negative Present I 180
negative prospective 211–12
negative subjunctive 90, 211, 217
negative verb 89–90, 148, 212, 216
neogrammatical 8
neuter 68, 100, 109, 113–14, 204
nisba 1, 56–58, 72, 88, 100, 120, 253, 263
nominal predicate 103, 105–6, 121–24, 191, 216, 262
nominalization, nominalized 79, 88–89, 91, 95, 97, 100, 107, 109–10, 112, 115, 146, 148, 166, 191, 193, 200, 201, 260
non-finite verbal form 73–74, 86, 98, 208, 216
non-initial clause, sentence, form 75, 78–80, 83, 84–85, 91, 94–96, 145, 148, 153, 161–68, 173–75, 179, 184–89, 193, 195–96, 209, 225–29, 231, 273
non-specific 70, 149, 158, 160–61, 176, 189–92, 202, 214, 218, 235
non-transformative verb 76
noun 9, 30, 52–63, 69, 72, 89, 99, 103–4, 106, 111–15, 119, 134–36, 146, 149, 157, 159, 173, 190,

212–13, 218, 224, 235, 262–63, 265, 276
noun clause, nominal sentence 64, 68, 100, 103–44, 146, 150, 152, 154–55, 157–58, 160, 162, 168, 175, 179, 184–85, 188–89, 191–92, 199–200, 204, 209, 214, 218, 231–32, 234, 253–54, 262, 268–69
noun phrase, nominal phrase 9, 69, 73, 103–4, 106, 109, 113, 117–20, 123, 134–38, 156, 161, 164, 170, 183, 199–202, 216–17
number (singular, dual, plural) 6, 52–53, 67–69, 73, 86, 106, 116, 118, 120, 133, 136, 141, 265, 267–68
numeral 7, 60, 71–72, 255, 267

oath 228
object 3, 64–66, 81–83, 88–89, 90, 92, 99–100, 106, 115, 121, 132, 134–35, 139, 153–54, 156, 159–60, 167, 174, 184, 188, 198–201, 203–4, 206, 217–18, 224, 254, 259, 268, 274–75
objective future 80, 94–95, 177, 222, 225
objectless 199, 205
Old Perfective 65–66, 74. *See also* pseudoparticiple, stative
omission
under agreement 156–61
under relevance 149, 153, 157, 161, 163, 186, 191, 198–99, 203, 205, 264, 270–71, 273, 275–76
Omotic 5
onset 45, 48, 248
optative 66, 83, 96, 125, 223
ordinal 71–72

palatal, *see* consonant, phoneme
parataxis, paratactic 79, 162–66, 174–75, 185–87, 189–90, 195–96, 221–25, 227
participle 53, 63, 66, 68, 72–74, 86–87, 88–90, 98, 106, 109, 113, 115–18, 125, 127, 130, 133, 135, 146, 158, 160, 202–8, 217–19, 234, 252, 259–60, 266–67, 275–76, 278
participial construction, pattern, predicate 57, 87, 183, 206, 234
participial statement 114, 153, 189, 198
particle 64–65, 70, 78–79, 81–82, 84, 89, 91–93, 98–101, 105, 108–9, 113–15, 121–27, 134, 144, 147–57, 162, 182, 184–88, 200, 208, 210–11, 221, 224, 229–30, 253–56, 261, 265–68, 271, 276–77
passive 53, 63–64, 66, 75–76, 83–88, 97–99, 106, 117, 184, 186–88, 190, 193, 195, 198–199, 202, 204–8, 211, 217, 219, 224–25, 253, 257, 273–76
past tense 53, 75, 77–78, 80, 85–86, 91–94, 97–98, 122, 124, 126, 162, 166, 175–76, 178, 186–87, 193–96, 199, 203, 207–11, 218–21, 224–28, 230–32, 234, 254, 261, 276–78
patient 63, 83–84, 86, 117, 134, 136, 198, 206–7
perfect 3, 66, 75–78, 80, 84–85, 188, 209, 256–57, 268, 274
Perfect I 221, 224, 227
Perfect II 232
perfectivity, perfective 66, 75–80, 84–88, 91, 93, 97–99, 117, 127, 151, 196, 201, 206–9, 217, 219, 221, 225, 233–34, 256, 267, 276, 278
"philosophy of writing" 14, 19
phoneme 1, 3, 5, 7, 11–16, 19–20, 28–50, 54, 60, 99, 211, 242, 245–49, 253
phonogram 12–16, 18, 20–21, 23, 125
pictogram, pictographic 12–16, 18, 20
plosive, *see* consonant
plural 1, 3–5, 37, 39, 45, 48, 54–55, 58–69, 72, 74, 81, 87, 97–98, 113, 224, 251–55, 260, 262, 272
plurisyllabic 39, 41, 44, 249
Polotsky, Hans Jacob 8–9, 116, 147, 192, 271, 278
polysynthetic 51, 92, 220
possessive 22, 55, 70–71, 103, 118, 120, 126, 136–39

posttonic 37, 39–40, 48–50, 55, 57, 249, 251–52, 257
postvocalic 35
pragmatics, pragmatic 3–4, 9, 103, 105–8, 115–17, 119, 124, 128, 130–32, 134–35, 140, 147–48, 154–55, 163, 165–66, 170–71, 179, 188–89, 194–200, 209, 213–15, 232, 258, 264, 271, 273
"pre-Coptic Egyptian" 7, 46, 61–62
predicate, *see* adjectival, adverbial, nominal, pseudoverbal, verbal predicate
prefix 1, 3, 7, 54, 72, 79, 81–82, 86–87, 90–91, 95, 170, 178, 220, 223, 229, 234, 259, 272
prefix conjugation 1, 4, 52
preposition 13, 58, 63, 66–67, 70–71, 73, 78–79, 83, 89, 93, 95, 99–101, 110, 118, 120, 123, 139–40, 144, 149–52, 155–57, 161, 166, 172–73, 176–77, 199, 201, 204, 208, 213, 217, 220, 223–24, 230, 254, 158, 260, 268, 276
prepositional phrase 66, 98, 132, 144–45, 148–49, 177, 198–99, 213–14, 229, 272
present 75, 77–80, 83, 85–86, 93–94, 103, 117, 122–24, 126, 147, 154, 178–79, 220–21, 228, 261
present perfect 77–78, 209
Present I 91–94, 166, 172–81, 221–22, 229
Present II 91, 232
preterite 75, 77, 86, 117, 134, 184, 186, 189, 209–10, 224–25, 232, 273
pretonic 48, 50
prevocalic 42, 44
proclitic 67, 93, 101, 108, 149, 162–64, 166
progressive present 80
promissive future 96, 230–31, 261
pronominal predicate 138
pronominalization 120
pronoun, *see* demonstrative, dependent, etc.
pronunciation 14, 16, 22–25, 28–29, 99, 242, 245, 278
prospective 66, 75, 79–88, 91, 94–97, 102, 118, 123–26, 134, 145, 147, 152, 166, 168–69, 176–77, 181, 184–85, 191, 193–95, 197, 199, 203, 206–12, 215–16, 222–24, 229–34, 259, 261, 263–65, 270, 274–76
pseudocleft sentence 104, 106, 117, 134–37, 198, 262
pseudoparticiple 65–66, 74. *See also* Old Perfective, stative
pseudoverbal clause, pattern, sentence 66, 77–78, 80, 84, 89, 93–94, 99, 110–11, 113, 125, 131, 144–82, 184–86, 188–89, 194, 199, 208, 213, 220, 232–35, 253, 269
Ptolemaic 6, 11–12, 19–20, 23–24, 26–27, 243

qabbālâh 24
qualitative, *see* stative
question 81, 116, 265, 273. *See also* interrogative

radical 52, 54, 73, 79, 81. *See also* root
rebus principle 12–13, 20, 255
reduplication 41, 44, 47–49, 54, 72, 79, 193, 200, 203, 208, 247, 277
reflexive verb 54
relative adjective, converter, element, pronoun 67–71, 91, 98–101, 109, 158, 160, 175, 178, 202–3, 212, 218, 232, 234, 259, 277
relative clause, conversion 70, 86–87, 98, 115, 128, 130, 132, 135–36, 158–61, 166–67, 171, 175, 179–80, 184, 190–91, 202–8, 214, 218–19, 226, 232–35, 258, 264, 269, 275
relative form 54, 63, 68, 73, 86–87, 89–91, 98–99, 106, 109, 113–15, 117, 133, 135, 144, 146, 158, 160, 166, 183, 198, 201–5, 208, 217–19, 231, 233–34, 259, 264, 267, 275–76, 278
relevance, *see* omission under relevance
replacing focus 117
resumptive 68, 70, 86, 111, 159–61, 191, 203, 258, 267, 270, 276
rheme, rhematic 107–8, 119, 124, 132, 195, 263

rhyme 36
root 1, 3, 32, 52–54, 72–76, 82, 86, 88, 97, 100, 113, 115, 149, 151, 167, 196, 250–51, 255, 259. *See also* radical
Rosetta Stone 26

Sahidic 14, 40–41, 45–47, 49–50, 136, 139, 224, 230–31, 235, 243, 247–49, 267, 272
script, *see* writing
"second tenses" 232–33, 278
semagram 13, 243
semantics, semantic 12–13, 20, 23, 30, 52, 54, 60, 66, 70, 74–76, 80, 82–85, 89, 97–98, 101, 104–8, 110–12, 114–20, 122–25, 128–31, 139–41, 144–49, 152–53, 155–56, 161, 165–68, 171–73, 177, 179, 183, 192, 197, 204–6, 209–11, 214, 218–19, 226–27, 231, 255, 266, 268, 271, 273–74, 276
semiconsonant, semiconsonantal 12–13, 36, 45, 50, 52, 57, 61–62, 81–82, 252–54. *See also* semivowel
Semitic 1–3, 5, 8, 11, 14, 29–32, 34–35, 37–38, 48, 50–52, 54, 56, 58, 63, 65–66, 71, 74, 79, 86, 89, 92, 99, 101, 123, 244–45, 255–57, 259, 268
Semito-Hamitic 1
"semitocentric" 51, 75, 250
semivowel, semivocalic 12, 16, 28, 39, 42, 52–54, 56, 58, 60, 66, 73, 251. *See also* semiconsonant
sentence conjugation 92, 94, 96, 177, 221, 222, 224–25, 227, 230
sequential 91, 93, 95, 178, 225–27, 230, 234, 272
Sethe, Kurt 8
sibilant, *see* consonant, phoneme
SOV-order 3
specificity, specific 70, 86, 98, 103, 105, 107, 139, 158, 160, 173, 176, 190, 202–3, 218, 224, 232, 235, 254, 258, 263
Standard theory 8–10, 79, 123, 147–49, 157, 163, 183, 188, 190, 192, 269–71, 273–74
state (vs. action) 150
stative 1, 30, 65–67, 73–74, 76–80, 84–85, 91, 93, 97, 110–11, 113, 125, 145, 149–50, 157, 161, 164, 170, 172–73, 176, 184, 187–88, 193, 207–8, 213, 220, 254, 257, 263, 272, 274, 277. *See also* Old Perfective, pseudoparticiple
Steindorff, Georg 8
stem 52–59, 62–63, 73–74, 77, 79, 81–82, 84, 86, 88, 94, 99, 220, 224, 251–52, 277
stress (phonological, pragmatic) 3, 35–49, 41, 43–50, 54–58, 64, 67, 81, 89, 99, 108, 117, 120, 135, 138, 140, 198, 210, 220, 224, 247, 249, 252, 257, 262
subject, *see* grammatical, logical
subjectless 73, 205
subjunctive 81–83, 85, 90, 95, 97, 102, 123, 152, 184–85, 193–94, 201, 210–13, 217, 224, 226, 229–31, 265, 270, 273, 275, 277
subordination, subordinate 77–79, 82, 91, 114, 125, 150–52, 155–58, 161–67, 174–75, 178–79, 183, 185, 189–90, 196–97, 200–1, 204, 217, 220, 225–27, 229–32, 234, 257, 270–71, 275, 277
suffix 1, 3, 6–7, 52–61, 65–66, 68–69, 72–74, 77, 81–82, 90, 97, 193, 254–55
suffix conjugation 1, 4, 52, 65–66, 73–74, 83, 205, 257, 275
suffix pronoun 31, 36, 63–67, 93, 95, 99, 107, 120, 128, 132, 138, 146, 156, 168, 173–75, 177, 191, 206–8, 213, 253–54
SVO-order 3, 5, 7, 51, 91
syllable, syllabic 14, 23, 36–41, 44–45, 47–50, 54–56, 59, 247–49, 252
"syllabic orthography" 14, 22, 38, 242
synthetic (vs. analytic) 4–7, 51–52, 54, 72, 84, 86, 90–91, 98–99, 138, 187, 213, 220, 224, 231–34

tense, temporal 4, 53, 74–80, 82, 84–86, 88, 91–95, 103, 117, 121–25, 134, 139, 144–45, 148–49, 152, 156, 164, 176, 184–85, 190, 193–

94, 196–97, 210, 215, 222, 226, 228, 230, 232, 254, 257, 259, 263
tenseless 256
thematic (morphology) 57, 59
theme (pragmatics) 107, 163, 192, 196, 199, 265
thematization, thematized 113, 115, 123–25, 196–98
thetic (vs. categorical) 109–12, 122, 153–55, 200, 216
time, *see* tense
topic, topical 4, 64, 84, 105, 111–12, 119, 121, 132, 141–42, 148, 150, 153–54, 187–88, 194, 197, 199, 274–75
topicalization, topicalized 77–79, 81, 84–85, 90–91, 97, 101, 105, 107–8, 111, 114–15, 117, 120, 124, 130–32, 135–36, 138, 141–42, 150–52, 155–57, 163, 168, 183–84, 187–88, 192–99, 206, 213, 215–16, 224, 226, 228, 230–32, 235, 262, 267, 269, 274–75, 277–78
transcription 11, 16–18, 24, 29–32, 34, 37–39, 43, 57–58, 63, 72, 81, 242, 245–46, 251, 259–60
transformative verb 76
transitive 63–66, 76, 83–84, 87–89, 117, 198, 204–5, 257
translation 16, 111, 155, 159, 199, 270
transliteration 8, 15–16, 25, 28, 30, 43, 125, 140
triconsonantal 1, 12, 52–54
triradical, triradicalism 3, 52, 54, 58, 77, 250, 252
trisyllabic 36
truth value 179
typology, typological 2, 4–5, 19, 41, 51–52, 66, 92, 103–4, 111, 114–15, 129, 133, 219–20, 254, 266–67, 269

unbound 127, 178
universal 117, 189
uvular, *see* consonant, phoneme

velar, *see* consonant, phoneme
verbal class, root, stem 36, 52, 54, 67, 72–74, 76–77, 85–86, 88–89, 97, 99, 115, 149, 167, 196, 220, 259
verbal clause, sentence 64, 66, 70, 77, 100–1, 106, 110–12, 115, 122–24, 126–27, 130, 140, 147–52, 154–60, 162–68, 172, 176, 179, 183–236, 262, 266, 272, 275–76
verbal form 5, 9, 37, 39, 52, 60, 63, 65, 72–75, 78, 80–81, 83–84, 86, 89–91, 97–98, 106, 118, 122, 125–26, 129–30, 144, 147–49, 156–57, 163, 169, 177–79, 181, 183–84, 189–90, 192–200, 202, 204–8, 210, 214–16, 220–21, 223, 227, 229, 231–32, 253–54, 263, 272–74
verbal phrase 9, 64–65, 73, 77–79, 81–85, 90, 99, 106–7, 112, 115, 117, 124, 135–26, 146–49, 156–57, 160, 163–64, 156, 166, 170–71, 174, 178, 180, 183–87, 190–93, 195–201, 204–5, 209, 213–14, 216, 219–21, 228, 231–32, 235
verbal predicate, predication 9, 75–76, 79, 83–84, 89, 91, 121–22, 134, 139, 149, 152, 154, 159–60, 188, 196–98, 200–2, 207–9, 213–15, 219, 229, 253, 275
"verbalistic" 9, 149, 183, 241
verbs of motion 77, 80
"virtual relative clause" 70, 128, 158–61, 166, 171, 175, 179, 184, 190–91, 202, 214, 218, 235, 264
vocalization, vocalized 29–30, 39, 47, 56, 77, 79, 81–82, 244, 251, 257, 259–60
vocative 68, 164
voice 53, 73–76, 83–88, 97–98, 184, 204, 225, 276. *See also* active, "middle," passive
vowel, vocalic 1, 3–4, 12, 14, 16, 28, 30, 35–53, 55–60, 64, 66, 72, 81, 86–87, 90, 99, 175, 210, 220, 224, 246–49, 252, 257, 261, 266
VSO-order 3, 6, 51, 91

weak (class, consonant, radical, root) 14, 52, 73, 77, 79, 81, 86, 88, 259
Westendorf, Wolfhart 8

wish (verbs of) 81–83, 85, 96, 123, 183–84, 201, 212, 217, 265, 275. *See also* mood
word 1, 11–14, 16, 18–23, 26, 28–30, 35–39, 41, 43–44, 48–53, 55–62, 71–72, 92, 120, 210, 241, 245–49, 251, 253, 255, 260, 263, 266, 277
word edge 36
word order 5, 91, 261
writing 11–28, 30, 35, 38, 45, 49–50, 62, 71, 81, 88, 119, 177, 210, 242, 246, 253, 255, 261, 263

Young, Thomas 26